Challenges of Party-Building in Latin America

Nearly four decades since the onset of the third wave, political parties remain weak in Latin America: parties have collapsed in much of the region, and most new party-building efforts have failed. Why do some new parties succeed while most fail? This book challenges the widespread belief that democracy and elections naturally give rise to strong parties and argues that successful party-building is more likely to occur under conditions of intense conflict than under routine democracy. Periods of revolution, civil war, populist mobilization, or authoritarian repression crystallize partisan attachments, create incentives for organization-building, and generate a "higher cause" that attracts committed activists. Empirically rich chapters cover diverse cases from across Latin America, including both successful and failed cases.

STEVEN LEVITSKY is David Rockefeller Professor of Latin American Studies and Professor of Government at Harvard University.

JAMES LOXTON is a Lecturer in Comparative Politics in the Department of Government and International Relations at the University of Sydney.

BRANDON VAN DYCK is Assistant Professor of Government and Law at Lafayette College.

JORGE I. DOMÍNGUEZ is Antonio Madero Professor for the Study of Mexico and Professor of Government at Harvard University.

Challenges of Party-Building in Latin America

Edited by

STEVEN LEVITSKY
Harvard University

JAMES LOXTON
University of Sydney

BRANDON VAN DYCK
Lafayette College

JORGE I. DOMÍNGUEZ
Harvard University

CAMBRIDGE
UNIVERSITY PRESS

CAMBRIDGE
UNIVERSITY PRESS

University Printing House, Cambridge CB2 8BS, United Kingdom

One Liberty Plaza, 20th Floor, New York, NY 10006, USA

477 Williamstown Road, Port Melbourne, VIC 3207, Australia

4843/24, 2nd Floor, Ansari Road, Daryaganj, Delhi - 110002, India

79 Anson Road, #06-04/06, Singapore 079906

Cambridge University Press is part of the University of Cambridge.

It furthers the University's mission by disseminating knowledge in the pursuit of education, learning and research at the highest international levels of excellence.

www.cambridge.org
Information on this title: www.cambridge.org/9781316601402

© Cambridge University Press 2016

First published 2016
First paperback edition 2017

A catalogue record for this publication is available from the British Library

Library of Congress Cataloging in Publication data
Names: Levitsky, Steven, editor.
Title: Challenges of party-building in Latin America / edited by Steven
Levitsky, Harvard University; James Loxton, University of Sydney;
Brandon Van Dyck, Lafayette College; Jorge I. Dominguez, Harvard University.
Description: New York, NY : Cambridge University Press, 2016. |
Includes bibliographical references and index.
Identifiers: LCCN 2016026214 | ISBN 9781107145948 (hardback)
Subjects: LCSH: Political parties–Latin America. | Party affiliation–Latin
America. | Latin America–Politics and government–21st century.
Classification: LCC JL969.A45 C46 2016 | DDC 324.2/1098–dc23
LC record available at https://lccn.loc.gov/2016026214

ISBN 978-1-107-14594-8 Hardback
ISBN 978-1-316-60140-2 Paperback

Publication of this book has been supported in part through the generosity of the David Rockefeller Center for Latin American Studies and the Weatherhead Center for International Affairs at Harvard University.

Contents

Figures

Tables

Contributors

Editors

Steven Levitsky is David Rockefeller Professor of Latin American Studies and Professor of Government at Harvard University. He is the author of *Transforming Labor-Based Parties in Latin America: Argentine Peronism in Comparative Perspective* (Cambridge University Press, 2003), co-author of *Competitive Authoritarianism: Hybrid Regimes after the Cold War* (Cambridge University Press, 2010), and co-editor of *Argentine Democracy: The Politics of Institutional Weakness* (2005), *Informal Institutions and Democracy: Lessons from Latin America* (2006), and *The Resurgence of the Latin American Left* (2011). He is currently writing a book on the durability of revolutionary regimes.

James Loxton is a Lecturer in Comparative Politics in the Department of Government and International Relations at the University of Sydney. He received his PhD from Harvard University in 2014. He is currently writing a book on conservative party-building in Latin America and co-editing the volume *Life after Dictatorship: Authoritarian Successor Parties Worldwide*.

Brandon Van Dyck is Assistant Professor of Government and Law at Lafayette College. He received his PhD from Harvard University in 2014. He is currently writing a book on the divergent trajectories of Latin America's new left parties. His research has appeared in *Comparative Politics*, *Latin American Politics and Society*, *Latin American Research Review*, and *Foreign Affairs Latinoamérica*.

Jorge I. Domínguez is the Antonio Madero Professor for the Study of Mexico and was Vice Provost for International Affairs at Harvard University, 2006–2015. He is the author of *Democratic Politics in Latin America and the Caribbean* (1998), *Cuba: Order and Revolution* (1978), *Cuba hoy: Analizando su pasado, imaginando su futuro* (2006). He is also author and co-editor of *Cuban Economic and Social Development: Policy Reforms and Challenges in the 21st Century* (2012). He is a past editor of the journal *Cuban Studies* and a past president of the Latin American Studies Association.

Chapter Authors

William T. Barndt is Assistant Professor of Political Studies at Pitzer College in Claremont, California. He received his PhD in Politics from Princeton University. His book manuscript, *Democracy for Sale: Corporation-Based Parties and the New Conservative Politics in the Americas*, demonstrates that particular business conglomerates are constructing their own parties and party factions throughout much of the Western hemisphere. He has published his research in *World Politics*, *Latin American Politics and Society*, *Journal of Politics in Latin America*, and in edited volumes.

Kathleen Bruhn is Professor of Political Science at the University of California, Santa Barbara. Her recent publications include "Electing Extremists? Party Primaries and Legislative Candidates in Mexico" (*Comparative Politics* 45 (4), 2013); "'To Hell with Your Corrupt Institutions!': AMLO and Populism in Mexico," in *Populism in Europe and the Americas: Threat or Corrective to Democracy?* (Cambridge University Press, 2012); and "Too Much Democracy? Primaries and Candidate Success in Mexico's 2006 National Elections" (*Latin American Politics and Society* 52 (4), 2010). She is the author of *Taking on Goliath: The Emergence of a New Left Party and the Struggle for Democracy in Mexico* (2004) and *Urban Protest in Mexico and Brazil* (Cambridge University Press, 2008), and co-author of *Mexico: The Struggle for Democratic Development* (2001 and 2006).

Eduardo Dargent is Associate Professor of Political Science at the Pontificia Universidad Católica del Perú. He earned his PhD in Government from the University of Texas at Austin. He is the author of *Technocracy and Democracy in Latin America: The Experts Running Government*

(Cambridge University Press, 2015) and *Demócratas precarios: Élites y debilidad democrática en América Latina* (2009). His research focuses on comparative public policy, democratization, and the state in the developing world.

Kent Eaton is Professor of Politics at the University of California, Santa Cruz. Focusing on territorial politics in Latin America, his research examines the causes and consequences of reforms that redistribute authority between national and subnational governments. His co-authored and co-edited works on decentralization include *Making Decentralization Work: Democracy, Development and Security* (2010), *The Democratic Decentralization Programming Handbook* (2009), and *The Political Economy of Decentralization Reforms: Implications for Aid Effectiveness* (2010). His recent articles have appeared in *Comparative Politics*, *Comparative Political Studies*, and the *Journal of Latin American Studies*.

Kenneth F. Greene is Associate Professor of Government at the University of Texas at Austin. His first book, *Why Dominant Parties Lose: Mexico's Democratization in Comparative Perspective* (Cambridge University Press, 2007), won the 2008 Best Book Award from the Comparative Democratization Section of the American Political Science Association. In addition to work on authoritarian regimes and democratization, he was principal investigator on the Mexico 2012 Panel Study, a multiwave public opinion project. His current work focuses on vote-buying in authoritarian and democratic contexts and on party systems in new democracies emerging from authoritarian rule.

Alisha C. Holland is Assistant Professor of Politics at Princeton University. She received her PhD from Harvard University in 2014. Currently, she is finishing a book on the politics of why governments choose not to enforce laws that the poor tend to violate. Her research has appeared in *American Journal of Political Science*, *American Political Science Review*, *Comparative Political Studies*, and *Latin American Research Review*.

Juan Pablo Luna is Associate Professor in the Instituto de Ciencia Política at the Pontificia Universidad Católica de Chile. His research focuses on political parties and democratic representation, the political effects of inequality, and the nature of state institutions. He is the author of *Segmented Representation: Political Party Strategies in Unequal Democracies* (2014) and co-author of *Latin American Party Systems* (Cambridge University Press, 2010). His dissertation was awarded the 2008 Juan Linz Best Dissertation Award by the Comparative Democratization Section of the American Political Science Association. His work has appeared in *Comparative Political Studies, Política y Gobierno, Revista de Ciencia Política, Latin American Politics and Society, International Political Science Review, Third World Quarterly, Journal of Latin American Studies, Journal of Democracy, Perfiles Latinoamericanos*, and *Democratization*. He has held visiting positions at Princeton University (2008), Brown University (2011), and Harvard University (2013).

Noam Lupu is Assistant Professor of Political Science and Trice Faculty Scholar at the University of Wisconsin–Madison. His book, *Party Brands in Crisis* (Cambridge University Press, 2016), explores how the dilution of party brands eroded partisan attachments in Latin America and facilitated the collapse of established parties. His ongoing projects examine the effects of inequality, violence, and corruption on mass attitudes and behavior, as well as the descriptive representation of the working class. Lupu's research has appeared in *American Journal of Political Science, American Political Science Review, Comparative Political Studies, Journal of Politics*, and *World Politics*, among others.

Raúl L. Madrid is Professor in the Department of Government at the University of Texas at Austin. He is the author of *The Rise of Ethnic Politics in Latin America* (Cambridge University Press, 2012) and *Retiring the State: The Politics of Pension Privatization in Latin America and Beyond* (2003), and is a co-editor of *Leftist Governments in Latin America: Successes and Shortcomings* (Cambridge University Press, 2010). His articles have appeared in *Comparative Politics, Electoral Studies, Journal of Latin American Studies, Latin American Politics and Society, Latin American Research Review, Political Science Quarterly*, and *World Politics*.

Paula Muñoz is Associate Professor of Social and Political Science at the Universidad del Pacífico. She earned her PhD in Government from the University of Texas at Austin. Her dissertation explores the use of electoral clientelism in Peru, a country with weak political parties. Her research focuses on political parties, electoral campaigns, subnational politics, and public policy.

Kenneth M. Roberts is Professor of Government at Cornell University, with a specialization in Latin American political economy and the politics of inequality. He is the author of *Changing Course: Party Systems in Latin America's Neoliberal Era* (Cambridge University Press, 2014) and *Deepening Democracy? The Modern Left and Social Movements* *in Chile and Peru* (1998), and the co-editor of *The Resurgence of the Latin American Left* (2011) and *The Diffusion of Social Movements* (Cambridge University Press, 2010). His current research explores the relationships among parties, populism, and social movements in contexts of economic crisis.

David Samuels is Distinguished McKnight University Professor of Political Science at the University of Minnesota. His most recent book (with Matthew Shugart) is *Presidents, Parties, and Prime Ministers: How the Separation of Powers Affects Party Organization and Behavior* (Cambridge University Press, 2010). He is also the author of the introductory textbook *Comparative Politics* (2012) and serves as the co-editor of *Comparative Political Studies*.

Mauricio Zavaleta holds an undergraduate degree in political science from the Pontificia Universidad Católica del Perú. He is the author of *Coaliciones de independientes: Las reglas no escritas de la política electoral en el Perú* (2014). He has published articles on subnational politics, political parties, and social conflict around mining activities in Peru.

Cesar Zucco Jr. is an assistant professor at the Fundação Getúlio Vargas' Brazilian School of Public and Business Administration. He was previously an assistant professor in the Political Science Department at Rutgers and has held visiting positions and postdoctoral fellowships at Princeton and Yale. He has published articles and chapters on electoral politics, political parties, executive–legislative relations, ideology, and social policy, and his work has appeared in the *American Journal of Political Science, Journal of Politics,* and *Legislative Studies Quarterly*.

Acknowledgments

We have incurred numerous debts in the development of this project. We are especially grateful to the Weatherhead Center for International Affairs (WCFIA) and the David Rockefeller Center for Latin American Studies (DRCLAS), both at Harvard University, which generously co-sponsored the Harvard conference out of which this book emerged. We are grateful to all who presented papers at that conference, for their substantive work and their collegial spirit. We thank Marina Ivanova of the WCFIA for her extraordinary work in organizing the conference.

We would also like to thank the numerous scholars who provided feedback on parts or all of the volume, particularly Candelaria Garay, Frances Hagopian, Henry Hale, Adrienne LeBas, Scott Mainwaring, Omar Sánchez, Hillel Soifer, Martín Tanaka, and Alberto Vergara.

Finally, we are grateful to Manuel Meléndez, a former Harvard undergraduate and budding political scientist, who provided invaluable research and editorial assistance at various stages of the project.

Abbreviations

Abbreviation	Original term	English term
AD M-19	Alianza Democrática Movimiento 19 de Abril	19th of April Movement Democratic Alliance
ADN	Acción Democrática Nacionalista	Nationalist Democratic Action
AMLO	Andrés Manuel López Obrador	
ANAPO	Alianza Nacional Popular	National Popular Alliance
ANSESAL	Agencia Nacional de Seguridad Salvadoreña	Salvadoran National Security Agency
AP	Acción Popular	Popular Action
APB	Autonomía para Bolivia	Autonomy for Bolivia
APP	Alianza para el Progreso	Alliance for Progress
APRA	Alianza Popular Revolucionaria Americana	American Popular Revolutionary Alliance
ARENA (Brazil)	Aliança Renovadora Nacional	National Renewal Alliance
ARENA (El Salvador)	Alianza Republicana Nacionalista	Nationalist Republican Alliance
AS	Alianza Social	Social Alliance
ASI	Alianza Social Indígena/ Alianza Social Independiente	Indigenous Social Alliance / Independent Social Alliance
ASP	Asamblea por la Soberanía de los Pueblos	Assembly for the Sovereignty of Peoples
BEPS	Brazilian Election Panel Study	
CBN	Cervecería Boliviana Nacional	National Bolivian Brewery

Abbreviation	Original term	English term
CC	Convergencia Ciudadana	Citizen Convergence
CD (Panama)	Cambio Democrático	Democratic Change
CD (El Salvador)	Convergencia Democrática	Democratic Convergence
CNOC	Coordinadora Nacional de Organizaciones Campesinas	National Coordinator of Peasant Organizations
CONAIE	Confederación de Nacionalidades Indígenas del Ecuador	Confederation of Indigenous Nationalities of Ecuador
CONALDE	Consejo Nacional Democrático	National Democratic Council
CONDEPA	Conciencia de Patria	Conscience of the Fatherland
COPEI	Comité de Organización Política Electoral Independiente	Independent Electoral Political Organization Committee
CPC	Chim Pum Callao	
CPSC	Comité Pro-Santa Cruz	Pro-Santa Cruz Committee
CR (Colombia)	Cambio Radical	Radical Change
CR (Peru)	Cambio Radical	Radical Change
CSUTCB	Confederación Sindical Única de Trabajadores Campesinos de Bolivia	Unitary Syndical Confederation of Bolivian Peasant Workers
CTC	Central de Trabajadores de Cuba	Cuban Labor Confederation
DEM	Democratas	Democrats
DM	Diretório municipal	Municipal office
DP-UDC	Democracia Popular – Unión Demócrata Cristiana	Popular Democracy – Christian Democratic Union
DPP	Democratic Progressive Party	
EG	Encuentro por Guatemala	Gathering for Guatemala
EJE	Eje Pachakuti	Axis of Pachakuti
ERP	Ejército Revolucionario del Pueblo	People's Revolutionary Army
ESEB	Estudo Eleitoral Brasileiro	Brazilian Electoral Study
FA	Frente Amplio	Broad Front
FARC	Fuerzas Armadas Revolucionarias de Colombia	Revolutionary Armed Forces of Colombia
FDNG	Frente Democrático Nueva Guatemala	New Guatemala Democratic Front
FDR	Frente Democrático Revolucionario	Democratic Revolutionary Front
FES	Función Económica y Social	Economic and Social Function

(*continued*)

Abbreviation	Original term	English term
FG	Frente Grande	Big Front
FIM	Frente Independiente Moralizador	Independent Moralizing Front
FMLN	Frente Farabundo Martí para la Liberación Nacional	Farabundo Martí National Liberation Front
FREDEMO	Frente Democrático	Democratic Front
FREPASO	Frente País Solidario	Front for a Country in Solidarity
FRG	Frente Republicano Guatemalteco	Guatemalan Republican Front
FS	Fuerza Social	Social Force
FSLN	Frente Sandinista de Liberación Nacional	Sandinista National Liberation Front
FULKA	Frente Unido de Liberación Katarista	United Front of Katarista Liberation
GANA (El Salvador)	Gran Alianza por la Unidad Nacional	Grand Alliance for National Unity
GANA (Guatemala)	Gran Alianza Nacional	Grand National Alliance
ID	Izquierda Democrática	Democratic Left
INRA	Instituto Nacional de Reforma Agraria	National Agrarian Reform Institute
IPSP	Instrumento Político por la Soberanía de los Pueblos	Political Instrument for the Sovereignty of the Peoples
ISI	Import substitution industrialization	
IU (Peru)	Izquierda Unida	United Left
IU (Bolivia)	Izquierda Unida	United Left
LAPOP	Latin American Public Opinion Project	
LCR	La Causa Radical	Radical Cause
LLV	Levitsky, Loxton, and Van Dyck	
MAS (Bolivia)	Movimiento al Socialismo	Movement toward Socialism
MAS (Venezuela)	Movimiento al Socialismo	Movement toward Socialism
MDB	Movimento Democrático Brasileiro	Brazilian Democratic Movement
MDS	Movimiento Demócrata Social	Social Democratic Movement
MIAJ	Movimiento Independiente Amauta Jatari	Amauta Jatari Independent Movement
MIP	Movimiento Indígena Pachakuti	Pachakuti Indigenous Movement
MIR	Movimiento de la Izquierda Revolucionaria	Movement of the Revolutionary Left

Abbreviation	Original term	English term
MITKA	Movimiento Indio Tupak Katari	Tupak Katari Indian Movement
MITKA-1	Movimiento Indio Tupak Katari-1	Tupak Katari Indian Movement-1
MKN	Movimiento Katarista Nacional	National Katarista Movement
MNI	Movimiento Nueva Izquierda	New Left Movement
MNR	Movimiento Nacional Revolucionario	Revolutionary Nationalist Movement
MODIN	Movimiento por la Dignidad y la Independencia	Movement for Dignity and Independence
MORENA (Mexico)	Movimiento Regeneración Nacional	National Regeneration Movement
MORENA (Panama)	Movimiento de Renovación Nacional	National Renewal Movement
MOVADEF	Movimiento por Amnistía y Derechos Fundamentales	Movement for Amnesty and Fundamental Rights
MR-8	Movimento Revolucionário 8 de Outubro	October 8th Revolutionary Movement
MRTK	Movimiento Revolucionario Tupak Katari	Tupak Katari Revolutionary Movement
MRTKL	Movimiento Revolucionario Tupak Katari de Liberación	Tupak Katari Revolutionary Liberation Movement
MUD	Mesa de la Unidad Democrática	Democratic Unity Roundtable
MUPP-NP	Movimiento Unidad Plurinacional Pachakutik – Nuevo País	Pachakutik Plurinational Unity Movement – New Country
MVR	Movimiento V República	Fifth Republic Movement
NPC	Nuevo Poder Ciudadano	New Citizen Power
ORDEN	Organización Democrática Nacionalista	Nationalist Democratic Organization
PAC	Partido Acción Ciudadana	Citizens' Action Party
PAIS	Política Abierta para la Integridad Social	Open Politics for Social Integrity
PAN (Guatemala)	Partido de Avanzada Nacional	National Advancement Party
PAN (Mexico)	Partido Acción Nacional	National Action Party
PCdoB	Partido Comunista do Brasil	Communist Party of Brazil
PCB	Partido Comunista Brasileiro	Brazilian Communist Party
PCC	Partido Comunista de Cuba	Communist Party of Cuba
PCN	Partido de Conciliación Nacional	Party of National Conciliation

(*continued*)

Abbreviation	Original term	English term
PD	Partido Demócrata	Democratic Party
PDC	Partido Demócrata Cristiano	Christian Democratic Party
PDS	Partido Democrático Social	Democratic Social Party
PDT	Partido Democrático Trabalhista	Labor Democratic Party
PED	Processo de Eleições Diretas	Process of Direct Elections
PEN	Partido Encuentro Nacional	National Encounter Party
PFL	Partido da Frente Liberal	Liberal Front Party
PH	Partido Humanista	Humanist Party
PIN	Partido de Integración Nacional	National Integration Party
PJ	Partido Justicialista	Peronist Party
PL	Partido Liberal	Liberal Party
PLD	Partido de la Liberación Dominicana	Dominican Liberation Party
PLN	Partido Liberación Nacional	National Liberation Party
PMDB	Partido do Movimento Democrático Brasileiro	Brazilian Democratic Movement Party
PMS	Partido Mexicano Socialista	Socialist Mexican Party
PNP	Partido Nacionalista Peruano	Peruvian Nationalist Party
PNS	Party Nationalization Score	
PODEMOS	Poder Democrático Social	Social Democratic Power
PP (Brazil)	Partido Progressista	Progressive Party
PP (Guatemala)	Partido Patriota	Patriotic Party
PP (Peru)	Perú Posible	Possible Peru
PPB-NC	Plan Progeso para Bolivia – Nueva Convergencia	Plan for Bolivia – New Convergence
PPC	Partido Popular Cristiano	Popular Christian Party
PPD	Partido por la Democracia	Party for Democracy
PPK	Peruanos por el Kambio	Peruvians for Change
PR	Proportional representation	
PRD (Mexico)	Partido de la Revolución Democrática	Party of the Democratic Revolution
PRD (Panama)	Partido Revolucionario Democrático	Democratic Revolutionary Party
PRD (Dominican Republic)	Partido Revolucionario Dominicano	Dominican Revolutionary Party
PRE	Partido Roldosista Ecuatoriano	Ecuadorian Roldosista Party
PRI	Partido Revolucionario Institucional	Institutional Revolutionary Party
PRIAN	Partido Renovador Institucional Acción Nacional	Institutional Renewal Party of National Action
PRO	Propuesta Republicana	Republican Proposal

Abbreviation	Original term	English term
PRSD (Chile)	Partido Radical Socialdemócrata	Social Democratic Radical Party
PRUD	Partido Revolucionario de Unificación Democrática	Revolutionary Party of Democratic Unification
PS (Chile)	Partido Socialista	Socialist Party
PS (Peru)	Partido Socialista	Socialist Party
PSB	Partido Socialista Brasileiro	Brazilian Socialist Party
PSC	Partido Social Cristiano	Social Christian Party
PSDB	Partido da Social Democracia Brasileira	Brazilian Social Democracy Party
PSN	Partido Solidaridad Nacional	National Solidarity Party
PSP (Cuba)	Partido Socialista Popular	Popular Socialist Party
PSP (Ecuador)	Partido Sociedad Patriótica	Patriotic Society Party
PSUM	Partido Socialista Unificado de México	United Socialist Party of Mexico
PSUN	Partido Social de Unidad Nacional / Partido de la U	Social Party of National Unity / Party of the U
PSUV	Partido Socialista Unido de Venezuela	United Socialist Party of Venezuela
PT	Partido dos Trabalhadores	Workers' Party
PTB	Partido Trabalhista Brasileiro	Brazilian Labor Party
PUSC	Partido Unidad Social Cristiana	Social Christian Unity Party
PV	Partido Verde	Green Party
PVEM	Partido Verde Ecológico de México	Ecologist Green Party of Mexico
RAICES	Reforma Regional Andina Integración Participación Económica y Social	Social and Economic Participation Integration Andean Regional Reform
RMF	Ricardo Martinelli Foundation	
RN (Chile)	Renovación Nacional	National Renewal
RN (El Salvador)	Resistencia Nacional	National Resistance
RN (Peru)	Restauración Nacional	National Restoration
SCST	Santa Cruz Somos Todos	We're All Santa Cruz
SP	Somos Perú	We Are Peru
UCC	Unión de Centro Centro	Union of the Centrist Center
UCEDE	Unión del Centro Democrático	Union of the Democratic Center
UCR	Unión Cívica Radical	Radical Civic Union
UCS	Unidad Cívica Solidaridad	Civic Solidarity Unity
UDC	Unión Demócrata Cristiana	Christian Democratic Union

(continued)

Abbreviation	Original term	English term
UDI	Unión Demócrata Independiente	Independent Democratic Union
UNE	Unidad Nacional de Esperanza	National Unity of Hope
UNO	Unión Nacional Odriísta	Odriísta National Union
UPP	Unión por el Perú	Union for Peru
URNG	Unidad Revolucionaria Nacional Guatemalteca	Guatemalan National Revolutionary Unity
VERDES	Verdad y Democracia Social	Truth and Social Democracy
VES	Villa El Salvador	
VV	Vamos Vecino	Let's Go Neighbor

Introduction

Challenges of Party-Building in Latin America

Steven Levitsky, James Loxton, and Brandon Van Dyck

Political parties are the basic building blocks of representative democracy. Political scientists have long argued that democracy is "unworkable" (Aldrich 1995: 3) or even "unthinkable" (Schattschneider 1942: 1) without them. Yet four decades into the third wave of democratization, parties remain weak in much of Latin America. Since 1990, major parties have weakened dramatically or collapsed altogether in Argentina, Bolivia, Colombia, Costa Rica, Ecuador, Guatemala, Peru, and Venezuela.[1] At the same time, most efforts to build new parties have failed. The regional landscape is littered with the corpses of new parties that either failed to take off or experienced brief electoral success but then fizzled out or collapsed.[2] Consequently, most Latin American party systems are more fluid today than they were two decades ago. Of the six party systems scored as "institutionalized" in Mainwaring and Scully's (1995) seminal work, one (Venezuela) has collapsed fully, three (Argentina, Colombia, Costa Rica) have collapsed partially, and a fifth (Chile) has arguably been "uprooted" (Luna and Altman 2011).[3] Of the four party systems that Mainwaring and Scully (1995) classified as "inchoate," only Brazil's has strengthened

---

[1] On party weakness and party system collapse in Latin America, see Roberts and Wibbels (1999), Sánchez (2009), Morgan (2011), Seawright (2012), and Lupu (2014, 2016).

[2] Examples include the United Left (IU), Liberty Movement, Independent Moralizing Front (FIM), and Union for Peru (UPP) in Peru; the Front for a Country in Solidarity (FREPASO), the Union of the Democratic Center (UCEDE), the Movement for Dignity and Independence (MODIN), and Action for the Republic in Argentina; the National Encounter Party (PEN) in Paraguay; the Guatemalan Republican Front (FRG), National Advancement Party (PAN), and Guatemalan National Revolutionary Unity (URNG) in Guatemala; and the M-19 Democratic Alliance (AD M-19) in Colombia.

[3] Uruguay's party system remains institutionalized.

over the last two decades. The Bolivian, Ecuadorian, and Peruvian party systems have only weakened further.[4]

These developments have generated a new pessimism about the prospects for party-building in Latin America. Scholars such as Levitsky and Cameron (2003) and Mainwaring and Zoco (2007) argue that changing structural conditions – particularly the spread of mass media technologies – have weakened incentives for party-building. If politicians no longer need parties to win elections, these scholars suggest, the era of stable mass party organizations may be over.

Yet the experience of party-building has not been universally bleak. Several new parties have, in fact, taken root in contemporary Latin America. These include the Workers' Party (PT) and Brazilian Social Democracy Party (PSDB) in Brazil; the Independent Democratic Union (UDI) and Party for Democracy (PPD) in Chile; the Farabundo Martí National Liberation Front (FMLN) and Nationalist Republican Alliance (ARENA) in El Salvador; the Party of the Democratic Revolution (PRD) in Mexico; the Sandinista National Liberation Front (FSLN) in Nicaragua; and the Democratic Revolutionary Party (PRD) in Panama.[5] These cases challenge sweeping claims that the era of party-building is over. Party-building, it seems, is difficult but not impossible in contemporary Latin America.

This volume seeks to explain variation in party-building outcomes in Latin America since the onset of the third wave of democratization (1978 to present). Why have some new parties established themselves as enduring political organizations while the vast majority of them have failed? This question has important implications for both the stability and quality of democracy. Where parties are weak, or where party systems decompose and are not rebuilt, democracies frequently suffer problems of governability, constitutional crisis, and even breakdown (e.g., Peru in the 1990s, Venezuela in the 2000s). In contrast, where parties remain strong, or where previously inchoate party systems become institutionalized, democracies tend to remain stable (e.g., Chile, Uruguay) or consolidate (e.g., Brazil, Mexico).

Despite the scholarly consensus around the importance of strong parties, we know relatively little about the conditions under which such parties emerge. Dominant theories of party and party system development are

---

[4] For a more optimistic perspective on the recent evolution of Latin American party systems, see Carreras (2012).

[5] For a complete list, see Table 1.1.

based mainly on studies of the United States and Western European countries.[6] Since almost all of these polities developed stable parties and party systems, much of the classic literature takes party-building for granted. Thus, while scholars such as Duverger (1954), Lipset and Rokkan (1967), Sartori (1976), Shefter (1994), and Aldrich (1995) help us understand the origins and character of parties and party systems in advanced industrialized democracies, they offer less insight into a more fundamental question: Under what conditions do stable parties emerge in the first place?

Building on recent research on party formation in Europe, Africa, Asia, the former Soviet Union, and Latin America,[7] this introductory chapter develops a conflict-centered approach to party-building. We argue that robust parties emerge not from stable democratic competition, but rather from *extraordinary conflict* – periods of intense polarization accompanied by large-scale popular mobilization and, in many cases, violence or repression. Episodes of intense conflict such as social revolution, civil war, authoritarian repression, and sustained popular mobilization generate the kinds of partisan attachments, grassroots organizations, and internal cohesion that facilitate successful party-building. We also argue that party-building is more likely to succeed where party founders inherit a brand and/or organizational infrastructure from social movements, guerrilla movements, or previous dictatorships.

Latin America is a useful region for analyzing variation in party-building. For one, it is almost uniformly democratic. Unlike Africa, Asia, and the former Soviet Union, nearly every country in Latin America has had three or more decades of regular, competitive elections. In addition, Latin American countries share broadly similar histories, cultures, and social structures, as well as broadly similar institutional arrangements (e.g., presidentialism, combined with proportional representation [PR] or mixed PR/plurality electoral systems). Yet party-building outcomes vary widely in the region, both cross-nationally and within countries over time. This empirical variation is crucial for understanding the determinants

---

[6] See, for example, Duverger (1954), Downs (1957), Lipset and Rokkan (1967), Panebianco (1988), Kitschelt (1989), Shefter (1994), and Aldrich (1995). Mainwaring (1999) makes a similar critique.

[7] On party-building in Europe, see Kitschelt (1989), Kalyvas (1996), Hug (2001), Tavits (2013), and Ziblatt (forthcoming); on Africa, see LeBas (2011), Arriola (2013), and Riedl (2014); on Asia, see Hicken (2009) and Hicken and Kuhonta (2015); on the former Soviet Union, see Moser (2001), Hale (2006), and Hanson (2010); on Latin America, see Mainwaring (1999), Levitsky and Cameron (2003), Van Cott (2005), Mainwaring and Zoco (2007), Mustillo (2007, 2009), Lupu and Stokes (2010), Vergara (2011), Luna (2014), and Lupu (2014, 2016).

of party-building: we cannot pinpoint the sources of successful party-building without also studying cases of failure.

DEFINING AND MEASURING
PARTY-BUILDING

The focus of this volume is *party-building*, which we define as the process by which new parties develop into electorally significant and enduring political actors.[8] We seek to explain not party formation, which is widespread across Latin America,[9] but instead cases in which new parties actually take root. Thus, our operationalization of successful party-building includes both electoral and temporal dimensions. To be considered a success, a new party must achieve a minimum share of the vote and maintain it for a significant period of time. It need not win the presidency, but it must, at a minimum, consistently receive a sizable share of the national vote. Our conceptualization thus excludes "flash parties," which perform well in one or two elections but then collapse (e.g., Front for a Country in Solidarity [FREPASO] in Argentina), as well as minor parties that persist over time but win only a small share of the vote (e.g., some Latin American communist parties).

We score party-building as successful when a new party wins at least 10 percent of the vote in five or more consecutive national legislative elections.[10] We add the condition that a successful new party must also survive the departure of its founding leader. Parties that are little more than personalistic vehicles may achieve success over multiple elections if their founding leaders remain active and at the head of the party ticket (e.g., Hugo Banzer's Nationalist Democratic Action [ADN] in Bolivia). While some of these parties eventually institutionalize (e.g., Peronism), most collapse after their founding leaders exit the political stage (e.g., ADN, Gustavo Rojas Pinilla's National Popular Alliance [ANAPO] in Colombia,

---

[8] Following Sartori (1976: 56), we define a political party as any political group that competes in elections with the goal of placing candidates in public office.

[9] Barriers to party formation are low throughout Latin America (Mainwaring 2006). Parties form easily, frequently, and for a variety of reasons. According to Mustillo, for example, 133 new parties formed in Bolivia and Ecuador alone during the third wave (2007: 2). Many of these parties were personalistic vehicles, created by and for a single candidate. On party formation, see Kitschelt (1989), Aldrich (1995), Hug (2001), and Van Cott (2005).

[10] National legislative elections must be held at least two years apart from one another. If elections are held in consecutive years (e.g., Guatemala in 1994 and 1995, Peru in 2000 and 2001), both elections are counted, but parties that participate in them must reach the 10-percent threshold in six consecutive elections to be considered successful.

Manuel Odría's National Odriísta Union [UNO] in Peru). In our view, such cases should not be viewed as cases of successful party-building.[11]

Based on this operationalization, we count eleven cases of successful party-building in Latin America since the onset of the third wave (see Table 1.1).[12] These successes represent a tiny fraction of the overall number of parties created in Latin America during this period. We compiled a list of all parties that emerged in eighteen Latin American countries between 1978 and 2005,[13] and which won 1 percent or more of the national legislative vote at least once (see Appendix I for the full list).[14] Using these somewhat restrictive criteria (many additional parties failed to capture 1 percent of the national vote), we counted 307 new parties. Of these, 244 are scored as unsuccessful because they: (1) failed to win 10 percent of the vote and then disappeared (N = 202); (2) failed to win 10 percent of the vote but survived as marginal parties (N = 20); (3) won 10 percent of the vote in at least one election (but fewer than five) and then collapsed (N = 20); or (4) won 10 percent of the vote in five consecutive elections but collapsed after their founding leader left the political scene (N = 2).

An additional fifty-two parties are scored as "incomplete" cases, either because they have yet to compete in five elections, or because they have competed in five elections but only recently reached the minimum 1 percent threshold for inclusion.[15] Of these fifty-two incomplete cases, twelve have won at least 10 percent of the vote in one or more elections and can thus be considered "potentially successful."[16] A few of these parties, such as Bolivia's

---

[11] Thus, personalistic parties that reach the 10-percent threshold in five consecutive elections but then collapse after the founding leader dies or otherwise ceases to be a viable presidential candidate are not scored as successful. The two parties excluded on these grounds are Hugo Banzer's ADN in Bolivia and Abdalá Bucaram's Ecuadorian Roldosista Party (PRE).

[12] Peru's *Fujimorismo* nearly qualifies as a success but is excluded because it failed to win 10 percent of the vote in the 2001 legislative election. Uruguay's Broad Front (FA), though discussed in Luna's chapter, is not included in our sample because it was formed in 1971, prior to the onset of the third wave.

[13] This includes all Latin American countries except Cuba.

[14] We include parties that won at least 1 percent of the vote in coalition with other parties. We exclude strictly provincial parties; thus, parties must compete in more than one province for seats in national legislative elections to be included.

[15] Most of these parties have not competed in five consecutive legislative elections. A few have competed in five elections but surpassed the 1 percent threshold for inclusion (e.g., Indigenous Social Alliance/Independent Social Alliance [ASI] in Colombia) or the 10-percent threshold for success (e.g., *Fujimorismo* in Peru) fewer than five elections ago.

[16] These are Bolivia's Movement toward Socialism (MAS); Colombia's Social Party of National Unity (PSUN/Party of the U); Costa Rica's Citizens' Action Party (PAC) and Broad Front (FA); Guatemala's Patriotic Party (PP), National Unity of Hope (UNE), and Grand National Alliance (GANA); Panama's Democratic Change (CD); Peru's

TABLE 1.1 *Cases of successful party-building in Latin America since 1978*[1]

Country	Party	Birth
Brazil	Workers' Party (PT)	1980
Brazil	Brazilian Social Democracy Party (PSDB)	1988
Brazil	Liberal Front Party (PFL)/Democrats (DEM)	1985
Chile	Independent Democratic Union (UDI)	1983
Chile	National Renewal (RN)	1987
Chile	Party for Democracy (PPD)	1987
El Salvador	Nationalist Republican Alliance (ARENA)	1981
El Salvador	Farabundo Martí National Liberation Front (FMLN)	1992
Mexico	Party of the Democratic Revolution (PRD)	1989
Nicaragua	Sandinista National Liberation Front (FSLN)	1979
Panama	Democratic Revolutionary Party (PRD)	1979

[1] A party is scored as successful if it wins at least 10 percent of the vote in five or more consecutive national legislative elections *and* survives after its founding leader has ceased to be a viable presidential contender (due to death, forced or voluntary retirement, or abandonment of the party). Elections must be held at least two years apart from one another. If two legislative elections are held within two years of one another (e.g., Guatemala in 1994 and 1995, Peru in 2000 and 2001), both elections count, but parties must win 10 percent or more of the vote in at least *six* consecutive elections. To be scored as successful, a party must receive 10 percent or more on its own in at least one national legislative election; once it has done so, subsequent elections in which it participates in alliances that win at least 10 percent of the vote are also counted.

Movement toward Socialism (MAS), the United Socialist Party of Venezuela (PSUV), and Costa Rica's Citizens' Action Party (PAC), are likely to become full cases of success. Most of the others, however, are already in decline and are thus unlikely to reach the 10-percent/five-election threshold. The other thirty-nine incomplete cases are parties that have never won 10 percent of the vote and are thus unlikely to succeed. Hence, our limited number of successful new parties is not simply due to their having had insufficient time to meet our five-election criterion. Beyond the PSUV, MAS, PAC, and perhaps Peru's *Fujimorismo* and Colombia's Social Party of National Unity (PSUN/ Party of the U), very few of the incomplete cases are poised to cross the 10-percent/five-election threshold in the years to come.

Of the 255 new parties that emerged in Latin America between 1978 and 2005 and can be scored definitively, then, only eleven (or 4 percent) actually took root. These results are similar to those generated

Fujimorismo, National Solidarity Party (PSN), and Peruvian Nationalist Party (PNP); and Venezuela's Fifth Republic Movement (MVR)/United Socialist Party of Venezuela (PSUV).

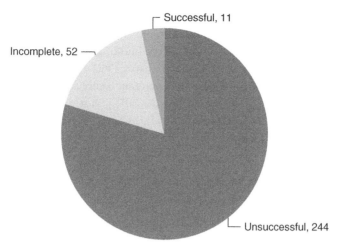

FIGURE 1.1 Party-building outcomes in eighteen Latin American countries, 1978–2005.

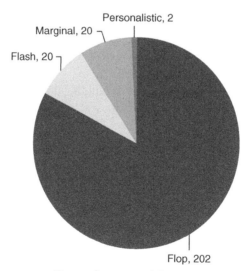

FIGURE 1.2 Types of unsuccessful party, 1978–2005.

by Mustillo's (2009) study of new party trajectories in Bolivia, Chile, Ecuador, and Venezuela. Of the 297 parties examined by Mustillo, 3.5 percent were successful (what he calls "explosive" or "contender" parties), while 89 percent died without achieving any success ("flops"), 4 percent achieved brief success but then collapsed ("flash" parties), and 3 percent remained marginal contenders ("flat" parties) (2009: 325).

Our eleven cases of successful party-building are diverse. They span the left (PT, PPD, FMLN, FSLN, Mexico's PRD) and right (UDI, RN, ARENA, PFL/DEM), and include insurgent successor parties (FMLN, FSLN), social movement-based parties (PT), authoritarian successor parties (UDI, ARENA, Panama's PRD), and parties born from schisms within established parties (PSDB, PFL/DEM, Mexico's PRD).

EXPLAINING SUCCESSFUL PARTY-BUILDING:
A CONFLICT-CENTERED APPROACH

Why have a handful of new parties established themselves as enduring electoral contenders in Latin America, while so many others have not? What factors enabled the PT, the FMLN, and the Mexican PRD to take root, while other new left-of-center parties, such as the United Left (IU) in Peru, FREPASO in Argentina, and the Democratic Alliance M-19 (AD M-19) in Colombia, collapsed? Likewise, what explains the success of the UDI in Chile and ARENA in El Salvador, when most other new conservative parties, such as the Union of the Democratic Center (UCEDE) in Argentina, the National Advancement Party (PAN) in Guatemala, and the Liberty Movement in Peru, failed?

Contemporary approaches to party-building do not adequately explain this variation. For example, scholars have argued that democracy itself, if uninterrupted, should encourage party development.[17] There are two versions of this argument. The top-down version focuses on how democratic institutions shape the incentives of individual politicians. In his seminal work on party formation in the United States, for example, John Aldrich (1995: 28–55) argues that under democracy, individual politicians have an incentive to "turn to parties" in order to achieve collective goals, such as winning elections and passing legislation, which, in turn, increase the likelihood of sustaining a long political career. Although Aldrich recognizes the coordination problems inherent in party formation (1995: 55–56), he argues that stable democracy creates "more or less continuous incentives for ambitious politicians to consider party organizations as a means to achieve their goals" (1995: 286).

The bottom-up version of the democracy-centered approach links regular elections to the development of partisan attachments (Campbell et al.

---

[17] See Aldrich (1995), Brader and Tucker (2001), and Lupu and Stokes (2010).

1960; Converse 1969; Tucker and Brader 2001; Lupu and Stokes 2010; Dinas 2014). Drawing on classic works such as Campbell et al. (1960) and Converse (1969), Lupu and Stokes argue that since voters cast ballots for parties, "the desire to resolve cognitive dissonance leads them to see themselves as partisans of this party, which in turn makes them more likely to cast votes for it in the future" (2010: 92).[18] Thus, "over time, as people have repeated opportunities to vote for parties and are exposed to their mobilizing efforts, they acquire partisan attachments" (Lupu and Stokes 2010: 102).

Yet evidence from Latin America suggests that elections and democracy are insufficient to induce politicians to invest in parties or to engender stable partisan identities. Nearly four decades since the onset of the third wave, new parties have taken root in only a handful of Latin American countries. Moreover, of our eleven successful cases, only one (Brazil's PSDB) was born under democracy. The other ten all emerged under authoritarian rule.[19] Outside of Brazil, then, no successful party-building occurred under democracy in Latin America between 1978 and 2005, despite the fact that many countries experienced two or more decades of uninterrupted electoral competition.

Another approach to party-building focuses on institutional design. Institutionalist approaches highlight how constitutional, electoral, and other rules shape incentives for politicians and voters to coordinate around or aggregate into national parties.[20] For example, scholars have examined the impact of electoral and other institutional barriers to entry on party formation in Latin America (Van Cott 2005). Likewise, scholars of Brazilian politics have argued that open-list PR electoral systems weaken parties by encouraging candidate-centered strategies (Mainwaring 1999; Ames 2001). These analyses have generated useful insights into how parties organize and how politicians operate in relation to those organizations. They are less useful, however, for explaining what enables parties to take root. Electoral rules may shape incentives for party formation, but they do not generate the partisan attachments or activist networks that are so essential to long-term party survival. In Latin America, institutional design has had a limited impact on party-building

[18] Dinas (2014) makes a similar argument, drawing on US electoral data.
[19] Brazil's PFL was born in 1985 in the last days of the Brazilian military regime, and Chile's RN and PPD were created in 1987 in anticipation of a transition to a more competitive regime.
[20] See Duverger (1954), Cox (1997), Mainwaring (1999), Moser (2001), Chhibber and Kollman (2004), and Hicken (2009).

outcomes. Empirical analyses find little, if any, relationship between electoral rules and party-building outcomes in the region. For example, Mustillo (2007: 80) found that electoral rules had a "rather trivial" impact on party-building. Among our cases, new parties succeeded in federal (e.g., Brazil, Mexico) and unitary systems (e.g., Chile, El Salvador), under powerful executives (e.g., Brazil, Chile) and more constitutionally limited ones (e.g., Mexico), and in electoral systems with high (e.g., Brazil) and low (e.g., Chile) district magnitudes. In some cases (e.g., Brazil), new parties consolidated in institutional contexts widely considered unpropitious for party-building (Mainwaring 1999), while in others (e.g., Peru), new parties failed despite repeated efforts to design institutions aimed at strengthening parties (Vergara 2009; Muñoz and Dargent, Chapter 7, this volume). Indeed, electoral rules have changed so frequently in much of Latin America that they may be best viewed as endogenous to, rather than determinative of, party strength (Remmer 2008).

What, then, explains variation in party-building outcomes in Latin America? New parties must generally do three things if they are to take root. First, they must cultivate strong partisan identities. To succeed over time, parties need partisans, or individuals who feel an attachment to the party and thus consistently turn out to support it. In his chapter for this volume and elsewhere (2014, 2016), Noam Lupu argues that the key to building a stable partisan support base lies in the development of a *party brand*. A party's brand is the image of it that voters develop by observing its behavior over time.[21] Parties with strong brands come to "stand for" something in the eyes of their supporters. According to Lupu (2014: 567), voter attachments to party brands are based on a sense of "comparative fit": in other words, "individuals identify with a party to the extent that they consider themselves similar to the party brand."

Establishing a party brand is no easy task. New parties must either carve out space for themselves vis-à-vis established parties or, where party systems are weakly institutionalized, compete with a plethora of other new parties. According to Lupu (2014, 2016), two factors are essential for brand development: interparty differentiation and intraparty consistency. In other words, a new party must distinguish itself from other parties, and its behavior must be consistent over time. If it becomes indistinguishable from other parties, or if its profile changes markedly from one election to the next, the perception of "comparative fit" will diminish

---

[21] The notion of party brand is similar to what Hale (2006: 12) calls "ideational capital," or the "cultivation of a *reputation* for standing for [certain] principles."

and its brand will be diluted. When a party's brand is diluted, its ability to maintain electoral support will depend more on its performance in office (Kayser and Wlezien 2011; Lupu 2014). For Lupu, then, a new party that both dilutes its brand *and* performs poorly in office is especially likely to collapse.

Whereas Lupu defines the concept of party brand in programmatic terms, we define it more broadly. The bases of partisan attachments vary. In Latin America, partisan identities have at times been rooted in socio-cultural (Ostiguy 2009a, 2009b) and even personalistic appeals. Indeed, many of the most successful and enduring party brands in Latin America (e.g., Radicalism and Peronism in Argentina, Colorados and Blancos in Uruguay, *Aprismo* in Peru, *Priísmo* in Mexico) have been programmatically ambiguous. Several of these parties emerged out of conflicts (e.g., populism/antipopulism) whose axes did not correspond to the standard left–right spectrum,[22] and their brands persisted for decades despite considerable programmatic inconsistency and internal heterogeneity. Thus, although brand development clearly contributes to the formation of partisan attachments, it is important to recognize that brands are built on diverse – and sometimes nonprogrammatic – bases.

A second element of successful party-building is the construction of a *territorial organization*.[23] Parties rarely survive in voters' minds alone. Rather, most durable parties have an organized presence on the ground, whether in the form of official branch structures, informal patronage-based machines, or social movements. Territorial organization contributes to the success of new parties in several ways. First, it enhances parties' capacity to mobilize electoral support. The boots on the ground provided by grassroots organization enable parties to disseminate their brand (Samuels 2006; Samuels and Zucco 2014), build and sustain clientelist linkages (Levitsky 2003; Stokes et al. 2013; Luna 2014), and mobilize voters on election day (Tavits 2013: 24–36). Second, territorial organization helps new parties survive crisis. Because the rank-and-file cadres who make up new party organizations tend to be ideologically committed activists, they are more prone to "stick it out" in the face of electoral setbacks and other early crises (Van Dyck, Chapter 5, this volume). Thus, new parties with organized activist bases have a built-in cushion against early failure. Third, a strong territorial organization

---

[22] On populism versus antipopulism and its relationship to the left–right axis, see Ostiguy (2009a, 2009b).

[23] See Tavits (2013) and Van Dyck (2014b, Chapter 5, this volume).

facilitates the capture of subnational office, which, by allowing parties to demonstrate a capacity to govern, can contribute to their longer-term success (Holland, Chapter 10, this volume).

In sum, parties with grassroots organizations are more sustainable than those without them. Although a handful of parties with weak territorial organizations have enjoyed enduring electoral success (e.g., PPD in Chile, PSDB in Brazil), such parties are the exception. Nearly all of the new parties that took root in Latin America since the onset of the third wave – from the PT and the FMLN on the left to ARENA and the UDI on the right – possessed extensive grassroots organizations.

A third element of successful party-building is a *robust source of organizational cohesion*. Organizational cohesion refers to the propensity of party leaders and cadres to hang together – especially in the face of crisis. Low cohesion is the Achilles' heel of many new parties; parties that suffer schisms during their formative periods usually fail. For example, Peru's IU, which emerged as a major electoral force in the 1980s, was decimated by a schism in 1989 and never recovered (Roberts 1998; Van Dyck 2014b). Similarly, the conservative UCEDE, which became Argentina's third largest party in the 1980s, collapsed after suffering a wave of defections to the government of Carlos Menem in the early 1990s (Gibson 1996). The Guatemalan PAN suffered a precipitous decline after founder Álvaro Arzú and presidential candidate Óscar Berger abandoned the party in the early 2000s, and Colombia's Green Party, which came out of nowhere to finish second in the 2010 presidential election, was crippled by defections – including that of its presidential candidate and best known figure, Antanas Mockus – following the election.

Although parties of all ages suffer schisms, new parties are especially vulnerable to them. For one, they tend to lack strong brands that, in established parties, raise the electoral cost of defection for losers of internal power struggles. Parties may use patronage to keep politicians in the fold (Muñoz and Dargent, Chapter 7, this volume), but patronage in the absence of strong partisan attachments tends to be a weak source of cohesion (Levitsky and Way 2012). Strictly patronage-based parties are prone to fragmentation, as politicians have an incentive to "jump ship" whenever their access to public office becomes imperiled. Indeed, many new patronage-based parties in Brazil, Ecuador, Guatemala, Panama, and elsewhere suffered debilitating schisms during the third wave.[24] Thus, new parties that possess an alternative source of cohesion, such as

---

[24] On party fragmentation in Brazil, see Mainwaring (1999).

a shared ideology (Hanson 2010), *esprit de corps* generated by intense polarization or threat (LeBas 2011; Levitsky and Way 2012), or perhaps charismatic leadership (Panebianco 1988), are less likely to suffer debilitating schisms.

New parties are thus most likely to succeed when they develop a clear brand, build a strong territorial organization, and acquire a robust source of organizational cohesion. Such tasks have proven difficult to accomplish in contemporary Latin America. Consider, for example, brand development. As Roberts (2014; also Chapter 2, this volume) argues, the 1980s and 1990s constituted a "neoliberal critical juncture" in Latin America, marked by severe economic crisis and far-reaching policy change. The 1982 debt crisis and subsequent emergence of a broad consensus around market-oriented policies hindered brand development in at least two ways. First, recession, fiscal crisis, and soaring inflation undermined government performance throughout the region, increasing the likelihood of policy failure. Second, the so-called Washington Consensus encouraged interparty convergence and intraparty inconsistency. Parties that had previously favored statist or redistributive programs engaged in abrupt programmatic reversals, abandoning leftist or statist programs in favor of macroeconomic orthodoxy and neoliberal reforms (Stokes 2001; Roberts 2014). As a result, many of these new parties experienced brand dilution (Lupu, Chapter 3, this volume).

The economic crisis of the 1980s and 1990s thus undermined brand development by increasing the likelihood that new parties would dilute their brands *and* perform poorly in office. As Roberts' chapter shows, several party-building projects in Latin America were derailed, at least in part, by the neoliberal critical juncture. For example, Argentina's FREPASO, which originated as a left-of-center party, diluted its brand by rapidly shifting to the center in the 1990s, and then collapsed after serving as junior partner in the disastrous government of Fernando de la Rúa (Lupu, Chapter 3, this volume). Left-of-center parties such as the Democratic Left (ID) in Ecuador and the Movement of the Revolutionary Left (MIR) in Bolivia were similarly weakened by periods in government in which neoliberal policies diluted their brands (Roberts, Chapter 2, this volume), and the embryonic brand of Pachakutik in Ecuador as an "ethnopopulist" party was diluted when its political ally, Lucio Gutiérrez, turned to the right after winning the presidency in 2002 (Madrid, Chapter 11, this volume). In contrast, new left parties that did not win the presidency in the 1980s and 1990s had the luxury of remaining opposed to neoliberalism during this period and could therefore maintain programmatic

consistency. Paradoxically, then, *losing* elections appears to have been critical for the survival of new left parties in the 1980s and 1990s.[25]

Organization-building also proved difficult in the contemporary
period. As Kalyvas (1996: 41) has observed, "Organization-building does
not come naturally or automatically to political actors. It is a difficult,
time-consuming, costly, and often risky enterprise." Given the costs of
organization-building, politicians who can win and maintain office *without* investing in territorial organization are likely to do so.[26] Hale (2006)
has shown, for example, that Russian politicians routinely deploy state
agencies and large business conglomerates as substitutes for party organization.[27] Other scholars have emphasized that mass media – especially
television – provide a quicker, easier route to electoral success than does
organization-building (Cameron and Levitsky 2003; Mainwaring and
Zoco 2007). As Mainwaring and Zoco (2007: 156–157) write:

> When television emerges as a major campaign vehicle before parties are well
> entrenched, political actors have less incentive to engage in party-building. It is
> easier and – in the short term – more effective to use the modern mass media than
> to build a party.

Drawing on such work, Van Dyck (Chapter 5, this volume) argues that the
third wave of democratization inhibited organization-building in Latin
America by providing office-seekers with unprecedented access to mass
media and state substitutes. His chapter shows that due to open electoral
competition and widespread media access, left-wing parties born under
democracy tended to underinvest in organization. Indeed, since the onset
of the third wave, Latin American politicians of diverse ideological backgrounds have either not invested seriously in territorial organization (e.g.,
AD M-19, FREPASO) or opted to forego party-building altogether in
favor of personalistic candidacies (e.g., Fernando Collor in Brazil, Alberto
Fujimori and Alejandro Toledo in Peru, Rafael Correa in Ecuador).

The Centrality of Conflict

Building on the classic work of Lipset and Rokkan (1967) and Huntington
(1968), we argue that it is not the ordinary politics of democratic competition but rather extraordinary times, marked by intense – and often

---

[25] This was arguably the case with the PT, the FMLN, the Mexican PRD, and the Uruguayan
Broad Front (FA).
[26] See Levitsky and Cameron (2003), Hale (2006), and Mainwaring and Zoco (2007).
[27] Levitsky and Zavaleta (Chapter 15, this volume) find a similar use of party substitutes
in Peru.

violent – conflict, that create the most favorable conditions for party-building.[28] Periods of extraordinary conflict, including armed revolutionary struggle, civil war, sustained popular mobilization, and authoritarian repression, are most likely to generate the partisan attachments, territorial organization, and cohesion that enable new parties to take root.

Extraordinary conflict contributes to party-building in several ways. First, it strengthens partisan attachments. As scholars such as Wood (2003), LeBas (2011), and Balcells (2012) have shown, experience with civil war, repression, and other forms of violence tends to generate enduring political identities.[29] Conflict also tends to produce the partisan differentiation that Lupu (Chapter 3, this volume) identifies as essential to brand development. In Latin America, civil war (e.g., nineteenth-century Colombia and Uruguay, twentieth-century El Salvador), revolution (Mexico, Nicaragua), and sustained conflict between populists and anti-populists (e.g., Peronism/anti-Peronism in Argentina) or leftists and right-wing dictatorships (e.g., Chile and Uruguay in the 1970s) often sharply divided societies along partisan lines. Parties that represented the poles of such conflicts were highly differentiated, which helped to crystallize partisan identities.

Conflict also encourages organization-building. Politicians have a greater incentive to invest in organization when their goals extend beyond the electoral arena, and particularly when they face severe extraelectoral threats (Kalyvas 1996; Roberts 2006). In his analysis of party-building under populist governments, for example, Roberts (2006) argues that Hugo Chávez built a more extensive organization than Alberto Fujimori because Chávez's leftist project triggered greater resistance from powerful actors – and thus required greater mobilizational capacity to defend – than Fujimori's neoliberal project. Several strong party organizations in contemporary Latin America were born of extraelectoral conflict. For example, both guerrilla movements seeking to seize power via armed struggle (e.g., FMLN, FSLN) and conservative parties seeking to defend the status quo in the face of a perceived revolutionary threat (e.g., ARENA, UDI) had strong nonelectoral incentives to organize at the grassroots level. Although these organizations were not initially created

---

[28] Our argument also draws on the work of Smith (2005), Hanson (2010), Slater (2010), LeBas (2011), Vergara (2011), Balcells (2012), and Levitsky and Way (2012).

[29] Wood (2003) argues that experience with military repression in El Salvador increased political identification with the FMLN. Similarly, Balcells (2012) shows that victimization during the Spanish Civil War was correlated with strong political identities in the post-Franco era.

for electoral purposes, they eventually contributed to parties' longer-term electoral success.

Conflict also facilitates organization-building by mobilizing activists. Grassroots organizations are networks of activists. Without the boots on the ground provided by such activists, formal party organizations are often little more than shells (Scarrow 1996; Van Dyck, Chapter 5, this volume). In established parties, grassroots party work may be carried out by party employees and patronage-seekers (Kitschelt 1989; Greene 2007). Because most new parties have limited access to state resources, however, they typically must rely on volunteer activists to build grass-roots organizations. Given the time, labor, and uncertain payoffs associated with building a new party organization, it is usually only the most ideologically committed activists – what Panebianco (1988: 26–30) calls "believers" – who are willing to engage in such work. The mobilization of believers, in turn, requires the existence of a "higher cause."[30] High-stakes conflicts such as civil wars, revolutions, populist movements, and antiauthoritarian struggles provide precisely such higher causes. For this reason, episodes of conflict often mobilize the initial generation of ideologically committed activists who are so vital to building grassroots organizations.

The organization-building consequences of conflict may be reinforced by a selection effect. Adversity and violent conflict deter less committed individuals from partisan participation, attracting only those whose convictions trump their risk aversion and short-term ambitions (Greene, Chapter 6, and Van Dyck, Chapter 5, this volume). Parties born in a context of violence or repression thus tend to be composed of an unusually large number of rank-and-file ideologues. While the presence of large numbers of "believers" may handicap parties' electoral performance by limiting their capacity to appeal to electoral majorities (Greene 2007, Chapter 6, this volume), their presence nevertheless facilitates organizational survival, for it ensures that the party's "boots" remain on the ground even in the face of major setbacks, such as electoral defeat (Van Dyck, Chapter 5, this volume).

Finally, conflict can be a powerful source of organizational cohesion. As Adrienne LeBas has argued, intense polarization hardens partisan boundaries by sharpening "us–them" distinctions, strengthening collective identities, and fostering perceptions of a "linked fate" among cadres (2011: 44–47). Where such polarization is accompanied by

[30] See Hanson (2010).

violent conflict, it often generates strong partisan loyalties (e.g., American Popular Revolutionary Alliance [APRA] after the 1930s; Peronism after 1955). For example, the conflict and repression that followed Perón's 1955 overthrow cemented Peronist loyalties for at least a generation (James 1988). For Peronists of the so-called Resistance era, "there was no doubt that the fundamental enemy was anti-Peronism whatever its different guises; and conversely the fundamental friend was another Peronist ... The Resistance saw no need for any internal differentiation."[31] The hardened partisan boundaries generated by violent polarization effectively "trap" potential defectors inside the organization (LeBas 2011: 46). Where the main partisan alternative is associated with an historic enemy (e.g., *gorilas* for Peronists, *Somocistas* for the FSLN, "communists" for ARENA), abandoning the party may be equated with extreme disloyalty and even treason (LeBas 2011: 47; Levitsky and Way 2012).

Conflict has long been a source of party-building in Latin America. As Domínguez reminds us in the Conclusion, many of the region's most historically successful parties were born or became consolidated during periods of violent conflict. For example, Uruguay's long-dominant parties, the Blancos and Colorados, "emerged as a product of war" (López-Alves 2000: 69), with partisan attachments and nationwide activist networks consolidating amid a series of civil wars in the nineteenth and early twentieth centuries (López-Alves 2000: 69–87). The Guerra Grande (Great War) (1838–1851) played a "decisive" role in crystallizing partisan identities, as the "horrors of a long and often ferocious war cemented popular loyalties" to such an extent that the parties "enjoyed more loyalty ... than the ... state" (González 1995: 140). Colombia's Liberal and Conservative parties were similarly forged in civil wars (López-Alves 2000: 117–134). The War of the Supremes (1839–1843) was a "watershed for party-building, shaping party subcultures and organizations" (López-Alves 2000: 127–128), and the series of (often brutal) civil wars that followed left partisan identities "deeply entrenched" (Archer 1995: 174). The Liberal and National parties in Honduras and the National Liberation Party (PLN) in Costa Rica were also forged in civil war, and historically dominant parties in Mexico and Bolivia trace their origins (Mexico's Institutional Revolutionary Party [PRI]) or consolidation (Bolivia's Revolutionary Nationalist Movement [MNR]) to revolutionary uprisings. Other major parties, including the Dominican

---

[31] Roberto Carri, "La Resistencia peronista: crónica por los resistentes," *Antropología del Tercer Mundo* (June 1972), quoted in James (1988: 96).

Revolutionary Party (PRD) in the Dominican Republic, the Radicals and Peronists in Argentina, Democratic Action (AD) in Venezuela, APRA in Peru, and the Broad Front (FA) in Uruguay, took root during periods of intense polarization and authoritarian repression.

Polarization and violence were also a major source of party-building during the third wave. Three of our eleven cases of successful party-building – the FMLN and ARENA in El Salvador and the FSLN in Nicaragua – emerged out of violent conflict. El Salvador, which is arguably the most striking case of party-building in Latin America since the onset of the third wave, experienced a bloody civil war during the 1980s. The civil war strengthened partisan identities, generated intra-party cohesion, and involved guerrilla and paramilitary structures that later served as organizational platforms for party-building (Wood 2003; Loxton, Chapter 9, and Holland, Chapter 10, this volume). The FSLN also emerged out of a violent revolutionary struggle in the late 1970s. The party's extensive grassroots presence, solid partisan support base, and striking level of internal cohesion have been widely attributed to *Sandinismo*'s guerrilla origins (Gilbert 1988: 49–55; Miranda and Ratliff 1993: 13–14). Three other successful new left parties – the PT, the PPD, and the Mexican PRD – were born in opposition to authoritarian rule, and their formative periods were shaped, to varying degrees, by polarization, protest, and repression (Van Dyck, Chapter 5, this volume). At the other end of the ideological spectrum, the formation of the UDI was powerfully shaped by perceptions of a Marxist threat in the polarized context of Augusto Pinochet's Chile (Loxton, Chapter 9, this volume). Finally, two new parties that appear likely to take root – *Chavismo* in Venezuela and the MAS in Bolivia – were also products of conflict. *Chavista* identities and organizations were strengthened by intense polarization, which culminated in the 2002 coup attempt and the large-scale mobilizations of late 2002 and early 2003 (see Roberts 2006). Likewise, the MAS was forged in the context of a massive wave of social protest that included the 2000 "Water War," the 2003 "Gas War," and violent regional autonomy protests of 2007–2008 (Anria 2013).

Conflict-centered approaches to party-building may be traced back to the classic work of Lipset and Rokkan (1967) and Huntington (1968). Huntington argued, for example, that robust ruling parties were often a "product of intense political struggle," such as revolutionary and violent anticolonial movements (1968: 415–417). Likewise, Lipset and Rokkan's (1967) seminal analysis of the origins of modern European party systems centers on the role of polarization and conflict.

Until recently, however, contemporary scholarship on party-building has largely neglected the role of conflict.[32] Although Lipset and Rokkan (1967) are widely cited, their work is often mischaracterized as attributing party formation to the mere presence of class, religious, or ethnic cleavages in society.[33] Based on this interpretation, scholars often conclude that a "social cleavage" approach has little explanatory power in Latin America.[34] In fact, Lipset and Rokkan (1967) made no such argument. For them, the "critical cleavages" that produced enduring partisan identities and organizations in Europe did not simply reflect underlying social structures. Rather, they were generated by *conflict*, either in the form of "movements of protest against the established national elite" or "organized resistance" to the expansion of state authority (Lipset and Rokkan 1967: 21–23, 42). Thus, it was not the growth of the working class, per se, that gave rise to strong socialist parties, but rather the sustained mass mobilization waged by working-class movements, which in many cases brought countries to the brink of civil war.[35] Indeed, Lipset and Rokkan's "critical cleavages" did not even require objective social bases. In the United States, for example, enduring partisan conflicts were based on "contrasting conceptions of public morality," not underlying social divisions (Lipset and Rokkan 1967: 12). If the primary impetus for party-building in Lipset and Rokkan (1967) is *actual conflict* rather than underlying social divisions, their ideas may have more contemporary relevance in Latin America than is often believed.

A potential critique of conflict-centered explanations is that the causal arrows may be reversed: perhaps polarization and conflict are endogenous to, rather than determinative of, party strength. Yet close examination of historical cases suggests that polarization creates strong parties, and not vice versa. In Colombia, Uruguay, Costa Rica, and El Salvador, for example, there is ample evidence that strong partisan identities and organizations emerged after – and as a consequence of – the onset of

[32] Recent exceptions include Smith (2005), Slater (2010), Lebas (2011), Levitsky and Way (2012), and Slater and Smith (2016).

[33] According to Mainwaring (1999: 21), for example, the social cleavage approach is "predicated on the idea that social identities such as class, religion, ethnicity, and region provide the bases for common interests and thereby create enduring partisan sympathies."

[34] See, for example, Dix (1989), Mainwaring (1999), and Van Cott (2005).

[35] See Lipset and Rokkan (1967: 21–22). Thus, in Austria, "extreme opposition between Socialists and Catholics ... ended in civil war" (22); in Finland, civil war and subsequent repression of the communists left "deep scars" on the party system (50); Italy was "torn by irreconcilable conflicts among ideologically distinct camps" (43); and Belgian parties emerged out of "continuing processes of economic, social, and cultural mobilization" (42).

civil war.[36] Similarly, the organizations and collective identities that undergirded Mexico's PRI and Nicaragua's FSLN were clearly products of revolutionary war. Indeed, at the outset of revolutionary violence in their respective countries, the PRI did not exist and the FSLN was a relatively small guerrilla organization. Likewise, populist parties such as Peronism and *Chavismo* were better organized and more societally rooted *after* periods of conflict than when populist governments assumed office.[37] For example, Peronist organizations and identities were almost certainly strengthened by the mobilization and repression that occurred in the wake of Perón's 1955 overthrow (James 1988; McGuire 1997). Although strong parties may in some cases help to generate polarization, as in Chile in the 1960s and 1970s,[38] it is more common for such parties to moderate over time. Indeed, comparative research on Latin American party systems suggests that societally rooted parties and party systems are associated with *lower* levels of polarization than are weak parties and inchoate party systems (Mainwaring and Scully 1995: 28–33). Hence, the claim that strong parties generate polarization, and not vice versa, lacks empirical support.

Conflict is neither necessary nor sufficient for successful party-building. Some new parties (e.g., PSDB in Brazil) take root in the absence of intense polarization, and as Eaton's chapter on the failure of Bolivia's eastern autonomy movement to produce a successful party shows, periods of conflict do not invariably lead to the emergence of strong parties. However, strong parties are more *likely* to take root when they emerge in contexts of extraordinary conflict.

A conflict-centered approach thus helps to explain why successful party-building is a relatively rare event – and why it has been especially uncommon in Latin America since the onset of the third wave. Latin America has been predominantly democratic since the 1980s, and most of the region's civil wars ended by the early 1990s. With the end of the Cold War, left–right polarization diminished across much of the region (Mainwaring and Pérez-Liñán 2013), and the level of programmatic differentiation between parties fell considerably.[39] In most respects, democratization, peace, and decreasing

---

[36] On Colombia and Uruguay, see López-Alves (2000). On El Salvador, see Wood (2003).
[37] On Peronism, see James (1988). On *Chavismo*, see Roberts (2006) and Hawkins (2010).
[38] On Chile, see Valenzuela (1978) and Scully (1992).
[39] There were exceptions. In some countries, particularly Bolivia and Venezuela, ideological polarization increased in the 2000s. It is worth noting that in these cases, polarization gave rise to parties (the MAS in Bolivia, *Chavismo* in Venezuela) that appear likely to take root.

polarization were desirable developments. They may, however, have inhibited party-building.

Organizational Inheritance

Conflict is not the only path to successful party-building. Another means of acquiring a party brand and grassroots organization is inheritance.[40] The costs and coordination problems inherent in party-building may be reduced where politicians can appropriate preexisting brands or organizations and deploy them for partisan ends. Studies of party-building in Europe (Kalyvas 1996; Ziblatt, forthcoming), Africa (LeBas 2011), and Latin America (Van Cott 2005; Vergara 2011) suggest that new parties are more likely to succeed where politicians build upon an infrastructure inherited from preexisting movements or organizations.

Several of the chapters in this volume highlight the importance of organizational inheritance. For example, Loxton's chapter shows how authoritarian successor parties in Chile and El Salvador benefited from organizational resources inherited from former dictatorships.[41] In Chile, the success of the UDI was facilitated by its inheritance of extensive clientelistic networks built by mayors appointed by the military authorities during the 1980s. In El Salvador, ARENA inherited much of its organizational muscle from the Nationalist Democratic Organization (ORDEN), a vast paramilitary group created by the country's previous military regime. Authoritarian successor parties may also inherit popular brands, particularly if the previous regime retains substantial public support. Thus, brands that were originally forged by authoritarian regimes (e.g., *Pinochetismo* in Chile, *Torrijismo* in Panama, *Fujimorismo* in Peru) may continue to appeal to part of the electorate, and thus attract voters to parties led by incumbents of the old regime (see also Levitsky and Zavaleta, Chapter 15, this volume).

As Holland's chapter demonstrates, insurgent successor parties may also benefit from organizational inheritance. Both the FMLN and the

---

[40] Conflict and organizational inheritance are not mutually exclusive. Intense conflict is often accompanied by organization-building in the form of powerful social movements, guerrilla or paramilitary organizations, or authoritarian regime structures. Such organizational infrastructure, in turn, can later serve as the platform for party-building (e.g., Chile, El Salvador, Nicaragua).

[41] On authoritarian successor parties and the phenomenon of authoritarian inheritance, see Loxton (2015).

FSLN were built upon established guerrilla movements with networks of activists and supporters throughout the national territory (Allison 2006a, 2006b).[42] In her chapter, Holland shows how the FMLN drew on these networks in order to win subnational office after democratization, which laid the bases for its subsequent growth at the national level. The FMLN and FSLN also inherited brands forged during armed struggle. Revolutionary brands were polarizing, which posed a challenge for insurgent successor parties at election time. However, they also provided voters with a clear sense of what those parties stood for (and how they differed from other parties), which allowed them to sidestep many of the challenges of brand development.

Organizational inheritance also contributed to the success of many movement-based parties. Recent scholarship has shown that unions (LeBas 2011), religious associations and churches (Kalyvas 1996; Ziblatt, forthcoming), and indigenous and other social movements (Van Cott 2005; Vergara 2011) often serve as mobilizing structures for new parties. Brazil's PT is a prime example. Unions and grassroots church organizations played a major role in the PT's initial organization-building efforts (Keck 1992; Van Dyck, Chapter 5, this volume). Moreover, as Samuels and Zucco argue in their chapter, the PT's later organizational expansion was based on a strategy of opening local offices in areas with high NGO density and mobilizing NGO activists for partisan work. Similarly, Madrid argues in his chapter that ethnic parties were more likely to succeed in Latin America where they built upon the infrastructure of preexisting indigenous movements, as did the MAS in Bolivia and Pachakutik in Ecuador. Finally, Eaton's chapter on the failure of party-building in the Bolivian East usefully illustrates the opposite scenario. According to Eaton, one of the reasons for the failure of the country's eastern autonomy movement to produce a viable party was the decline of the once powerful Pro-Santa Cruz Committee (CPSC).

Barndt's chapter on corporation-based parties examines a less conventional platform for party-building: private firms. According to Barndt, corporations have the potential to provide crucial resources for party-building, including finance, physical infrastructure, and personnel. In Panama, Ecuador, and elsewhere, individual corporations have not

---

[42] The FSLN qualifies as both an insurgent successor party and an authoritarian successor party, since it transformed into an authoritarian ruling party after seizing power in 1979.

merely financed existing parties, but have actually created their own new parties. While many corporation-based parties are personalistic vehicles, Barndt argues that some of them have the potential to institutionalize and endure.

* * *

In sum, extraordinary conflict creates more favorable conditions for party-building than do elections and democracy. By strengthening partisan attachments, inducing elites to invest in organization, mobilizing ideologically committed activists, and generating robust sources of organizational cohesion, episodes of intense (and often violent) conflict create conditions that are more favorable for party-building than those generated by democratic institutions alone. Party-building is also more likely to succeed where politicians inherit infrastructure and collective identities from nonelectoral organizations or previous authoritarian regimes.

Table 1.2 scores our eleven successful cases on the two main variables discussed in this section. In terms of conflict, it is worth highlighting that only one of our successful parties (the PSDB) emerged under stable democracy. By contrast, three successful parties emerged in a context of civil war or insurgency, and seven emerged under authoritarian rule.[43] Of the seven parties born under (or amid transitions from) authoritarianism, five emerged under bureaucratic authoritarianism,[44] a regime type widely associated with large-scale popular mobilization, intense polarization, and high levels of repression (O'Donnell 1973; Valenzuela 1978; Collier 1979).

In terms of organizational inheritance, six of our eleven successful cases were authoritarian successor parties, and two were insurgent successor parties.[45] Two other parties, the PT and the Mexican PRD, were built upon social movements (Van Dyck, Chapter 5, this volume). Only the PSDB and the PPD lacked a clear organizational inheritance.

---

[43] As noted above, Brazil's PFL was formed in 1985, shortly before the country's transition to democracy, and Chile's RN and PPD were formed in 1987 in anticipation of a transition.

[44] See O'Donnell (1973) and Collier (1979). Although there is much debate on the concept and theory of bureaucratic authoritarianism, four authoritarian regimes in South America are commonly viewed as falling into this category during the 1960s and/or 1970s: Argentina, Brazil, Chile, and Uruguay.

[45] The FSLN can be scored as both an authoritarian successor party and an insurgent successor party.

TABLE 1.2 *Cases of successful party-building: birth environment and organizational inheritance*

Party	Year of formation	Birth environment	Organizational inheritance
PT (Brazil)	1980	Bureaucratic authoritarianism	Social movements
PSDB (Brazil)	1988	Democracy	None
PFL (Brazil)	1985	Bureaucratic authoritarianism[1]	Authoritarian successor
UDI (Chile)	1983	Bureaucratic authoritarianism	Authoritarian successor
RN (Chile)	1987	Bureaucratic authoritarianism[1]	Authoritarian successor
PPD (Chile)	1987	Bureaucratic authoritarianism[1]	None
ARENA (El Salvador)	1981	Civil war/insurgency	Authoritarian successor
FMLN (El Salvador)	1992	Civil war/insurgency	Insurgent successor
PRD (Mexico)	1989	Authoritarianism	Social movements
FSLN (Nicaragua)	1979	Civil war/insurgency	Insurgent successor[2]
PRD (Panama)	1979	Authoritarianism	Authoritarian successor

[1] Created during final years of military rule in anticipation of a transition.
[2] The FSLN may also be scored as an authoritarian successor party.

Table 1.3 presents data on the regime conditions under which the 255 new parties listed in Appendix I were born.[46] Between 1978 and 2005, Latin American countries (excluding Cuba) collectively spent 318 years under electoral democracy,[47] eighteen of which can be considered populist[48]; ninety years under authoritarian rule, thirty-one of which

[46] Here we examine only the parties that can be definitively scored. Thus, our fifty-two "incomplete" cases are excluded.
[47] For the sake of simplicity, we define electoral democracy in minimalist terms, thereby including borderline or hybrid cases such as the Dominican Republic, Paraguay, and Guatemala in the early 1990s. Although major insurgency may occur under democracy (or authoritarianism), we treat these categories as mutually exclusive. Thus, cases of civil war/insurgency are excluded from the democracy and authoritarianism categories.
[48] Following Levitsky and Loxton (2013), we define populism as cases in which elected presidents (1) are political outsiders, (2) are elected via explicitly antiestablishment appeals that target the entire political and/or economic elite, and (3) establish a personalistic linkage to voters. It should be noted that this is a more demanding definition than those employed by scholars such as Roberts (1995) and Weyland (1996, 1999). For example, it excludes cases such as Carlos Menem in Argentina and Fernando Collor in Brazil, since neither president was a true political outsider.

TABLE 1.3 *Polarization and conflict and party-building outcomes in Latin America, 1978–2005*

Level of polarization and conflict	Total country-years	Successful party-building cases
Civil war/major insurgency	78	3
All authoritarianism	90	7
Bureaucratic authoritarian	31	5
Other authoritarian	59	2
All electoral democracy	318	1
Populist presidency	18	0
Nonpopulist presidency	300	1
Total	486	11

were under bureaucratic authoritarianism[49]; and seventy-eight years under civil war or major insurgency (see Appendix II for coding of cases). Strikingly, 318 years of electoral democracy produced only one successful party. By contrast, seventy-eight country-years of civil war or major insurgency gave rise to three successful parties, and ninety country-years under authoritarianism produced seven successful parties. If we examine only bureaucratic authoritarian regimes, the numbers are even more suggestive: five successful new parties were born during thirty-one years of bureaucratic authoritarian rule.[50] Finally, although eighteen years of populism produced no new parties that are scored as successful, this outcome may be a product of how recently populism occurred in the relevant cases. For example, *Chavismo* and *Fujimorismo* are parties of recent populist origin that, in our view, stand a good chance of crossing the volume's threshold for successful party-building in the future.

    A true empirical test of the argument developed here would require an analysis of the effects of a range of variables – including party system characteristics, electoral rules, economic conditions, state capacity, and contingent factors such as party strategies and leadership decisions – on all of the 255 parties listed in Appendix I. Such an analysis is

[49] Following Collier (1979: 3–5), and using our start date of 1978, country-years scored as bureaucratic authoritarian are Argentina (1978–1983), Brazil (1978–1985), Chile (1978–1990), and Uruguay (1978–1984).

[50] It is important to note that these new parties were not born during the most closed, repressive periods of bureaucratic authoritarian rule, but rather during periods of regime liberalization (Brazil's PT, Chile's UDI) or in the lead-up to democratic transitions (Brazil's PFL and Chile's PPD and RN).

beyond the scope of this introductory chapter.[51] Nevertheless, the data presented here suggest two important points. First, successful party-building is rare under all political conditions. Second, the clustering of successful cases in the civil war and bureaucratic authoritarian categories suggests the plausibility of our conflict-centered approach to party-building.

We do not claim that authoritarianism always favors party-building. Authoritarian regimes vary widely, and many of them are clearly not conducive to party-building. In some cases, authoritarianism weakens or destroys parties (Mainwaring 1999), and some dictatorships are so repressive that even clandestine organization-building is virtually impossible (e.g., Cuba). Thus, with the exception of insurgent successor parties (e.g., the FMLN), party-building under authoritarianism is most likely to occur under particular conditions, such as electoral authoritarian rule (e.g., Mexico under the PRI) or periods of authoritarian liberalization (e.g., Brazil in the late 1970s and early 1980s, Chile in the late 1980s). Liberalizing authoritarian regimes appear particularly conducive to party-building, since they combine a degree of space for political activity with higher levels of popular mobilization and violence than are typically found under stable democracy.

NEW DEBATES AND ISSUES FOR RESEARCH

The chapters in this volume engage several important debates regarding the causes of successful and failed party-building – and draw attention to several new ones. This final section examines some of these debates, specifically the effects on party-building of (1) regime type, (2) the state, (3) leadership, and (4) populism.

Democracy, Authoritarianism, and Party-Building

As noted above, democracy is widely believed to be more fertile terrain for party-building than authoritarianism. Electoral and legislative institutions are said to encourage politicians to "turn to parties" (Aldrich 1995), and to foster the development of mass partisan attachments (Brader and Tucker 2001; Lupu and Stokes 2010). At the same time, freedom of association lowers the cost of partisan activism.

---

[51] Mustillo (2007) undertakes a large-n test of contending explanations of new party success and failure. However, his analysis yields few substantive results.

As this chapter has shown, however, strikingly few successful parties in Latin America have emerged under stable democracy. Van Dyck offers one possible explanation for this outcome. Because parties born in opposition to authoritarian rule (e.g., Brazil's PT, Mexico's PRD) lacked access to the state and mass media, he argues that their leaders faced strong incentives to invest in territorial organization, which in turn enhanced their long-term durability. By contrast, parties that emerged under democracy (e.g., Argentina's FREPASO) could substitute mass media appeals for organization-building, which left them vulnerable to collapse. Loxton's chapter also links successful party-building to authoritarianism, albeit in a different way. He shows how conservative parties that built upon the brands, organizations, clientelist networks, and business ties inherited from previous dictatorships (e.g., Chile's UDI, El Salvador's ARENA) were more likely to succeed than conservative parties with stronger democratic credentials (e.g., Argentina's UCEDE, Guatemala's PAN). Thus, although strong parties may be critical for democracy, many of them, paradoxically, find their roots in periods of authoritarian rule.

At the same time, authoritarianism may also inhibit party-building (Mainwaring 1999; Mustillo 2007; Lupu and Stokes 2010). Greene's chapter highlights the *costs* of building parties under authoritarian rule. He argues that opposition parties with virtually no possibility of winning elections – such as the PRD and National Action Party (PAN) under PRI rule in Mexico – tend to attract mainly diehard ideologues, since pragmatists interested in advancing their careers are likely to join the dominant party. As a result, they evolve into what he calls "niche parties," which are characterized by ideological extremism and high barriers to entry for new members. Niche parties are well suited to survive under the hardships of authoritarianism. However, Greene argues that their organizational "birth defects" tend to persist and shape their behavior after democratization in ways that are detrimental to their electoral prospects. Thus, rather than targeting the median voter, niche parties such as Mexico's PRD tend to remain at the ideological extremes, thereby limiting their capacity to win elections.

Greene and Van Dyck's arguments may be more complementary than they initially appear. Origins under authoritarianism may simultaneously hinder parties' electoral performance *and* contribute to their long-term survival. It may be true that parties born under authoritarianism are more ideologically extreme, and as Greene shows, such niche orientations often persist after democratization. Both Mexico's PRD and Brazil's PT were slow to adopt vote-maximizing strategies after democratization, which contributed to successive electoral defeats. Yet an ideological activist base may also benefit new parties. Committed cadres are often more willing to make the sacrifices necessary to build a robust territorial organization and, crucially, are more likely to "stick it out" during hard times. Thus, niche origins may have left the PT and PRD better positioned to take root and survive over the long term (and in the case of the PT, eventually win national office). For Van Dyck, then, the PRD should be viewed as a case of successful party-building. While its niche orientation contributed to a series of electoral setbacks, the party's activist-based organization also enabled it to survive those setbacks. Indeed, although the PRD failed to win the presidency through 2012, it was one of the few new left parties to take root in Latin America during the third wave.

Party-Building and the State: A Double-Edged Sword?

As Martin Shefter's (1977, 1994) seminal work showed, the state can have a powerful impact on party-building.[52] Both the relationship of parties to the state and the character of the state itself may affect politicians' incentives and capacity to invest in party organization. Yet, as the chapters in this volume make clear, the state's effects on party-building are decidedly double-edged.

On the one hand, the state has long been a key resource for Latin American party organizations.[53] Maintaining a territorial organization is costly, and most Latin American parties' access to private sources of finance such as business has historically been limited (Gibson 1996: 216–220; Schneider 2010). Thus, the activists and cadres who compose parties' grassroots organizations in the region have often been compensated with public sector jobs or access to other state resources (Morgan 2011; Grindle 2012; Gingerich 2013).[54] Indeed, as Domínguez reminds us in the Conclusion, nearly all of Latin America's most successful and enduring parties were (or evolved into) patronage-based machines. The chapter by Muñoz and Dargent highlights the degree to which party organization in Colombia and Peru had traditionally depended on patronage resources.

---

[52] On the state and party-building, see also Zolberg (1966), Mainwaring (1999), Hale (2006), Mainwaring (1999), and Slater (2010).

[53] See, for example, Hagopian (1996), Mainwaring (1999), Greene (2007), Mustillo (2007), Dargent and Muñoz (2011), Morgan (2011), Morgan et al. (2011), Grindle (2012), and Gingerich (2013).

[54] On how state corruption may be used to sustain party organizations, see Gingerich (2013).

In both countries, political reforms that limited national politicians' capacity to distribute patronage resources not only weakened existing parties, but also inhibited subsequent party-building efforts.[55]

Holland's chapter also highlights how the state may contribute to party-building. In the case of El Salvador, she argues that election to local office facilitated the FMLN's successful transition from guerrilla movement to party during the 1990s. Governing at the local level helped the FMLN to strengthen its organization (by providing career opportunities for cadres) and to establish a reputation for good governance. In contrast, Holland attributes the failure of Colombia's AD M-19 to the fact that it never seriously pursued subnational office.

State resources may remain central to party-building even if economic liberalization and state reform ultimately limit Latin American politicians' ability to deploy patronage resources for partisan ends.[56] In some cases, for example, public finance has emerged as a key alternative type of state resource. As Bruhn's chapter shows, public financing played a major role in sustaining Mexican party organizations beginning in the late 1990s (perhaps contributing to the PRD's consolidation), and it appears to have strengthened party organizations in Brazil (Samuels and Zucco, Chapter 12, this volume).

On the other hand, access to the state also has clear negative consequences for party-building. Politicians who hold major office can use the state as a "substitute" for parties (Hale 2006). Instead of making costly investments in organization-building, such politicians can use public resources to fund their campaigns and deploy government workers to do their campaign work (Hale 2006; Van Dyck, Chapter 5, this volume). In short, access to the state weakens politicians' incentive to construct the kind of grassroots organization that facilitates long-term party survival. Thus, although state resources may provide a useful electoral shortcut, they ultimately result in weaker organizations and less durable parties. Indeed, as Van Dyck's chapter shows, it was the new left parties that lacked access to the state during their formative periods, such as the PT and the Mexican PRD, which built the most durable grassroots organizations in third wave Latin America.[57]

---

[55] Morgan (2011) makes a similar argument about party collapse in Venezuela.
[56] See Greene (2007) and Hagopian et al. (2009). For more skeptical views on the decline of patronage, see Levitsky (2003), Grindle (2012), and Gingerich (2013).
[57] Similarly, Tavits' study of postcommunist parties found that organization-building was most likely among parties that were "left out of government" (2013: 155–156).

A second, less studied way in which the state may affect party-building is through its impact on governance. As Mainwaring (2006) has argued, state capacity has a powerful impact on government performance, which in turn affects governing parties' electoral performance. Where states are weak, as in much of the Andean region, government performance invariably suffers. Limited tax capacity means less revenue to spend on health care, education, infrastructure, social policy, and other public services; weak state bureaucracies yield public services that are plagued by uneven coverage, inefficiency, and corruption; and ineffective justice systems and police forces result in widespread perceptions of impunity and insecurity. Under conditions of state weakness, then, it is difficult for *any* party to govern effectively. When governments repeatedly fail to deliver the goods, the result is often a crisis of political representation, characterized by widespread voter rejection of established parties (Mainwaring 2006). It is very difficult to build a successful new party under such circumstances.

Thus, where states are weak, as in much of Central America and the Andes, new parties are more likely to fail. During the contemporary era, governing took a devastating toll on new parties such as the ID and the Ecuadorian Roldosista Party (PRE); ADN in Bolivia; Possible Peru (PP) and the Peruvian Nationalist Party (PNP) in Peru; and the Guatemalan Republican Front (FRG) and PAN in Guatemala. In each of these cases, weak states contributed to widespread perceptions of corruption and/or ineffective government performance, which eroded public support and contributed to party-building failure.

Party-building is more likely to succeed where state capacity is high. Where states possess a minimum level of tax capacity and bureaucratic effectiveness, parties that win public office have an opportunity to govern well and carry out policies that strengthen their brands. Indeed, seven of the eleven new parties that took root in Latin America after the onset of the third wave did so in countries with relatively effective states: Chile, Brazil, and Mexico.

The Role of Party Leaders

Dominant personalities and charismatic leaders are widely viewed as inimical to party-building (Mainwaring and Scully 1995; Weyland 1996, 1999). Politicians who mobilize support based on personalistic appeals are often reluctant to invest in party structures that could limit their power and autonomy. Moreover, because such appeals tend to be non-programmatic, personalistic parties and campaigns are generally viewed as unfavorable for partisan brand development. Indeed, Latin American history offers numerous examples of personalistic leaders who abandoned, destroyed, or seriously weakened their own parties.

Yet scholars have paid insufficient attention to the ways in which leaders may contribute to party-building. Popular or charismatic leaders can strengthen new parties in at least two ways. First, they win votes. As Samuels and Shugart (2010) have shown, presidential systems compel parties to nominate politicians with broad popular appeal. Parties without viable presidential candidates rarely become electorally competitive, and noncompetitive parties rarely endure. In Latin America, which is uniformly presidentialist, founding leaders or leading presidential candidates have often played a decisive role in getting new parties off the ground by making them electorally viable.[58] In extreme cases, dominant personalities lay the basis for an enduring partisan brand, as in the cases of Peronism, *Fujimorismo*, and *Chavismo*. Yet even in the case of more institutionalized parties such as Popular Action (AP) and APRA in Peru; the PLN in Costa Rica; AD and the Independent Electoral Political Organization Committee (COPEI) in Venezuela; the PRD and Dominican Liberation Party (PLD) in the Dominican Republic; and, more recently, ARENA, the PT, the PSDB, and Mexico's PRD, founding leaders played an indispensable role in early efforts to mobilize popular support.

Individual leaders may also act as a source of party cohesion. As Van Dyck (2014b) argues, party leaders who combine external appeal and internal dominance may help bind new parties together during the critical formative period. Party founders with undisputed internal authority, such as Víctor Raúl Haya de la Torre in APRA, Lula in the PT, Roberto D'Aubuisson in ARENA, Jaime Guzmán in the UDI, and Cuauhtémoc Cárdenas in the Mexican PRD, were able to adjudicate conflict within their parties, as their word was effectively law. In such cases, the leader's external electoral appeal further reduced the likelihood of schism, as the prospect of competing without the leader's coattails discouraged other party elites from defecting. In effect, then, charismatic leaders may substitute for established partisan brands and institutional mechanisms of dispute resolution during parties' formative periods (Van Dyck 2014b).

Most theories of party-building downplay the role of leaders. Political scientists often avoid placing individual leaders at the center of their analyses for fear of excessive voluntarism. In presidential democracies, however, the electoral appeal of individual leaders can be a crucial means of mobilizing the support necessary for new parties to take off. Popular leaders hardly ensure party institutionalization; in fact, they often hinder it. But

---

[58] Dix (1989) makes a similar point.

without a popular leader at the top of the ticket, new parties are unlikely to take off in presidential democracies, making long-term success unlikely.

The Paradox of Populism

Populism, in which personalistic outsiders use plebiscitary means to mobilize mass electorates against the entire political and/or economic elite,[59] is also widely viewed as inimical to party-building (Hawkins 2010; Mainwaring and Scully 1995; Weyland 1996, 1999). Populists often adopt an explicitly antiparty appeal (Barr 2009; Weyland 1996, 1999). As presidential candidates, for example, Argentina's Perón, Peru's Fujimori, Venezuela's Chávez, and Ecuador's Correa attacked established parties as corrupt and unrepresentative entities that stood in the way of "true" or "authentic" democracy, and in power took steps to weaken existing parties. Moreover, populists tend not to invest in building strong parties, preferring personalistic vehicles instead. Perón, Fujimori, Chávez, and Correa relied heavily on personalistic and plebiscitary appeals, and at times circumvented, undermined, or discarded their own parties.

Yet if populists weaken parties in the short run, they may – however indirectly and unintentionally – strengthen them in the long run. Successful populism almost invariably polarizes societies, and in many cases, it generates sustained social and political conflict.[60] Successful populists such as Perón, Haya de la Torre, Fujimori, and Chávez earned intense support among large (usually lower-income) sectors of society, while at the same time triggering the intense opposition of other (usually middle- and high-income) sectors (de la Torre 2000; Hawkins 2010). In Argentina, Peru, and more recently Venezuela, the result was intense, prolonged, and sometimes violent polarization between populist and antipopulist movements that eventually created the bases for strong partisan identities and organizations.[61]

Thus, although populist experiences do not immediately give rise to strong parties, they may create the raw materials for party-building in the future. Intense polarization between populist and antipopulist forces tends to produce clear (if personalized) brands, powerful partisan identities and subcultures, and large activist bases that, even if initially organized as loosely structured "movements," may eventually form the basis for mass

---

[59] This definition draws on Barr (2009) and Levitsky and Loxton (2013).
[60] See James (1988), Collier and Collier (1991), de la Torre (2000), and Hawkins (2010).
[61] On the case of Argentine Peronism, see James (1988), McGuire (1997), Levitsky (2003), and Ostiguy (2009b).

party organizations. This process clearly occurred in the case of Peronism, is likely to occur in the case of *Chavismo*, and may be occurring in the case of *Fujimorismo* (Levitsky and Zavaleta, Chapter 15, this volume).

The volume is organized as follows. Part I presents three perspectives on the development of party–voter linkages and party brands in contemporary Latin America. Chapter 2, by Kenneth M. Roberts, examines how the neoliberal critical juncture of the 1980s and 1990s reshaped the axes of party system competition and, consequently, opportunities for party-building in the region. Roberts finds that because of the dramatic region-wide shift toward market-oriented policies during this period, and the pressures that this put on left-leaning parties in office to engage in "bait-and-switch" tactics to implement such policies, one of the keys to success for new left parties, paradoxically, was losing elections and remaining in the opposition. Chapter 3, by Noam Lupu, introduces a new theory of party brand development that focuses on the centrality of programmatic differentiation and consistency. It then applies this theory to the cases of FREPASO in Argentina and the PT in Brazil in the 1990s and 2000s, showing why brand development failed in the former but succeeded in the latter. Chapter 4, by Juan Pablo Luna, argues that in the context of high levels of inequality and social fragmentation, successful parties must appeal to diverse socioeconomic groups through what he calls "segmented, harmonized linkages," whereby they simultaneously employ a range of programmatic, clientelistic, and symbolic appeals.

Part II examines challenges of organization-building in contemporary Latin America, focusing on the role of the state and political regimes. Chapter 5, by Brandon Van Dyck, argues that, paradoxically, in third wave Latin America, successful new left parties were more likely to emerge in adverse, authoritarian contexts than under stable democracy. Left parties born under authoritarianism lacked regular access to the media and the state during their formative periods and thus had incentives to build strong organizations, which increased the likelihood of long-term party survival. Chapter 6, by Kenneth F. Greene, examines the flipside of being born under conditions of adversity. Greene argues that parties born in opposition to dominant party regimes (e.g., the Mexican PRD) tend to become ideologically extreme "niche parties" that have difficulty appealing to electoral majorities after democratization. Chapter 7, by Paula Muñoz and Eduardo Dargent, highlights the continued importance of patronage resources in Latin America. The chapter shows how political reforms that limited party leaders' access to patronage in Colombia and Peru not only weakened old party organizations, but also hindered the construction of new ones. Chapter 8, by Kathleen Bruhn, examines the impact of public financing, offering some initial evidence that generous public financing – as exists in Brazil and Mexico – may help new party organizations consolidate.

Part III examines the role of organizational inheritance. Chapter 9, by James Loxton, focuses on authoritarian successor parties. Drawing on an analysis of new conservative parties in Chile and El Salvador, Loxton argues that new parties that inherit brands, organizations, and other resources from outgoing dictatorships are more likely to succeed than ideologically similar parties of more democratic origin. Chapter 10, by Alisha C. Holland, examines insurgent successor parties in Colombia and El Salvador. Holland argues that such parties were more likely to take root when they used their inherited resources to capture local office, since this allowed them to consolidate their organizations and build a reputation for good governance. Chapter 11, by Raúl L. Madrid, looks at the obstacles to ethnic party-building in Latin America. Madrid argues that limited resources and fluid ethnic identities make ethnic party-building difficult, but that ethnic parties are most likely to succeed when they inherit the organization of preexisting indigenous movements and make inclusive appeals that he calls "ethnopopulism." Chapter 12, by David Samuels and Cesar Zucco Jr., examines the success of the PT in Brazil in forging large numbers of partisan identifiers, and argues that one of reasons for the party's success in this area was its strategy of recruiting civil society activists and opening branches in areas of high NGO density. Chapter 13, by William T. Barndt, examines the increasingly widespread phenomenon of corporation-based parties, or parties that are built upon the finance, infrastructure, and brand of large private firms.

Part IV examines two failed cases of party-building and one prospective case. Chapter 14, by Kent Eaton, examines the failure of Bolivia's eastern autonomy movement to produce a viable conservative party in the 2000s. Eaton's explanation focuses on the Morales government's successful wooing of eastern economic elites and the decline of the Pro-Santa Cruz Committee (CPSC), the once powerful civil society organization that might have served as the backbone of such a party. Chapter 15, by Steven Levitsky and Mauricio Zavaleta, asks why no successful party-building has occurred in post-Fujimori Peru. The chapter argues that party system collapse had a path-dependent effect, whereby politicians learned how to win elections without parties and developed a set of informal institutions that effectively substituted for party organization. Chapter 16, by Jorge I. Domínguez, examines party-building scenarios in a hypothetical posttransition Cuba. Domínguez argues that party-building outcomes are likely to be heavily shaped by the fate of the Communist Party of Cuba (PCC) and the character of the transition itself.

The Conclusion, also by Domínguez, places the volume's chapters in historical perspective by reexamining the sources of success and failure in earlier generations of Latin American parties.

Appendix I

New Parties Formed in Latin America, 1978–2005[1]

Outcomes	Number of cases
Successful[2]	11
Unsuccessful	244
Flop[3]	202
Marginal[4]	20
Flash[5]	20
Personalistic[6]	2
Incomplete	52
Successful[7]	12
Marginal[8]	40
Total	307

[1] We include all parties created between January 1, 1978 and December 31, 2005 that received at least 1 percent of the vote, by themselves or in coalition, in at least one national legislative election. Parties must be national in orientation, competing for seats in more than one province. We include parties created via schisms from preexisting parties, as well as new parties created via the fusion of two or more preexisting parties. However, we exclude preexisting parties that changed their name between 1978 and 2005 but otherwise remained intact (e.g., Brazil's Democratic Social Party [PDS], formerly the National Renewal Alliance [ARENA]), as well as preexisting parties that divided into two parties but reunited between 1978 and 2005 (e.g., the Chilean Socialist Party). A party's birth year is the year of its creation, not the year legal status was granted. In a few cases in which we could not obtain information about the birth year, we use the first year the party competed in elections. Cuba is excluded.

[2] A party is scored as successful if it wins at least 10 percent of the vote in five or more consecutive national legislative elections *and* survives after its founding leader has ceased to be a viable presidential contender (due to death, forced or voluntary retirement, or abandonment of the party). Elections must be held at least two years apart from one another.

If two legislative elections are held within two years of one another (e.g., Guatemala 1994 and 1995, Peru in 2000 and 2001), both elections count, but parties must win 10 percent or more of the vote in at least *six* consecutive elections to be scored as successful. A party must receive 10 percent or more on its own in at least one national legislative election; once it has done so, subsequent elections in which it participates in alliances that win at least 10 percent of the vote are treated as meeting the 10-percent threshold.

3 A party is scored as a flop if, either by itself or in coalition, it wins between 1 percent and 10 percent of the vote in at least one national legislative election but subsequently dissolves, merges into another party, or falls below 1 percent of the vote prior to reaching five consecutive national elections. We borrow the term "flop" from Mustillo (2009).

4 A party is scored as marginal if, either by itself or in coalition, it wins between 1 percent and 10 percent of the vote in five or more consecutive national legislative elections *or*, over the course of five consecutive elections, it wins between 1 percent and 10 percent, falls below 1 percent, and then returns to between 1 percent and 10 percent. Elections must be held at least two years apart from one another. If two legislative elections are held within two years of one another, both elections count, but parties must win 1 percent or more of the vote in at least *six* consecutive elections to be scored as marginal.

5 A party is scored as a flash party if it wins 10 percent or more of the vote in at least one but fewer than five consecutive national legislative elections, and then falls permanently below the 10-percent threshold.

6 A party is scored as unsuccessful (personalistic) if it wins at least 10 percent of the vote in five consecutive national legislative elections, but then collapses or becomes marginal soon after its founding leader has ceased to be a viable presidential contender (due to death, forced or voluntary retirement, or abandonment of the party).

7 A party is scored as incomplete (successful) if it has won at least 10 percent of the vote in one or more consecutive national legislative elections, including the most recent one, but has not yet reached the five-election threshold.

8 A party is scored as incomplete (marginal) if, by itself or in coalition, it has won at least 1 percent of the vote in one or more consecutive national legislative elections, including the most recent one, but has not yet competed in five consecutive elections.

Argentina

Party	Birth	Outcome
Unión del Centro Democrático (UCEDE)	1982	Unsuccessful (flop)
Movimiento al Socialismo (MAS)	1982	Unsuccessful (flop)
Partido Humanista (PH)	1984	Unsuccessful (marginal)
Partido Blanco de los Jubilados (PBJ)	1987	Unsuccessful (flop)
Fuerza Republicana (FR)	1988	Unsuccessful (flop)
Movimiento por la Dignidad y la Independencia (MODIN)	1990	Unsuccessful (flop)
Frente Grande (FG)	1993	Unsuccessful (flop)
Frente País Solidario (FREPASO)	1994	Unsuccessful (flash)
Política Abierta para la Integridad Social (PAIS)	1995	Unsuccessful (marginal)
Nueva Dirigencia (ND)	1996	Unsuccessful (flop)
Acción por la República (AR)	1997	Unsuccessful (flash)
Izquierda Unida (IU)	1997	Unsuccessful (flop)
Partido Unidad Federalista (PAUFE)	1999	Unsuccessful (flop)
Afirmación para una República Igualitaria (ARI)	2001	Unsuccessful (marginal)

Party	Birth	Outcome
Polo Social	2001	Unsuccessful (flop)
Autodeterminación y Libertad (AyL)	2001	Unsuccessful (marginal)
Recrear para el Crecimiento (Recrear)	2002	Unsuccessful (flop)
Propuesta Republicana (PRO)	2005	Incomplete (marginal)

Bolivia

Party	Birth	Outcome
Ofensiva de la Izquierda Democrática (OID)	1978	Unsuccessful (flop)
Movimiento de Izquierda Nacional (MIN)	1978	Unsuccessful (flop)
Frente Revolucionario de Izquierda (FRI)	1978	Unsuccessful (flop)
Partido Barrientista Revolucionario (PRB)	1978	Unsuccessful (flop)
Partido de Vanguardia Obrera (VO)	1978	Unsuccessful (flop)
Movimiento Indio Túpac Katari (MITKA)	1978	Unsuccessful (flop)
Partido Socialista-1 (PS-1)	1979	Unsuccessful (flop)
Acción Democrática Nacionalista (ADN)	1979	Unsuccessful (personalistic)[1]
Movimiento Indio Túpac Katari-1 (MITKA-1)	1980	Unsuccessful (flop)
Alianza de Fuerzas de la Izquierda Nacional del MNR (AFIN-MNR)	1980	Unsuccessful (flop)
Movimiento Nacionalista Revolucionario Unido (MNRU)	1980	Unsuccessful (flop)
Movimiento Revolucionario Túpac Katari de Liberación (MRTKL)	1985	Unsuccessful (flop)
Frente del Pueblo Unido (FPU)	1985	Unsuccessful (flop)
Movimiento Bolivia Libre (MBL)	1985	Unsuccessful (flop)
Conciencia de Patria (CONDEPA)	1988	Unsuccessful (flash)
Frente Unido de Liberación Katarista (FULKA)	1989	Unsuccessful (flop)
Izquierda Unida (IU)	1989	Unsuccessful (flop)
Unidad Cívica Solidaridad (UCS)	1989	Unsuccessful (flash)
Eje del Acuerdo Patriótico (EAP)	1993	Unsuccessful (flop)
Vanguardia Revolucionaria 9 de Abril (VR-9A)	1989	Unsuccessful (flop)
Alternativa del Socialismo Democrático (ASD)	1993	Unsuccessful (flop)
Alianza Renovadora Boliviana (ARB)	1993	Unsuccessful (flop)
Nueva Fuerza Republicana (NFR)	1995	Unsuccessful (flop)
Movimiento al Socialismo (MAS)	1995	Incomplete (successful)
Vanguardia Socialista de Bolivia (VSB)	1997	Unsuccessful (flop)
Movimiento Indígena Pachakuti (MIP)	2000	Unsuccessful (flop)
Partido Libertad y Justicia (PLJ)	2002	Unsuccessful (flop)
Frente de Unidad Nacional (FUN)	2003	Incomplete (marginal)
Alianza Social (AS)	2005	Unsuccessful (flop)

[1] ADN won at least 10 percent of the vote for more than five consecutive national legislative elections, but collapsed after the death of its founder, Hugo Banzer, in 2002.

Brazil

Party	Birth	Outcome
Partido Democrático Trabalhista (PDT)	1979	Unsuccessful (marginal)
Partido dos Trabalhadores (PT)	1980	Successful
Partido Trabalhista Brasileiro (PTB)	1981	Unsuccessful (marginal)
Partido Liberal (PL)	1985	Unsuccessful (flop)
Partido da Frente Liberal/Democratas (PFL/DEM)	1985	Successful
Partido Verde (PV)	1986	Incomplete (marginal)[1]
Partido da Social Democracia Brasileira (PSDB)	1988	Successful
Partido da Reconstrução Nacional (PRN)	1989	Unsuccessful (flop)
Partido Trabalhista Renovadora (PTR)	1990	Unsuccessful (flop)
Partido de Reedificação da Ordem Nacional (PRONA)	1990	Unsuccessful (flop)
Partido Progressista Reformador (PPR)	1993	Unsuccessful (flop)
Partido Progressista (PP)	1993	Incomplete (marginal)
Partido Progressista/Partido Progressista Brasileiro (PP/PPB)[2]	1995	Unsuccessful (marginal)
Partido Social Cristão (PSC)	2002	Unsuccessful (flop)
Partido Socialismo e Liberdade (PSOL)	2004	Incomplete (marginal)

[1] Although the PV formed in 1986, it did not cross the 1-percent threshold until the 2002 general election. Thus, we score the PV as incomplete (marginal).
[2] The PPB formed in 1995 as a merger of the PP and PPR (both est. 1993). In 2003, the PPB changed its name to PP.

Chile

Party	Birth	Outcome
Unión Demócrata Independiente (UDI)	1983	Successful
Partido Humanista (PH)	1984	Unsuccessful (marginal)
Renovación Nacional (RN)	1987	Successful
Partido por la Democracia (PPD)	1987	Successful
Unión de Centro Centro (UCC)	1990	Unsuccessful (flop)
Alianza Nacional de los Independientes (ANI)	2002	Unsuccessful (flop)
Partido de Acción Regionalista (PAR)	2003	Unsuccessful (flop)

Colombia

Party	Birth	Outcome
Frente por la Unidad del Pueblo (FUP)	1978	Unsuccessful (flop)
Nuevo Liberalismo (NL)	1979	Unsuccessful (flash)

Party	Birth	Outcome
Frente Democrático (FD)	1982	Unsuccessful (flop)
Unión Patriótica (UP)	1985	Unsuccessful (flop)
Movimiento Nacional Conservador (MNC)	1986	Unsuccessful (flop)
Frente Popular (FP)	1991	Unsuccessful (flop)
Alianza Democrática Movimiento 19 de Abril (AD M-19)	1990	Unsuccessful (flash)
Movimiento Unión Cristiana (MUC)	1991	Unsuccessful (flop)
Movimiento de Salvación Nacional (MSN)	1991	Unsuccessful (flop)
Laicos por Colombia (LC)	1991	Unsuccessful (flop)
Alianza Social Indígena/Alianza Social Independiente (ASI)	1991	Incomplete (marginal)[1]
Compromiso Cívico y Cristiano por la Comunidad (C4)	1994	Unsuccessful (flop)
Fuerza Progresista (FP)	1994	Unsuccessful (flop)
Movimiento Comunal y Comunitario (MCC)	1997	Unsuccessful (flop)
Movimiento Cívico Seriedad por Colombia (MCSC)	1998	Unsuccessful (flop)
Movimiento Ciudadano (MC)	1998	Unsuccessful (flop)
Convergencia Popular Cívica (CPC)	1998	Unsuccessful (flop)
Nueva Fuerza Democrática (NFD)	1998	Unsuccessful (flop)
Cambio Radical (CR)	1998	Unsuccessful (marginal)
Movimiento Independiente de Renovación Absoluta (MIRA)	2000	Incomplete (marginal)
Movimiento Unionista (MU)	2002	Unsuccessful (flop)
Movimiento Voluntad Popular (MVP)	2002	Unsuccessful (flop)
Convergencia Ciudadana (CC)	2002	Unsuccessful (flop)
Movimiento Integración Regional (MIR)	2002	Unsuccessful (flop)
Movimiento Integración Popular (MIP)	2002	Unsuccessful (flop)
Movimiento Nacional (MN)	2002	Unsuccessful (flop)
Nuevo Liberalismo (NL)	2002	Unsuccessful (flop)
Movimiento de Renovación Acción Laboral (MRAL)	2002	Unsuccessful (flop)
Movimiento de Participación Popular (MPP)	2002	Unsuccessful (flop)
Movimiento Progresismo Democrático (MPD)	2002	Unsuccessful (flop)
Movimiento Popular Unido (MPU)	2002	Unsuccessful (flop)
Colombia Siempre (CS)	2002	Unsuccessful (flop)
Equipo Colombia (EC)	2002	Unsuccessful (flop)
Apertura Liberal (AL)	2002	Unsuccessful (flop)
Por el País que Soñamos (PPS)	2002	Unsuccessful (flop)
Partido Colombia Democrática (PCD)	2003	Unsuccessful (flop)
Polo Democrático Alternativo (PDA)	2005	Incomplete (marginal)
Partido Social de Unidad Nacional (PSUN/Partido de la U)	2005	Incomplete (successful)
Partido Verde (PV)	2005	Incomplete (marginal)

[1] Although the ASI was formed in 1991, it did not cross the 1-percent threshold until the 2010 general election. Thus, we score the ASI as incomplete (marginal).

Costa Rica

Party	Birth	Outcome
Pueblo Unido (PU)	1978	Unsuccessful (flop)
Partido Acción Democrática Alajuelense/ Alianza Patriótica (PADA/AP)	1978	Unsuccessful (marginal)
Partido Alianza Nacional Cristiana (PANC)	1981	Unsuccessful (flop)
Movimiento Independiente Nacional (MIN)	1982	Unsuccessful (flop)
Partido Nacional Democrático (PND)	1982	Unsuccessful (flop)
Partido Acción Laborista Agrícola (PALA)	1990	Unsuccessful (flop)
Fuerza Democrática (FD)	1992	Unsuccessful (flop)
Movimiento Libertario (ML)	1994	Incomplete (marginal)
Partido de Integración Nacional (PIN)	1995	Unsuccessful (flop)
Partido Renovación Costarricense (PRC)	1995	Incomplete (marginal)
Partido Demócrata (PD)	1997	Unsuccessful (flop)
Partido Acción Ciudadana (PAC)	2000	Incomplete (successful)
Frente Amplio (FA)	2004	Incomplete (successful)
Restauración Nacional (RN)	2004	Incomplete (marginal)
Partido Accesibilidad sin Exclusión (PASE)	2004	Incomplete (marginal)
Patria Primero (PP)	2005	Unsuccessful (flop)

Dominican Republic

Party	Birth	Outcome
Unidad Democrática (UD)	1978	Unsuccessful (flop)
Partido de Trabajadores Dominicanos (PTD)	1980	Unsuccessful (flop)
Fuerza Nacional Progresista (FNP)	1980	Unsuccessful (flop)
Partido Acción Constitucional (PAC)	1982	Unsuccessful (flop)
Partido Popular Cristiano (PPC)	1982	Unsuccessful (flop)
Partido del Pueblo Dominicano (PPD)	1984	Unsuccessful (flop)
Partido Revolucionario Independiente (PRI)	1985	Unsuccessful (flop)
Partido Demócrata Institucional (PDI)	1986	Unsuccessful (flop)
Bloque Institucional Social Demócrata (BIS)	1989	Unsuccessful (flop)
Alianza Social Dominicana (ASD)	1991	Unsuccessful (flop)
Alianza por la Democracia (APD)	1992	Unsuccessful (flop)
Partido Renacentista Nacional (PRN)	1994	Unsuccessful (flop)
Partido de Unidad Nacional (PUN)	2001	Unsuccessful (flop)
Partido Revolucionario Social Demócrata (PRSD)	2004	Unsuccessful (flop)

Ecuador

Party	Birth	Outcome
Movimiento Popular Democrático (MPD)	1978	Unsuccessful (flop)
Izquierda Democrática (ID)	1978	Unsuccessful (flop)

Party	Birth	Outcome
Partido Demócrata (PD)	1978	Unsuccessful (flop)
Pueblo Cambio y Democracia (PCD)	1980	Unsuccessful (flop)
Partido Roldosista Ecuatoriana (PRE)	1982	Unsuccessful (personalistic)[1]
Coalición Nacional Republicana (CNR)	1984	Unsuccessful (flop)
Liberación Nacional (LN)	1989	Unsuccessful (flop)
Movimiento Unidad Plurinacional Pachakutik – Nuevo País (MUPP-NP)[2]	1995	Unsuccessful (flop)
Movimiento Independiente Liberación Provincial (MILP)	1998	Unsuccessful (flop)
Movimiento Ciudadana Nuevo País (MCNP)	1998	Unsuccessful (flop)
Cambio y Dignidad (CD)	1998	Unsuccessful (flop)
Movimientos Sociales Independientes (MSI)	1998	Unsuccessful (flop)
Acuerdo Provincia por Nuevo País (APNP)	1998	Unsuccessful (flop)
Gente Nueva (GN)	1998	Unsuccessful (flop)
Partido de Libertad (PL)	2001	Unsuccessful (flop)
Movimiento Patria en Solidaridad (MPS)	2002	Unsuccessful (flop)
Movimiento Integración Provincial (MIP)	2002	Unsuccessful (flop)
Transformación Democrática (TD)	2002	Unsuccessful (flop)
Partido Sociedad Patriótica 21 de Enero (PSP)	2002	Incomplete (marginal)
Partido Renovador Institucional Acción Nacional (PRIAN)	2002	Incomplete (marginal)

[1] The PRE was the personalistic vehicle of Abdalá Bucaram (Freidenberg 2003), who was removed from the presidency for reasons of "mental incapacity" in 1997 and subsequently went into exile in Panama. The PRE remained above 10 percent of the vote through the 2002 election, as Bucaram promised his imminent return to Ecuador. However, following his abortive return to Ecuador in 2005, and after being refused amnesty on multiple occasions, the likelihood of Bucaram returning to Ecuador and seriously contending for the presidency became exceedingly slim. He ceased to be a significant political actor after 2006, and as a result, the PRE declined into marginality. Given the PRE's failure to remain viable after its leader's political exit, we score it as unsuccessful (personalistic).

[2] Often called simply "Pachakutik."

El Salvador

Party	Birth	Outcome
Alianza Republicana Nacionalista (ARENA)	1981	Successful
Acción Democrática (AD)	1981	Unsuccessful (flop)
Partido de Orientación Popular (POP)	1981	Unsuccessful (flop)
Partido Auténtico Institucional Salvadoreño (PAISA)	1982	Unsuccessful (flop)
Partido Liberación (PL)	1985	Unsuccessful (flop)
Convergencia Democrática (CD)	1987	Unsuccessful (flash)
Movimiento Auténtico Cristiano (MAC)	1988	Unsuccessful (flop)
Frente Farabundo Martí para la Liberación Nacional (FMLN)	1992	Successful

(*continued*)

Party	Birth	Outcome
Movimiento de la Unidad (MU)	1993	Unsuccessful (flop)
Partido Renovador Social Cristiano (PRSC)	1994	Unsuccessful (flop)
Partido Liberal Democrático (PLD)	1994	Unsuccessful (flop)
Partido Demócrata (PD)	1995	Unsuccessful (flop)
Partido Unión Social Cristiana (USC)	1997	Unsuccessful (flop)
Centro Democrático Unido (CDU)	1998	Unsuccessful (flop)
Partido Popular Republicano (PPR)	2001	Unsuccessful (flop)
Movimiento Renovador (MR)	2002	Unsuccessful (flop)
Fuerza Cristiana (FC)	2002	Unsuccessful (flop)
Acción Popular (AP)	2003	Unsuccessful (flop)
Cambio Democrático (CD)	2005	Incomplete (marginal)

Guatemala

Party	Birth	Outcome
Partido Nacional Renovador (PNR)	1978	Unsuccessful (flop)
Partido Socialista Democrático (PSD)	1978	Unsuccessful (flop)
Movimiento Emergente de Concordancia (MEC)	1982	Unsuccessful (flop)
Partido Democrático de Cooperación Nacional (PDCN)	1983	Unsuccessful (flop)
Unión del Centro Nacional/Unión del Cambio Nacionalista (UCN)	1984	Unsuccessful (flash)
Acción Democrática (AD)	1984	Unsuccessful (flop)
Frente Cívico Democrático (FCD)	1984	Unsuccessful (flop)
Movimiento de Acción Solidaria (MAS)	1986	Unsuccessful (flash)
Partido de Avanzada Nacional (PAN)	1989	Unsuccessful (flash)
Frente Republicano Guatemalteco (FRG)	1989	Unsuccessful (flash)
Alianza Popular Cinco (AP-5)	1990	Unsuccessful (flop)
Partido Reformador Guatemalteco (PREG)	1991	Unsuccessful (flop)
Unión Democrática (UD)	1993	Unsuccessful (flop)
Desarrollo Integral Auténtico (DIA)	1993	Unsuccessful (flop)
Partido Progresivo (PP)	1994	Unsuccessful (flop)
Partido Libertador Progresista (PLP)	1994	Unsuccessful (flop)
Frente Democrático Nueva Guatemala (FDNG)	1995	Unsuccessful (flop)
La Organización Verde (LOV)[1]	1995	Unsuccessful (flop)
Movimiento Reformador (MR)[2]	1995	Unsuccessful (flop)
Unidad Revolucionaria Nacional Guatemalteca (URNG)	1998	Incomplete (marginal)
Movimiento Principios y Valores (MPV)[3]	1999	Unsuccessful (flop)

Party	Birth	Outcome
Partido Patriota (PP)	2001	Incomplete (successful)
Unidad Nacional de Esperanza (UNE)	2002	Incomplete (successful)
Partido Unionista (PU)	2002	Incomplete (marginal)
Gran Alianza Nacional (GANA)[4]	2002	Incomplete (successful)
Alianza Nueva Nación/Alternativa Nueva Nación (ANN)	2003	Incomplete (marginal)
Democracia Social Participativa (DSP)	2003	Unsuccessful (flop)
Transparencia	2003	Unsuccessful (flop)
Centro de Acción Social (CASA)	2003	Unsuccessful (flop)

[1] Formerly the Unión Reformista Social.
[2] Formerly the Partido Laborista Guatemalteco.
[3] Formerly Acción Reconciliadora Democrática.
[4] Formerly the Partido Solidaridad Nacional (PSN). In 2003, the PSN, along with the PP and the MR, formed a coalition called GANA. The PP and the MR subsequently left the coalition, and in 2005 the PSN – the only remaining member – renamed itself GANA.

Honduras

Party	Birth	Outcome
Partido Unificación Democrática (PUD)	1992	Unsuccessful (marginal)

Mexico

Party	Birth	Outcome
Partido Demócrata Mexicano	1979	Unsuccessful (flop)
Partido Socialista Unificado de México (PSUM)	1982	Unsuccessful (flop)
Partido Verde Ecológico de México (PVEM)	1986	Unsuccessful (marginal)
Partido del Frente Cardenista de Reconstrucción Nacional	1987	Unsuccessful (flop)
Partido Mexicano Socialista (PMS)	1988	Unsuccessful (flop)
Partido de la Revolución Democrática (PRD)	1989	Successful
Partido del Trabajo	1990	Unsuccessful (marginal)
Movimiento Ciudadano (MC)[1]	1998	Incomplete (marginal)
Partido Democracia Social (PDS)	1999	Unsuccessful (flop)
México Posible	2003	Unsuccessful (flop)
Partido Socialdemócrata (PSD)[2]	2005	Unsuccessful (flop)
Partido Nueva Alianza	2005	Incomplete (marginal)

[1] Formerly Convergencia por la Democracia.
[2] Formerly the Partido Alternativa Socialdemócrata y Campesina.

Nicaragua

Party	Birth	Outcome
Movimiento Democrático Nicaragüense (MDN)	1978	Unsuccessful (flop)
Frente Sandinista de Liberación Nacional (FSLN)	1979	Successful
Partido Conservador Demócrata (PCDN)	1979	Unsuccessful (flop)
Partido Socialdemócrata (PSD)	1979	Unsuccessful (flop)
Alianza Popular Conservadora (APC)	1984	Unsuccessful (marginal)
Partido Demócrata de Confianza Nacional (PDCN)	1986	Unsuccessful (flop)
Partido de Acción Nacional (PAN)	1987	Unsuccessful (flop)
Partido Neoliberal (PALI)	1987	Unsuccessful (marginal)
Partido Liberal Independiente de Unidad Nacional (PLIUN)	1987	Unsuccessful (marginal)
Partido Nacional Conservador (PNC)	1989	Unsuccessful (flop)
Partido Integracionista de América Central (PIAC)	1989	Unsuccessful (flop)
Acción Nacional Conservadora (ANC)	1989	Unsuccessful (flop)
Partido Conservador Nicaragüense (PCN)	1991	Incomplete (marginal)
Unión Demócrata Cristiana (UDC)	1992	Incomplete (marginal)
Partido Resistencia Nicaragüense (PRN)	1993	Incomplete (marginal)
Proyecto Nacional (PRONAL)	1995	Unsuccessful (flop)
Movimiento de Renovación Sandinista (MRS)	1995	Incomplete (marginal)
Camino Cristiano Nicaragüense (CCN)	1996	Unsuccessful (flop)
Movimiento de Unidad Cristiana (MUC)	1997	Incomplete (marginal)
Alianza por la República (APRE)	2004	Unsuccessful (flop)
Alianza Liberal Nicaragüense (ALN)	2005	Unsuccessful (flash)

Panama

Party	Birth	Outcome
Partido Revolucionario Democrático (PRD)	1979	Successful
Movimiento Liberal Republicano Nacionalista (MOLIRENA)	1981	Unsuccessful (flash)
Partido de Acción Popular (PAPO)	1982	Unsuccessful (flop)
Partido Nacionalista Popular (PNP)	1983	Unsuccessful (flop)
Partido Liberal Auténtico (PLA)	1988	Unsuccessful (flash)
Partido Renovación Civilista (PRC)	1992	Unsuccessful (flop)
Partido Misión de Unidad Nacional (MUN)	1992	Unsuccessful (flop)
Movimiento de Renovación Nacional (MORENA)	1993	Unsuccessful (flop)
Movimiento Papa Egoró (MPE)	1993	Unsuccessful (flop)
Partido Solidaridad (PS)	1993	Unsuccessful (flash)

Party	Birth	Outcome
Partido Liberal Republicano (LIBRE)	1994	Unsuccessful (flop)
Unión Democrática Independiente (UDI)	1994	Unsuccessful (flop)
Partido Panameñista Doctrinario (PPD)	1994	Unsuccessful (flop)
Partido Liberal Nacional (PLN)	1997	Unsuccessful (flop)
Cambio Democrático (CD)	1998	Incomplete (successful)

Paraguay

Party	Birth	Outcome
Partido Patria Libre (PPL)	1990	Unsuccessful (flop)
Partido Encuentro Nacional (PEN)	1991	Unsuccessful (flash)
Partido País Solidario (PPS)	1996	Incomplete (marginal)
Movimiento de Renovación Nacional (MORENA)	1998	Unsuccessful (flop)
Partido Patria Querida (PPQ)	2001	Incomplete (marginal)
Unión Nacional de Ciudadanos Éticos (UNACE)	2002	Incomplete (marginal)
Frente Amplio (FA)	2002	Incomplete (marginal)

Peru

Party	Birth	Outcome
Partido Revolucionario de los Trabajadores (PRT)	1978	Unsuccessful (flop)
Unión de Izquierda Revolucionaria (UNIR)	1980	Unsuccessful (flop)
Izquierda Unida (IU)	1980	Unsuccessful (flash)
Unidad de Izquierda (UI)	1980	Unsuccessful (flop)
Frente Democrático de Unidad Nacional (FDUN)	1984	Unsuccessful (flop)
Izquierda Socialista (IS)	1989	Unsuccessful (flop)
Obras	1989	Unsuccessful (flop)
Fujimorismo[1]	1990	Incomplete (successful)
Frente Independiente Moralizador (FIM)	1990	Unsuccessful (flash)
Frente Popular Agrícola del Perú (FREPAP)	1990	Unsuccessful (flop)
Renovación Nacional (RN)	1992	Unsuccessful (marginal)
Unión por el Perú (UPP)	1994	Unsuccessful (marginal)
País Posible/Perú Posible (PP)	1994	Unsuccessful (marginal)
Renacimiento Andino (RA)	1996	Unsuccessful (flop)
Somos Perú (SP)	1997	Unsuccessful (marginal)
Partido Solidaridad Nacional (PSN)	1999	Incomplete (successful)
Avancemos	2000	Unsuccessful (flop)
Avanza País (AP)	2000	Unsuccessful (flop)

(*continued*)

Party	Birth	Outcome
Solución Popular (SP)	2001	Unsuccessful (flop)
Partido Humanista (PH)	2001	Incomplete (marginal)
Proyecto País	2001	Unsuccessful (flop)
Todos por la Victoria (TV)	2001	Unsuccessful (flop)
Alianza para el Progreso (APP)	2001	Incomplete (marginal)
Fuerza Democrática (FD)	2004	Unsuccessful (flop)
Justicia Nacional (JN)	2004	Unsuccessful (flop)
Cambio Radical	2004	Incomplete (marginal)
Partido Nacionalista Peruano (PNP)	2005	Incomplete (successful)
Restauración Nacional (RN)	2005	Incomplete (marginal)
Partido Socialista (PS)	2005	Incomplete (marginal)

[1] *Fujimorismo* has changed its name multiple times since its formation in 1990. Originally Cambio 90, it subsequently competed under the labels Nueva Mayoría (1995), Perú 2000 (2000), Vamos Vecino-Sí Cumple (2001), Alianza por el Futuro (2006), Fuerza 2011 (2011), and Fuerza Popular (2016).

Uruguay

Party	Birth	Outcome
Nuevo Espacio	1994	Unsuccessful (flop)
Partido Independiente (PI)	2002	Incomplete (marginal)

Venezuela

Party	Birth	Outcome
Nueva Alternativa	1978	Unsuccessful (flop)
Independientes con el Cambio (ICC)	1983	Unsuccessful (flop)
Convergencia	1993	Unsuccessful (flash)
Movimiento V República/Partido Socialista Unido de Venezuela (MVR/PSUV)	1997	Incomplete (successful)
Patria Para Todos (PPT)	1997	Incomplete (marginal)
Apertura a la Participación Nacional	1997	Unsuccessful (flop)
Proyecto Venezuela	1998	Unsuccessful (flash)
Integración y Renovación Nueva Esperanza (IRENE)	1998	Unsuccessful (flop)
Renovación	1998	Unsuccessful (flop)
Un Nuevo Tiempo (UNT)	1999	Incomplete (marginal)
Primero Justicia (PJ)	2000	Incomplete (marginal)
Por la Democracia Social (PODEMOS)	2002	Incomplete (marginal)
Unidad Popular Venezolana (UPV)	2004	Unsuccessful (flop)
Movimiento Revolucionario Tupamaro (MRT)	2004	Unsuccessful (flop)

Appendix II

*Level of Conflict/Polarization in Eighteen Latin
American Countries (1978–2005)*

Argentina
1978–1983 – Authoritarianism (bureaucratic authoritarianism [BA])
1983–2005 – Democracy

Bolivia
1978–1982 – Authoritarianism (non-BA)
1982–2005 – Democracy

Brazil
1978–1985 – Authoritarianism (BA)
1985–2005 – Democracy

Chile
1978–1990 – Authoritarianism (BA)
1990–2005 – Democracy

Colombia
1978–2005 – Civil war/major insurgency

Costa Rica
1978–2005 – Democracy

Dominican Republic
1978–2005 – Democracy

Ecuador
1978–1979 – Authoritarianism (non-BA)
1979–2002 – Democracy
2002–2005 – Populism

El Salvador
1978–1980 – Authoritarianism (non-BA)
1980–1992 – Civil war/major insurgency
1992–2005 – Democracy

Guatemala
1978–1996 – Civil war/major insurgency
1996–2005 – Democracy

Honduras
1978–1982 – Authoritarianism (non-BA)
1982–2005 – Democracy

Mexico
1978–2000 – Authoritarianism (non-BA)
2000–2005 – Democracy

(*continued*)

Nicaragua
1978–1979 – Civil war/major insurgency
1979–1981 – Authoritarianism (non-BA)
1981–1989 – Civil war/major insurgency
1989–2005 – Democracy

Panama
1978–1989 – Authoritarianism (non-BA)
1989–2005 – Democracy

Paraguay
1978–1989 – Authoritarianism (non-BA)
1989–2005 – Democracy

Peru
1978–1980 – Authoritarianism (non-BA)
1980–1992 – Civil war/major insurgency[1]
1992–2000 – Populism
2000–2005 – Democracy

Uruguay
1978–1985 – Authoritarianism (BA)
1985–2005 – Democracy

Venezuela
1978–1998 – Democracy
1998–2005 – Populism

---

[1] From 1990 to 1992, Peru simultaneously experienced insurgency and populist government. Since major insurgencies tend to be more polarizing than populism, we score Peru as a case of civil war/major insurgency, not populism, during this period.

PART I

PARTY–VOTER LINKAGES AND CHALLENGES OF BRAND-BUILDING

2

Historical Timing, Political Cleavages, and Party-Building in Latin America

Kenneth M. Roberts

Theorists of democracy routinely assert that party systems perform a series of vital functions for representative governance. If that is the case, "third wave" democracies – those born through the spread of representative institutions to new countries and regions since the mid-1970s (Huntington 1991) – would appear to be in serious trouble, as many are characterized by weak, volatile, or fragile party systems. At the elite level, political entrepreneurs in many "third wave" democracies form, discard, and switch parties at a dizzying pace, offering voters little continuity on the "supply side" of the political marketplace. At the mass level – the "demand" side – voters often neither trust nor identify with political parties, and they refrain from developing durable partisan loyalties, much less joining party organizations. Not only are voters "mobile," switching their partisan preferences from one election cycle to the next, but in many contexts they are prone to support independent "outsiders" or populist figures whose primary appeal seems to be their detachment from established party organizations. Not surprisingly, prominent voices have expressed concerns that weak party systems may jeopardize the stability of new democratic regimes, or at least diminish the quality of democratic representation (Mainwaring and Zoco 2007).

It is possible, of course, that party system weakness is a temporary phenomenon that is destined to pass as new democratic regimes consolidate and partisan loyalties congeal over time. Much theorizing on the subject suggests that this should be the case. Converse (1969), for example, argues that party system stability only develops over time as political learning and socialization occur, allowing voting behavior and partisan identities to become "habituated" (see also Zuckerman, Dasović, and Fitzgerald 2007). Recent research on new democratic regimes and party systems in postcommunist Eastern Europe lends some support to this proposition, as electoral volatility in the region tapered off over time after reaching exceedingly high levels in the early election cycles that followed regime transitions (Powell and Tucker 2009).

The Latin American experience during the "third wave" of democratization, however, casts a dark cloud over such guardedly optimistic expectations. Partisan instability in the region during the first decade of redemocratization in the 1980s was hardly unexpected; after all, party systems had to be revived or, in some cases, reconstituted following extended periods of military rule, political proscription, and often violent repression in the 1960s and 1970s. Traditional partisan networks had been deactivated or shredded by military repression, and large numbers of new voters entered the electorate in the 1980s without established partisan identities. Adding to the tumult, the region experienced its most severe economic crisis in half a century during the 1980s, forcing new democratic regimes and their party systems to grapple with the political costs of debt-induced recessions, hyperinflation, austerity measures, and market-based structural adjustments. The depth of the crisis made anti-incumbent voting patterns virtually universal in the region (Remmer 1991), and would have posed a serious challenge to even the most institutionalized of party systems. Given the region's historical pattern of pendular swings between democracy and authoritarianism, the most pressing issue in the 1980s was not whether party systems would stabilize, but whether fledgling democratic regimes would survive.

With relatively few exceptions, however, Latin America's new democratic regimes proved to be remarkably and unexpectedly resilient in the face of such challenges (Mainwaring and Hagopian 2005). Given this resilience, scholars expressed optimism that party systems would stabilize as democratic elections were routinized and voters sorted themselves into rival partisan camps (Dix 1992). Economic recovery – in particular, the defeat of hyperinflation throughout the region by the early to mid-1990s – provided additional grounds for optimism about the potential for institutionalizing partisan competition. Paradoxically, however, routinized democratic competition and economic recovery did *not* stabilize party systems in the 1990s; to the contrary, electoral volatility actually *increased* across the region during the second decade of the "third wave." Further confounding expectations, as shown in Figure 2.1, volatility continued to increase during the first decade of the twenty-first century – that is, the third decade of the "third wave," a period of relative economic

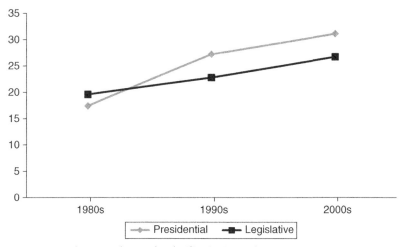

FIGURE 2.1 Average electoral volatility in Latin America, 1980–2010.

Source: Author's calculations of the Pedersen Index of Volatility (1983) from data provided in Nohlen (1993, 2005), and Georgetown University's *Political Database of the Americas* (http://pdba.georgetown.edu/).

abundance thanks to a new global commodity boom and rapidly declining external debt. Entire party systems largely or completely decomposed in Peru and Venezuela in the 1990s and Colombia, Bolivia, and Ecuador in the early 2000s, with established parties being displaced by populist figures or new political movements with questionable staying power.

In short, democratic regimes persevered during Latin America's "third wave," and they institutionalized electoral contestation as the route to political power. On average, however, party systems *de*-institutionalized over time. Converse's process of voter habituation clearly was not functioning as hypothesized. Neither did trends in the region conform to rational choice assumptions that voters would develop name brand loyalties to established party organizations in order to provide information shortcuts and lower the costs of voting (see Aldrich 2011). And with electoral volatility rising over time, the fragility of ties between parties and voters could no longer be attributed to the short-term perturbations associated with the regime transitions and economic hardships of the 1980s.

Latin America's puzzling rise in electoral volatility, however, seemingly lends credence to a provocative alternative explanation advanced by Mainwaring and Zoco (2007) for the instability of "third wave" party systems. This explanation centers on a reinterpretation of the relationship between partisanship and time. Time matters, they argue, not because its linear passage habituates voters and institutionalizes partisanship, but rather because of the period and sequencing effects of party-building activities at different moments in world historical time. Party systems born in the "third wave" are not fragile because they are young; they are fragile because they came along too late to develop the types of encapsulating mass party organizations that stabilized West European party systems by the early decades of the twentieth century. Such mass party organizations were anchored in class cleavages, and they integrated voters and social blocs into dense partisan and civic associations that forged strong collective identities, thus limiting individual voter mobility (Bartolini and Mair 1990).

Timing matters for Mainwaring and Zoco, however, because this integrative and encapsulating mode of partisanship is not universally available to party-builders. Indeed, the model was specific to a stage of world historical development in which electoral mobilization was a labor-intensive affair that required mass-based organization, strong local branches, and extensive grassroots participation. It thrived, then, in a period when labor movements were on the ascendance – providing the social and organizational bases for at least one side of the standard cleavage alignment – and telecommunications had not yet revolutionized electoral campaigns by reducing the dependence of political entrepreneurs on mass party organizations to mobilize voters. The sequencing of party system development in the "third wave," then, came too late to form encapsulating party organizations. So conceived, tenuous partisanship is a congenital defect of new party systems that will not be corrected with the passage of time; it is a function of period and sequencing effects, rather than age per se. As Schmitter (2001) pithily stated, "parties are not what they once were."

Although Mainwaring and Zoco's argument is theoretically compelling and backed by considerable empirical evidence, this chapter suggests that it is overly deterministic in its sequencing postulates. The generalizable patterns that they identify mask considerable cross-national variation, and major anomalies to these general patterns reveal a number of important contingencies and conditional effects. Even if encapsulating mass party organizations are a fading memory, it does not necessarily follow that party systems will be electorally unstable; as Chapter 1 by Levitsky, Loxton, and Van Dyck makes clear, a number of successful new parties were founded during Latin America's "third wave," and in several countries new party *systems* emerged and stabilized over time. Intriguingly, the region also offers examples of much older party systems with encapsulating traditions that quite suddenly broke down in the "third wave." Recent work on Eastern Europe (Tavits 2013) and Africa (Riedl 2014) likewise finds substantial variation in the strength and stability of third wave party systems.

In Latin America, this variation cannot be understood merely by studying the attributes of individual parties. It is essential as well to explore the systemic properties under which individual parties compete – in particular, the competitive axes or cleavage alignments that structure national party systems. This systemic perspective suggests that the success of party-building efforts in Latin America's "third wave," and the broader stability or volatility of national party systems, was not predetermined by historical timing or sequencing effects. Instead, these outcomes rested on the more contingent effects of national critical junctures during the epochal "dual transitions" to political democracy and market liberalism in the 1980s and 1990s.[1] Political battles over these dual transitions either aligned or dealigned party systems along a programmatic axis of competition anchored by well-defined leftist and rightist alternatives. As Levitsky, Loxton, and Van Dyck suggest, polarized conflicts between the left and right over regime preferences and market reforms helped to align party systems programmatically, producing institutional legacies of relatively stable partisan competition, whether parties and party systems were new or old. Indeed, successful party-building efforts were far more likely where partisan competition was programmatically aligned along the left–right spectrum. Conversely, where the dual transitions did not sharply polarize the left and right over regime and economic policy preferences, partisan competition was weakly structured by programmatic differences, and programmatic dealignment ensued. Dealigned party systems were susceptible to highly disruptive "reactive sequences" – including mass social protest – in the aftermath of the dual transitions, bequeathing legacies of electoral instability and organizational decay. Causal processes are traced through a comparative historical analysis of these critical junctures in three "new" party systems – those of Brazil, Ecuador, and El Salvador – and one much older party system in Venezuela.

---

[1] This chapter extends the critical juncture framework developed in Roberts (2014) by giving more systematic attention to historical timing and sequencing effects in party system development. It also elaborates on the role of regime transitions and regime preferences in the structuring of party system programmatic alignments in Latin America's "third wave."

LINKAGES, CLEAVAGES, AND PARTY SYSTEM
ALIGNMENTS

In an effort to understand stable partisanship, scholars have tried to identify different types of societal linkages that generate partisan identities and bind voters to specific party organizations. Kitschelt (2000), for example, identifies three principal types of party–voter linkages: those based on clientelism, programmatic preferences, and charismatic appeal (see also Lawson 1980). Clearly, strong linkages can be a source of stable partisanship, and may well be a precondition for it. In the process of forming societal linkages, however, parties inevitably construct cleavages as well; that is, they differentiate their supporters from those of their rivals, as parties, by definition, only represent a "part" of the body politic. If strong linkages are important to stable partisanship, so also are deep cleavages, for the simple reason that they "anchor" voters or limit individual voter mobility. The wider and deeper the divide between rival partisan camps, the less likely voters are to cross that divide from one election cycle to the next; hence the emphasis in Chapter 1 on the party-building effects of conflict and polarization. Not surprisingly, then, the classic scholarly work on the development of West European party systems has emphasized the role of well-organized sociopolitical cleavages – especially those anchored in class conflict – in the stabilization of partisan and electoral competition (Bartolini and Mair 1990; Lipset and Rokkan 1967).

The European scholarly tradition presumes that cleavages are grounded in sociological distinctions of class, ethnicity, religion, or region. As such, cleavages have a structural foundation upon which to build collective identities (their cultural or ideational dimension) and encompassing party and civic organizations. Partisan alignments in much of the world, however, are not clearly anchored in rival social blocs. Myriad social distinctions exist in any society, and the process that determines which, if any, get "politicized," or translated into axes of partisan contestation, is historically contingent. The existence of extreme class inequalities in Latin American societies, for example, has not ensured that partisan competition will be structured along class lines (see Roberts 2002). Partisan cleavages, therefore, are social and political constructs, not structural requisites, and they are heavily conditioned by historical patterns of social conflict, political mobilization, and identity formation – that is, by social processes that parties themselves often shape through their ideology, strategic behavior, and political agency.

The relatively shallow sociological grounding of competitive alignments is surely one of the reasons why party systems elsewhere have
found it difficult to replicate West European levels of electoral stability.
Nevertheless, any competitive party system must "cleave" the electorate
as rival parties mobilize support, and cleavages constructed in the political arena between rival party organizations – without reference to social
group distinctions – are not necessarily unstable alignments. The absence
of strong class cleavages has not prevented the US party system from having a remarkably stable competitive axis – or political cleavage – between
Republicans and Democrats. This cleavage is grounded in parties' programmatic brands or "reputations," and it sorts voters into rival partisan camps according to their policy preferences (Sniderman and Stiglitz
2012), even if such preferences have weak sociological foundations.

Indeed, the Latin American experience – until quite recently – provided
examples of highly stable competitive alignments between nineteenth-century oligarchic parties that did not clearly differentiate their supporters
on the basis of social class *or* programmatic preferences. In countries like
Uruguay and Colombia, traditional oligarchic parties built exclusive clientelist networks that aligned and stabilized the electorate in the political
sphere in the absence of well-defined social cleavages or programmatic
distinctions (Gillespie 1991; Hartlyn 1988). Patron-clientelism allowed
elite-based parties to cultivate vertical linkages to lower-class voters by
selectively distributing particularistic benefits in exchange for political loyalty – in the process, impeding the development of horizontally organized,
class-based parties that tried to mobilize popular support through programmatic commitments to broader redistributive policies. Once voters
were incorporated into a patronage machine and the social networks that
helped sustain it, crossing to the "other side" could be prohibitively costly,
as it might jeopardize access to public resources that were controlled by
party brokers. Economic dependency thus combined with the discretion-
ary allocation of public resources to create stable organizational loyalties,
as well as vigorous rivalries against other parties that also sought control
over state resources in order to reward their own clientele networks.

In Latin America's "third wave" of democratization, however, partisan
alignments grounded in rival clientelist networks have progressively weakened. Several party systems with roots in nineteenth-century oligarchic
divides have broken down (Colombia) or been transformed by the rise of
newer leftist rivals (Uruguay). Only Honduras and Paraguay continue to
be dominated by nineteenth-century oligarchic parties, and these parties
are under pressure from emerging leftist rivals in both countries. Patterns

of state and market reform that limit the availability of state resources to nourish partisan clientelist networks have undoubtedly contributed to this decline of oligarchic party machines (see Muñoz and Dargent, Chapter 7, this volume). So also has the growing success of leftist parties in mobilizing popular constituencies behind more programmatic, redistributive platforms in the aftermath to market liberalization. Indeed, the generalized strengthening of leftist alternatives in the region since the late 1990s – following the crisis-induced technocratic convergence around market liberalization in the 1980s and 1990s – has restructured partisan and electoral competition along a more programmatic, left–right axis in many countries. Although this realignment has not always been grounded in well-defined, much less well organized, class cleavages, it has clearly revived partisan competition around programmatic linkages and differences.

Party systems, however, have varied widely in their ability to manage and withstand this revival of left–right programmatic contestation. In some countries – most notably, Brazil – it helped to stabilize party systems that were notorious for their fragility and inchoateness, or even newly formed during the "third wave" itself (see Mainwaring 1999). In others, like Venezuela, it contributed to the decomposition of longstanding and highly institutionalized party systems (Coppedge 1994). Such variation was not determined by the historical timing or sequencing of party system formation. Neither was it determined by deep historical development patterns associated with industrialization and the early construction of welfare states, which Kitschelt et al. (2009) see as the foundation for the programmatic structuring of party systems in the region. Instead, contemporary alignments have been heavily conditioned by the impact on party systems of two more recent but fundamental transitions in the 1980s and 1990s – regime transitions from authoritarianism to democracy, and economic transitions from statist to neoliberal development models. These transitions shaped national critical junctures that either aligned or dealigned party systems along a left–right axis of contestation during the "third wave." In the process, they bequeathed party systems that were more or less resilient in the face of strengthening societal pressures for redistributive measures and social citizenship rights in the aftermath to market-based economic adjustment.

CRITICAL JUNCTURES AND PARTY SYSTEM ALIGNMENT

Whether cleavages are anchored in social group distinctions or simply constructed in the political arena through partisan rivalries, they only possess meaningful programmatic content under three basic conditions: (1) individual parties must adopt clear and relatively cohesive programmatic stands on issues that divide the body politic; (2) these programmatic stands must differentiate a party from its competitors; and (3) parties elected into public office must pursue policies that largely conform to the principles and platforms on which they ran. In short, as Lupu argues in Chapter 3 in this volume, meaningful party "brands" require that parties adopt programmatic stands that are internally consistent and recognizably different from those of their rivals. Slippage along any of these dimensions will weaken programmatic linkages or brand name identities and make cleavage alignments more fluid. Brand dilution, therefore, narrows the gulf between rival parties and makes individual voters more mobile, at least on the basis of their programmatic preferences. The opposite is true where programmatic differences crystallize, anchoring voters – those with programmatic preferences, at least – in their partisan camp. This can be readily seen in the recent US experience, where the much maligned ideological polarization between Republicans and Democrats – whatever its impact on effective governance – has increasingly "sorted" voters into rival camps and stabilized voting behavior (Aldrich 2011; Hetherington 2011; Sniderman and Stiglitz 2012).

Clearly, the level of programmatic structuration varies across party systems, and also across time in any given party system. It is not, in other words, a fixed property of party systems, even if it is conditioned by historical development patterns (Kitschelt et al. 2009). What determines, then, why some party systems are more programmatically aligned than others? And why does the level of programmatic structuration vary longitudinally in a given party system?

In Latin America, partisan alignments during the "third wave" were heavily shaped by patterns of political contestation associated with the two major societal transitions of the late twentieth century – that is, the dual transitions to political and economic liberalism. These transitions were profound in their effects and sweeping in their scope; between the late 1970s and early 1990s, every country in the region adopted market-based structural adjustment policies (Morley, Machado, and Pettinato 1999), and all except Costa Rica, Colombia, and Venezuela experienced a regime transition from authoritarianism to democracy.[2] Party systems mapped onto these transitions in strikingly diverse ways, however, generating well-defined left–right cleavages in some countries, but diffusing or

---

[2] Mexico's gradual regime transition was not complete until somewhat later, arguably the 2000 election that produced the first partisan alternation in power.

dealigning such cleavages in others. These differences had major implications for successful party-building and the institutionalization of partisan and electoral competition.

In other work (Roberts 2014), I have argued that the transition from state-led development to market liberalism was a critical juncture for Latin American party systems. The authoritarian regimes and regime transitions that generally (though not always) preceded market reform were, however, "conditioning causes" that "predispose[d] cases to diverge" in specific ways during the critical juncture (Slater and Simmons 2008: 8). These regime effects were two-fold: they determined whether left–right alignments were reinforced by a regime cleavage between authoritarians and democrats, and they shaped the balance of power between conservative and leftist forces. As explained below, these conditioning factors played an important role in the configuration of partisan alignments during the critical juncture of market reform.

In many countries, democratic transitions in the late 1970s and 1980s brought traditional political parties back onto center stage. In others, major new parties emerged during the transition period, and party systems were largely reconstituted. Whether party systems were old or new, however, regime transitions varied in the extent to which they cleaved partisan competition between authoritarians and democrats – or, at least, between supporters and opponents of authoritarian regimes. In some countries – primarily those where right-wing military dictatorships governed in the 1960s and 1970s[3] – authoritarian successor parties anchored one side of the central political divide following regime transitions (see Loxton, Chapter 9, this volume). In Honduras, Paraguay, and, more ambiguously, Uruguay,[4] these were traditional parties of the right that had supported or collaborated with military rulers. In Brazil, Chile, Bolivia, and El Salvador, military rulers and their civilian allies forged new parties of the right during transition periods to safeguard the political and economic interests of authoritarian coalitions following the restoration of democratic competition. Such parties generally tried

---

[3] The exceptions were Mexico and Panama, where successor parties were derived from authoritarian regimes that historically possessed both conservative and populist tendencies, thus diffusing left–right cleavages based on regime preferences. In Nicaragua, the regime transition that followed the 1990 defeat of the Sandinistas included a revolutionary successor party that aligned the party system on a left–right axis.

[4] In Uruguay, conservative sectors of the two traditional parties, the Colorados and Blancos, had collaborated with the military dictatorship after 1973, while other factions of these parties supported redemocratization. The leftist Frente Amplio (Broad Front) was a staunch opponent of military rule and a target of its repression.

to defend elite economic interests and shield military institutions from political retribution or prosecution for human rights violations. As such, they sought to preserve the "reserve domains" of military influence or other "authoritarian enclaves" that placed institutional constraints on popular democratic majorities (see Valenzuela 1992). These parties thus anchored the right side of partisan cleavage alignments following democratic transitions, generally facing off against leftist rivals that were fierce opponents of military regimes (as were, less consistently, centrist parties in these countries).

Authoritarian successor parties were not formed, however, in Peru and Ecuador, where left-leaning military regimes governed in the 1970s, or in Argentina, where the military's authoritarian project was too thoroughly discredited to spawn an electorally competitive conservative successor. In these latter countries, cleavages between authoritarians and democrats were not a major factor in aligning partisan competition following regime transitions. Even where major parties of the left and right existed – as in Peru and Ecuador – they tended to share an opposition stance toward military rulers, albeit for different reasons.

Although conservative successor parties were prevalent in the region, they did not always produce strong left–right programmatic alignments around regime preferences following democratic transitions. In Honduras and Paraguay, for example, leftist parties were miniscule and electorally noncompetitive, allowing right-wing successor parties to compete in conservative-dominated regimes that reproduced much of the authoritarian political order. Where a major party of the left was present, however, to compete with conservative successor parties – in particular, in Brazil, Chile, El Salvador, and Uruguay – deep cleavages over regime loyalties reinforced left–right programmatic alignments that were grounded in economic ideology and rival preferences toward redistributive reforms. In these countries, authoritarian legacies weighed heavily on the partisan alignments that emerged during the regime transitions that ushered in the "third wave."

Authoritarian legacies and regime transitions were also important because of the power balances they created between rival forces, which ultimately influenced partisan alignments around the process of market reform. In particular, authoritarian regimes that empowered conservative actors made it more likely that they could take the lead in the adoption of structural adjustment policies. Market reforms that were adopted by conservative or centrist actors, whether parties or military rulers, and consistently opposed by a major party of the left, helped to align partisan competition programmatically. This pattern of "contested liberalism" prevailed in the four aforementioned cases where strong left–right regime cleavages also existed – Brazil, Chile, El Salvador, and Uruguay.[5] Contested liberalism made conservative actors the champions and defenders of market reform, while channeling societal opposition toward institutionalized parties on the left.

Conversely, where conservative actors were not strong enough to lead the process of market reform following regime transitions (or under established democratic regimes), structural adjustment policies were often adopted by center-left or populist parties – as in Argentina, Bolivia, Costa Rica, Ecuador, and Venezuela – or by an independent populist figure like Alberto Fujimori in Peru. In these countries, market liberalization dealigned party systems programmatically. "Bait-and-switch" patterns of market reform were led by political actors who ran for office on other platforms and often criticized neoliberal adjustment measures, producing a reform dynamic that Stokes (2001) called "neoliberalism by surprise." In so doing, they left party systems without an effective institutional channel for societal opposition to the neoliberal model. In contrast to the aforementioned alignment of contested liberalism, bait-and-switch reforms produced a pattern of "neoliberal convergence," whereby all the major parties led or supported the process of market liberalization.

In the short term, this policy convergence may have ameliorated partisan conflict and broadened the political base for technocratic market reforms. Over the longer term, however, it stripped much of the programmatic content from partisan competition, thus dealigning party systems programmatically. In Lupu's terms (Chapter 3, this volume), bait-and-switch reforms undermined intraparty consistency, while the convergence of major parties on variants of market liberalism eroded interparty differentiation. Indeed, this convergence left party systems vulnerable to forms of social and political backlash by marginalized groups that lacked institutionalized channels for the articulation of dissent from neoliberal orthodoxy. Such backlashes – the "reactive sequences" (Mahoney 2001) to neoliberal critical junctures – took a variety of different political forms, from mass social protest to electoral protest movements, including

[5] Elsewhere (Roberts 2014), I add Mexico, Nicaragua, and the Dominican Republic to the set of cases with aligning critical junctures, where market reforms were led by conservative actors and opposed by a major party of the left. Argentina, Bolivia, Costa Rica, Ecuador, Peru, and Venezuela are coded as cases of programmatic dealignment, where major populist or center-left parties played a central role in the reform process.

the election of antiestablishment populist outsiders or new "movement parties" that emerged organically from protest cycles.

These reactive sequences could be highly destabilizing for party systems – both old and new – that were not programmatically aligned along a left–right axis of competition during the dual transitions to political and economic liberalism in the 1980s and 1990s. Where such alignment occurred, however, reactive sequences in the aftermath to market liberalization were moderated considerably; as societal resistance to market insecurities intensified, it strengthened established parties of the left, rather than extrasystemic populist and leftist alternatives. The fate of party systems, then, hinged more on the aligning and dealigning effects of these dual transitions, rather than the age of party systems or the historical timing and sequencing of their formation. Indeed, new parties – of the left or the right – were *not* predestined to weakness or evanescence in the third wave if they emerged in party systems that experienced aligning critical junctures. Of the eleven parties that Levitsky, Loxton, and Van Dyck categorize as successful cases of party-building during the third wave, ten (all but the Democratic Revolutionary Party [PRD] in Panama) were founded in the seven party systems that I elsewhere identify as having experienced aligning critical junctures (Roberts 2014). Beyond the attributes of individual parties, then, systemic properties weighed heavily on the prospects for new parties. The dynamics and consequences of programmatic alignment and dealignment are explored in greater depth in the comparative case studies below.

PROGRAMMATIC (DE)ALIGNMENT AND PARTY SYSTEM INSTITUTIONALIZATION IN COMPARATIVE PERSPECTIVE

Latin America's political landscape during the "third wave" of democratization provides examples of both relatively stable and unstable party systems. This variation, however, does not readily map onto the categories of "old" and "new" party systems, or to any historical periodization of formative experiences. Of the four countries analyzed here, only one – Ecuador – conforms to expectations of organizational volatility and inchoateness for party systems formed during the "third wave." The other three cases defy the hypothesized relationship in fundamental but different ways: Venezuela, because an older and highly institutionalized party system decomposed during the 1990s, and Brazil and El Salvador, because new party systems progressively consolidated and stabilized over

the course of the "third wave." Although these divergent outcomes cannot be explained by party system age or founding periods, they correspond closely to patterns of programmatic alignment and dealignment
during the dual transitions to political and economic liberalism of the
late twentieth century.

Of the four cases, only Venezuela entered the period of the "third
wave" with an intact party system. Indeed, Venezuela was not, properly
speaking, a case of "third wave" democratization, as its democratic transition occurred earlier, in the late 1950s. When other Latin American
countries were struggling to restore democratic rule in the late 1970s and
1980s, Venezuela stood out for the strength and stability of its democratic
institutions, and its earlier "pacted transition" often served as an implicit
model for aspiring democratizers in the region (Karl 1987; O'Donnell
and Schmitter 1986). Venezuela's party system dated to an earlier episode of postwar democratization in the 1940s, during the period that
Mainwaring and Zoco (2007) characterize as the global high point of
mass party organization. In the other three cases, party systems were
largely reconstituted during the "third wave" itself, and are thus para-
digmatic examples of the new party systems that Mainwaring and Zoco
allege to be singularly prone to underinstitutionalization.

The dual transitions to democracy and market liberalism during the
"third wave" aligned (or dealigned) these four party systems in strikingly diverse ways, however. Clearly, the "third wave" did not generate
a regime cleavage in partisan competition in the Venezuelan case, given
the preexisting character of the country's democratic regime and the close
collaboration of the two leading parties – Democratic Action (AD) and
the Independent Electoral Political Organization Committee (COPEI) –
in forging the political and economic pacts that undergirded the 1958
democratic transition. Although these parties were at loggerheads in the
1940s, when COPEI emerged as a conservative response to a left-leaning, labor-backed AD government between 1945 and 1948, ten years of
military dictatorship drove the two parties into a tacit alliance in support
of a democratic transition in the late 1950s. The two parties moderated
their ideological differences and formed the organizational linchpin of
the post-1958 democratic regime, increasingly dominating the electoral
arena and alternating in national executive office until their demise in the
1990s (Coppedge 1994).

Likewise, Ecuador's democratic transition in the late 1970s did not
forge a well-defined regime cleavage in partisan competition. In contrast to
most countries in the region, Ecuador – like Peru – experienced a socially

reformist, left-leaning period of military rule in the 1970s, and the military regime did not spawn a civilian successor party to defend its legacy under democratic rule. Conservative political and business elites distrusted the military regime and generally supported a regime transition, as they opposed the military's statist policies and chafed at their exclusion from policymaking arenas (see Conaghan and Malloy 1994). Populist and leftist actors were likewise excluded under military rule and hoped to capitalize on a restoration of democratic channels for participation and representation. Consequently, although parties differed in their economic policy preferences, they converged in their support of regime change. These actors were organizationally fragmented and inchoate, however, as Ecuador entered its 1978–1979 democratic transition with a party system in a state of considerable flux. The traditional oligarchic conservative and liberal parties were nearing the end of a secular decline, and the aging populist *caudillo* and five-time president José María Velasco Ibarra was in the final stages of a storied political career that left no significant partisan descendant. A fluid set of relatively new conservative (Social Christian Party, or PSC), centrist (Popular Democracy – Christian Democratic Union, or DP-UDC), populist (Concentration of Popular Forces, or CFP, and the Ecuadoran Roldosista Party, or PRE), and leftist (the Democratic Left, or ID) party organizations thus emerged to compete in the electoral arena as the democratic transition got underway. No central cleavage between authoritarians and democrats structured partisan competition, however.

As in Ecuador, party systems were also reconstituted during "third wave" democratic transitions in Brazil and El Salvador. In contrast to Ecuador, however – not to mention Venezuela – these new party systems were sharply cleaved by a central divide between erstwhile supporters and opponents of military regimes. Conservative successor parties were founded in both Brazil and El Salvador to defend the legacies of right-wing military regimes and protect the interests of their elite supporters following the restoration of democratic competition (see Loxton, Chapter 9, this volume). Similarly, major parties of the left emerged in both countries out of the social movements and activist networks that had been the primary targets of military repression. Polarizing and violent political conflict occurred in both countries, including a civil war in El Salvador, an urban guerrilla insurgency in Brazil, and severe military repression in both countries.

In Brazil, the 1964–1985 military regime dissolved established political parties, repressed those with populist and leftist tendencies, and created an "official" two-party system out of the state and local political networks of the more conservative traditional parties. As stated by Power (2000: 55), the military regime's institutional manipulation forged "a political cleavage that would characterize Brazilian politics for a generation or more: authoritarians versus democrats." Brazil's party system would eventually be reconstituted around the axis of competition formed by this central cleavage. During a protracted democratic transition, the official promilitary party, the National Renewal Alliance (ARENA) – which dominated most state and local governments and their patronage networks under the military regime (Hagopian 1996) – gave rise to an authoritarian successor party, the Liberal Front Party (PFL), that consolidated a position as the most important party on the conservative side of the political spectrum. Prodemocratic forces, on the other hand, joined the official "opposition" party to the military regime, the Brazilian Democratic Movement (MDB), which became the centrist catchall party, the Party of the Brazilian Democratic Movement (PMDB) during the democratic transition and spawned a major spin-off, the Brazilian Social Democracy Party (PSDB), in the late 1980s. Meanwhile, the labor and social movements that protested against military rule formed a new partisan vehicle of the socialist left, the Workers' Party (PT), which steadily grew over the course of the 1980s and 1990s.

Brazil's newly reconstituted party system, therefore, was initially built around a central left–right cleavage that demarcated the supporters and opponents of military rule and sorted them into rival ideological camps. To be sure, the political salience of this regime cleavage gradually faded as the new democratic regime whittled back authoritarian restrictions (Hunter 1997), consolidated its authority, and grappled with chronic hyperinflationary pressures. By the 1990s, the centrist, prodemocratic PSDB had moved into an alliance with conservative forces to implement stabilization and structural adjustment policies, over the opposition of the PT and other leftist forces. Centrist forces, in short, shifted from a tacit prodemocratic alliance with the left to an explicit promarket alliance with the right as economic stabilization displaced regime transition as the dominant issue on the political agenda. The tactical repositioning of the center, however, did little to alter the basic configuration of conservative, centrist, and leftist blocs, with a left–right cleavage over economic policy that redefined but largely reproduced the original cleavage rooted in regime differences.

In El Salvador, as well, a regime cleavage forged by authoritarianism and civil war spawned a new party system during the 1980s and 1990s. Prior to the 1979–1992 civil war, party system development was impeded by virtually uninterrupted military rule and highly irregular electoral competition; the traditional right-wing party was allied to military rulers, while the centrist Christian Democrats led opposition forces. During the civil war, when direct military rule gave way to a US-backed civilian government, these parties were overtaken by new party organizations that grew directly out of the rival armed combatants. On the right, the Nationalist Republican Alliance (ARENA) was formed in 1981 out of the military intelligence and paramilitary networks organized by former army major Roberto D'Aubuisson, with financial backing from Salvadoran business elites at home and abroad (Stanley 1996; Wood 2000a: 67–70; also see Loxton, Chapter 9, this volume). On the left, an umbrella revolutionary movement known as the Farabundo Martí National Liberation Front (FMLN) was founded in 1980, and subsequently evolved into a party of the same name as it negotiated its entry into the political system at the end of the civil war (see Holland, Chapter 10, this volume). These two parties, firmly located on opposite ends of the ideological spectrum, would dominate the electoral arena following the inauguration of a more inclusive democratic regime in 1992.

The regime cleavages between authoritarians and democrats – or revolutionaries – that initially structured partisan competition along a left–right axis in El Salvador and Brazil progressively faded in significance as new democratic regimes were consolidated. Crucially, however, the left–right cleavage was subsequently reinforced in both countries by the alignment of partisan actors around the process of market liberalization. In both countries, conservative parties or coalitions with strong business support were empowered to lead the process of market reform, while a major party of the left was present to channel popular resistance. In Brazil, tentative market reforms began, in a hyperinflationary context, under President José Sarney of the PFL in the late 1980s. More ambitious structural adjustment measures were then adopted by the maverick conservative leader Fernando Collor de Mello, and finally consolidated in the mid-1990s by President Fernando Henrique Cardoso of the PSDB, who governed in alliance with the PFL and other centrist and conservative parties. The labor-backed PT spearheaded opposition to neoliberal reforms, with its leader Luiz Inácio "Lula" da Silva finishing second in three consecutive presidential elections in 1989, 1994, and 1998. In El Salvador, neoliberal reforms began when ARENA first captured the presidency behind the leadership of businessman Alfredo Cristiani in 1989. The model continued under his three ARENA successors, with the FMLN positioned on the left at the head of opposition forces.

Between them, these two cases of aligning critical junctures account for five of the eleven examples of successful party-building identified by Levitsky, Loxton, and Van Dyck in Latin America's third wave – PFL, PSDB, and PT in Brazil, and ARENA and FMLN in El Salvador. In both countries, party systems provided well-defined and clearly differentiated options on the left and right that arrayed themselves on opposite sides of the political divide that formed around the process of market liberalization in the 1990s. Surveys of party legislators clearly attested to this interparty, left–right programmatic cleavage; on a scale of 1 (left) to 10 (right), PFL legislators gave their party an average score of 8.29 in 1999, while legislators from their centrist ally PSDB scored their party at 5.23, and those from the opposition PT gave their party an average score of 3.4 (Mendoza and de Oliveira 2001). The cleavage was even more pronounced in El Salvador, as ARENA legislators scored their party at 8.6 in 1998, whereas FMLN legislators located their party at 1.9 (Artiga González 2001: 143, 161).

Partisan alignments around the process of market liberalization in Venezuela and Ecuador were strikingly different. Venezuela was an archetypal case of bait-and-switch market reform – not once, but twice. The first major attempt at structural adjustment began in 1989 following the election of Carlos Andrés Pérez of AD – a populist figure from a traditionally labor-based, center-left party. A second major push occurred under the administration of Rafael Caldera and his Planning Minister Teodoro Petkoff from 1996 to 1998. Although Caldera was a historic leader of the conservative, promarket party COPEI, he broke with the party to run an independent campaign for the presidency in 1993, adopting a highly critical stance toward the neoliberal reforms implemented under Pérez. Petkoff, meanwhile, was the historic leader of the former guerrilla movement and leftist party Movement toward Socialism (MAS). Both reform episodes, therefore, were launched in contravention to the electoral mandates and programmatic commitments that ushered leaders into office.

In Ecuador, a succession of political leaders from across the ideological spectrum tried to impose market reforms – often with limited success – between the mid-1980s and early 2000s. Although conservative presidents like León Febres Cordero and Sixto Durán Ballén were ambitious reformers, major liberalization initiatives were also adopted by presidents from the country's leading leftist (Rodrigo Borja of ID) and populist (Abdalá Bucaram of the PRE) parties, as well as the independent populist figure Lucio Gutiérrez after 2002, who had been elected with the support of the left-leaning indigenous party, Pachakutik (see Madrid, Chapter 11, this volume). As such, bait-and-switch reform dynamics were prevalent in Ecuador, undermining any left–right programmatic structuring of partisan and electoral competition.

In short, party systems in both Ecuador and Venezuela were programmatically dealigned by the process of structural adjustment, and essentially left without an institutionalized partisan vehicle for the articulation of dissent from market orthodoxy. In Venezuela, where the two major historic parties, AD and COPEI, both supported market reforms after 1989, legislators from AD located their party at 4.5 on a left–right, 1–10 scale in 1995, while legislators from COPEI located their party at 5.7 (Molina et al. 2003). This relatively narrow gap – far smaller than those seen in Brazil and El Salvador – was indicative of the programmatic convergence that occurred as the major party "brands" ceased to represent distinctive programmatic alternatives, even as Venezuela embarked on a course of dramatic and controversial market restructuring. Likewise, left–right programmatic structuration was relatively weak in Ecuador, where the conservative PSC, the center-left ID, and the populist PRE all took turns leading the process of market reform. In 1998, legislators of the PSC located their party at 7.4 on the left–right scale, while those of the ID and the PRE located their parties at 4.2 and 4.4, respectively (Freidenberg 2003).

In contexts of bait-and-switch reform and programmatic dealignment, societal resistance to market liberalization was more likely to be channeled into extrasystemic forms of social and/or electoral protest – the "reactive sequences" (Mahoney 2001), so to speak, to neoliberal critical junctures. In Venezuela, this took the form of the mass urban riots known as the Caracazo that greeted the initial adoption of adjustment measures by Pérez in February 1989, unleashing a powerful process of political deinstitutionalization from which the party system – and the post-1958 political order – never recovered. Pérez weathered two military coup attempts before being impeached on grounds of corruption in 1993, while voters abandoned the two major parties to support a series of independent and leftist "outsiders" – first Caldera and the leftist Radical Cause (LCR) in 1993, and finally Hugo Chávez in 1998.

In Ecuador, an indigenous movement that adopted a staunch antineoliberal line gathered steam over the course of the 1990s, eventually joining forces with other popular actors in a series of mass protests that directly or indirectly toppled three consecutive elected presidents in 1997, 2000, and 2005 (Silva 2009; Yashar 2005). Established parties were displaced after 2000 by independent populist figures, culminating in the election of the left populist outsider Rafael Correa in 2006. Similar patterns of bait-and-switch reform also culminated in mass protest movements, the overthrow of elected presidents, and partial or complete party system decomposition in Bolivia and Argentina, providing further evidence of the unstable institutional legacies of neoliberal critical junctures that programmatically dealigned party systems. In Bolivia, Venezuela, and Ecuador, the election of populist outsiders or new leftist "movement" parties led to plebiscitary expressions of popular sovereignty that produced sharp breaks with regime institutions, as well as major departures from neoliberal orthodoxy. New leftist leaders convoked constituent assemblies, refounded regime institutions, and experimented with a broad range of statist, nationalist, and redistributive development policies.

Reactive sequences to market liberalization in Brazil and El Salvador were far less institutionally disruptive. Both countries turned toward the left politically in the postadjustment period, but they did so by electing institutionalized and increasingly moderate parties of the left that had remained in opposition throughout the period of market reform. The PT and the FMLN provided institutional outlets for the articulation of dissent from market orthodoxy, moderating social protest movements and stabilizing their respective party systems. The "left turns" that occurred with the election of the PT in 2002, 2006, 2010, and 2014 and the FMLN in 2009 and 2014 did not produce efforts to refound regime institutions, and new administrations adopted moderate redistributive social reforms without dramatic departures from macroeconomic orthodoxy. The same was true in Chile and Uruguay, where institutionalized parties of the left also strengthened and came into power in the aftermath to market reforms that had been adopted by conservative rulers (see Roberts 2014).

PROGRAMMATIC ALIGNMENTS AND PARTY SYSTEM STABILITY

The programmatic alignment and dealignment of partisan competition during the dual transitions to political and economic liberalism had powerful implications for the stability of party systems in the aftermath to market reforms. Debt and hyperinflationary crises during the 1980s and 1990s had weakened labor unions, disarticulated popular movements, and limited the policy options of elected governments. Following structural adjustment and the stabilization of inflationary pressures across the region by the mid-1990s, however, diffuse societal opposition to

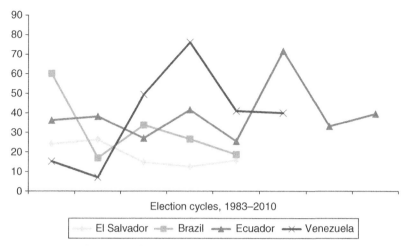

FIGURE 2.2 Electoral volatility in presidential elections, 1983–2010 (Pedersen Index of Volatility).

Source: Calculated from electoral data provided in Nohlen 2005 and Georgetown University's *Political Database of the Americas* (http://pdba.georgetown.edu/). The years of the first election cycle in each country varied with the timing of democratic transitions.

neoliberal reforms often congealed around new forms of social mobilization and political articulation. The political channeling and party system effects of this opposition in the postadjustment period varied dramatically, depending not on the age of party systems but rather on their programmatic alignment or dealignment. As seen above, where bait-and-switch reforms dealigned party systems, opposition was more likely to be expressed through mass social protest and antiestablishment forms of electoral protest that severely destabilized party systems. Conversely, where market reforms aligned party systems programmatically, opposition was channeled into institutionalized parties of the left rather than extrasystemic forms of social or electoral protest.

These distinct institutional legacies of reform alignments are readily apparent in the four cases analyzed here. As seen in Figure 2.2, longitudinal patterns of electoral volatility in the four party systems diverged sharply. Venezuela's long-standing, highly institutionalized party system was electorally stable in the 1980s, but increasingly volatile following its bait-and-switch process of structural adjustment. According to the Pedersen index of volatility, a basic measure of vote shifts from one election cycle to the next, volatility in Venezuelan presidential elections averaged a mere 11.1 percent in the 1980s, then jumped to 62.8 percent in the 1990s and 40.6 percent in the first decade of the twentieth century. Volatility in Ecuador's much younger, dealigned party system started high and then spiked when voters abandoned established parties after the mass protests that toppled President Jamil Mahuad in 2000. Volatility peaked in 2002 at 71.6 percent.

In El Salvador, on the other hand, the volatility trend line moved in the opposite direction from that in Venezuela and Ecuador: the new party system became *more* stable over time, once the FMLN was incorporated into the electoral arena and partisan competition was clearly aligned along a left–right axis. Volatility in presidential elections averaged 25.1 percent between 1984 and 1994, then dropped to an average of 14.2 percent between 1994 and 2009, well below the regional average. Indeed, electoral volatility in presidential elections in El Salvador after 2000 was the third lowest in Latin America, and the country boasted the lowest level of volatility in the region in legislative elections after 2000. Equally dramatic, in Brazil's new party system – once notorious for its fluidity and underinstitutionalization (Mainwaring 1999) – electoral volatility was extremely high at the beginning of the democratic period, but fell sharply after structural adjustment brought hyperinflation under control and reinforced left–right programmatic structuration. Brazil recorded a volatility score of 60 between the 1989 and 1994 presidential elections, but more moderate scores of 16.8, 33.7, 26.5, and 18.6 thereafter. The Brazilian and Salvadoran cases clearly demonstrate that party systems founded during the "third wave" are not fated to remain volatile and weak where they are cleaved along a left–right axis of competition marked by meaningful and consistent programmatic distinctions (see Hagopian, Gervasoni, and Moraes 2009).

The very high levels of electoral volatility recorded in Venezuela and Ecuador are even more striking when one considers that they became increasingly extrasystemic rather than intrasystemic. Volatility, that is, was not attributable to vote shifts from one established party to another. Instead, massive vote shifts occurred from traditional parties toward independent personalities or new political movements, on both the right and the left sides of the ideological spectrum. Indeed, the vote for independent figures or new parties formed after 1990 reached 100 percent in presidential elections in Venezuela after 2000 and in Ecuador (as well as Bolivia) in 2009. Even in legislative elections, where volatility based on leadership personality is lower and established parties are more likely to retain a hold on portions of the electorate, the shift away from traditional parties to new challengers was dramatic in Venezuela and Ecuador. This can be

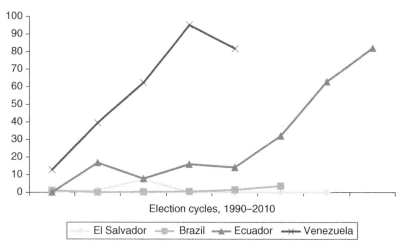

FIGURE 2.3 Percentage of legislative seats held by parties formed after 1990.
Source: Nohlen (2005) and Georgetown University's *Political Database of the Americas* (http://pdba.georgetown.edu/).

seen in Figure 2.3, which tracks the cumulative growth in the percentage of legislative seats captured by parties formed after 1990 across successive election cycles from 1990 to 2010. This percentage gradually rose, reaching over 80 percent in Venezuela after 2006 and Ecuador in 2009 as new parties and movements displaced traditional parties in national legislatures. In both countries, as in Bolivia, the new parties that emerged on the left out of the social backlash against a dealigned partisan establishment have, to date, demonstrated considerable electoral resiliency, with Chávez, Correa, and Morales all achieving reelection with record vote percentages. New party formation on the right in these postcollapse settings has been more tenuous, with opposition forces remaining dependent on fluid electoral fronts rather than new party organizations.

In Brazil and El Salvador's programmatically aligned party systems, on the other hand, the trend line for this indicator of new party seats has been remarkably flat. Indeed, the vote for parties or movements formed after 1990 as part of a backlash against neoliberalism was virtually nonexistent; post-1990 parties averaged a mere 1.8 percent of legislative seats in Brazil after 2000, and zero in El Salvador during the same period. Clearly, parties formed during the democratic transitions of the 1980s consolidated their positions and closed off the electoral marketplace to new competitors. Rather than triggering an electoral backlash against the established party system, societal resistance to market liberalization translated into a progressive strengthening of institutionalized leftist parties, the PT in Brazil and the FMLN in El Salvador. Furthermore, centrist and conservative parties that led the process of market reform in these two countries remained major power contenders, even after losing ground electorally to their leftist rivals in the postadjustment period. El Salvador's ARENA and Brazil's PSDB, in particular, continued to represent business and middle-class interests that supported market liberalization, placing significant institutional constraints on new leftist governments. This was in sharp contrast to the pattern in Venezuela and Ecuador, where conservative parties abdicated leadership of the market reform process to a bewildering array of populist, leftist, and personalist alternatives, and were subsequently swept aside in the generalized societal backlash against a dealigned partisan establishment.

The dynamics found in these four countries closely conform to the larger patterns seen across the region. Parties of the left that remained in opposition during the period of structural adjustment were often able to channel social discontent, broaden their electoral base, and come into power in the postadjustment period. Labor-based populist or center-left parties that governed during the critical juncture generally paid a severe price – either for avoiding structural adjustment and absorbing the political costs of hyperinflation (the Bolivian left and APRA in Peru), or for adopting bait-and-switch reforms and being outflanked and displaced on the left by new populist figures or movement parties (the fate of the MNR in Bolivia, the ID in Ecuador, and AD in Venezuela). The exceptions in the bait-and-switch category were the PLN in Costa Rica, which was outflanked on the left by a new rival but displaced the conservative Social Christian Unity Party (PUSC) in order to remain electorally competitive, and the *sui generis* case of the Peronists in Argentina, who led the process of market reform in the 1990s and then veered left to channel the social backlash against it when the neoliberal model collapsed under the watch of their rivals during the 2001–2002 financial crisis. In these dealigning cases, the major conservative or centrist parties that abdicated leadership of the reform process to populist or center-left rivals eventually collapsed electorally: COPEI in Venezuela, PUSC in Costa Rica, Nationalist Democratic Action (ADN) in Bolivia, PSC in Ecuador, the Radical Civic Union (UCR) in Argentina, and Popular Action (AP) and the Popular Christian Party (PPC) in Peru. By contrast, in the aligning cases where conservative actors led the process of market reform against staunch leftist opposition, conservative parties remained major competitors in the aftermath period, even where the left replaced them in public office.

These patterns indicate that programmatic alignment and dealignment are *systemic* phenomena, referring to the presence or absence of programmatically coherent and differentiated parties to anchor voters on rival sides of the competitive axis. The destabilizing reactive sequences that followed in the wake of dealigning structural adjustment did not concentrate their effects on the individual parties or leaders that implemented bait-and-switch reforms; bystanders who stood on the sidelines and watched or cheered paid electoral costs as well when partisan competition became detached from programmatic alternatives during a period of fundamental policy change.

CONCLUSION

Although the era of mass party organizations with encapsulated voters anchored in social cleavages may have passed, it does not necessarily follow that new party systems formed during the "third wave" of democracy are destined to be fragile and volatile. The recent Latin American experience suggests that the stability of party systems is not strictly determined by their age or historical period of foundation. Indeed, more contingent patterns of cleavage alignment or dealignment during recent periods of regime transition and market-based structural adjustment often trump the effects of historical period or timing effects. Well-defined left–right cleavages forged by the alignment of partisan competition around regime loyalties and economic policy preferences can exert a stabilizing effect on party systems – even relatively new ones formed during the "third wave." In Latin America, at least, the relative volatility of party systems during the "third wave" is less a function of their age, or the age of the democratic regimes in which they compete, than it is a function of widespread programmatic dealignment during the dual transitions to political and economic liberalism. Such dealignment is neither permanent nor irreversible, however, providing a ray of hope for those who believe that strong political parties are vital for democratic governance, but fear that the historical opportunity for the construction of such parties lies in the distant past.

3

Building Party Brands in Argentina and Brazil

Noam Lupu

Successful mass parties need to build a stable base of partisans, citizens who feel an affinity with the party. Around the world, voters are much more likely to support the party with which they identify (e.g., Campbell et al. 1960; Green, Palmquist, and Schickler 2002; Lupu 2015a). Partisanship also stabilizes elections and protects parties from volatile shifts in public opinion. Even when a party fails to fulfill its campaign promises, or oversees a period of economic decline, partisans are willing to give their party the benefit of the doubt (Kayser and Wlezien 2011). To use Hirschman's (1970) terms, partisans will support their party out of loyalty. And loyalty "can serve the socially useful purpose of preventing deterioration from becoming cumulative, as it so often does when there is no barrier to exit" (79).

Research on mass partisanship has nevertheless focused little on how partisan attachments emerge. That is partly because studies of partisanship focus largely on established democracies, where parties and partisan attachments are already widespread and stable.[1] Scholarship

For their advice and suggestions, I thank the editors, the anonymous reviewers, Frances Hagopian, Henry Hale, and participants at the conference on "Challenges of Party-Building in Latin America" at Harvard. I also thank David Samuels, Cesar Zucco, and the Center for the Study of Public Opinion at the State University of Campinas for generously sharing data. A previous version of this chapter was presented at the 2014 annual meeting of the American Political Science Association. I gratefully acknowledge the support of the Center for Advanced Study in the Social Sciences at the Juan March Institute. Sebastián Lavezzolo provided excellent research assistance. Replication material available on the author's website.

[1] Extrapolating from these cases, Converse (1969) posits that mass partisanship will necessarily emerge over time in new democracies, but leaves unanswered the question of which parties will attract partisans.

about partisanship in these settings typically turns on whether partisan attachments are stable predispositions or instead fleeting attitudes (Bartle and Bellucci 2009; Budge, Crewe, and Farlie 1976). Evidence of partisan stability is thought to support theories that conceive of partisanship as a social identity (e.g., Green, Palmquist, and Schickler 2002), while evidence of unstable partisanship is thought to support a more rationalistic interpretation of partisanship as a 'running tally' of performance evaluations (e.g., Thomassen 1976). But these studies tell us little about the circumstances under which parties successfully grow their partisan base.

A handful of studies took up the reverse question – why partisanship erodes – when, in the 1970s and 1980s, scholars of advanced democracies observed aggregate declines in reported partisan attachments. Most offered structural explanations that emphasized the spread of education, emerging mass media, or public financing of parties (Dalton 1984; Flanagan and Dalton 1984; Inglehart 1977; Katz and Mair 1995; Ward 1993). Yet these arguments found little empirical support in analyses of aggregate and individual-level data (Albright 2009; Arzheimer 2006; Berglund et al. 2006; Huber, Kernell, and Leoni 2005; Schmitt-Beck, Wieck, and Christoph 2006; Schmitt and Holmberg 1995).[2] More recently, scholars of developing democracies have also begun to grapple with trends of partisan erosion (Lupu 2014, 2016; Morgan 2011; Seawright 2012). But theories of partisan erosion do not necessarily tell us about partisan emergence.

As a result, we still know little about where mass partisanship comes from, a crucial question for understanding how and when party-building succeeds. Developing democracies – where parties are nascent or partisan attachments weakened by authoritarian interludes – offer opportunities for studying how partisanship emerges. In these settings, some new parties successfully cultivate mass attachments whereas others do not. How do we explain these divergent outcomes?

I argue that one important determinant of whether new parties succeed in building a partisan base is their ability to develop a strong and broad-based *party brand* (see Lupu 2014, 2016). Party brands

---

[2] Even the observation of partisan erosion in these countries has been contested (Bartels 2000; Green, Palquist, and Schickler 2002; Hetherington 2001; Schmitt and Holmberg 1995).

give voters an idea of the type of citizen a particular party represents. When parties offer a demonstrably consistent brand that appeals to a substantial swath of the electorate, voters attracted to that brand are more likely to form lasting attachments. When parties are inconsistent, constantly shifting positions, such attachments are unlikely to form. At the same time, partisanship also depends upon voters' ability to distinguish among competing parties. If the differences between the parties are trivial, voters will fail to form strong attachments to one party over another. Voters will form attachments to a party when they see important differences between their party and its competitors.

Branding alone does not ensure that citizens form lasting partisan attachments; parties must also make themselves known to a citizenry that may have little experience with parties and often pays little attention to politics (Brader and Tucker 2008; Delli Carpini and Keeter 1996). Often, parties need a presence in local communities to become a salient category of identification for voters (Samuels and Zucco 2015; also Chapter 12, this volume). But a strong party brand is a necessary condition – even if not, on its own, a sufficient one – for party success (Levitsky, Loxton, and Van Dyck, Chapter 1, this volume).

This chapter argues that branding helps to account for the emergence – and, in one case, decline – of partisan attachments with new parties in Argentina and Brazil. In Argentina, the Front for a Country in Solidarity (FREPASO) emerged in 1994 and successfully developed a leftist brand in opposition, one that it subsequently diluted when its coalition government pursued neoliberal policies. As a result, attachments with FREPASO grew in the late 1990s and plummeted during the early 2000s. During the 1990s, Brazil's Workers' Party (PT) gradually adopted a more broad-based, moderate leftist brand and benefited from the rightward shift of its main rival. As a result, its partisan base grew throughout this period. Despite vast differences between the two-party systems, party brands appear to have played a critical role in building the partisan bases that helped determine the electoral fortunes of these new parties.[3] Analyses of survey data from Brazil further corroborate the underlying expectation that individuals who perceive differences between the parties are more likely to form partisan attachments.

---

[3] Van Dyck (Chapter 5, this volume) also studies the diverging eventual fates of FREPASO and the PT. I am primarily interested in the similar ways these parties successfully built partisan bases, though an implication is that the same factor – party brand strength – may help to explain FREPASO's demise.

PARTY BRANDS AND MASS PARTISANSHIP

Scholars disagree about whether partisanship is a psychological attachment and social identity (e.g., Campbell 1960; Green, Palmquist, and Schickler 2002) or a product of voters maximizing their expected utilities (e.g., Achen 1992; Fiorina 1981). Empirically, much of the debate between these contrasting perspectives – especially among comparative scholars – has focused largely on the question of partisan stability over time (Bartle and Bellucci 2009; Budge, Crewe, and Farlie 1976). Evidence that partisanship is stable over time is taken to support the social identity perspective (e.g., Green, Palmquist, and Schickler 2002), that partisanship is an "unmoved mover." Conversely, evidence of partisan volatility is considered inconsistent with such theories (e.g., Thomassen 1976). The underlying logic is that while voters' evaluations of party performance fluctuate from year to year, social identities form in childhood or adolescence – whether by socialization or learning – and stabilize thereafter.

Yet, the implication that partisanship must be stable if it is a social identity assumes that the objects of identity (i.e., parties) are themselves stable. The possibility that parties are themselves moving parts is rarely noted. This gap is no doubt partly the result of the overwhelming empirical focus of partisanship research on advanced democracies, the US in particular. In these contexts, the same parties tend to persist and their reputations are slow to change (e.g., Baumer and Gold 1995). But in developing democracies, political parties are often new and may undergo dramatic transformations. In these contexts, the implications of existing theories of partisanship are not immediately apparent. What can they tell us about the rise and decline of mass partisanship in developing democracies? Answering this question requires building upon existing theories about the origins of mass partisanship.

We can think of party attachments as group identities, akin to the attachments people form to social groups.[4] They are based on the stereotypes people have about each group (see Baumer and Gold 1995; Green, Palmquist, and Schickler 2002; Rahn 1993; Sanders 1988). People have an idea about what the prototypical poor person looks like, or how the prototypical banker behaves, and they categorize themselves into group identities by comparing themselves to the group prototype. Individuals identify as a poor person or a banker if they think they resemble, or *fit*, that prototype (Hogg et al. 1995;

---

[4] For a formal statement of my argument, see Lupu (2013). I present my theory in social identity terms, though a similar model could be written from the rationalistic perspective (e.g., Grynaviski 2010). My aim here is not to adjudicate among these perspectives.

Turner et al. 1987). And they also feel closest to a group when they think other groups' prototypes look very different from them, a concept social psychologists call *comparative fit* (Hogg et al. 2004; Turner 1999).

As with other social identities, a voter feels closest to the party whose prototype she thinks she most resembles, relative to all other parties. Voters form perceptions of party prototypes based on what the parties say and do over time.[5] Party elites may profess their support for a particular set of policies, they may pass certain legislation, or they may associate themselves with well-known individuals who suggest what kind of voter they represent. As Przeworski and Sprague highlight, "parties appeal to the middle classes, women, or ecologists by presenting themselves as representatives of their interests and values, by evoking appropriate symbols, and by offering specific policy proposals" (1986: 82). Voters thus learn what to associate with the prototypical partisan by observing what politicians say and do. So the prototypical Democrat might be seen as a worker if the Democratic Party is perceived to be the party that looks out for labor interests. These prototypes comprise what I call a party *brand*. Voters constantly update their perceptions of parties' brands, incorporating new observations into their prior beliefs about the parties.

Perceptions of party prototypes are necessarily noisy, so we can characterize party brands as weak or strong depending on how precisely voters can pinpoint them. When voters see a party sending clear signals, they develop a clearer image of its prototypical partisan, and the brand becomes stronger. As their uncertainty about the party's position increases, the party appears to be more heterogeneous, perhaps containing multiple prototypes, and the brand becomes diluted.

These learned party brands form the basis of voters' attachments. A voter will feel the greatest affinity with the party whose prototypical partisan she thinks she most resembles, relative to all other parties. As with other social identities, partisan identity is determined partly by the resemblance, or fit, between the voter's self-image and her image of the party prototype. Party attachments, therefore, increase as voters perceive they more closely fit with the party. The more strongly a voter identifies as a worker, the more strongly she will identify with the party whose prototype is the worker. But when voters are uncertain about what a party's

---

[5] Of course, we never observe other people's vote choices, so citizens rely on other heuristics, including the actions of party elites, to determine what kind of voter a party serves. The party whose elites regularly meet with African American interest groups, march in civil rights protests, and support policies considered to benefit the African American community, is also more likely to be seen as the party of African Americans.

prototype really is – when it is unclear whether a party really looks out for us unionized workers – the less certain they will be about their resemblance to the prototype and the weaker their attachments will be.

These attachments also depend on comparative fit, the degree to which a voter feels she resembles the prototype of one group and differs from that of another group. As Kirchheimer (1966: 192) noted, "There is need for enough brand differentiation to make the article plainly recognizable, but the degree of differentiation must never be so great as to make the potential customer fear he will be out on a limb." Thus, a voter feels most attached to a party when its prototype most resembles her *and* the prototypes of other parties seem very different. The worker identifies with the party for labor most when it is also clear that rival parties look out for opposing constituencies, like business owners.

Conceiving of mass partisanship in this way implies that the behaviors of parties can affect voter attachments (Lupu 2013). In particular, parties can build their brands through consistency and differentiation.[6] When disciplined party elites present a consistent message, voters become increasingly certain about the party brand. Similarly, a party that maintains consistent positions from year to year increases citizens' certainty about its brand. Voters who are attracted to that brand will be more likely to identify with the party the more certain they are about what that brand really is. The more Democratic elites consistently seem to represent the interests of workers, the more certain voters will be in their perception of the Democratic prototype as a worker. Greater certainty means that workers will be more likely to identify as Democrats.

Parties must also differentiate themselves from prominent rivals in order to build a strong brand and attract partisans. They may offer very different policies from their opponents, or they may clearly demonstrate their opposition to the positions of rival parties. As they do, voters come to realize that the parties represent very different constituencies, and they become more likely to identify with the one they most resemble.[7] Even

---

[6] Elsewhere (Lupu 2014, 2016), I examine what this theory of partisanship tells us about the kinds of party behaviors that dilute party brands, erode partisanship, and lead established parties to break down. Here, I study the reverse phenomenon: what kinds of party behaviors strengthen party brands, grow and sustain mass partisanship, and bolster new parties. As I note below, reversing the implications highlights the fact that in order for new parties to build nationally successful brands, they need to be consistent and differentiated, but also broadly appealing.

[7] This may be why more successful parties tend to form in opposition or in contexts of adversity (LeBas 2011; Van Dyck, Chapter 5, this volume), where the distinction between them and the ruling party is most stark.

when voters are certain about two party brands, they will form stronger bonds with one over the other if they perceive substantial differences between them. It is not enough for Democratic elites to consistently look out for labor interests to attract workers; it must also be the case that Republican elites consistently seem to look out for business interests.

Partisanship thus emerges when parties are consistent and differentiated, but only among those voters who think they resemble the party prototype. So parties seeking a broad, national base must also appeal to a substantial swath of the electorate. A party may have a strong brand borne of consistency and distinguishing itself from competitors, but if that brand represents a minority of voters, its partisan base will be limited. New parties seeking a broad partisan base must, therefore, develop a broadly appealing, consistent brand that differs from rival party brands.

Doing so does not guarantee party success; grassroots organizations, voter experience, and mass attention are likely also necessary (Brader and Tucker 2008; Samuels and Zucco 2015; Chapter 12, this volume). But building a strong and appealing brand is a necessary, if not sufficient, condition for party success (Levitsky, Loxton, and Van Dyck, Chapter 1, this volume). Indeed, cases of failed party-building often falter because they fail to develop clear brands.[8]

Through different trajectories, both Argentina's FREPASO and Brazil's PT achieved broad-based, strong brands that yielded growing partisan bases. Unlike the PT, however, FREPASO quickly diluted its brand in office, eroding its mass partisanship.

Building and Diluting the FREPASO Brand in Argentina

When Argentine president Carlos Menem was elected in 1989, he promised massive wage increases and price controls to stem hyperinflation. As the leader of the Peronist Party (PJ), Menem had the backing of labor unions and poor voters attracted by his commitments to state largesse and social justice. But on taking office, he shocked Argentine voters by instead pursuing a staunchly neoliberal set of economic policies (Campello 2015; Gerchunoff and Torre 1996; Stokes 2001). His first package of economic

---

[8] Whether maintaining a strong party brand is necessary for the survival of parties once they become more established is a separate question. Indeed, parties that already have strong brands and widespread partisan attachments occasionally choose to dilute those brands for electoral gain (Lupu 2016). The fact that these parties sometimes succeed electorally does not imply that weakening their brand has no impact on their partisan base (Domínguez, Chapter 17, this volume).

policies sharply devalued the currency and made deep cuts to government spending. He then set about reversing traditional Peronist commitments by privatizing state-owned companies, defying union demands and antagonizing labor leaders, and pardoning military officers convicted of committing crimes during the 1976–1983 dictatorship.

These reversals created divisions within the PJ and two prominent defections. In the first, twenty prominent PJ legislators defected from the PJ in early 1990 in protest over both the neoliberal economic agenda and the military amnesty laws (Abal Medina 2009; Novaro and Palermo 1998). Known as the Group of Eight for their eight leaders, they eventually formed a coalition with small leftist parties that became known as the Big Front (FG). The second prominent defection was that of Mendoza senator José Octavio Bordón in September 1994. Bordón had been a vocal critic of Menem's economic agenda for years, leading an internal opposition faction. But he was eventually sidelined within the party and decided to form a new party, Open Politics for Social Integrity (PAIS).

By the time Menem faced reelection in 1995, the two defector parties had united behind Bordón's candidacy, forming FREPASO. Bordón criticized not only the manner in which Menem's economic reforms were passed and the allegations of corruption surrounding the administration, but also the reforms themselves and the neoliberal economic agenda. Menem's economic successes made him difficult to beat, and he won reelection with nearly 50 percent of the vote. But FREPASO demonstrated it had quickly become a nationally competitive force.[9]

FREPASO had staked out a clear and consistent center-left position and had become the clear alternative to the Menem administration's economic agenda. Although it did not argue for reversing all of Menem's reforms, FREPASO leaders emphasized the social costs of neoliberal policies on unemployment, poverty, and inequality, and promised to work to address them. By March 1996, FREPASO was viewed by a plurality of survey respondents as the party that best represented an alternative to Menem's economic project.[10]

The result was that mass attachments to FREPASO increased significantly. Figure 3.1 plots the proportion of respondents across various opinion polls between 1994 and 2003 who said they identified with FREPASO. From 1994 to 1997, as FREPASO increased its national

[9] Bordón left FREPASO and returned to the PJ in 1996.
[10] Author's calculations from survey of 505 adult residents of Greater Buenos Aires conducted by Römer & Associates. The questions asked, "What politician or political party do you think today represents the clearest opposition to the government?"

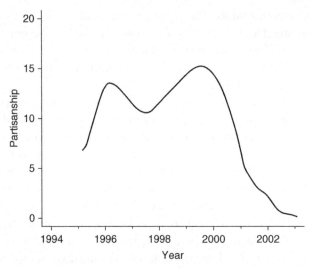

FIGURE 3.1 FREPASO partisanship in Argentina, 1994–2003.

Notes: Lines represent proportions of respondents from nineteen surveys who said they identified with FREPASO. These are moving averages generated by locally weighted (LOESS) regressions ($\alpha = 0.3$, $\lambda = 1$).

Sources: Carlos Fara & Associates; Gallup International; Mansilla, Delich, & Associates; Romer & Associates; Sofres-Ibope.

prominence and as it staked out a consistent position in opposition to Menem and the PJ, it attracted the adherence of leftist voters. Some of these partisans had previously been supporters of Argentina's second largest party, the Radical Civic Union (UCR) (Calvo and Escolar 2005). Nevertheless, FREPASO lacked grassroots organizations beyond the city centers and its leaders viewed this as the party's primary electoral obstacle (Abal Medina 2009; Van Dyck, Chapter 5, this volume). Bordón's votes in 1995 were concentrated in the urban centers and the party won only three senate seats.

The UCR's presidential candidate came in third in 1995, in one of the party's worst electoral defeats in history. For decades, the UCR and PJ had competed fiercely. Whereas the PJ promoted heavy state intervention in the economy and drew its electoral support from the rural poor and urban working classes (Levitsky 2003; Lupu and Stokes 2009; McGuire 1997), the UCR appealed to the upwardly mobile middle classes with promises of labor flexibility and greater market openness (Mora y Araujo 1995). But the UCR had diluted its brand as the alternative to Peronism (Lupu 2014, 2016). In the past, the party had taken centrist or center-right economic positions, proposing some of the very market-oriented policies Menem pursued. In late 1993, UCR leader Raúl Alfonsín signed a pact with Menem calling for a constitutional reform that would allow Menem to seek reelection (García Lema 1994; Grindle 2000: ch. 7; Jones 1996; Negretto 2001).

It was not long before the UCR and FREPASO began exploring the possibility of an electoral alliance. Unlike FREPASO, the UCR had spent decades building an organizational presence in rural provinces. An alliance with the UCR offered FREPASO an instant grassroots organization. But it also meant compromising some of its principles. After all, the UCR was ideologically to the right of FREPASO and had become quite indistinguishable from Peronism.[11] FREPASO leaders like Carlos "Chacho" Álvarez voiced concern about the effects of a pragmatic alliance on the new party's burgeoning "identity" (Álvarez and Joaquín Morales 2002: 69).

Still, leaders in both parties were aware that they could not win a three-way presidential contest in 1999. So in August 1997, the UCR and FREPASO formed an alliance to present joint lists in legislative elections that year. The Alliance for Work, Justice, and Education (Alianza) promised to make "corrections" to the economic model, particularly to address social issues and unemployment. In the October election, it garnered a plurality of the votes (though not a plurality of congressional seats), setting the stage for an Alianza presidential victory in 1999 (Cheresky 2003).

Such a victory, though, would require arduous reconciliation between the two parties. In a hard-fought primary battle, the UCR's Fernando de la Rúa won out, but the parties agreed to make FREPASO leader Álvarez his running mate (Novaro and Palermo 1998). De la Rúa handily won the presidency, but tensions persisted, both within and between the two parties, over their incongruent, if pragmatic, alliance.

Socioeconomic policy had been one of the primary sources of conflict between the UCR and FREPASO on the campaign trail. Meanwhile, financial crises in Asia and Brazil put pressure on the Argentine economy. On taking office, De la Rúa announced tax increases and austerity measures, including cuts in education and social services, the very areas the Alianza had promised to reinforce.[12] The cuts were deeply criticized

---

[11] The University of Salamanca has been conducting surveys of legislators across Latin America since the late 1990s. They ask legislators about their perceptions of the ideological positions of the parties, and these results are instructive. In May–June 1998, legislators on average placed the PJ at 7.8 on a 1–10 left–right scale, the UCR at 7.6, and FREPASO at 4.6.

[12] The justification offered by the administration was that the federal government's fiscal situation was worse than previously thought. Álvarez later argued that, "we were prisoners of the recession and the deficit" (Álvarez and Morales Solá 2002: 105).

by FREPASO legislators and cabinet members. Although the Alianza held
a majority in the Chamber of Deputies, the dissent of some FREPASO
legislators made it difficult for the De la Rúa administration to gain support for its legislative agenda (Jones and Hwang 2005). In a telling sign
of the conflicts within the Alianza, De la Rúa resorted to legislating by
presidential decree (Mustapic 2005).

De la Rúa also resorted to making decisions without consulting Álvarez
or the rest of FREPASO. Throughout 2000, the conflict between the president and vice president became increasingly heated and public. In June,
journalists began to uncover evidence that certain senators had been paid
bribes by the administration in return for their support of a labor reform
bill. Álvarez and FREPASO had spent years accusing the Menem administration of corruption and demanded that the Alianza hold itself to a
higher standard. But De la Rúa refused to open investigations, leading
Álvarez to announce his resignation.[13]

FREPASO stayed in the Alianza,[14] but relations with De la Rúa and
the UCR were strained beyond repair. In early 2001, De la Rúa appointed
a committed neoliberal as Minister of the Economy and announced new
spending cuts to education, a direct contradiction of one of the foundations of FREPASO's program. The reaction from FREPASO was swift.
Party leaders spoke out against the administration with unrestrained
vehemence. Within weeks, the Radical president decided he could no
longer govern with FREPASO and began to rely instead on the architect
of Menem's neoliberal reforms, Domingo Cavallo, and his backers in the
PJ. By the end of 2001, economic pressures forced De la Rúa to resign the
presidency (Levitsky and Murillo 2003).

Argentines' attachments to FREPASO declined precipitously during
the Alianza administration (see Figure 3.1). The incongruence of the UCR-
FREPASO alliance was not immediately obvious, particularly while the
Alianza was in opposition in the final years of Menem's second term. But
once in office, it became increasingly clear that FREPASO had allied itself
with a party willing to implement the very policies FREPASO emerged
to oppose. Forced to make difficult governing decisions, FREPASO abandoned its brand completely. Álvarez had been right to worry about the

---

[13] Álvarez's resignation was apparently celebrated within the administration (Novaro
2009: 587). A few months later, Álvarez also resigned from FREPASO.
[14] Would a formal break with the administration have helped FREPASO preserve its
brand? A great deal of damage was already done by 2001, so it might have been too late.
Moreover, FREPASO had been so critical in getting De la Rúa elected that it is unlikely
that a procedural break would have done much to dissociate the two in the minds of
Argentines.

effects of the alliance on the fledgling party's identity. FREPASO would come to be seen as indistinguishable from the UCR and the PJ; all three seemed to the public to be supporting the same kinds of economic policies. The Alianza administration diluted the brand FREPASO had built in the mid-1990s and Argentines abandoned the party.

Building the PT Brand in Brazil

Scholars of Latin America long listed Brazil's party system among the region's weakest and most fragmented (Mainwaring and Scully 1995). Among its perceived flaws, mass partisanship in Brazil appeared to be fairly weak and limited (Mainwaring 1999). But since redemocratization, the Brazilian party system appears to have coalesced in some ways (Hagopian, Gervasoni, and Moraes 2009; Lyne 2005; Power and Zucco 2009), and partisan attachments appear to have become more widespread and more meaningful (Samuels 2006; Samuels and Zucco 2010, 2015, also Chapter 12, this volume; Sousa Braga and Pimentel 2011).

Most of that development has been driven by the PT, initially a radical socialist party that emerged in the 1970s out of social movements and independent unions (Keck 1992; Meneguello 1989). Unlike other parties in Brazil, the PT was widely regarded as programmatic, disciplined, and organizationally rooted (Hunter 2010). In an open-list electoral system that fosters candidate-centered voting, the PT promoted the party label and consistently attracted more party line votes than its competitors (Samuels 1999).[15] Its leader, Luiz Inácio Lula da Silva, became a recurring contender for president after the transition, and the PT soon emerged as the leading national party of the Brazilian left (Melo and Câmara 2012).

Within a few years of democratization, presidential elections became races between the PT and its main rival, the Brazilian Social Democracy Party (PSDB). The PSDB splintered from the successor of the military-sanctioned opposition party, the Brazilian Democratic Movement Party (PMDB). Originally conceived as a center-left party like European social democratic parties, the PSDB shifted decisively to the right during the neoliberal administration of Fernando Henrique Cardoso (1994–2002) (Fernandes Veiga 2011; Power 1998, 2008). Yet, while the PSDB has become the main national rival of the PT (Melo and Câmara 2012), it remains weakly institutionalized as a decentralized coalition of state-level

---

[15] Hunter (2010: 58) reports that in a 2002 poll, 93 percent of respondents associated the PT or Lula with the number it is assigned in the Brazilian ballot system, whereas less than 1 percent correctly associated other parties with their numbers.

personalities with loose organizational ties and few links to civil society (Roma 2002, 2006).

Whereas the PSDB shifted its ideological position to the right during the 1990s, the PT shifted rightward in the late 1990s and early 2000s. After Lula's second defeat in 1994, the party began to rethink its radical leftist program and perception. Its close association with unions and organized social movements meant that it rarely attracted votes from the poor Northeast of the country despite its promises of land reform and redistribution (Hunter 2010). Lula and other party pragmatists pushed the party to moderate its program to attract center-left votes, particularly once that political space was abandoned by the PSDB (Samuels 2004; Ribeiro 2014). Their efforts gained particular momentum after Lula's third defeat in 1998. Even Lula's image got a makeover that entailed "coaching his speech and inducing him to don a suit and tie, crop his beard, lose weight, whiten his teeth, and stop chain-smoking" (Hunter 2010: 111).

By the end of Lula's second term in office, the PT had repositioned itself as a center-left party opposing the center-right platform of the PSDB. Its partisans were now more centrist (Fernandes Veiga 2011) and poorer (Samuels and Zucco 2010), and Lula's support came increasingly from poorer regions (Hunter and Power 2007; Zucco 2008). In 1997, few poor survey respondents viewed the PT as the party that most closely represents their interests.[16] But by 2006, many more did; in fact, when asked which party most protects them, poor respondents in 2006 were far more likely to choose the PT than any other party.[17] In 2010, when survey respondents were asked to locate national figures on a 0–10 scale of closeness to the poor, they placed Lula's successor, Dilma Rousseff, closer to the poor and the PSDB's José Serra closer to the rich.[18]

Over the course of the 1990s and 2000s, the shifting positions of the PT and PSDB entailed changes to their brands and, potentially, to their distinctiveness. Since these two parties largely head up the major legislative blocs and regularly contend for the presidency, they are the most prominent parties in Brazilian voters' minds. The PSDB had always held a moderate ideological position, so its shift to the center-right should have altered the makeup of its support base without necessarily increasing it.

---

[16] Based on author's calculations from a November 1997 national survey of 2,700 adults conducted by the Fundação Perseu Abramo.

[17] Based on author's calculations from a March 2006 national survey of 2,379 adults conducted by the Fundação Perseu Abramo.

[18] Interestingly, the perceived differences between the parties increased over the course of the 2010 election campaign.

In fact, such a shift might have weakened the party's brand in the short term by confusing voters (see Lupu 2014, 2016). But the consistently weak institutionalization of the PSDB, its subordination to individual leaders, and its decentralized organization have doubtless helped prevent the party from fostering a strong partisan base, either as a center-left party early on or as a center-right one since the Cardoso presidency.

On the other hand, the PT stood to gain significant partisan appeal from both its own rightward shift and from that of its rival. As Hunter notes, "The party's ideological moderation brought it closer to the center of the distribution of popular preference" (Hunter 2010: 38), making the PT brand seem closer to the interests of a larger swath of the electorate. That brand would need to be diluted somewhat to make the party's shift credible; in 2002, for instance, Lula's electoral coalition included a party of the right for the first time.[19] And any shift in program entails some inconsistency between the party's past promises and its new ones. But the PT maintained its commitment to egalitarian social policies even while it adopted more moderate economic ones (Hunter 2010). It also maintained its deep links to civil society organizations (Amaral 2011; Samuels and Zucco, Chapter 12, this volume). Moreover, the PT benefited from its high level of internal discipline and from the pragmatism of its leaders, which allowed it to stake out a new ideological position without provoking internal conflicts like those experienced by FREPASO.

Party brands become weaker by confusing citizens when parties shift positions. But some shifts may move a party closer to or farther from portions of the electorate. Both proximity and uncertainty matter for partisanship, so some party shifts can generate countervailing individual-level effects. The PT's rightward shift likely confused some Brazilians about the party's brand and weakened their attachments. But the party's moderation made it more appealing to a broader swath of the Brazilian electorate, who could now see themselves in the party prototype. In the aggregate, the positive effect swamps the negative one. This is no doubt partly because the PT's moderation was relatively slow, deliberate, and characterized by little intraparty conflict, in contrast with the rapid, conflict-ridden shift by FREPASO.[20]

---

[19] Unlike the FREPASO-UCR alliance, the PT's alliances with right-wing parties were far less prominent. Although these alliances were necessary to secure a legislative majority, most Brazilian voters were unaware of the alliances and few recognize these small right-wing parties.

[20] Samuels and Zucco (2014, Chapter 12, this volume) attribute the growth of PT partisanship to the party's unique grassroots organizational structure and links with local civil

The PT brand was also strengthened by the fact that its rightward shift did not entail completely converging with a rival major party. By the time of the PT shift, the PSDB had already abandoned the center-left. That meant that the PT's moderation did not reduce the differences between these parties. By some measures, the overall ideological distance between the PT and the PSDB actually grew somewhat during the 1990s and 2000s (Zucco and Lauderdale 2011), particularly given the time that elapsed between the PSDB's rightward shift under Cardoso and the PT's subsequent moderation following his reelection. Other measures reveal little to no overall change in the differences between the two parties (Power 2008; Power and Zucco 2009). Either way, the PT seems to have struck the kind of balance between differentiation and appeal that Kirchheimer encouraged. That meant that the PT developed a strong, moderate brand over the course of the 1990s and 2000s. Along with its other grassroots efforts (e.g., Samuels and Zucco 2014, Chapter 12, this volume; Van Dyck 2014a), the more widely appealing PT brand made it possible for the party to grow its partisan base.

Aggregate survey data largely corroborate these expectations. Figure 3.2 plots the proportion of respondents to national Datafolha polls who said they identified with the PT between 1989 and 2011. Attachments to the PT have increased dramatically since 1989. As the ideological distance between the PT and PSDB increased over the course of the 1990s, and even as the PT began to shift its own position, identification with the PT grew significantly. PT partisanship then grew dramatically after 1998, once the party substantially moderated and staked out a position that appealed to many more Brazilians. The upward trend in PT partisanship suffered somewhat during Lula's first term, perhaps because of the corruption scandal that engulfed the party (Hunter and Power 2007), or alternatively because the PT's ideological compromises in office somewhat weakened its brand. Still, the overall trend of growing PT partisanship seems to correlate closely with the party's shift to a more appealing brand and its differences with the rival PSDB.

society organizations. In their reading, and following Levitsky, Loxton, and Van Dyck (Chapter 1, this volume), these organizational attributes provide avenues for citizens to participate in party affairs, in turn generating party attachments. But the mechanism by which grassroots organization generates partisanship may be informational rather than participatory. It may be that grassroots organization and close ties with local civil society help a party successfully reach citizens with credible information about what it stands for. As citizens learn this information, they will start to form attachments to it, as long as it also has a clear and appealing brand.

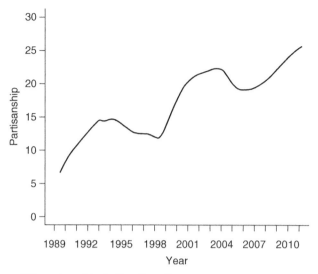

FIGURE 3.2 PT partisanship in Brazil, 1989–2011.

Notes: Lines represent proportions of respondents from seventy-five national surveys who said they identified with the PT. These are moving averages generated by locally weighted (LOESS) regressions (α = 0.2, λ = 2).
Source: Datafolha.

Interestingly, the PSDB has not similarly benefited – in terms of its partisan base – from its national prominence and consistent ideological differences with the PT. Why this is the case remains an open question. Relative to the PT, the PSDB is far less institutionalized, far less disciplined, and far more decentralized, which may mean that its brand seems more ambiguous to voters. Another possibility is that while the PSDB has an equally strong brand, it has not engaged in grassroots efforts to attract partisans, whereas the PT has (Samuels and Zucco, Chapter 12, this volume). A strong party brand may be a necessary condition for building a partisan base, but it is not on its own sufficient, and the PSDB may be lacking the additional efforts needed to attract partisans.

PARTY PERCEPTIONS AND PARTISANSHIP: TESTING INDIVIDUAL-LEVEL EXPECTATIONS

The experiences of FREPASO in Argentina and the PT in Brazil are consistent with the notion that distinguishable party brands are a necessary condition for building partisanship. But the observed correlations between aggregate attachments and party polarization do not tell us whether individuals who perceive the parties to be more polarized are those who form a party attachment. They also cannot confirm whether the relationship between these variables is causal.

Unfortunately, individual-level data from the late 1990s in Argentina is sparse, and I know of no survey that asked voters about their perceptions of party positions. But such data is available for Brazil, where a national election study, the Brazilian Electoral Study (ESEB), was conducted in 2002, 2006, and 2010. These national surveys asked respondents to place the major Brazilian parties on a 0–10 left–right scale.[21] I use these responses to construct a measure of a respondents' perception of how polarized the party system in her country is. I measure perceived polarization as the mean distance a respondent places between the parties. So, for a respondent who placed five parties on the left–right scale, I take a weighted average of the twenty distances between each pair of parties (see also Lupu 2015b).[22]

If perceiving a distinguishable party brand matters for partisanship, then I should find that respondents who perceive more polarization among Brazil's parties will be more likely to identify with the PT. To test this hypothesis, I estimated probit models for each survey year that relate perceived polarization with the likelihood of identifying with the PT. These models also control for other individual characteristics that might affect a respondent's propensity to develop a party attachment. We expect that individuals who place themselves close to a party on the

---

[21] The surveys asked respondents about six to nine parties; given Brazil's fragmented party system, this means that some relevant national parties were left out. Specifically, the 2002 survey asked respondents to place the PT, PSDB, Liberal Front Party (PFL), PMDB, Brazilian Socialist Party (PSB), Labor Democratic Party (PDT), Brazilian Labor Party (PTB), and Liberal Party (PL). The 2006 survey asked about the PMDB, PT, PSDB, PFL, PDT, PTB, and Socialism and Freedom Party (P-SOL). The 2010 survey asked about the PT, PMDB, PSDB, Republic Party (PR), Democrats (DEM), PSB, Progressive Party (PP), PDT, and PTB. The parties covered represented 86.6 percent of the lower house vote in 2002, 64 percent in 2006, and 79.6 percent in 2010. This means that my measure of perceived polarization is imperfect, particularly in 2006.

[22] Put formally:

$$P_i = \sum_{k=1}^{m-1} \sum_{j=1}^{m} \frac{w_j + w_k}{m - 1} \mid p_j - p_k \mid,$$

where j and k are different parties, w_j and w_k are the positions the respondent assigned parties j and k, p_j and p_k are their vote shares, and m is the number of parties the respondent placed. Note that this means that only respondents who placed two or more parties are included in my analysis.

left–right scale are more likely to identify with it. I measure an individual's proximity to the PT as the left–right distance between her position and the position she assigns the PT. I also control for demographic characteristics, including education level, household income (except in 2006), age, and gender.[23]

Figure 3.3 presents the results of this analysis. The figure illustrates the predicted probability that a respondent identifies with the party, based on shifting each variable from its sample 25th to 75th percentile, with all other continuous variables held at their sample means and ordered variables held at their sample medians. Consistent with my expectations, the results across the Brazilian election studies suggest that individuals who perceived the parties to be further apart are indeed more likely to identify with the PT.

Still, these associations fail to identify the causal relationship between perceived polarization and party attachments. The ESEB surveys measure both perceived polarization and partisanship in the context of the same interview. Thus, these associations may indicate the reverse causal direction, or perhaps a feedback loop between perceived polarization and partisanship.

One way to address this problem and identify the causal relationship between perceived polarization and partisanship is through repeated interviews of the same survey respondents. Indeed, part of the definition of a cause is that it occurs prior to an outcome (Finkel 1995). Panel surveys allow us to test whether perceptions of party polarization affect changes in partisanship within the same individuals over time, helping to identify the causal link (Bartels 2006). Fortunately, researchers conducted a Brazilian Election Panel Study (BEPS) in 2010 in which they asked respondents, in three interviews over the course of the election campaign, about their party attachments and their perceptions. Although perceptions about parties and voter partisanship may change slowly in more established democracies, the fragmentation and fluidity of the Brazilian party system offers a case where voters are likely to learn about the parties during election campaigns and shift their perceptions quite rapidly.

Compared to the ESEB, the BEPS asked slightly different questions about voter perceptions. Rather than asking about parties, the BEPS

---

[23] These estimates are weighted using the design and demographic weights provided by the ESEB.

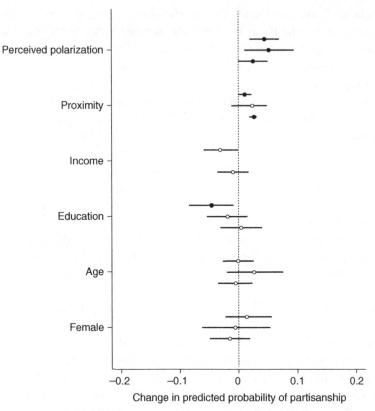

FIGURE 3.3 Perceived polarization and PT partisanship in Brazil.

Notes: Values represent changes in the predicted probability that a respondent identifies with the PT, based on shifting each variable from its sample 25th to 75th percentile, with all other continuous variables held at their sample means and ordered
variables held at their sample medians. Solid lines show the simulated 95 percent
confidence interval. Black dots represent values that are significant at 95 percent
confidence, white dots those that fall short of that threshold. For each variable, the
top value represents the result from the 2002 survey, the middle value the 2006 survey, and the bottom value the 2010 survey. These predicted values are based on the
estimates from probit models presented in Appendix Table A1 (2002: N = 1,512,
R^2 = 0.024; 2006: N = 484, R^2 = 0.024; 2010: N = 1,026, R^2 = 0.026).

Source: ESEB (2002, 2006, 2010).

asked respondents about the positions of presidential candidates. That
means that we have to assume that respondents generally perceived
agreement between a party and its presidential candidate. What is useful
about the BEPS questions is that they asked respondents to place the
candidates on a dimension other than the ideological left–right. There

are good reasons to think that different Brazilian voters understand the left–right scale differently (Zechmeister 2015), so it would be better to use a measure of voters' perception on a more politically salient dimension, like class. The BEPS asked respondents to what extent they thought the PT and PSDB presidential candidates (Dilma Rousseff and José Serra, respectively), each "defends the interests of the poor" on a 1–10 scale.[24] I use the difference in a respondent's placement of these candidates to measure how far apart she perceives these parties to be on the poor–rich class dimension.

To analyze the causal effect of perceived polarization on partisanship, I specify a cross-lagged structural equation model frequently used by scholars of US public opinion working with panel survey data (e.g., Highton and Kam 2011; Layman and Carsey 2002; Lupu 2015b). This approach uses simultaneous equations to model current partisanship and current vote intention as functions of prior partisanship and prior vote intention. The logic behind cross-lagged causality is that a variable X is said to cause another variable Y if prior observations of X are associated with current observations of Y, holding constant prior observations of Y (Finkel 1995: 25–26). In this context, we want to know whether prior perceived polarization affects current partisanship while taking account of preexisting partisan commitments.[25] My models again control for individual demographic characteristics: household income, education, age, and gender. Since there are multiple waves in the BEPS, I pool observations of respondents in each two-wave dyad and cluster standard errors by respondent.

The results reveal a causal effect of perceived polarization on partisanship. Figure 3.4 reports estimates from the cross-lagged model. The left panel shows that both prior perceived partisanship and prior partisanship positively affect current partisanship. This suggests that partisanship is somewhat stable over the course of the panel (see also Lupu 2015a). But the fact that prior perceptions of polarization affect current

---

[24] The survey question stated, "People say that some politicians defend the interest of the poor, whereas others defend the interests of the rich. I would like to rate the following politicians from 1 to 10 on whether they defend the interests of the poor, where 1 means they don't defend the poor and 10 means they defend the poor a lot."

[25] This means simultaneously estimating the equations:

$$\text{Partisanship}_{i,t} = \alpha_1 + \beta_1 \text{Partisanship}_{i,t-1} + \gamma_1 \text{Perceivedpolarization}_{i,t-1} + \varepsilon_1$$

$$\text{Perceivedpolarization}_{i,t} = \alpha_2 + \beta_2 \text{Partisanship}_{i,t-1} + \gamma_2 \text{Perceivedpolarization}_{i,t-1} + \varepsilon_2$$

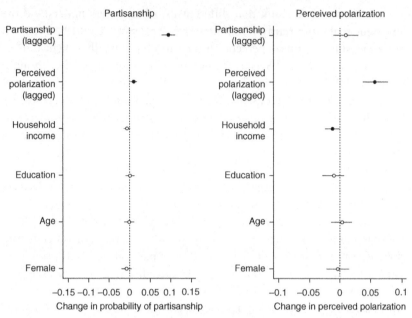

FIGURE 3.4 Perceived polarization and PT partisanship in Brazil, panel survey.

Notes: Values represent changes in the predicted probability that a respondent identifies with the PT or perceives polarization between the parties, based on shifting each variable from its sample 25th to 75th percentile, with all other continuous variables held at their sample means and ordered variables held at their sample medians. Solid lines show the simulated 95 percent confidence interval. Black dots represent values that are significant at 95 percent confidence, white dots those that fall short of that threshold. These predicted values are based on cross-lagged structural equation estimates presented in Appendix Table A2 (N = 1,208).

Source: BEPS (2010).

partisanship is evidence that voters become more partisan as they perceive more polarization in Brazil.

I find no evidence of reverse causation in the BEPS data. The right panel in Figure 3.4 reports the estimated effects of prior perceptions of polarization and prior partisanship on current perceptions of polarization. Prior perceptions of polarization increase the likelihood of perceiving polarization currently, suggesting that perceptions of polarization, like partisanship, are somewhat stable over time. The concern that partisanship affects perceptions of polarization, on the other hand, finds no support. Prior partisanship does not have a statistically significant effect on current perceptions of polarization.

Survey data for Brazil thus confirm my individual-level expectations. In both Argentina and Brazil, aggregate trends in partisanship and party polarization correlated by and large as I hypothesized. But these aggregate trends could be misleading about the individual-level relationships or the direction of causality. If distinguishable party brands are a necessary condition for partisanship at the level of individual voters, then we should be able to uncover such a relationship with appropriate survey data. Indeed, national surveys from Brazil show just such a relationship, and allow us to identify the causal effect of perceiving party differences on partisanship.

PARTY BRANDS, TIMING, AND THE SUCCESS OF NEW PARTIES

New political parties regularly come and go in multiparty systems. But some succeed in becoming major competitors in national elections. To achieve that level of success, new parties must build a broad partisan base that cushions the party against rapid shifts in public opinion. Because partisans give their party the benefit of the doubt, successful mass parties need to build a base of partisans to rely on in unfavorable times.

Building a broad base of partisans requires an appealing, consistent, and differentiable party brand. Parties must stake out a position that signals that they represent a large swath of the electorate, and they must send that signal consistently to voters. If voters observe mixed signals from the party and its leaders, they will see an ambiguous brand and fail to form strong attachments. In addition, strong party brands require that parties differentiate themselves from their competitors. If voters see negligible differences between the parties, they are unlikely to form lasting attachments to one over the other. Instead, when voters unambiguously perceive a party that represents citizens like them, in stark contrast to its rivals, they are far more likely to identify with it.

Argentina's FREPASO and Brazil's PT both succeeded in building such a brand. In the mid-1990s, FREPASO adopted a consistent and prominent center-left stance in opposition to the social costs of Menem's neoliberal economic reforms. At a time when Menem's PJ and its traditional rival, the UCR, had converged on the reform agenda, FREPASO became a credible alternative. The PT pursued a similar tack. Eschewing the radical left-wing platform of its origins, the party shifted to the center-left just as Cardoso's PSDB implemented its neoliberal program. Appealing to a broader swath of Brazilians, the PT, like FREPASO, led the national center-left opposition at a time when the social costs of the Washington Consensus were being felt by millions of voters. Indeed, those Brazilians who saw more differences between the parties were most likely to identify with the PT. Despite the vast differences between the Argentine and Brazilian party systems, these new parties developed strong brands and built growing bases of partisan support. Comparing their successes shows that appealing, consistent, and differentiated party brands help parties attract mass attachments.

The comparison of FREPASO and the PT also suggests that, at least during the 1990s heyday of the Washington Consensus, new left parties did better when they remained out of office than when they won elections (see also Roberts 2015; Chapter 2, this volume). New left parties could stake out clear brands on the ideological left as long as they were not required to govern. Once in office, however, they confronted economic constraints that forced them into compromising those positions and eroding their partisan base (Lupu 2014, 2016), as the case of FREPASO demonstrates. Had FREPASO not pragmatically allied itself with the UCR, it would likely have remained in opposition for some time, strengthening its brand and expanding its partisan base. Instead, FREPASO entered a coalition government whose policies increasingly contradicted its brand, eroding the party's fledgling base.

By the time the PT won the presidency, in contrast, the Washington Consensus had waned and rising commodity prices provided leeway for leftist administrations to abandon neoliberal prescriptions (see Levitsky and Roberts 2011). That allowed the PT to maintain its center-left position on redistribution and social programs without sacrificing macroeconomic stability. The PT had gradually abandoned aspects of its more radical early brand, but it did so without abandoning its entire platform, as FREPASO did. The PT's inconsistency also brought it closer to mainstream Brazilian voters, increasing its potential appeal. It seems one crucial reason for the PT's success in building a partisan following was its repeated national electoral defeats; had Lula won the presidency in 1989, his party's fate would likely have looked more like FREPASO's.

Appendix

TABLE A1 *Perceived polarization and PT partisanship in Brazil*

	2002	2006	2010
Perceived polarization	0.129** (0.037)	0.149* (0.060)	0.084* (0.043)
Proximity	0.047 (0.025)	0.057 (0.039)	0.142** (0.029)
Household income	−0.062* (0.031)		−0.020 (0.033)
Education	−0.091* (0.039)	−0.081 (0.076)	0.010 (0.042)
Age	−0.000 (0.003)	0.005 (0.005)	−0.001 (0.003)
Female	0.057 (0.076)	−0.028 (0.131)	−0.070 (0.081)
Constant	−0.129 (0.270)	−0.885 (0.511)	−1.137** (0.344)
Observations	1,512	484	1,026
Pseudo-R^2	0.024	0.024	0.026
ePCP	0.54	0.48	0.58

Notes: Robust standard errors in parentheses; ** $p < 0.01$, * $p < 0.05$.
Source: ESEB.

TABLE A2 *Perceived polarization and PT partisanship in Brazil, panel survey*

Variable	
Partisanship	
Prior partisanship	0.377** (0.032)
Prior perceived polarization	0.088** (0.027)
Household income	−0.043 (0.030)
Education	0.013 (0.031)
Age	0.000 (0.029)
Female	−0.030 (0.026)
Constant	0.400** (0.119)
Perceived polarization	
Prior partisanship	0.027 (0.029)
Prior perceived polarization	0.239** (0.034)
Household income	−0.064 (0.033)
Education	−0.037 (0.036)
Age	0.014 (0.031)
Female	−0.013 (0.028)
Constant	0.945** (0.134)
Observations	1,208
Respondents	815
Log-likelihood	−18360.69

Note: Clustered standard errors in parentheses; ** $p < 0.01$, * $p < 0.05$.
Source: BEPS 2010.

4

Segmented Party–Voter Linkages

The Success of Chile's Independent Democratic Union and Uruguay's Broad Front

Juan Pablo Luna

This chapter seeks to explain the success of two recently formed parties in Latin America: Uruguay's Broad Front (FA) and Chile's Independent Democratic Union (UDI).[1] The FA and UDI differ in a number of ways. The FA is a left-wing, union-based party that spent most of its formative years in clandestine opposition to Uruguay's right-wing military dictatorship (1973–1984). The UDI is a conservative party with strong ties to the Chilean economic elite and deep roots in the Pinochet military dictatorship (1973–1989). The UDI's party organization is coherent and hierarchical, while the FA's is much more diverse and confrontational. Despite these differences, the FA and UDI are both clear cases of successful party-building, according to the definition and operationalization used in Chapter 1 of this volume. Both parties have passed the 10 percent threshold in five consecutive congressional elections and today are the most electorally successful parties in their respective countries. In Uruguay, the FA has won at least a plurality of votes in every national election since 1999, and it won the presidency (and a legislative majority) in 2004, 2009, and 2014. In Chile, the UDI has won the largest congressional bloc in the last four elections (2001, 2005, 2009, and 2013). What explains the success of these two highly dissimilar political parties?

---

[1] The FA was established in 1971, and the UDI was established in 1983. Because the FA was created in 1971, prior to the onset of the third wave of democratization, it is not included in the sample presented by Levitsky, Loxton, and Van Dyck (Chapter 1, this volume).

In this chapter, I argue that the FA and the UDI, despite their differences, succeeded for the same basic reason: they established segmented, harmonized linkages to distinct electoral constituencies. Both parties developed in unequal, socially fragmented societies and, in order to succeed electorally, had to appeal simultaneously to distinct socioeconomic groups: in the FA's case, to both unions and informal/unemployed workers, and in the UDI's case, to both the economic elite and the poor. The FA and the UDI succeeded, I argue, because they established different *types* of linkages to their distinct constituencies; I refer to this process as the *segmentation* of electoral appeals. Both parties also successfully coordinated their candidates' behavior in order to minimize potential tensions between their distinct electoral appeals; I refer to this process as *harmonization*. Segmentation and harmonization gave the FA and the UDI an electoral edge over rival parties that were either unable to segment their appeals to different constituencies or unable to harmonize their segmented appeals. Segmentation and harmonization thus facilitated the consolidation of both the FA and the UDI, and played a key role in their success in party-building.

The segmentation of electoral appeals is not a new discovery.[2] Taylor-Robinson (2010) has even recently presented an explicit argument on segmentation.[3] However, the implications of electoral

[2] See, for example, Calvo and Murillo (2007), Coppedge (1998), Gibson (1992, 2005), Hagopian (2009), Levitsky (2003), Magaloni et al. (forthcoming), Morgan (2011), Taylor-Robinson (2010), and Valenzuela (1977). As Coppedge (1998) writes, "Before we can assess more accurately how ideological Latin American parties and party systems are, it is necessary to clarify three issues. First, personalism and ideology are not necessarily mutually exclusive qualities. Some of the most rigidly ideological parties in the world have been closely identified with, and tightly controlled by, strong personalities, and parties that are known primarily as vehicles for strong personalities may nevertheless stake out clear ideological positions. Second, clientelism and ideology are not necessarily mutually exclusive. Many successful parties all over the world trade personal favors for political support. Even in supposedly highly ideological Chile, party officials of all tendencies engaged in the same sorts of clientelistic activities (Valenzuela 1977: 166). Clientelism is merely a means to build and maintain a power base; ideology, where it exists, is what guides what that power is used for. Many parties are to some degree clientelistic, to some degree personalistic and to some degree ideological; these three qualities vary independently" (552).

[3] According to Taylor-Robinson (2010), "Clientelism may help a legislator to represent both rich and poor constituents. The rich may want national policies that the poor cannot monitor, or that poor people view as unlikely to be implemented in a timely fashion or to directly affect them (e.g., increasing the safety of bank deposits or regulating private school tuition). In that case a legislator can address the rich person's national policy preferences without the poor person wanting to sanction him. Meanwhile, the legislator can deliver clientelistic benefits to poor people. Clientelistic benefits may be the policy/service package the poor person desires because they are cheap to monitor and their value is clear.

segmentation for the emergence and success of new parties are still poorly understood.

The argument I present in this chapter suggests that segmented electoral appeals are an enduring characteristic of contemporary party systems. The structure of segmentation and the types of electoral appeals that get segmented change over time, in line with parties' adaptation to different opportunity structures. Historical and contextual conditions and the patterns of social inequality shape the relative sizes and profiles of different social constituencies, which are differentially prone to becoming mobilized electorally through diverse strategies.[4] Different partisan endowments give individual parties greater or lesser capacity to develop complex linkage strategies and to adapt (or fail to adapt) to new opportunity structures that emerge with the passage of time. For that reason, segmentation strategies that work at a given time and place might not work in a different context. However, electoral segmentation itself is ubiquitous and can be structured in terms of socioeconomic categories, territorial dimensions, or both. In ethnically divided societies, this type of segmentation can also be implemented along ethnic or religious lines.

This chapter contributes to the analysis of party-building by analyzing the mobilization strategies pursued by two new parties that successfully deployed segmented linkage strategies in order to grow electorally. In doing so, the chapter illustrates how new and small parties that emerge with strong ties to a relatively small electoral constituency can, over time, expand their electoral base by deploying segmented linkages to new electoral constituencies. Both parties' strategies relied on the

The legislator's clientelistic work could also win favor with the rich person who receives the contract to build a local public works project. In this scenario, poor and rich people do not have incompatible policy preferences; they are interested in different things and representing both should be feasible, unless the government's budget is so limited that it cannot afford to fund both policies and services" (48). Although its implications are in some respects similar, my argument differs from Taylor-Robinson's in several ways. First, in my framework, parties eventually have the capacity to avoid "structural determinism" and mobilize "poor voters" programmatically, provided that favorable structural conditions and favorable partisan agency exist. Second, in my framework, the agent could either be a party or an individual candidate. I therefore place equal emphasis on the need to segment linkages and to harmonize mobilization strategies at the partisan (collective) level. Last, but not least, my argument considers not only programmatic and clientelistic linkage strategies. Other linkage strategies, some of which are not contingent on short-term interactions between a party and its voters (e.g., party identification, which is usually built on a long-term relationship between the party and its identifiers), are also crucial in understanding the strategies that parties pursue.

[4] For a recent argument and evidence on the structure of inequality and its effects on voters' distributive preferences, see Lupu and Pontusson (2011).

specific endowments that each of the two organizations carried from its inception.

The chapter is organized as follows. I begin by presenting two general arguments. First, I argue that to explain party-building, it is useful to sequence and combine arguments focused on party origin and party consolidation. Second, I argue that in unequal and socially fragmented societies, segmentation and harmonization are critical for electoral success. I then illustrate the latter argument through an examination of the very different cases of Uruguay's FA and Chile's UDI. My discussion of both cases is brief and stylized but based on more systematic and documented analyses presented elsewhere (Luna 2007, 2010, 2014). After my case discussions, I compare the FA and the UDI systematically, engaging the main arguments developed in Chapter 1 and other chapters of the book. A brief conclusion follows.

SEQUENCING EXPLANATIONS OF PARTY ORIGINS AND CONSOLIDATION

Political parties can be understood as either exogenous or endogenous institutions. Understanding parties as exogenous institutions does not necessarily neglect that parties are complex organizations, formed by different individuals with distinct and sometimes competing preferences and goals (see Kitschelt 1989, 1994; Levitsky 2003; Panebianco 1988). Yet, in this view, parties impose constraints that shape the incentives that those ambitious politicians face when seeking to advance their political careers. Alternatively, parties could also be conceived of as epiphenomenal to the choices and preferences of individual actors in pursuit of specific interests (e.g., election and reelection). This latter conception also understands parties as complex and collectively created organizations (see Aldrich 1995). Yet that approach focuses more on modeling the action of different clusters of individual actors (i.e., candidates, MPs) on the basis of their often narrowly conceived "interests."

Conceiving parties as either endogenous to the choices of ambitious politicians, or alternatively, as exogenous constraints, yields specific analytical payoffs (and blind spots). For instance, seeking answers to the question of "why (not) parties?" by understanding parties as exogenous institutions might lead to functional arguments on the virtues of political parties for democracy. Chapter 15 by Levitsky and Zavaleta (this volume) illustrates the analytical payoffs to be gained by shifting the focus to politicians' incentives in a context of no parties and competitive elections in order to explain the persistent absence of parties. Yet, conceiving parties exclusively as endogenous institutions might lead us to underestimate key organizational traits that become pivotal for success once parties are formed (see, e.g., Chapter 12 by Samuels and Zucco (this volume) on the rise and evolution of the Workers' Party in Brazil).

The argument I present in this chapter suggests that sequence matters, not only substantively, but also analytically.[5] In my view, an endogenous understanding of political parties is crucial to understanding party formation. However, once parties are formed, treating them as exogenous constraints that partially structure politicians' behavior makes better sense.[6]

The moment of party formation is crucial in infusing parties with a collective identity, with high levels of party elite cohesiveness, and with a core electoral constituency. In other words, party formation determines parties' DNA (Panebianco 1988). The two cases I analyze in this chapter suggest, in line with Levitsky, Loxton, and Van Dyck (Chapter 1, this volume), that times of conflict and political and social turmoil, as well as adverse prospects regarding immediate electoral victory (or survival), are crucial contextual conditions that explain party formation.[7]

The moment of party formation is also pivotal in determining the different sets of resources that the new party will have at its disposal (from material benefits, to funding for electoral campaigns, to symbolic resources such as a party's programmatic reputation, "epic," or party ID). If authoritarian successor parties may be endowed with organizational and financial resources (Loxton, Chapter 9, this volume), parties born out of instances of mass mobilization may inherit a strong base in organized civil society (Madrid, Chapter 11, and Van Dyck, Chapter 5, this volume), as well as a strong party identity and/or programmatic brand (on the latter, see Lupu, Chapter 3, this volume).

---

[5] For analyses of the substantive importance of sequencing and timing, see Roberts (Chapter 2, this volume), Eaton (Chapter 14, this volume), and Mainwaring and Zoco (2007).

[6] This is not to deny the relevance of an endogenous understanding of parties over time. Although not merely an externality of agents' pursuit of their individual goals, over time political parties benefit from (or are disadvantaged by) the predominant strategies that their candidates pursue while trying to win elections. In short, depending on context, party resources may further some forms of electoral appeals more than others, and, *ceteris paribus*, some kinds of candidate appeals contribute more than others to strengthening parties as collective organizations over time. In fact, reliance on candidate-based appeals has precisely the opposite effect.

[7] See also Van Dyck (Chapter 5, this volume). For negative cases, see Eaton (Chapter 14, this volume) and Levitsky and Zavaleta (Chapter 15, this volume).

It follows that in a given party system at a given time, individual parties carrying a specific DNA will face different strategic situations regarding the suitable and feasible mobilization strategies that they should follow in pursuit of electoral expansion. Parties' strategic situation is thus contingent on their own characteristics and historical trajectories, but also on the interaction between parties' own features and the electoral and systemic context in which they compete (see Roberts, Chapter 2, this volume).[8] In short, a party's DNA yields unique resources and constraints for electoral growth and survival.

If this latter argument holds, explanations for party survival and electoral growth might be highly contextual (i.e., equifinal and/or multifinal). In other words, what works for one political party might be detrimental for others, and vice versa. The relevance of (programmatic) brands is a case in point (Lupu, Chapter 3, this volume). Branding was pivotal for the electoral consolidation of the FA outside its core constituency, while brand dilution was equally pivotal for the electoral growth of the UDI beyond its original electoral strongholds. On a different note, both parties analyzed in this chapter (one on the left, the other on the right) relied on municipal governments as a way to "clean" their image and moderate their perceived programmatic stance (see Holland, Chapter 10, this volume).

In sum, the argument on the role of segmentation and harmonization of electoral appeals that I introduce in this chapter should not be

---

[8] Given the importance of parties' historical trajectories, new parties might lack access to critical resources. Yet, especially in the context of rising discontent with established parties, being a newcomer might in itself be a powerful competitive resource. There might also be a mismatch between parties' resources and strategic needs. For instance, due to its particular trajectory in a party system, a party could command disproportionate access to a decentralized network of activists. This is typical of mass-based electoral parties that consolidated their organizations in the early and mid-twentieth century. Whereas such a network might remain an important resource for pursuing electoral mobilization on the basis of clientelism or party identification, it might have become less useful for the pursuit of other types of linkages that nowadays can be pursued at a distance and "by air" (e.g., programmatic, leader-based appeals). If a mass party pursues one of those types of appeals, its network at the grassroots level is certainly not a key resource, and might even become a hindrance (e.g., fueling grassroots discontent with leaders who have "abandoned" their bases). As argued by Muñoz and Dargent (Chapter 7, this volume), state reforms and decentralization have resulted in the weakening of political parties that relied on patronage to mobilize voters in both Peru and Colombia. Moreover, in contexts where individual candidates are allowed to raise funds for their electoral campaigns in a decentralized manner, the value of party-provided funds decreases. Their value further decreases in contexts where parties, as collective institutions, have less access to campaign financing. In sum, though valuable in principle, the electoral payoffs to be derived from party-provided resources are subject to significant contextual variation. See Bruhn (Chapter 8, this volume) for evidence of the role of public finance in party-building.

confused with a given set of predefined electoral tactics. Segmentation and harmonization constitute a feasible overall strategy for electoral growth and party survival by allowing new parties to expand beyond their core constituencies while drawing on resources inherited through the party's DNA. Yet, segmented and harmonized strategies go hand-in-hand with (successful) electoral mobilization tactics that are more fruitfully analyzed on a case-by-case basis. In other words, while consistent with the idea of an overarching *segmented and harmonized strategy*, the cases I analyze here do not necessarily hint at precise mobilizational tactics that travel across space or time.

LINKAGE SEGMENTATION AND HARMONIZATION: A FRAMEWORK

Parties can build linkages to voters through three main types of appeal.[9] First, they can support public policies that distribute resources to large groups of citizens (e.g., pensions for unionized workers). Second, they can give or promise activists and voters access to private, excludable goods (e.g., government jobs, clientelistic handouts). And third, they can make symbolic or cultural appeals. For simplicity, I call the first type of linkage *programmatic*, the second *clientelistic*, and the third *symbolic*.

Programmatic parties compete by publicizing their policy platforms and implementing them in government, with voters making electoral choices based on their own programmatic proximity to the parties. Clientelistic parties compete by securing access to state or private resources (e.g., government jobs, corporate finance) and channeling these resources to activists, voters, and constituency groups, with activists providing information on which individual voters or constituency groups should be targeted (Calvo and Murillo 2007; Stokes 2005). Parties reliant on symbolic linkages may build support in numerous ways, such as personalistic or charismatic appeals; identification with a particular cultural group or set of values; development of a strong internal party subculture; and historical association with a major period of conflict and polarization.

Segmented Appeals in Unequal, Fragmented Societies

In societies with high levels of economic inequality and class fragmentation, exclusive reliance on *programmatic* linkages is problematic for

---

[9] This section summarizes the theoretical framework of Luna (2014).

party-building. In such societies, parties must gain the support of distinct socioeconomic constituencies in order to build winning coalitions. But if they seek to attract distinct constituencies by making multiple, simultaneous programmatic appeals, they run a significant risk of programmatic incoherence or contradiction. They can solve this problem by segmenting their appeals, using, for example, programmatic appeals to attract one constituency and a different type of appeal (clientelistic or symbolic) to attract another.

As an illustration, consider the following hypothetical scenario. A leftist party emerges and successfully courts middle-class unions by promising to protect formal sector pensions and social benefits. Over time, social fragmentation increases. Market reforms weaken the clientelistic networks of the party's political rivals, creating a new constituency of informal workers and unemployed people available for electoral capture. The party must capture this new constituency in order to build a winning electoral coalition, as unions are too small to provide a sizable plurality. But the programmatic appeals that the party has traditionally used to attract the unionized middle sectors are unlikely to attract informal and unemployed workers, whose distributive preferences differ from – and often run counter to – formal sector union preferences. In order to confront this strategic scenario, the party pursues electoral expansion by remaining prounion in programmatic terms, but simultaneously using clientelistic and personalistic tactics to attract unemployed and informal workers. This is a stylized account of the electoral strategy implemented by the FA in Uruguay.

Or, imagine a conservative party that, in exchange for financial resources from the economic elite, represents elite interests in the legislature. Since economic inequality is high, and since economic elites, by definition, represent a miniscule percentage of the population, the party will be condemned to a minority position in the party system if it depends on the electoral support of upper-class voters alone. In order to increase its vote share, the party uses its considerable financial resources to channel clientelistic benefits to the poor. In return, poor voters give the party the numbers it needs to succeed electorally. This electoral success then enables the party to "pay back" the economic elite more effectively, as more legislative seats translate into greater policy influence. This is a stylized account of the electoral strategy implemented by the UDI in Chile.

Both examples illustrate the general argument of the chapter. Political parties often seek to establish an electoral base by making programmatic appeals to a particular constituency. But in unequal, fragmented societies, a single programmatic constituency (e.g., unions) rarely suffices to build a winning electoral coalition. Because distinct programmatic appeals can lead to incoherence, party-building in unequal, fragmented societies is more likely to succeed when parties *segment* their electoral appeals – that is, when they simultaneously deploy different types of electoral appeals (programmatic, clientelistic, symbolic) to attract distinct constituencies.[10]

To be sure, not every process of electoral expansion results from segmentation. "Catchall parties," for example, simply diffuse their ideological profiles in an effort to expand their electoral constituencies (Kirchheimer 1966). Nevertheless, this chapter shows that segmented strategies have been critical for successful party-building in two very different Latin American parties: the left-wing, union-based FA in Uruguay and the right-wing, elite-based UDI in Chile.

The Challenge of Harmonization

Although segmentation helps parties solve the problem of attracting distinct constituencies, a separate challenge remains: that of coordinating the actions of party candidates, or *harmonizing* the party's overall electoral strategy. Parties differ in the degree to which their appeals are party-centered or candidate-centered. When party-centered appeals predominate, parties tend to be centralized and disciplined, with all party candidates implementing the party strategy on pain of expulsion. When candidate-centered appeals predominate, parties may be decentralized and undisciplined. In these cases, there is no "party line": candidates pursue their electoral strategies individually and independently of the party.

The use of party-centered appeals facilitates harmonization and thus contributes to party-building. Where party-centered appeals predominate, individual politicians sacrifice autonomy, but in exchange, they receive access to valuable campaign resources from the party. A virtuous cycle ensues, as candidates' dependence on centralized

---

[10] Edward Gibson's (1992, 1997) approach to electoral coalition-making in Latin America provides a useful guide. According to Gibson, the analysis of conservative party strategies should begin by distinguishing between the core and noncore constituencies. The core constituency provides ideological and financial resources, and is the most important group in defining the party's identity. However, the core constituency does not provide enough votes to make the party electorally viable. Conservative parties therefore need to make inroads into noncore constituencies. The electoral strategy for attracting noncore constituents is necessarily different from the one directed at core supporters, and usually entails deemphasizing ideological (class-based) appeals. Such parties thus face the challenge of harmonizing segmented electoral strategies to craft multiclass social bases.

party resources strengthens the party organization and enhances party leaders' capacity to coordinate candidate appeals.[11] Uruguay's FA fits this description.

In contrast, the use of candidate-centered appeals makes harmonization difficult and thus undermines party-building. Where candidate-centered appeals predominate, party candidates do not depend on centralized party resources or coordinate with each other across districts. In fact, they may even compete with each other if they are on the same list. In these cases, internal inconsistencies and contradictions are more likely to emerge, and party organizations have diminished value, as they have relatively little to offer to their candidates. Not only do such conditions undermine party-building, they also make established parties more likely to decompose. After Chile's 1990 transition to democracy, many established parties came to rely increasingly on candidate-centered appeals, which has undermined harmonization and contributed to the uprooting of the party system (Luna 2014).[12]

A more complex scenario arises when parties pursue electoral strategies that combine both party-centered and candidate-centered appeals. Here, strategic harmonization is difficult but feasible. Parties must take the resources generated by their partial reliance on party-centered appeals and use them efficiently in order to harmonize both party- and candidate-centered appeals at the party level. Parties often fail to meet this challenge, but sometimes they succeed. Chile's UDI is one successful case.

---

[11] Strategic harmonization should not be confused with the notion of strategic coordination, which deals with different types of party system outcomes regarding the coordination of supply (strategic entry) and demand (strategic voting) under different electoral formulas (Cox 1997; Duverger 1951). Strategic harmonization is also conceptually different from party system nationalization (Caramani 2006; Chhibber and Kollman 2004; Mainwaring and Jones 2003; Morgenstern and Potthoff 2005) and vertical integration (Hicken 2009). Party system nationalization and vertical integration refer to the evenness in the geographical distribution of electoral support for the party. Strategic harmonization, in contrast, refers to the party's capacity to implement segmented linkages across constituencies in ways that reduce possible trade-offs and enhance synergies among distinct mobilization attempts. Such strategies should exploit the party's competitive advantages and target specific constituencies, which may be more or less evenly distributed across districts. If the key electoral constituencies of a party implementing a segmented and coordinated strategy were territorially concentrated in a small set of districts, such a party could both display low levels of nationalization (or vertical integration) and high levels of strategic harmonization.

[12] Harmonization is not especially problematic for Uruguay's traditional parties. Those parties' main challenge was to maintain their historical levels of linkage segmentation (Luna 2014).

THE ARGUMENT AT WORK:
THE CASES OF CHILE AND URUGUAY

The sections that follow illustrate the chapter's theoretical argument in the cases of the UDI and the FA. While the two parties differ in many ways, both of them succeeded by establishing segmented linkages to distinct electoral constituencies and harmonizing their segmented appeals. Specifically, both parties gained an initial electoral following by making programmatic appeals to a core constituency: the UDI to the economic elite, the FA to unions, urban middle classes, and the leftist intelligentsia. Since Chile's economic elite and Uruguay's unions were too small to deliver national pluralities, the UDI and FA reached beyond their core constituencies and established ties to new, peripheral constituencies: the poor in the case of the UDI, and informal and unemployed workers in the case of the FA. Given the programmatic tensions between rich and poor in Chile, and between unionized and informal/unemployed workers in Uruguay, the UDI and the FA did not use programmatic appeals to reach these peripheral constituencies. Instead, they relied on clientelistic and symbolic appeals. These segmentation strategies were successful: both the UDI and the FA forged stable, multiclass coalitions that enabled them to rise to electoral prominence and eventually establish themselves as the leading parties in their respective countries.

Analyzing the social bases of political parties and their connection to specific party strategies is extremely complicated. On the one hand, information about actual electoral behavior is aggregated into districts or municipalities. The analysis of such information thus confronts the risks of ecological fallacy. Those risks are multiplied in diachronic analyses because, among other things, people move across districts between elections, older people die, and new voters are added to the electoral register. On the other hand, isolating the specific impact of a given mobilizational strategy on observed electoral results is virtually impossible, particularly in the case of broad multiclass coalitions.[13]

For these reasons, the data that I present below on the relative electoral growth of the UDI and FA should be taken, at best, as a plausibility test for my argument, which is based on intensive fieldwork across a diverse set of electoral districts in both countries (see Luna 2014 for details). Although Tables 4.1 and 4.2 present the complete historical series of

---

[13] For instance, Uruguay's FA displays a pattern of continuous electoral growth across all segments of the population. It is impossible, however, to discern which strategies (or contextual factors) are the cause of a given result in a specific electoral cross-section.

TABLE 4.1 *Lower chamber (1989–2009) and municipal election (2008) results per electoral pact and mainstream parties*

	Lower chamber elections						Municipal elections				
	1989	1993	1997	2001	2005	2009	1992	1996	2000	2004[1]	2008[1]
Main electoral pacts											
Concertación	51.50	55.40	50.51	47.90	51.77	40.4[2]	53.30	52.13	52.13	46.35[2]	28.27[1]
Alianza	34.18	36.68	36.26	44.27	38.7	39.58[3]	29.67	32.47	40.09	38.12	38.35
Main political parties											
Pact: Concertación											
DC	25.99	27.12	22.98	18.92	20.78	12,95	28.93	26.03	21.62	20.90	15.97
PS	10.40	11.93	11.05	10.00	10.02	9	8.53	10.70	11.28	11.41	10.25
PPD		11.84	12.55	12.73	15.44	11.56	9.21	11.71	11.41	8.23	7.73
Pact: Alianza											
UDI	9.82	12.11	14.45	25.18	22.34	21	10.19	3.36	15.97	19	17.58
RN	18.28	16.31	16.77	13.77	14.12	16.22	13.44	13.60	15.54	14.97	14.66
Other parties											
Communist	4.38	4.99	6.88	5.22	5.14		6.55	5.09	3.24	3.93	

[1] Average of electoral support in municipal council and mayoral elections, which were held separately for the first time in 2004.

[2] Elections in which Concertación and Juntos Podemos (Together We Can) united to form electoral alliances ("*pacto por omisión*").

[3] Election in which the Alianza pact was branded the "Coalición por el Cambio" (Coalition for Change), as it included other minor parties.

Source: Own construction on the basis of information contained in www.elecciones.gov.cl.

TABLE 4.2 *Electoral results 1971–2004 (percentages)*

	Colorado Party	Blanco Party	FA	Nuevo Espacio	Others	Total
1971	41.0	40.2	18.3		0.6	100
1984	30.3	35.0	21.3		0.0	100
1989	30.3	38.9	21.2	9.0	0.6	100
1994	32.3	31.2	30.6	5.2	0.7	100
1999	32.7	22.2	40.3	4.6		100
2004	10.4	34.3	50.7		2.5	100

Source: Own construction on the basis of information contained in Buquet (2005).

electoral results obtained for each party since their inception and until their arrival into executive office (as part of the Alianza coalition in the case of the UDI), the graphs that I present below focus on the period in which each party witnessed its most significant electoral growth (from 1997 to 2005 in the case of the UDI, and from 1984 to 2004 in the case of the FA). The graphs show the relative electoral performance of each party across different socioeconomic strata in order to display the particular pace and rate of electoral growth of the UDI and FA across different constituencies. Although admittedly suboptimal, my description of each party's electoral evolution across different socioeconomic strata closely resembles the results obtained by other researchers, who relied on different techniques to analyze their electoral performance.[14]

The Case of the UDI

The UDI is a relatively new party, with strong ties to the former military regime (1973–1990) headed by General Augusto Pinochet.[15] Today, the UDI has more seats in Chile's Congress than any other party. The UDI's involvement with the Pinochet regime[16] and its ties to business and socially conservative interests (such as Opus Dei and the Legionnaries of Christ) help explain its strong electoral performance since 1989 within its core constituency: the upper socioeconomic segments of Chilean society (Fontaine 2000).

[14] For Chile, see Altman (2004) and Morales (2008). For Uruguay, see Moreira (2000, 2005) and Mieres (1994).

[15] An expanded version of this case study is available in Luna (2010) and Luna (2014).

[16] For more on the UDI's status as an authoritarian successor party, see Loxton (Chapter 9, this volume).

However, the UDI has also become more successful than other parties at recruiting voters among the poorest segments of Chilean society, including historical strongholds of the left. This strategy has enabled the Chilean right to show a "new face," downplaying factors (i.e., its authoritarian past) that still hinder its electoral growth in noncore social groups (Garretón 2000). Considering the levels of hostility and suspicion that the UDI continues to provoke among much of the Chilean population, the party's capture of a sizable noncore constituency is analytically puzzling.

To explain the UDI's electoral growth, I argue that the party has pursued a dual representational strategy by extracting economic resources from its "vote-poor/resource-rich" core constituency in exchange for ideological and interest representation, and then using those resources to capture the vote of its noncore "vote-rich/resource-poor" constituency.[17] This has been accomplished by developing a powerful grassroots network structuring nonprogrammatic linkages with poor constituents.[18] During the dictatorship, the UDI was able to penetrate local politics and build local machines using state resources (Huneeus 2000; Klein 2004; Morales and Bugueño 2001; Pollack 1999). By contrast, since the transition to democracy, the party has relied on private donations to feed its local networks. The electoral growth in the party's noncore constituency was also triggered by the emergence of a popular leader (and presidential candidate in 1999–2000 and 2005): Joaquín Lavín. Lavín mobilized supporters with an "antipolitics" appeal that distinguished him from traditional politicians.

The UDI's strong showing in the presidential elections of 1999–2000 and in the congressional elections of 2001 were thus the cumulative

---

[17] See Kitschelt (2000) for a discussion of these sorts of "dual-representation strategies." As one UDI leader put it, "Our leaders convinced business elites that the party would be able to protect the market-oriented model introduced under Pinochet, aided by the special majority requirements that Jaime [Guzmán] included in the 1980 Constitution [...] We tell our friends: 'to represent you, we should get more votes in the popular sectors, not at the elite level where we cannot get more.' So we ask them for their financial support, but we also ask them to abstain from showing up with us; in the snapshot, we will always be with the poor, not with them [...] It was hard for them to understand that we needed to appeal to the poor, but that's where there are more votes to grasp" (anonymous UDI national leader, personal interview, 2008).

[18] According to UDI legislator María Angélica Cristi, "Poor people need you more frequently, at every moment ... They don't know where to go, how to do things. They don't get the paperwork done; they need medical exams; they need to place a child in a given school [...] And that's where we come in ... The truth is that the greatest benefit from being a deputy is that you can pick up the phone and ask: 'Can we solve this?'" (personal interview, 2003).

result of both contextual and endogenous factors. Public discontent with
the governing Concertación coalition in the aftermath of the 1998 Asian
financial crisis provided a crucial opportunity for the electoral growth
of opposition parties. Drawing on its unique organizational matrix and
strategic vision, as well as the development of a charismatic leadership
and the availability of economic resources, the UDI was able to profit
from this situation.

In 2005 and 2009, the UDI still received the most votes at the congressional level. However, its presidential candidate in 2005 came in third
place, and in 2009, it supported the candidacy of Sebastián Piñera of the
National Renewal (RN) party. The weakness of the UDI's leadership led
to its poor showing in the 2004 and 2009 presidential races. Despite its
presidential misfortunes, the party's grassroots political machine enabled
it to perform surprisingly well in the 2004 and 2009 congressional races.

Two additional factors helped the UDI in the posttransition period.
First, after the transition to democracy, Chilean partisan identities and
traditional political apparatuses weakened, reducing traditional parties'
ability to mobilize support in popular communities (Oxhorn 1995; Posner
1999, 2004; Roberts 1998). As a result, and in contrast to the linkage
dynamic observed in wealthy neighborhoods, grassroots activities, constituency service, and particularistic exchanges became central elements
for electoral mobilization. Successful politicians tended to be those who
were able to pay a household's utility bill during the campaign period,
offer legal or medical assistance, or distribute TV sets, food boxes, opti-
cal lenses, equipment for a neighborhood soccer club, or cakes for Bingo
parties organized by community organizations.[19] In sum, politicians
who developed personal contact with members of poor communities –
structuring efficient problem-solving networks or distributing "*cosas*"
(stuff) – came to enjoy a competitive advantage over more personally
distant candidates. Given the decline of partisan identities and national
party apparatuses, local networks have become structured around individual candidates and incumbent congress members and mayors, who
have strategically chosen to downplay their partisan identities. The UDI's
main ally, RN, remains a party of cadres that lacks a well-developed and
competitive party apparatus at the local level (Barozet and Aubry 2005).

The UDI, in contrast, has used grassroots organization and nonprogrammatic appeals to win what party strategists call the "soft vote": the
vote of nonpartisan, nonideological members of Chile's popular sectors.

---

[19] Personal interviews with local council members and former and current members of
Congress in 2002 and 2003.

The UDI has progressively expanded a disciplined party organization, which has captured more campaign resources than its competitors and deployed those resources strategically through an extensive grassroots political machine. The UDI's financial edge stems from its association with the new economic policies implemented under the Pinochet dictatorship; these policies favored economic elites, who, after democratization, came disproportionately to support the UDI (see Loxton, Chapter 9, this volume). The UDI's success at developing a grassroots political machine stems from sustained efforts to expand its territorial organization into urban peripheries by recruiting, training, and financially supporting the campaigns of young activists – usually from the upper class. These activists, deployed strategically in specific districts with favorable electoral conditions (e.g., where an RN incumbent decided not to run for reelection), have engaged in community service and run personalistic and "apolitical" campaigns, seeking to distance themselves from traditional politicians and, crucially, from the UDI's own brand. At the same time, the party has developed a leadership class capable of moderating the party's image while creating empathy among disillusioned voters. Among this group of voters, women have been especially attracted to the party, and to Lavín's leadership in particular.[20] Once again, efforts have been made to dilute the party's conservative brand among its noncore constituency supporters, and to portray leaders like Lavín as nontraditional candidates who care about people's "real problems."

Figure 4.1 displays the UDI's electoral growth in districts of six different poverty deciles, taking electoral returns in 1997 as base 100. Although electoral growth (particularly in 2001) was evident across the board, the party's biggest electoral gains were in the poorest two strata. There were also modest increases in areas associated with the historical base of the party (top 10 percent districts), where previous RN support has migrated to the UDI. The party has gained less in middle-class districts, however.

Table 4.3 characterizes the linkage strategies used by the UDI to mobilize different socioeconomic constituencies. The party mobilizes upper socioeconomic segments of Chilean society on the basis of programmatic and interest representation, as well as on the basis of the party's identification with the economic model implemented by the dictatorship headed by General Pinochet.[21] Meanwhile, the party also mobilizes voters in the

---

[20] For more information, see Altman (2004) and Morales (2008).
[21] According to UDI legislator Julio Dittborn, his district (23) "is a very peculiar one ... 90 percent of the people who live there are not expecting me to solve a specific problem for them. Nor are they expecting me to visit their home, give them something, or solve a

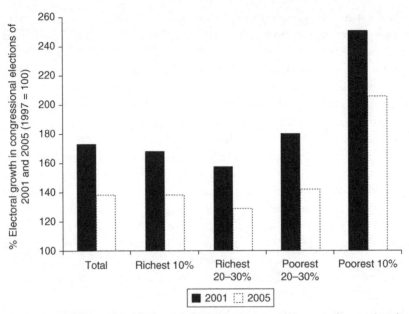

FIGURE 4.1 Electoral evolution of the UDI across social strata (lower chamber elections; 1997 is Base 100 for the index).

Source: Own construction based on data from the Observatorio Electoral of the Universidad Diego Portales.

poorest segments of Chilean society by combining candidate trait and clientelistic strategies. The latter focuses on the distribution of material goods to individuals and small groups, as well as on the work of social helpers providing medical or legal help.

Regarding strategic harmonization, the UDI is more internally coherent and disciplined than other Chilean parties. This result is achieved through top-down harmonization (via party leadership), facilitated by the greater relative amounts of symbolic and material resources available to the party's hierarchy. Moreover, the 1991 assassination of UDI founder Jaime Guzmán contributed to a decentralization of power among his

social problem for them. What they expect is that I represent their opinions in the media. And that in Congress I vote like they would, if they were in my seat. Therefore, it is a district with almost no fieldwork activity ... And as an economist, what I do is to appear frequently on the media speaking about those topics that are interesting and important for my voters. And the rest comes from their identification with the UDI, which represents the hard core of the Pinochet regime. These are the people that see the UDI as some kind of perpetuator of the military regime's heritage. That's the basis of our strength in this district. And I have the joy that in my district rightist supporters are many and that I don't have to convince them (personal interview, 2003).

TABLE 4.3 *Socioeconomic linkage segmentation in the electoral strategy of the UDI*

Agent making the appeal	Resources used in the appeal		
	Symbolic	Material: Public policies	Material: Private or club goods
Candidate	Candidate traits (popular sectors)[1],[2]	Electoral platform	Particularistic
Party	Partisan identity	Programmatic (upper classes)[1],[3]	Clientelistic (popular sectors)[1],[2]

[1] Predominant linkage strategies.
[2] Links to peripheral constituency.
[3] Links to core constituency.

disciples in the party elite, none of whom was considered Guzmán's sole natural heir. Guzmán's successors responded by creating an informal but highly disciplined "collegial" leadership. This collegial body strategically concentrated and allocated resources to help the UDI grow and socialize new leaders, without having to face internal conflicts derived from their individual political ambition.

The Case of the FA

In October 2004, the Uruguayan left, led by the FA, came to power, putting an end to 175 years of electoral dominance by the country's traditional parties.[22] In addition to winning the presidency, the FA won, for the first time since 1966, an absolute majority (50.7 percent) in Congress, marking a political watershed in Uruguayan history (Altman and Castiglioni 2006; Buquet 2005; Lanzaro 2004).

The FA's successful electoral bid was the result of the party's transition from a predominantly urban, labor-based, center-left, mass party to an increasingly catchall, professional electoral organization. Operating within an opportunity structure marked by the crisis of Uruguay's state-centric sociopolitical matrix (Cavarozzi et al. 2002) and the decreasing capacity of both traditional parties to satisfy and retain their historical constituents, the FA successfully moderated its platform while consistently opposing market reform. The party thereby mobilized its core constituency through programmatic appeals, defending the state-centric model and its stakeholders' social interests.

[22] An expanded version of this case study is available in Luna (2007) and Luna (2014).

This programmatic stance allowed the FA to maintain its core constituency in middle-class segments and organized labor. However, it was a complex intertwining of personality-based, community service linkages and localized efforts to enhance the social organization and political awareness of lower-class constituencies that enabled it progressively to win over an electorally critical noncore constituency.

The party also developed two powerful charismatic leaderships that helped it broaden its appeal: those of Tabaré Vázquez and José Mujica. Vázquez and Mujica moderated and broadened the FA's electoral appeals. Under their leadership, the FA ran several candidacies in the interior in 2005. The party's territorial activists also took up brokerage roles and particularistic problem-solving activities. The FA's capacity to develop and sustain a devoted network of partisan activists in every locality of the country was pivotal in this latter regard, especially when traditional party structures atrophied.[23]

From 1990 onward, the FA municipal government in Montevideo – home to approximately half of the electorate – contributed decisively to the FA's successful electoral coalition-building in 2004. The municipal government promoted moderation, proved the party's capacity to govern effectively, helped the FA penetrate strongholds of Uruguay's traditional parties (the Colorados and Blancos) in Montevideo's periphery, and catalyzed the charismatic leadership of the FA's first elected president, Tabaré Vázquez. Widespread public discontent with the Colorados and Blancos, coupled with the growing perception of the FA as a viable alternative to the traditional parties, significantly boosted the FA's national electoral prospects.

As a result, the FA was able to establish a double support base in Uruguayan society, composed of its original constituency – urban middle sectors with ties to the old import substitution industrialization (ISI) model – and a new constituency of informal, poor, and/or rural voters. These new constituents had grown disenchanted with the traditional party elite as a result of economic hardship and the decline of traditional clientelism. To reach these distinct constituencies simultaneously, the FA employed a strategy of segmentation. On the one hand, the FA mobilized its traditional social base by drawing on strong partisan identities and the pursuit of programmatic mobilization. To some degree, the FA also used

---

[23] According to FA legislator José Mahía, "We have learned a lot from the traditional parties and we are currently doing things that we used to underrate. We now have a structure of local leaders, each one of them a *caudillo* in his place, working with a team [...] trying to help people to solve their most immediate needs" (personal interview, 2002).

such strategies to mobilize new lower-class and informal constituents.[24] However, it relied even more on the priming of candidate traits and the pursuit of clientelistic mobilization.[25] The latter usually took the form of "social promotion" activities and constituency service rather than individual "giveaways." In short, as an opposition party, the FA succeeded in articulating an electoral strategy that gradually allowed it to grow in sectors of the population that had historically supported the traditional parties, without alienating its traditional leftist constituency.[26]

As Figure 4.2 shows, during the 1984–2004 period, the FA grew significantly stronger in all three social strata and geographical units. Nonetheless, in Montevideo, the FA's electoral growth was especially concentrated in the lower social strata, where its emergent constituency was consolidated in the election of 1999.[27] Importantly, the greatest surge in support from this sector occurred not in 2004, when support from the other two segments rose,[28] but in 1994, soon after the FA's election to

[24] According to FA activist Omar Álvez, "We analyzed this on the basis of Census data, and we reached the conclusion that in Artigas, 80 percent of the families depend on income coming from public sources, either national or municipal. In Bella Unión, the proportion was reversed, with only 20 percent living from direct or indirect state transfers. And political behavior correlates with that; the left does well where people are not dependent on the state. You cannot develop a classical leftist strategy where people are fearful of the power holder. And that happens when they depend on them for their jobs. Here, the municipality was not paying employer's contributions to the pension system. That is money from the employees that was illegally appropriated by the municipality, hindering their future pension. In fact, they even lost access to credit because they showed up as debtors. We publicly denounced this situation, asking municipal employees to support a legal claim against the mayor. We have 1200, 1300 employees in this municipality. Do you know how many of them signed up? Eleven. In Bella Unión, people are more able to resist, and that facilitates our task of ideological and political formation" (personal interview, 2003).

[25] According to FA leader Lucía Topolanski, "We usually have someone [a traditional *caudillo* with a local political network] acting as a bridge, and then we go and try, very slowly, to talk to the people. We reach the Blancos with a 'ruralist' and 'Artiguist' discourse. And they also like our rebellious past as 'Tupamaros' because that is the root of Blanco identity. Meanwhile, we reach the Colorados by talking about the old Batlle. However, if you tell them about Marx and Lenin, or about *Frenteamplismo*, forget it" (personal interview, 2003).

[26] To do so, the party also embraced programmatic and electoral alliances with traditional party splinter groups and the centrist Nuevo Espacio (a faction of the FA that defected but eventually returned to the party), while preserving party discipline.

[27] Significant differences between lower strata and both middle and upper ones were obtained when comparing FA's electoral growth rates, taking 1984 and 1989 as a baseline, using one-way ANOVA.

[28] As one FA leader eloquently put it, in 2004 the party grew significantly stronger in all social strata due to public discontent with the economic crisis: "This campaign [2004] is one of the easiest ones that we have had [...] You just need to step on the corner

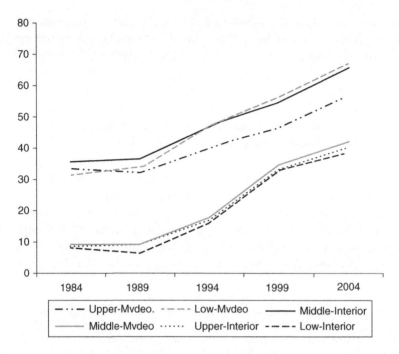

FIGURE 4.2 Electoral growth of the FA across socioeconomic and geographic segments.

Sources: Own construction on the basis of Moreira (2000, 2005), Kaztman (1999), Mieres (1994), and data from the Corte Electoral 2004.

Montevideo's municipal government (in 1989). Quite notably, in 1994 the party was able to capture traditional clientelistic strongholds of the Colorado and Blanco parties in Montevideo's periphery (Mieres 1994).

For instance, in Zone 17 (Cerro, Casabó, Pajas Blancas, and Santa Catalina), where the poverty rate reached 47.1 percent (and where 75.8 percent of residents voted for the FA in 2004), a 15 percentage point increase in electoral share in favor of the FA was observed between 1989 (42.3 percent) and 1994 (57.7 percent). This is further illustrated by a correlation analysis of vote shares over time in each zone, which demonstrates significant inconsistencies (lower correlations) between the vote shares of 2004 and those of 1984 (.36) compared to those of

and ask: 'Who is responsible for this mess?' Then you start distributing printed ballots in the street [...] Today, the Frente Amplio is the hope of the poor, of business people, and of the rural sector" (Eleuterio Fernández Huidobro, interviewed in *Página 12*, September 13, 2004).

2004 and 1989 (.79**).[29] Since 1994, except for inertial electoral growth witnessed in each zone, relative electoral returns have been very stable, with highly significant and strong correlations obtained (1994 = .97**, 1999 = .96**). It is therefore clear that the most significant realignment of lower sector support for the FA occurred between 1984 and 1994.

Although it began with a higher electoral support base in the middle strata in 1984, the FA's performance with this group presents a growth trend similar to that observed in the lower strata, thus illustrating the party's capacity to maintain and expand its hold on social sectors closer to its historical constituency, while also expanding its support among new ones. In 2004, in the aftermath of the harsh economic crisis of 2002, the FA grew almost evenly across all three social strata, making significant inroads in upper social sectors that were most likely alienated by economic malaise. For instance, in Zone 5 (Pocitos, Punta Gorda, Buceo), where only 3.4 percent of households were poor in 2004 and where the FA had increased its electoral share by only 6.7 percent in all previous elections (winning 33 percent in 1984 and 39.7 percent in 1999), support for the party grew by almost 10 percent in 2004 (to 49.4 percent).

Figures from the country's interior complement this portrait. Although electoral support for the FA was still lower in the interior than in the capital in 2004, the data illustrates the progressive consolidation of the FA as a national party. In this regard, taking 1984 as a baseline, the party's electoral growth rates were significantly higher in the interior than in Montevideo. FA's performance in 2004 was relatively homogeneous across different social strata, with middle sectors presenting only slightly higher levels of support for the party than upper and lower strata. Although no significant differences of means were obtained, the evolution of the party's social base in the interior appears to have been the opposite of that observed in Montevideo. Moreover, although the FA expanded its share of the lower strata vote more markedly in 1999 than it had in 1984, 1989, or 1994, the absolute vote share the party obtained in this segment remained the smallest, in stark contrast to Montevideo, where the FA won the municipal government.

As an opposition party, the FA successfully articulated a mixed linkage strategy that gradually allowed it to win support among segments of the population that had historically supported the traditional parties,

---

[29] Reported coefficients correspond to Spearman's correlations of electoral returns in Montevideo's eighteen zones. Source: Raw data reported by Moreira (2005: 37–41).

TABLE 4.4 *Socioeconomic linkage segmentation in the electoral strategy of the FA*

Agent making the appeal	Resources used in the appeal		
	Symbolic	Material: Public policies	Material: Private or club goods
Candidate	Candidate traits[1,2]	Electoral platform	Particularistic
Party	Partisan identity[1,2,3]	Programmatic[1,2,3]	Clientelistic[1,2]

[1] Predominant linkage strategies.
[2] Links to peripheral constituency.
[3] Links to core constituency.

while not alienating its traditional leftist constituency. In so doing, the FA changed from a Marxist mass party to an electoral professional one, pursuing a segmented electoral strategy, while still providing consistent opposition to neoliberal reforms. This allowed it to pool and channel social discontent with the other parties in the system. Moreover, the FA's programmatic realignment around *Batllismo* (a prostatist ideology historically associated with the Colorados) allowed it to increase the level of programmatic linkages between the party and poor constituents. This was based on a strategy of opposing incumbents (and their policy choices) in the media, while penetrating the clientelistic strongholds of the traditional parties with its activist base. Table 4.4 summarizes the segmented linkage strategies deployed by the FA.

In addition, the FA's factionalized structure helped it broaden its electoral appeal at a time when the appeals of the two traditional parties were growing increasingly narrow. Notwithstanding its factionalization, the FA was able to retain the presidency in 2009 and again in 2014. Its strong partisan identification, as well as the successful development (and alternation) of charismatic leaderships, have enabled the pursuit and maintenance of a harmonized electoral strategy to mobilize different segments of the Uruguayan population on the basis of segmented linkages.

COMPARING THE CASES

Notwithstanding their substantial differences, Chile's UDI and Uruguay's FA both succeeded in segmenting and harmonizing voter linkage strategies. In this respect, they differed from their partisan rivals. In the case of other parties in Chile, segmentation was possible, but harmonization was not achieved. Consequently, Chilean parties progressively weakened as institutions (Luna and Rosenblatt 2012). In the case of traditional parties in Uruguay, segmentation was constrained by the erosion of clientelistic linkages and by the programmatic "cornering" of both parties in an unpopular proreform stance. Moreover, the scarcity of clientelistic side payments, the erosion of both parties' symbolic resources (i.e., the decay of previously very strong partisan identities) and the prospects of electoral defeat also hindered traditional parties' capacity to harmonize their electoral strategies.

Both the UDI and FA drew on resources provided by their core constituencies in order to pursue electoral expansion. While the nature of their core constituencies and the associated resources were markedly different – financial resources provided by business interests (UDI) versus activist networks and a strong partisan identity provided by labor unions, students, cooperatives, and middle-class voters (FA) – both parties used their core constituencies' resources to the same end: to segment and harmonize their linkage strategies.

Both the UDI and the FA cleaved to their core constituencies. While in opposition, they relied on available institutional resources, such as their growing congressional representation. The UDI also relied on the "authoritarian enclaves" (Garretón 2003) of the Chilean Constitution in order to act as guardian of the market reforms carried out by the military regime – even without commanding many congressional seats. The FA relied on its capacity to mobilize large segments of the electorate around direct democracy initiatives to block legislation promoted by the governing parties. Moreover, drawing on their disproportionate access to particular resources, both parties were able to carve out a peripheral constituency, penetrating previous strongholds of their rival parties.

Both parties were also able to limit the eventual electoral trade-offs and internal conflicts that their segmented linkage strategies might have produced. Contextual factors such as social segmentation and differences across districts (particularly in Chile) proved instrumental in reducing the risks of pursuing a segmented linkage strategy. Yet, partisan endowments and explicit strategies were also crucial for achieving strategic harmonization. Strong partisan identifications (especially in the case of the FA), a sense of mission (especially in the case of the UDI), the development of charismatic leaderships capable of cementing a heterogeneous social and political coalition (particularly in the FA), and the allure created by the prospects of winning presidential office proved pivotal in both cases.

TABLE 4.5 *A comparative analysis of the UDI and FA in terms of their brand, territorial organization, and sources of elite cohesion*

	UDI	FA
Brand	Significant for mobilizing electoral and financial support from the party's (small) core constituency; hidden when mobilizing peripheral constituencies	Significant for massive electoral mobilization through different types of linkages (i.e., PID, programmatic)
Territorial organization	Top-down, selective territorial reach contingent on elite's electoral strategizing	Bottom-up, decentralized. Relevant for internal politics of the party
Elite cohesion	Collegiate of *coroneles* formed under Jaime Guzmán's leadership; elite controls key resources for leadership formation and electoral expansion and enforces top-down decision making	Leadership and factional disputes pivotal for internal competition in the party; institutionalization of party statute for conflict resolution regarding programmatic debate and candidate selection

Finally, the UDI and FA both succeeded in developing effective brands, strong territorial organizations, and sources of cohesion – the three key conditions for successful party-building outlined in Chapter 1. Nevertheless, they did so in very different ways, as summarized in Table 4.5.

The "party brand" of the UDI is usually hidden when seeking to mobilize large segments of the population (and the party's more numerous noncore constituency). In this respect, the party only taps into its identification with the legacy of the Pinochet regime when seeking to raise funds from business and conservative elites. In the case of the FA, the party brand is pivotal for electoral mobilization. Yet, such a brand combines programmatic stances, strong partisan identities, and a direct relationship to certain leaders that came to represent the epitome of *Frenteamplismo*.

The territorial organizations of both the UDI and the FA played a functionally equivalent role. First, they enabled both parties to establish solid and extensive linkages to civil society. Second, they created room for ambitious politicians to develop a career within the party without immediately triggering leadership disputes for access to a single prize (i.e., the presidential nomination). Third, both parties' access to municipal office was pivotal for engaging in "municipal branding," showcasing "new governing styles" to campaign for national office (Hunter 2010; Pasotti 2010).[30]

Despite such commonalities, there are significant differences in the anatomy and functioning of each party's territorial organization. In the case of the UDI, the territorial organization grew out of elite electoral strategizing. In this respect, the party elite decided where to field candidates and in which districts to invest in expanding its reach. Further, although the party had local activists, the central party leadership usually selected and sent UDI youngsters to incubate the new party branches. Moreover, the territorial organization, even if partisan by design and finance, works on the basis of personalistic linkages between the UDI's "delegate" and local civil society.

In the case of the FA, *comités de base* (base-level party structures) emerged as a result of both bottom-up processes and a top-down strategy to expand across society in a homogenous manner. Thus, the territorial organization of the FA grew more organically, but also became more uniformly present in the country. Although the *comités* gradually became the locus of factional competition within the party, the territorial organization remained "partisan" – associated with the party, not with a specific leader or faction. Finally, the territorial organization of the party plays a strong statutory role in programmatic debate and candidate selection (Yaffé 2005). For this reason, power and resources are much more dispersed in the FA than in the UDI.

With respect to elite cohesion, the UDI displays much higher levels of elite consensus and homogeneity. Several of the party's key leaders were personally trained by UDI founder Jaime Guzmán and are a highly disciplined group (*"los coroneles"*). Guzmán's sudden death (via assassination) in 1991, as well as the party's inauspicious electoral prospects after Chile's transition to democracy, helped tame individual ambitions and unite lower leaders. Access to pivotal financial resources, as well as the *coroneles'* collective role in recruiting, forming, and promoting new party cadres, have undoubtedly played a significant role in enforcing elite cohesion and loyalty among the UDI's rank-and-file to the *coroneles*.

Factional competition, in turn, is part of the FA's DNA. The party emerged as a coalition of different groups, which, while preserving their original identity, joined forces to compete against the traditional parties under the double simultaneous vote (DSV) electoral rule.[31] Leadership

---

[30] On the importance of subnational office for party-building, see Holland (Chapter 10, this volume).

[31] The DSV means that voters vote simultaneously for a party and for a specific set of candidates (*lema*) within the party, though they have to select a list – which cannot be

disputes have also run rampant in the party, especially after the emergence of Tabaré Vázquez as a contender for national leadership against Líber Seregni, the party's historical leader. In spite of these characteristics, the FA organization has managed to stick together for at least three reasons: first, the consolidation of a powerful and overarching *Frenteamplista* identity, which solidified under political persecution during the authoritarian regime;[32] second, the rapid routinization of clear rules for arbitrating conflicts among factions and leaders on issues such as candidate selection, programmatic discussion, and party discipline;[33] and third, the "failed" experience of Nuevo Espacio (New Space), a faction of the FA that defected in order to contest power on its own. The failure of Nuevo Espacio had a significant demonstration effect, such that after 1989, factions and their leaders understood that the "whole" had become "more than the sum of its parts," and that defection would likely result in political oblivion.

I have argued throughout that parties that segment their linkage strategies more than competitors while still ensuring harmonization have a better chance of success in unequal societies. Drawing on the DALP Project's Dataset, Table 4.6 tests this general causal claim by looking at the composition of systemic and individual party strategies in my two case studies.[34] For each case, Table 4.6 displays the nonweighted average score for each linkage type obtained by all parties included in the expert survey in both Chile and Uruguay, against the score obtained by the recently most successful party in each case (the UDI and FA). Table 4.6 shows each party and system's 1–4 point average for each of the four pure linkage strategies included in the survey. Those questions asked country experts

modified – from among those presented by rival factions within each party. Once they choose the party, they have as many options as there are lists presented by the party. An obvious consequence of voting for a party is that split tickets are not allowed. The party that obtains a plurality of the votes is the winner; and the winner of a plurality within that party becomes president. From 1934 until the electoral cycle of 1999–2000, all elections occurred at the same time. This simultaneity obviously reinforced the effects of the ban on split tickets. The DSV vote, reinforced by the proportional representation (PR) electoral system, provided incentives for emerging leaderships in the party to compete with established ones by opening a parallel electoral list (*sub-lema*) within the overall *lema*.

[32] On the effects of being born under conditions of adversity, see Greene (Chapter 6, this volume) and Van Dyck (Chapter 5, this volume).

[33] The institutionalization of party statutes did not eliminate conflict, but it did provide accepted procedures for dealing with them.

[34] The Project is called "Democratic Accountability and Citizen-Politician Linkages around the World," and was directed by Herbert Kitschelt at Duke University. I thank Herbert Kitschelt for granting access to this dataset at an early stage of the research. I also thank Yi-Ting Wang for assistance in working with the database.

TABLE 4.6 *Electoral segmentation in Chile and Uruguay: the UDI and FA in comparison to other parties in each party system*

	Leadership appeals	Programmatic appeals	Targeted appeals	Party ID appeals	Party's average
Chile					
PDC	2.8	3.4	2.8	3.5	3.1
PRSD	1.8	2.5	1.7	2.8	2.2
PPD	3.1	3.1	2.5	2.7	2.9
PS	2.8	3.3	2.5	3.4	3.0
RN	3.2	3.0	2.6	2.5	2.8
UDI	**3.8**	**3.2**	**3.1**	**2.8**	**3.2**
System's average	2.9	3.1	2.5	3.0	
Uruguay					
Colorados	2.4	3.3	1.9	3.6	2.8
Blancos	2.8	3.4	1.9	3.6	2.9
FA	**3.0**	**3.8**	**1.7**	**3.7**	**3.0**
System's average	2.8	3.5	1.9	3.6	

Source: Own construction on the basis of DALP Project.

to rank the extent to which relevant parties sought to mobilize support by engaging in four types of strategies: "featuring a party leader's charismatic personality," "emphasizing the attractiveness of the party's positions on policy issues," "emphasizing the capacity of the party to deliver targeted benefits to its electoral supporters," and "drawing on and appealing to voters' long-term partisan loyalty ('party identification')."[35] On each item, experts were asked to assess parties' reliance on this set of strategies on a four-point scale ranging from 1 ("not at all") to 4 ("to a great extent"). As Table 4.6 shows, in both cases, the most successful party (the UDI and the FA) segmented its appeals more than other parties in the system, by combining different types of appeals at a greater "dosage."

CONCLUSION

This chapter has argued that segmented, harmonized appeals contributed to the success of two very different parties in Latin America: the FA in Uruguay and the UDI in Chile. This argument is not intended as a

---

[35] A fifth strategy was included in the survey with the following phrasing: "emphasizing their general competence to govern and bring about or maintain economic, social and political stability." Although this item was designed to capture valence competition, in my view respondents might interpret this as ambiguously reflecting either programmatic or personalistic traits. The inclusion of this fifth item would not have altered the obtained results for each case and system.

comprehensive explanation of the two parties' success. Indeed, a comparison of the UDI and FA suggests the importance of several additional factors. Three, in particular, are worth highlighting. First, both the UDI and the FA benefited from their (very different) positions during the military-authoritarian period (see Van Dyck, Chapter 5, and Loxton, Chapter 9, this volume). In Chile, the UDI's close ties to the Pinochet regime gave it an edge, after the transition, in representing the views of Chilean economic and conservative elites – who, as already noted, made important financial contributions to the party (Loxton, Chapter 9, this volume). In Uruguay, a *Frenteamplista* partisan identity crystallized as the party resisted political persecution under military rule. This partisan identity became pivotal for successful electoral strategizing and organizational development in the postauthoritarian period.

Second, both parties benefited from structural economic shifts that weakened established rivals. In Chile, structural shifts eroded the grassroots linkages of the governing center-left coalition, the Concertación, and also led to the progressive consolidation of an antiparty and antipolitical mood. In this context, the UDI campaigned against traditional politicians and employed a highly personalized, "apolitical," and "innovative" governing style. In Uruguay, the territorial organizations of both traditional parties weakened due to the implementation of austerity measures and the longer-term context of economic decline. Moreover, public discontent with the traditional parties grew as Colorado and Blanco presidents perpetually alternated in office, and both parties regularly engaged in congressional deal-making. In this context, the FA's territorial organization reached sectors of the population with a declining traditional party presence. Moreover, at the national level, the FA consolidated its programmatic stance in perpetual opposition to the market reform agenda proposed by the Blancos and Colorados.

Third, and finally, both parties developed in competition with strong and relatively stable parties. Consequently, the UDI and the FA grew slowly and incrementally, losing several elections after democratization. This "disadvantage" translated into party-building efforts specifically devised to deal with structural adversities. Moreover, both parties' initially inauspicious prospects contributed to lengthening the time horizons of party elites. Leaders competed in many elections, knowing that the elections were not "winnable," but using them as a means to build the party and progressively expand its reach. Present-day party leaders often claim that in the early races, the party sacrificed short-term opportunities (e.g., participation in broad coalitions that would have led to rapid electoral success) for long-term goals, and powerful leaders also sacrificed for the party.[36] In other words, over time, the party's "epic" became one in which the collective organization consolidated as more than the sum of its parts (i.e., individual candidates). The power of this narrative helped generate cohesion: individual leaders or factions who exited – or considered exiting – the party would likely be electorally punished for doing so.[37]

As a contrasting illustration, we might consider contemporary party systems in the Andean region. These party systems are either completely open (e.g., Peru) or dominated by a quasihegemonic incumbent (e.g., Ecuador, Bolivia, and Venezuela). In both contexts, ambitious politicians can achieve electoral success without investing in party-building. In Peru, almost anyone can win a national election. In Ecuador, Bolivia, and Venezuela, myriad opposition candidates can vie to become the main opposition figure in the first round and then attempt to rally the support of an otherwise fragmented opposition. In such a context, time horizons are compressed, and confrontational dynamics and fragile, opportunistic electoral pact-making tend to prevail. As Hale (2006) and Van Dyck (Chapter 5, this volume) suggest, party-building is more likely when easy, short-term routes to office are not available. This chapter's analysis thus suggests that in contemporary Latin America, and in contexts of open democratic contestation more broadly, new parties are more likely to succeed when confronting established parties in gradual decline.

---

[36] The decision of the group in Chile known as the *gremialistas* to split from the newly formed and larger party, RN, in order to go it alone as the UDI, is a case in point.

[37] The case of the Nuevo Espacio split in Uruguay is a case in point.

PART II

CHALLENGES OF ORGANIZATION-BUILDING

5

The Paradox of Adversity

New Left Party Survival and Collapse in Brazil, Mexico, and Argentina

Brandon Van Dyck

The "neoliberal turn" of the 1980s and 1990s created profound, long-term challenges for the Latin American left. With the collapse of import substitution industrialization (ISI) and the emergence of an elite neoliberal consensus, the left's traditional economic platform (e.g., industrial protectionism, price controls, nationalization of key industries) became politically infeasible in much of the region; and with the decline of labor unions and rise of the informal sector (a product of trade liberalization and deindustrialization), the left's capacity to mobilize the popular classes weakened (Roberts 1998; Levitsky and Roberts 2011). Despite these challenges, five new left-wing parties have taken root in Latin America since the onset of the third wave of democratization in the region in 1978. Six others, after initially rising to prominence, promptly collapsed and disintegrated.[1] Interestingly, most of the new left parties that took root were born in adversity. Brazil's Workers' Party (PT) and Mexico's Party of the Democratic Revolution (PRD) formed in electoral opposition to authoritarian regimes, while El Salvador's Farabundo Martí National Liberation Front (FMLN) and Nicaragua's Sandinista National Liberation Front (FSLN) emerged from armed conflict. In contrast, most of the new left parties that collapsed after liftoff were born in democracy, under less adverse circumstances (e.g., Argentina's Front for a Country in

---

[1] The five cases of success are Brazil's Workers' Party (PT), Chile's Party for Democracy (PPD), El Salvador's Farabundo Martí National Liberation Front (FMLN), Mexico's Party of the Democratic Revolution (PRD), and Nicaragua's Sandinista National Liberation Front (FSLN). The six cases of failure are Argentina's Front for a Country in Solidarity (FREPASO), Colombia's Democratic Alliance April 19 Movement (AD M-19), El Salvador's Democratic Convergence (CD), Guatemala's New Guatemala Democratic Front (FDNG), Paraguay's National Meeting Party (PEN), and Peru's United Left (IU).

Solidarity [FREPASO], Peru's United Left [IU]). How do we make sense of this paradox?

The chapter argues that, paradoxically, adverse circumstances may facilitate party-building. New parties tend to collapse because, in most cases, they do not have *strong territorial organizations* and *committed activists* and, consequently, do not survive early electoral letdowns and crises. A central theoretical claim of the chapter is that new parties with strong territorial organizations and committed activists tend to emerge under adverse conditions – specifically, conditions of limited access to (1) state resources (Shefter 1994) and (2) mass media.[2] Office-seekers with limited state and media access have no choice but to undertake the slow, labor-intensive, and non-vote-maximizing work of organization-building. At the ground level, organization-building is laborious, largely unremunerated, sometimes risky, and, typically, unlikely to bear electoral fruit in the short term. Consequently, the process selects for "believers" (Panebianco 1988: 26–30), or ideologically committed activists. Limited access to state resources and mass media thus may facilitate successful party-building – and, notably, is characteristic of office-seekers engaged in antiauthoritarian struggles. Thus, the chapter's takeaway argument is that party-building is more likely to succeed in authoritarian contexts (provided that repression is not too extreme) than under democracy.

The chapter is organized in two sections. The first presents the theoretical argument that low state and media access – a set of adverse conditions associated with opposition to authoritarian rule – facilitates party-building. The second illustrates this argument through a comparison of three new left parties in Latin America: two that formed in opposition to authoritarian regimes, built durable party organizations, and weathered early electoral crises (Brazil's PT, Mexico's PRD), and one that formed under democracy, did not build a durable party organization, and collapsed after an early electoral crisis (Argentina's FREPASO).

THE ARGUMENT: THE PARADOX OF ADVERSITY

With few exceptions, political parties must establish strong partisan brands in order to become institutionalized (Lupu 2016; Chapter 3, this

---

[2] In his seminal analysis of party-building in America and Europe, Martin Shefter argues that political parties founded by leaders "without positions of power in the prevailing regime" must build mass party organizations in order to "bludgeon their way into the political system" (1994: 5). The theory presented in this chapter incorporates and builds on Shefter's insight.

volume). It is rare, though, for parties to be born with strong brands (see Levitsky, Loxton, and Van Dyck, Chapter 1, this volume). Most new parties must first go through a process of brand development, in which they differentiate themselves from other parties and, crucially, demonstrate internal consistency over time (Lupu 2016; Chapter 3, this volume). During this embryonic period, new parties commonly experience electoral setbacks and crises. New parties tend to disintegrate not only because they face such challenges, but also because they are unable to survive them.

New parties are much more likely to survive early challenges if they have strong territorial organizations and committed activists (Cyr 2012; Tavits 2013). Building a strong territorial organization, however, is no easy task. It requires significant time and work, as the party must recruit members, establish local offices, and train local organizers to do this work; develop institutions for internal decision making and conflict resolution; and procure financing for basic party infrastructure, transportation, and salaries, often through small dues and donations. These processes are slow and depend on volunteer labor. Organization-building also reduces elite nimbleness and flexibility. Large rank-and-file memberships are likely to demand internally democratic procedures that prolong party decision making, and to insist on candidates and programs that alienate sectors of the electorate. For all these reasons, new parties that invest in organization typically make slow electoral progress, at best.

Office-seeking elites thus only have a strong electoral incentive to invest in organization if they cannot win office by quicker, easier, or more vote-maximizing means. Two such means are (1) the use of the state (i.e., public money, infrastructure, personnel) for electoral purposes (Hale 2006) and (2) mass media appeals (Mainwaring and Zoco 2007). Consequently, only when office-seekers *lack* access to state and media do they have a strong electoral incentive to invest in party organization.

State, Media, and Incentives for Organization-Building

In many developing countries, politicians in office have opportunities to use the state as a "substitute" for party organization (Hale 2006). Such politicians can siphon public money to finance their campaigns, deploy government employees (e.g., hospital workers, army members) as campaigners, recruit candidates from government agencies, and use public buildings as campaign offices. Investing in party organization takes longer, requires more fundraising, and imposes tighter constraints on elite nimbleness and flexibility. Thus, it is often electorally rational for elites in office to forego party-building and use state resources to win elections (Hale 2006). An extended period in the opposition, then, may actually serve as a blessing in disguise for party-builders. In the opposition, office-seekers cannot use the state for electoral purposes. Effectively, they lack access to a major party substitute that has hindered party-building in numerous developing countries.

Importantly, though, in recent decades, office-seekers in the opposition often have not needed to invest in parties in order to obtain a mass following. Given the extensive reach of television and radio in most countries today, media-savvy political entrepreneurs can win major elections (including presidential elections) through mass media appeals, with little or no party organization behind them. They can appeal to millions of voters instantaneously, autonomously, and without the need for canvassing. Consequently, the rise of broadcast media has reduced elite incentives for party-building and weakened or prevented the emergence of strong parties in many present-day polities (Mainwaring and Zoco 2007: 156–157). Brazilian ex-president Fernando Henrique Cardoso memorably observed in the late 1980s that for office-seekers, "a TV channel is worth more than a party" (quoted in Mainwaring 1999: 150).

Yet, where large segments of the opposition lack access to mass media, the only new opposition parties capable of achieving electoral success are those that build strong organizations. In many electoral authoritarian regimes today, restrictions on freedom of the press deprive new opposition parties of media access. Such parties must invest heavily in territorial organization if they wish to contend for national power.

Mobilizing Structures and the Means for Organization-Building

Elites who have incentives to invest in organization must also have the means to build strong organizations. Access to civil society feeder organizations, or "mobilizing structures" (Tarrow 1998: ch. 8), significantly reduces the costs of organization-building by supplying new parties with readymade activist networks, trained elites and cadres, and physical infrastructure (e.g., offices, phones, computers). Historically, most strong party organizations have been built on trade unions, social movements, local church associations, guerrilla armies, and other organizational platforms (see, e.g., Kitschelt 1989; Kalyvas 1996; LeBas 2011).[3]

---

[3] In some cases, the state apparatus itself has served as an organizational platform for party-building. See Shefter (1994) on internally mobilized parties.

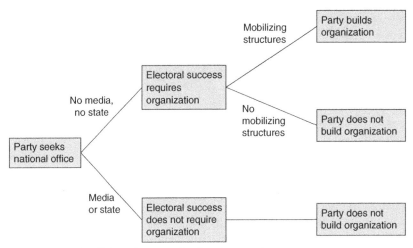

FIGURE 5.1 Conditions for organizational strength.

Adversity and Activist Commitment

A strong territorial organization, though necessary to cushion new parties against collapse, is not sufficient. To survive major setbacks, new parties, even those with territorial organization, require high levels of activist commitment. Conditions of low state and media access not only create incentives for organization-building, they also select for committed activists. As observed earlier, new parties with low state and media access tend to make slow electoral progress, at best. Under these circumstances, elites cannot offer selective incentives (e.g., public or party jobs) to most activists in the short term. The unavailability of selective incentives weeds out careerists and patronage-seekers. As a rule, only ideologically committed activists – Panebianco's "believers" (1988: 26–30) – are willing to donate their time and labor to a new party with weak, uncertain electoral prospects (Shefter 1994; Greene 2007; Hanson 2010).

The Role of Authoritarianism

Low state and media access thus facilitates party-building by creating incentives for territorial organization and selection pressures for committed activists. Critically, new parties with low state and media access are more likely to be found in authoritarian contexts than democratic ones. In authoritarian systems, the ruling elite excludes the opposition from the state, either by not holding elections, or by holding elections but significantly handicapping the opposition through fraud, repression, excessive spending, and numerous other means.[4] Many authoritarian regimes handicap opponents by limiting their access to media. Through selective licensing, bribes, sanctions, and outright ownership, they ensure that major media outlets support the regime and ignore or defame the opposition.

Authoritarian contexts can facilitate opposition party-building in two additional ways. First, although in extreme cases, authoritarian repression undermines party-building by deterring even the most committed regime opponents from organizing, in less extreme (and more typical) cases, such repression strengthens opposition selection pressures by weeding out activists unwilling to face the risk of violence or imprisonment. Second, the large-scale mobilization of believers, naturally, requires the existence of a higher cause. Antiauthoritarian movements tend to furnish such higher causes. They are struggles against political exclusion and, sometimes, state violence. Consequently, they stir passions, helping mobilize the founding generation of activists who are so vital to building resilient party organizations.

Under democracy, by definition, civil liberties such as freedom of speech, press, association, and protest are broadly protected, and in the contemporary era, opposition parties have access to broadcast media. Consequently, new opposition parties under democracy are, on average, more capable than their antiauthoritarian counterparts of quickly penetrating the state. In many important respects, this ease of opposition access to state and media is desirable, but it weakens the incentives and selection pressures that are critical for party-building.

THE ARGUMENT AT WORK: NEW LEFT PARTY SURVIVAL AND COLLAPSE IN BRAZIL, MEXICO, AND ARGENTINA

The rest of the chapter illustrates the above argument through a comparison of three Latin American new left parties: Brazil's PT (est. 1980), Mexico's PRD (est. 1989), and Argentina's FREPASO (est. 1994). These parties share several analytically relevant features. Not only were they born on the political left during the same general period, they emerged in opposition to their governments' neoliberal economic policies. Throughout

---

[4] For more on these hybrid, "competitive authoritarian" regimes, see Levitsky and Way (2010).

their formative periods, they had limited access to state resources and strong ties to nationally organized mobilizing structures. Finally, they all suffered early electoral crises. The PT experienced a major letdown in its first election; the PRD suffered crushing defeats in its first two national elections; and FREPASO had a disastrous election in 2001. Yet, while the PT and PRD survived and took root, FREPASO disintegrated. The case studies below provide evidence that, paradoxically, the PT and PRD weathered their crises because of their origins under authoritarian rule. Deprived of access to mass media, both parties initially invested in organization and, when crisis struck, were equipped to survive. In contrast, FREPASO's founders began their party-building project under democracy, with access to independent mass media. Consequently, they did not invest in organization and were not equipped to survive.

The PT in Brazil

Brazil's PT was established in 1980 and spent its first half-decade as a leading opponent of Brazil's military regime (1964–1985). Its founders came from the civil society organizations leading Brazil's prodemocracy struggle at the grassroots level: the autonomous labor movement, or "new unionism", in collaboration with the Catholic and Marxist left.

PT Organization-Building: State, Media, and Mobilizing Structures
During its first decade of existence, the PT had virtually no access to state resources or private finance. In a country with a federal government, over twenty state governments, and over 4,000 municipal governments, the PT, on creation, did not hold a single executive post. Not until 1989 did the PT occupy its first major executive position, the mayoralty of São Paulo. Annual party revenue was below US$ 200,000 until 1986 and $1.1 million until the mid-1990s (Ribeiro 2010: 111).[5] Such meager patronage and financial resources were grossly insufficient to grease the wheels of a major party machine, especially in a country of Brazil's size.

The early PT also lacked access to mass media. During the years of Brazil's military dictatorship, television ownership and access increased substantially, and control of popular local and regional TV stations became essential for congressional and subnational political success. Brazil's military presidents systematically awarded broadcasting concessions to local and regional bosses on political grounds, in implicit

[5] Adjusted for 2010 inflation levels.

exchange for progovernment media coverage, "creating the new phenomenon of electronic [clientelism]" (Porto 2003: 294). This pattern, which harmed the new unionism and PT during the late military period, continued after the 1985 transition to civilian rule under presidents José Sarney (1985–1990) and Fernando Collor de Mello (1990–1992), who were both opponents of the PT. During Sarney's term, the distribution of local television and radio licenses on political grounds "reached a new level" (Porto 2012: 63), and through Collor's abbreviated tenure, "political favoritism" remained "the only criterion" for awarding broadcasting concessions.[6]

Throughout the PT's gestation period and formative years, a single network – Globo – held a monopoly in television news and systematically omitted, distorted, and manipulated its political coverage in order to weaken and defame the left-wing opposition (Porto 2012). Globo's most flagrant breach of journalistic neutrality occurred in 1989, when the network's flagship news program, *Jornal Nacional*, heavily edited presidential debate segments in order to improve the image of right-wing candidate, Fernando Collor, and portray the PT's leader, Lula da Silva, as radical and dangerous. In 1993, Lula identified Globo's media monopoly as a central impediment to full democratization in Brazil (*Beyond Citizen Kane*).

Out of power and off the airwaves, the early PT depended almost exclusively on grassroots activism for electoral gain – a reality not lost on early PT organizers.[7] While low access to material resources and media made organization-building electorally necessary, the PT's ties to civil society made such organization-building possible. The early PT built an extensive party infrastructure by tapping into three main feeder groups: new unions, the Catholic left, and the Marxist left. New unions not only supplied the PT's top leaders but also provided the PT with more cadres, activists, members, and office locales than any other civil society feeder organization (Keck 1992: 77–79). The Catholic left, however, also played a vital role in early PT organization-building. With the rise of the new unionism in the late 1970s, Catholic base-level communities became heavily involved in the autonomous labor struggle and, later, the PT. The Catholic left's strength in rural and peripheral urban areas, where the new unionism was generally weak, extended the early PT's organizational reach (Keck 1992: 78–79). Finally, many elites and cadres from

---

[6] Quoted in BBC documentary, *Beyond Citizen Kane*.
[7] See Van Dyck (2014b: chapter 2).

Brazil's three leading Marxist parties[8] defected to join the PT instead of the larger, more established, center-left Brazilian Democratic Movement Party (PMDB), and the PT also absorbed a group of more radical Marxist organizations such as the Trotskyist Workers' Faction (Secco 2011: 47–49; Keck 1992: 79–81).

During the 1980s, the PT established an extensive organizational presence in several areas of Brazil, particularly the urban, industrialized Southeast and South and several rural states (e.g., Acre, Pará). In 1980 and 1981, PT membership and formal branch presence skyrocketed and, thereafter, expanded steadily. By 1989, the PT had 625,000 members (Keck 1992: 110) and formal branches in nearly half of Brazil's municipalities (Ribeiro 2010: 24). By the mid-1990s, PT membership approached 1 million (Ribeiro 2010: 244).

Selection Effects and Activist Commitment

PT founders describe the organization-building of the 1980s as an extremely difficult undertaking requiring immense effort.[9] The difficulty stemmed primarily from the need to recruit and register hundreds of thousands of party members in hundreds of municipalities, and to train an army of activists to do this organizing work. Organizers worked without pay and, in some exceptional cases, under threat of repression.[10] Such conditions, together with the early PT's electoral marginality, shaped the profile of the party's early joiners. By and large, those who joined the early PT did so out of a commitment to the party's cause, platform, and participatory ethos.

Surviving Crisis in 1982

The PT's strong organization and committed activists fortified it amid early electoral crisis. In the 1982 municipal, state, and congressional elections, the PT suffered a major letdown. The party had entered the electoral season with optimism due to the "great energy of struggle"[11] and unexpectedly large rally audiences during the PT's 1982 campaigns (Keck 1992: 141–144; Bom 2008: 96). Most activists believed that Lula

---

[8] Namely, Partido Comunista Brasileiro (PCB – Brazilian Communist Party), Partido Comunista do Brasil (PcdoB – Communist Party of Brazil), Movimento Revolucionário 8 de Outubro (MR-8 – October 8 Revolutionary Movement).

[9] See, for example, Bom (2008: 90). Also see Van Dyck (2014b: ch. 2).

[10] Anti-left violence in the late 1970s and 1980s affected agricultural workers primarily (Petit 1996: 142), and Marxist activists and industrial workers secondarily. Several new unionists were killed by local authorities, including Manoel Fiel Filho in 1976 and two strikers in Leme, São Paulo in the mid-1980s.

[11] Author's interview with Antônio Donato, May 4, 2010.

would win the São Paulo governorship, the most important of the offices
contested (Bom 2008: 96). Lula placed a distant fourth, though, and in
a country with over 4,000 municipalities, the PT won only two small
mayoralties. In Brazil's congress, the PT received a paltry 3.5 percent of
the seats. Keck (1992: 149, 152–153, 156) calls the 1982 results a "profound shock and disappointment to the PT," which "the PT experienced
as a severe defeat," and after which "deep disappointment and a kind of
collective depression" set in.

Nevertheless, the PT quickly rebounded at the base level. In intraparty dialogues after the election, party leaders assessed that the 1982
campaigns had distanced the party from its civil society roots. The party
thus initiated a "return to the base" and a renewed emphasis on "social
action" (Keck 1992: 197). With no elected offices to occupy, top party
leaders, including Lula, rededicated themselves to the new unionism. In
1983, they founded the umbrella new union confederation, the Unified
Workers' Central (CUT), beginning a successful effort to expand the
autonomous labor movement. The PT's renewed focus on social action
came to involve other civil society actors as well, particularly landless
workers. On the strength of the PT's grassroots leadership (Secco 2011:
113), Brazil's 1983–1984 movement for direct elections (Diretas Já)
became the largest mass mobilization in the country's history.

The PT performed unexpectedly well in the mayoral elections of
November 1985. The party ran campaigns in nearly every state capital,
and PT candidates reported breakout performances across the country.
The PT won the mayoralty of Fortaleza (then Brazil's fifth largest city),
and unlike in 1982, PT candidates finished second or third in a number
of other major municipal contests, including São Paulo's. In part, the PT's
performance reflected its new civil society ties, developed since 1982. In
addition, though, the PT had begun to solidify a distinctive party brand.
The PT's boycott of the January 1985 presidential election – following
the Brazilian Congress's rejection, months earlier, of the amendment
for direct elections – had consolidated its image as a party of principle,
less willing to compromise for short-term political gain than the PMDB
(Secco 2011: 119). This helped the PT attract and cement Brazil's left-
wing vote. By the second half of the 1980s, the PT dominated the left side
of Brazil's electoral spectrum.[12]

---

[12] Talk by PT historian Lincoln Secco at PT zonal office in Pinheiros, São Paulo. Accessed
on December 16, 2014, www.youtube.com/watch?v=D3wlv-Y5tOw and www.youtube.
com/watch?v=kW2FEfwmsx4.

The Institutionalization of the PT

The PT's evolution from the late 1980s to the 2010s is well known and widely studied.[13] In 1989, Lula da Silva burst onto the national political scene and almost won the presidential election, significantly raising the PT's national profile. In 1994 and 1998, though, Lula suffered successive presidential defeats, largely because the PT ran too far to the ideological extreme, as "niche parties" often do (Greene, Chapter 6, this volume; Hunter 2010). As in 1982, these setbacks (especially Lula's 1994 loss) dashed party members' and supporters' expectations. Nevertheless, the PT – as it had done before – survived to "play another day." In fact, in contrast to the early 1980s, the PT of the 1990s, even as it lost repeated presidential elections, never ran a serious risk of collapse. Below the presidential level, the PT made steady electoral gains. After winning only two mayoralties in 1982, the PT won 36 in 1988, 54 in 1992, 115 in 1996, and 187 in 2000 (Hunter 2010: 202). In 1989, the PT won the São Paulo mayoralty, one of Brazil's most important executive posts after the presidency. In 1990, the PT crossed the 10 percent threshold in the lower house of congress and continued to gain in 1994 and 1998 (see Figure 5.2). In 1994, the PT won its first two governorships (Espírito Santo, Brasília), and in 1998, it won three (Acre, Mato Grosso do Sul, Rio Grande do Sul). In short, while Lula was losing presidential elections, the PT was steadily growing and becoming institutionalized as a major national party.

During the first two decades of the twenty-first century, the PT became Brazil's most successful party. At the national level, the party finally "adapted," embracing macroeconomic orthodoxy and modernizing its campaign tactics (Samuels 2004; Hunter 2010). These adaptations paved the way for Lula's 2002 presidential victory and enabled the PT to follow Lula's 2002 victory with repeat victories in 2006, 2010, and 2014. Between 1994 and 2014, the PT regularly won 10–20 percent in the lower house of congress, and in 2014, it captured four governorships.

What is critical, however, is that the PT survived the formative years. The 1980s tested the PT's durability, as the party suffered a major electoral setback in 1982 and operated on the margins of national electoral politics for nearly a decade. The PT survived this difficult period and could subsequently take root because of its durable party organization, built under adverse, authoritarian conditions.[14]

---

[13] See Samuels (2004), Hunter and Power (2007), Hunter (2010), Ribeiro (2010), Secco (2011), Power and Zucco (2013), Zucco (2013), and Samuels and Zucco (2014, 2015).

[14] Nogueira-Budny (2013) advances a related argument about the PT, which he refers to as the "no pain, no gain" thesis. Nogueira-Budny shows that the PT's formative experiences

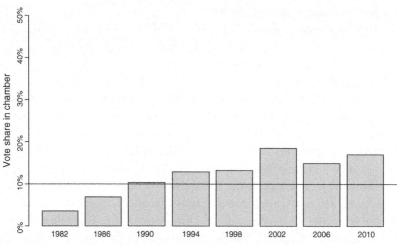

FIGURE 5.2 PT vote share in lower house of Congress.

The PRD in Mexico

Mexico's (PRD) is another case of an opposition party that formed under adverse, authoritarian circumstances, built a strong organization with committed activists, survived early electoral crisis, and took root. The PRD was born in 1989 under the authoritarian rule of the hegemonic Institutional Revolutionary Party (PRI). It grew out of a mass movement to elect Cuauhtémoc Cárdenas, leftist PRI defector, president of Mexico in 1988. After Carlos Salinas of the PRI defeated Cárdenas in an election widely viewed as fraudulent, the left-wing movement that had backed Cárdenas strengthened, and from it, the PRD emerged in 1989.

PRD Organization-Building: State, Media, and Mobilizing Structures
The PRD was born with no governors and only a handful of mayors in small, poor municipalities. It did not win a single governorship or major mayoralty until the late 1990s, in contrast to the conservative National Action Party (PAN), the PRI's other main opposition party. The PRD also lacked major sources of private funding and thus suffered from chronic "financial shortages" and a lack of "resources to invest in electoral campaigns ... and professional cadres" (Borjas 2003: 297). At the local level, early PRD candidates often financed and ran their own campaigns. As

under bureaucratic authoritarian rule ultimately contributed to its success by facilitating its adaptation from Marxism-Leninism to market liberalism.

late as the mid-1990s, the national PRD organization could only afford fifty permanent staff (Bruhn 1997: 189). One party activist and scholar summarized that as late as the mid-1990s, "there was nothing [i.e., no patronage] to distribute."[15]

In contrast, the PRI had vast financial resources (public and private) at its disposal, which it used to outspend the PRD by overwhelming margins during the first half of the 1990s (Greene 2008: 107–114). The Salinas administration (1988–1994) also created and implemented a major poverty relief program, PRONASOL (National Solidarity Program), which targeted electorally strategic municipalities across Mexico and helped the PRI co-opt or divide many local electorates and civil society organizations previously sympathetic to Cárdenas (Molinar and Weldon 1994).

The early PRD also lacked access to mass media. Lawson (2002) has shown that until the late 1990s, the owners of Mexico's major media conglomerates, in exchange for preferential treatment by the government, systematically set the public agenda in accordance with PRI priorities, omitted politically disadvantageous developments from news programming, favorably covered the PRI, and cast PRI opponents in a negative light. At the center of Mexico's PRI-dominated media establishment lay the Televisa conglomerate (est. 1973). By the 1990s, Televisa, much like Brazil's Globo network, monopolized Mexico's television market, commanding over 80 percent of Mexico's television audience (Lawson 2002: 29). In a telling quotation from the mid-1990s, Televisa's chief executive, Emilio Azcarragá Jr., called himself a "soldier of the PRI" and described his network as "part of the governmental system" (quoted in Lawson 2002: 30).

Unsurprisingly, the early PRD suffered from systematic media hostility and blacklisting. During the 1988 presidential campaign, Cárdenas received under nine hours of airtime on Televisa's primetime cable news program, *24 Horas* (*24 Hours*), while Salinas received over 140 hours (Rodríguez 2010: 190). In the lead-up to the 1994 presidential campaign, PRI candidate Ernest Zedillo received forty-six times more airtime than Cárdenas and the PAN's Diego Fernández de Cevallos combined (Bruhn 1997: 280). According to several analyses, unfair media treatment significantly harmed the PRD in both the 1991 congressional election and 1994 general election (Gómez 1997: 16; Borjas 2003: 430–431, 513–515, 571, 587).

---

[15] Author's interview with Adriana Borjas, July 11, 2011.

The PRD thus relied on grassroots volunteers to reach voters, and like Brazil's PT, the PRD was able to build a strong activist-based organization because of its ties to civil society. The early PRD drew primarily from three groups: the traditional Marxist left, the "social" (or "extra-parliamentary") left, and ex-PRI networks. In late 1988, Mexico's then largest left party, the Socialist Mexican Party (PMS), dissolved itself so that the PRD could adopt its registry and absorb its members and offices. Thus, on creation, the PRD inherited several thousand ex-PMS leaders and cadres, a disproportionate number of whom would rise to positions of national leadership or win major office (Martínez 2005). The social left, however, provided the PRD with a much larger number of early members and activists.[15] This sector encompassed organizations and movements that eschewed electoral politics, detested the PRI, had "iron-willed activist bases," and sometimes engaged in "warlike (including armed) forms of struggle" (Martínez 2005: 53, 55). Among social left actors, rural unions in the southern states and urban popular movements in Mexico City (particularly the Neighborhood Assembly, or Asamblea de Barrios) played the most important role in supplying PRD members and establishing local PRD branches (Rodríguez 2010: 257–258; Bruhn 1998: 225). Finally, large networks of defecting PRI cadres and activists fed into the PRD, particularly in Michoacán and Tabasco, the home states (respectively) of the PRD's most prominent PRI defector, Cuauhtémoc Cárdenas, and fellow PRI defector and future PRD presidential candidate, Andrés Manuel López Obrador (AMLO).[16]

PRD organizational-building quickly resulted in a high degree of territorial implantation. Within a few years of its birth, the PRD had established a strong presence in several parts of Mexico, especially Mexico City and several of the country's poor southern states (e.g., Michoacán, Guerrero, Tabasco). By the middle of the 1990s, the PRD had over 1 million members and offices in over half of Mexico's more than 2,000 municipalities (Borjas 2003: 371).

Selection Effects and Activist Commitment

Joining the early PRD typically required a willingness to do party work without a salary or the prospect of a likely election victory or government

---

[15] Interview with Cuauhtémoc Cárdenas in Borjas (2003, vol. II: 410–411).
[16] Guillermo Correa, "Muñoz Ledo: "El gran dilemma de 1994 es democracia o dictadura", *Proceso*, no. 820, July 18, 1992. Also, Borjas (2003: 519, vol. II: 74).

job. In one member's words, the early PRD "couldn't be a business."[17] As late as the second half of the 1990s, activism also required, in many cases, a willingness to put one's own safety at risk (Rodríguez 2010: 284). In fact, in proportional terms, the number of left-wing activists killed in Mexico during this period – estimates range from 250 to 600[18] – exceeded the number killed in Brazil under military rule (Rodríguez 2010: 297). The realities of political work without pay, dim electoral prospects, and threats of violence discouraged careerists from joining the early PRD. For the most part, only individuals with sincere ideological commitments to the PRD joined as active members during the party's formative years.

Surviving Crisis in 1991 and 1994

Organizational strength and activist commitment fortified the PRD amid early electoral crisis. The PRD suffered major setbacks in its first two national elections, the 1991 congressional election and 1994 general election. Before the 1991 election, PRD "leaders and activists shared ... a certainty" that the PRD would win "broad representation" in the legislature despite the resource asymmetries, media bias, and repression of the campaign (Borjas 2003: 388). The party performed abysmally, though, unexpectedly losing seats and finishing a distant third with only 8 percent of the vote. The result dashed member expectations and threatened the party's survival. Some prominent social left leaders, in protest of the PRI's hostile campaign tactics, advocated that the PRD withdraw from the electoral sphere. Cárdenas would later describe 1991 as the most challenging episode in the PRD's history: "The objective of the '91 midterms was the real, effective liquidation of the PRD ... [T]his was the PRD's hardest electoral moment" (quoted in Borjas 2003, vol. II: 408).

In fact, however, the 1991 crisis galvanized much of the PRD base. The PRD's twenty-year commemorative volume states: "1991 represented for the PRD its first political setback but at the same time the consolidation of an iron-willed base" (González et al. 2010: 66). When asked why the PRD did not fold after the 1991 elections, one founding activist from the radical left replied that the PRI had murdered scores of activists and committed widespread fraud; thus, the PRI's victory was seen as illegitimate and did not discourage most party activists. Another founder with social left origins expressed a similar sentiment, stating that the PRI's hostility

---

[17] Author's interview with Silvia Gómez, July 4, 2011.
[18] González et al. (2010: 66), Zambrano (2010: 284), Bruhn (1997: 202), Borjas (2003: 45, 341, 436), Rodríguez (2010: 284).

only motivated the base – that most PRD activists did not even enter-
tain the thought of giving up after 1991.[19] The gubernatorial election
results of 1992 and 1993 demonstrated the PRD's base-level resilience, as
the party received large (though not winning) vote shares in Michoacán,
Guerrero, Nayarit, Veracruz, and Zacatecas (Borjas 2003: 490–491).

In the 1994 presidential election, the PRD suffered a second major setback. Contesting the presidency for a second time, Cuauhtémoc Cárdenas
ran too far to the left of the median voter (Greene 2007) and lost in a
landslide, receiving just 17 percent of the vote and finishing a distant
third. The lopsidedness of the outcome was not anticipated; in fact, many
PRD members had believed that Cárdenas would prevail (González et al.
2010: 66; Borjas 2003: 507). Moreover, the prospect of a Cárdenas presidential victory in 1994 – and, with it, both the completion of Mexico's
transition to democracy and a historic victory for the Mexican left – had
animated PRD members since the party's founding. That Cárdenas not
only lost, but received under one-fifth of the vote, deflated hopes, led to
anger, disillusionment, and recriminations, and damaged the party's credibility and self-conception as a serious contender.

As in 1991, though, most PRD activists – more radical, on average,
than the party moderates who blamed Cárdenas's defeat on ideological
intransigence – remained unfazed. They viewed the 1994 result, like the
1991 result, as an illegitimate outcome based on fraud, overwhelming
financial advantage, media corruption, and brutal repression. The defeat,
in their view, was merely another lost battle in a longer-term war with
the PRI. Many PRD members had been killed during the 1994 campaign,
and one PRD founder, when asked by the author what enabled the PRD
to rebound from the 1994 presidential defeat, responded, "We were at
war."[20] Thus, as had occurred after the 1991 congressional election, PRD
activist networks regrouped, directing their energies toward upcoming
subnational campaigns and, in Tabasco, postelection civil resistance
(Borjas 2003, vol. II: 94, 599–600).

In sum, then, despite suffering electoral crises in both 1991 and 1994,
the PRD survived and pressed forward. In a 2010 interview, party founder
and early federal deputy, Carlos Navarrete, eloquently summarized the
PRD's early spirit of resistance:

[PRD president Carlos Salinas's 1988–1994 term] was a very hard time ... They
were times of persecution, of hundreds of dead activists. They were times in which

---

[19] Author's interview with Paco Saucedo, July 9, 2011.
[20] Author's interview with Salvador Nava, July 9, 2011.

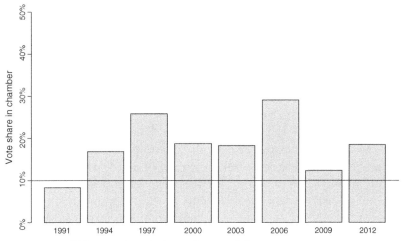

FIGURE 5.3 PRD vote share in lower house of Congress.

they stole elections from us, covering the width and depth of the country. They were times in which the government besieged us. They were times of *resistance, fundamentally, of not giving up, of maintaining and raising our flags.* (Navarrete 2010: 265; emphasis not in the original)

The Institutionalization of the PRD

The PRD's development during the second half of the 1990s and first two decades of the twentieth century is well known and widely studied.[21] During the 1990s and first two decades of the twenty-first century, the PRD became institutionalized as Mexico's third major party. In 2006 and 2012, the PRD's Andrés Manuel López Obrador (AMLO) came close to winning the presidency. Between 1994 and 2015, the PRD elected at least 10 percent of Mexico's congress members in every election (see Figure 5.3), with a higher average vote share than Brazil's PT. The PRD also won over a dozen governorships between 1998 and 2015, and it held the Mexico City mayoralty – perhaps the second most important elected office in the country – continuously from 1997 to 2015.

The PRD's success since the mid-1990s stems from several factors, including media liberalization (Lawson 2002), the PRD's co-optation and absorption of regional PRI elites and their machines, and the party's increased use of paid activists such as the Sun Brigades (Van Dyck 2014b: ch. 4). Above all, though, the PRD's gains reflect the

[21] See Borjas (2003), Martínez (2005), Rodríguez (2010), Mossige (2013).

solidification and expansion of its brand. Since 2000, most Mexicans have been able to locate the PRD party symbol, an Aztec Sun, on the left-right spectrum,[22] and PRD partisans in the electorate have guaranteed the PRD a solid electoral floor nationally.

For the PRD, collapse remains unlikely despite the recent defections of Cuauhtémoc Cárdenas, the party's founder, and AMLO, the party's 2006 and 2012 presidential candidate.[23] The PRD's "hardcore vote" (*voto duro*) virtually guarantees a high baseline level of access to office and the associated patronage. It also guarantees access to financial resources; the landmark electoral reforms of 1996, which tied generous public financing to parties' performance in congressional elections, have filled PRD coffers since the late 1990s. Additionally, the PRD's committed activist base remains an important source of electoral capacity and resilience.

The PRD has paid an electoral price for catering to its base (Greene 2007; Chapter 6, this volume). In particular, the presidency continues to elude the PRD, and in this sense, the PRD has failed where Brazil's PT has succeeded. In fact, many scholars treat the PRD as a failure or underachiever, citing the party's repeated presidential defeats and internal dysfunction (Bruhn 1998; Greene 2007; Chapter 6, this volume; Mossige 2013). Yet, like the PT, the PRD has established itself as a perennial contender for national power, something very few new parties in Latin America, left or otherwise, have achieved. In short, the achievements of the PRD have received far too little emphasis. Viewed in comparative perspective, the PRD is an unmistakable case of successful party-building.

In explaining this success, what is critical is that the PRD survived its formative period. The Salinas years, and especially the PRD's defeats in 1991 and 1994, seriously tested the party's durability. Like Brazil's PT, the PRD ultimately took root because it managed to survive early crisis, and like the PT, the PRD drew its early strength and resilience from a committed, organized activist base forged in the crucible of authoritarianism.

---

[22] 2000 Mexico Panel Study. Accessed on Dec. 16, 2014. http://web.mit.edu/clawson/www/polisci/research/mexico06/Papers.shtml#TSAccordionHead296290.

[23] AMLO left the PRD shortly after his loss in the 2012 presidential election. He now leads the National Regeneration Movement (MORENA), a left party in Mexico that became officially registered in 2014. Cuauhtémoc Cárdenas left the PRD in late 2014, citing a range of unresolved differences with the current party leadership.

FREPASO in Argentina

In contrast to the PT and PRD, Argentina's FREPASO is a case of an opposition party that formed under democratic, relatively advantageous conditions, did not invest in organization, and collapsed after suffering an early electoral crisis. FREPASO's origins lie in a 1990 schism within Argentina's then governing party, the historically populist Peronist Party (PJ). In 1989, president Carlos Menem (PJ) reneged on populist campaign promises and implemented extensive neoliberal reforms, provoking opposition from a bloc of left-leaning PJ congressmen. Eight of these congressmen, known as the "Group of Eight" and led by Carlos "Chacho" Álvarez, defected from the PJ in mid-1990. The initial electoral vehicles that they created failed, but political opportunity struck after the congressional elections of October 1993. In November 1993, Raúl Alfonsín, the leader of the PJ's main opposition party, the Radical Civil Union (UCR), signed the Olivos Pact, which pledged UCR support for a controversial constitutional amendment allowing Menem to run for reelection in 1995. The UCR's perceived "subordination" to Menem's institutional tampering provoked a backlash among its own middle-class constituency (Jozami 2004: 56, 19). Álvarez and the Group of Eight, now leading the center-left party, the Big Front (FG), quickly became the public face of opposition to *Menemismo* and UCR complicity (Pazos and Camps 1995: 180, 215). In the April 1994 constituent assembly elections, the FG made an electoral breakthrough, winning 13 percent of the national vote, up almost 10 percentage points from the congressional election just months earlier (Abal Medina 2009: 368). This result marked the beginning of the FG's meteoric, five-year path to national power. From the mid- to late 1990s, Álvarez and fellow FG elites forged a succession of increasingly centrist alliances, making anticorruption and ethics the centerpiece of their platform and backtracking on their original opposition to neoliberalism (Jozami 2004: 26–27, 123–139; Lupu 2016). In late 1994, the FG joined forces with center-right ex-governor of Mendoza province, José Octavio Bordón, and his new party, Open Politics for Social Integrity (PAIS), to create the center-left party FREPASO. In 1995, FREPASO's Bordón/Álvarez ticket[24] placed second in the presidential election, behind Menem, and FREPASO placed third in the congressional election, behind the PJ and UCR. In 1997, FREPASO moved further to the center by

---

[24] FREPASO held an open primary to nominate its presidential candidate, and Bordón won a surprise victory largely due to his organizational base in Mendoza.

forming an electoral coalition with the UCR, the Alliance for Justice, Work, and Education. In 1997, the Alliance won control of the congress, and in 1999, the Alliance won both the congress and the presidency, with Fernando de la Rúa (UCR) and Chacho Álvarez (FREPASO) on the winning presidential ticket. In the span of five years, then, FG/FREPASO rose from electoral marginality to national power. How was this achieved?

FREPASO's Organizational Weakness: State, Media, and Mobilizing Structures

Mass media, and especially television, were the "primary engine" of FG/ FREPASO's meteoric growth (Novaro and Palermo 1998: 117). Party leaders made "efficient and intense use" of mass media, constantly holding televised press conferences, participating in interviews with broadcast outlets and major newspapers, and making TV-tailored "political displays" (Novaro and Palermo 1998: 117, 150–151). Chacho Álvarez, in particular, was a "media phenomenon" who "charmed the media with [his] irreverence toward the traditional rituals of politics, [his] ease of manner and speed" (Abal Medina 2009: 369). According to one ex-FG member, Álvarez's political genius lay in his ability to anticipate public opinion shifts, and in his recognition of "the importance of media, above all television" (quoted in Pazos and Camps 1995: 263). Álvarez's media charisma crystallized in late 1993, when he became the most visible antagonist of *Menemismo* and corruption during the Olivos negotiations and backlash (Pazos and Camps 1995: 180, 215). From late 1993 onward, Álvarez "began to be required by the press" due to his charisma, eloquent critiques, and rapid responses to events (Pazos and Camps 1995: 179).

Álvarez and the FREPASO leadership considered media a highly desirable, even necessary, alternative to organization-building. Throughout the 1990s, FREPASO's founders were engaged in a near-permanent campaign, competing in national elections in 1991, 1993, 1994, 1995, 1997, and 1999. The recruitment and training of activists and development of a nationwide organizational infrastructure would have consumed energy and resources while important national elections loomed (Novaro and Palermo 1998: 116). As one party member succinctly put it: "There was no time to build an organization."[25] Chacho Álvarez provided the same assessment in a 1997 interview, stating that he and fellow party leaders

---

[25] Author's interview with Héctor Mazzei, July 12, 2012.

could not devote energy to organization-building with major elections constantly on the horizon.[26]

FREPASO leaders also recognized that, if a party organization was established, internal decision-making procedures would slow elite response time. FREPASO prized the capacity for rapid response. A party observer recalled that Álvarez wanted to "move nimbly."[27] Contemporary politics required speed, he said, as journalists often appeared with a microphone and FREPASO had to respond. According to an ex-FREPASO member, party leaders "always fought to have freedom of action, hoping not to be tied down by institutional procedures when making decisions ... [T]he party's nucleus ... considered Álvarez's speed of response an important requirement" (Abal Medina 2009: 360).

Moreover, a large activist base would have denied FREPASO leaders, especially Álvarez, ideological and tactical flexibility. Through the 1990s, Álvarez and other party elites had ties to left-wing mobilizing structures with national reach, including several radical left parties and, most importantly, Argentina's two largest anti-Menemist union confederations, the Argentine Workers' Central (est. 1991) and the Teachers' Confederation of the Argentine Republic. FREPASO's leaders, however, consciously refrained from incorporating these groups into the party and using them as a platform for organization-building (Van Dyck 2014b: ch. 7). A party organization composed of such groups might have selected unelectable candidates or pressured FREPASO candidates to refuse centrist alliances and take extreme policy positions. Such decisions would have satisfied the base but alienated the middle-class voters that FREPASO was successfully targeting. By keeping the organized left at arm's length, Álvarez and fellow elites could make the most electorally rational decisions on program, coalitions, and party candidacies without consulting members (Pazos and Camps: 263–264). In the words of one former member, the "hypercentralization" of decision making within FREPASO allowed for "extreme operational flexibility."[28]

In short, FREPASO leaders recognized that by relying on mass media and restricting decision-making power to a tiny elite (often to Álvarez alone), FREPASO could quickly and easily attain national visibility, adapt nimbly to circumstances, and make electorally optimal ideological and tactical choices. Organization-building, by consuming scarce time and

---

[26] Álvarez's interview with Steven Levitsky, July 29, 1997.
[27] Author's interview with Aldo Gallotti, August 3, 2012.
[28] Author's interview with Edgardo Mocca, August 5, 2012. See also Abal Medina (2009: 361).

resources and placing procedural, ideological, and tactical constraints on elite decision making, would have prevented FREPASO from rapidly progressing in perpetually imminent elections. For these reasons, after 1991, "[t]he idea of building a solid and stable party organization was never in [the] minds" of "Álvarez and his followers" (Abal Medina 2009: 360).

Thus, by the end of the 1990s, FREPASO dominated the left side of the Argentine political spectrum, but it had a vanishingly small party apparatus and a "practically non-existent" base-level organization (Abal Medina 2009: 364). The party never employed more than five staff (Abal Medina 2009: 363). In 1998, party members Novaro and Palermo noted that "the FG and then FREPASO seem to have an almost ghostlike existence outside of the media arena" (1998: 151). One campaign strategist for the Alliance described FREPASO simply: "There was no organization."[29]

Crisis and Collapse in 2001

Like the PT and PRD, FREPASO faced an early electoral crisis. Upon entering office in December 1999, the Alliance government inherited a rapidly contracting economy and a ballooning national debt, and its orthodox policies did not stem the tide. The Alliance's problems magnified in late 2000 when a senate corruption scandal erupted, implicating several Alliance senators and two Alliance ministers (including one from FREPASO). Through September of 2000, Álvarez maintained public support for De la Rúa but privately urged him to fire the two implicated ministers. After De la Rúa refused, Álvarez tendered his resignation in October 2000. Following Álvarez's resignation, Argentina's economic and fiscal crises worsened, and in the 2001 midterm congressional elections, voters harshly punished the Alliance. The PJ retook the lower house, and the Alliance's vote share plummeted to 23 percent, down nearly half from 44 percent in 1999. For FREPASO, the outcome was especially dire. Whereas the UCR lost slightly more than a quarter of its congressional seats (from eighty-nine to sixty-five), FREPASO lost over half of its seats (from thirty-seven to fifteen). Two months later, amid riots triggered by a national bank freeze, President De la Rúa resigned, and the PJ returned to the presidency in late December 2001.

In 2001, then, both the UCR and FREPASO suffered electoral crisis. An important difference between the two parties, however, was that the UCR had a national grassroots organization, while FREPASO did not. On the strength of its territorial organization, the UCR survived,

---

[29] Author's interview with Francisco de Santibañes, August 2, 2012.

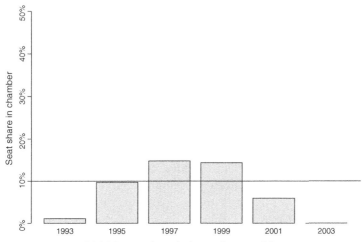

FIGURE 5.4 FREPASO seat share in lower house of Congress.
Note: Since FREPASO ran together with the UCR from 1997 to 2001, specific vote share figures for FREPASO are not available.

albeit in diminished form, and to this day remains a major player in Argentine politics, currently holding more than 20 percent of the seats in the Chamber of Deputies and more than 15 percent of the seats in the senate. In contrast, FREPASO, at the time of the 2001 crisis, was nothing but a small elite network, entirely dependent on voter identification with its brand. Thus, according to a former member, "when FREPASO lost its image, it lost everything."[30] After the 2001 election, FREPASO's members defected in order to preserve their careers. Most returned to the PJ, to smaller left parties, or to PJ satellite parties. In the words of one ex-FREPASO member, "each [member] returned home."[31] Summarizing FREPASO's collapse, an Alliance campaign consultant invoked a common metaphor: "Building an image through the media is like building with mud."[32]

CONCLUSION

This chapter has highlighted the critical importance of organization for successful party-building. The PT and PRD built strong grassroots

---

[30] Author's interview with Héctor Mazzei, July 12, 2012.
[31] Author's interview with Héctor Mazzei, July 12, 2012.
[32] Author's interview with Francisco de Santibañes, August 2, 2012.

organizations composed of committed activists, and this enabled them to rebound from early crisis and eventually take root. FREPASO lacked a grassroots organization and thus collapsed amid early crisis.

One might object that FREPASO's electoral crisis occurred in a radically different (and significantly worse) context than the PT and PRD crises. The PT and PRD, after all, were mere opposition parties when they experienced crushing electoral defeats, while FREPASO was a *governing* party whose national brand failed due to the party's disastrous performance in office. One could argue that this contextual difference mattered more for the parties' divergent trajectories than the internal, organizational differences emphasized in this chapter. For a few reasons, this argument is unpersuasive – or at least should not be overstated. First, it is not obvious, in theory, that new parties in the opposition should have an easier time regrouping from electoral crisis than new governing parties. To be sure, new parties that fail in government face a difficult test, as they must rebuild their brands and maintain party morale despite internal perceptions that a short-term return to power is impossible. However, crushing electoral defeats suffered by new parties in the opposition bring great challenges of their own, dashing member expectations, curbing activist enthusiasm, and generating a sense of internal pessimism or hopelessness. The PT and PRD are cases in point. Moreover, even if we assume that FREPASO's electoral crisis was more severe than the PT's and PRD's, it does not follow that FREPASO's subsequent collapse was inevitable; only that it was more likely, other things equal. This leaves room for the possibility that, if FREPASO had invested in territorial organization and an activist base before 1999–2001, it still would have been able to survive, in some form, after its disastrous performance in government and the crushing 2001 election. Finally, and relatedly, the electoral resilience of Argentina's UCR at the congressional and subnational levels since the 2001 election provides some evidence that governing parties can survive the electoral fallout from a disastrous performance if they are territorially organized. As discussed above, the UCR was FREPASO's senior partner in the coalition that governed Argentina from 1999 to 2001, and like FREPASO, the UCR suffered massive losses in the 2001 legislative election. In contrast to FREPASO, however, the UCR survived – albeit in diminished form – and, at present (2015), remains a major player in Argentine politics, currently holding more than 20 percent of the seats in the Chamber of Deputies and more than 15 percent of the seats in the senate.

Given this chapter's focus on organizational strength, one might ask what role brand development, which is largely independent of organization, played in the cases of party-building examined. In his chapter for this volume, Lupu highlights the role of brand dilution in explaining the divergent trajectories of the PT and FREPASO. On his account, FREPASO diluted its brand by moving sharply to the right on economic policy during the second half of the 1990s. For Argentine voters, this made FREPASO both internally inconsistent over time and, by the late 1990s, almost indistinct from other Argentine parties, particularly the UCR. In contrast, the PT, even as it moderated in the 2000s, preserved more of its left-wing brand than FREPASO did, largely due to its social policy initiatives. The PT also, unlike FREPASO, remained well to the left of its main competitors (e.g., the Party of Brazilian Social Democracy [PSDB]). Lupu (2016) argues that new parties with diluted brands, like FREPASO, depend exclusively on strong government performance. It follows, on his account, that the Argentine economic crisis and corruption scandal of the late 1990s and early 2000s – over which FREPASO presided, in coalition with the UCR – put the nail in FREPASO's coffin.

This chapter emphasizes, however, that parties do not exist in voters' minds alone (see Levitsky, Loxton, and Van Dyck, Chapter 1, this volume). Indeed, FREPASO's collapse illustrates how fragile new parties are *if* they exist in voters' minds alone. The formative period of party development is critical precisely because most parties, early on, are still in the process – like FREPASO was in the 1990s – of crafting, expanding, and solidifying their brands. The PT and PRD, early in their development, did not have strong brands. They also lacked governing responsibilities. Both had disastrous first elections, reflecting considerable brand weakness. The PT and PRD survived these crises because they existed on the ground, not just in voters' minds. By the time crisis struck, they had established strong activist networks in much of the national territory, and these activists stuck it out.

Committed activists, of course, are not uniformly positive in their effects. As Greene aptly observes in Chapter 6, this volume, parties with organizations composed of ideologues, or "niche parties," often eschew vote-maximizing behavior long after birth, as the PT did throughout the 1980s and 1990s, and the PRD did throughout the 1990s and 2000s. But committed activists are also critical for early survival, and thus are best seen as a mixed blessing for new parties.

Importantly, the antiauthoritarian struggles that generate strong organizations and committed activists do not last forever; the antiauthoritarian struggles in Brazil and Mexico provide cases in point. How do parties provide incentives to activists and cadres once these struggles end? As Chapter 1, this volume, suggests, access to the state may be critical for the longer-term survival of political parties. Even if state resources do not produce strong party organizations, they may help sustain party organizations or even expand them. Party leaders can use state patronage to attract new activists and retain the services of old ones. Bruhn (Chapter 8, this volume) provides evidence that generous public financing helped the PRD sustain its large party organization after the formative period, from the late 1990s onward. There is also evidence that both the PT and PRD have used public monies to expand their organizational reach after the formative period (Samuels and Zucco, Chapter 12, this volume; Van Dyck 2014a).

In short, the conditions for party survival change over time. As parties exit the formative period, access to patronage and public finance often become critical, greasing the wheels of party machines and facilitating long-term consolidation. But in the beginning, adversity is critical.

6

The Niche Party

Authoritarian Regime Legacies and Party-Building in New Democracies

Kenneth F. Greene

This chapter focuses on an insidious legacy of party-building under author-itarianism for party fortunes in subsequent democratic contexts. "Niche parties" arise as electoral vehicles for severely disadvantaged political out-siders in systems that bias elections in favor of the incumbent party, such as hybrid autocracies.[1] Niche parties are animated by conflicts between the regime and its opponents, but the unlevel playing field makes them into hermetic, inward-looking organizations focused on cultivating an identity of difference. Rather then following a logic of expansion to win elections like parties in fully competitive democracies, niche parties follow a logic of survival in the face of their slim chance of winning elections, few fungible resources, and vulnerability to state-sponsored repression. These attributes make niche parties robust, but poorly suited to compete on a level playing field after transitions to fully competitive democracy.

Niche parties are interesting objects of study for four reasons. First, they are successful in the sense described by this volume's editors: they create partisans in the electorate, establish territorial organizations, and generate internal cohesion.[2] Yet their origins as besieged outsiders force the creation of a narrowly defined identity that produces small groups of intense partisans but fails to align majoritarian constituencies, establishes territorial organizations in geographically proscribed areas but fails to expand across the national territory, and generates internal cohesion by

---

[1] Niche parties also arise in dominant party democracies. See Greene (2007). I use the term "niche party" consistent with Greene (2007) but distinct from Meguid (2008) and Adams et al. (2005).

[2] For an argument about the potential benefits of the adverse conditions that give rise to niche parties, see Van Dyck (Chapter 5, this volume).

recruiting like-minded activists from specific feeder organizations in society rather than recruiting broadly.

Second, niche parties challenge rationalist arguments about party adaptation, showing that party origins can cast a long shadow on their organizations and policy proposals. They are designed to endure authoritarianism, not primarily to thrive in democracy and thus can exhibit tremendous path dependency long after the restrictive conditions that gave rise to them have changed. Third, niche parties' peculiar organizations mean that they often suffer from unexpected intraparty struggles over organization and program. Whereas party leaders in fully competitive democracies typically focus on winning elections and may conflict with more ideologically oriented activists (May 1973), these actors' preferences can be flipped in parties that challenge systematically advantaged incumbents. Finally, niche parties can persist long past their usefulness, creating unexpected pathologies in new democracies exiting from competitive authoritarian or electoral authoritarian rule. If they achieve elected office, such parties can act more like vanguards than representatives and they can make legislative majorities difficult to reach, encouraging gridlock in congress.

In the first section of this chapter, I conceptualize niche parties and show how they resolve key organizational problems in ways that differ from existing party types. The second section makes sense of niche parties' peculiar organizational design. The third section characterizes Mexico's rightist National Action Party (PAN) and leftist Party of the Democratic Revolution (PRD) as niche parties during the long period of authoritarian single-party dominance under the Institutional Revolutionary Party (PRI) and, more surprisingly, *after* democratization when there were numerous advantages to adopting a broader organizational form. The fourth section compares the absence of major organizational change in the PAN and PRD to the higher degree of moderation and adaptation of Brazil's Workers' Party (PT). The conclusion discusses the implications of niche parties for politics in Mexico, the limits of rationalist theories of party organization, and relates this chapter's argument to those of other chapters in this volume.

NICHE PARTY ORIGINS

Niche parties are generated by political outsiders in systems that permit genuine electoral competition among multiple partisan options but where challengers have a very low chance of winning office and opposition party members pay high costs for their activism. Such parties are a main electoral vehicle for independent opposition forces in long-term regimes[3] that permit partisan competition but so dramatically tilt the partisan playing field in their favor that only a subset of highly motivated prospective politicians who are deeply antagonistic to the incumbent regime are actually willing to oppose it.[4] Niche parties are thus most likely to emerge in competitive authoritarian regimes (Levitsky and Way 2002, 2010) and electoral authoritarian regimes (Schedler 2002) that permit meaningful competition. Although not the focus of this chapter due to its geographic restriction to Latin America, niche parties are also likely to emerge in dominant party democratic regimes (Greene 2007) that Sartori (1976: 194) referred to as "predominant" party systems, where elections are tremendously biased in favor of the incumbent.

Niche parties form where genuine partisan competition makes them useful vehicles for opposition actors but where "normal" opposition parties could not survive. Their emergence depends on the opportunities for partisan competition created by the incumbent regime. Where autocrats choke off the electoral arena by prohibiting all but one challenger, opposition forces will likely coalesce into a broad front rather than separate niche parties. Where autocrats make the environment even more difficult by harshly repressing large numbers of challengers, opponents will forego parties and mobilize through social movements or revolutionary organizations. As a result, niche parties do not exist in fully closed authoritarian regimes or where partisan competition is a sham. Niche parties thus only form where they are a useful tool for opposing the incumbent party at the polls and not just as a vehicle for expressing dissatisfaction with the regime.

Niche parties can form but are unlikely to endure in fully competitive democracies with free *and fair* electoral competition. Third parties in the United States rise and fall periodically as they fail to gain electoral traction and lose the support of donors and activists (Rosenstone et al. 1984). Niche-like parties in Western Europe frequently challenge specific policies and then either melt away after these fights are settled (Hug 2001; Meguid 2008) or expand into broad-based "normal" parties like the Greens (Kitschelt 1989). Movement parties such as ethnic parties in

---

[3] Short episodes of competitive authoritarianism, such as in Nicaragua 1985–1990 and Peru 1995–2000, are usually too brief to spawn niche challengers.

[4] Some regimes create "satellite" parties that are brand-differentiating devices for the incumbent party or nominally independent but co-opted by the regime. These parties are not independent of the regime and do not qualify as niche parties.

Latin America (Van Cott 2005) are too fragile to count as niche parties and either return to their movement origins over time or expand into "ethnopopulist" parties with broader appeal and autonomous organizations (Madrid 2008).

Niche parties differ from existing party types. Aldrich (1995) and Kitschelt (2000) usefully categorize parties by their solutions to three central problems: the social choice problem of getting members to agree on a package of public policy issues the party seeks to institute, the internal collective action problem of inducing prospective activists and politicians to work for the party, and the external collective action problem of getting citizens to support the party at the polls.

Existing party types can generate separate solutions to these three problems, and this separation affords them important flexibility. Where parties can offer prospective activists side payments or the possibility of meaningful nominations for public office that they might actually win, the parties can reserve the use of their platforms to make strategic appeals to voters. For instance, catchall parties (Kircheimer 1966) and electoral-professional parties (Panebianco 1988) offer activists a reasonable probability of obtaining office, or the spoils derived from public office, and these benefits help maintain coalitions of members that only loosely agree on policy. Strategically minded politicians can then craft the party's policy offer to maximize its electoral appeal. Similarly, clientelist parties (Kitschelt 2000) recruit members with selective benefits but do not coordinate members' social choice preferences. Although these parties may win many of their votes through vote buying, their candidates are also free to craft wide-ranging platforms that they think will help them win elections. In addition, separate solutions to the internal collective action and social choice problems also allow politicians competing in different constituencies to tailor their messages to voters' particular tastes.

Niche parties cannot resolve the internal or external collective action problems through traditional means. They can offer only a handful of activists access to meaningful nominations because their chance of winning all but a few down-ballot offices is extremely slim. They also cannot offer side payments because incumbents typically monopolize access to state resources, and potential donors in society are usually unwilling to support challenger parties for fear of retribution by an incumbent that controls access to government contracts and licenses, the enforcement of the tax code, and the repressive apparatus of the state (Greene 2007; Levitsky and Way 2010). Niche parties' resource poverty also means that they cannot advertise in the mass media or hire armies of canvassers, and thus cannot solve the external collective action problem for more than a narrow slice of the electorate.

Niche parties are thus forced to use their ideologies (i.e., their solution to the social choice problem) to address their internal and external collective action problems. For losing parties under threat of extinction, overcoming the internal collective action problem means that the ideological benefits of working for the opposition must be powerful. Ideologies become more powerful when they are well defined and clearly differentiated from the existing partisan options. Challengers to systematically advantaged incumbents thus face an interesting trade-off. As they construe their ideologies more narrowly, they are better able to recruit activists (i.e., solve the social choice problem for a portion of the potential activists in the population); however, narrowness not only forces them to recruit fewer activists but also diminishes the strategic flexibility that candidates have when appealing to voters. The very ideology that creates the party's internal life also constrains its appeals to a small slice of the electorate.

Niche party's ideologies are thus endogenous to the environment in which they compete. As the probability of winning falls (because the incumbent claims greater advantages) and the costs of joining the opposition rise (because the incumbent engages in more brutal and widespread repression), niche parties' ideologies narrow and they become smaller organizations populated by more anti-status quo activists who appeal to thinner slices of the electorate. Thus, niche parties should be somewhat "less" niche-oriented in dominant party democratic regimes where incumbents benefit from dramatic advantages but do not repress challengers, and somewhat "more" niche-oriented in competitive authoritarian and electoral authoritarian regimes where the costs of opposition are substantially higher. Niche parties can also arise in other regimes where incumbents benefit from dramatic advantages and challengers must "claw" their way into the system from the outside, such as in Brazil, where the PT organized as a niche party during the protracted transition to fully competitive democracy.

NICHE PARTY ORGANIZATION AND ADAPTATION

Niche party organizations are designed to protect and reinforce their party's identity and design mechanisms to distribute their meager fungible resources. As a result, niche parties are built as closed and hierarchical organizations that resist innovation, recruit from specific feeder groups, promote leaders who best embody the party's identity and past rather than its long-term future goals, and nominate candidates who represent limited core constituencies in the electorate rather than a broad base of popular support. These parties are built less for winning elections today than they are for surviving to compete another day.

Niche parties create high barriers to new activist recruitment that isolate them from society's mainstream but serve five purposes. First, they ensure that activists are "good types" who reflect and perpetuate the party's identity. Recruiting from known feeder organizations gives a shortcut for identifying prospects and diminishing the time–cost of training. Second, activists who join despite high barriers are likely more committed to the party's cause than those who would enter easily. More committed activists work harder and ask for fewer tangible benefits. Third, activists who are ideologically "pure" are more likely to remain in the party over the longer term. Challengers to autocratic incumbents must constantly worry that the costs of activism will encourage their members to abstain or that the appeal of greater benefits will cause exit to the incumbent party. Fourth, activists who must struggle in order to join are likely to be higher quality. They affiliate with the opposition not because they want a career in politics per se but because they are driven to oppose the incumbent through force of conscience and ideology. They are likely to be thoughtful and energetic citizens with significant time that they can devote to the party's cause. Finally, high barriers ensure that the activist corps will remain relatively small, thus giving the party fewer mouths to feed with its nearly empty coffers.

Niche parties are also miserly with promotions. Talented youngsters rarely skyrocket up the ranks to become party leaders due to their organizational skills or receive nominations for public office due to their wide appeal with voters. Rather, leaders and candidates tend to have long histories of activism and have thus endured the deepest sacrifice. They have paid high opportunity costs and may have lived under the threat of real or potential repression by the state. Only after having paid their dues can they ascend. One might expect that impoverished parties that cannot offer meaningful nominations would instead offer titles – everyone gets to be a vice president! But promoting the most committed imbues leadership with meaning that it otherwise would not have. Niche party leaders do not command many fungible resources and their candidates have only the slimmest chance of winning. Such positions are meaningful not because they translate into power outside the party but because they yield moral authority over the activist corps. It is a badge of honor to rise in a niche party, one that signifies a life well lived, fighting the good fight for longer and with more sacrifice than others. Promoting the most committed also further guards the party's identity.

Finally, niche parties are hierarchical and bureaucratic organizations. A bureaucratized hierarchy enforces the status differences between leaders and activists, insulates the party's identity and resources from recent recruits, and creates an organizational training ground for those who one day hope to take control of the state. Niche party members do not seek to conquer the state like revolutionary organizations or dissolve it and institute anarchical politics; rather, they seek to run the state (typically as a democracy). Preparation for running the state can be aided by running a bureaucratic organization.

High barriers to affiliation and advancement as well as a bureaucratic and hierarchical organizational structure help protect the one resource that besieged niche parties can use to attract members and voters: their identities. Niche parties do not create hermetic and inward-looking organizations that are obsessed with the purity of their identities and the morality of their goals because they believe these will propel them to victory. Rather, they do so because it is the only party-building path open to severely disadvantaged challengers. Without adopting a self-protective posture, no party could materialize to challenge incumbents in systems with tremendously biased competition. At the same time, this necessary organizational form forces opposition parties to rely on small activists corps, narrowly defined core constituencies, and ideologies that are far out of the mainstream, helping them lose at the polls.

Niche party organizations are designed to protect and reproduce their identities, making them remarkably insulated from external influences. Even when changes in the competitive environment could yield advantages for broadening appeals, high barriers to recruitment and advancement end up recruiting like-minded activists and socializing them in the parties' traditions and practices.

Yet not all niche parties are shackled by their past. Some, such as Brazil's PT, manage to adapt as democratization enhances the benefits of moderation and organizational openness. Whether they do so depends not only on the strength of external influences (spatial, institutional, ideological), but also on the balance of power between party leaders and candidates for high-level office. Unlike leaders in competitive parties that tend to mirror the preferences of voters under specifiable conditions (Downs 1957; May 1973), leaders in niche parties tend to be the most committed to reproducing the party's appeals and thus resist transforming into catchall-style competitors, even when the structure of competition encourages them to do so. In contrast, *high-level* candidates who run in large single-member districts, such as presidential and gubernatorial candidates, typically prefer broader appeals because it is their only potential path to victory. Much depends then on party leaders' control over these high-level candidates. Rules and practices that give national party leaders jurisdiction over resources and nominations, including centralized party finance systems, prohibitions on reelection, and the preponderance of closed-list seats in legislative elections, make party leaders into central figures and mean that adaptation can only occur through them (Levitsky 2003). Where leaders are less powerful, either high-level candidates (Samuels 2004) or moderate activists (Kitschelt 1994) can force adaptation.

To this point, I have made four main arguments about niche parties. First, they should emerge as partisan vehicles for political outsiders in conditions of highly unequal multiparty competition that occurs in many (but not all) competitive and electoral authoritarian regimes and in some dominant party democratic regimes. Second, their organizations differ from existing party types, especially in how they recruit activists and promote leaders. Niche parties seek to recruit known "good types" who share the party's identity and they have limited resources for identifying such prospective activists. As a result, they tend to recruit from a small number of feeder organizations in society. In addition, because promotion comes from a long history of activism and closely reflecting the party's identity of difference, leaders and lower-level candidates should hold more anti–status quo policy preferences than activists. Third, where niche parties take root during long periods of undercompetitive politics, their self-protective organizations can help them persist even if the regime transitions to a fully competitive multiparty democracy and conditions encourage them to become more like catchall competitors. Finally, niche parties can (and some do) transform into catchall parties where external incentives for change are strong and national level leaders are subordinated to presidential candidates or grassroots activists who favor broadening appeals.

NICHE PARTIES IN MEXICO UNDER PRI DOMINANCE BEFORE 2000

Niche parties have existed in a variety of competitive systems that bias elections in favor of the incumbent party; however, thoroughly describing them requires a wealth of primary data that I have collected only for Mexico. In this section, I show that the rightist PAN and leftist PRD can be characterized as niche parties during the period of PRI dominance before 2000. In the following section, I examine the persistence of niche-oriented characteristics after the transition to fully competitive democracy in 2000. Because the two sections focus on similar elements of party organization, some data presented in this section help sustain the argument in the next.

From 1929 until 2000, Mexico is best described as a dominant party authoritarian regime (Greene 2007), a subset of competitive authoritarian regimes (Levitsky and Way 2002, 2010) and electoral authoritarian regimes (Schedler 2002). The PRI won every presidential election and held a supermajority in congress until 1988. It was not until 1997 that it lost its simple majority in the lower house, and 2000 that it ceded the presidency to Vicente Fox of the PAN. During this long period of single-party dominance, the electoral arena was open and even satisfied some criteria for minimally free elections (Schumpeter 1947). Opposition forces were permitted to form parties and compete in elections. Despite periods when multiple opposition parties emerged, forces on the right mostly coalesced around the PAN, founded in 1939 as an alliance of social and fiscal conservatives (Loaeza 1999). On the left, the PRD was founded in 1989 by bringing together a handful of high-level leftist defectors from the PRI and generations of activists who had participated in small socialist, communist, and independent parties, as well as intellectual clubs and social movements (Bruhn 1997). Surveys conducted in 1999 show that nearly half of the party's leaders and activists were previously affiliated with parties and movements of the independent left and not the PRI (Greene 2007: 153).

Despite the minimally free electoral arena, competition was maximally unfair (Greene 2007; Schedler 2002). Challenger parties had a very low probability of winning elections and their activists paid high opportunity costs as well as high repressive costs for their participation. The small and uncertain benefits of activism coupled with the high and certain costs of joining an opposition party meant that challengers were constantly under threat. As a result, they created niche party organizations focused on survival.

These parties tended to reproduce themselves over time through an iterative recruitment process. Once formed by members who largely favored niche party-building strategies, subsequent generations of recruits were selected in part because they reflected the values of the niche organization. That these parties continue to build as niche organizations, even after democratization, implies that such new members put their preferences into practice; however, quite a lot may intervene between preferences and actions, and this chapter does little to fill that space.

Recruitment and Advancement Practices

Niche parties impose high barriers to activist recruitment that create closed organizations as one way of protecting their identities. Relying on allied feeder organizations in society to supply known "good types" ensures that activists share the party's ideals, makes them cheaper to mold in the party's image, and helps generate a higher quality and committed activist corps.

Both the PAN and the PRD created procedures designed to recruit "good types" from known core constituencies who were ideologically pure, even though they did so in different ways. From its beginnings in 1939, the PAN considered itself as a party of "excellent minorities" (Loaeza 1999) where membership was restricted to ideologically compatible and committed activists. Founding party president Manuel Gómez Morín viewed the PRI's sectoral organizations among labor, peasants, and urban middle sectors as inimical to democracy and the free expression of individual preferences. As a result, the PAN eschewed relations with major social organizations and relied exclusively on individual affiliation. This decision limited the PAN to a minority base because the PRI's sectors included the major social groups of the early and mid-twentieth century.

Ensuring that the PAN's minority base was "high quality" required strict control over affiliation. Until 1996, prospective members had to be sponsored by an existing activist in good standing and then get approval from both the local party as well as the National Members' Registry that was controlled by the twenty- to thirty-member National Executive Committee. The committee also determined whether a recruit met the standard of having "an honest way of life,"[5] and it sometimes delayed affiliation decisions for up to a year (Mizrahi 2003). Activists were also required to pass an exam on the party's history and basic principles that typically required a preparation course. The exam helped train new recruits but it also ensured that members were ideologically like-minded, committed to the cause, and literate. According to Mizrahi, these safeguards "demonstrate the party's reluctance to include a heterogeneous and ideologically diverse population in its ranks" (2003: 56).

[5] PAN statutes, Article 8.

The PAN's high barriers to affiliation became a point of pride. One story told to me by the party president and others during separate interviews involved a high-level PRI member who wanted to run as a PAN candidate. But because the would-be PANista had not gone through the standard approval process, he was not allowed to join the party or run under its label, even though party leaders thought he could win. Eventually, he met the requirements by going through the standard process, ascended to a position in the National Political Council and, according to one party leader, "became one of the foremost authorities on the party's doctrine."[6] This story typifies how many PAN leaders think about the relationship between the party and potential activists: the party molds them more than they mold the party.

The concern over ideological dilution ran so deep that members were willing to sacrifice electoral victories for purity. When asked whether they would prefer to move their party to the center at the risk of mimicking their competitors or differentiate the PAN ideologically at the risk of losing elections, over 60 percent chose the latter.[7] This emphasis on party identity seems almost fantastical from the perspective of theory that expects parties to act as rational vote maximizers.

By the mid-1990s, the PAN's membership stood at about 50,000 in a country with some 37 million voters. Its member-to-voter ratio of 0.13 percent was dwarfed by the PRI's score of 18.7 percent.[8] Nevertheless, the party was unwilling to give up on its high barriers to affiliation for fear of diluting its identity. A compromise was put in place that created a two-tier membership structure, beginning in 1996. Activists with the ability to participate in party forums and vote on issues open to membership input would continue to go through the same burdensome affiliation procedure. A new group called "adherents" could sign up easily, but would be limited to auditing party proceedings. The path from adherent to activist would still run through the same procedures as newly affiliating activists.

The parties of the independent left and the PRD approached the question of affiliation differently, but they ended up with strikingly similar results. Unlike the PAN, these parties did not impose formal barriers to affiliation but they did use strict informal barriers. Parties of the independent left were based on dissident labor organizations, peasant groups, and radical intellectual clubs (see Bruhn 1997; Greene 2007). In contrast

[6] Author interviews, 1999.
[7] Mexico Party Personnel Surveys, 1998–1999.
[8] Internal documents, PRI National Executive Committee.

to the PAN, individual affiliation in the left was almost unknown and advancement without the support of an organized social group was practically impossible.

The group basis of intraparty politics on the left migrated into the PRD when it formed in 1989. Formally, the PRD had an open affiliation procedure designed to incorporate broad segments of civil society. Party leaders hoped that low formal barriers would help expand on Cuauhtémoc Cárdenas's huge appeal in his 1988 presidential campaign and that they would be able to ride this wave of opposition sentiment to the presidency in the following election. Yet despite formal openness, recruitment was de facto regulated by factions comprised of partisan groups, social movements, and nongovernmental organizations (Sánchez 1999: 100).

Based on in-depth interviews, I counted twenty-two important intraparty factions, known as *corrientes*, between the party's founding in 1989 and 2000. Sánchez (1999: 79–87) reports more than 30. These factions tended to be fluid but ever present, and they were so central to intraparty life that internal documents routinely measured the preelectoral force of candidates for party offices through the identity of local social and partisan organizations that supported each faction rather than through head counts, polls, or prior internal election results.

Membership in base-level social and partisan groups and in the broader factions that coordinated them at the state and national levels served as the analytical equivalent of formal barriers to entry in the PAN. Factions operated as filters to ensure that only recruits who were known to share the party's ideological line played a role in local leadership and party conventions. According to Agustín Guerrero Castillo, then President of the PRD in the Federal District, "The *corrientes* are responsible for most of the growth of the party. Without their structure, there are no activists, because every activist belongs to a *corriente*" (quoted in Sánchez 1999: 100).

The factional structure of the PRD and its role in regulating activist recruitment and advancement has not disappeared with Mexico's transition to democracy. When asked if they belonged to a faction, 65 percent of the delegates to the party's 2004 National Congress said they were affiliated with one of forty-two distinct groupings inside the party.[9]

Creating high barriers to recruitment implies that niche parties should put a premium on identifying "good types" who are like-minded. If they

---

[9] Survey of delegates to the PRD's 2004 National Congress conducted by Olivares Plata Research.

have already proven that they share the party's identity and can be trusted as loyal and long-lasting members, then they will be cheaper to recruit. As a result, niche parties should rely on a small set of feeder organizations in society to supply activists, if such organizations are available.

Reliance on Feeder Organizations

The PAN's focus on "excellent minorities" and the PRD's use of gate-keeper factions rooted in local sociopolitical groups limited recruitment to core constituencies. That was precisely the idea: challenger party organizations were initially designed to generate tightly knit activist corps that would help the parties survive when they had little chance of winning and when the costs of participation were high.

The political biographies of individual party elites show that both the PAN and PRD relied heavily on nonparty feeder groups associated with their core constituencies to provide new activists at least until the 1990s, after which time relevant data are scarce. PAN elites who joined in the 1960s belonged to an average of more than five feeder organizations, including professional membership societies, Catholic lay organizations, and family values groups (see also Mabry 1973). But by 1999, recent recruits belonged to an average of just 1.5 feeder organizations.[10] Thus, although the PAN was significantly reliant on core constituencies to provide new activists for decades, it had broadened its recruitment sources by the late 1990s.

A similar pattern of recruitment occurred in the PRD. Elites that joined organizations of the independent left in the 1960s were members of more than four nonparty feeder organizations, primarily in working-class groups and neighborhood organizations. There is a slight increase in the 1970s, probably because the PRI's use of repression in that era forced many leftists underground (Greene 2007). But by 1999, new recruits held an average of just three nonparty organization memberships.[11] The PRD remained somewhat more reliant on specific feeder groups than the PAN, but the direction of change was the same.

In both parties, shifts in the social and political environment did result in less reliance on core constituencies over time; however, those processes were gradual and, as described below, did not significantly affect the composition of leadership in either party.

[10] Mexico Party Personnel Surveys, 1998–1999.
[11] Mexico Party Personnel Surveys, 1998–1999.

Moving Up: Differences among Activists, Leaders, and Candidates

Niche parties promote from within and select from among the longest serving (and longest suffering) activists to become leaders. Indeed, the national leaders in the PAN who were interviewed in 1998 joined the party, on average, in 1979, whereas activists who served as delegates to the party's National Convention in 1999 joined an average of a decade later.[12] In the PRD, national leaders interviewed in 1999 joined a leftist party or movement in the mid-1980s that was eventually absorbed into the PRD, whereas activists did not affiliate, on average, until the early 1990s.[13]

Niche parties also promote those that most closely reflect the parties' programmatic identity of difference from the incumbent and this creates a surprising distinction in policy preferences between leaders and activists. Standard theory predicts that candidates and party leaders should mirror the preferences of the largest mass of voters in order to maximize their chances of winning office, whereas activists, who are assumed to participate in politics for ideological reasons, should have preferences that deviate from the mainstream (May 1973). In Mexico, this would imply centrist leaders and candidates and polarized activists. (For a detailed discussion of why centrism is a plausible best response programmatic strategy for the peripheral parties [i.e., PAN and PRD], see Greene [2007, 2008].)[14] Yet my argument about niche party development largely implies the opposite: activists in the PAN and PRD should hold policy preferences that deviate somewhat from the status quo on the right and left, respectively, whereas leaders should deviate more. Candidates should be of two types: against the predictions of standard theory, lower-level candidates should be the most extreme in their views; however, high-level candidates who compete in single-member districts and can only win through very broad appeals, including gubernatorial and presidential candidates, are likely to conform to existing theory and hold preferences that mirror those of the median voter.

---

[12] Mexico Party Personnel Surveys, 1998–1999. Statistically significant difference at the .001 level.

[13] Mexico Party Personnel Surveys, 1998–1999. Statistically significant difference at the .001 level. For a discussion of affiliation year with the PRD's predecessors, see Greene (2007).

[14] Arguments that predict cycling in three-party unidimensional competition (a scenario that describes Mexico) rely on the assumption of unrestricted party mobility in the competition space, including leapfrogging, without adverse reputational effects. Without these highly restrictive assumptions, peripheral parties should squeeze the interior party's market.

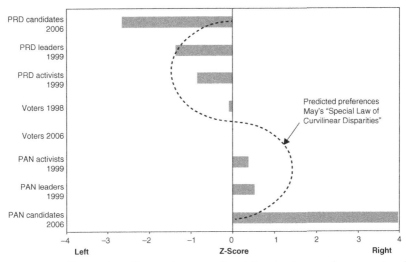

FIGURE 6.1 Economic policy preferences of activists, leaders, and congressional candidates in Mexico's PAN and PRD.

Sources: Data on activists and leaders come from the Mexico Party Personnel Surveys using questions on privatization, the extent of the social safety net, and the control of capital flows. Data on candidates come from the Mexico 2006 Candidate Surveys, using questions on privatization, the extent of the social safety net, and the extent of commercial relations with the United States. Data on voters come from the 1998 Latinobarometer survey for Mexico and the Mexico 2006 Panel Study, Wave 1. Both voter surveys use questions on privatization and the extent of the social safety net.

Figure 6.1 shows the economic policy preferences of voters as well as activists, leaders, and (lower-level) congressional candidates in the PAN and PRD who ran in single-member district elections in 2006. The underlying dimension is built from questions about the desirability of privatization, the extent of social welfare programs, and the free flow of capital across borders, thus capturing an overall preference for state- or market-led development policy. The positions are expressed as Z-scores to facilitate comparability. Voters surveyed in 1998 and again in 2006 held remarkably centrist preferences in the aggregate. Thus, May's "Law" would predict that candidates should also prefer centrism as depicted with the dotted line in the figure. In fact, we see just the opposite. Preferences for noncentrist economic policies increase with status in both parties. Activists are the most centrist and closest to the median voter (not shown). Party leaders are less centrist than activists. But the most striking finding is that congressional candidates are by far the least centrist. Not only are they distant from the median voter, they are to the extreme of their identified voters.

The large distance between lower-level candidates' and voters' policy preferences is surprising for two reasons. First, it runs counter to the intuition that candidates should want to position themselves close to the largest mass of voters to win elections. It is certainly possible that candidates expressed personal views when we interviewed them but they use their platforms in strategically rational ways when campaigning. I find this possibility somewhat far-fetched considering that interviews were conducted by professional pollsters over the phone during the heat of the campaigns and with no offer of anonymity. It would have been foolish for candidates to give us personal policy preferences that are at great variance from the content of their campaigns.

These findings could also be an artifact of aggregation that comes from candidates across multiple districts with different local median voters. (Note that it is not an artifact of Mexico's mixed-member electoral system because the data are only from candidates who must win plurality races in their districts.) However, Bruhn and Greene (2009) examined district-level candidate–voter dyads and showed that PRD and PAN candidates adopted positions that were significantly to the left and right, respectively, of voters in their constituencies.[15]

The second striking element concerns the timing of the interviews. We spoke with candidates in the run-up to the 2006 elections, a long six years after PRI dominance finally ended and free and fair elections were firmly established. The conditions that gave rise to niche parties had disappeared during Mexico's protracted transition to democracy, punctuated by the PRI's loss in 2000. One would expect candidates to take advantage of the level partisan playing field to expand their ranks, open to society, and represent broader sectors than their traditionally constrained core constituencies. In fact, broadening their appeal would seem overdetermined. By 2000, a plurality of voters identified as independent. The PAN and PRD should have acted quickly to attract these "floating" voters and cement a long-term winning coalition. They did not, remaining instead niche-oriented parties with specialized appeals that were out-of-step with the average voter's preferences.

---

[15] Candidates and officeholders in the United States are sometimes significantly off the median on important policy issues, but much of this apparent extremism actually responds to voters' preferences in their districts (Erikson 1978).

AFTER THE FALL: WHY NICHE PARTIES PERSIST
IN DEMOCRATIC MEXICO

When the PRI lost the presidency in 2000 and Vicente Fox of the PAN formally took office the following year, Mexico experienced the first nonviolent transition of power to a rival political group in its history. Elections became definitively free and fair by international standards, the PRI's *federal* patronage machine was disbanded, most of its authoritarian cronies left power, political decentralization took on real meaning, Congress became a legitimate player in national political life, press freedom and access to information expanded, and reform of state institutions proceeded apace. (Clearly, there remains much to do, but, overall, fully competitive democracy has taken root.) Yet the PAN and PRD – the very parties that spearheaded democratization – have been among the slowest institutions to reform. In fundamental ways, neither party has moved beyond its niche orientation.

What accounts for this surprising lack of adaptation? Why did these parties fail to take advantage of the level playing field to expand their ranks, open to society, and build on the generations of sacrifice by their activists? Not only does this make good common sense, it makes good sense based on social science theory. Multiple arguments about party organization based on rational choice calculations suggest that these parties should have transformed into catchall competitors (for a summary, see Greene 2007). The basic notion that parties are teams and should want to win election contests (Schlesinger 1991) points toward expansion. Arguments that highlight the role of candidates in selecting party strategies would predict expansion (May 1973; Alesina and Spear 1988). Wright's (1971) claim that party organizations adopt the "rational-efficient" form similarly predicts moving from a niche toward a catchall approach. Yet what should be easy cases for these arguments are in fact deviant ones.

Both the PAN and PRD have maintained fundamental aspects of their niche orientation because niche party organizations are designed to reproduce themselves. They do so by recruiting like-minded activists who subscribe to the party's existing identity rather than its possible future goals. They also promote those who have most deeply imbibed this identity and thus seek to recreate it. As a result, niche parties can demonstrate tremendous path dependency even when the conditions that gave rise to their hermetic organizational profiles have disappeared.

In this section, I show that the PAN and PRD have maintained niche-oriented organizations many years after democratization. In addition to the data on candidates' noncentrist policy preferences in 2006 shown in the prior section, I present information here on (1) the party-building preferences of party personnel, (2) the geographic concentration of party members and supporters in the electorate, and (3) conflicts between niche-oriented party leaders and presidential candidates who tried but largely failed to "pry open" their party organizations.

Party-Building Preferences

To characterize party-building preferences, I use survey data that taps the opinions of activists, leaders, and candidates in the PAN and PRD. Specifically, I asked respondents to rate the importance of three trade-offs in party-building strategy: appeal to new voters (catchall) or core constituencies (niche); open recruitment to maximize the number of activists (catchall) or restrict it to higher-quality recruits (niche); and adapt the platform to voters' preferences (catchall) or remain loyal to the party's traditional platform (niche). Figure 6.2 shows a simple additive index of these three items, rescaled from zero (catchall) to one (niche). The same questions were asked on all six surveys with only very minor changes in wording that would not likely affect responses.

The results are immediately striking. Not only do preferences lean in favor of niche party-building over expanding each party's reach, but the degree of preference for creating niche parties actually increases the further up the leadership ladder. Activists in both parties are the most willing to open their party organizations whereas leaders more jealously guard the traditional inward-looking organization.[16] Even more notable is that candidates who must actually win votes to achieve office were, by a wide margin, the most dedicated to building niche parties.

The interviews with candidates took place in the run-up to the 2006 general elections, indicating that niche party-building preferences persisted among the group least likely to hold them – from the perspective of standard party theory – for at least six years after the onset of fully competitive democracy. In free and fair democratic competition, one would expect candidates – especially candidates in plurality elections – to prefer armies of canvassers who can reach out to noncore constituencies rather than passionate proselytizers who can only preach to the

---

[16] Differences are statistically significant at the .05 level or better.

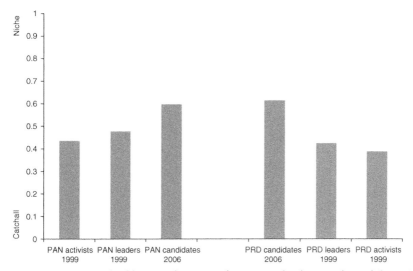

FIGURE 6.2 Party-building preferences of activists, leaders, and candidates in Mexico's PAN and PRD.
Notes: Data for activists and leaders come from the Mexico Party Personnel Surveys (see Greene 2007). Data for congressional candidates come from the Mexico 2006 Candidate Survey (see Bruhn and Greene 2009). Number of interviews: activists PAN 511, PRD 184; leaders PAN 126, PRD 151; congressional candidates PAN 40, PRD 47.

converted. Large and competitive districts with low levels of party identification and highly persuadable independents (Greene 2011) mean that there are few advantages to mobilizing the base at the cost of attracting independents.

The preference for niche party-building, especially among candidates for public office, cannot be explained as a standard rational vote-getting strategy; rather, it comes from the PAN and PRD's long-term niche-oriented approach to party-building. Having recruited committed and ideological activists from feeder organizations in society and promoted those with the longest sacrifice to their parties, they created candidates who prefer to reproduce inward-looking habits rather than respond to the incentives of the electoral marketplace.

Membership and Partisanship

These niche party-building preferences appear to be associated with concrete outcomes regarding party membership. In previous work

(Greene 2007: ch. 6), I showed that despite different recruitment practices, both the PAN and PRD tended to recruit new activists from
specific geographic areas over time until the late 1990s. Yet even if
this niche-oriented mode of expansion persisted before 2000, one
would expect the formerly opposition parties to grow rapidly after
the end of PRI dominance. After all, the PAN held the presidency
from 2000 to 2012 and the PRD was on a dramatic upward swing
in electoral support, with PRD presidential candidate Andrés Manuel
López Obrador narrowly losing in 2006 and again performing well
in 2012. Presumably, prospective politicians would join these parties,
recognizing the value of their labels, benefit-seekers in search of jobs
in the public bureaucracy would obtain membership cards, and citizens that had long identified with these parties but were dissuaded
from joining due to the potential dangers of membership would flock
to their ranks.

To be sure, membership rolls for both parties did increase substantially. The PRD claimed nearly 2.1 million members on the eve of
democratization in 1999 but boasted a whopping 6.9 million in 2006.
The PAN had just over 612,000 members in 1999 and grew to almost
1.9 million by 2012. But these numbers can be deceiving for two reasons. First, they may not represent the true size of either party. The
PRD's membership records are haphazard at best. The PAN maintains a
much more professionalized approach to recruitment and closely tracks
data on members. Yet in true niche party style, party leaders became
concerned that its rapid expansion was an illusion and needed rein-
ing in. In 2013, it forced all current members to reaffiliate in person
through a municipal party committee. The results were striking. Just
62.2 percent of activists and 12 percent of "adherents" went to the
trouble of affirming their membership. As a result, the PAN's official
membership roll dropped to 401,000, its lowest point since 1998 and
reversing a trend of growth since 1993.[17]

Second, neither party's membership has become more nationalized
since the transition to fully competitive democratic elections. I calculate the Party Nationalization Score (PNS), using the method described
by Jones and Mainwaring (2003) and employing Mexico's thirty-one

---

[17] Author's calculations using party membership data supplied by the Registro Nacional de
Miembros, Comité Ejecutivo Nacional del PAN. Data on PRD membership after 2000
was graciously provided by Professor Kathleen Bruhn.

states and the Federal District as the units of analysis.[18] A party with equal membership across geographic units would achieve a PNS of one whereas a party that is concentrated in only one unit would shrink toward zero. In 2006, the PRD reached a PNS of 0.41.[19] Not only is this score quite low in absolute terms and even lower in conceptual terms when one considers that Mexico features only three major parties, it is virtually the same as the party's PNS since 1996. During the last twenty-five years, the PAN has always maintained broader nationalization than the PRD; however, it too has failed to expand geographically since democratization. In 2013, its PNS reached 0.62, a number that is slightly lower than the party's nationalization level in 1996. Even if we were to use the 2012 numbers that party leaders thought were sufficiently fake to shed nearly 80 percent of its membership during its reaffiliation drive, the PNS would have reached just 0.65.[20] In short, neither party has expanded beyond its traditional geographic strongholds and thus both parties likely persist in attracting members with the same profile as they did before democratization.

Despite limited and geographically concentrated formal membership, the PAN and PRD could have used their well-defined identities and platforms to create partisans in the electorate. From the perspective of voters, the transition from single-party dominance to multi-party competition was a process of partisan dealignment from the PRI. Indeed, in 1983, the first year for which reliable public opinion surveys of partisanship are available, and just after the government presided over a devastating economic crisis, 59 percent of voters identified with the PRI (Domínguez and McCann 1996: 88). Just prior to the PRI's loss of the presidency in 1999, 38 percent of voters identified with the incumbent party (Moreno 2003: 32–33), and in the run-up to the 2012 elections, that number had fallen to just over 25 percent (Greene et al. 2012). Partisan dealignment and democratization went hand-in-hand. Realigning these voters would be a clear sign that the PAN and PRD had moved beyond their narrowly defined constituencies to broader society-wide appeals. But neither party succeeded in doing so. Instead, voters increasingly identified as independents: 24 percent in 1983, 31 percent in 1999, and 40 percent in 2012. By the end of the 2012 general election campaigns, the PAN had 14 percent

[18] PNS is the complement of the Gini coefficient, also known as the Gini index. Gini is a measure of statistical dispersion of a unit of value; it is the most commonly used measure of inequality but here it is used to measure geographic disperson of party membership.

[19] Data were provided by Professor Kathleen Bruhn; calculations by the author.

[20] Current (but not past) data are available at www.rnm.mx/estrados.

of identified voters (7.1 percent strongly) and the PRD had 10.7 percent (5.8 percent strongly) (Greene et al. 2012). But nearly half of these voters should be considered tantamount to independents. As I show in prior work, only strong partisans behave like the literature on partisanship expects them to by successfully resisting the partisan campaign messages of opponents (Greene 2011). Overall, the PAN and PRD have created few real partisans, largely failing to realign the electorate.

Conflicts between Presidential Candidates and Party Leaders

If both the PAN and PRD have remained geographically proscribed and are staffed by personnel who hold noncentrist policy preferences, on average, how can we make sense of the PAN's two successful presidential bids in 2000 and 2006, as well as the PRD's narrow loss in 2006 and second place finish in 2012? Presidential candidates in Mexico who must win a plurality of the votes in a single nationwide district are the most interested in pursuing vote-maximizing strategies and the tension between such candidates and their parties may be endemic in presidential systems (Samuels 2002). What is surprising in Mexico is not that such tension exists but that presidential candidates are forced to fight so viciously with party leadership to spearhead strategies of expansion. In addition, presidential candidates typically lose these battles and are forced to establish extraparty organizations to support their candidacies.

Hierarchical organizational structures entrenched niche-oriented leaders and set the stage for showdowns with presidential candidates. The clearest example comes from the PAN. In the run-up to the 2000 presidential elections, PAN leaders possessed polling data suggesting that a relative newcomer to the party, Vicente Fox, had a real chance of beating the PRI's likely candidates. Polling also showed that it would take a miracle for longtime PAN insider Diego Fernández de Cevallos to become competitive. Yet party leaders very nearly prevailed in their attempts to block Fox's nomination and scuttle what turned out to be their successful bid to end seventy-one years of single-party dominance. Fox only survived the battle that took place behind closed doors among the party's 300-member National Council because he had begun campaigning as if he were the party's nominee over a year beforehand and had created a parallel party structure called *Amigos de Fox* (Friends of Fox) that was so large, it outshined the PAN in many areas of the country. This structure also gave Fox access to much more money than previous PAN

candidates had been able to invest in election bids. It may be coinciden-
tal, but Fox's money-man spent the afternoon of the Council meeting
lobbying the small group's members in the hotel lobby just beyond the
secretive meeting's closed doors (author's observation, 1999). In the end,
Fox squeaked through but never seemed to forgive his own party for its
gatekeeper approach to the nomination that almost brought his rising
star crashing down.[21]

The story behind Andrés Manuel López Obrador's ascent shows a different path marked by similar challenges. As President of the PRD from
1996 to 1999, he was much more of an insider than was Fox in the PAN.
Yet it is a testament to the importance of overcoming intraparty inertia that López Obrador spent years working to dominate his factional
rivals and outshine the PRD's favorite son and two-time presidential
contender, Cuauhtémoc Cárdenas. Even after López Obrador had all but
decimated his potential challengers by molding the PRD in his image,
he still found it necessary to go beyond the party. Much as Fox had
done, López Obrador created a broad nonparty support organization
called MORENA (Movimiento Regeneración Nacional). Subsequently
he became so frustrated with organizational inertia that he voluntarily
exited the PRD in 2012 and transformed MORENA into its own political party in 2014, vowing to build a broader movement that will sweep
him to the presidency in 2018.

Whether a party should be thought of as niche-oriented is principally
a question of its organizational style, its recruitment and advancement
practices, and the content of its appeals, not its vote share in specific
electoral contests. Niche parties do create the conditions for losing
against broader rivals in fully free and fair elections; however, parties' electoral success should be measured against the viability of their
adversaries. In 2000 and 2006, the PRI was in a state of disrepair, it
nominated lackluster candidates, and it gave those candidates tepid
support. The high barriers to new party entry in Mexico meant that
plausible alternatives to the PAN, PRI, and PRD would not emerge
over the short term. Thus, as the PRI lost votes, the other two parties
stood to gain. That their candidates managed to gain only after cowing
party leaders and going to great lengths to create nonparty support
organizations is the real indicator of the continuing niche orientation
of the PAN and PRD.

---

[21] For an expanded discussion of Fox's nomination, see Greene (2007), Bruhn (2004), and
Shirk (2005).

NICHE PARTIES IN OTHER COUNTRIES

In other work I have described the emergence and operation of niche parties in other competitive authoritarian regimes (Taiwan, Malaysia, and Botswana) and in dominant party democratic regimes (Japan, Italy, India, and Israel) (see Greene 2007, 2011). Beyond Mexico, other countries in Latin America have not experienced long-term competitive authoritarian or dominant party regimes, with the possible exception of Paraguay, for which there is too little literature to craft an argument from secondary sources. However, Brazil offers an interesting case. From at least the 1979 electoral reform under military rule that permitted multiparty competition for the direct election of lower house representatives until the first direct election of the president in 1989/1990, Brazil shared many features with hybrid autocratic regimes. One could even push the start date back to 1974, when the military allowed two-party competition for the presidency but forced all opposition politicians to join the officially sanctioned Brazilian Democratic Movement (MDB). During this eleven- to sixteen-year period, the military and its civilian allies held substantial advantages in elections; opposition forces could compete but did so at a severe disadvantage.

In this context, leftist forces associated with Brazil's large industrial trade unions as well as leftist intellectuals launched the PT in 1980 with the objective of winning electoral power and instituting socialist policies. From its founding until the mid-1990s, the PT organized as a niche party. According to Hunter, it "pursued a radical leftist program and concentrated on building a strong organization rather than maximizing votes" (2007: 449). The PT's perennial presidential candidate, trade union leader and self-described socialist, Luiz Inácio "Lula" da Silva went so far as to proclaim that "We must not let electoral concerns take over the party's agenda" (quoted in Hunter 2007: 450). The PT was so concerned about diluting its ideological stance that it refused to make alliances with other parties, even in regions where it lacked a presence. In organizational terms, the PT prioritized ideological cohesion among its activists and discipline among its legislators. It also exacted "tight scrutiny" over prospective candidates (Hunter 2007: 462), presumably to ensure that they were ideologically "pure." Indeed, the party held such sway over individual politicians that officeholders were required to donate a portion of their salaries to the cause. In electoral terms, the PT focused on appealing to core constituencies, including unionists, Christian base communities associated with liberation theology, and members of the rural landless people's movement (Hunter 2007: 455). In short, the PT demonstrated all key aspects of the niche party type: prioritizing a noncentrist policy agenda over a vote-seeking strategy, recruiting activists and winning votes from narrowly defined core constituencies, tightly controlling nominations, and jealously guarding the party's identity against outside influences.

Starting in the mid-1990s, the PT transformed aspects of its structure into a catchall-style organization.[22] After formally giving up on the goal of socialism, it accepted the major tenets of the market and even recognized a role for the International Monetary Fund. In a counterpoint to Lula's dogged defense of the party's ideological agenda over electoral concerns in the 1980s, influential party leader and eventual party president José Genoino argued in 2002, "It's now time to win, not just to stake out our ground" (quoted in Hunter 2007: 456). The PT also entered into regional pacts with rightist and clientelist parties to help extend its reach. And whereas Lula had campaigned as a party man in the past, he now campaigned as a broader figure by emphasizing his personality, leadership traits, and moderate policy stances.

What accounts for the PT's greater adaptation compared to Mexico's former opposition parties? Whereas Lula managed to transform the PT from within, Fox and López Obrador were forced to create extraparty movements to extend their electoral appeal. Both Mexican candidates met with stiff resistance from entrenched party leaders that were able to partially thwart the attempt to pry these parties open. The difference owes to the party's organizational structures. Leaders with niche-oriented preferences in the PAN and PRD controlled recruitment and advancement practices and dominated their own candidates. The PT, by contrast, exhibited much more intraparty democracy, thus making it susceptible to change from below. As Brazil's political arena opened, new activists with more moderate preferences found it plausible to join the PT. In addition, PT candidates began to win more local-level offices and many of them adopted more moderate preferences as a practical matter for governing (Samuels 2004). Both of these forces existed in the PAN and PRD but they were too marginalized by entrenched leaders to affect the core of these parties. In the PT, by contrast, Lula's moderate faction found

---

[22] For a discussion of changes and continuities within the PT, see Samuels and Zucco (Chapter 12, this volume).

support from among new voices and, taking advantage of the party's more porous structure, this coalition successfully opened the party.

The key question then becomes, what explains the PAN and PRD's greater organizational centralization compared to the PT? One plausible argument is that the prohibition on reelection and use of closed-list proportional representation for 40 percent of seats in Mexico's lower house gives the PAN and PRD much more control over candidates than Brazil's open-list system. This is undoubtedly true; however, Taiwan's Democratic Progressive Party remains a closed, niche-oriented party despite the use of the candidate-centered single nontransferable vote system. Another explanation concerns the duration of hybrid autocracy and the timing of party formation. The PAN and the independent left that eventually formed the PRD were created generations before Mexico's democratization. This long period of outsider status forced these parties to adapt their structures for survival over the long term. The generation that formed the PT likely had much shorter time horizons because Brazil's military regime was in the process on transitioning to a competitive democracy. Although a full exploration is beyond the scope of this chapter, it is plausible that different party structures owe to distinct regime legacies. Whereas long-term competitive authoritarian rule spawns hermetic niche challenger parties that have great difficulty overcoming their past at the onset of democratization, shorter-term authoritarian "situations" (Linz 1973) and those in transition generate challengers that may demonstrate some important niche-like qualities, but without these characteristics being so deeply embedded that they cannot be overcome when the competitive environment opens.

CONCLUSION

Niche parties are unique. Unlike existing party types that were conceptualized to help scholars think about partisan dynamics in the context of fully free and fair elections, niche parties emerge to compete against entrenched and hugely advantaged incumbents in regimes that may reach minimal procedural levels for free elections but where the playing field is far from fair. As a result, niche parties organize in ways that may appear perverse from the perspective of existing theory. Instead of opening themselves broadly to attract members from multiple social groups, they prize the purity of their identity and differentiate it from that of the incumbent. They thus create closed organizations that are inward-looking and self-protective. Such organizations are the only ones that could attract members and survive in the harsh conditions in which challengers to advantaged incumbents live. Yet these organizations are also relatively unresponsive to changes in the partisan environment and can endure even after the incumbent has lost and elections become fully free and fair.

The idea that regime outsiders are driven to create well-structured partisan groups whose members are joined by ideological affinity is not new. Revolutionary organizations ranging from Leninist parties to Maoist insurgencies and guerrillas inspired by Ché's notion of *foquismo* have long used ideology as their core organizing tool. Social movements that hang together in defiance of Mancur Olson's predictions about the fragility of collective action also use ideology to appeal to their members (Chong 1991). Shefter's (1994) work on outsider political parties also implies that organizations tend to be stronger and more coherent among parties that emerge from society rather than from within government. As argued in Chapter 1 of this volume, such coherence and sense of purpose can benefit parties because they hold them together in times of adversity, create tight bonds to certain groups of voters, and their programmatic differentiation from other parties create the basis for building partisan identification.

Yet whereas niche parties are successful survivors, they are also often hampered by their origins. They challenge entrenched incumbents at the ballot box when no other organizations could form to do so, but their organizations can block further expansion when conditions change and elections become fully free and fair. Brazil's PT successfully made the shift to a more catchall form of organization in the mid-1990s, about a decade after democratization. It has remained an internally coherent party that commands more partisan identifiers than its competitors, even as it has broadened its programmatic appeal to much larger groups of voters (Hunter 2007). The PAN and PRD have not yet adapted some fifteen years after democratization and, in Mexico's case, niche parties have outlived their usefulness.

This chapter has argued that niche party organizations demonstrate path dependence. Scholars often debate which actors should behave as standard rational choice theories predict. Yet few question that political elites benefit from sufficient information and incentives to act strategically in pursuit of their interests. From the perspective of standard rationalist assumptions, niche parties behave in irrational ways. One can clearly reconstruct politicians' utility functions in ways that bring niche parties into line with rationalist expectations for periods when they are severely disadvantaged (Greene 2007). However, if parties remain

niche-oriented when partisan competition becomes fully free and fair and
standard predictions point toward openness, expansion, and strategic
position-taking toward the mass of centrist voters, then scholars need to
think more rigorously about path dependence in parties' organizational
development. This chapter has taken one step; providing a more general
theory to account for variation in adaptation across cases remains to be
done in future work.

Because niche parties can persist long past their usefulness, they can
create unexpected pathologies in new democracies exiting from competitive authoritarian or dominant party democratic rule. In the case of
Mexico, the PAN and PRD might be thought of as the heroes and the
antiheroes of democratization. They are the heroes because without
the bravery, sacrifice, and simple stubbornness of their activists over
the course of generations, no parties would have opposed the PRI.
Without pressure at the ballot box, Mexico's democratization may not
have occurred at all. At the very least, it probably would have occurred
through regime breakdown rather than a peaceful and protracted transition through elections. In addition, the strength of these parties has
created a structure for democratic party competition and has possibly
limited the expansion of revolutionary movements. Despite its limitations, few question that Mexico's democracy is well down the path to
consolidation.

The PAN and PRD are also the antiheroes of democratization
because their continued niche orientations have played a role in representational failure, partisan gridlock, and the return of the PRI in the
2012 presidential elections. There are, of course, numerous plausible
explanations for the PRI's return, ranging from economic difficulties to
mass casualties in the war on drugs and the campaign blunders of at
least one of the leading contenders. Yet, in addition, the niche orientation of the PAN and PRD should be taken into account. Both parties'
presidential candidates started from a very small base of support in the
electorate and ceded policy space to the centrist PRI candidate. This
was not a unique election, but the crowning failure in a pattern that
previously helped PRI candidates win in a plurality of state elections
after national-level democratization. Thus, niche parties not only help
defeat dominant incumbents, they also help them come back.

7

Patronage, Subnational Linkages, and Party-Building

The Cases of Colombia and Peru

Paula Muñoz and Eduardo Dargent

A critical component of party-building is the establishment of durable linkages between national and subnational organizations. If parties
cannot recruit and retain local politicians, territorial organizations will
be difficult to sustain. Although parties are often assumed to be bound
together by programmatic linkages, in much of Latin America the primary glue linking national and subnational politicians has been the flow
of patronage resources. In the absence of such flows, the linkages between
national parties and subnational politicians may erode, with negative
consequences for party-building.

This chapter argues that political reforms that limit parties' control over the distribution of subnational patronage resources may pose
a threat to party-building. Such reforms are often aimed at fostering
programmatic competition, enhancing democratic representation, and
improving democratic governance. However, by eroding subnational
party linkages, they may have the unintended effect of both weakening
existing party organizations and inhibiting the construction of new ones.
These political reforms affecting the control of patronage resources are
especially harmful to party aggregation in countries with weak programmatic cleavages.

The chapter examines two cases, Colombia and Peru, in which political elites undertook major reforms aimed at improving democratic representation and governance in a context of political crisis. The chapter
argues that by failing to take into account the role of patronage resource
distribution in linking national and subnational organizations, reformers in both countries undermined party-building efforts. In Colombia,
the reforms weakened intermediate-level politicians who had previously

served as "gatekeepers," linking national and local party factions. In Peru, democratizing reforms dispersed resources away from national parties, weakening an already inchoate party system and further reducing incentives for party-building. Colombia and Peru are good cases to observe the effects of subnational patronage resources on party-building because currently other types of political capital, such as ideology, or preexisting organization, have strongly diminished.[1] As the chapter shows, postreform party-building efforts in both countries were largely unsuccessful.

The chapter is organized as follows. The first section argues that robust linkages to subnational organizations are critical to building and sustaining national parties, and it explores the role of patronage resources in sustaining those linkages. In this section we also explain how political reforms can be harmful to these patronage linkages, especially in the absence of other linkages keeping parties together. The chapter then examines political reform processes in Colombia and Peru, showing how reforms that limited national party brokers' access to patronage resources unintentionally weakened party aggregation and hindered efforts to build new parties. It then examines several cases of party formation in Colombia and Peru to highlight the difficulties of party-building once subnational linkages are severed. First, it examines Colombia's Green Party (PV) and Peru's Nationalist Party (PNP), two parties with attractive brands but little control over subnational patronage resources that failed to translate short-term electoral success into long-term party-building. Second, it examines Chim Pum Callao (CPC) and the Alliance for Progress (APP) in Peru and the National Integration Party (PIN) in Colombia, three parties in which local politicians used subnational patronage resources to build local party organizations but were unable to scale up to create viable national parties. We conclude by specifying the scope conditions of our argument and discussing some additional implications of our findings.

PATRONAGE, SUBNATIONAL LINKAGES, AND PARTY-BUILDING

Party aggregation is critical for building strong national parties with territorial roots. By party aggregation, we refer to the process of coordination

---

[1] Both Colombia and Peru experienced insurgencies in the 1980s, but neither the Revolutionary Armed Forces of Colombia (FARC) nor the Shining Path in Peru enjoyed enough support to provide the bases for party-building. Beyond these insurgencies, programmatic polarization was relatively low in both countries.

among national, regional, and local politicians in a single national party-building effort.[2] Strong parties must attract competitive candidates for local and national positions and maintain their loyalty over time.

Classic theories of party development emphasize the role of factors such as social cleavages, institutions, and ideology.[3] Such accounts often treat the programmatic dimension (e.g., brands, ideology) as central to linking parties to both voters and politicians. In practice, however, patronage and the distribution of other selective benefits – what Hale (2006) calls "administrative capital" – often play a major role in sustaining party organizations. The distribution of patronage resources, such as the partisan allocation of public jobs, can be a critical source of party cohesion, particularly where programmatic linkages are weak.[4] In Latin America, public employment has long been an important means of compensating local cadres and activists for party work (Grindle 2012). Indeed, many of the most durable parties in Latin American history, including the PRI in Mexico, the Liberals and Conservatives in Colombia, the Blancos and Colorados in Uruguay, and the Liberals and Nationals in Honduras, have been predominantly patronage-based (see Domínguez, Chapter 17, this volume). Control of public sector jobs, pork barrel projects, campaign funds, and other public resources allow parties to attract – and retain the loyalty of – local candidates and activists through the distribution of selective benefits. To the extent that party leaders control the vertical flow of such resources, they can maintain subnational linkages by structuring the careers of local politicians.

Given the centrality of patronage resources in maintaining parties' subnational linkages, political reforms that disrupt the flow of such resources can pose a major challenge to existing party organizations and also impede efforts to construct new parties.[5] While the decline of patronage is often viewed as contributing to the emergence of more programmatic politics (Hagopian, Gervasoni, and Moraes 2009), it may in fact contribute to party breakdown. Political reforms that undermine party leaders' gatekeeping capacity as the distributors of selective incentives, or that provide local politicians with independent access to resources,

---

[2] Hicken (2009: 8) defines party aggregation as "the extent to which electoral competitors from different districts come together under a common party banner."

[3] See Duverger (1954), Lipset and Rokkan (1967), and Aldrich (1995).

[4] Recent work that highlights the role of patronage resources in holding parties together includes Hale (2006), Harbers (2009), Greene (2007), Morgan (2011), and Dargent and Muñoz (2011).

[5] The following account draws heavily on Dargent and Muñoz (2011).

may unintentionally sever subnational party linkages, thereby weakening national parties and making future party-building more difficult.

Two types of political reform appear especially likely to undermine party aggregation. One is decentralization. By allowing local politicians to attain office through direct election rather than being centrally appointed, decentralization reduces their dependence on national party leaders. It also creates demand for local-level campaign funds that national parties often cannot meet (Morgan 2011). The consequent use of self-financed campaigns in turn reduces local politicians' dependence on national parties. When mayoral or regional offices are won by self-financed local politicians who then assume control over those offices' patronage resources, national parties' control may be seriously threatened. This is particularly true when local elections are not held concurrently with national ones, as local politicians will have no incentive to seek national coattails or coordinate with national party leaders.

Second, political reforms that undermine the gatekeeping power of intermediate party leaders can also weaken subnational linkages. Intermediate party leaders are crucial for binding together national organizations because they are the link between the national leadership and local committees. Reforms that effectively cut such leaders out of the resource distribution process may thus sever parties' subnational linkages. An example is the elimination of legislators' prerogative to approve budgets for public projects in their districts.

Once the resource flows that previously bound national and subnational organizations are altered or discontinued, future party-building becomes more difficult. As noted in Chapter 1, territorial penetration is critical to party-building. In Latin America, most territorial organizations are patchwork quilts of local organizations that are held together by patronage resources. Stitching together such organizations requires resources.[6] And to ensure coordination among subnational politicians, such that they aggregate into a single party, national party leaders must control resource allocation *at the subnational level*. Where they do not, building successful new parties is likely to be difficult, especially where programmatic competition is weak, as in Colombia and Peru.

It is important not to overstate the importance of patronage resources for party-building. As Chapter 1 argues, intense polarization – ideological

---

[6] Possible alternatives to patronage include legal public finance (Bruhn, Chapter 8, this volume) and private finance (Barndt, Chapter 13, this volume). Many new parties in Latin America, however, lack sufficient access to either of these sources.

or otherwise – may create alternative (and more effective) bases for successful party-building.[7] As we discuss in the conclusion, the negative effects of a reduction in patronage resources or decentralization for party-building seems conditional on the absence of these programmatic cleavages. When these cleavages are present, decentralization may even help parties to build across territory. Thus, in Brazil, the decline of patronage resources – in a context of increased programmatic competition – appears to have contributed to the emergence of robust programmatic parties (Hagopian, Gervasoni, and Moraes 2009), and in Bolivia, intense polarization facilitated party aggregation despite decentralization (Vergara 2011). Something similar occurred in the case of the FMLN in El Salvador. In the context of intense ideological polarization, the FMLN took advantage of decentralization in order to strengthen its territorial organization without diluting its radical brand at the national level (Holland, Chapter 10, this volume). Polarization also spurred investments in subnational politics in the case of Chile's UDI, a conservative party whose core constituency was the country's economic and conservative elites. Access to patronage resources (in this case, provided by private donors) allowed the UDI to segment its party–voter linkage, appealing to poorer voters through clientelism while linking to its elite core constituency with a programmatic appeal (Luna, Chapter 4, this volume).

In the absence of polarization, however, access to state resources may be the best available means for linking national parties and subnational politicians. In the sections that follow, we show how political reforms aimed at enhancing democratic representation and participation in Colombia and Peru undermined existing parties and inhibited the construction of new territorial organizations by reducing party leaders' control over subnational resources.

THE UNINTENDED CONSEQUENCES OF DEMOCRATIC REFORMS

In the 1990s and 2000s, Colombia and Peru, respectively, carried out far-reaching reforms with the aim of improving the quality of their democracies. At the time these reforms were carried out, the two countries differed greatly in their levels of party system institutionalization. Colombian parties were among the oldest in Latin America (Hartlyn 1988; Gutiérrez

---

[7] See also see Hagopian, Gervasoni, and Moraes (2009), Vergara (2011), and Roberts (Chapter 2, this volume).

2007). The country's two-party system of Liberals and Conservatives was viewed as one of Latin America's most institutionalized, although scholars noted that national party elites exercised only weak control over local politicians (Mainwaring and Scully 1995). In contrast, Peru experienced a dramatic and unprecedented party system collapse in the 1990s (Tanaka 1998; Lynch 1999; Seawright 2012). Even before the collapse, the Peruvian party system was weakly institutionalized (Mainwaring and Scully 1995), although it was ideologically structured and highly competitive (Cameron 1994). Despite these differences, both countries experienced acute political crises that prompted elites to implement reforms.

In Colombia, reformist elites had long been concerned about the erosion of political legitimacy caused by rampant clientelism.[8] The backdrop for this erosion of legitimacy was a political arrangement known as the National Front, whereby Liberals and Conservatives agreed to share power and exclude other political forces.[9] This arrangement gave the Liberal and Conservative parties a monopoly on political positions in Colombia, which in turn enabled them to use state resources to shore up their clientelistic support bases (Archer and Shugart 1997; Dávila and Delgado 2002: 320–322). The parties were strengthened by their ability to distribute patronage resources, such as jobs, public works projects, scholarships, and handouts. This arrangement reinforced the position of intermediate actors within the parties. Control over patronage resources allowed regional barons to gain power and gradually contest the authority of national party leaders (Dávila and Delgado 2002: 320–326). These mid-level regional actors played a crucial role in party aggregation by structuring political careers within regions and linking local and national politics. Although presidents had the formal power to unilaterally appoint governors and mayors, they generally consulted with regional-level party factions in making these appointments (Pizarro 2002: 371).

Yet the National Front also created serious problems for Colombia's traditional parties. During this time, programmatic differences between the Liberals and Conservatives faded, and corruption became rampant. Eventually, the high levels of corruption associated with this system led to intraparty disputes between clientelistic leaders and more

[8] The following account draws on Dargent and Muñoz (2011).
[9] The National Front was introduced in Colombia in 1958, following a decade of violence between Liberals and Conservatives. Key components of the arrangement were alternation of the presidency between the two parties every four years and strict parity in Congress, the cabinet, and other governmental posts. Formally, the arrangement lasted until 1974, though aspects of it continued until 1986. See Hartlyn (1988).

programmatically oriented ones (Gutiérrez 2007: 148–165), as well as to high levels of popular dissatisfaction. A mounting sense of illegitimacy finally led to the adoption of decentralizing reforms (Eaton 2006; Falleti 2010) and the elimination of the partisan ballot in the late 1980s (Pizarro 2002: 374–375; Gutiérrez 2007: 256). Several scandals, including the discovery of links between politicians and drug lords and the assassination of three presidential candidates during the 1990 election campaign, brought the system to a crisis point. In December 1990, in an attempt to defuse this crisis, elections were held for a constituent assembly (Archer and Shugart 1997; Segura and Bejarano 2004). Liberal candidates won a plurality of seats (twenty-five of seventy), while Conservative factions won twenty seats, and the AD M-19, a new party rooted in a recently demobilized leftist guerrilla group, won nineteen seats.[10] Many of those elected were programmatically oriented politicians opposed to the traditional patronage-based system. The result was that reformists dominated the constituent assembly and were thus able to design the new rules of the game (Botero 2006; Rodríguez 2006; Gutiérrez 2007: 255–260).[11]

Reformers in the constituent assembly shared a diagnosis of the main problem of Colombian politics: weak programmatic linkages due to corruption in the traditional political parties. In their view, clientelistic politicians not only damaged democracy through corruption and policy immobility, but also impeded the emergence of programmatic parties. Thus, in an attempt to improve the quality of Colombian democracy, these reformists carried out several far-reaching measures aimed at putting an end to such practices. In the absence of pervasive clientelism, they believed, programmatic linkages would grow organically. In designing these reforms, however, they seem to have simply taken party aggregation for granted. In their attempt to reduce the pernicious effects of clientelism and corruption, they paid little heed to the crucial role of subnational patronage for maintaining strong national parties. The 1991 Constitution included two major types of reform:

[10] On the rise and fall of the AD M-19, see Holland (Chapter 10, this volume).

[11] Two additional factors explain why reformers dominated the constituent assembly and pursued significant institutional change. First, the seventy assembly members were elected in a single national district, which favored candidates with national appeal over regional based ones (Falleti 2010: 136–137). Second, the regional barons decided to remain on the sidelines, largely due to a rule banning members of the constituent assembly from running for office through 1994 (Gutiérrez 2007: 255–260). The degree of electoral abstention reached a historic high of 74 percent, since voters were not mobilized through the clientelistic means typically used in rural areas. Consequently, urban voters, who were more prone to vote for programmatically oriented politicians, were overrepresented in the constituent assembly.

1. Fiscal and Electoral Reforms Designed to Weaken Regional Barons

The constituent assembly abolished so-called "*auxilios parlamentarios*," or budget resources allocated individually to senators and members of the lower chamber. In addition, elections at the three different levels of government (national, regional, and local) would be conducted on different dates in order to discourage coordinated mobilization of electoral machines (Pizarro 2002: 371–373). The Constitution also adopted a national district for the election of senators, thus weakening regional barons (Gutiérrez and Dávila 2000: 6). Finally, electoral reforms opened the system to new political groups and indigenous minorities.[12]

2. Decentralization Reforms Granting More Autonomy and Resources to Municipalities and Instituting Elections for Regional Governors

The constituent assembly sought to strengthen municipal rather than regional governments. Thus, the Constitution and subsequent laws gave municipalities greater responsibility in the provision of social services (Eaton 2006; Falleti 2010: 143–146). Municipalization was conceived of as a way to bring government closer to the people and improve efficiency, while also reducing clientelism (Gutiérrez 2007: 258). In designing this particular form of decentralization, assembly members also pointed to the failed experience of Colombian federalism in the nineteenth century, which they used to discard the possibility of a decentralization model based on stronger regions (Faletti 2010: 138–139).

After the constituent assembly, the traditional parties found themselves challenged by new electoral groups and independent candidates. Nevertheless, they continued to dominate national politics for some time. Electoral barons also fought to regain some of their patronage resources through special budget allocations, and they continued to target their campaigns to specific geographical areas (Crisp and Ingall 2002; Rodríguez 2002). Based on this situation, some observers concluded that Colombia's traditional parties had managed to resist the reformist challenge, successfully adapting to the new rules of the game and maintaining control over clientelistic resources (Gutiérrez and Dávila 2000).

Eventually, however, the traditional parties began to weaken. In 2002, an independent candidate, Álvaro Uribe, won the presidency. Uribe campaigned on a hardline antiguerrilla and promilitary platform. Despite

---

[12] For an analysis of these electoral reforms, see Pizarro (2002) and Botero and Rodríguez (2008).

being a former member of the Liberal Party and governor of the wealthy region of Antioquia, he portrayed himself as an enemy of traditional politics who was capable of reforming the corrupt political system. With Uribe surging in the polls, even the incumbent Conservative Party realized that its chances of winning were nil and endorsed him. Uribe won 53 percent of the vote. He was reelected in 2006 with a whopping 62 percent. Uribe's rise helped to partially upend the traditional party system and, as such, seemed to open the way for the building of new parties. In the sections below, we will examine two attempts at party-building in this altered context, and look in particular at the impact of the reforms of the 1991 Constitution in impeding such attempts.

In Peru, the most important events prior to the enactment of reforms took place during the presidency of Alberto Fujimori (1990–2000). In 1992, Fujimori carried out a "self-coup" (*autogolpe*) and subsequently installed a competitive authoritarian regime (Levitsky and Way 2010; Tanaka 2005a). This was to have serious consequences for Peruvian parties, weakening existing ones and making it more difficult for new ones to emerge. Two policies were particularly consequential. First, Fujimori concentrated resources in the executive. He dissolved elected Regional Assemblies and appointed administrative officials, while also creating a powerful Ministry of the Presidency that gave him direct control of most public resources (Planas 1998; Zas Fris 2005). Without institutional counterbalances, Fujimori invested heavily in distributive politics to bolster his popularity among low-income voters (Graham and Kane 1998; Roberts 1995; Schady 2000).

Second, Fujimori deepened municipalization in order to undermine potential opponents. In 1993, a new constitution was approved by an elected constituent assembly. The 1993 Constitution eliminated the distinction between local district municipalities and mid-level provincial governments (Muñoz 2005: 37), which had formerly provided provincial mayors with a visible platform from which to challenge Fujimori (Tanaka 2002: 13). In addition, fiscal decentralization redistributed resources away from the capital city and toward poorer rural areas (Araoz and Urrunaga 1996) and district municipalities (Muñoz 2005: 41), thereby further reducing the influence of the provincial level (Nickson 1995).[13]

---

[13] Prior to 1994, provincial municipalities were responsible for distributing transfers to their districts. District municipalities' budgets had to be approved by provincial councils. Consequently, all district mayors had to negotiate the amount of their transfers with their provinces (Nickson 1995: 244–245).

These changes in the distribution of power and resources weakened the financial incentives for joining national parties in two ways. First, with the dissolution of elected regional governments and the weakening of provincial municipalities, mid-level politicians lost the limited power and resources they had possessed. Second, lower-level authorities now received their own resources and therefore had no incentive to negotiate with upper-level political bodies. Given Fujimori's substantial resource advantage and the discrediting of the country's political parties, party leaders suddenly had little to offer local candidates. Moreover, Fujimori was not personally interested in party-building (Roberts 2006; Tanaka 2002). Consequently, between 1995 and 2000, Peru saw the rise of independent politicians (Levitsky and Cameron 2003; Lynch 1999).

In late 2000, Fujimori's competitive authoritarian regime collapsed after a video that exposed the extent of the regime's corruption was leaked to the press. During the transition to democracy that followed, politicians focused on dismantling many of the institutions associated with Fujimori's regime (Vergara 2009). The reformers who led this process, however, did not give adequate thought to the issue of party aggregation. In fact, not only did they fail to appreciate the negative implications of Fujimori's reforms for party aggregation, they actually carried out even more radical decentralizing reforms. One reason was that, for many Peruvian intellectuals, centralization and authoritarianism were intrinsically linked. Many scholars erroneously characterized Fujimori's regime as centralizing (Contreras 2004; Zas Fris 2005) or even hypercentralist (Planas 1998), failing to recognize that fiscal decentralization under Fujimori had increased municipal autonomy. Based on their misreading of this particular aspect of the Fujimori regime, decentralization became a synonym for democratization.[14]

The problem was exacerbated by the inexperience of President Alejandro Toledo, who was elected in 2001 and quickly called regional elections (Tanaka 2002; Vergara 2009: 28). The timing of this announcement mattered in two ways. First, it left little time to review and legislate the decentralization process (Zas Fris 2005: 197–198). While there was ample consensus among politicians and civil society about the need to decentralize after the transition (Vergara 2009), there was no agreement on the particular details of regionalization (Tanaka 2002). Second, decentralization preceded and subsequently shaped other reforms such as the

---

[14] See, for instance, Planas (1998).

Parties Law (Vergara 2009). Three key sets of reforms were implemented in Peru after the transition to democracy:

1. *Administrative and Institutional Reforms Aimed at Preventing Political Manipulation of the State Apparatus for Partisan Use*

Technocratic controls over budgeting decisions were strengthened and procedures to enhance transparency were created. Civil society participation in public policymaking was also encouraged through the creation of institutionalized forums and citizen participation in local and regional budgeting (Remy 2004). The aim of these reforms was to prevent politicians from using the state as a "party substitute," as President Fujimori had done.[15]

2. *Decentralizing Reforms that Further Dispersed Power and Resources, but Without Creating a Clear Hierarchy Among Levels of Government*

Instead of creating a smaller number of larger political units, the reforms superimposed elected regional governments on the existing departments, to which the national government began transferring functions and responsibilities. However, reformers did not reestablish a distinction between provincial and district municipalities (Muñoz 2005: 59). The result was the coexistence of three different levels of subnational government that did not depend on one another either functionally or financially. In 2001, reformers approved a bill granting regional and municipal governments a share of tax revenue on mineral extraction, thereby further reinforcing the nonhierarchical character of the system.

3. *New Laws Affecting Parties and Elections*

In 2000, Congress reestablished multiple districts for legislative elections. In 2003, the Party Law gave political parties a legal monopoly over national-level candidacies. The law also established a set of tough requirements for registering parties and identified procedures that parties had to follow when electing their authorities. In 2005, a minimum electoral threshold of 5 percent was established in order to gain representation in Congress.

In sum, in both Colombia and Peru, reformers carried out a number of far-reaching institutional changes in an attempt to improve their

---

[15] On party substitutes, see Hale (2006) and Levitsky and Zavaleta (Chapter 15, this volume).

democracies. In both countries, however, reformers failed to adequately consider how resulting changes in the distribution of resources would affect party aggregation. In the following section, we examine the unintended effects of these reforms on subsequent party-building efforts.

PROBLEMS OF PARTY-BUILDING WITHOUT SUBNATIONAL LINKAGES

By redistributing power and resources, democratizing reforms in Colombia and Peru hindered party aggregation and impeded subsequent party-building efforts. In Colombia, the institutional changes reduced the resource asymmetries that had assured the dominance of regional-level intermediate party leaders. As reformers had anticipated, decentralization successfully weakened the power bases of regional bosses, especially senators, and increased the autonomy of local politicians. After decentralization, elected authorities in municipalities and governorships owed less to senators,[15] and legislators now depended more on mayors (Willis, Garman, and Haggard 1999: 226). Fiscal decentralization also reduced partisan control over the distribution of resources; local budgets nearly tripled, increasing from 2.4 percent of GDP in 1990 to 6.2 percent in 2006 (Fedelino 2010: 50–55). This reallocation of resources benefited municipalities: while the share of total government expenditures at the municipal level increased from 10.5 percent in 1980 to 17.3 percent in 1990, the departmental level saw its share reduced from 16.7 percent to 15.7 percent (Willis et al. 1999: 13). The 1991 Constitution's elimination of *auxilios parlamentarios* (legislators' fixed budget) and the creation of a national electoral district for the senate also both weakened regional barons. Although the regional barons initially responded – with some success – by campaigning in their traditional geographical strongholds (Crisp and Ingall 2002; Rodríguez 2002), they eventually lost ground to candidates who ran national campaigns.[16] Ultimately, the regional barons failed to adapt to the changing conditions of political competition (Pizarro 2002: 376–380).[17]

---

[15] Authors' interview with Boris Zapata, former subsecretary of the Liberal Party, Bogotá, June 4, 2008.
[16] Authors' interview with Víctor Renán Barco, senator for Cauca, Bogotá, May 17, 2006.
[17] Authors' interview with Otto Morales Benites, former Liberal Party leader, Bogotá, June 4, 2008.

At the same time that institutional reforms weakened regional barons, they made it easier for local politicians to sustain their own support bases. The result was that mayors now emerged as political bosses.[18] Health and education resources were funneled directly to local communities, which increased possibilities for patronage spending (Gutiérrez and Dávila 2000; Eaton 2006: 545).[19] The upshot is that the reforms did not end clientelism, as intended by the authors of the reforms, but instead merely "deconcentrated" it. In other words, the "franchises" gained financial autonomy (Dávila and Delgado 2002; Pizarro 2002). Local clientelistic networks were further bolstered by the influx of illegal money from drug traffickers and paramilitary groups (Gutiérrez 2007: 259–260 and ch. 9).

In sum, the Colombian reforms had the intended effects of weakening regional barons and granting more autonomy and resources to municipal governments. However, they have also had a major unintended effect: the partial deinstitutionalization of the traditional party system (Boudon 2000; Muñoz and Dargent 2011). Independent candidacies and party-switching became more common, and traditional parties lost considerable power, although they remained relevant actors, particularly at the subnational level (Dargent and Vergara 2012; Gamboa 2010). This void has not been filled by new parties. Lacking the resources necessary to take root outside of major cities and to avoid internal splits, would-be party-builders have faced an uphill battle, as will be seen in the discussion of the PV. Thus, while the traditional parties have found it increasingly difficult to maintain their previous level of strength in the aftermath of reform, the construction of new parties in Colombia has also proved to be extremely difficult in the postreform environment.

In Peru, democratizing reforms dispersed power and resources – beyond what Fujimori had done in the 1990s – without empowering national or intermediate-level political actors. Consequently, the reforms ended up *increasing* the barriers for party aggregation in several ways. First, they provided additional sources of resources for subnational politicians, increasing their autonomy vis-à-vis national politicians. Due to Peru's booming economy in the 2000s, municipalities began to administer significantly more resources than they had in the 1990s. For example, between 1999 and 2008, shared revenues transferred to municipalities

---

[18] Authors' interview with Boris Zapata, former subsecretary of the Liberal Party, Bogotá, June 4, 2008.
[19] Authors' interview with Mauricio Santa María, former deputy director of the National Planning Department, Bogotá, February 25, 2008.

increased by 143 percent (CAD 2008). Moreover, when mineral prices increased in the mid-2000s, the budgets of subnational governments in mining areas grew exponentially. However, the bulk of these transfers to subnational governments came *after* parties had ceased to be important actors at the subnational level.

Second, reforms simultaneously weakened parties. The 2003 Parties Law established more stringent requirements for national parties than for regional and local movements, and its implementation encountered enforcement problems (Tanaka 2007; Vergara 2009). For instance, even though direct public financing of parties is included in the Parties Law, this provision has never been implemented. Likewise, the creation of elected regional governments in 2002 further reduced the incentives to join national parties, favoring instead ephemeral regional coalitions formed solely to contest elections (Zavaleta 2014a).

Third, better administrative controls made it more difficult for national parties to access resources that they could offer local politicians or employ to finance their activities between elections. Technocratic controls, new transparency procedures, and media awareness made it more difficult to politically manipulate the national executive (Muñoz 2013: 63–64). They also made it more difficult for politicians to repay favors, which increased resentment among local political operators.[20] Within this context, the relationship between national party leaders and local politicians underwent an important shift. Rather than offering resources to congressional candidates, political parties began to recruit local politicians who could fund their own campaigns and contribute money to the party, in exchange for a slot on the ballot (see Levitsky and Zavaleta, Chapter 15, this volume).

Finally, despite the creation of elected regional governments, the institutional changes did not fully empower regional political actors. Local politicians benefited from running together for office but lacked sufficient incentives to build durable regional parties. Indeed, most of the parties or "regional movements" that emerged were better characterized as "coalitions of independents" (Zavaleta 2014a). Thus, even though regional politicians could access state resources through office, regional movements tended to be weakly organized.

This relative weakness of intermediate-level politicians was largely due to the coexistence of three levels of subnational government that did not depend, either administratively or financially, on one another. Regional

---

[20] Authors' interview with Guido Lucioni, *Fujimorista* ex-candidate for Congress, Lima, February 5, 2010.

governments did not have any leverage over provincial municipalities, which in turn could not influence district politics. In fact, mayors and regional presidents spent more time trying to negotiate additional resources from the national government than they did coordinating among themselves (Muñoz 2007).

In short, democratizing reforms made it even more difficult to rebuild Peru's collapsed party system. The alleged "rebirth" of parties in the 2000s (Kenney 2003) proved to be not only partial but brief. Partisan labels remained so discredited that local candidates believed that they would hinder rather than help their electoral prospects (de Gramont 2010; Levitsky 2013; Zavaleta 2014a). In this new institutional context, parties had neither reputations nor resources to offer local politicians, leaving local politicians without incentives to join them (Levitsky and Zavaleta, Chapter 15, this volume).

In both Colombia and Peru, then, political reforms undermined party-building by reducing incentives for party aggregation. As a result, new parties in both countries were little more than loose coalitions of candidates. In the following sections, we analyze the challenges facing politicians seeking to build party organizations in this postreform environment.

FAILED NATIONAL PARTY-BUILDING: BRANDS WITHOUT RESOURCES

Without access to subnational resources, new parties struggle to translate national electoral surges into local-level penetration and effective party-building. Even when parties develop a strong brand and perform well in a national election, if they cannot channel resources to local politicians and thereby assure their loyalty over time, their party-building efforts are unlikely to succeed. In what follows, we illustrate the challenges of party-building without subnational resources through two cases, the PV in Colombia and the PNP in Peru.

The Green Party in Colombia

The experience of the Colombian Green Party (PV) illustrates how new parties may surge at the national level but, in the absence of subnational resources, face difficulty penetrating the local level, where machine politics thrive. Created in 2005, the PV took off in 2009, when three former popular mayors of Bogotá – Antanus Mockus, Enrique Peñalosa, and Luis Eduardo Garzón – joined it. The PV nominated Mockus as its

2010 presidential candidate. Although President Uribe's successor, Juan Manuel Santos, was heavily favored, Mockus surged in the polls in the months before the election. His impressive first-round performance led to widespread media coverage of the "green wave" and Mockus's highly original campaign (Wills-Otero and Benito 2012). The PV sought to position itself as a centrist party, promising citizens an end to corruption and other abuses and a strengthening of the rule of law. This platform was crucial for mobilizing younger and independent voters (Rincón 2011). Indeed, Mockus's campaign triggered the most important cyberactivist movement in Latin America (Rincón 2011).

However, the PV's actual performance on election day illustrated the difficulty of national party-building without local organization, especially when clientelism is well established at the subnational level. The "green wave" was largely a virtual phenomenon: the PV did not have an established social constituency and an organized party apparatus to mobilize its voters (Rincón 2011). Although Mockus qualified for the presidential runoff with 21 percent of the first-round vote, he lost to Santos by a margin of 40 percentage points in the second round. Without a solid territorial organization, the PV won less than 5 percent of the legislative vote (Wills-Otero and Benito 2012), most of which was concentrated in the big cities.[21]

The PV also performed poorly in subnational elections the following year, again illustrating the limits of its party-building effort. The party won only two of thirty-two governorships and fifty-one of 1,101 municipalities. Ultimately, it failed to position itself as a sufficiently viable alternative to attract competitive candidates and appeal to voters. This was due to several factors. First, partisan (collective) resources continued to be important for competing in local elections (Botero and Alvira 2012; Gamboa 2010; Wills-Otero, Battle, and Barrero 2012). Thus, viable contenders in subnational elections would look for partisan endorsement and join the party that offered the most benefits (Botero and Alvira 2012: 145–146).[22] As a new party with little administrative capital, the PV found it difficult to attract competitive local candidates.

Second, traditional party brands continued to hold value in local elections (Botero and Alvira 2012; Gamboa 2010; Wills-Otero, Battle, and Barrero 2012). However, contrary to Lupu's (Chapter 3, this volume)

---

[21] "¿Qué Pasó con la Ola Verde?," *La Silla Vacía*, January 3, 2010, www.lasillavacia.com/historia/15107.

[22] The situation differs markedly in Peru, where party endorsements are of very little value. See Levitsky and Zavaleta (Chapter 15, this volume).

conception of brands, in Colombia these tended not to be programmatic in nature. Local platforms in Colombian subnational elections were typically not consistent with parties' overall programmatic positions, since candidates decided them based on local considerations and without consulting the party organization (Botero and Alvira 2012: 156). Instead, party brands at the local level were rooted in historical party identification and in the reputation for solving problems (Gamboa 2010). This posed a major challenge for a new party like the PV, since it could not draw on either of these sources of brand identification.

Third, traditional parties retain important geographical strongholds in which they dominate local elections and maintain close relations with powerful elites (Gamboa 2010; Wills-Otero, Battle, and Barrero 2012). As explained above, democratizing reforms did not eliminate clientelism in Colombia but instead deconcentrated it. Although regional barons, particularly senators, lost clout, mayors and governors became local bosses. The consolidation of political machines at the local level reduced the incentive to compete, given that other parties had low odds of winning subnational elections (Wills-Otero, Battle, and Barrero 2012: 91). In fact, during the 2010 elections, the only nontraditional parties that made significant electoral inroads were the Social Party of National Unity (PSUN), a party created by President Uribe and later used by Juan Manuel Santos, and Radical Change (CR), the PSUN's ally in Congress. Both parties attracted local and national politicians with previous links to traditional parties, and in both parties members used illegal resources for local party-building.[23] Without access to subnational resources or the endorsement of the national incumbent, the PV found it extremely difficult to compete with local machines for the support of rural voters.

Finally, the 2011 election confirmed the PV's lack of institutional mechanisms for solving internal conflicts and overcoming its heavy reliance on individual personalities. As Dávila (2013) explains, during the 2011 regional and municipal elections, "[t]he personalism and egos of the former mayors destroyed what little organization they had been able to build ... [The PV] reproduced and exacerbated personalism in politics. It served as an electoral umbrella for antipolitics turncoats [*tránsfugas*]." From the beginning, the PV was dominated by a handful of strong

---

[23] Both the PSUN and CR were later implicated in the so-called parapolitics scandal when it was discovered that some of their legislative representatives and local authorities had ties to right-wing paramilitary groups accused of human rights violations and drug trafficking. See López et al. (2010).

personalities, who often did not see eye-to-eye. The party's strong electoral performance in the Department of Santander, for example, was primarily the result of the personal traits of one important PV leader, Sergio Fajardo.[24] Similarly, Enrique Peñalosa's ambition to win back the mayoralty of Bogotá resulted in his acceptance of former President Uribe's controversial endorsement of his candidacy. This decision sent a confusing message to the party's core constituency, which valued the PV's programmatic stance against "politics as usual" (Dávila 2013).[25] Peñalosa's defeat in Bogotá's municipal election and the party's poor overall performance constituted a serious setback for the PV. Moreover, the decision to accept Uribe's endorsement caused intense internal disagreement in the party. These internal disputes ended with the resignation of the PV's most popular leader and 2010 presidential candidate, Antanus Mockus. The PV's more recent "left turn" has further exacerbated internal tensions and sent an ambiguous message to its original centrist constituency.[26]

In sum, although the PV presented a novel brand during the 2010 election, it did not have access to the kinds of subnational resources and territorial organization necessary to compete with consolidated local machines in congressional and subnational elections. The result was a poor electoral showing and a serious obstacle to effective organization-building. Moreover, the party was not able to control its leaders' personal ambitions and assuage their disagreements, which in turn diluted its innovative centrist and "clean" brand. For these reasons, the PV's future electoral prospects appear bleak.

The Nationalist Party in Peru

The experience of the Nationalist Party (PNP) in Peru similarly illustrates the difficulty of building a national party organization without control over the distribution of subnational patronage resources. It also shows how easy access to national office may weaken incentives to invest in party-building (Van Dyck, Chapter 5, this volume). Founded in 2005

---

[24] For a discussion of Fajardo's campaign, see "Fajardo, la estrella de los verdes, pero lejos del partido," *La Silla Vacía*, November 8, 2011, http://lasillavacia.com/historia/fajardo-la-estrella-de-los-verdes-pero-lejos-del-partido-29324.

[25] In September 2012, PV spokesperson Luis Eduardo Garzón joined President Juan Manuel Santos's cabinet.

[26] In September 2013, the PV forged an alliance with the left-leaning Progressive Movement. Since then, the Progressives have gained considerable influence in the PV leadership, displacing moderates such as Enrique Peñalosa.

by populist former military officer Ollanta Humala, the PNP quickly emerged as a major electoral force. In 2006, Humala nearly captured the presidency with a left-wing populist campaign (Cameron 2009), and the PNP – in alliance with the Union for Peru (UPP) – won a legislative plurality, with 21 percent of the vote. Support for Humala outside Lima was impressive: he won a majority of votes in 130 out of 195 provinces.

PNP party-building efforts soon stalled, however. The PNP's legislative ticket was little more than a shortlived alliance among local politicians (see Levitsky and Zavaleta, Chapter 15, this volume). As a result, the party's legislative faction lacked even a minimum of cohesion. Thus, the PNP's alliance with the UPP collapsed soon after the 2006 election, and over the next few years, several other PNP legislators abandoned the party for other parliamentary groups that they deemed to be more electorally viable. The PNP's original parliamentary group was progressively dismembered, falling from forty-five members in 2006 to twenty-five in 2011. Only sixteen of the original forty-five PNP legislators ran for reelection in 2011, and nine of those sixteen ran with *other parties*. The upshot is that the PNP not only found it difficult to attract competitive local candidates, but it also struggled to retain candidates' loyalty after elections.

Obstacles to PNP party-building were particularly manifest at the local level. Lacking administrative capital, the PNP was unable to attract strong local-level candidates. Without Humala on the ticket, the PNP's brand was ineffective. With no real territorial organization and few resources to offer, the party's nationalist-leftist platform failed to attract competitive local candidates. Fearing a poor performance in the absence of viable candidates, the PNP opted to remain largely on the sidelines in the 2010 local and regional elections.[27] The only exception was Cusco's regional presidential election, in which the PNP backed a popular mayor, Jorge Acurio, who won. Overall, the PNP won only ten of 195 provincial governments and none of Peru's twenty-five regional governments (except for its ally's victory in Cusco). As a result, the party failed to establish a significant local-level presence to complement Humala's national-level electoral appeal.

The PNP's failure to establish a foothold at the local and regional levels inhibited organization-building even as the party's national electoral

---

[27] Authors' interviews with Alberto Adrianzén, member of Andean Parliament and former member of Gana Perú Alliance, Lima, November 9, 2013; and Verónika Mendoza, congresswoman and former member of the Nationalist Party, Lima, November 21, 2013.

fortunes soared. Humala won the presidency in 2011, and the PNP captured a legislative plurality, this time with 26 percent of the vote. However, *Humalismo* again failed to channel this national-level electoral success into party-building, for several reasons. First, the PNP lacked the resources to build and sustain an activist base. Humala's electoral success in 2011 attracted a large number of new activists, the vast majority of whom were patronage-seekers. As Humala rose in the polls, new activists flooded, indiscriminately, into the party.[28] After Humala's victory, these activists demanded access to patronage and other state resources.[29] Although the PNP was able to provide some activists with jobs in central government agencies (most of them located in Lima),[30] the party's failure to capture local and regional office left it unable to meet public employment demands in the interior.[31] After the 2002 decentralization reforms became effective, regional governments controlled most of the patronage appointments in their regions, leaving the national government with limited patronage resources outside of Lima.[32] Because the PNP controlled very few local and regional governments, the party could not meet members' widespread demands for patronage in the interior.[33] Consequently, serious intraparty conflict erupted in many regions, including Arequipa, Cusco, Ayacucho, Ancash, Junín, Puno, and others, and

[28] Authors' interview with Verónika Mendoza, congresswoman and former member of the Nationalist Party, Lima, November 21, 2013.
[29] Authors' interviews with Alberto Adrianzén, member of Andean Parliament and former member of Gana Perú Alliance, Lima, November 9, 2013; Verónika Mendoza, congresswoman and former member of the Nationalist Party, Lima, November 21, 2013; and anonymous activists from the Nationalist Party from Ayacucho and Ancash, Lima, November 29, 2013.
[30] See, for instance, "Los financistas pasan por caja," *Revista Velaverde*, July 15, 2013, www.revistavelaverde.pe/?p=3705.
[31] See also "Ruido político: La verdadera crisis en el nacionalismo," *Spacio Libre*, January 31, 2012, www.spaciolibre.net/ruido-politico-la-verdadera-crisis-en-el-nacionalismo/; "Dirigentes regionales del Partido Nacionalista reclaman cargos estatales," *Diario Correo*, July 10, 2013, http://diariocorreo.pe/ultimas/noticias/6545815/dirigentes-regionales-del-partido-nacionalis.
[32] Authors' interviews with Paula Vilca, former Vice Minister of Interculturality during Humala's government and expert in regional politics, Lima, November 11, 2013; and Alberto Adrianzén, member of Andean Parliament and former member of Gana Perú Alliance, Lima, November 9, 2013. The national government possesses only a limited number of positions for special projects and decentralized public offices, as well as the right to appoint *gobernadores* (national government representatives in the regions), which have limited power and resources.
[33] Authors' interview with Alberto Adrianzén, member of Andean Parliament and former member of Gana Perú Alliance, Lima, November 9, 2013.

many dissatisfied activists abandoned the party.[34] Ultimately, then, winning the presidency did not facilitate organization-building – and may in fact have undermined it.

The PNP's lack of control over subnational resources was particularly evident in Cusco. Although new regional president Jorge Acurio was nominally a PNP ally, he was in fact a self-financed independent politician who owed virtually nothing to the national party. In the face of a surge in demand, regional government jobs among campaign activists who campaigned for the PNP alliance, Acurio ignored national party recommendations and instead appointed his own friends and supporters.[35] Unwilling to be bound by the national party, Acurio spearheaded a dissident faction that divided the PNP in Cusco.[36]

Personalism posed another obstacle to organization-building. President Humala and his wife, Nadine Heredia, thoroughly dominate both the national government (Dargent and Muñoz 2012) and the party

[34] See "Partido Nacionalista con futuro incierto al 2014," *Diario Correo*, October 14, 2013, www.larepublica.pe/14-10-2013/partido-nacionalista-con-futuro-incierto-al-2014; "Acurio reconoce que Partido Nacionalista se dividió y ya no tiene la misma solidez," *Diario Correo*, January 31, 2013, www.larepublica.pe/30-01-2013/acurio-reconoce-que-partido-nacionalista-se-dividio-y-ya-no-tiene-la-misma-solidez; "División política dentro del partido de Ollanta Humala," *Diario Jornada*, July 10, 2013, www.jornada.com.pe/regional/598-division-politica-dentro-del-partido-de-ollanta-humala; "Nacionalistas exigen trabajo y toman local del programa Juntos," *Diario Correo*, July 18, 2012, http://diariocorreo.pe/ultimas/noticias/513357/nacionalistas-exigen-tranbajo-y-toman-local-de; "Nacionalistas se enfrentan en plenario regional," *Huaraz Noticias*, March 1, 2012, www.huaraznoticias.com/titulares/nacionalistas-se-enfrentan-en-plenario-regional; "Chimbote: militancia nacionalista se reduce por diferencia entre Nena Escalante y Fredy Otárola," *Radio Santo Domingo*, July 1, 2013, www.rsdenlinea.com/noticias/todas-las-noticias/12384-chimbote-militancia-nacionalista-se-reduce-por-diferencia-entre-nena-escalante-y-fredy-otarola; "Bronca nacionalista por designación de puestos laborales," *Diario Correo*, July 15, 2012, http://diariocorreo.pe/politica/bronca-nacionalista-por-designacion-de-puestos-250529/; "Militantes de Puno atacan con huevos a dirigente Luis Aliaga," *La República*, March 29, 2012, www.larepublica.pe/29-03-2012/militantes-de-puno-atacan-con-huevos-dirigente-luis-aliaga; "Militantes del partido de Ollanta decepcionados por no ocupar puestos de trabajo," *Radio Pachamama*, May 15, 2012, www.pachamamaradio.org/15-04-2012/militantes-del-partido-de-ollanta-decep-cionados-por-no-contar-con-puestos-de-trabajo.html; and authors' interview with Paula Vilca, former Vice Minister of Interculturality during Humala's government and expert in regional politics, Lima, November 11, 2013.

[35] Authors' interview with Verónika Mendoza, congresswoman and former member of the Nationalist Party, Lima, November 21, 2013.

[36] In 2013, Acurio declared that in Cusco, the PNP "only exists as a registered party, but it is not a solid organization." See "Acurio reconoce que Partido Nacionalista se dividió y ya no tiene la misma solidez," *Diario Correo*, January 31, 2013, www.larepublica.pe/30-01-2013/acurio-reconoce-que-partido-nacionalista-se-dividio-y-ya-no-tiene-la-misma-solidez.

organization.[37] Thus, in the face of regional factional disputes, Humala did not turn to the party structure for solutions, but rather appointed his former bodyguard, a retired policeman, to head a commission in charge of restructuring the party organization in the southern part of the country.[38] Indeed, Humala's orientation toward party-building is at best ambiguous.[39] Although he purports to favor strengthening the party structure, he shows little desire to be held accountable to an autonomous organization or confront divergent opinions.[40] Given that Humala was elected president without a strong party organization, he may believe that it is now unnecessary to build one.

In short, despite its striking national-level electoral success in 2006 and 2011, the PNP advanced very little in terms of organization-building. The PNP leadership possesses neither the means (i.e., subnational resources) nor the incentive to strengthen the party's territorial structure. Although it is too early to draw conclusions about the PNP's party-building prospects, the evidence thus far suggests that the party is unlikely to consolidate.[41]

---

[37] Authors' interviews with Alberto Adrianzén, member of Andean Parliament and former member of Gana Perú Alliance, Lima, November 9, 2013; and Verónika Mendoza, congresswoman and former member of the Nationalist Party, Lima, November 21, 2013.

[38] "Jefe del Partido Nacionalista en el sur purgó cárcel por delito de homicidio simple," *La República*, December 16, 2011, www.larepublica.pe/16-12-2011/jefe-del-partido-nacionalista-en-el-sur-purgo-carcel-por-delito-de-homicidio-simple; "Nacionalistas piden la cabeza de Luis Aliaga que purgó cárcel por homicidio," *La República*, December 16, 2011, www.larepublica.pe/16-12-2011/nacionalistas-piden-la-cabeza-de-luis-aliaga-que-purgo-carcel-por-homicidio. The move was criticized within the party ranks as an autocratic imposition. See "Ruido político: La verdadera crisis en el nacionalismo," *Spacio Libre*, January 31, 2012, www.spaciolibre.net/ruido-politico-la-verdadera-crisis-en-el-nacionalismo.

[39] Authors' interviews with Alberto Adrianzén, member of Andean Parliament and former member of Gana Perú Alliance, Lima, November 9, 2013; and Verónika Mendoza, congresswoman and former member of the Nationalist Party, Lima, November 21, 2013.

[40] Authors' interview with Verónika Mendoza, congresswoman and former member of the Nationalist Party, Lima, November 21, 2013.

[41] Some scholars contend that Fuerza Popular, the current *Fujimorista* party, offers a more successful example of top-down party-building (Levitsky and Zavaleta, Chapter 15, this volume; Meléndez 2014). *Fujimorismo* is a stronger political force precisely due to the factors highlighted in the volume's Chapter 1. In particular, the *Fujimorismo/* anti-*Fujimorismo* cleavage strengthened *Fujimorismo* as a political identity. In addition, *Fujimorista* leader Keiko Fujimori is a presidential frontrunner for 2016. As a result, *Fujimorismo* is poised to attract better subnational and congressional candidates than other parties. From a comparative perspective, however, *Fujimorismo* is still far from a successful case of party-building, especially on the territorial dimension on which this article focuses. *Fujimorismo* lacks a strong national organization and has won few local governments in recent regional and local elections (in 2014, it won 3 of 25 regional presidencies and 4 of 195 provincial governments). Thus, even if Fuerza Popular is Peru's

As the cases of Colombia's PV and Peru's PNP demonstrate, new parties without access to subnational patronage resources often have difficulty penetrating the local level, even when they possess an attractive brand and achieve national-level electoral success. During national elections, a party can campaign based on its candidate's personal traits and diffuse its brand through the media (Boas 2005). Local elections, however, require traditional campaigning and, consequently, a greater investment in party organization or substitutes (Muñoz 2014; Szwarcberg 2012; Zavaleta 2014a). Access to subnational patronage resources is thus critical for establishing subnational linkages and holding together coalitions of local politicians. Without territorial organization, it is difficult for new parties to sustain a solid electoral performance over time.

FAILED AGGREGATION: WHEN (LOCAL) RESOURCES ARE NOT ENOUGH

If party-building is difficult without access to subnational patronage resources, subnational parties based exclusively on the distribution of patronage resources face an alternative set of obstacles. While such parties may flourish in their own subnational pockets, if they do not have some means of scaling up to the national level, they are unlikely to become true cases of successful party-building. This section examines the limitations of party-building based on subnational resources alone. We first discuss the cases of Peru's Chim Pum Callao (CPC) and the Alliance for Progress (APP), two relatively successful (and thus atypical) experiences that illustrate both the advantages and limitations of relying primarily on subnational resources for party-building. We then turn to the experience of Colombia's Citizen Convergence (CC), later renamed the National Integration Party (PIN). This party is an extreme case, in which party aggregation was based on subnational resources obtained, through both legal and illegal means, by local elites.

Chim Pum Callao in Peru

CPC is one of the few Peruvian parties that managed to establish stable linkages with voters following the collapse of the national party system. Legally, CPC is registered as a "regional movement" in the port region

strongest party, the *Fujimorismo*/anti-*Fujimorismo* cleavage does not appear sufficient to facilitate the construction of strong subnational linkages.

of Callao, which means that it can only compete in subnational elections in that district. Since its creation in the mid-1990s, CPC has achieved extraordinary success in municipal and regional elections (Rojas 2011). According to its founder, former Callao regional president Alex Kouri, much of this success can be explained by its efficacy in office: it delivers public works while addressing the most pressing needs of the poor.[42]

In contrast to most local parties in Peru, CPC is more than just a personalistic vehicle or a temporary coalition of candidates. It is a regional machine that is hegemonic in Callao, with a reputation for delivering the goods (Rojas 2011). CPC is built primarily on subnational state resources. According to Kouri, CPC's organization is so intertwined with the subnational state apparatus that the two are difficult to distinguish.[43] CPC uses subnational state resources to distribute patronage to loyal supporters and deliver goods and services to the poor. Thus, for example, municipal and regional directors command networks of paid local brokers who, in turn, mobilize poor voters for political activities (Rojas 2011). In electoral terms, CPC has been strikingly successful, winning all regional elections and the bulk of district-level elections since the 2002 decentralization.

Although CPC's success demonstrates that party-building through the use of patronage resources is still a viable strategy in Peru (Muñoz and García 2011; Rojas 2011), it also demonstrates the limits of bottom-up party-building in a decentralized context. Decentralization imposes an electoral ceiling on party-builders using subnational state resources: the regional level. Politicians cannot use subnational resources outside of their electoral district. Thus, although regional political entrepreneurs may consolidate power in their districts, as Kouri did, they lack resources to offer candidates in other regions. This is especially the case with regional patronage machines like CPC, which lack an attractive brand or a charismatic national-level candidate. Thus, CPC failed to extend beyond Callao or establish itself as a national-level platform for Kouri. Without a national party, Kouri was forced to turn to another organization, Radical Change (CR), to run (unsuccessfully) for Congress in 2011. After Kouri's entry into national politics, CPC grew increasingly factionalized and experienced a schism in 2012.[44] Its future is therefore uncertain.

---

[42] Authors' interview with Álex Kouri, Chim Pum Callao founder, Lima, January 10, 2011.

[43] Authors' interview with Álex Kouri, Chim Pum Callao founder, Lima, January 10, 2011.

[44] Authors' interview with Álex Kouri, Chim Pum Callao founder, Lima, January 10, 2011. Also "Chim Pum Callao rechaza chuponeo y confirma expulsión de Sotomayor," *Radio Programas del Perú*, March 29, 2012, www.rpp.com.pe/2012-03-29-chim-pum-callao-rechaza-chuponeo-y-confirma-expulsion-de-sotomayor-noticia_466563.html.

Alliance for Progress in Peru

Peru's APP constitutes another moderately successful attempt at subnational party-building. Founded in 2001 by wealthy businessman César Acuña, the APP began a serious party-building effort after Acuña was defeated in the 2006 congressional elections and decided to focus on the subnational level (Zavaleta 2014a). The APP was initially a corporation-based party (see Barndt, Chapter 13, this volume), financed almost entirely by Acuña's private resources. Acuña used his consortium of private universities based in northern Peru as a source of selective benefits to distribute to activists and candidates and to finance candidates' campaigns (Barrenechea 2014; Meléndez 2011). After winning the Trujillo mayoralty in 2006, Acuña used municipal resources to cement the APP's organization in the region of La Libertad (of which Trujillo is the capital). Nevertheless, most of the party's resources come from Acuña's universities, in the form of salaries, scholarships, and others selective benefits. These resources, together with (Acuña-sponsored) charity programs that engage in private clientelism (Barrenechea 2014; Meléndez 2011), enabled the APP to consolidate a powerful territorial organization in La Libertad, establish a solid presence in neighboring regions such as Lambayeque,[45] and eventually compete in districts across the country. In 2010, the APP fielded candidates in ten of twenty-five regional presidential elections and 126 mayoral elections. It won 7.7 percent of the national vote, capturing two regional presidencies (Ayacucho and Lambayeque) and fourteen mayoralties (Barrenechea 2014).

Despite its modest success in scaling up, the APP's party-building strategy faces serious limitations. National party-building based on clientelism is difficult. A clientelistic reputation is easier to achieve at the local level; creating a national brand is far more challenging. The APP has no clear ideology or program, and Acuña lacks the charisma to be a strong national candidate. For these reasons, the APP has relied almost entirely on the distribution of Acuña's private resources. Although these resources helped the party recruit local candidates in various parts of the country, the APP has not developed an electoral appeal that extends beyond its local clientelistic networks. This helps to explain why the APP's success has thus far been limited to subnational elections.[46] A clientelistic party-building strategy based on private resources is, moreover, very

---

[45] Acuña's brother, Humberto, won the regional presidency of Lambayeque in 2010.
[46] The APP did not run a presidential candidate in 2011, but rather backed Pedro Pablo Kuczynski, who finished third.

costly. Although the strategy was successful in Acuña's home region in the north, it appears difficult to replicate nationally.[47] Indeed, the strategy may be viable only in the north, where Acuña's private universities are well endowed with resources (Barrenechea 2014), and only in the context of the kind of economic boom that Peru experienced in the early 2000s.

Indeed, there are signs that the APP's national party-building efforts may not be sustainable. For example, many of the local and regional candidates it recruited in 2010 have not remained in the party. Most notably, Wilfredo Oscarima, who won the Ayacucho regional presidency in 2010 under the APP label, refused to cooperate with the party leadership after taking office and eventually departed. To date, then, the APP remains strongest and best organized in the north; indeed, it is only there that it has shown a capacity to systematically recruit candidates and retain them over time.

Citizen Convergence in Colombia

In Colombia, the most successful case of bottom-up party-building emerged out of "parapolitics," or politicians with ties to paramilitary and other illicit groups. By opening up the political system to new groups and independent politicians, Colombia's political reforms allowed numerous politicians with ties to paramilitaries and other illegal groups to win local office (López 2010; Romero 2011). These new local elites used public office to capture rents and advance their interests in various ways, but in some cases, they deployed subnational resources to build new political organizations (López 2010).

The most prominent example of such party-building was Citizen Convergence (CC), which later renamed itself the National Integration Party (PIN). A regionally based party created in 1997, the CC/PIN was always closely linked to "parapolitics."[48] The party was created by local elites in the department of Santander who were interested in expanding their political and economic power at the subnational level (López 2010). These elites sought paramilitary assistance in order to increase their chances of capturing state rents (López 2010; Romero 2011). In exchange for the logistical and organizational support that paramilitary

---

[47] As Barndt (Chapter 13, this volume) shows, however, such strategies have achieved some national-level success in Panama, Ecuador, and elsewhere.

[48] During the late 2000s, Colombia was rocked by a major political scandal when several congressmen were accused of having close ties to (and being financed by) paramilitaries.

groups provided, they received a share of rents, as well as protection and coverage of their criminal activities.

The CC quickly consolidated itself as a regional machine, using sub-national resources to channel patronage and clientelistic benefits to allies and voters, and using regulatory powers to assure impunity for its armed allies and the extraction of further rents. A few years after its creation, the CC defeated the Liberal Party in Santander, a traditional Liberal bastion, and won the governorship. In the 2003 local elections, the CC won several municipalities with a strong paramilitary presence (Universidad de los Andes 2010). In 2002, the party jumped into national politics, winning a seat in the senate and two seats in the lower chamber.[49] Once in Congress, it became part of President Uribe's governing coalition (López 2010). After the "parapolitics" scandal broke, several CC leaders (e.g., Luis Alberto Gil, Hugo Aguilar, Alfonso Riaño, Juan Carlos Martínez) were prosecuted for their ties to paramilitary groups (Universidad de los Andes 2010). Yet the CC continued to grow.[50] Even after its main leaders were imprisoned, the party won nine seats in the senate and eleven in the lower chamber in the 2010 election, and it won thirty-five municipalities in the 2011 subnational elections.[51]

Although the CC does not meet this volume's criteria for a successful new party, it nevertheless became a significant congressional force. It did so, in large part, through the deployment of subnational state and private resources. As with other parties that depend primarily on subnational patronage resources, however, the CC largely failed to transcend the limits of its regional stronghold. This was particularly true after the "parapolitics" scandal discredited the party's national brand. Unlike Peru's patronage-based parties, the CC routinely deployed violence, intimidation, and other criminal activities as means to consolidate local power. Violence and crime, however, limited the CC's ability to scale up to the national level. The party's blatantly illegal character marred its national brand, which damaged its electoral prospects.

In sum, although party-building strategies based solely on access to subnational resources proved modestly successful in building durable subnational party organizations in Peru and Colombia, successful

---

[49] "El fin de Convergencia Ciudadana," *Verdad Abierta*, January 18, 2012, www.verdadabierta.com/component/content/article/63-nacional/3798-el-fin-de-convergencia/.

[50] In 2010, after its label was discredited by this process, the CC made an alliance with other controversial groups and formed the PIN to compete in congressional elections.

[51] "El PIN reniega de su ADN," *La Silla Vacía*, October, 6, 2010, http://lasillavacia.com/historia/18524.

subnational party machines such as CPC, APP, and the CC had difficulty scaling up to the national level. Subnational resources (whether public or private) facilitate the construction of powerful clientelist machines at the local level, but in a postreform environment in which patronage resources are dispersed, clientelism has not proven to be viable party-building strategy at the national level.

CONCLUSION

This chapter highlighted the importance of patronage resources for establishing durable linkages between national and subnational party organizations. Our main contention was that subnational patronage resources, and the way that they are distributed within the territory, have significant implications for party-building. We compared two countries, Colombia and Peru, in which political reforms that limited national parties' control over the distribution of subnational patronage resources made party-building more difficult. We first examined the cases of two parties with attractive brands but little control over subnational patronage resources. These parties failed to translate national electoral surges into successful organization-building. We then examined the mirror image of such cases: parties in which local politicians with access to patronage resources consolidated local party organizations but were unable to scale up and become viable national parties.

As mentioned earlier, the impact of political reforms affecting the control and distribution of patronage resources on party-building should not be overstated. This chapter argues that the dispersion of subnational resources away from party control is likely to make party-building more difficult. However, as discussed in Chapter 1, the presence of facilitating structural conditions, such as polarization and conflict, limits the impact of such reforms on party aggregation. The negative effects of decentralization on party-building, for example, seem conditional on the absence of such cleavages. When such cleavages exist, decentralization may help parties to build across territory. Decentralization reforms could contribute to bottom-up party-building, with political groups using municipal governments as stepping stones to national politics. Similarly, national parties exploiting these cleavages could use local elections to parachute across national territory. In the absence of such social and political cleavages, institutional reforms, such as those implemented in Colombia and Peru, are quite harmful to existing party linkages – and to party-building more generally.

The cases of Bolivia and Brazil, two countries in which party-building has been facilitated by political reforms similar to the ones discussed above, allow us to highlight this point. In Brazil, market reforms reduced the availability of patronage resources, while decentralization reforms strengthened municipalities in relation to state governorships. Nevertheless, parties transformed from loose patronage machines at the regional level to more programmatically coherent organizations (Hagopian, Gervasoni, and Moraes 2009). As Hagopian et al. argue, market reforms created a programmatic cleavage in the country that allowed for party-building. The reduction of patronage resources affected traditional clientelistic politicians but did not affect the new, emerging programmatic party brands. Furthermore, national parties, particularly the PT, used local governments to extend across the territory.

Similarly, a strong antimarket cleavage helped the Movement toward Socialism (MAS) in Bolivia to become a national party (Vergara 2011).[52] The party's antimarket discourse helped the party to win seats in Congress, and eventually the presidency. Furthermore, political decentralization efforts in the nineties made the party's growth across territory possible, facilitating victories at both the regional and local levels. Once in power, the MAS used distributive strategies to consolidate its control, reinforcing its programmatic appeal with the administrative resources gained through the control of national and local governments.

What practical lessons can we derive from this analysis? An obvious lesson for reformers interested in party-building is that they should pay more attention to the role of patronage resources in party aggregation, especially in decentralized polities where local actors enjoy greater autonomy than in the past. Today, transparency laws, anticorruption agendas, and better administrative controls limit parties' ability to control resources. Obviously, we are not suggesting that corruption or low transparency should be tolerated in order to build up parties. But other ways in which parties can access resources are worth exploring. For example, while it may not be enough to ensure successful party-building, public funding of political parties may reinforce party aggregation by providing parties additional resources to attract competitive candidates. In fact, Bruhn's chapter shows that increased party system institutionalization is associated with higher levels of public funding (Bruhn, Chapter 13, this volume).

---

[52] See also Madrid (Chapter 11, this volume).

Another lesson may be that some decentralizing reforms are less harmful for party aggregation than others. For example, extreme municipalization such as that adopted in the Andean region seems to have been especially harmful for party-building, particularly when those reforms dispersed resources without establishing a clear hierarchy among levels of government. In contrast, decentralization that creates incentives for coordination among levels of government may be less harmful for party-building. If regional authorities retain significant hierarchical control over local governments, they are more likely to maintain partisan linkages. If the regional governments created in Colombia had been given more power over municipalities, for example, perhaps party dispersion might have been less acute, and governors might have become new intermediate party leaders. This argument may also apply to Peru.

In conclusion, while partisan control of subnational patronage resources is hardly a necessary or sufficient condition for successful party-building, it clearly facilitates this challenging enterprise. At the very least, we hope to have shown that the relationship between patronage resources and party-building requires more attention than it has received.

8

Money for Nothing?

Public Financing and Party-Building in Latin America

Kathleen Bruhn

There are two things that are important in politics. The first is money, and I can't remember what the second one is.

– *Mark Hanna (1895)*

Since the early 1990s, many Latin American governments have invested an increasing amount of public money to subsidize political parties. Yet we have little sense of what they get for it. Do public subsidies strengthen parties' organizational capacity, legitimacy, and stability? Or do they merely fuel media-based campaigns that permit parties to bypass the tedious work of forging ties with civil society? The authors of this volume argue that successful new parties are most likely to emerge in contexts of intense polarization and conflict. Systems of public finance rarely exist in such contexts.

Yet more than half of the successful new parties discussed in Chapter 1, this volume,[1] emerged or survived in countries with strong public finance systems. This chapter will argue that public finance can play a key role in successful party-building. The fact that a given party has survived for five or more electoral cycles (part of this volume's definition of successful new parties) cannot automatically be attributed to the conditions of its formation alone: other factors – including the later adoption of public finance laws – may contribute to parties' survival. Public finance provides parties with predictable sources of funding that enhance the chances they will remain electorally competitive. "Successful" new parties are therefore more likely in these contexts.

---

[1] I exclude those in El Salvador, Nicaragua, and Panama, whose systems of party finance are not covered in this chapter.

Moreover, systems of public finance promote stronger organizational development by all parties, old and new. Typically, such systems require parties that receive funds to create a basic territorial and bureaucratic structure as a condition of funding, and they give them the financial means to do so. New parties in particular benefit from these incentives.

To develop this argument, the first section of the chapter presents data on correlations between the generosity of public financing in nine Latin American countries and changes in party system institutionalization, comparing Mainwaring and Scully's original 1995 rankings with updated 2010 rankings. In general, the greater the generosity of funding, the stronger the expected impact on party system institutionalization. This section is followed by a longitudinal case study of one of the book's successful new parties, Mexico's Party of the Democratic Revolution (PRD).

THEORIZING ABOUT THE IMPACT OF PUBLIC
FINANCING ON POLITICAL PARTY SYSTEMS

Latin American countries were the earliest innovators of public financing systems. Uruguay instituted limited reimbursement of campaign expenditures as early as 1928, followed by Costa Rica in 1956. Germany and other European countries did not follow suit until later. Nevertheless, theorizing about the effects of public financing of parties has reflected largely European concerns. The most well-known argument in this respect is the characterization of public party financing as contributing to a system of "cartel parties," in which existing parties collude to exclude new competitors by voting themselves ever increasing state subsidies (Katz and Mair 1995). Moreover, public financing undermines the need for parties to draw financial resources from supporters, and "has fostered the centralization of party structures and the professionalization of political activities, thus widening the gap between the apparatus and the grassroots" (Mendilow 1996: 331).[2]

Scholars of newer democracies, in contrast, argue that public funding of political parties can provide critical insurance against anarchic and unstable party systems (Booth and Robbins 2010; Casas Zamora 2005; Nassmacher 2009; van Biezen 2004; van Biezen and Kopecký 2007). Most European democracies introduced public finance when they had established party systems with strong mass parties. Third Wave

---

[2] See also Hopkin (2004: 640), Ignazi et al. (2010: 203), Mendilow (1996), Nassmacher (2009), van Biezen (2000: 336–337).

democracies rarely begin with even one such party. The "centralization of party structures and the professionalization of political activities" may be more helpful than harmful when the alternative is not strongly rooted parties accountable to mass members, but instead personalistic movements of convenience accountable to no one.

The most widely cited study of public financing in Latin America reaches few conclusions about its overall impact.[3] The comprehensive presentation of data on rules governing public financing is an invaluable contribution, but the sheer number of factors (and the limited number of cases) leaves us with more descriptive than theoretical accounts.

This chapter focuses primarily on the generosity of public subsidies as an independent variable, and on party system institutionalization as a dependent variable. It argues that public financing can contribute to successful party-building through two principal causal mechanisms. First, public finance increases the likelihood that new parties which reach the 10-percent threshold (this volume's threshold for "success") will continue to receive resources to campaign effectively and therefore survive electorally. And second, public financing gives all parties (including new parties) both the incentive and the means to invest in organization – the "building" part of party-building.

Public finance systems systematically reward electoral success with resources for future electoral campaigning in a way that private financing does not. Virtually all public finance systems base current subsidies on previous electoral results. In so doing, they reward larger parties and stabilize party systems: parties that did well in the last election get proportionately more resources than parties that did worse, and are therefore more likely to remain competitive. Private donors, in contrast, choose how to allocate their money without respect to how well the party did previously. Indeed, private donors, other things being equal, should be less likely to donate to a new party, due to uncertainty. With only one electoral result to go on, no one can reliably predict a new party's future performance. Under these circumstances, public financing is a crucial bet on the survival of a new party. Unlike private donors, the state is obligated to provide the new party with funds in proportion to its *past* performance,

---

[3] See Gutiérrez and Zovatto (2011). Aspects covered include electoral rules, whether candidates or parties receive the funds, whether funds go to all party activities or only campaigns, whether there are electoral thresholds to receive funding, and how easy it is to register new parties. For other sources, see Aguiar (1994), Austin and Tjernstrom (2003), Burnell and Ware (1998), Nassmacher (2009), Posada Carbó and Malamud (2005) and – on the post-communist systems – Roper and Ilcstens (2009).

as if certain that its future performance will match it. This gives a new party resources with which to campaign regardless of whether they get private money. Public financing thus tends to insulate political parties from dependence on private donors (del Castillo 2005; Roper 2008).

Private donors may, of course, bet on a new party if they are strongly motivated. Loxton (this volume) discusses one such example. In the case of the UDI, inherited business support gave it resources to outspend other parties at election time and maintain its clientelist networks. The parties discussed by Barndt (Chapter 13, this volume) are even more strongly linked to the personal ambition of the CEO: when the founder of Bolivia's Civil Solidarity Union (UCS) died, his less politically ambitious heirs sold off the company's interests and the party withered away. Private donors may also be motivated by sinister purposes, as in the case of illicit enterprises, such as drug cartels; in such cases, however, the donor relies on threats as well as rewards to secure cooperation and alternative sources of financing are often not enough to persuade targets to act contrary to the cartels' interests. Due to the hidden nature of this income, as well as the concomitant use of threats, it is nearly impossible to gauge the impact of black money, though we know it is pervasive in several Latin American cases, including Mexico.

Patronage is another important potential source of resources for party-building and maintenance. Muñoz and Dargent's chapter (Chapter 7, this volume) is particularly illuminating regarding the implications of cutting off the flow of patronage resources linking national and subnational politicians. They note, for instance, that "decentralization ... creates demand for local-level campaign funds that national parties often cannot meet. The consequent use of self-financed campaigns in turn reduces local politicians' dependence on national parties." Without patronage resources, national parties had little to offer local bosses. But subnational parties could not scale up based on subnational resources alone. A more generous system of public financing might have helped national parties in Colombia bridge the gap created by lost patronage funds. New parties in particular have to cross a much higher threshold to get access to patronage resources – actually winning executive office, often at multiple levels – than they do to win access to public finance. Public finance would therefore potentially help new parties more than patronage in most cases.

Finally, public finance has specific implications for organization. While all parties have an incentive to reach out to voters if they want to survive electorally, the means by which they do this may vary. One popular strategy is the mass media campaign: parties can hire professional marketing consultants to design modern advertising campaigns, purchase media time, and use polls and focus groups to make sure the messages work. Alternatively, parties can use public subsidies to buy (or attempt to buy) votes in clientelistic exchanges, offering voters a basket of food or a loan in exchange for electoral support. Finally, parties might invest in organization, hiring full-time staff to provide constituent service in order to secure loyalty to the party brand, building local party offices and expanding outreach to civil society organizations.

Mass media campaigns, however, have different implications for party-building than either clientelistic exchanges or investments in organization. As Van Dyck notes (Chapter 5, this volume), Argentina's Front for a Country in Solidarity (FREPASO) successfully used the mass media to become an overnight success in Argentina – but it did not invest in territorial organization and, as a result, quickly collapsed after suffering its first major electoral setback: "[The] rise of broadcast media has reduced elite incentives for party-building and either weakened or prevented the emergence of strong parties in many present-day polities."

It is thus significant that public financing gives parties an incentive as well as the means to invest in organization. Public finance laws typically require parties to meet a common set of standards to qualify for funding, often including the submission of formal statutes, lists of officers or members, addresses of offices and contact information, and the establishment of a territorial organization in a specified minimum of states and localities. Moreover, parties have to submit annual financial reports on their income and expenditures, which requires them to hire professional staff and accountants. Public finance systems also stabilize party incomes over time, giving parties the financial predictability and security to hire full-time staff. In short, parties with public finance are more likely to create complex and permanent party organizations independent of elections and candidates. Private finance does not create similar incentives to invest in organization; indeed, such investments may be seen as wasteful (see Barndt, Chapter 13, this volume).

These two causal mechanisms – stabilization through reporting and auditing requirements and stabilization through proportionality of income to previous electoral success – point toward a prerequisite for the adoption of public finance systems: the existence of two or more viable competitors. A hegemonic party in control of the state could, of course, vote itself a public subsidy, but such a law would make visible what it would most wish to hide: its unfair resource advantage over other parties. Moreover, parties that divert state resources to their political advantage or take money under the table from special interests do not make these sources of income public. Only when two or more competitors have a reasonable chance of winning will they establish a public finance law sharing resources or require each other to release an annual audit of their finances. When party competition collapsed in Venezuela during the late 1990s, one of the first casualties was public finance, eliminated in the 1999 constitution aimed at consolidating Chávez's power. Similarly, as Eaton's chapter (Chapter 14, this volume) makes clear, the elimination of public finance in Bolivia became part of a strategy to prevent the emergence of a united conservative opposition party.

To sum up, systems of public financing encourage organizational development and support the survival of larger parties, thus promoting predictability of the major players in the political system. In many ways, these characteristics should improve democratic governability. Voters get to know the parties over a longer period of time. Parties develop reputations, both with the voters and with each other, allowing them to engage in legislative coalition-building over time and to be held accountable from one election to the next. Yet none of these causal mechanisms suggests that public financing will force parties to develop affective ties with voters or to invest in representative linkages with civil society. Parties *may* do so, but they may also limit their contact with voters to election campaigns. As we shall see, this has critical implications for one significant aspect of party-building: loyalty.

MEASURING PUBLIC FINANCE AND PARTY SYSTEM INSTITUTIONALIZATION

My analysis of the nine largest Latin American democracies demonstrates a wide range in terms of levels of public financing and party system institutionalization. With respect to the independent variable, three countries currently have no public funding for parties: Venezuela, Bolivia, and Peru.[4] Chile remains largely privately financed, though with a limited system of campaign reimbursement since 2003. The remaining countries all introduced or significantly expanded public financing in the 1990s,[5] but

---

[4] Venezuela constitutionally prohibited public funding in 1999. Bolivia distributed public funding in two national elections (1997 and 2002), though it did not formally end the public finance system until 2008 (Romero Ballivián 2011). Peru, though it approved a law in 2003 providing public funding to parties, did not require funding; as of 2011, the law remained an unfunded mandate (Tuesta Soldevilla 2011: 454).

[5] Argentina introduced public financing in 1961 and revived its system after the democratic transition. Brazil introduced its current system in 1995. Bolivia had a system of public

TABLE 8.1 *Public financing for political parties in Latin America (presidential elections)*

	Total financing	Per party	Per registered voter	Election year
Mexico	$375,123,221	$46,890,403	$5.26	2006
Brazil	279,985,560	10,768,675	2.06	2010
Argentina	26,663,879	533,278	0.92	2011
Uruguay	16,068,444	4,017,111	6.27	2009
Colombia	13,286,974	2,214,496	0.45	2010
Bolivia	9,405,783	1,175,723	2.26	2002
Chile	6,383,010	1,595,753	0.77	2009
Average	$103,845,267	$8,399,430	$2.57	

differed in the generosity of subsidies (see Table 8.1).[6] While Argentina spends over $26 million on subsidies, it distributes this money among so many regional labels and alliances (fifty in the 2011 national elections and an astounding 247 in 2010) that it ends up spending very little per party. Mexico, in contrast, has been easily the biggest spender, at least through 2008.

With respect to the dependent variable, we have an approximate estimate of party system institutionalization prior to the expansion of public financing systems in the 1990s from Mainwaring and Scully's now classic (1995) work.[7] Four countries begin with high party system institutionalization, two with medium levels of institutionalization, and three with low levels of institutionalization. Table 8.2 describes each country in

financing between 1997 and 2008, though it was operational only in 1997 and 2002. Chile introduced a system of limited campaign reimbursement in 2003. Colombia introduced public finance in 1991. It substantially increased public funding in 2004, but also substantially raised the requirements for parties to get funded. Mexico had a very limited public finance system in 1977, which expanded dramatically in 1996. Peru created a public finance system in 2003 that has never been funded. Uruguay's public finance system is the oldest, dating to 1928, but funds doubled in 1994. Venezuela's public finance system lasted from 1973 to 1998. See Gutiérrez and Zovatto (2011: 551); see also www.tse.jus.br/transparencia/relatorio-cnj/fundo-partidario.

[6] Data about the size of public subsidies are surprisingly hard to get, especially for past elections. Estimates presented here reflect the most recent presidential election year for which data about public subsidies were available. I chose to use presidential election years because subsidies are highest for presidential election years, and because two countries – Chile and Uruguay – offer subsidies only in the form of reimbursement for campaign expenditures. Since countries did not hold elections in the same year, I translated all values in national currencies into US dollars of that election year, using the currency converter OANDA, at www.oanda.com/currency/converter/.

[7] Most of these rankings are based on data ending in 1993 at the latest.

TABLE 8.2 *Institutionalization and public subsidies*

	Level of public subsidies to parties	Initial institutionalization (Mainwaring and Scully 1995: 17)
Uruguay	High	High
Mexico	High	Medium
Brazil	High	Low
Colombia	Moderate	High
Argentina	Moderate	Medium
Bolivia	Moderate→none	Low
Chile	None→low	High
Venezuela	None (since 1999)	High
Peru	None	Low

terms of its initial level of party system institutionalization and classifies the countries – based on the data in Table 8.1 – as adopting a subsequent level of high, moderate, or low/no public spending on parties.

The pattern of variation is fortunate for testing our hypothesis. Of the three high-spending countries, one was highly institutionalized prior to 1995, one moderately institutionalized, and one weakly institutionalized (inchoate). Of the three countries that spent the least, two were highly institutionalized. If public finance helps, we should see improvement in Mexico and Brazil. Conversely, we should see deterioration in Chile and Venezuela. Although public financing for parties did not prevent the collapse of the Venezuelan party system in 1998, the lack of public finance after 1999 should make it harder for new parties to survive despite the presence of some of the other conditions – including authoritarianism, polarization, and conflict – hypothesized to favor new parties.

The next order of business is to evaluate party system institutionalization since the establishment of public financing. In this task, I depend on the template laid out by Mainwaring and Scully, who classified Latin American party systems according to four criteria.

1. Regularity in patterns of party competition (low/moderate electoral volatility)

I measure this criterion, as did Mainwaring and Scully, using Pedersen's index of electoral volatility: the shift in support for political parties from one election to the next, summing all of the gains and losses and dividing by two. I calculated average electoral volatility over the four most recent national legislative elections.

2. Party penetration of society

In order to measure "how deeply parties penetrate society," Mainwaring and Scully calculate the difference between presidential voting and legislative seats, assuming that, "where parties are key actors in shaping political preferences, this difference should be less pronounced" (Mainwaring and Scully 1995: 9). In my view, comparing presidential *votes* to legislative *seats* introduces an unnecessary element of error in that it includes the impact of different electoral formulas for translating votes into seats. My calculations therefore compare presidential voting to legislative voting as a more direct measure of voting consistency. I averaged this indicator over the three most recent national elections.[8]

3. Party system legitimacy

The third criterion emphasizes that "citizens and organized interests must perceive that parties and elections are the means of determining who governs, and that the electoral process and parties are accorded legitimacy" (Mainwaring and Scully 1995: 14). Using expert evaluations, they gave each party system a score ranging from 1 (low legitimacy) to 3 (high legitimacy), with medium-high being 2.5, medium being 2, and medium-low being 1.5. I refer to this hereafter as an MS score.

To measure party system legitimacy without expert evaluations, I used two regional surveys which have become available since 1995, the Latinobarometer and the Latin American Public Opinion Project (LAPOP). The question closest to the intent of this factor asks whether parties are necessary for the functioning of democracy.[9] However, since legitimacy requires confidence in political parties and in democracy as a

[8] I refer to national presidential and legislative elections that are held concurrently. Nonconcurrent elections are bound to produce larger average differences. Mainwaring and Scully also draw on expert evaluations of party ties to organized interests in classifying party systems' penetration of society. I do not attempt to replicate this measure. However, such ties have weakened everywhere in Latin America.

[9] In LAPOP, the question reads, "La democracia puede existir sin los partidos políticos. ¿Hasta qué punto está de acuerdo o en desacuerdo con esta frase?" ("Democracy may exist without political parties. To what extent do you agree or disagree with that statement?"). Answers range from "muy en desacuerdo" ("strong disagreement") (1) to "muy de acuerdo" ("strong agreement") (7) www.vanderbilt.edu/lapop/index.php. In

whole, I included questions about these aspects to construct an index.[10] I assigned an MS score based on responses to the questions in each survey and averaged them to create an overall legitimacy score for each party system.

4. Strong party organization

The final criterion looked for evidence of strong party organization, based on information about whether "political elites are loyal to their parties and party discipline in the legislature is reasonably solid. Parties are well organized, and ... have a presence at the local and national levels" (Mainwaring and Scully 1995: 16). Again, Mainwaring and Scully used expert evaluations and assigned an MS score. I based my updated estimates on multiple indicators along three separate dimensions. Multiple indicators give us a more reliable measure than any single indicator, but not all indicators give us information of equal weight or value, and therefore do not belong in a single index.[11] I averaged these three dimensions to produce an estimate of party organizational levels for each of the nine countries.

The first dimension is the average age of all parties that received at least 10 percent of the vote in the most recent legislative election. Mainwaring and Scully count party age as evidence of the ability of parties to penetrate society. I place it under the rubric of organizational stability; that is, older parties are more likely to have a bureaucratic organization (e.g., Huntington 1968; Michels 1962; Panebianco 1988).

Latinobarometer, the question reads, "Hay gente que dice que sin partidos políticos no puede haber democracia, mientras que hay otra gente que dice que la democracia puede funcionar sin partidos. ¿Cuál frase está más cerca de su manera de pensar?" ("There are people who say that there can be no democracy without political parties, while there are other people who say that democracy may work without parties. Which expression is closer to your way of thinking?") www.latinobarometro.org/latino/latinobarometro.jsp. I calculated mean scores from the raw data for each survey, assigned each survey an MS score (high to low institutionalization), and averaged the two MS scores.

[10] Specifically, I used a question about satisfaction with democracy, rather than the more traditional question about whether democracy is the best form of government. This question is more likely to reflect evaluations of the existing political system.

[11] For example, the dimension of party age gives us more information than a single question about how many parties have working websites and thus should not be placed in an additive index. Moreover, separating out organizational complexity from other dimensions substantiates the argument that requirements associated with public finance laws promote organization.

The second dimension looks at evidence of party organization obtained from party websites and statutes.[12] I collected information on four questions: (1) What percentage of parties in the country have working websites? (2) What percentage of parties have a national executive leadership divided according to functional roles (e.g., secretaries of organization, labor relations, etc.)? (3) How many functional organizations exist within the parties? (4) What percentage of parties have statutes that specify a maximum number of years between meetings of the parties' top authority (a Congress or an Assembly)?

Having a working website where party statutes and other information are available to average voters indicates an expectation of permanence; that is, communication with the public is not limited to elections. Organizational complexity in the form of differentiation of roles reflects specialization and professionalization of party functions beyond electoral performance. Finally, I argue that parties which limit the discretion of national leaders by requiring periodic meetings of the leadership have stronger party organizations.

The third dimension draws on assessments of party organizational strength by the legislators of each country's major parties, from the Observatorio de Élites Parlamentarias de América Latina,[13] based on several questions: (1) whether legislators believe that parties are necessary for democracy; (2) whether legislators think that the country's parties are generally active, inactive, or active only during elections; and (3) whether their *own* party is continuously active or active only during elections.[14]

---

[12] In cases where a party had no working website, I relied on several other websites that collect party statutes, including the Observatorio de Partidos Políticos de América Latina (http://americo.usal.es/oir/opal/documentos%20partidistas.htm), and the Inter-American Development Bank (www.iadb.org/research/geppal/page.cfm?artID=7360). The individual electoral authorities of some countries (especially Mexico and Brazil) also have good websites for this purpose.

[13] This invaluable collection of information is housed at the University of Salamanca under the direction of Miguel Alcántara Saez. Basic data can be accessed at http://americo.usal.es/oir/elites/, and more detailed data are available upon request from the project organizers.

[14] Question 1 asks: "Hay gente que dice que sin partidos no puede haber democracia. ¿Hasta qué punto: mucho, bastante, poco, o nada, está Ud. de acuerdo con esta afirmación?" ("There are people who say that there can be no democracy without political parties. To what extent do you agree with this statement – a lot, enough, little, or not at all?"). Question 2 asks: "¿Cómo calificaría Ud. la participación popular en la vida de los partidos de su país: escasa y marginal, escasa y marginal excepto en elecciones, o intensa y constante?" ("How would you rate political participation in the life of your country's parties: little and marginal, little and marginal except during elections, or intense and constant?"). Question 3 asks: "En su opinión, ¿La estructura de su partido es continua o

Table 8.3 compares Mainwaring and Scully's 1995 evaluations with my contemporary measures. For each column, I have converted the raw data into MS scores. It is immediately evident that the past two decades have been tough on Latin American party systems. Only Uruguay now ranks as highly institutionalized (i.e., with an aggregate score over ten), compared to four countries in 1995. However, as anticipated, Brazil and Mexico did improve, while Chile and Venezuela have deteriorated.

HOW PUBLIC FINANCE WORKS

Although there are too few cases for meaningful statistical analysis, there is a rough but unmistakable correspondence between countries with more generous systems of public financing and party systems that improved or at least held steady (see Figure 8.1). The best performers have been Brazil and Mexico, which are also the most generous in public financing per party. Brazil has risen out of the inchoate category to achieve moderate institutionalization, and Mexico has both improved its overall score and seen the institutionalization of a new and significant party on the left. Chile, Argentina, and Colombia, with less public financing, lost ground.

The poorest performers since 1995 had little or no public financing. The collapse of Venezuela's party system in 1998 occurred because its traditional political parties were completely discredited. Public financing, indeed, turned into a form of life support that contributed to popular perceptions that parties survived only as parasites of the state. Once Chávez took power and ended state funding he effectively starved out not only the traditional parties but also any new challengers to his authority

The case of Bolivia is more interesting. Bolivia's improved party institutionalization score depends in part upon a manufactured difference: in 1995, Bolivia received a relatively low score on party penetration of society based upon the difference between presidential vote and legislative seats. At the time, ironically, voters could not split their tickets (choose a different party for the legislature and the presidency). The difference resulted from the fact that votes were used to assign legislative seats according to different legislative formulas depending on the election, and different formulas resulted in varying degrees of over- or

meramente electoral?" ("In your opinion, is your own political party organization continuous or merely electoral?"). Because each country's legislature meets during a different period, the exact dates differ. For most questions, the most recent information came from roughly 2009. However, Question 3 on party activity seems not to have been asked after about the mid-2000s.

TABLE 8.3 *Party system institutionalization in Latin America*

	Volatility[1]	Consistency	Legitimacy	Organization	Overall 2012	Overall 1995	
Uruguay	2.5	3	2.9	2.6	11	11.5	↑
Chile	3	2	1.9	2.4	9.3	11.5	→
Mexico	2.5	2.5	1.4	2.4	8.8	8.5	←
Brazil	2.5	1.5	2	2.2	8.2	5	↑
Colombia	1.5	1	1.7	2.2	6.4	10.5	→
Bolivia	.5	2.5	1.5	1.5	6	5	←
Argentina	1	1	1.6	2.3	5.9	9	→
Venezuela	.5	1	2.3	1.7	5.5	10.5	→
Peru	.5	1	1.4	1.4	4.3	4.5	→
Average	1.6	1.9	1.9	2.2	7.6	8.3	→

[1] In special recognition of their outrageous levels of electoral volatility, I gave Bolivia, Peru, and Venezuela only .5 rather than the minimum of 1 in the original Mainwaring and Scully study.

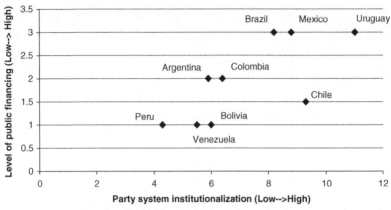

FIGURE 8.1 Public financing and party system institutionalization.

underrepresentation. Thus, consistency scores did not reflect party penetration of society at all, but rather, electoral system design. Ticket splitting remains next to impossible in the contemporary period, giving rise to
high consistency scores when comparing the presidential and legislative
vote. However, it is not unfair to place Bolivia among countries that have
parties with strong social roots: the Movement toward Socialism (MAS),
at least, fits this description.

Public finance systems do not prevent new parties from forming. In
2010, roughly 41 percent of the parties in the countries with generous
public finance and 44 percent of the parties in the countries with moderate
public finance had emerged since 1995. In countries with no public finance,
95 percent of the parties were new.[15] Public finance systems also do not give
existing parties eternal life. Around 23 percent of the parties in countries
with generous public finance and 33 percent of parties in countries with
moderate public finance systems disappeared between 1995 and 2010; in
countries with no public finance, 94 percent of parties disappeared.

From an actuarial standpoint, however, public finance systems do not
promote the survival of all parties equally. Rather, a party's level of financial support is tied proportionately to its previous level of electoral support. Any other approach – such as equal support to all parties – creates
perverse incentives for new party proliferation and fragmentation and
actually destabilizes the party system. According to one analysis, liberal
rules of access to public financing and few limits on the registration of
new parties led to the "virtual liquefaction suffered by the Colombian
political party system" (Casas and Zovatto 2011: 27).

---

[15] I count parties with at least 2 percent of the vote.

Likewise, private systems of financing do not reward parties in a systematic, rational way. The idea that private donors reward parties for past success assumes that donors expect those parties to persist. If parties are likely to disappear, or new parties are constantly emerging, donors may instead see better prospects to buy influence in a start-up – or, in fact, start up their own party, over which they have absolute control (see Barndt, Chapter 13, this volume).

In Latin America as a whole, the average age of parties with more than 10 percent of legislative seats declined from 58 years to 49 years over the last two decades, but in countries with strong public finance systems these parties tended to survive. The average age of parties in Brazil more than doubled, despite high levels of party birth and death (54 and 45 percent, respectively).

Is public finance related to greater party longevity, and if so, how? One possibility is that parties used public money to invest in strong ties to social organizations and civil society, holding membership drives, and building an activist base to give themselves an advantage over their electoral competitors. This is the classic image of "party-building": an institutionalized party system means that parties become strongly rooted in society, can express the desires and demands of social groups, can symbolically identify the people with the state, can allow people to trust and have confidence in the government, and stabilize democracy.

Except that most of the time, parties do not appear to have used public money to do any of these things, Brazil's Workers' Party (PT) being perhaps a significant exception (see Samuels and Zucco, Chapter 12, this volume). One of the most direct measures of social rootedness asks people whether they sympathize with any political party. In developed democracies, partisan identities are important predictors of vote choice and highly stable over time. In new democracies, questions about party identity often reflect only attitudes toward candidates in the most recent election.

Table 8.4 draws upon biennial surveys carried out by LAPOP. First, we look at whether respondents "sympathize" with any political party. To compensate for the possibility that a survey done in an election year might artificially raise party sympathizer rates for one country, we average responses over several waves of the survey.[15] We further test the stability

---

[15] Specifically, Table 8.4 draws upon surveys from 2008, 2010, and 2012. I use LAPOP rather than the alternative Latinobarometer questions because I prefer the scaling and wording of the LAPOP questions about party identification ("simpatiza," which is stronger identification, rather than "hay un partido hacia el cual se siente más cercano" in Latinobarometer).

TABLE 8.4 *Party identification in Latin America*

	Identifiers	Stability of ID (2008–2010)	Percentage that identify with (2010)	
Uruguay	56.7	93.4	71	FA
			19	Partido Nacional
Venezuela	37.9	98.5	61.7	PSUV (Hugo Chávez)
			16.3	Un Nuevo Tiempo (anti-Chávez)
Mexico	32.1	93.1	52.8	PRI
			28.7	PAN
Colombia	30.6	79.3	41.9	Partido de la U (Álvaro Uribe)
			18.9	Partido Liberal
Brazil	29	96.3	60.9	PT
			16.2	PMDB
Bolivia	25.5	88	77.8	MAS (Evo Morales)
			6.5	Partido Popular
Argentina	23.8	93.3	48.8	PJ
			17.2	UCR
Peru	18.9	91.1	24.3	APRA
			15.4	Partido Nacionalista (PNP)
Chile	15.6	95.6	31.3	Renovación Nacional
			25.4	Partido Socialista
Average	30	92.1		

of partisan identification by looking at the changes in the percentage of respondents who identify with a specific political party between two waves of the survey.

From Mexico on down, two-thirds of citizens in these countries claim no party loyalty; Venezuela performs just a hair better, and only in Uruguay does a majority identify with a party. By way of comparison, 63.3 percent of US citizens sympathized with a party in the 2012 wave of LAPOP. Public financing appears to have no impact on levels of partisan identification. Venezuela, with no public financing, has a slightly higher level of party identification than generous Mexico. Brazil, Argentina, and Bolivia – with high, moderate, and no public financing respectively – have similar levels of party identification.

Parties in countries with strong public finance systems do seem to be more likely to spend money on professional organizations. Public money comes with strings attached. In order to receive public finance, for example, Brazilian parties must provide the state with membership lists, party statutes, and regular reports on income and expenditures. Parties must spend 20 percent of their budget to support an institute for policy research and political education, and at least 5 percent of their budget to promote women's participation.[16] Samuels and Zucco (Chapter 12, this volume) report that "all of Brazil's main parties have a local-level organizational presence in at least 78% of the country's 5500+ municipalities." Even if many of these local organizations – particularly in the case of conservative parties – are established as provisional committees and have few civil society roots, the fact remains that the idea of Brazilian parties finding it necessary to invest in *any* kind of presence in local municipalities would surely have astonished most Brazilianists of the early 1990s, and seems principally due to the requirements of Brazil's electoral law. Parties like the PT that always wanted to invest in organizational expansion finally got the financial resources to do so from the reform law which tripled the amount of taxpayer money going into the party fund (Samuels and Zucco, Chapter 12, this volume), but other parties, either to compete with the PT or to comply with reporting requirements, expanded their territorial organizations as well. The resulting organizations did not have equal implications for electoral outcomes, but the public finance system does seem to have contributed to the expansion of partisan loyalties for the PT and encouraged organizational development in other Brazilian parties.

More generally, in terms of the four elements of organizational complexity (working websites, high-level functional leadership, specialization, and regularly scheduled leadership elections), the three countries with the highest levels of organizational development across all political parties are Mexico, Brazil, and Chile. In Brazil, party finance laws probably provided a strong push toward organizational development. In Mexico, one cannot attribute the Institutional Revolutionary Party's (PRI) organizational development to the public finance law. The National Action Party (PAN), likewise, was well organized prior to 1996, although the size and professionalization of its organization has expanded dramatically since it began to accept public finance. The PRD, however, as

---

[16] Summary from the 1995 Law of Political Parties, Articles 38–44, www.tse.jus.br/transparencia/relatorio-cnj/fundo-partidario.

discussed below, expanded its organizational infrastructure significantly as its public financing grew. In Chile, the organizational development of the main parties also predates any adoption of public finance. Curiously absent from this group is Uruguay, among the top countries in terms of public financing. However, Uruguay allocates financing in the form of reimbursement for campaign expenditures only, not for ordinary party expenses. The effect of public finance on party organization may therefore be limited.

Although often seen as negative, party bureaucracy has at least two potential benefits: a professional party organization can serve as a damper against takeover by reckless adventurers, and it can ease the transition from a founding party leader to subsequent generations. Bureaucracies, if nothing else, are slow to move and change direction. Procedures become routinized. Increasingly large staffs cannot be overseen by just one person, making room for the development of mid-level leaders.

Still, it is not clear that the primary contribution of public finance systems to party longevity goes through organizational development. After all, parties survive in democracies by winning elections, not by building bureaucratic organizations. Typically, parties spend most of their money on campaigns. Indeed, by tying funding levels to previous electoral performance, public finance systems stimulate the already powerful incentives for parties to focus on elections. Some public finance systems even limit funding to campaign spending reimbursement; the success of Uruguay with just such a system suggests that the resource advantages provided to larger parties explain at least some of the correlation between public finance and party system stabilization. Beginning with a highly institutionalized party system, Uruguay protected this system by ensuring that parties that win electoral support can compete effectively in elections. This method particularly helped the Broad Front (FA), which – as both a newer party and a left party – might otherwise have lacked the resources available to Uruguay's traditional parties, who could get support from private economic elites, the military, and elites embedded in the state.

When parties receive regular nondiscretionary stipends to support their electoral campaigns, overall electoral volatility may decline, stabilizing party systems. Clearly, electoral volatility may decline for other reasons. Brazil's remarkable reduction in electoral volatility, from an average of 40 percent prior to 1995, to an average of 13.9 percent in the four elections preceding 2012, surely owes much to the greatly improved record of economic performance registered by the governments of the Brazilian Social Democracy Party (PSDB) (1994–2002) and PT (2002 to 2016), who earned repeated reelection from Brazilian voters. Nevertheless, many other Brazilian parties also reduced their vote swing without occupying national executive office.

Public finance – if awarded to national parties – can also strengthen the links between national and local party offices, giving presidents stronger party organizations to work with in the legislature. National parties that have something to offer local organizations are in a better position to enforce legislative discipline. At the least, national parties with public finance have more influence over legislative campaigns, highlighting the party label. The difference between presidential and legislative votes tends to be lower in systems with strong public finance – 7.1 percent versus 27.6 percent in systems with no or low public finance. The difference between the presidential and legislative votes went down in Chile after it adopted a system of public finance (although the electoral system did not change), but went up over time in every other country with moderate or no public financing for parties.

However, to trace the full impact of public financing, we need to look at parties over time. For this reason, I now turn to the case of Mexico – the most generous public financing system – and specifically, to the case of a successful new party, the leftist PRD.

MEXICO AND THE PRD

The 1996 electoral reform dramatically changed Mexico's system of public financing, originally established to keep small parties afloat and provide credibility to the illusion of electoral competition. Public subsidies of parties totaled roughly twenty-seven million dollars in 1994 – a presidential election year – versus 200 million dollars in 1997, which was not. Over the next thirteen years, Mexico would spend roughly three billion dollars on parties. 72.5 percent of this money went to the three largest parties, which collectively garnered over 90 percent of the vote. 15.4 percent went to two smaller parties that survived from 1997 to 2010, and an additional 12 percent was spread out over a variety of parties with shorter life spans.[17]

---

[17] Of the thirteen parties founded after the 1996 electoral reform, eleven lasted for only one national election. Convergencia, founded in 1999, dissolved in 2011. The Partido Alianza Social, also founded in 1999 with the support of the powerful teachers' union, existed through the 2012 presidential election. For further information on funding of Mexican parties, see Lorenzo Córdova Vianello (2011) and www.ife.org.mx.

However, two of the three main parties had survived since the 1930s without public financing. The conservative PAN actually refused to take public money until the late 1980s; the ruling PRI, of course, was created by the state in 1929 and never needed any other source of funding besides state resources during seventy years of hegemonic rule. More interesting is the example of the PRD, founded in 1989 as the fusion of various popular movements and leftist parties, most notably the Mexican Socialist Party (PMS), whose party registration it took, as well as dissidents from the PRI led by Cuauhtémoc Cárdenas. Cárdenas, in a very real sense, was the PRD's *raison d'être*. In late 1987, frustrated by the neoliberal direction of the ruling party's economic policies and his own inability to influence the presidential succession, Cárdenas left the PRI and ran an independent campaign for president. When he nearly won, forcing the PRI into fraud on an unprecedented scale to salvage victory, he judged that the time was ripe to launch a new left party.[18]

The new party immediately ran into trouble. Most of its 1988 allies deserted, bought off by PRI promises of financial assistance or scared off by repression and intimidation. PRD electoral victories were stolen, its activists were threatened, arrested, or murdered, and it had few resources to conduct campaigns. Its national headquarters, formerly the property of the PMS, were located in a modest building near the bustling Metro Insurgentes station. It had one working bathroom on the main floor. Reception consisted of a long table and folding chairs. Municipal party committees, even in some cities, often met in members' homes. Campaigns were do-it-yourself affairs, using makeshift sound systems and borrowed pickups to hold grueling rounds of small-town rallies. Volunteer labor and donated materials to paint the candidate's name on local landmarks supplemented limited media time.

In this way, the PRD built a territorial organization, relying largely on preexisting networks of activists, as Van Dyck (Chapter 5, this volume) argues. The party became more strongly established in states where a bigger chunk of the PRI organization broke away to follow a top defector. The pattern continued through the first two decades of the PRD's existence: if the PRD recruited a high-profile PRI dissident to run as its gubernatorial candidate, he or she brought along not only a voting base but also an activist network that the party could use. Leftist parties contributed smaller networks because they had fewer activists.

---

[18] For a more complete account of the foundation of the PRD, see Bruhn (1997).

Yet the overall result of these activities often did not look very organized or very electorally effective. In Michoacán, for example, two of Cárdenas's lieutenants spent over a decade fighting each other for candidacies, for control of the state party, and for the governorship. They cheated in internal elections, worked at cross-purposes, and duplicated or undermined each other's efforts. Their supporters even came to blows. Their squabbling caused the party to lose many local elections.

More generally, lines of authority within the PRD were driven by personal rather than party loyalties. When in doubt, competing factions appealed to Cárdenas instead of elected party leaders for definitive decisions and many party committees remained empty shells. In general, many of the founders of the PRD saw themselves more as movement leaders than as party-builders (see also Mossige 2013). In contrast to the PAN, which required prospective members to be sponsored by a current member, to take classes in party doctrine, and to go through a period of apprenticeship before being admitted to full membership, the PRD imposed few if any requirements on recruits. Application for membership was simple and immediately qualified one to vote in party elections. The party did not collect dues, require attendance at meetings, or keep up-to-date membership lists.

The PRD's seeming aversion to rules reflected two factors. For one thing, unlike the Brazilian Worker's Party, where labor unions dominated, no single group held a majority. None of the numerous and shifting PRD factions could make or enforce party rules. Rules were to be changed or ignored according to the temporary balance of power. Second, any organizing the party did was driven primarily by elections. It would be nice to have an accurate membership list, or to expand the party organization into areas where it was weak, but now, this week, the party needed to submit a list of poll-watchers for all of the polling stations in the local elections in Guerrero, and find experienced people to train them, and order the ballots to select candidates for the local congressional elections in November's elections in Tabasco, or – even better – avoid them by negotiating some unity candidacies, and so on. Mexico's PRI during its authoritarian regime deliberately staggered the country's electoral calendar such that every year, every month, opposition parties had to spend their limited resources to prepare for (or protest) an election somewhere in Mexico. And so, broader organizational development took a back seat.

In the PRD's first years, activists clung to the hope that Cárdenas would win the 1994 presidential election and make party-building unnecessary, or at least easier, by supplying them with the vast patronage resources of the presidency. Polarization during these years and the fallout from the 1988 fraud helped establish a strong party brand for the PRD, as Van Dyck suggests (Chapter 5, this volume). The PRD was the resistance, the victim of the fraud, the party that would not sell out to Salinas or the neoliberals, the protesters in the streets.

Polarization also nearly destroyed the PRD electorally. In 1991, the party got just 7.9 percent of the vote, a tiny fraction of Cárdenas's official vote in 1988 and barely more than the historic vote of the independent left. With Cárdenas a candidate again in 1994, the PRD improved to 16 percent, but the PAN took over second place in national preferences and the PRI surged back to a comfortable 49 percent. Cárdenas's aura as the man of destiny was gone.

In the absence of any further changes to the electoral system, the PRD might have managed to get above 10 percent of the vote in 1997, even though it failed in 1991. Mexico experienced an economic crisis in 1995 and 1996 which turned voters away from the PRI. Yet the PRD also benefited in 1997 from two electoral reforms that had nothing to do with the difficult conditions of the PRD's emergence or its grassroots networks: first, the PRI allowed elections to determine the mayor of Mexico City, which meant that Cárdenas could be a candidate again, giving the PRD's legislative candidates his long coattails. When Cárdenas won control of Mexico City (which the PRD has held ever since), he gained some ability to hold the party's factions together by virtue of the patronage resources he then controlled. Second, the expansion of public finance in 1996 opened up a new path to electoral consolidation for the PRD.

In 1994, the PRD received $3,123,446 to fund its presidential and legislative campaigns. In 1997, it got $37,009,432 for congressional campaigns alone. Just as critically, the party that initially saw itself more as a movement than a party began to become professionalized. Today, the PRD has specialized offices devoted to electoral analysis, polling, and tracking data on turnout and registration. Between 1998 and 2010, "ordinary permanent" expenditures, which cover salaries and benefits for employees as well as buildings and utilities, accounted for 78.4 percent of all PRD expenditures.[19] The party has a new national headquarters, in a better neighborhood, with multiple elevators, bathrooms, and media-equipped

---

[19] Spending for state and local campaigns does not fall under the responsibility of the national party. From 1998 to 2008, parties received twice as much money during national election years for campaign spending only. Thus, spending on campaigns amounted to half of all funds received during national election years (2000, 2003, 2006).

rooms for press conferences.[20] As Mexican public finance law requires, the PRD established a research institute and a publication house that produces a newspaper, videos, and content for its website. Paid staff expands enormously during campaign season, but a sizable permanent staff maintains party activity in the intervals between national elections. A parallel system of public finance at the state level helps state parties do the same. As of 2010, the PRD spent nearly 40 percent of its income on salaries, compared to 39 percent for the PAN, 30 percent for the PRI, and an average of 12.9 percent for the smaller parties. These resources enable the PRD to compete with the PAN and PRI in national campaigns on a more even footing, to maintain a robust organizational presence in between campaigns, and to produce policy research, enhancing not only its chances of survival but also its contribution to Mexican democracy.

Moreover, public financing proved significant in keeping the always fractious PRD from bolting the political system even when internal conflicts challenged the willingness of key party factions to abide by the rules of the democratic game. When the PRD's populist leader Andrés Manuel López Obrador led protests in response to his narrow defeat in the 2006 presidential election, told PRD congressmen not to take their seats in the legislature, and threatened to deny Calderón the ability to govern, the paid leaders of the PRD continued to work, took the party into the legislature, selected candidates for upcoming local and state elections, and quietly cashed their checks from the state. When López Obrador left the PRD after losing the 2012 presidential election, he did not mount an external challenge to the state, but instead announced his intention to form a new political party using the registration of an existing party. Meanwhile, the publicly financed PRD agreed to cooperate with the PRI and the PAN to enact economic reforms, select candidates for upcoming elections, and cash its public funding checks.

In contrast to Brazil's PT, however, the PRD did not successfully turn public financing into an expanded grassroots organization or growing partisan loyalties; in fact, public financing helped distance the party base from an increasingly bureaucratized party elite, which no longer depended on an active membership base to supply financial contributions or to volunteer labor as a replacement for media access. Mexican law limits private donations to parties, including in-kind donations, to

---

[20] The PAN, too, upgraded from its original modest national headquarters to a large new headquarters in a more centrally located neighborhood. Vicente Fox celebrated his election as president from this new headquarters in 2000.

no more than 10 percent of party income. As a result, parties have little incentive to cultivate connections to supporters.

This loosening resource dependence (as well as Mexico's traditional rules against reelection, in effect until the 2018 elections) may contribute to the representation gap between party leaders and party sympathizers. As Bruhn and Greene (2007) show, legislative candidates are not only distinctly more extreme than the average sympathizer *of their own party*, they seem unaware of the difference, and are confident that they could persuade voters to their own view even in the case of normally strongly held views such as attitudes toward abortion. This is a picture of candidates who are in the habit of consulting party leaders, not voters.

Moreover, the PRD's original reliance on a volunteer activist base has been increasingly supplemented by paid vote mobilizers, starting with the "Sun Brigades" in 1997, who went house to house to recruit and turn out potential PRD voters in Mexico City. Although the PRD has continued to rely on a campaign strategy organized around plaza rallies more than either the PAN or PRI, it has not focused on setting up new permanent party offices, like the PT, but rather mobilized only during electoral campaigns, limiting the impact of mobilization efforts on the development of long-term party loyalties. Indeed, since many of these campaigns led to subsequent protests that alienated some middle-class voters, one can even track a decline in PRD partisanship over time. As of 2012, the PRD had fewer partisans than either the PRI or the PAN.

CONCLUSIONS

Public financing can help parties develop organizationally. It can stabilize party systems by rewarding larger parties and bribing more extreme parties to remain in the institutional game. But the Beatles were right: money cannot buy you love. In fact, even in relatively stable party systems, there is not much love to spare. As Table 8.4 demonstrates, among party identifiers, one party typically dominates. The leading party in Latin America has on average 34 percent more identifiers than the second place party. In Uruguay and Brazil – two of the more institutionalized party systems – the gap is 52 percent and 45 percent respectively.

The leading parties have historical socialization in their favor (PRI, Argentina's Peronist Party [PJ]), union or social movement ties (PT, PRI, PJ, Bolivia's MAS), or charismatic leadership (the United Socialist Party of Venezuela [PSUV], MAS, PT, Colombia's Party of the U). But all have a mobilizational past or present. Money can make a party brand visible during the campaign season, but political ads are apparently about as memorable and persuasive as toothpaste or catfood commercials. They do not lead voters to identify with the product.

The contrast between this chapter's findings and the overall argument of the editors of this book raises a rather striking paradox. Scholars have long imagined that the four dimensions of party system institutionalization laid out by Mainwaring and Scully go together – that is, parties with strong social roots result in lower electoral volatility, higher system legitimacy, and more strongly organized political parties. But this constellation of "system goods" may be, at the very least, temporally inaccurate (see also Luna and Altman 2011). If, in fact, the development of social roots requires a period of polarization and conflict, mobilization and instability, the stabilization of voting patterns through public finance may come at the cost of developing social roots and even popular legitimacy. The potential benefit is that if parties last longer, voters can develop an understanding of their policy positions. They can more easily locate them with respect to their own preferences, and choices may become more connected to policies. Even if voters feel indifferent toward parties, clarity of electoral choice can enhance the representative quality of elections. The risk is that voters may fail to see themselves reflected in any of the choices offered to them and run off with the first populist candidate to win their hearts.

Indeed, electoral reforms in Mexico allowing candidates to run as independents for the first time produced a shocking rejection of the traditional parties in the 2015 midterm elections. Most spectacularly, in the key border state of Nuevo León, independent candidate Jaime "El Bronco" Rodriguez whipped his PRI rival by more than two to one, with a campaign focused largely on the themes of corruption and drug violence. Nevertheless – and far more quietly – the new Mexican congress took office with only two unaffiliated legislators seated. The three major parties – PRI, PAN, and PRD – together controlled just over 85 percent of the seats in the lower house of the congress, and an additional 5.4 percent of seats went to a party (Mexico's Ecological Green Party [PVEM]) that had run in close coalition with the PRI. Despite significant voter discontent, and the opening up of the ballot to independents, the new congress would remain in the hands of the traditional parties (at least, for now). Yet despite the inertia embedded in Mexico's electoral and political system, one cannot help but suspect that somewhere out there lurking is Mexico's Chávez, its Morales, its Correa, waiting to be revealed in a future presidential election. And when that happens, the first thing to go will be public finance for parties.

PART III

ORGANIZATIONAL INHERITANCE: ALTERNATIVE PLATFORMS FOR PARTY-BUILDING

9

Authoritarian Successor Parties and the New Right in Latin America

James Loxton

On September 11, 1990, a delegation of party leaders from the Independent Democratic Union (UDI) presented General Augusto Pinochet, the Chilean army commander-in-chief and former dictator, with a letter of gratitude.[1] The letter had been signed by 20,000 UDI supporters, and thanked him and other former members of the military junta for their "liberating military action" seventeen years earlier against the government of Salvador Allende. The UDI expressed its conviction that Pinochet would go down in history as one of Chile's "great patriots," and that the coup would be remembered forever as one of the military's "most unequalled glories." This letter, which was accompanied by public celebrations, was provocative. During the period of military rule (1973–1990) that the UDI was celebrating, approximately 3,000 people had been killed or "disappeared," and tens of thousands more had been tortured or exiled. With the transition to democracy having occurred just six months earlier, the memories of this period were still raw. Moreover, the date chosen could not have been more symbolic: it was on the same day in 1973 that the military had carried out its coup.

In the context of democracy, one might predict that a party with such obvious links to a former dictatorship, or what I call an *authoritarian successor party* (Loxton 2015), would not have much of a political future. In contemporary Latin America, however, such a prediction would be wrong. The UDI not only went on to cross this volume's threshold for party-building by winning 10 percent or more in five consecutive

---

[1] "General (R) Gustavo Leigh Guzmán: 'El Pronunciamiento Militar Fue Inevitable y Bien Hecho,'" *El Mercurio*, September 11, 1990; "General Pinochet Dijo que en Situación Similar al Año 73 Actuaría de la Misma Forma," *El Mercurio*, September 12, 1990.

legislative elections, but by 2001, it had become the single most-voted-
for party in Chile – a status that it has held in all subsequent legislative
elections. The UDI was not unique. In fact, six of the eleven cases of successful party-building in Latin America since 1978 (see Levitsky, Loxton,
and Van Dyck, Chapter 1, this volume) were authoritarian successor
parties: the UDI and National Renewal (RN) in Chile; the Nationalist
Republican Alliance (ARENA) in El Salvador; the Liberal Front Party
(PFL) in Brazil; the Democratic Revolutionary Party (PRD) in Panama;
and the Sandinista National Liberation Front (FSLN) in Nicaragua.
Authoritarian successor parties were not an exclusively right-of-center
phenomenon. The FSLN grew out of a leftist revolutionary regime, and
the PRD emerged from the military "populist" regime of General Omar
Torrijos. The UDI, RN, ARENA, and PFL, however, were all conservative parties. These four parties, in turn, were the only cases of successful
party-building among what has been called Latin America's "new right."[2]
In short, most (but not all) successful new authoritarian successor parties were conservative parties, and *all* successful new conservative parties
were authoritarian successor parties.

What explains the surprising success of so many authoritarian successor parties, and their disproportionate success among new conservative parties in particular? In this chapter, I argue that much of the
reason was owing to what I call *authoritarian inheritance*.[3] While roots
in dictatorship are likely to make such parties unattractive in the eyes
of many voters, they may also endow parties with a number of valuable resources that can help them to flourish under democracy. These
resources may include the three core determinants of party-building identified in Chapter 1: (1) a party brand, (2) territorial organization, and (3)
a source of cohesion. Two other common forms of authoritarian inheritance are (4) clientelistic networks and (5) a source of party finance.
While these resources would be useful for any new party, I argue that
they are especially useful for conservative parties, helping them to overcome the central challenge of conservative party-building: the construction of a multiclass electoral coalition. In the following pages, I present a
theory of authoritarian inheritance and illustrate it through an examination of the two most dramatic instances of conservative party-building
in Latin America since the onset of the third wave: the UDI in Chile and
ARENA in El Salvador. I show that each party emerged from its country's

---

[2] See, for example, Durand (1997) and Gibson (1992).
[3] For earlier versions of this argument, see Loxton (2014a, 2014b).

previous military dictatorship, and argue that this authoritarian geneal-ogy, rather than serving as an impediment to a strong performance under democracy, was the key to its success.

CHALLENGES OF CONSERVATIVE PARTY-BUILDING

With the onset of the third wave in the late 1970s, it seemed possible that a new era of conservative party strength was dawning in Latin America. Historically, conservative parties had been weak in much of the region, which scholars identified as a key source of democratic instability (Di Tella 1971–1972; Gibson 1996). Lacking strong parties to represent it at the ballot box, the right frequently knocked on the barracks door instead. The low point came in the 1960s and 1970s, when "most of the groups included under the Right were clearly antidemocratic" (Chalmers et al. 1992: 4). The third wave, however, altered this dynamic by bring-ing intense international pressure to abide by democratic norms.[4] With the coup option no longer viable, rightist actors in several countries responded by forming new conservative parties. Many observers began to speak of a "new right" in Latin America – one that was less beholden to land-owning elites, less institutionally tied to the Catholic Church, more interested in reaching out to the popular sectors, and above all, more committed to the tenets of neoliberalism.[5]

Yet these new parties faced severe challenges – some generic to party-building as such, others specific to conservative party-building in particular. As Chapter 1 argues, party-building entails three main challenges: development of a party brand, construction of a territorial organization, and avoidance of debilitating schisms. Conservative par-ties, like all parties, must grapple with these challenges. However, they face an additional challenge peculiar to their condition as conservative parties: the construction of a multiclass electoral coalition. Following Gibson's (1996: 7) influential formulation, conservative parties can be defined as "parties that draw their core constituencies from the upper strata of society."[6] The concept of core constituencies is central to this

---

[4] See Huntington (1991) and Mainwaring and Pérez-Liñán (2005).

[5] See Durand (1997) and Gibson (1992).

[6] In this chapter, I use the terms "conservative parties" and "parties of the right" inter-changeably. Not all scholars accept Gibson's (1996) sociological definition of conserva-tive parties, preferring to use an ideological definition instead. Luna and Rovira (2014: 4), for example, define the right as "a political position distinguished by the belief that the main inequalities between people are natural and outside the purview of the state." There

definition: "A party's core constituencies are those sectors of society that are most important to its political agenda and resources. Their importance lies not necessarily in the number of votes they represent, but in their *influence* on the party's agenda and capacities for political action" (Gibson 1996: 7).[7] To be sure, all parties must build coalitions in order to win elections, including parties of the left (Przeworski 1985). For conservative parties, however, the challenge is acute, given the small size of their core constituencies. Economic elites, by definition, represent a miniscule percentage of a country's population. In order to be successful, then, conservative parties must go well beyond their elite core constituencies and attract the vast majority of their votes from other sectors of society. As a result, "[t]he study of conservative party politics is ... the study of the construction of polyclassist coalitions" (Gibson 1996: 8).

In order to construct a multiclass electoral coalition, conservative parties must pursue a peculiar logic of electoral mobilization. While it is to the advantage of leftist parties to emphasize class cleavages and advocate economic redistribution, conservative parties must downplay the importance of class and appeal to voters on other grounds. One strategy is *clientelism*, in which individuals receive direct material benefits in exchange for their votes.[8] Instead of dividing society on the basis of class, clientelism divides voters into "ins" and "outs," with the former receiving payouts in exchange for their support. A second strategy is to emphasize *crosscutting identities* such as religion, region, or nation. As Gibson (1992: 20) explains: "Catholics, Bavarians, Correntinos, southerners, and the nation are some of the collective identities counterposed by conservative movements to the class-based appeals of the Left." Instead of dividing society along class lines, then, this strategy divides it according to identities that cut across class, such as Christians and non-Christians. Finally,

---

is a strong elective affinity between these definitions: a party that draws its core constituency from the upper strata of society is likely to oppose large-scale redistribution, and a party that opposes large-scale redistribution is likely to be especially attractive to the upper strata of society. The two main parties examined in this chapter – the UDI in Chile and ARENA in El Salvador – meet both the sociological and ideological definitions, as do the failed cases mentioned below, including the Union of the Democratic Center (UCEDE) in Argentina, the Liberty Movement in Peru, and the National Advancement Party (PAN) in Guatemala. In cases of parties where the sociological and ideological definitions do not align – such as *Fujimorismo* in Peru – I make a note of this.

[7] In the case of conservative parties, potential core constituencies include "the owners and managers of major business firms, large landowners, and finance capitalists," as well as the "descendants of aristocratic or socially prominent families, rentier groups, and high-income members of the liberal professions" (Gibson 1996: 12).

[8] On clientelism as a strategy for linking parties and voters, see Kitschelt (2000).

conservative parties can emphasize *valence issues*, or issues about which virtually all voters agree, such as corruption, economic growth, public security, and national defense.[9] Valence issues cast an even wider net than crosscutting identities like religion or region, potentially encompassing the whole of society. Because voters already agree on the importance of these issues, winning votes through this strategy is not a matter of staking out a distinct position along a spectrum of policy alternatives, but rather about making the case – credibly – that one's party is the most effective vehicle for delivering the policy good in question.

The combination of the generic challenges of party-building, and the specific challenge of constructing a multiclass coalition, means that new conservative parties face an uphill battle. If a party wishes to develop a brand based on valence issues,[10] for example, it must make the case to the electorate that it is uniquely capable of providing these goods. But if its leaders have never held power, it is unlikely to appear credible when making such promises. Similarly, if a party wishes to win support through clientelism, this requires a robust territorial organization, or what Hale (2006) calls "administrative capital."[11] As parties with elite core constituencies, however, conservative parties usually do not have access to the kinds of mass-based mobilizing structures often used by leftist parties, such as labor unions and social movements (Van Dyck, Chapter 5, and Madrid, Chapter 11, this volume).[12] While it might seem that they would at least have ready access to material resources, conservative parties in Latin America have traditionally had a hard time winning the support of business (Gibson 1996: 216–220; Schneider 2010). In the face of these challenges, some party leaders will feel tempted to abandon the party in its early years in favor of other options, resulting in devastating party schisms. Since the third wave, the temptation to defect has become particularly acute, given new opportunities to reach voters directly via the mass media (Mainwaring and Zoco 2007; Van Dyck, Chapter 5, this volume), the adoption of neoliberalism by some nonconservative parties (Stokes 2001; Roberts, Chapter 2, and Lupu, Chapter 3, this volume),

---

[9] On the difference between "valence issues" and "position issues," see Stokes (1963).

[10] For Lupu (2014; Chapter 3, this volume), in order to have a strong brand, a party must stake out a distinct and consistent position on some continuum, such as the left–right spectrum. Thus, party brands for Lupu are defined in terms of what Stokes (1963) calls "position issues." I use the concept of party brand more loosely, allowing for the possible existence of brands based on different kinds of reputation, including valence issues.

[11] See also Kitschelt (2000) and Levitsky (2003).

[12] For important exceptions, see Kalyvas (1996) and Ziblatt (forthcoming).

and the proliferation of various forms of "party substitute" (Hale 2006; Levitsky and Zavaleta, Chapter 15, this volume).

Given the challenges of conservative party-building, it is perhaps no wonder that scholars went from predicting a new era of conservative party strength in the 1980s and 1990s to highlighting a "conservative party deficit" in the 2000s (Roberts 2006). Argentina has seen no less than three failed attempts at conservative party-building in the two decades since its 1983 transition to democracy: the Union of the Democratic Center (UCEDE), Action for the Republic, and Recreate for Growth. The UCEDE, in particular, was met with great fanfare, with many believing that it would become Argentina's "long-sought democratic mass conservative party" (Gibson 1990: 180). The party had virtually no presence outside of Buenos Aires, however, and was racked by constant infighting. When Peronist Carlos Menem made a sharp turn to the right after being elected president in 1989, UCEDE leaders and supporters abandoned the party *en masse* in favor of the new president. Peru's Liberty Movement, which was created by novelist Mario Vargas Llosa in 1987 and inspired excitement similar to that of the UCEDE, suffered a similar fate. Though the party performed well in the 1990 general election, it collapsed after newly elected President Alberto Fujimori veered to the right and implemented much of its economic program.[13] Even the National Advancement Party (PAN) in Guatemala, which performed strongly in the 1990s and nearly crossed this volume's threshold for party-building, collapsed in the wake of devastating internal schisms in the early 2000s.

Not all new conservative parties failed, however. Indeed, four of the eleven cases of successful party-building in Latin America identified in Chapter 1 are conservative parties: the UDI and RN in Chile; ARENA in El Salvador; and the PFL in Brazil. These four parties, in turn, shared a startling similarity: all of them had deep roots in dictatorship.

A THEORY OF AUTHORITARIAN INHERITANCE

Although it might seem that roots in dictatorship would be a liability for a party in the context of democracy, I argue that such roots can in fact be the key to successful party-building. In order to understand why this is the case, it is first necessary to define authoritarian successor parties. Authoritarian successor parties are *parties that emerge from authoritarian*

---

[13] For an account of Menem and Fujimori's implementation of "neoliberalism by surprise," see Stokes (2001).

regimes, but that operate after a transition to democracy (Loxton 2015). There are two parts to this definition. First, these are parties that operate *after* a transition to democracy. This means that ruling parties of existing authoritarian regimes are excluded, even if the regime in question holds somewhat competitive elections, as in the case of "competitive authoritarian" (Levitsky and Way 2010) or "electoral authoritarian" (Schedler 2006) regimes. To be sure, many authoritarian successor parties begin their lives as authoritarian ruling parties. After democratization, however, they become – if they survive – authoritarian successor parties. To illustrate, we can say the Institutional Revolutionary Party (PRI) in Mexico was an authoritarian *ruling* party until the country's transition to democracy in 2000; thereafter, it became an authoritarian *successor* party. An important implication of this part of the definition is that in order to win votes, party leaders cannot rely on the "menu of manipulation" (Schedler 2002) used by electoral authoritarian regimes, such as coercion, fraud, or the massive abuse of state resources. Authoritarian successor parties can, and often do, enjoy success under democracy. To be considered authoritarian successor parties, though, they must broadly abide by the democratic rules of the game.

Second, authoritarian successor parties emerge from authoritarian regimes. This can happen in one of two ways, corresponding to two distinct subtypes of authoritarian successor party. The first are *former authoritarian ruling parties*. Many authoritarian regimes in the twentieth century – both civilian and military – used "official" parties as instruments of rule.[14] In some regimes, this involved a formal one-party arrangement, in which all parties but the ruling party were legally proscribed; in others, it occurred through a hegemonic-party system, in which opposition parties theoretically could contest for power but in which competition was severely constrained.[15] Following transitions to democracy, such parties often continued to exist (though they sometimes changed their names), thus becoming authoritarian successor parties. Examples in Latin America include Brazil's Democratic Social Party (PDS), Mexico's PRI, Nicaragua's FSLN, and Panama's PRD.

The second subtype are what I call *reactive authoritarian successor parties*. As the name suggests, these are parties created in *reaction* to a transition to democracy, either by high-level authoritarian incumbents

---

[14] There is a large literature on this subject. For a useful review, see Levitsky and Way (2012).

[15] On the distinction between "hegemonic" and "one-party" arrangements, see Sartori (1976).

in anticipation of an imminent transition, or by former incumbents shortly after a transition. By high-level incumbents, I mean figures such as heads of state, ministers, and key members of the security apparatus.[16] While authoritarian successor parties of this type have received less scholarly attention than former authoritarian ruling parties, they are a widespread phenomenon. As discussed in the case studies below, both the UDI and ARENA were reactive authoritarian successor parties. The UDI was formed in 1983 by high-level incumbents of the Pinochet regime – most notably, Jaime Guzmán, a prominent political advisor and architect of the regime's 1980 constitution – in reaction to an economic and political crisis that they feared would result in democratization. ARENA was founded in 1981 by Major Roberto D'Aubuisson, the former deputy director of intelligence under military rule and notorious "death squad" leader during the 1980s, in reaction to a palace coup in 1979 that eventually set in motion a transition to democracy. Other examples of reactive authoritarian successor parties in Latin America include Bolivia's Nationalist Democratic Action (ADN) and the Guatemalan Republican Front (FRG), which were founded (and continued to be led under democracy) by former military dictators Hugo Banzer and Efraín Ríos Montt, respectively.

It should be noted that authoritarian successor parties are not exclusive to Latin America. They are a worldwide phenomenon, playing prominent roles in democracies in Africa, Asia, Europe, and the Americas (Loxton 2015). Nor are they found exclusively on the right. While the categories of authoritarian successor party and conservative party sometimes overlap *empirically*, as in the cases of the UDI and ARENA, they are *analytically* distinct. Thus, some authoritarian successor parties are left-of-center (e.g., Nicaragua's FSLN, Panama's PRD), and others have no clear-cut ideological profile (e.g., Mexico's PRI, Guatemala's FRG). This means that while I focus here on authoritarian successor parties of the right in Latin America, the findings of the chapter have broader implications.

---

[16] In dictatorships that survive for long periods, much of the population is often implicated in the regime in some way. In order to prevent the concept from being stretched to an excessive degree, the definition excludes parties founded by individuals who held low-level positions in the old regime. In Guatemala, for example, the PAN was founded in 1985 by Álvaro Arzú, who had served under military rule as the director of the state tourism institute. However, because this position in no way made him a significant figure in the military regime, the PAN would not be considered an authoritarian successor party.

What explains the prevalence of authoritarian successor parties, and their success among new conservative parties in Latin America in particular? Much of the reason, I argue, is authoritarian inheritance. New parties are not all created equal. Instead, they vary dramatically in terms of what Hale (2004: 996) calls their "starting political capital," or "the stock of assets they possess that might be translated into electoral success." Some parties are born with large endowments of starting political capital; others are born with little and thus must start virtually from scratch. The idea that the inheritance of preexisting resources is a crucial determinant of party-building is one of the most robust findings in the parties literature. In his seminal study of Christian Democratic parties in Europe, for example, Kalyvas (1996) highlights the role played by Catholic associations. Similarly, in her work on opposition parties in Sub-Saharan Africa, LeBas (2011) argues that one of the main determinants of success was the presence of "mobilizing structures," particularly corporatist labor unions. In all of these cases, parties that inherited large stocks of starting political capital were better equipped to succeed than those born with less.

The idea that parties born with greater stocks of starting political capital would have a better chance of success than parties born with less is not particularly surprising. What is perhaps more surprising is that this could be inherited from authoritarian regimes. I call this type of starting political capital *authoritarian inheritance*. The argument is straightforward: just as Christian Democratic and socialist parties may inherit valuable resources from Catholic associations and labor unions, respectively, so too may authoritarian successor parties inherit valuable resources from authoritarian regimes. While such inheritance is potentially valuable for all new parties, it is particularly valuable for conservative parties, since it can help in the construction of a multiclass electoral coalition. As discussed above, conservative parties have several options for building such a coalition, including clientelism, crosscutting identities, and valence issues. Many new conservative parties collapse, however, before these strategies can be implemented because their leaders and supporters abandon the party while it is still in its embryonic phase – often in favor of party substitutes. Authoritarian successor parties may be spared this fate. They may simply inherit the resources necessary to carry out these strategies, and thus hit the ground running. Potential forms of authoritarian inheritance include the three determinants of party-building identified in Chapter 1: (1) a party brand, (2) territorial organization, and (3) a source of cohesion. In addition, parties may inherit (4) clientelistic networks and (5) a source of party finance.

Party Brand. The first resource that authoritarian successor parties may inherit from dictatorships is a brand. The idea that a brand derived from a dictatorship could be popular is counterintuitive. Many authoritarian regimes in Latin America in the 1960s and 1970s were highly repressive. They imprisoned, tortured, and killed thousands of their own citizens, and were widely denounced as human rights violators. Nevertheless, it is undeniable that some dictatorships enjoy considerable popular support. In Chile, for example, when citizens were given the opportunity in 1988 to vote on whether to extend Pinochet's rule, 44 percent voted in favor. One possible reason is clientelism, as authoritarian regimes try to buy popular support through materialistic payouts. Another is performance: if authoritarian regimes provide goods that people value, such as economic growth or political stability, they may win the support of much of the population despite their repressive activities.[17] These factors are likely to be especially prized by the population if the authoritarian regime is preceded or followed by (or both) a period of political and economic chaos. Dictatorships that provide these valued goods may end up developing a brand that many find attractive. If authoritarian successor parties succeed in transferring these brands to themselves, they inherit a valuable resource. This form of authoritarian inheritance is particularly valuable for conservative parties, since they often campaign on the basis of valence issues. If a party's leaders have a history in government – even if this occurred under authoritarianism – and actually managed to provide these valued goods while in office, the party is more likely to be seen as credible than a party without such experience.

Territorial Organization. The second resource that authoritarian successor parties may inherit is a territorial organization. Parties that are able to build upon preexisting mobilizing structures have an advantage over parties that must build from scratch.[18] The reason is straightforward: "Organization building does not come naturally or automatically to political actors. It is a difficult, time-consuming, costly, and often risky enterprise" (Kalyvas 1996: 41). Authoritarian regimes are one potential

---

[17] This argument is similar to Grzymala-Busse's (2002: 5) concept of a "usable past" in her seminal study of ex-communist parties in East Central Europe, which she defines as "the historical record of party accomplishments to which the elites can point, and the public perceptions of this record." Of course, not all authoritarian regimes perform well in office. Some are disastrous, such as the military regime in Argentina from 1976 to 1983 – which, not surprisingly, did not give rise to a viable authoritarian successor party at the national level.

[18] See Kalyvas (1996), LeBas (2011), and Van Dyck, Chapter 5 and Madrid, Chapter 11, this volume.

source of mobilizing structure. While many authoritarian regimes prefer a demobilized population, they may nevertheless invest in grassroots organization as an instrument of control. El Salvador's military regime, for example, constructed a vast paramilitary network called the Nationalist Democratic Organization (ORDEN), which it used for spying, extrajudicial executions, and for getting out the vote in undemocratic elections (discussed later). While it might seem that organizations initially designed for repression would be of little use to a party operating in a democracy, in practice they have demonstrated remarkable versatility. If an authoritarian successor party inherits such a territorial organization, it is born with one of the key determinants of party-building – and one that conservative parties, in particular, often find elusive.

Source of Party Cohesion. The third resource that authoritarian successor parties may inherit is a source of party cohesion. Many new parties collapse in the face of devastating schisms during the early years of the party-building effort. Having some source of cohesion that can decrease the likelihood of schisms is thus of paramount importance. According to Levitsky and Way (2012: 870), one of the most robust sources of party cohesion is a history of "sustained, violent, and ideologically driven conflict." When party activists have fought in the trenches together, they are more likely to feel a strong affective attachment to the party, to develop an ethos of internal discipline, and to confer high levels of legitimacy on party leaders. They are also less likely to consider defecting to opposition parties that, until recently, were literally their mortal enemies.[19] While Levitsky and Way (2012) mainly have in mind revolutionary struggles, there is good reason to believe that counterrevolutionary struggles can have similar effects (Slater and Smith 2016). While most observers view the regimes that gave rise to authoritarian successor parties like the UDI and ARENA as murderous dictatorships, the protagonists of these regimes, unsurprisingly, see themselves differently. In their view, they were soldiers on the front line of the Cold War struggling bravely, and at great personal cost, to save the fatherland from the imported ideology of Marxism. If such memories of struggle and sacrifice can be passed to an authoritarian successor party, it inherits a powerful source of cohesion.

Clientelistic Networks. In addition to these three core ingredients of party-building, authoritarian successor parties may also benefit from two other forms of authoritarian inheritance. First, they may inherit clientelistic networks. In order for clientelism to be effective, it is necessary

---

[19] See also LeBas (2011).

to have a clientele – that is, a group of individuals locked into a stable relationship of dependency with their patron. For this, the patron must become known to his clients and be viewed as reliable, and clients must come to expect and depend on payoffs from their patron. As Hagopian (1996) demonstrates in her classic work on traditional politics in Brazil, patrons are sometimes able to retain their clientelistic networks after a regime transition, and subsequently to lend their support to incumbents of the new regime. In similar fashion, authoritarian successor parties may inherit clientelistic networks forged under authoritarianism. Few authoritarian regimes seek to hold on to power through coercion alone; instead, they attempt to build popular support through various means, including the selective distribution of material goods. When authoritarian successor parties succeed in transferring these clientelistic networks to themselves, they inherit a valuable resource. This is particularly important for conservative parties, since clientelism is one of the key strategies available to such parties for building a multiclass electoral coalition.

Source of Party Finance. Finally, authoritarian successor parties may inherit a source of party finance. All parties need money to operate. In Latin America, however, the most obvious source of party finance for conservative parties – business – has often proved elusive. As Gibson (1996: 216) notes, "Historically, Latin American business has remained an aloof ally in the electoral struggles of conservative parties." Dubious about the prospects of conservative party start-ups, the "portfolio of business investment in politics" (Schneider 2010) has often tilted toward other types of political action, such as lobbying and outright corruption.[20] Authoritarian successor parties have the potential to disrupt this pattern. In countries where business was part of the social coalition backing the old regime, such parties may inherit a reputation as trustworthy allies. Alternatively, parties may earn the support of business indirectly by performing well in early elections as a result of other forms of authoritarian inheritance (brand, etc.), thereby demonstrating to business that they are worth betting on. Authoritarian successor parties that inherit the support of business are likely to have greater access to financial resources for organizational upkeep, campaign spending, and in some cases, the maintenance of clientelistic networks (Luna 2010; Chapter 4, this volume).

---

[20] For a discussion of a new tool in the portfolio of business investment in politics – the creation of parties by individual corporations, or "corporation-based parties" – see Barndt (Chapter 13, this volume).

To conclude, there are strong theoretical reasons to explain why authoritarian successor parties of the right often enjoy success under democracy. As a result of authoritarian inheritance, they may be born with some of the key determinants of party-building in general, and conservative party-building in particular. Yet roots in dictatorship are hardly an unalloyed good. For many voters, the idea of voting for an authoritarian successor party will be anathema, particularly if the regime from which the party emerged was responsible for large-scale human rights violations or proved incompetent in office. If the valuable resources bequeathed by authoritarian regimes can be thought of as *authoritarian inheritance*, the opposite can be thought of as *authoritarian baggage* (Loxton 2015). In some cases, the baggage may be so great that outgoing authoritarian incumbents do not even bother to form a party, since its chance of success would be nil.[21] It is more common, however, for authoritarian regimes to produce some mix of inheritance and baggage. Thus, a core challenge for authoritarian successor parties is to manage this mix in such a way as to reap the maximum benefits of authoritarian inheritance, while minimizing the damaging effects of authoritarian baggage.[22] While authoritarian baggage undoubtedly creates complications for authoritarian successor parties, it need not damn a party's prospects. Indeed, as I show below in my examination of Chile's UDI and El Salvador's ARENA – authoritarian successor parties and also Latin America's two most successful new conservative parties – roots in dictatorship can be the key to successful party-building.

CHILE'S UDI

The UDI was founded on September 24, 1983, against the backdrop of the military regime headed by General Augusto Pinochet. Chile had been under military rule since the 1973 coup against the leftist Popular Unity government of Salvador Allende. The founders of the UDI had been key actors in the military regime – most notably Jaime Guzmán, the

---

[21] This may help to explain why no authoritarian successor party emerged in Greece and Argentina after the collapse of military regimes in 1974 and 1983, respectively – regimes notable for their repressiveness and poor performances in office (among other things, both lost wars to geopolitical archrivals).

[22] There are various strategies that authoritarian successor parties can pursue in an attempt to offset the damaging effects of authoritarian baggage, such as expressing contrition for the past, obfuscating their origins, or scapegoating particular figures from the old regime (Loxton and Levitsky 2015).

main political advisor to the military junta during the first several years
of the dictatorship and the architect of the regime's 1980 constitution,
and Sergio Fernández, the interior minister and *de facto* head of cabinet between 1978 and 1982.[23] The UDI brought together representatives of two of the dictatorship's most important civilian factions: the
"*gremialistas*," a group of Catholic conservatives led by Guzmán, and
the "Chicago Boys," a group of free-market technocrats named for
their links to the economics department at the University of Chicago.
For nearly a decade, the *gremialistas* and the Chicago Boys had served
as the dictatorship's "political team" and "economic team" (Huneeus
2000: 461), respectively. They had played a crucial role in developing the
regime's long-term project of "protected" democracy and neoliberal economics. They had also occupied important positions within the administrative apparatus of the state, from the cabinet to municipal government.

   Yet the UDI was not the official ruling party of the military regime.
While some supporters had urged Pinochet to form a party, he refused
out of fear that this would degenerate into "populism."[24] The UDI was
formed in the wake of the severe economic crisis that hit Chile in 1982–
1983. In response to the crisis, Pinochet decided to introduce more statist
economic policies and initiate a political "opening." In April 1982, as part
of this policy shift, "[t]he emblematic figures heading the two groups in
charge of official policy since 1978, Gremialista Sergio Fernández and
Chicago Boy Sergio de Castro, were thrown out of the cabinet" (Huneeus
2007: 363). In this context of economic depression, mounting opposition
protests, and policy moderation by the regime, a transition to democracy
(such as the one then occurring in neighboring Argentina) seemed like a
real possibility. In order to pressure the regime to correct course, and to
protect its original policy project in a possible democratic future, the UDI
was formed. As Fernández (1994: 195) later explained, the goal of the
party was "to give permanence and projection to the new ideas that ...
had been expressed in the cabinet of 1978," i.e., that of the *gremialistas*
and Chicago Boys. The UDI was thus a reactive authoritarian successor
party, founded by former high-level authoritarian incumbents in reaction
to the possibility of an imminent transition to democracy.

   In the mid-1980s, the relationship between the UDI and the military regime again became very close. Many of those purged returned
to positions of influence, including UDI founder Fernández, who was

[23] See Valenzuela (1995: 44–46) and Huneeus (2007: 196, 225–270).
[24] See Valenzuela (1995: 61) and Huneeus (2007: 225–226).

reappointed interior minister in 1987. As Pinochet shifted the regime back to its original project of protected democracy and neoliberalism, the UDI once again became his most enthusiastic supporter. Following a short-lived merger with other incipient conservative parties to create National Renewal (RN),[25] the UDI regained its independence and created an organization called the "UDI for the Yes" to campaign for Pinochet in the 1988 plebiscite on the continuation of his rule. Following Pinochet's defeat and the subsequent transition to democracy, the UDI made no attempt to hide its past. On the contrary, it proclaimed, loudly and proudly, its roots in the old regime. A pamphlet from Jaime Guzmán's successful 1989 bid for the senate, for example, shows a photo of Pinochet and the candidate embracing, below which is written: "Jaime Guzmán has col-laborated patriotically with the current [military] government, being one of the main creators of the new democratic institutions."[26] Similarly, in an August 1990 op-ed entitled "The Example of Pinochet," Guzmán thanks the general for "having led the liberation of the fatherland," and gushes about his "mixture of military valor and Christian humility, which testify in an exemplary manner to the true greatness of his soul."[27] In the early 1990s, the number of former high-level incumbents of the dictatorship in the UDI swelled, with emblematic exministers like Hernán Büchi and José Piñera joining the party's ranks. This influx of new members prompted the UDI's secretary general at the time, Joaquín Lavín, to boast: "We have the group most representative of the work of the military government."[28]

The UDI's status as an authoritarian successor party did not prevent it from succeeding under democracy. On the contrary, it easily crossed the threshold for party-building used in this volume by winning more than 10 percent in five consecutive legislative elections. In the founding election of 1989, it won 9.8 percent of the vote for the lower house of Congress; in 1993, this rose to 12.1 percent; in 1997, it rose again to

---

[25] Between 1987 and 1988, the UDI was part of RN, which was created as an umbrella party for the right. In 1988, however, Jaime Guzmán was expelled and took the bulk of UDI members with him. The rump RN continued to exist and became a successful party after the transition to democracy. Like the UDI, RN was an authoritarian successor party, given that some of its founders were prominent figures from the military regime, such as former interior minister Sergio Onofre Jarpa (Huneeus 2007: 443–445, 470, 487). Unlike the UDI, however, the party was also home to more democratic figures, such as Sebastián Piñera and Andrés Allamand.

[26] "Jaime Guzmán: Chile necesita un gran senador," campaign pamphlet from Guzmán's 1989 senate bid.

[27] "El ejemplo de Pinochet," *La Tercera*, August 26, 1990.

[28] "La cosecha de la UDI," *Qué Pasa*, April 29, 1991.

14.5 percent; in 2001, it spiked to 25.2 percent; in 2005, it won 22.3 percent; in 2009, it won 21.0 percent; and in 2013, it won 19.0 percent. In 2001, 2005, 2009, and 2013, the UDI was the single most-voted-for party in Chile. The UDI has managed to obtain these impressive results by building the kind of multiclass electoral coalition that so many new conservative parties find elusive, winning support well beyond its upper-class core constituency (Luna 2010; Chapter 4, this volume). While the UDI's self-description as a "poor people's party"[29] may be something of an exaggeration, its support among the popular sectors is undeniable.

What accounts for the UDI's success? A major cause, I argue, was authoritarian inheritance. Although its roots in the military regime undoubtedly made it unappealing to many voters, they also provided it with a number of valuable resources. First, the UDI inherited a popular brand in the form of *Pinochetismo*. The 1988 plebiscite demonstrated that most Chileans did not support Pinochet; however, it also showed that a large minority did. There were two major reasons for this. One was that the experience of the Allende government (1970–1973) had been traumatic for many Chileans.[30] Hyperinflation, shortages of basic goods, constant political mobilization, and fear of Marxist dictatorship meant that many welcomed the coup when it finally occurred. The second reason was the regime's strong economic performance. It is true that talk of the "Chilean miracle" was always somewhat exaggerated, with Chile suffering the worst recession in Latin America during the 1982–1983 debt crisis (Domínguez 1998). Nevertheless, Chile's average 1 percent annual growth from 1981 to 1990 was exceptionally good by regional standards of the day, and growth was extremely high during the second half of the 1980s. These two factors help to explain why 44 percent of Chileans voted for Pinochet in the 1988 plebiscite. In interviews, UDI leaders routinely point to the popularity of the military regime as a cause of their party's success.[31] This interpretation is supported by survey data, which show that UDI supporters are far more likely to hold a positive view of the dictatorship than the general population (Huneeus 2003). In short, the UDI, as the party most associated with the military regime, benefited from its inheritance of a brand with significant appeal – the brand of *Pinochetismo*.

[29] Since its earliest days, the UDI's has described itself as a "*partido popular*," which could be translated either as "popular party" or "poor people's party." The UDI has always used it in this latter sense, portraying itself as a party uniquely capable of representing the interests and aspirations of Chile's most vulnerable sectors.

[30] See Power (2002).

[31] Author's interviews.

Second, the UDI inherited a territorial organization. By the time of democratization, the UDI possessed a significant grassroots organization, particularly in urban slums (*poblaciones*). This had been constructed during the 1980s by a party entity called the Departamento Poblacional (Slum Department), whose aim, in the words of one UDI slogan, was "to fight the Communists, inch by inch, in every *población* in the country."[32] The UDI focused its attention on the greater metropolitan area of Santiago, forming small cells of party activists in virtually every slum in the city. This organizational structure helped the party to stage a number of attention-grabbing events, such as proregime demonstrations during the 1982–1983 economic crisis and a petition with tens of thousands of signatories "against communism" in 1984.[33] While part of the UDI's success on the organizational front was the product of sheer tenacity, it did not have to construct its organization from whole cloth. Instead, it inherited networks linked to a regime organization called the National Youth Secretariat, created in the 1970s to educate young people about the ideals of the military regime, and which provided various forms of social assistance to regime supporters. The National Youth Secretariat was thoroughly dominated by the *gremialistas* and "covered the whole country, having a branch in each province and most municipalities" (Huneeus 2007: 249). The UDI also benefited from assistance from sympathetic mayors – many of whom were *gremialistas* – and from leniency by the military authorities, despite the fact that parties were technically illegal until 1987. While opposition parties faced the risk of violent repression, the UDI was able to operate largely unimpeded, since, as one party founder put it, "for people that were in some way inside the government, there was not the same prohibition that there was for others."[34] The UDI's strong organization has continued to pay electoral dividends to the present day, playing a crucial role in the distribution of clientelistic goods (Luna 2010; Chapter 4, this volume).

Third, the UDI inherited a source of cohesion rooted in a history of joint struggle. The UDI's internal discipline has received much commentary, with the party said to possess "a high level of party discipline ... difficult to find outside Leninist structured left-wing parties" (Pollack 1999: 118). Even more impressive than its internal discipline, however, is the more basic fact that the UDI has never suffered a schism. There were

---

[32] See Pinto (2006) and Soto (2001).
[33] See Pinto (2006: 178–179) and Soto (2001: 16).
[34] Author's interview, November 10, 2011.

at least three moments when a less cohesive party may well have splintered: in the mid-1980s, when the estrangement of the UDI and Pinochet came to an end; in 1987–1988, when the UDI merged into RN, and then saw Guzmán expelled; and in the early 1990s, when the UDI was still weaker than two potential rivals, RN and the Christian Democrats. Yet UDI leaders and supporters remained loyal to the embryonic party. Part of this cohesion probably stemmed from the cultural homogeneity of UDI leaders, most of whom had attended Catholic schools and universities (Joignant and Navia 2003). However, as Valdivia (2008) has argued, the UDI's founders also understood themselves as "political warriors." As such, their "homogeneity [was] based not only on common sociocultural origins ... but on a common political perspective that was articulated to an important extent in the fires of the struggle against the Popular Unity [government]" (Valdivia 2008: 145). This perception of struggle continued under the dictatorship and, indeed, after the transition to democracy. The climax came in 1991, when Guzmán, now a senator, was assassinated by leftist extremists. By all accounts, rather than tearing the UDI apart, this act of "martyrdom," as UDI members describe his murder, only increased their resolve and drew them closer together.

Fourth, the UDI inherited extensive clientelistic networks. During the military regime, a large amount of power was transferred to appointed mayors as part of a process of "municipalization."[35] Municipal governments now found themselves the locus of key policy areas, such as health and education, and came to play an important role in the administration of antipoverty subsidies, emergency employment schemes, and low-income housing. While the most significant social policy development was simple retrenchment,[36] "[t]he military government was far from oblivious to the plight of the poor, and Pinochet championed policies aimed at helping the neediest" (Constable and Valenzuela 1991: 230). These antipoverty programs "provide[d] lifelines under increasingly harsh economic and social conditions" (Klein 2004: 308). Given the extreme poverty suffered by much of the population during these years, the fact that mayors controlled the levers of social policy gave them a powerful tool for building clientelistic networks (Klein 2004; Luna 2010). This was particularly important for the *gremialistas*, since many of them were appointed mayors in the country's most important municipalities, such as Santiago and Valparaíso. At the time of the transition to democracy, at least 150 of

---

[35] See Klein (2004: 304–309).
[36] See Castiglioni (2001).

the country's mayors – roughly half of the total – were UDI members.[37] The UDI's domination of municipal government paid electoral dividends in the founding election of 1989, when ten of the fourteen deputies that the party elected were former mayors running in the very municipalities that they had administered during the dictatorship. In interviews, these mayors-cum-deputies readily admit that the fact that they had been mayors was critical for getting elected to Congress. In the words of one party founder, the early success of the UDI "can be explained through the mayors, because the mayor, with the entire municipal apparatus, can reach the entire municipality, and that can be translated into votes ... So, I think the big [electoral] result of the UDI is due to the mayors and due to Pinochet. Poor people were *Pinochetista*, so they supported *Pinochetista* mayors."[38]

Finally, the UDI inherited a source of finance in the form of business connections. Business had been an active supporter of the 1973 coup. Afterwards, it became a pillar of support for the military regime, both because it had been traumatized by the Allende experience (Frieden 1991), and because the regime gave it a role in the economic policy-making process during the 1980s (Silva 1996). In the 1988 plebiscite, "business support for Pinochet ... was nearly universal" (Barrett 2000: 8). This close relationship between business and the military regime benefited the UDI for a few reasons. First, as the party most closely associated with the regime and its economic model, the UDI was seen as a trustworthy ally. Second, many in the business community had held public posts during military rule, where they established connections with UDI members. As such, the "UDI and the dominant business groups that emerged after economic restructuring in the 1980s shared close informal ties based on common origins in the dictatorship" (Fairfield 2010: 51–52). Finally, once it became clear that the UDI was not only the most programmatically attractive option but also a viable electoral contender – a fact demonstrated by the party's strong performances in the 1989 founding election and subsequent elections – many businesspeople began to shift their support away from the more compromise-prone RN, and toward the more hardline, doctrinaire UDI.[39] As a result of this business support, the UDI was able to spend more lavishly than other parties at election time, and to maintain its clientelistic networks through privately donated resources (Luna 2010; Chapter 4, this volume).

[37] "Enrostraron a la UDI Militancia de 150 Alcaldes Designados," *El Mercurio*, June 27, 1991.
[38] Author's interview, May 17, 2012.
[39] See Barrett (2000: 10).

In sum, the UDI has benefited from several forms of authoritarian inheritance, which were crucial for its success under democracy. The UDI is the most *Pinochetista* party in Chile, and it is also the most-voted-for party in Chile. While its association with the military regime no doubt makes it unappealing to many Chileans, it has nevertheless managed to eke out the consistent support of a slim plurality of the electorate. Many voters supported the party because they found its inherited brand attractive, while others were drawn to it because of clientelistic payouts. These strategies allowed the UDI to build a multiclass electoral coalition, and were facilitated by the party's additional inheritance of a strong territorial organization, party cohesion rooted in a history of struggle, and the financial backing of the business community. In recent years, with public opinion turning decidedly against the dictatorship,[40] the UDI has finally begun to downplay its origins. Many UDI leaders, however, have refused to go along with this shift,[41] and even for those who have, the shift has been more a matter of emphasis than of substance. In the words of one prominent UDI leader: "We changed discourse without renouncing what we had been. We have never renounced it. Instead, we have moved it discreetly to the background."[42] An even more successful case of conservative party-building, and also an authoritarian successor party, is El Salvador's ARENA.

EL SALVADOR'S ARENA

ARENA was born on September 30, 1981, against the backdrop of a half-century of military rule. The Salvadoran military had created a highly institutionalized system of authoritarian rule, which Stanley (1996) famously described as a "protection racket." In this system, the "the military earned the concession to govern the country ... in exchange for its willingness to use violence against class enemies of the country's relatively small but powerful economic elite" (Stanley 1996: 6–7). But the regime did not maintain itself through coercion alone. It also held regular

---

[40] See CERC (2013).

[41] In June 2012, for example, UDI deputy Iván Moreira wished the deceased Pinochet a happy Father's Day on Twitter – because, in his words, Pinochet was "the father of the nation" – and assured him that "your faithful children remember you fondly." See "Diputado Iván Moreira envió saludo a Pinochet en día del Padre," *Emol.com*, June 17, 2012: www.emol.com/noticias/nacional/2012/06/17/546058/diputado-moreira-saluda-a-pinochet-en-dia-del-padre-tus-fieles-hijos-te-recuerdan-con-carino.html. Accessed January 12, 2014.

[42] Author's interview, March 8, 2012.

elections, in which the military candidate of the official party – first called the Revolutionary Party of Democratic Unification (PRUD), and later called the Party of National Conciliation (PCN) – always won the presidency. Both the coercive and electoral components of the regime were supported by a mass-based, nationwide entity called ORDEN.[43] ORDEN, whose members were mostly exmilitary conscripts in rural areas, served "not only as a paramilitary but also as a para-political organization" (McClintock 1985: 212), helping to spy, carry out repression, and turn out the vote for the official party on election day. ORDEN, for its part, was under the mandate of a regime entity called the Salvadoran National Security Agency (ANSESAL), which served as "the nerve center of the combined intelligence networks of the security system, and in particular the coordinator of intelligence flowing in from the tens of thousands of ORDEN members" (McClintock 1985: 219).

ARENA was born at a moment when this system was breaking down. The catalyst for party formation was a palace coup by a group of reformist junior officers in October 1979, who replaced the sitting military president with a left-leaning Revolutionary Governing Junta. The new junta promptly declared its opposition to "the ancestral privileges" of "the dominant classes," and promised to carry out land reform, increase benefits to the poor, and strengthen ties to the revolutionary socialist regime in neighboring Nicaragua.[44] It also ordered the dissolution of ORDEN and ANSESAL. The 1979 coup did not put an immediate end to military rule, but it caused a regime shake-up that was even more serious than the one that would occur in Chile in the wake of the 1982–1983 economic crisis (discussed previously). Changes at the top, however, did not have the downstream effects intended by the new military rulers. Officially, ORDEN and ANSESAL ceased to exist, and the state was now friendly toward centrist and even leftist political forces.[45] However, the new junta could not enforce its edicts: ORDEN and ANSESAL continued to exist extraofficially, and the security apparatus unleashed a vicious campaign of violence against suspected "subversives."[46] Between 1980 and 1992, El Salvador descended into a full-scale civil war in which the

[43] The acronym ORDEN spells the word "order" in Spanish.

[44] For the text of this proclamation, see Loveman and Davies (1997: 203–206).

[45] The Revolutionary Governing Junta initially had several civilian members drawn from the country's various opposition political forces. These civilians included not just centrist Christian Democrats, but also social democrats and even communists (Stanley 1996: 134).

[46] See Stanley (1996: 178–217).

security apparatus and allied paramilitaries were pitted against leftist guerrillas from the Farabundo Martí National Liberation Front (FMLN). During the war, tens of thousands of Salvadorans were killed, the vast majority of them civilians.

One of the key figures in the country's violence was Major Roberto D'Aubuisson, the former deputy director of ANSESAL described by one US ambassador as a "pathological killer."[47] During his twenty-year military career, D'Aubuisson had been a protégé of General José Alberto Medrano, the founder of ANSESAL and ORDEN and the man sometimes referred to as the "father of the death squads."[48] Medrano, in turn, referred to D'Aubuisson and two other close associates as "my three murderers."[49] Following the October 1979 coup, D'Aubuisson resigned from the military and absconded with the bulk of ANSESAL's files, which contained detailed information on suspected "subversives" in El Salvador.[50] He made personal copies of many of the files, and helped to transfer ANSESAL (now under a new name) from the presidential palace to a military compound. Using information from these files and his connections in the armed forces and ORDEN (also under a new name), D'Aubuisson helped to unleash a campaign of terror against "communists," understood in the broadest possible sense.[51] In a series of televised appearances in 1980, D'Aubuisson would read off lists of "subversives" and provide detailed information about them. In many cases, their mutilated bodies would later turn up in garbage dumps or on the side of the road. As General Medrano, D'Aubuisson's old boss, explained matter-of-factly: "D'Aubuisson was pointing out the communists so the troops could kill them."[52] Some of these killings were carried out by paramilitary forces (some of which were rooted in ORDEN), but the bulk seem to have been carried out by the armed forces themselves.[53] D'Aubuisson became the public face of the "death squad" phenomenon. He not only provided information about people to be killed, but also helped to

---

[47] Robert White, quoted in Paige (1997: 34).

[48] Quoted in Lindo-Fuentes and Ching (2012: 77).

[49] Quoted in LeoGrande (2000: 48).

[50] See Pyes (1983) and Stanley (1996: 150).

[51] For example, D'Aubuisson believed that Christian Democrats were "Communists." He would illustrate this at campaign rallies by cutting open watermelons with a machete, since, like watermelons, Christian Democrats (whose party color was green) were "green on the outside, but red on the inside" (ARENA 2011: 40–41).

[52] Quoted in Nairn (1984: 28).

[53] See Nairn (1984: 25). For more on ARENA's connection to death squad violence based on declassified United States intelligence, see Arnson (2000).

coordinate specific operations, including the March 1980 assassination of Archbishop Óscar Romero.[54]

ARENA was born in 1981 as the "aboveground alter ego" (Pyes 1983: 1) of El Salvador's death squad networks. It was also an authoritarian successor party. As the former deputy director of ANSESAL, D'Aubuisson had occupied a high-level position in the old regime. While his preference seems to have been a simple return to the *status quo ante* – something he attempted to bring about through at least one coup attempt in 1980[55] – D'Aubuisson turned to party-building after intense pressure from the United States for El Salvador to hold new elections foreclosed this option. Thus, like the UDI, ARENA was a reactive authoritarian successor party. It was not a former authoritarian ruling party,[56] but rather was formed in reaction to an imminent transition to democracy, and, as discussed below, would draw heavily on the ORDEN apparatus of the old regime.[57]

ARENA's origins did not prevent it from enjoying electoral success. On the contrary, the party was a major electoral force from the very beginning. In its debut election, the 1982 election for a constituent assembly, it came in second place with 29.3 percent. In the 1985 legislative election, it again came in second place with 29.7 percent, and in 1988, it came in first place with a whopping 48.1 percent. Although El Salvador was not a full democracy in the 1980s, in the democratic "founding election" of 1994, ARENA again came in first place with 44.3 percent. In the 1997, 2000, 2003, 2006, 2009, 2012, and 2015 legislative elections, ARENA oscillated between 31.9 and 39.8 percent of the vote, easily crossing the threshold for party-building used in this volume. ARENA won the presidency in 1989 and held onto it without interruption for the next twenty years. In terms of its performance in both legislative and presidential elections, ARENA was not only the most successful new conservative party in Latin America – it was the region's most successful new party of any sort.

---

[54] This was one of the findings of the UN Truth Commission for El Salvador (1993) conducted after the end of the civil war. See also Laurie Becklund, "Lots Reportedly Drawn to Kill Salvador Archbishop," *The Los Angeles Times*, April 15, 1983.

[55] See McClintock (1985: 272–273) and Stanley (1996: 201–202).

[56] The PCN, the former ruling party of the old regime, continued to exist and enjoyed moderate electoral support after the country's transition to democracy, though it was far less successful than ARENA.

[57] Remarkably, D'Aubuisson's turn to party-building did not mean a turn away from death squad violence. On the contrary, even after being elected president of the Constituent Assembly in 1982, D'Aubuisson continued to direct a team of civilians and active duty members of the armed forces that, according to the United States Central Intelligence Agency, was engaged in "abduction, torture and murder" (quoted in Arnson 2000: 96).

What explains ARENA's spectacular success? A major cause, I argue, was authoritarian inheritance. Like the UDI in Chile, ARENA's connections to the old regime – and, moreover, its association with death squad violence – undoubtedly made it unattractive to many voters. Yet, also like the UDI, ARENA's past simultaneously bequeathed to it a number of valuable resources that helped it to flourish under democracy. First, ARENA inherited a territorial organization from ORDEN. ORDEN was a massive organization, and to a very real degree, it had been the organizational heart of the old regime.[58] By the time of its official dissolution, it is estimated to have had as many as 100,000 members[59] – an extraordinary number, considering that the entire population of El Salvador at the time was less than five million. Moreover, it had a truly nationwide presence, "penetrat[ing] every hamlet in the country" (Americas Watch 1991: 5). When ARENA was formed, "ORDEN was the organizational core of the new party" (Stanley 1996: 232). As one ARENA founder explained: "D'Aubuisson's obsession was to reorganize all those who had been members of ORDEN," for the simple reason that "that organization had grown to have 100,000 members, who knew and admired [him]."[60] Given his former position in ANSESAL, which had overseen ORDEN, D'Aubuisson had ORDEN contacts throughout the country and was able to incorporate much of this mobilizing structure into ARENA. The party was thus born with a tremendous resource: "ARENA always had a presence in all of the national territory, becoming a true mass party … [F]rom the beginning, ARENA had activists in the entire country, both in urban and rural areas" (Artiga 2001: 140).[61] In short, ARENA was able to inherit from the pre-1979 military regime the kind of mass-based, nationwide territorial organization that most new conservative parties can only dream of.

Second, ARENA inherited a party brand. D'Aubuisson may have been a "pathological killer," but he was a popular pathological killer. As in

---

[58] It was arguably even more important than the regime's official party. This was especially true in the late 1970s, when the PCN "was in almost complete disarray, especially in rural areas, where it had been largely supplanted by the paramilitary elements of ORDEN and the 'territorial' militias" (Stanley 1996: 127).

[59] See White (1973: 207), Nairn (1984: 23), and McClintock (1985: 208).

[60] Fernando Sagrera, quoted in Galeas (2004: 12).

[61] One reporter covering the 1982 election commented with surprise that ARENA, despite having been formed only a few months before, "appears to have out-organized the other seven [parties] in the race," running candidates for every available post and campaigning across the country. See "Candidate Favoring Napalm Use Gains in Salvador," *New York Times*, February 19, 1982.

Chile, the Salvadoran military regime appears to have had the support of at least a large minority of the population.[62] This support came not just from elites, but also from many poor peasants. Because of conscription and the semimandatory character of ORDEN, many experienced a political socialization that made them supportive of the *status quo* and distrustful of anything that smacked of "communism."[63] The October 1979 coup threatened to disrupt this familiar order. When D'Aubuisson appeared on television and forcefully denounced these changes, many greeted him as a popular hero. In making these denunciations, he spoke with the authority of someone who, until recently, had been near the top of the security apparatus. D'Aubuisson's widespread popularity was one of ARENA's main electoral assets. Indeed, a "large part of ARENA's appeal was a muscular, violent anti-Communist nationalism that D'Aubuisson, who struck a defiantly macho pose in campaigns, could embody better than anyone else" (Paige 1997: 36). This popularity was illustrated in the second round of the 1984 presidential election, when D'Aubuisson, as ARENA's candidate, won 46.4 percent of the vote. In 1985, ARENA began to modify its image, replacing D'Aubuisson with Alfredo Cristiani, a mild-mannered businessman, as party leader. However, ARENA never turned its back on D'Aubuisson. To this day, the image of "The Major," as he is known, is ubiquitous at party events, offices, and publications.[64] While the brand of *D'Aubuissonismo* was particularly important for winning votes in the party's early years, ARENA has continued to evoke memories of its founder in order to bolster its reputation for "*mano dura*," or "tough on crime" (Holland 2013).

Third, ARENA inherited a source of cohesion rooted in a history of joint struggle. Even more than in the UDI, the founders of ARENA viewed themselves as part of an epic struggle to save their country from international communism. As reflected in the title of a book written by one ARENA founder, they saw themselves as "warriors of liberty."[65] D'Aubuisson had devoted his life to this struggle. This was also true of ORDEN members, given the explicitly anticommunist nature of the organization. With the outbreak of civil war in 1980, the struggle reached

---

[62] All elections under military rule were unfair. In the 1960s and early 1970s, however, the regime began to liberalize, with elections becoming somewhat competitive (Webre 1979). While the regime still used dirty tricks to win elections, it nevertheless demonstrated an impressive capacity to mobilize voters on its behalf.

[63] See White (1973: 205–206) and McClintock (1985: 34).

[64] Author's field observations.

[65] See Panamá (2005).

a new level of intensity. While the vast majority of victims of violence were perceived leftists,[66] the right also suffered casualties. In February 1982, D'Aubuisson himself was shot (and survived), as were other top ARENA leaders at various points, such as Hugo Barrera, Ricardo Valdivieso, and Guillermo Sol Bang. In June 1989, José Antonio Rodríguez Porth, a cabinet minister and prominent ARENA leader, was assassinated. In the late 1970s and 1980s, leftist guerrillas carried out an assassination campaign against ORDEN members in the countryside, killing several hundred in 1980 alone (Stanley 1996: 206). In eastern El Salvador, "the situation was so bad that refugee camps had to be established for members of ORDEN and their families" (Dunkerley 1982: 175). These experiences allowed ARENA to craft a compelling origin story, in which the party had struggled and sacrificed in order to save the fatherland from an implacable enemy. In the words of one ARENA founder: "We were an opposition party, born in terrible conditions of persecution."[67] This history has served as a powerful source of cohesion. While some leaders have defected from ARENA over the years, most of them eventually returned to the party, and they were generally unsuccessful in taking a significant portion of the rank-and-file with them.[68] In short, ARENA's history of struggle has helped it to avoid the kinds of schisms that have contributed to the death of other new parties.

Finally, ARENA inherited a source of party finance in the form of business connections. Business associations in El Salvador had long been loyal "defenders of the authoritarian ancién regime" (Johnson 1998: 123), and in exchange, they were granted a prominent role in the economic policy-making process. The October 1979 coup upended this relationship, leaving business "politically orphaned" (Gaspar 1989: 44). As the reformist juntas, and later the Christian Democratic government of José Napoleón Duarte (1985–1989), enacted land reform and expropriated key assets, business turned elsewhere for assistance. As a prominent symbol of

---

[66] The UN Truth Commission for El Salvador (1993) found that the leftist FMLN had been responsible for approximately 5 percent of deaths. The rest were attributed to the state and allied paramilitaries.

[67] Guillermo Sol Bang quoted in Galeas (2011: 102–103).

[68] Examples include Free Fatherland, which was created by ARENA founder Hugo Barrera in 1985, and the Republican People's Party, which was formed by ARENA founder Gloria Salguero Gross in the early 2000s. Both new parties failed, and Barrera and Salguero Gross returned to ARENA. In 2010, in the wake of ARENA's loss in that year's presidential election, the party finally experienced a serious schism, with twelve ARENA deputies splitting from the party to create the Grand Alliance for National Unity (GANA).

intransigent opposition to reform,[69] D'Aubuisson began to receive substantial funding from disgruntled elites, particularly those in exile in Guatemala and Miami. Business support for ARENA increased after the party demonstrated that it was a viable entity by performing well in the 1982, 1984, and 1985 elections. The intimate relationship that developed between business and ARENA has allowed the party's spending at election time to be "in a different league" (Wood 2000b: 249) from that of other parties. For example, "ARENA used about three times more funds on ads in the campaigns of 1994, 2004, and 2006 than the main opposition party, FMLN" (Koivumaeki 2014: 278).

To conclude, much of ARENA's success can be attributed to authoritarian inheritance. ARENA was born as the partisan extension of El Salvador's death squads, which in turn were rooted in the security and paramilitary apparatus of the pre-1979 military regime. These death squads killed tens of thousands of civilians; they also laid the basis for the most successful new conservative party in Latin America. While many Salvadorans were no doubt put off by the party's past, this very past allowed it to inherit crucial ingredients of party-building. Like the UDI in Chile, ARENA eventually began to downplay its origins, particularly after Cristiani became party leader. Yet, also like the UDI, ARENA has never renounced its past. D'Aubuisson continues to be the undisputed hero of the ARENA pantheon, and is routinely referred to in party literature as "our maximal leader." ARENA's school for training party activists is called the Major Roberto D'Aubuisson Institute, and every year the party commemorates him in full-page newspaper advertisements on the date of his death (February 20). To this day, ARENA's party anthem – which party members sing with great enthusiasm at campaign events – contains the lines "liberty is written in blood" and "El Salvador will be the tomb where the Reds meet their end."

CONCLUSION

In this chapter, I examined conservative party-building in Latin America since the onset of the third wave, and argued that the key to success was authoritarian inheritance. New conservative parties that were also authoritarian successor parties, I argued, were often born with key

---

[69] According to Stanley (1996: 121), D'Aubuisson's rabid anticommunism and high-level position within ANSESAL meant that he was already well known among some economic elites prior to the 1979 coup.

determinants of party-building, including a brand, territorial organization, a source of cohesion, clientelistic networks, and a source of party
finance. While such resources would be of use to any new party – and,
indeed, there are examples of left-of-center authoritarian successor
parties in Latin America – I argued that authoritarian inheritance was
particularly useful for conservative parties. This is what explains the
seemingly paradoxical fact that the only cases of successful conservative
party-building since the region's transition to democracy – the UDI in
Chile and ARENA in El Salvador, as well as RN in Chile and the PFL in
Brazil – all had deep roots in dictatorship.

What are the implications for new efforts at conservative party-building in Latin America? Based on my theory of authoritarian inheritance,
such efforts would appear to have little chance of success. Over the past
three decades, Latin America has become unprecedentedly democratic,
and those authoritarian regimes that do exist tend to be on the left (e.g.,
Cuba, Venezuela). While the decline of authoritarianism is undoubtedly
a positive development for the region, my theory would predict that this
has also lessened the probability of successful new conservative parties emerging in the future. A potential exception is *Fujimorismo*,[70] the
party that emerged from the competitive authoritarian regime of Alberto
Fujimori in the 1990s, and which today is the strongest party in Peru
(Levitsky and Zavaleta, Chapter 15, this volume).[71] Yet, if *Fujimorismo*
does eventually cross the threshold for party-building, it will be the pro-
verbial exception that proves the rule: an authoritarian successor party
that emerged from a right-of-center authoritarian regime in an era when
such regimes are a nearly extinct species.

[70] The other major possible exception is the Social Party of National Unity (PSUN) in
Colombia, the party founded by President Álvaro Uribe (2002–2010). However, after
ex-defense minister Juan Manuel Santos became president in 2010 and embarked on a
policy course different from that of his former mentor, Uribe left the party and became
Santos's most strident critic. Because Uribe was the party's main asset – a fact indicated
by its informal name, the Party of the U – its future, as of this writing, is very much
in doubt.

[71] While *Fujimorismo* would qualify as a party of the right based on an ideological definition, it probably would not meet Gibson's (1996) sociological definition, since, to date,
Peruvian elites have been wary of the party. However, given its right-of-center programmatic orientation, and evidence that it is in the process of institutionalizing, it is not hard
to imagine it evolving into a vehicle of elite interest representation.

10

Insurgent Successor Parties

Scaling Down to Build a Party after War

Alisha C. Holland

We should have had ten mayors rather than ten congressmen.
— *Carlos Franco, former commander and*
party director of AD M-19[1]

Municipal government is like the letter of introduction [to voters].
— *Óscar Ortiz, Vice President of El Salvador*
and former Mayor of Santa Tecla[2]

The bonds of war can form powerful bases for political parties. But wartime solidarities can also dissipate. Fighters demobilize, commanders
retire, and those that remain in politics fail to inspire or deliver in office.
As with most new political parties, insurgent successor parties, or political
parties that emerge from groups that use violence to challenge an established government, have a checkered record of success. Some parties have
endured and achieved national power, such as El Salvador's Farabundo
Martí National Liberation Front (FMLN) and Nicaragua's Sandinista
National Liberation Front (FSLN), while others have flopped, such as
Colombia's Democratic Alliance M-19 (AD M-19) and Guatemala's
National Revolutionary Unit (URNG). Why do some armed actors transition to form successful political parties? And why do others fail?

This chapter explores what happens to armed organizations after
they sign peace agreements and disarm. Insurgent successor parties are
marked by an inherent tension. On the one hand, they often inherit the

[1] Quoted in Boudon (1997: 154).
[2] Quoted in Manning (2007: 267).

building blocks for successful party-building identified in Chapter 1 of this volume: a territorial organization, recognizable brands, and a source of cohesion among former fighters. On the other hand, the past use of violence, ideological extremism, and subculture of armed organizations tend to repel moderate voters. As Lupu (2013, 2016; Chapter 3, this volume) emphasizes, partisanship is strengthened by voters' ability to distinguish among the major parties, but also by identification with the prototypical party member. Without changing the image of a party member from a highly ideological former fighter to a committed democrat, insurgent organizations risk electoral marginalization, much like the niche parties discussed by Greene (Chapter 6, this volume). Former insurgents thus face pressure to whitewash the past and policy ideals that animate their core members, while maintaining distinct party brands.

My argument is that a *subnational electoral strategy* can help insurgent successor parties navigate this dilemma and build durable parties. Subnational office-seeking provides several concrete advantages: (1) a reputation for governance, (2) career incentives for former fighters, (3) information about the electoral capabilities of former fighters, and (4) ways for politicians without battlefield experience to enter and reform the party. On the one hand, subnational office holding can build partisan identification because voters see former insurgents exercise power in their local communities. Winning local elections creates a *demonstration effect* that makes voters more likely to identify with and support an insurgent successor party in national elections. On the other hand, the nonideological nature of local politics means that insurgent successor parties do not need to alter their oppositional stances and strong identities to appeal to voters. Therefore, subnational office holding allows insurgent successor parties to shift their image and boost electoral appeal without diluting their party brand.

While investments in subnational elections assist in party-building, they are hardly the only determinants of success. I reinforce existing work on former insurgent groups, and the broader themes of this volume, concerning the importance of organizational inheritances and polarization for party-building. How leaders engineered their insurgent organizations shapes the likelihood that party projects succeed, and polarization provides a motivation for party leaders to invest in parties as an alternative route to power.

This chapter illustrates the argument through the comparison of two former insurgent groups, the FMLN in El Salvador and AD M-19 in Colombia. These cases are selected because they are representative of important variation in the organizational legacies of insurgent groups. Although born with different endowments, both parties held substantial promise during their formative stage. In 1994, its first election, the FMLN won 21 percent of the presidential vote and a quarter of legislative seats. The party had a large ground organization, but it was a hodgepodge of five insurgent groups that proceeded to splinter and shed their more moderate elements. At the time, the FMLN's protection of its leftist identity was widely considered a mistake and even a threat to democracy, given the mismatch between a centrist electorate and a strong leftist party (Barnes 1998: 64). In contrast to the FMLN's extensive base organization, AD M-19 united a small cadre of insurgents. The group's promise came in its moderation: it calculated its electoral appeal as a social democratic, antiestablishment alternative to oligarchic political machines. Indeed, AD M-19 began on an auspicious path, winning 13 percent of the presidential vote in its first showing in 1990 and becoming the second largest party in the Constituent Assembly after the Liberal Party, beating Colombia's other traditional party, the Conservative Party. The parties thus entered electoral politics with different advantages – a grassroots base for the FMLN and a popular platform for AD M-19. Their success was an open question.

Twenty years on, the FMLN has proved a solid democratic contender in one of the most stable party systems in Latin America. It took the presidency in 2009 and again in 2014, after building its strength in local and legislative elections. AD M-19 has disappeared as a party. Its main actors have resurfaced under multiple party labels over the years. AD M-19's collapse underscores that moderate branding serves short-term electoral goals at the cost of party-building. Conversely, the FMLN's endurance provides yet another example of the importance of inherited organizations, particularly those constructed under adversity, for party-building. Within-case causal process observations demonstrate the importance of subnational office holding in understanding these outcomes. Drawing on electoral data, I show that the FMLN's vote share in presidential elections was 7 percentage points higher in municipalities where it won local office in the 1990s, all else equal. In contrast, AD M-19 endured the longest as a party in cities where it invested in subnational elections, suggesting that the neglect of, albeit smaller, subnational networks hastened the party's collapse.

The main contribution of this chapter is to identify a reputational mechanism through which subnational office holding assists with party-building. Typically, local office is considered a boon for party-building because it gives new parties access to local patronage, which they can distribute to supporters in exchange for votes, campaign work, and donations. My argument emphasizes, in contrast, that local office also gives parties an opportunity to govern effectively and thereby strengthen their brand. It also challenges theories that posit a detrimental impact of political decentralization on party-building. The effects of political decentralization are conditional on the party system context: when parties are born with polarizing brands, the limited ideological nature of local politics can help strengthen party durability and partisan attachments.

This chapter proceeds in five parts. The first section discusses the concept of insurgent successor parties, and argues that while such parties are often born with some of the key ingredients of party-building, they also face unique challenges related to their history of violence. The second section presents the argument for why subnational strategies can help them to succeed. The third examines the polarizing branding decisions and stellar subnational record of the FMLN. The fourth traces the failure of AD M-19 to the decision to dilute its national brand and disregard subnational politics. The fifth concludes by showing how the subnational argument sheds light on the trajectories of other parties in the region, such as Guatemala's URNG.

INSURGENT SUCCESSOR PARTIES

Insurgent successor parties can be defined as political parties that emerge from groups that use violence to challenge an established government. Their distinguishing characteristic is that they can trace their roots to armed groups, but now contest for power peacefully through elections. The study of insurgent successor parties matters due to their importance for postconflict outcomes. Conflict reoccurrence is found to be less likely when former militant groups participate in elections as political parties (Lyons 2005; Matanock 2014). Yet, there is wide variation in whether armed groups transition to become political parties, take up arms again, or disappear altogether. Of 127 militant groups operating in Latin America from 1980 until 2010, fifteen attempted to form political parties (Matanock 2014: 7). According to the threshold proposed in this volume, only two durable parties, Nicaragua's FSLN and El Salvador's FMLN, formed, uniting eight former insurgent groups.

Given their history of armed struggle, insurgent groups tend to enter politics with organizational infrastructure, recognizable brands, and a source of cohesion. This section outlines how along each of these dimensions, the need to transform organizations engineered for violent opposition into those that can succeed in electoral politics creates common challenges.

Organization

Insurgent successor parties have a critical organizational advantage in the form of leaders and members who were once willing to risk their lives for a cause. Much like authoritarian successor parties (Loxton, Chapter 9, this volume), formerly armed actors inherit preexisting territorial organizations that can allow them to circumvent the difficult work of building an organization from scratch. Insurgent groups, of course, vary in size and discipline. A number of scholars have noted that the most successful insurgent successor parties are those that can draw on powerful preexisting mass organizations (De Zeeuw 2008; Lyons 2005; Manning 2004, 2007; Soderberg Kovacs 2007).

Unlike other new parties, insurgent successor parties face a unique organizational challenge due to disruptions caused by disarmament and demobilization. Demobilization can damage preexisting organizational infrastructure as fighters scatter and rebuild their civilian lives. Daly (2016: ch. 4), for instance, argues that organizations that recruit and deploy soldiers in a dispersed manner, and allow soldiers to return home or displace to other locations, risk losing their organizational strength.

Even if organizations remain intact, insurgent successor parties must redefine organizational rules about how power and resources will be allocated. As Manning (2007) points out, while success on the battlefield leads to promotions during war, new rules for advancement must be defined for peacetime politics. This transition is difficult because insurgent successor parties tend to suffer from the same pathologies identified by Greene (Chapter 6, this volume) for niche parties. To convince armed groups to take political and physical risks, armed groups learn to protect their identities. They recruit from within and promote candidates who embody organizational loyalty. Avoiding electoral marginalization in the postconflict period thus requires former insurgents to craft new rules to structure politicians' careers and favor electorally viable candidates over those who best represent the organization's past.

Branding

Insurgent groups are recognized to stand for clear principles, or brands. Particularly for insurgencies that mobilize members through nonmaterial payoffs, overcoming collective action problems to risk violence requires that ideologies are distinct from political alternatives. Acts of violence and peace talks also catapult armed groups into the media's eye so the public can recognize the demands of former insurgents.

While identifiable, however, insurgent ideologies tend to be more radical than the platforms preferred by the median voter. Insurgent successor parties thus face a branding dilemma. On the one hand, if parties construe their ideologies more broadly, they sacrifice the identity that creates the party's internal life and risk alienating activists. The idea that a party will "throw away" its ideals for short-term electoral goals seems like a betrayal for participants who risked their lives and lost friends in conflict. On the other hand, the gap between the median voter and insurgents' ideological positions is often large. If former fighters willing to take up arms, use violence against civilians, and defend extreme positions populate insurgent successor parties, then civilians also may doubt their similarity to prototypical party members. The demands of electoral competition suggest moderation, fresh faces, and a rejection of military symbols and rhetoric to stand a shot at office.

In addition to a branding dilemma, insurgent successor parties face a credibility problem. Civilians generally reject violence, and even affinity with a broad cause may not lead civilians to trust ex-combatants' influence over civilian affairs. A common concern about insurgents is that they have no political experience. If anything, former fighters seem like they would make shoddy politicians who are unwilling to compromise or play by the rules. Voters may doubt that the skills needed to lead on the battlefield parallel those needed to govern in a democracy. Insurgent successor parties thus must not only shift their ideological positions and prototypical members to come closer to average civilians, they also must establish a reputation for democratic governance.

Cohesion

Insurgent successor parties benefit from a source of cohesion in shared symbols, experiences, and history in war. Having been socialized in an insurgency's subculture, the bonds between members and leaders may be more durable. Intense polarization and violent struggle can harden group loyalties and cultivate military-style mechanisms of organizational discipline (LeBas 2011; Levitsky and Way 2013; Loxton, Chapter 9, this volume). As Levitsky and Way (2013: 9) argue in the case of revolutionary organizations, participants in prolonged struggle often come to see party membership in terms of morality and loyalty. Former fighters share affective ties to an organization that will prevent them from exiting a party even when they have instrumental reasons to do so.

Nevertheless, wartime ties do not guarantee agreement or commitment to a shared democratic political agenda or unity among different insurgent groups. Fighters unite *against* a common enemy and cause, but not necessarily on a package of public policies that a democratic version of their organization seeks to institute (Manning 2004). Marxist-Leninist insurgent groups, in particular, have splintered over how to transform revolutionary principles into platforms consistent with representative democracy and a market economy. Insurgent groups also often demobilize as part of broad processes that incorporate multiple groups. While organizations may maintain internal cohesion, heterogeneous coalitions can strain new parties, as LeBas (2011) documents among prodemocracy movements that fuse multiple actors into a single party. Some insurgent successor parties like the URNG dissolved in part due to schism, while others like the FMLN suffered fractures, but managed to survive because members remained loyal to the idea of a unified opposition (Allison and Martín Álvarez 2012).

In short, insurgent successor parties are often born with some of the key ingredients of party-building: a territorial organization, a recognizable brand, and a source of elite cohesion due to their origins in armed conflict. Their challenge is to build political platforms and reputations for democratic governance that appeal to voters without estranging members and elite factions. This transition process can try even bonds forged through decades of shared struggle. The next section details how investments in subnational politics can help insurgent successor parties navigate these tensions.

SUBNATIONAL STRATEGIES

The spread of electoral decentralization across Latin America during the 1980s and 1990s has increased the number and stakes of subnational elections. Many scholars argue that electoral decentralization has harmful effects on party-building (e.g., Brancati 2007; Chhibber and Kollman 1998; Harbers 2009; Muñoz and Dargent 2011; Sabatini 2003; Ziegfeld 2016). Two features of local elections are thought to weaken parties. First, subnational races involve competition around issues with limited ideological content. Decentralization can lead to the development of "unique" party systems at the local or regional level. Voters also may fail to differentiate party labels on national issues when they vote for those same parties proposing seemingly similar local or regional platforms. Second, electoral decentralization can lead politicians to defect from major parties when they gain access to independent sources of patronage (Muñoz and Dargent, Chapter 7, this volume). Politicians do not need parties to attract supporters when they have the political and financial autonomy to strike out on their own.

My argument is that the distinctive features of subnational politics – limited ideological content and administrative autonomy – can interact positively with polarizing party brands by transforming a party's reputation for governance and internal composition. The reputational capital provided by subnational office holding frees parties to defend differentiated ideological positions at the national level. A subnational electoral strategy thus allows insurgent successor parties to improve their electoral prospects without converging on centrist positions that can dilute a party's brand and demobilize its core supporters. I focus on the case of insurgent successor parties here, but the theoretical logic applies more broadly to parties that form under conditions of adversity, such as those formed to oppose authoritarian regimes or hegemonic parties.

To begin, I define subnational electoral strategies as concerted investments in the pursuit of elected offices at the municipal, provincial, or regional level. Empirically, a subnational electoral strategy can be identified in several ways: parties run high-quality candidates for most subnational offices, allocate financing and staff to subnational races, rely on parallel party governance structures at the national and subnational levels, and achieve similar (if not higher) vote shares at the local rather than the national level. This concept is broader than measures of party system nationalization that consider the degree to which parties obtain similar vote shares across districts, such as the measure advanced by Jones and Mainwaring (2003). Outcome-based measures ignore whether parties make an effort to seek subnational office in the first place. A subnational electoral strategy also differs from grassroots activities in that it aims for the control of government, rather than cultivating members to win national office.

Subnational electoral strategies provide four specific advantages. First, and most importantly, experience in local government helps parties attach themselves to a reputation for governance. Local government does not involve grand ideological issues; instead, it requires pragmatic problem solving. The ability to engage in these tasks can transform the image of former insurgents into "normal" politicians capable of democratic governance. This reputational capital then allows voters to update their beliefs about a party's ability to govern and their prototypical supporters. From a party's perspective, the goal is to produce what I call a *demonstration effect*, whereby voting for former insurgents for local office or experience with their governance lessens the perceived risk of a similar choice for national office.

Voters are more likely to trust former insurgents first at the local level due to the inherently less ideological nature of subnational politics and the availability of crosscutting personal ties at lower levels of politics. It is easier to cross partisan lines when grand ideological issues are not at stake. Voters also may be more willing to elect a former insurgent who is known by alternative social markers in the community, such as the child of a community member, a responsible neighbor or a sports star (Daly 2016).

This reputational channel thus differs from arguments that stress that subnational offices help provide parties with access to patronage and public funding to reward activists with selective incentives, or what Hale (2006) calls administrative capital. While local politics is never pristine, the reputational capital from subnational office holding for ideologically extreme candidates often comes through attempts to downplay clientelistic linkages. In addition, a reputational argument explains why local politics remain valuable to parties even in weak states where office holding entails limited financial incentives. Salvadoran mayors, for example, received minimal state resources in the postwar period. They spent substantial time seeking outside funding to undertake projects and employ basic staff, not milking local government coffers and employing party activists. Still, there was an important impact on party-building because it established the FMLN's ability to hold executive power, albeit at a local level.

Second, subnational offices provide an arena for former fighters to build their political careers. Insurgent organizations want fighters to disarm and commit to democracy, but they do not necessarily want fighters to abandon their political project. As Aldrich (1995) argues, a main function of political parties is to regulate political careers. Local political offices are more numerous than national positions and thus parties can integrate former fighters into politics more directly through support for subnational office seeking. Relying on a multitiered electoral strategy also avoids internal conflict over limited national posts. For instance, both AD M-19 and the URNG disintegrated in part because of infighting over nominations for congressional list positions. The parties gave very little support to those running for municipal offices, and therefore could not diffuse elite tensions by channeling leaders toward subnational posts.

A third related advantage is that subnational office holding provides party leaders information about *which* former rebels and even nonfighters should rise through the party ranks and pursue national political office. Some former insurgents will inevitably fail as mayors, governors, and city councilors. A record in local office provides information to party-builders about former rebels who can translate their battle skills into electoral ones. Without this knowledge, insurgent successor parties promote former guerrillas based on their wartime records, which is a noisy indicator of an individual's potential in an executive or legislative role.

Lastly, subnational office holding incrementally can help inject new "blood" and policy ideas into insurgent successor parties. If the only route to advancement comes through past service to an insurgent group, then politicians who did not fight will see little incentive to build their career within the organization. In contrast, if success at the subnational level is taken as an alternative indicator of service to the party, insurgent successor parties gradually can renovate their leadership and composition. Local office holding also can shift the perspective of former insurgents as they become accountable to an electorate and engage in policy experimentation, rather than simply acting as critics of the governing party (on this point in the context of Brazil's PT, see Samuels 2004).

In order to understand why some parties pursue subnational electoral strategies, I underscore two factors. First, insurgent successor parties that enter the democratic period with a large or geographically concentrated territorial organization are more likely to continue to invest in local politics. As Van Dyck argues for new left parties more generally (Chapter 5, this volume), parties with minimal organization find it more attractive to use media appeals, and by extension, focus on national races where media outlets penetrate. The opportunities for subnational party-building thus depend on how armed groups were constructed.

Second, as time passes and demobilization uproots fighters, the choices of elites about how to preserve and institutionalize connections with constituencies matter. As Chapter 1 of this volume emphasizes, polarization and threat are more likely to encourage party investments in organization. This motivation extends to subnational electoral investments. Where political polarization is higher, parties are more likely to seek alternative political arenas where they can control government and differentiate their positions.

The next sections demonstrate the argument through a comparison of El Salvador's FMLN and Colombia's AD M-19. These are radically different guerrilla groups in terms of size, structure, and ideology, which allows me to examine the relative importance of territorial organization and median branding. However, these parties also are similar along several dimensions. Both benefited from electoral openings for the left and for local politics. El Salvador transitioned to democracy and allowed for contestation of municipal office. While not part of a democratic transition, Colombia implemented a new constitution and legislation that introduced direct elections for a host of new subnational positions, and attempted to weaken the traditional parties that had governed for most of the twentieth century. The FMLN and AD M-19 formed as opposition parties that confronted more established, well-greased political machines and conditions of continuing violence, in the form of death squads and crime in El Salvador and paramilitary violence in Colombia. But both parties entered a political space in which traditional right-leaning parties garnered waning ideological sympathy. El Salvador and Colombia are highly unequal societies that lacked major social democratic political parties. And, of course, both insurgencies could claim to have defended these leftist ideals with more than the usual political bluster, but rather, with their lives.

FMLN: BRAND REINFORCEMENT AND SUBNATIONAL STRATEGY

The FMLN formed from a mass-mobilizing insurgency with committed leaders and grassroots activists. Despite this organizational advantage, FMLN leaders fought over the party platform, candidates, and alliances. Ultimately, party leaders privileged ideological discipline and legislative opposition over electoral success. This position frustrated moderate voters and politicians. However, the FMLN complemented its polarizing national branding with an emphasis on subnational politics. Deliberate investments in local politics helped the FMLN build a reputation for competent governance, allowed politicians to develop their careers, and shifted the internal system of party advancement.

Origins and Inheritance

Civil war ravaged El Salvador from 1979 to 1992. The origins of the war lie in the country's yawning social and economic inequalities. Since the early 1930s, military authorities used violence to maintain labor-repressive agriculture. Fifty years of conservative military rule broke down when junior military officers launched a coup in 1979 and proclaimed a

"Revolutionary Governing Junta" intended to stave off a Nicaragua-style revolution (Dunkerley 1982; Stanley 1996). The left-leaning military government attempted to undertake major structural reforms, including land reform, banking system nationalization, and a reorganization of security forces. The actions threatened economic and security elites, who accelerated their repression of leftist guerrilla groups and formed "death squads" (see Loxton, Chapter 9, this volume). The deepening violence catalyzed the formation of a united movement of armed leftist revolutionary groups, the FMLN. The country plunged into civil war.

The FMLN engaged in intense popular mobilization during the war. It recruited from civil society organizations, particularly ecclesiastical base communities, unions, and student and teacher organizations. The vast majority of insurgent combatants were from poor rural backgrounds (McClintock 1998). Insurgent activism carried tremendous risks: more than 75,000 people (in a country of five million) died in the civil war, and more than 85 percent of serious acts of violence were carried out by state agents against suspected insurgents (UN Truth Commission for El Salvador 1993). As Wood (2003: 89) argues, convincing peasants to engage in such high-risk activism required shifting beliefs and political identities so peasants realized their very humanity was at stake. The FMLN forced landlords and the military to retreat from significant areas of the countryside, eventually controlling about a fifth of the national territory. It fought the US-trained and funded military to a stalemate. The civil war finally ended in a negotiated settlement and the signing of the Chapultepec Accords in 1992.

The FMLN came close to experiencing the most auspicious historical conditions for party-builders: it had extensive base participation and deep societal cleavages that made it unlikely for individuals to switch between partisan camps. In the run-up to the founding elections of 1994, polls consistently showed the FMLN with the support of a quarter of the electorate, compared to 30 percent for the main conservative party, ARENA (IUDOP 1994).

Despite a large base of former fighters and sympathizers, it remained unclear whether an organization with such a history of violence could be successful at attracting popular support beyond its immediate network of fighters. Roughly half of the electorate did not identify with either the FMLN or ARENA (IUDOP 1994–2000). While the FMLN performed better in the zones that it controlled during the war, it did not capture a plurality of the vote in any single department in the 1994 elections (Allison 2010). Given concerns about whether the government would respect the election results, the FMLN agreed to run a moderate candidate, Rubén Zamora, in coalition with the center-left Democratic Convergence (CD) party in the founding election. Zamora had not fought for any of the FMLN's constituent groups, but he had important wartime credentials as the founder of the Democratic Revolutionary Front (FDR), a leftist party that had been severely repressed in the early years of the war. Zamora forced the presidential election to a runoff, but lost by a wide margin to ARENA. The FMLN took twenty-one seats in the legislature compared to just one for CD, which underscored that electoral sympathies lay with a possibly reformed FMLN.

Internal divisions within the party complicated questions about how to expand its appeal to voters. The FMLN grouped together five former insurgent organizations that only loosely allied during the war. No single charismatic personality existed to rally together the groups, and leaders held divergent views about the party's future. Loosely put, the FMLN divided into what has been labeled an orthodox (or revolutionary socialist) and reformist (or social democratic) faction. Factional divisions were in part ideological, but more fundamentally they were rooted in different views on the role of alliances. In stating its ideological positions, the party used vague terms with multiple interpretations, such as defining the FMLN as a "revolutionary" party committed to "socialism" in its statutes. The orthodox faction interpreted this phrase to involve the construction of a socialist economy involving substantial (if not total) state ownership of property, while the reformist faction equated it with a general commitment to economic equality (Zamora 2003: 68). In terms of alliances, the orthodox faction privileged the "purity" of the organization over electoral goals. In contrast, the reformist faction believed that the left needed to expand beyond its base to appeal to moderate voters, as well as the business community, for support. It preferred immediate convergence on a platform closer to median voter preferences (Allison and Martín Álvarez 2012; Zamora 2003).

In addition to the risk of schism, the FMLN faced an external challenge, given that ARENA had built a formidable political apparatus over the course of a decade. Party-building began under US pressure to hold "demonstration elections" (Herman and Brodhead 1984). The exercise inadvertently prodded ARENA to transform into a real political party ahead of the left, which had rejected the elections as a tool of US imperialism (Karl 2004). At the war's end, ARENA penetrated both urban and rural areas, and had transformed its paramilitary networks into a vast territorial organization with a mass popular base (Loxton, Chapter 9, this volume). Moreover, ARENA had the support of the country's main business chambers, and leveraged its media access to stoke popular fears that destabilization would occur in the event of an FMLN victory (Wantchekon 1999; Wolf 2009). More than a quarter of survey respondents believed that the military would be justified to take power if the FMLN won the presidency (AmericasBarometer 1991, 1999). The FMLN thus faced an uphill battle to unite its large base organization, gain electoral support, and convince voters that it could hold power without destabilizing the country.

Branding

The FMLN took steps to preserve its opposition brand due to the polarized political environment. The party's choice to protect its identity, rather than expand its electoral appeal, is seen most clearly through its refusal to make alliances, its decisions to maintain tight legislative discipline, and its selection of presidential candidates.

First, despite its willingness to join with the CD in the founding election, FMLN legislators proceeded to divide on whether to continue such alliances. In 1994, several FMLN senators drawn from the more moderate insurgent groups that composed the FMLN, the People's Revolutionary Army (ERP) and National Resistance (RN), agreed to cooperate with ARENA in exchange for positions on the congressional executive committee. More broadly, ERP leader Joaquín Villalobos believed that the FMLN needed to strike agreements with moderate factions and business leaders to advance a social democratic agenda and gain electoral support. The dominant orthodox faction rejected the idea of associating with ARENA, and viewed cooperation in moral terms, calling the legislators "traitors," "opportunists," and "antidemocratic" (Zamora 2003: 101). The FMLN protected its brand. It expelled the legislators, losing a third of their congressional bloc and alienating moderates.

This schism challenges the idea that shared experiences of war bind leaders together. Nonetheless, tracing the fate of moderate politicians who defected from the FMLN reinforces the importance of base-level cohesion and polarization in party-building. The dissident legislators attempted to form a rival party, the Democratic Party. But the split proved a severe miscalculation due to the intense loyalties of the FMLN's supporters. The Democratic Party's share of valid votes did not surpass 1.2 percent for the 1997 legislative and mayoral elections. The party even flopped in the ERP's historic stronghold of Morazán, where most voters viewed the

ERP leadership's decision to break from the FMLN as a betrayal of what they had fought for and a risk to the unity necessary to obtain political power (Wood 2003: 261). The Democratic Party's failure (combined with CD's weak legislative showing) reified the perceived electoral dangers of centrist positions (Allison and Martín Álvarez 2012).

Second, the FMLN sacrificed electoral appeal, and even policy goals, to maintain opposition in the legislature. In the late 1990s and early 2000s, as Roberts describes (Chapter 2, this volume), the FMLN gained popular support for its rejection of a series of neoliberal reforms, including privatizations, trade deals, and the dollarization of the economy. The FMLN had achieved its greatest electoral gains in the 2001 legislative election, when it became the single largest party in Congress. With thirty-one of eighty-four seats, it held veto power on legislation that required a two-thirds majority. The FMLN leadership decided to vote against the 2002 budget, which would block government funding and thus undermine support for ARENA prior to the presidential election. But a massive earthquake had buffeted El Salvador, and the budget included approval for international loans for reconstruction. Reformist party members argued that a vote for the budget would rebuild the country and help those harmed by the earthquake. Six moderate legislators voted with ARENA to release the reconstruction funds. The FMLN leadership expelled the dissidents. In so doing, the FMLN lost is veto power and appeared to compromise its defense of the poor harmed by the earthquake. But exacting legislative discipline remains central to the FMLN's strategy of brand preservation. Surveys show that 78 percent of FMLN legislators believe a party should always require legislative discipline, and 54 percent agree that legislators should be expelled for voting against the party line (University of Salamanca 2013).

Third, the FMLN reinforced its brand through its choice of candidates. Although the FMLN supported Zamora in the founding elections, the party subsequently eschewed such moderate choices. The clearest example comes from the debates over Héctor Silva, the FMLN-aligned mayor of San Salvador. In 1999, polls showed that Silva was the most popular politician in the country ahead of all of ARENA's potential candidates. The FMLN's orthodox faction, nonetheless, rejected Silva. The FMLN finally did nominate a social democratic candidate, but one with extensive battlefield experience and service to the party, Facundo Guardado. Guardado garnered little support outside the party ranks and was easily pinned as a former guerrilla. Yet even Guardado was accused of being "distanced from revolutionary principles" and "morally corrupt" by the orthodox faction (Puyana Valdivieso 2005). Infighting, as well as Guardado's limited appeal, meant that he received just 29 percent of the presidential vote, even less than in the FMLN's opening salvo.

The concern over ideological dilution ran so deep that the FMLN continued to sacrifice electoral victory for purity in the 2004 presidential cycle. Amid frustration with the economic policies of ARENA and major subnational gains for the FMLN, many analysts expected the FMLN to take power. Silva had served another term as mayor of San Salvador and was favored for president. However, Silva, a gynecologist by training, brokered a resolution to a health sector strike that had paralyzed the government. The orthodox faction declared the mediation an "act of treason."[3] The FMLN instead ran the unpopular longtime Communist Party head, Schafik Handal. Handal repelled moderates, professing a commitment to socialism, democratic revolution, and resistance to imperialism.[4] When asked in the abstract about which party respondents supported, ARENA and FMLN were neck and neck. The gap grew to 12.5 percentage points when asked about which candidate voters supported (UTEC 2003). ARENA won easily in the first round of voting.

Nevertheless, at the same time that the orthodox faction dominated national politics, important shifts were afoot locally. Popular subnational politicians expanded the ranks of the reformist faction. Following the fractious candidate selection process in 2003, the reformist faction, led by then mayor of Santa Tecla, Óscar Ortiz, and a San Salvador city councilor, Carlos Rivas Zamora, threatened to leave the party.[5] In response, FMLN leaders rewrote the party statute so that the executive committee would pick the presidential ticket to be submitted to the base for ratification (FMLN Statutes, Article 64). For the first time, the new process allowed party leaders to split the ticket between the orthodox and reformist factions. Well ahead of the 2009 presidential elections, the FMLN leadership agreed to run a moderate presidential candidate with no wartime experience, or even party ties, Mauricio Funes. However, it would pair Funes with the leader of the orthodox faction, Salvador Sánchez Cerén, as vice president. The goal was to win the presidency with a centrist candidate in 2009 and then reverse the formula in 2014. As intended, Funes won in

---

[3] "Para el FMLN está claro que él ya no es candidato," *La Prensa*, November 2, 2002; "Muere Héctor Silva, el presidente que nunca fue," *El Faro*, December 8, 2011.

[4] "Ortodoxos presentan candidatos a dirigencia," *La Prensa Gráfica*, August 30, 2004; "La mitad del FMLN quiere que no gane Schafik," *El Diario de Hoy*, September 4, 2003.

[5] One segment of reformist members had already left in November 2004, including two mayors, three FMLN deputies, and several hundred local leaders. See Puyana Valdivieso (2005) and Manning (2007).

2009, and Sánchez Cerén won with the leader of the mayoral dominated reformist faction, Ortiz, as his running mate in 2014.

In retrospect, the FMLN's emphasis on maintaining clear opposition and spatial distance from ARENA can be appraised as farsighted calculus. The rate of partisan identification with the FMLN actually grew after the war.[6] But brand preservation came at the cost of locking the party out of executive power and reducing its legislative influence for more than a decade. Moreover, the selection of a centrist candidate came only after the growth of a wing of subnational politicians who were able to extract compromises from orthodox party leaders and promote a ticket that centrist voters could support. As I discuss next, the FMLN was able not only to reform internally, but also to avoid electoral marginalization due to its subnational electoral strategy.

Subnational Territorial Strategy

El Salvador may seem an odd country to emphasize subnational politics: it is a small and centralized country with only 262 municipalities. Compared to large federal countries, Salvadoran mayors have limited budgets and administrative powers to control service provision. Nonetheless, mayors receive 10 percent of the budget and can also broker agreements with international institutions and NGOs to fund development projects (McIlwaine 1998; Van der Borgh 2004). Salvadoran citizens have high levels of knowledge and respect for local government. When surveyed, 77 percent of respondents could name their mayor, and 18 percent had contacted their mayor (AmericasBarometer 1999).

The FMLN's large organization and ideological commitment to grassroots democracy gave the party an advantage in pursuing local office, but increases in subnational vote shares did not occur casually or in the absence of party investments. For one, party names and partisanship matter less in subnational elections. Even in the immediate aftermath of war, only 3 percent of respondents said that being from their political party was an important quality for a mayor (AmericasBarometer 1991, 1995). Limited partisan voting initially harmed the FMLN. In 1994, it won only 15 of 262 municipalities, even though it ran candidates on its own or in alliance in 241 municipalities (Artiga 2006: 63). Internal

---

[6] On average, 21 percent of the Salvadoran population identify as FMLN supporters, though some polls showed this as high as 40 percent with Funes in office. Meanwhile, 9.7 percent of the population identifies with ARENA, down from highs of more than 30 percent during the transition (AmericasBarometer 2006–2010).

displacement and demobilization also complicated local elections. More than 750,000 citizens were displaced during the civil war, more than a million Salvadorans migrated abroad, and two-thirds of the FMLN's leaders lived in metropolitan areas (Zamora 1998: 244).

After an underwhelming first performance, the FMLN put a greater emphasis on its subnational base in 1997. The FMLN established a separate National Secretary for Municipal Affairs to coordinate the campaigns and create a common municipal platform for the party. As the former head, Orestes Ortez, explains, the objective was to win areas where the FMLN had been influential in the civil war and urban areas where the party enjoyed growing support.[7] The campaign material straddled these two demographics. On the one hand, the municipal campaign was the first time that the FMLN used its wartime logo and tried to run former insurgents in rural areas. On the other hand, the propaganda used images of informal sector workers, such as flower and candy vendors on city streets, and appealed to local concerns.[8] The strategy seemed to work. The FMLN had a meteoric rise to a near tie with ARENA, winning 32.6 percent of the total vote compared to 36.7 percent for ARENA in 1997 and some of the country's most populous municipalities.

The FMLN also won the grand prize of San Salvador. The San Salvador mayoral race highlights that the FMLN's subnational success was both a deliberate strategy and a byproduct of foreclosed national opportunities. The orthodox faction's dominance pushed moderate politicians to seek other channels of influence. Silva viewed the FMLN's future in a post-Soviet world as a social democratic party that solved the poor's daily problems. Rather than "fighting among itself about the past, about revolution," Silva understood that the left "had to show the country that we could govern."[9] Silva won with a plan for managing the waste facility in San Salvador and renovating the city's historic center, hardly the stuff of grand ideological debate.[10] He gained broad support as he worked with businesses, citizens, and organized groups to relocate street vendors who had clogged the capital and extend public services to poor neighborhoods.[11]

---

[7] Leonel Herrera. "El FMLN ha replanteado toda su estrategia de gestión municipal," *Diario CoLatino*, May 29, 2007.
[8] "Las elecciones del 16 de marzo de 1997: quiebre de la hegemonía de ARENA," Centro de Información, Documentación y Apoyo a la Investigación, *ECA* 581.
[9] Author interview with Héctor Silva, San Salvador, July 17, 2009.
[10] "Candidatos a alcalde en primer debate televisivo," *Efe*, February 19, 1997.
[11] Ismael Moreno, "Entrevista con Héctor Silva," *Envío* 222, September 2000.

The experience of FMLN mayors, and particularly Silva, became a selling point for the party. In 1999, Guardado emphasized the party's responsible management of San Salvador on the campaign trail. The party ran on the slogan "governing at the service of the people," and stressed the model of civic participation exemplified by Silva.[12] In the 2000 municipal elections, the party expanded its subnational penetration and governed half of the population at the local level. Table 10.1 shows the party's solid showings in local politics throughout the 2000s.

The FMLN relied on dissatisfaction with ARENA's governance, grassroots networks, and alliances with international NGOs to make headway in subnational elections. Even in the 1990s, the party remained relatively resource-poor and depended heavily on its members for on-the-ground operations. According to FMLN press releases, 90,000 members go house to house in the days prior to municipal elections. Members are expected to put up posters and banners for their local candidates, as well as to help organize and attend rallies for the FMLN municipal candidates. In exchange, mayoral candidates must have been party members for at least two years, and donate 15 percent of their salary to the FMLN (FMLN Statutes, Article 266). Roberto Lorenzana, the FMLN's Communication Secretary, explains that each municipal candidate receives backing from the local party office and can design her own platform, but "nonetheless, the FMLN has a generic municipal proposal, that encompasses our point of view … we believe that it is necessary to give the people more power in the taking of decisions."[13]

The FMLN also recruited prominent politicians to run for subnational office as part of its strategy, particularly in growing urban areas. Take the example of Vice President Ortiz. Ortiz was a student movement leader and then directed FMLN forces in the department of Usulután during the war. After demobilization, Ortiz was assigned to organize the party in the department of La Libertad, where he served as a congressman from 1993 to 2000. But in 2000, the FMLN tapped Ortiz to run for mayor of Santa Tecla, a burgeoning city in San Salvador department. Ortiz won. He now touts city government as a way to transform the party's image: "The parties are becoming aware that the best way to sell their programs and to improve their image is increasingly at the level of municipal government … [and mayors] have demonstrated how to work efficiently" (quoted in

[12] Ismael Moreno, "Notable derrota de ARENA y triunfo relative del FMLN," *Envío* 217, April 2000.
[13] "El FMLN está listo para arrancar la campaña de Alcaldes y Alcaldesas," FMLN Press Release, February 9, 2012.

TABLE 10.1 *Election results in El Salvador, 1994–2014*

	Mayoral				Legislative				Presidential	
	ARENA		FMLN		ARENA		FMLN		ARENA	FMLN
	Seats	% Vote	Seats	% Vote	Seats	% Vote	Seats	% Vote	% Vote	% Vote
1994	207	44.5	15	20.5	39	45.0	20	21.4	68.4	31.7
1997	160	39.5	52	34.7	28	38.0	27	35.5		
1999									52.0	29.1
2000	127	36.0	69	35.9	29	36.0	31	35.2		
2003	111	36.4	62	34.9	27	33.3	31	35.5		
2004									57.7	35.7
2006	147	39.5	54	40.1	34	39.2	32	39.3		
2009	122	39.7	75	36.8	32	38.5	35	42.6	46.7	51.3
2014									49.9	50.1

Note: There are eighty-four seats in Congress, 262 mayors, and results are shown for the second round presidential race.

Source: Tribunal Supremo Electoral de El Salvador, TSE.

Manning 2007: 267). Ortiz invested massively in infrastructure, parks, and citizen participation, which the FMLN has called its "model for the country."[14] In so doing, Ortiz associated the FMLN with effective management, pushed the party past wartime associations, and helped build the party's popularity. Prior to the 2014 presidential race, 33 percent of the electorate actually favored Ortiz for president, compared to 16 percent for Sánchez Cerén and 26 percent for ARENA's candidate Norman Quijano (IUDOP 2012). Ortiz's place on the presidential ticket was critical to the victory of the orthodox faction's leader, Sánchez Cerén.

More generally, local government has become an important way to build a political career within the FMLN. When it formed, the FMLN chose candidates based on battlefield command positions and based on quotas for the five separate insurgent groups (Zamora 1998). The party continues to consider "historic roles," but it now weighs performance in local and department offices as additional criteria for candidate selection and appointments. In the 2009 legislative session, for example, a third of legislators report experience in municipal government (as mayors or members of municipal councils) in their official biographies. For comparison, roughly another third of legislators also report being founding members or fighters in one of the FMLN's constitutive organizations. These legislative trajectories suggest that local government can be an important way for the FMLN to structure political careers. As Ortiz puts it, the "second generation of the FMLN does not necessarily have experience in battle, but they have experience on the ground in local politics."[15] Hence, a subnational electoral strategy has contributed both to the party's external reputation and its internal transformation.

The Demonstration Effect

To test whether subnational office holding contributed to the FMLN's reputation for governance, I analyze municipal election results. My theory suggests that voters should be more likely to support the FMLN in presidential elections if the FMLN held office in their local municipality, all else equal. I therefore examine whether the FMLN's presidential vote share is higher in municipalities that elected an FMLN mayor in the early electoral cycles of 1994 and 1997 (*Early Demonstration*) or ever elected

---

[14] "Las obras: su carta de presentación," *Comunica*, June 27, 2008.
[15] "Oscar Ortiz abierto a candidatura presidencial para 2014 por el FMLN," *La Página*, January 15, 2012.

TABLE 10.2 *Subnational electoral victory and presidential vote share*

	2004 FMLN presidential vote share	
	1	2
Early Demonstration	0.0683* (5.57)	
Demonstration		0.0174* (2.54)
FMLN03	0.280* (6.39)	0.278* (6.05)
FMLN00	0.0490 (0.99)	0.0556 (1.05)
FMLN99p	0.0689 (1.96)	0.0565 (1.53)
FMLN97	0.112* (2.23)	0.174* (3.42)
Urban	−0.145 (−0.96)	−0.237 (−1.50)
Poverty	0.0928* (2.69)	0.0852* (2.37)
War	0.604 (0.50)	2.090 (1.71)
Observations	261	261
R^2	0.673	0.642

Note: *t*-statistics in parentheses; * $p < 0.05$.

an FMLN mayor (*Demonstration*).[16] Of course, municipalities that elect FMLN mayors may be generally more sympathetic to the FMLN than those that do not. I therefore control for the FMLN vote share in all prior municipal and presidential elections to account for differences in the municipality's underlying ideological support. The FMLN also tends to have higher levels of electoral support in municipalities that are more urban, poorer, and that experienced more wartime violence. Thus, I include measures of the population share in an urban area (*Urban*) and the percent of families below the poverty line (*Poverty*), using reports from the state's local development fund (*Fondo de Inversión Social para el Desarrollo Local*). I also control for the number of civil war deaths reported to the UN Truth Commission per 1,000 residents (*War*).

Table 10.2 shows the results of an ordinary least squares regression for the 2004 presidential elections. Having an FMLN mayor take office in a previous election cycle is positively associated with the 2004 presidential vote share, even controlling for all past electoral support for the FMLN. The election of an FMLN mayor in a single period is associated with 2 percentage points more support for the FMLN's 2004 presidential candidate. An early election of an FMLN mayor has an even more substantial

[16] All electoral data comes from El Salvador's national election authorities (*Tribunal Supremo Electoral*). I use data on the 2004 presidential election rather than the 2009 race because the demonstration effect should be most important when the FMLN runs extreme candidates, rather than the more moderate Mauricio Funes in 2009.

positive effect: having elected an FMLN mayor in 1994 or 1997 is associated with 7 percentage points more support for the FMLN in the 2004
presidential election. For perspective, an early experience with an FMLN
mayor is predicted to increase the vote share for the FMLN by roughly
the same amount as an 8-percentage-point increase in the municipal poverty rate. Admittedly, inferences about individual voting decisions from
aggregate outcomes raise ecological inference problems, and there may
be unobserved differences in the ideological predispositions of communities. But changes in voting patterns do provide suggestive evidence that
experiences with an FMLN mayor make voters more willing to vote for
the FMLN for president.

AD M-19: BRAND DILUTION AND NATIONAL STRATEGY

Colombia's AD M-19 pursued the opposite strategy from the FMLN.
AD M-19 selected positions popular with voters, downplayed the unsa-
vory bits of its violent past, and looked for ways to expand its resources
through alliances with the government in power and the incorporation of
candidates that it claimed to oppose. This centrist strategy failed. Voters
soon perceived few differences among parties and limited gains from
supporting a less well known party. Party strategists also ignored subnational elections, which left the party with no way to rebuild after poor
national showings or to structure the political careers of former fighters.

Origins and Inheritance

The insurgent organization M-19 has roots in La Violencia, the civil war
that followed the assassination of populist leader Jorge Eliécer Gaitán
in 1948. The fighting ended with a 1957 pact between the Liberal and
Conservative Parties to share power through an arrangement known as
the National Front. Most M-19 leaders got their start during this period,
joining the communist youth, and the political forces led by Gustavo
Rojas Pinilla, the military dictator of Colombia from 1953 to 1957.
Rojas Pinilla and his party, the ANAPO, emerged as a political movement
opposed to the National Front in the early 1960s. ANAPO made impressive inroads with the urban poor, particularly among recent migrants and
informal sector workers. While focused on a single personality, ANAPO
tried to build a genuine party apparatus with neighborhood-level organizations, membership cards, mass rallies, and a centralized command

structure. The movement combined populist rhetoric and appeals to social justice. Rojas Pinilla received 39 percent of the vote in the presidential election on April 19, 1970. By M-19's account, he only lost due to fraud (Dix 1979).

The allegedly stolen election catalyzed M-19's formation. The party's full name – 19th of April Movement – makes reference to the date of the supposed fraud against Rojas Pinilla. Rojas Pinilla did not incite his followers to violence, but the socialist branch of ANAPO, joined by leaders of the several budding insurgent organizations, students, and labor unions, decided that armed rebellion would be required to open Colombia's political system. The organization launched at a party conference in 1973 (Villamizar 1995).

M-19 had a distinctly urban, democratically oriented ideology compared to Colombia's other major guerrilla groups, such as the Revolutionary Armed Forces of Colombia (FARC) and the National Liberation Army (ELN). M-19 emphasized nationalism, "Colombian socialism," and "true" democracy. It drew on images and rhetoric from the assassinated Gaitán, as well as Rojas Pinilla's platform. Its core proposals included the direct election of governors, agrarian reform, and free education and medical care (Villamizar 1995). As party leader Antonio Navarro Wolff put it in an interview, "Our motivation was never to establish a revolution in Colombia, in the style of Cuba, but rather to achieve a democratic opening in a nation defined by a bipartisan system" (Navarro Wolff and Iragorri 2004).

M-19 never built a dense organization with territorial roots, despite what Van Dyck (Chapter 5, this volume) would label conditions of adversity that effectively blocked it from the pursuit of political power. In 1978, it did build a small military organization in the countryside with "mobile guerrillas" to add to its urban cells. The group also had weak mechanisms of internal discipline: it had no uniforms and no punishment for defection. Its leaders rejected an "apparatist" view that citizens had to engage in military organization to gain political consciousness. Instead, leaders viewed themselves as "armed propagandists" seeking to publicize the people's interests (Durán, Grabe, and Patiño 2008).

M-19 engaged in flashy acts of violence aimed to attract public attention through urban terrorist cells. The group conducted disturbances in the name of social democracy, such as robbing milk trucks and kidnapping drug traffickers to distribute loot in poor neighborhoods. It also executed highly visible acts of symbolic violence. The group stole Simón Bolívar's sword, entered the Dominican Republic's Embassy, and, most controversially, seized the Palace of Justice in 1985. While many of the group's actions garnered public sympathy, the palace siege ended with ninety-five people losing their lives after the government counterattacked. It decimated the group's reputation and motivated M-19 to seek peace as a way to recover popular support (Navarro Wolff 2001).

M-19 demobilized in 1988 in exchange for amnesty and political aperture. President Virgilio Barco led a peace initiative that paved the way for M-19's recognition as a political party, but left Colombia's largest guerilla groups in arms. M-19 demobilized with only 791 combatants (Nasi 2007). Nonetheless, M-19 quickly formed a political party. In 1989, AD M-19 formed and drafted its only real platform. The document called for participatory democracy, political decentralization, social justice, environmental protection, and diversified international relations (*Nuestro Compromiso con Colombia*).

As part of peace talks, M-19 achieved progress on some of its main objectives to open the electoral system. These reforms gained traction in part because they received support from important factions of the traditional parties who sought allies against entrenched regional interests (Shugart 1992a). President César Gaviria convened a constituent assembly to draft a new constitution in 1990. Critically, representatives were elected from a single nationwide district of seventy seats. This process circumvented the regional districts used to elect Congress, which favored regional political machines. AD M-19 flourished under the alternative electoral formula: it won 26.8 percent of the vote and nineteen seats with almost a million votes, beating even the Conservative Party, one of Colombia's two traditional parties.

Given its leadership position, AD M-19 played a central role in drafting constitutional provisions to guarantee social and economic rights, decentralize political and administrative power, and create a more equitable electoral system. The creation of elected subnational posts, as well as a single national congressional district, was intended to break regional political brokers' hold on power and aid new parties like AD M-19 (Shugart 1992b). Indeed, as Muñoz and Dargent describe (Chapter 7, this volume), the reforms weakened political brokers and accelerated the decline of the traditional political parties. These reforms, however, did not lead AD M-19 to develop into a durable party, as the former insurgents had hoped.

Branding

AD M-19 faced two basic options about how to build its electoral appeal after demobilizing. The party could move to the center where it faced competition from Colombia's traditional parties (and particularly dissident factions of the Liberal Party), or to the left where it risked association with still-armed guerrilla groups and electoral marginalization. Much like the FMLN, factions of the party were divided on the optimal course. Yet, AD M-19 followed the opposite path from FMLN in converging on a moderate platform that downplayed its leftist credentials.

AD M-19's strategy was to seek a new constituency of Colombians disaffected with the practices of traditional parties. It would emphasize clean, anticlientelistic politics and whitewash its leftist roots. For many Colombians who condemned the group's violence, AD M-19 nonetheless represented an attractive political principle: to break the traditional parties' stranglehold on power.

Unlike the FMLN, AD M-19 freely allied with other parties in exchange for power and policy influence. At the Constituent Assembly, AD M-19 worked with a breakaway faction of the Conservative Party, which shared many of its ideas about political decentralization and citizen participation and allowed the party to gain a leadership position. In so doing, the party appeared to sacrifice its ideals. The press mocked AD M-19's party leader, Antonio Navarro, as the "head of the new Colombian right."[17]

In addition, Navarro was appointed health minister in the Liberal government of César Gaviria in 1992 in exchange for AD M-19's legislative cooperation. The position provided AD M-19 with an opportunity to advance some of its social justice goals, and Navarro did propose the creation of a national health system and the expansion of coverage to marginalized populations. However, the proposals came during Colombia's economic liberalization and the Gaviria administration cut health funding. While Navarro repeatedly threatened to withdraw AD M-19 from the government unless the health and social spending budget was increased – which might have restored the party's credibility as a social democratic alternative – it ultimately withdrew to protest renewed attacks against guerrilla groups still active in the country.[18] The party also struggled to maintain its reputation for clean government due to frequent

[17] "En la asamblea se habla de Antonio Navarro como del jefe de la nueva derecha," *El Tiempo*, July 1, 1991.
[18] "AD M-19 se va del gobierno," *El Tiempo*, November 24, 1994.

(and arguably politicized) administrative investigations into whether AD M-19 used the Ministry to channel funds to aid the reinsertion of guerrillas (Boudon 1997: 130). AD M-19 could not offer credible opposition, as it participated in the cabinet of a government that implemented neoliberal economic reforms that, in theory, it opposed. The party also seemed more concerned with an unpopular defense of guerrilla groups than social democracy. This led to a decline in its popularity: while Navarro took 12.5 percent of the 1990 presidential vote and led in the polls at moments in the early 1990s, he captured just 3.8 percent in 1994.

Even AD M-19 leaders attribute their rapid demise to the party's unwillingness to provide clear opposition to neoliberal reforms. Some party members criticized the party's alliance with the Gaviria government from the beginning, but found themselves in the minority (Boudon 1997: 154–155). For instance, former party vice president Pedro Bonnet lamented the decision not to reinforce the party's leftist positions: "The angst of marginalized zones of the country has little to do with civil service reform, or the right to protect constitutional rights (*tutela*). Where was the concern to expose the errors of the government and its policies of economic liberalization?"[19] While the message of social democratic opposition has a natural latent constituency in a deeply unequal society like Colombia, just as in El Salvador, AD M-19 restrained its opposition to the government's economic model and talk of social democracy.

AD M-19 also reduced interparty differentiation through its choice of candidates. In an attempt to broaden its appeal, AD M-19 allowed politicians of diverse backgrounds to run on its centrist banner. The party soon became home to opportunists who capitalized on the antitraditional politics mood. In the press, the party was derided as a *sancocho*, the traditional Colombian stew of meats and vegetables, because of its eclectic mixture of candidates. Navarro insists that there was no other way to gain the popular support that the party needed than opening party ranks: "We could not have remained reduced to a group of ex-guerrillas … this was a *sancocho* of optimal quality, according to the tradition of M-19" (Navarro and Iragorri 2004: 138). Other AD M-19 leaders promoted an insular strategy to favor candidates who had participated in the armed group and derided the "movement of candidates" (Boudon 2001: 78, 80). The inclusion of diverse candidates also encouraged the party's

[19] "La AD M-19 se da la pela," *El Tiempo*, November 17, 1991.

fragmentation by leading to a proliferation of legislative lists by the 1994 elections.

The sharp decline in AD M-19's popularity can be viewed as a classic case of brand dilution. A 1993 poll found that 40 percent of Colombians could not distinguish between AD M-19 and the traditional parties, and that an even greater number found minimal differences (Boudon 1997: 154). Table 10.3 charts AD M-19's rapid fall. The columns depict the number of mayoral offices and seats in the senate, and the share of the presidential vote won by each party.

Subnational Territorial Strategy

AD M-19 did even worse in subnational elections than in national ones. The party had a weaker organizational base to draw on than the FMLN. However, AD M-19 also ignored the organizational networks that it could have nurtured and developed. This decision was largely motivated by the fact that AD M-19 gained near immediate access to national power and willingly partnered with the government in a less polarized political context.

AD M-19 did not benefit from a large grassroots organization like the FMLN. However, it did have four networks that it could have cultivated as a source of support in subnational elections. First, prior to demobilization, M-19 opened more than two hundred "peace houses" (*Casas de Paz*) that were intended to help former guerrillas transition to civilian life and to build a political movement (Villamizar 1995). Party vice president Pedro Bonnet proposed that the "peace houses" become schools to train militants as low- and mid-level politicians and inculcate them in the party's platform. As part of peace negotiations, the government agreed to social investments in these key geographic areas as a form of "peace dividends" that AD M-19 could capitalize on for electoral purposes. But the party saw the peace houses as a lower priority to national campaigning and closed them (Patiño 2000). Second, AD M-19 initially encompassed the remnants of ANAPO in large part through its alliance with Rojas Pinilla's grandson, Samuel Moreno. The sense of thwarted representation continued to motivate a distinct identification with ANAPO among older urban voters, which later would be drawn on to launch a new party in Colombia's major cities (*Polo Democrático Alternativo*). Third, AD M-19 initially proposed to represent what party founder Carlos Pizarro referred to as "nonconformist" segments of civil society that lacked political representation, such as labor leaders, indigenous groups, and

TABLE 10.3 *Election results in Colombia, 1990–1998*

	Mayoral			Senate			President		
	Liberal	Con.	AD M-19	Liberal	Con.	AD M-19	Liberal	Con.	AD M-19
1990	527	371	–	66	38	–	47.8	23.7	12.5
1990 C.A.				25	15	19			
1992	400	290	1	59	26	9			
1994	490	293	3	59	32	–	45.3	44.9	3.8
1998	457	203	3	59	29	–	34.6	34.3	–

Notes: In 1994, I list Pastrana as the Conservative candidate, although he ran on an independent label "Andres Presidente." I count the Conservative Party as both the Movimiento de Salvation Nacional and the Partido Social Conservador, and show the first round presidential results in order to see AD M-19's vote share.

Source: Registraduría Nacional del Estado Civil.

evangelicals (Beccassino 1989: 110). These organized groups that were never incorporated in other corporatist political projects could have formed an organizational base. Lastly, AD M-19 could have concentrated on making inroads in urban areas, where it had retained cells for decades and attracted sympathizers. More than half of AD M-19's votes in 1990 and 1991 came from urban areas (Archer and Shugart 1997: 148). Yet AD M-19 ignored all of these possible bases.

The potential for a subnational strategy centered on urban areas is clear from the one city where AD M-19 did support a local candidate, Barranquilla. Barranquilla had been one of M-19's urban bases, and gave Navarro a remarkable 41.1 percent of the vote in 1991 (Hoskin 1998: 104). In 1992, AD M-19 backed an independent Roman Catholic priest, Bernardo Hoyos, who won the mayor's office. Barranquilla became an anchor for the party's strength in the Atlantic region, and the party successfully supported municipal council and lower chamber campaigns there (Boudon 2001: 80–83). Although the counterfactual is unknown, more urban strongholds like Barranquilla could have helped AD M-19 improve its reputation for governance and keep its former activists mobilized.

The decision not to invest in city politics is surprising, given that AD M-19 had agreed to a provision making all participants in the Constituent Assembly ineligible to run for Congress (Archer and Shugart 1997: 148). This meant that some of the party's brightest stars could have devoted their talents to building the party as governors or mayors, rather than simply sitting out the election cycle. Nonetheless, AD M-19 only ran a handful of subnational candidates, and won a single mayoral office in 1992.

Only as AD M-19 flopped on the national stage did it try to refocus on a local agenda. Navarro ran for mayor of Pasto and won in 1994 after his failed presidential bid. Carlos Franco, then AD M-19 president, redirected efforts to subnational elections and announced that the party was investing in thirty candidates for mayor in 1997: "The strategy consists of prioritizing the struggle for local power in order to develop the autonomy to which the enemies of the past and clientelism were opposed."[20] But it was too late. The party had lost most of its following by then and took only two mayoralties.

AD M-19's weaker territorial organization and the limited polarization of Colombian politics reduced the perceived viability of investing in

---

[20] "La AD M-19 inicia su reestructuración," *El Tiempo*, May 31, 1997.

subnational politics. Moreover, unlike the FMLN, AD M-19 had always been a media-savvy organization. Party members believed that they could persuade voters by publicizing their moderate program. The party's near immediate electoral success reinforced the perception that organizational investments were unnecessary (Boudon 1997, 2001). As one party member put it, "No one wanted to be a mayor or a representative to the House, everyone aspired to the Senate ... Each one preferred to imagine an electoral base that did not exist" (Buenahora Febres-Cordero 1997: 373). The case of AD M-19 therefore underscores that there is an affinity between choices to pursue platforms preferred by the median voter and a shallow territorial strategy focused on national office.

CONCLUSION

This chapter demonstrates how subnational office-seeking can help parties build reputational capital and thus contribute to party-building. For parties launched out of violent struggle, such as the FMLN, or otherwise burdened by public distrust and repellent brands, the nonideological nature of subnational politics can be a valuable way to demonstrate governance potential. Subnational elections allow insurgent successor parties to retain their oppositional positions in the legislative arena, while complementing this image with a reputation for democratic governance at lower levels of politics.

In comparing organizations with different organizational endowments, this chapter reinforces the volume's theme that large territorially rooted organizations, such as that of the FMLN, have an advantage over parties that lack them, such as AD M-19. In hindsight, the success of the FMLN was overdetermined by its expansive network of fighters, deep popular roots, chance to counterbalance an identifiable conservative party, and subnational electoral investments. Nonetheless, within-case evidence suggests that a subnational electoral strategy strengthened the FMLN. A statistical analysis of election results demonstrated that the FMLN garnered stronger support in national races after it won locally. Critical transformations in the party, such as the decision to nominate palatable presidential tickets, also responded to pressure from subnational politicians. To use Zamora's phrase (2003: 68), a new generation of mayors helped the FMLN "escape from the [leftist] ghetto," while at the same time maintaining a clear voice as a political opposition.

Future research may demonstrate the applicability of the argument to other parties born with polarizing brands. For example, Guatemala's

URNG arguably is the most similar case to the FMLN, given that it also entered politics after negotiating an end to civil war and united four guerrilla groups.[21] But, as with AD M-19, the URNG converged on a centrist branding strategy and invested little in subnational elections. The URNG formed an alliance with a preexisting center-left party, and supported a social democratic candidate, Álvaro Colom, for president in 1999. The press nicknamed the coalition "strange and light" (Sichar 1999: 65). Colom took 11 percent of the presidential vote, but the alliance won just seven mayoralties across the country. Given a concentration on national office-seeking, the URNG had no way to incorporate its former fighters into politics and build the party, particularly after the alliance collapsed due to divisions over how to share power (Allison 2006a: 85). While the counterfactual is unknown, local office holding could have allowed former fighters to remain involved in politics without compromising the party's brand. Instead, despite shared struggle, the URNG fragmented.

Looking beyond insurgent successor parties, subnational electoral strategies have been credited with the success of parties that formed with strong party brands to oppose authoritarian regimes. For instance, the PT in Brazil engaged in important social policy experimentation at the subnational level, which strengthened its reputation for the defense of the poor within market-oriented institutions (Hunter 2010: ch. 4). Even more orthodox party members moved to the center once they were responsible for solving constituents' problems at the subnational level (Samuels 2004). On the opposite side of the political spectrum, the UDI in Chile pitched the party to a national audience based on its reputation as a capable municipal administrator. When UDI candidate Joaquín Lavín, a former mayor, ran for the presidency in 2000, he "municipalized" national politics, casting problems in terms of their immediate technocratic solutions rather than in ideological terms (Altman 2012: 250). Hence, it may be necessary to temper some of the scholarly pessimism about the impact of political decentralization on party-building. When parties have strong brands, they can use local office holding as a way to transform their image and organization. For parties unwilling to sacrifice their identities and polarizing brands like the FMLN – or looking to the future, the yet-to-demobilize FARC – city hall can be a critical stepping-stone to the national stage.

---

[21] The similarities should not be overstated: while the FMLN fought the government to a stalemate, the URNG was decimated in the 1980s and demobilized less than 3,000 guerrilla troops (Sichar 1999: 60).

11

Obstacles to Ethnic Parties in
Latin America

Raúl L. Madrid

The history of ethnic parties in Latin America is not an impressive one. Although numerous ethnic parties have emerged in the last couple of decades, only two of them, the Movimiento al Socialismo (MAS – Movement toward Socialism) in Bolivia and the Movimiento Unidad Plurinacional Pachakutik-Nuevo País (MUPP-NP – Pachakutik Plurinational Unity Movement-New Country) in Ecuador, have won a significant share of the vote. Most ethnic parties have failed miserably. Indeed, the typical ethnic party in Latin America has won less than 3 percent of the vote nationwide and disappeared after one or two elections. By contrast, ethnic parties in other regions of the world have registered much greater success.

What explains the relative absence of successful ethnic parties in Latin America? And why have a couple of ethnic parties succeeded (at least temporarily) in a region where most ethnic parties have failed?[1]

This chapter argues that ethnic parties have been hindered by the low level of ethnic consciousness and the fluidity and ambiguity of race and ethnicity in the region. Widespread *mestizaje*, along with social discrimination against Afro-Latinos and indigenous people, has meant that many people who are wholly or mostly of African or indigenous descent do not explicitly identify as such. This has made it difficult for ethnic parties to mobilize people based upon race or ethnicity. To worsen matters, many of the ethnic parties that have arisen have not reached out to other ethnic groups or adopted broad-based platforms. Instead, they have

---

[1] As discussed below, neither the MAS nor Pachakutik meets the strict measure of successful party-building laid out in Chapter 1 of this volume: capturing 10 percent of the vote in at least five consecutive national legislative elections. Nevertheless, compared to the other ethnic parties in the region, these parties have been quite successful.

concentrated on trying to mobilize members of their own ethnic group through narrow, ethnocentric, and, at times, exclusionary appeals.

Ethnic parties have also suffered from significant resource disadvantages. Indigenous and Afro-Latino parties have typically been founded by groups or individuals that lack the resources to fund national electoral campaigns. They have been largely unable to carry out television advertising, hire campaign advisors or staff members, distribute clientelist handouts, or carry out polling. As a result, they have been at a significant disadvantage vis-à-vis the traditional parties.

The ethnic parties that have succeeded have overcome these disadvantages in two main ways. First, they have reached out to members of other ethnic groups, wooing them through traditional populist strategies. This approach has enabled them to win the support not only of people who self-identify as indigenous, but many people who self-identify as white or mestizo as well. Ethnopopulism thus has been the most effective brand for ethnic parties in the last few decades. Second, the successful ethnic parties in Latin America compensated for their lack of resources by relying heavily on in-kind contributions by members of the indigenous movement, as well as various other social movements with which they have allied. These movements have provided free labor, meeting places, food, transportation, and campaign propaganda, among other goods. The social movements have thus helped the incipient parties overcome the financial and organizational deficits that new parties typically face.

This chapter explores these arguments through an analysis of four parties: the MAS and the Movimiento Indígena Pachakuti (MIP – Pachakuti Indigenous Movement) in Bolivia; the MUPP-NP (or simply Pachakutik) in Ecuador; and Winaq in Guatemala. These parties all faced similar challenges, but they varied considerably in terms of their performance. Whereas the MAS grew steadily over time and transformed itself into the dominant party in Bolivia, the MIP and Winaq never managed to catch on among most voters in their countries. Pachakutik, meanwhile, fared quite well in the first three elections in which it competed, but it shifted in a more ethnocentric direction beginning in 2006 and declined rapidly.

This chapter is organized as follows. The first section discusses the poor performance of most ethnic parties in Latin America and compares them to ethnic parties in other parts of the world. The second section explores how resource disadvantages and the low level of ethnic consciousness in Latin America have impeded the success of ethnic parties in the region. The subsequent two sections examine how the MAS and Pachakutik were able to overcome these obstacles. In the third section,

I describe how the MAS and Pachakutik overcame their resource disadvantages in part by relying on the human and material resources provided by social movements. In the fourth section, I discuss how the MAS and, initially, Pachakutik built multiethnic support by reaching out to members of other ethnic groups and adopting a broad, populist platform. The fifth section examines the electoral performance of the MIP in Bolivia and Winaq in Guatemala. It argues that the lack of success of these two parties can partly be explained by their failure to employ ethnopopulist strategies and to mobilize broad-based social movements behind them. The conclusion summarizes these arguments and discusses the future of ethnic parties in the region.

THE PERFORMANCE OF ETHNIC PARTIES IN LATIN AMERICA

By my count, at least eighteen ethnic parties have emerged in Latin America during the last few decades. This figure includes only those parties that have competed in presidential elections – if I included parties that competed in legislative or regional elections, the number would be much higher. I categorize as ethnic parties those parties that prioritize the interests of an ethnic group and make explicit ethnic appeals in order to win the support of members of that group. Ethnic parties, however, may be exclusionary or inclusive, and, as we shall see, the most successful ethnic parties in Latin America have been inclusive (Madrid 2012).

Most of the ethnic parties that have emerged in Latin America have fared quite poorly. As Table 11.1 indicates, the vast majority of ethnic parties competed in only one or two elections and won a very small portion of the vote. Only two parties, the MAS in Bolivia and Pachakutik in Ecuador, have performed well in some elections and even these two parties have not fared well in enough elections to be considered a success by the strict criteria laid out by Levitsky, Loxton, and Van Dyck in Chapter 1. The MAS has triumphed in three consecutive presidential and legislative elections (2005, 2009, and 2014), but it has not yet survived the passing of its founding leader (Evo Morales), nor has it yet won more than 10 percent of the vote in five legislative elections.[2] Thus, the MAS might best be classified as an apparent success.

---

[2] Nevertheless, the MAS has won more than 10 percent of the vote in four consecutive legislative elections (2002, 2005, 2009, and 2014) in addition to the 2006 elections for the Constituent Assembly.

Pachakutik in Ecuador also fared quite well for a time, but it was unable to sustain these results. It won at least 15 percent of the presidential vote in the first three elections in which it competed, and in 2002 it captured the presidency in alliance with Lucio Gutiérrez and his party, the Partido Sociedad Patriótica (PSP – Patriotic Society Party).[3] Pachakutik also won 10.8 percent of the legislative vote in 1996, 9.2 percent in 1998, and 12.1 percent in 2002.[4] Support for Pachakutik, however, declined dramatically beginning in 2006, dropping to approximately 4.1 percent of the valid vote and it has remained low since that time. Pachakutik might therefore be best classified as a temporary or aborted success.

By contrast, ethnic parties in other regions have fared much better.[5] According to a data set compiled by Holmsten, Moser, and Slosar (2009), ethnic parties have won an average of 7.2 percent of the seats of the lower chamber of the legislature in recent elections in Europe. (These figures only include ethnic parties that seek to represent ethnic minorities.) Ethnic parties have fared particularly well in Belgium, Bulgaria, Latvia, Macedonia, Romania, and Slovakia, winning more than 10 percent of the seats in each of these countries. Ethnic parties have also fared well in many Asian countries, winning 24.1 percent of parliamentary seats in India and 12.4 percent in Sri Lanka in recent elections, according to Holmsten, Moser, and Slosar (2009).[6] Ethnic parties are, perhaps, most successful in Sub-Saharan Africa, but systematic data on their share of the vote or seats in this region are unavailable.[7] What is clear, however, is that ethnic parties in Latin America have had a more difficult time winning support than ethnic parties in other regions.

---

[3] It should be noted, however, that Freddy Ehlers and Lucio Gutiérrez, the candidates that ran on Pachakutik's presidential tickets in 1996, 1998, and 2002, were not members of Pachakutik, but rather headed allied parties or movements.

[4] The figures provided for 1996 and 1998 refer to Pachakutik's results in the elections for national (at-large) deputies to the Ecuadorian legislature. The figures provided for 2002 refer to Pachakutik's results in the elections for provincial deputies (deputies elected from each province to the national legislature) because Ecuador did not hold elections for national deputies in 2002. Pachakutik and its allies won approximately 6.3 percent of the vote for provincial deputies in 1996 and 7.4 percent in 1998, although the exact national-level figures were not released by the Tribunal Supremo Electoral (Supreme Electoral Tribunal) and the numbers provided here should be regarded as estimates.

[5] Of course, what share of seats or votes is accounted for by ethnic parties will vary depending on what indicators are used to decide whether a party is ethnic. See Chandra (2011) for a comparison of different indicators.

[6] These figures would be much higher if they included ethnic parties that aim to represent majority ethnic groups, such as the Bharatiya Janata Party in India.

[7] See Dowd and Driessen (2008).

TABLE 11.1 *The performance of ethnic parties in presidential elections in Latin America, 1979–2011 (percentage of valid vote)*

	1979	1980	1985	1989	1993	1996	1997	1998	2002	2005	2006	2007	2009	2010	2011
Bolivia															
MITKA	1.9	1.2													
MITKA-1		1.3													
MRTK			1.1												
MRTKL			2.1	1.6											
FULKA				1.2											
MKN					0.8										
EJE					1.1										
IU-ASP							3.7								
MIP									6.1						
MAS-IPSP									20.9	53.7			64.2		
AS										2.2			2.3		
PULSO													0.3		
MUSPA													0.5		
Colombia															
ASI											1.2				
ASA														0.1	
Ecuador															
MUPP-NP						20.6		14.8	20.8		2.2				
MIAJ									0.9						
Guatemala															
Winaq												3.1			3.3

OBSTACLES TO ETHNIC PARTIES IN LATIN
AMERICA

Some scholars have attributed the paucity of successful ethnic parties
in Latin America to institutional obstacles, such as registration requirements, which have made it difficult for indigenous movements to form
parties (Birnir 2004; Rice 2006; Van Cott 2005). Birnir (2004: 14), for
example, maintains that spatial registration requirements prevented the
Ecuadorian indigenous movement from establishing a party prior to 1995.
According to Birnir (2004), an indigenous party in Ecuador emerged only
after the constitution was changed to allow the participation of independent movements in elections. Similarly, Van Cott (2005: 113) argues
that in both Bolivia and Ecuador, "restrictive party registration requirements were the main impediment to the formation of ethnic parties."
Indeed, various efforts to form indigenous parties in these countries as
well as in Peru have foundered when the would-be creators of the parties
were unable to obtain the requisite number of signatures.

An institutional explanation for the lack of success of ethnic parties
in Latin America is problematic for several reasons, however. First, there
is no systematic evidence that institutional obstacles to party registration
are greater in Latin America than in other regions of the world. Indeed,
the relatively high levels of party system fragmentation and electoral volatility that exist in Latin America suggests that the barriers to creating
new parties may be lower in Latin America than in other regions of the
world (Madrid 2005; Payne et al. 2002; Roberts and Wibbels 1999).
Second, many ethnic parties have managed to get on the ballot in spite
of the barriers to party registration in Latin America. Indigenous groups
in Bolivia, for example, borrowed the registration of long-defunct left-
wing parties in order to compete in elections in that country. Third and
finally, even if onerous registration requirements can help explain why
some would-be parties have not managed to gain access to the ballot,
they cannot easily explain why those parties that did register fared poorly
in elections. Indeed, the real puzzle is not the dearth of ethnic parties in
Latin America, but the absence of *successful* ones.

A more persuasive explanation for the absence of successful ethnic
parties in the region would focus in part on resource deficits. The groups
that have formed ethnic parties in Latin America, the indigenous population and the Afro-Latino population, have lacked access to the resources
that are typically necessary for parties to fare well in national elections.
By contrast, in many other regions of the world, ethnic parties have been

formed not just by groups at the bottom of the socioeconomic hierarchy, but by groups at the middle and even the top. Indeed, many of the most successful ethnic parties in the world have been formed by socioeconomically advantaged (or at least not disadvantaged) ethnic groups. These include parties that represent the Flemish in Belgium, Afrikaners in South Africa, Hindus in India, and East Indians in Trinidad, Suriname, and Guyana.

The indigenous and Afro-Latino populations in Latin America are clearly at the bottom of the socioeconomic hierarchy. Indigenous people are significantly poorer than whites and mestizos in the region. A 2002 survey in Bolivia found that 73.9 percent of indigenous people lived below the poverty line, compared to 52.5 percent of nonindigenous people (Jiménez Pozo, Landa Casazola, and Yáñez Aguilar 2006: 48). Similarly, in Ecuador, 80.2 percent of indigenous people fell below the poverty line in 2003, compared to 57.9 percent of nonindigenous people (Larrea and Montenegro Torres 2006: 84). Indigenous people are also less educated than the nonindigenous population and they tend to live disproportionally in rural areas where there is less access to jobs and educational and health services. According to one study, indigenous people had on average between two and four fewer years of schooling than nonindigenous people in Bolivia, Ecuador, Guatemala, Mexico, and Peru (Hall and Patrinos 2006: 247).

There is less data on the Afro-Latino population in the region, but the available studies suggest that this population also suffers from a substantial education and earnings gap. A 2003 study by the Colombian census bureau found that Afro-Colombians were more likely than whites and mestizos to be located in the lowest income quintiles, to be unemployed, and to lack social insurance (Sánchez and García 2006: 36). Afro-Colombians also had below-average rates of secondary and postsecondary education (Sánchez and García 2006: 40). Similarly, white males earned more than twice as much as black and brown (*pardo*) men in Brazil during the 1990s, and white females earned three times the amount earned by black and brown women (Telles 2004: 123). In addition, Brazilians between twenty-five and ninety years of age who self-identified as white averaged two more years of schooling than Brazilians in the same age category who self-identified as black or brown (Telles 2004: 127).

The high levels of poverty and low levels of education in indigenous and Afro-Latino communities have undermined ethnic parties in the region. In Latin America, candidates for office usually fund their own campaigns. It is difficult for the indigenous and Afro-Latino candidates of ethnic parties to self-fund, however, because they typically come from lower-class backgrounds. In the 1996 Ecuadorian legislature, for example, nearly two-thirds of Pachakutik's legislative delegation came from the lower classes, as opposed to only four percent of the candidates from the other three largest parties (Mateos Díaz and Alcántara Sáez 1998: 23). Not only are the candidates of ethnic parties in Latin America typically poorer and less educated than candidates from traditional parties, but the communities they come from are usually poorer and more marginalized as well. As a result, these candidates and parties often have relatively few local resources upon which they can draw, and they typically lack the social contacts that would enable them to raise funds from others more easily. The candidates of ethnic parties therefore have scant access to the sources of private finance that have sustained the "corporation-based parties" that Barndt (Chapter 13, this volume) discusses.

The dearth of resources has made it difficult for indigenous and Afro-Latino parties to compete on the national level and even the departmental level. They have typically lacked the highly trained and experienced advisors necessary to create sophisticated and comprehensive platforms and to develop complex campaign strategies. Moreover, they have lacked the funds necessary to advertise on television, to produce slick campaign materials, to carry out polls, to hire field operatives, to distribute goods at campaign rallies, and to build sophisticated voter turnout machines. In addition, they often have lacked the contacts necessary to gain media attention, to hold campaign events throughout the country, and to create an optimal list of candidates for a variety of elected positions. All of these factors have consistently undermined the performance of ethnic parties at the ballot box. Indeed, as we shall see, the leaders of ethnic parties have frequently complained about their lack of resources.

The most significant obstacle to the success of indigenous and Afro-Latino parties, however, is the low level of ethnic consciousness in the region. Ethnic consciousness in the region has been hindered in part by *mestizaje* or ethnic/racial mixing. *Mestizaje* refers to a biological process in which people of European and indigenous or African descent produced mixed-race children, but also a cultural process in which people of indigenous or African descent shed their traditional customs and adopted mestizo identities. *Mestizaje* began from the earliest days of the conquest, but in the nineteenth and early twentieth centuries, some Latin American nations promoted *mestizaje* as a means to whiten the population and build national unity. They portrayed their countries as mestizo nations and encouraged their citizens to identify with a mestizo national culture, rather than distinct racial or ethnic groups. Some countries went so far as to ban or avoid the use of the term "Indian" or other ethnic or racial terms in official discourse (Loveman 2014; Morner 1967; Yashar 2005).

Widespread social discrimination against indigenous people and Afro-Latinos has also encouraged *mestizaje* and inhibited the formation of ethnic consciousness in the region. Various scholars have described Latin American countries as pigmentocracies because of the strong correlation between skin color and socioeconomic status in the region (Morner 1967; Sidanius, Peña, and Sawyer 2001; Telles 2014). Because of this social discrimination, many people who are mostly or wholly of indigenous or African descent have preferred to self-identify as mixed or to eschew ethnic or racial identification altogether (Bailey 2009; Morner 1967; Telles 2004). Many of these self-identified mestizos grew up in an indigenous or Afro-Latino community and engage in some traditional practices of those communities, but are nevertheless reluctant to identify as indigenous or Afro-Latino because of prejudice against those groups.

As a result of these processes, the percentage of people who self-identify as mestizo has come to far outnumber the percentage of people who self-identify as indigenous or black in most Latin American countries. In Ecuador, for example, only 6 percent of the population self-identified as indigenous in the 2001 census, even though the indigenous movement has long claimed that indigenous people represent at least 25 percent of the population. By contrast, 78 percent of Ecuadorians self-identified as mestizo and 11 percent as white in this census. In Bolivia, surveys by the Latin American Public Opinion Project (LAPOP) have found that less than 20 percent of the population self-identifies as indigenous, even though approximately half of the population speaks an indigenous language (Seligson et al. 2006: 18).[8] By comparison, more than 60 percent of the population has typically self-identified as mestizo in these surveys. These data suggest that indigenous consciousness is relatively low among people of indigenous descent in Bolivia.

The percentage of the population that is willing to identify as indigenous has increased in some countries in recent years, however. Resurgent indigenous movements have promoted indigenous pride and traditions and encouraged indigenous self-identification. In Bolivia, for example, the percentage of people who self-identify as indigenous increased by

---

[8] The 2001 census in Bolivia found that 62 percent of the population identified with some indigenous ethnolinguistic category (mostly Aymara or Quechua), but the census was widely criticized for not allowing people to self-identify as mestizo.

10 percentage points between 2000 and 2008, according to LAPOP surveys (Moreno Morales et al. 2008: xxxiii). The percentage of the population that self-identifies as indigenous has also increased significantly in Brazil in recent decades owing in large part to decisions by people of indigenous descent to embrace their indigenous heritage (Perz, Warren, and Kennedy 2008). Nevertheless, even today most people of indigenous descent do not identify as such.

Censuses have also found that only a small portion of the population is willing to self-identify as black or Afro-Latino, even in countries where the Afro-Latino population is thought to be quite large. According to the 2005 census in Colombia, only 10.6 percent of the population self-identified with some Afro-Colombian category, although estimates have placed the Afro-Colombian population at anywhere from 15 to 35 percent. In Brazil, meanwhile, only 7.6 percent of the population self-identified as black in the 2010 census, as opposed to 47.7 percent who self-identified as white and 43.1 who self-identified as brown (*pardo*). In a recent survey in Brazil, only 50 percent of people who identified as black agreed with the statement that "what happens to members of my racial group influences my own life" (Telles 2014: 195). Bailey (2009: 215), meanwhile, finds that Brazilians "embrace racial ambiguity" and that "interests are not primarily interpreted along racial boundaries in Brazil."

The low level of ethnic consciousness in Latin America makes it difficult for indigenous or Afro-Latino parties to mobilize large numbers of people based on their race or ethnicity. Candidates are often reluctant to identify themselves as indigenous or Afro-Latino and to make explicit ethnic appeals. Voters, meanwhile, often do not respond well to such appeals when they are made. Even those people who self-identify as black or indigenous may focus mostly on nonethnic considerations, such as class, region, ideology, or candidate characteristics, when deciding how to vote. As a result, ethnic parties in Latin America have a difficult time winning support if they rely on ethnic appeals alone.

As we shall see, however, a couple of ethnic parties, namely the MAS in Bolivia and Pachakutik in Ecuador, managed to surmount the resource deficits they faced as well as the low level of ethnic consciousness in the region. They did so in part by building coalitions of social movements that provided them with numerous human resources as well as in-kind material contributions. These social movements provided the territorial organization that the new parties would have otherwise lacked. Perhaps more importantly, they developed broad and ethnically inclusive populist platforms that enabled them to win support from whites and mestizos as well as self-identified indigenous voters.

OVERCOMING RESOURCE DEFICITS

As Chapter 1 makes clear, territorial organization is crucial to long-term party success, and new parties often lack such organization. Social movements, however, may provide new parties with the organizational resources they lack, as the chapters by Samuels and Zucco (Chapter 12, this volume) and Van Dyck (Chapter 5, this volume) attest. Not surprisingly, successful ethnic parties have relied heavily on the assistance of social movements to help them surmount their resource deficits. The most successful ethnic parties that have arisen in Latin America, namely the MAS in Bolivia and Pachakutik in Ecuador, did not emerge from a vacuum. Rather, they sprang from strong indigenous movements that provided them with a variety of human and material resources that enabled them to jumpstart their campaigns.[9] The indigenous movements in Bolivia and Ecuador did not have sufficient resources at their disposal to carry out effective national campaigns, however. The MAS and Pachakutik therefore formed alliances with a variety of social movements, from neighborhood organizations to unions and trade associations. These social movements provided the fledgling parties with a variety of resources that helped them win votes in urban areas and other parts of the country where the indigenous movement had little presence.

Ecuador has traditionally had the strongest and most densely organized indigenous movement in the region. A plethora of indigenous organizations emerged over the course of the latter half of the twentieth century, and in 1986 some of these organizations came together to create a unified confederation, the Confederación de Nacionalidades Indígenas del Ecuador (CONAIE – Confederation of Indigenous Nationalities of Ecuador). Soon thereafter CONAIE demonstrated its strength, carrying out several important nationwide protests during the 1990s in which it managed to block policies that it opposed and extract concessions from the government. Many leaders of CONAIE viewed the creation of an indigenous party as the next logical step in its evolution as it moved from "protests to proposals." After considerable debate, CONAIE voted

[9] For detailed analyses of indigenous movements in Bolivia and Ecuador, see Albó (2002), Lucero (2008), and Yashar (2005).

in 1995 to create an indigenous party, Pachakutik, to compete in the 1996 elections.[10]

CONAIE provided Pachakutik with a number of important organizational resources (Madrid 2012: 85–86). First, it supplied the fledgling party with candidates who were well-known in indigenous areas. Most of the party's leaders and candidates for top positions have come directly from the indigenous movement. Second, the indigenous movement provided the party with a network of activists in indigenous areas who could distribute propaganda, give speeches, coordinate campaign events, and round up supporters. Third, although it had no funds that it could offer Pachakutik, CONAIE made substantial in-kind contributions to the cash-starved party, including food, transportation, meeting venues, and campaign materials. Fourth and finally, CONAIE provided Pachakutik with its seal of approval, which was particularly influential within indigenous communities.

Outside of indigenous areas, however, CONAIE had little in the way of resources it could offer the party. Pachakutik offset this shortcoming by building alliances with a variety of nonindigenous social movements from the outset. For example, it forged ties to the Coordinadora de Movimientos Sociales (Coordinator of Social Movements), which was an umbrella organization that brought together unions, women's groups, human rights agencies, environmental organizations, and neighborhood associations. Other nongovernmental organizations, such as teachers' and professional associations and the organization of rural social security affiliates, also subsequently joined the party's campaigns. These social movements provided important material and human resources, including campaign workers and meeting venues, in the cities and regions where the indigenous movement was traditionally weak. Thus, they played an important role in Pachakutik's initial success in urban areas.

Social movements also played a key role in the success of the MAS in Bolivia. The MAS originated in the Quechua-speaking coca growers' unions of rural Cochabamba. These unions, which carried out a wave of protests against US-sponsored coca eradication efforts beginning in the 1980s, gradually became the most powerful social movement in Bolivia. By the early 1990s, they had gained control of Bolivia's most important indigenous federation, the Confederación Sindical Única de Trabajadores

---

[10] There are a number of good studies of the origins of Pachakutik (e.g., Andolina 1999; Birnir 2004; Collins 2006; Van Cott 2005; Guerrero Cazar and Ospina Peralta 2003; Mijeski and Beck 2011; Sánchez López and Freidenberg 1998).

Campesinos de Bolivia (CSUTCB – Unitary Syndical Confederation of Rural Workers of Bolivia) and pushed the organization to establish a political party. In 1995, the CSUTCB along with the women's peasant federation, the Federación Nacional de Mujeres Campesinas "Bartolina Sisa" ("Bartolina Sisa" National Federation of Peasant Women), and an organization of migrant peasants, the Confederación Sindical de Colonizadores Bolivianos (Syndical Confederation of Bolivian Colonizers), established a precursor of the MAS, the Asamblea por la Soberanía de los Pueblos (ASP – Assembly for the Sovereignty of the Peoples), which competed under the party registration of a largely defunct left-wing party, Izquierda Unida (IU – United Left).[11]

These organizations provided the IU-ASP and, subsequently the MAS, with badly needed organizational resources in some rural indigenous areas. As Levitsky, Loxton, and Van Dyck argue in Chapter 1, conflict can help forge strong identities, promote organization-building, and create an activist base. Not surprisingly, the repressive coca eradication campaigns that the coca growers' unions endured in the 1980s and 1990s led them to develop an impressive ethos and organizational apparatus. The coca growers' unions aggressively defended coca growing in the region and in some areas they grew to become a virtual government, disciplining and taxing their members, and providing public works. The coca growers' unions vigorously supported the IU-ASP as the political arm of this movement, supplying the fledgling party with a lot of its initial staff and candidates, as well as its campaign materials. Nevertheless, these unions had relatively little influence or organizational resources outside of rural Cochabamba. As a result, the IU-ASP fared poorly outside of the coca-growing areas of rural Cochabamba.

In 1998, however, the IU-ASP split up and Evo Morales, who was the most powerful of the coca grower leaders, founded a new party, the Instrumento Político por la Soberanía de los Pueblos (IPSP – Political Instrument for the Sovereignty of the Peoples). In order to compete in elections, the IPSP borrowed the registration of another defunct left-wing party, the MAS. In the years that followed, Morales and the MAS established a broad network of alliances with social movements throughout the country. The MAS forged ties to many unions and neighborhood associations, as well as organizations of truck drivers, artisans, street vendors, teachers, and pensioners. It also reached out to numerous indigenous

---

[11] Numerous studies have examined the origins of the MAS (e.g., Muñoz-Pogossian 2008; Stefanoni and Do Alto 2006; Collins 2006; Rice 2006; Harnecker, Fuentes, and Ramírez 2008; Van Cott 2005).

organizations outside of Cochabamba. These social movements gave the MAS an organizational base outside of its regional stronghold. They supplied the MAS not only with candidates and campaign organizers who had local influence and contacts, but also with food, campaign materials, meeting spaces, and transportation. The MAS's expanding network of alliances helped it win votes in areas where it was traditionally weak, enabling it to dramatically expand its share of the national vote beginning in 2002.

Thus, the MAS and Pachakutik used their strong ties to social movements to help overcome the severe resource deficits they faced. The social movements did not have funds they could give to the parties, but they provided them with the human and material resources necessary to carry out a nationwide campaign, including in areas where the indigenous movement was relatively weak.

APPEALING ACROSS ETHNIC LINES

As discussed in Chapters 1 and 3 of this volume, successful party-building depends on the development of a party brand. This brand must appeal to a significant number of voters and it must distinguish the party from other parties (Lupu 2013). Both the MAS and, initially, Pachakutik, developed a successful brand, which I have referred to elsewhere as ethnopopulism (Madrid 2008, 2012). This brand enabled them to overcome the low level of ethnic consciousness in the region and attract the support of a large number of voters of diverse ethnic backgrounds.

The ethnopopulist brand had a couple of key components. First, it emphasized ethnic appeals, but in a highly inclusive manner. Both the MAS and Pachakutik sought to appeal to indigenous people by recruiting prominent indigenous leaders as candidates, forging ties with indigenous organizations, invoking indigenous symbols, and embracing traditional indigenous demands. Rather than focusing narrowly on the indigenous population, however, the parties stressed the inclusive nature of their projects and reached out to whites and mestizos. The high level of *mestizaje* in Latin America made this strategy feasible by blurring ethnic boundaries and reducing ethnic polarization. In a more ethnically polarized region, ethnic parties would be unlikely to win support across ethnic lines, but in Latin America, the inclusive strategies of the MAS and Pachakutik worked, enabling both parties to gain numerous white and mestizo as well as indigenous votes (Madrid 2008, 2012).

Second, the ethnopopulist brand stressed the use of traditional populist strategies to attract voters of all ethnic backgrounds. Both the MAS and, initially, Pachakutik sought out charismatic candidates and built their campaigns around them. They employed antiestablishment rhetoric and focused their campaigns on the lower classes. They adopted highly nationalist and state interventionist platforms. This campaign strategy, which is an example of what Luna (Chapter 4, this volume) refers to as a segmented linkage strategy, appealed to indigenous and nonindigenous people alike. It enabled the MAS to build a winning electoral coalition by fusing traditional populist constituencies, namely urban mestizo lower-class voters, to its rural indigenous core.

The MAS and its precursors initially concentrated on attracting indigenous voters. During the 1990s, the vast majority of the party's candidates were indigenous and its platform focused mostly on ending the US-sponsored coca eradication programs that mainly affected indigenous coca growers. As a result, the party's support was largely limited to indigenous people. The precursors of the MAS won only 3.0 percent of the national vote in 1995, 3.7 percent in 1997, and 3.3 percent in 1999, and the vast majority of those votes came from coca-growing regions.

Beginning in the early 2000s, however, the MAS reached out to whites and mestizos. It recruited white and mestizo candidates for a variety of important positions. For example, it nominated Antonio Peredo and Álvaro García Linera as its vice-presidential candidates in 2002, 2005, and 2009. It recruited other prominent mestizos, such as Filemón Escobar and Ana María Romero, as senatorial candidates. Whereas in 1997 all of the MAS's legislators were indigenous, by 2005 whites and mestizos represented more than half of the MAS's legislative contingent (Madrid 2012: 61). During this period, the MAS also forged ties to numerous urban-based, mestizo-dominated organizations. In 2005, for example, the MAS forged an alliance with the Movimiento Sin Miedo (Movement without Fear), an important mestizo-dominated left-of-center party, which was based in La Paz.

To win the support of white and mestizo voters, the MAS also broadened its platform, adopting populist rhetoric, strategies, and policy proposals. It built its campaigns around Evo Morales, the party's charismatic and down-to-earth leader. Morales and other leaders of the MAS denounced the traditional parties and elites whom they accused of being corrupt and self-serving, and they focused on winning the support of the poor. They criticized the neoliberal policies that Bolivia had adopted beginning in the 1980s, and they called for increased state intervention in the economy and income redistribution. Morales and other leaders of the MAS also railed against foreign intervention in Bolivia and advocated the nationalization of their countries' natural resources.

It is important to note that the MAS broadened its appeal not by forsaking its initial base and party principles, but rather by addressing new constituencies and issue areas. Throughout the 2000s, the MAS continued to vociferously defend indigenous rights and coca growing, but it also embraced a whole range of new issues that appealed to new constituencies, such as urban mestizos. The MAS's position on these new issues was hardly moderate. Indeed, the MAS's nationalist, antineoliberal, and antiestablishment rhetoric was downright radical at times. Thus, much like the parties that originated from former guerrilla movements in El Salvador and Nicaragua, the MAS did not make the mistake of moderating excessively.[12]

The MAS's ethnopopulist appeals were largely successful. The MAS finished second in the 2002 presidential elections with 20.9 percent of the vote, but then won the presidential elections in a landslide in 2005, 2009, and 2013. Whereas the MAS (or its predecessors) had received almost exclusively indigenous votes during the 1990s, the party earned the support of many whites and mestizos beginning in 2002. Indeed, the MAS won 32 percent of the white vote and 51 percent of the mestizo vote in the 2005 elections, according to a 2006 survey by the LAPOP. (Most of these self-identified mestizos, however, came from indigenous backgrounds and spoke indigenous languages.) Support from whites and mestizos was crucial to the MAS's victory in 2005, 2009, and 2013. Self-identified whites and mestizos represented almost 70 percent of the MAS's total vote in the 2005 presidential elections, according to the 2006 LAPOP survey (Madrid 2012: 61–62).

Pachakutik, by contrast, started out as a highly inclusive party. The indigenous movement played the lead role in the creation of Pachakutik, but various mestizo-dominated organizations helped found the party. White and mestizo leaders also occupied key positions in the party from the outset. Indeed, initially about one-third of the party's top leadership and legislative contingent was nonindigenous, and by 2002 half of the party's legislative delegation was white or mestizo (Madrid 2012: 90). Moreover, the party allied with nonethnic parties and supported white or mestizo candidates for president in the first three elections in which it competed. In 1996 and 1998, the party allied with the Movimiento Ciudadano Nuevo País (Citizens' Movement for a New Country) and nominated its leader, Freddy Ehlers, for president. In 2002, the party allied with the PSP and nominated its leader, Lucio Gutiérrez, as the

---

[12] On such "insurgent successor parties," see Holland (Chapter 10, this volume).

alliance's presidential candidate. In addition, the party forged a variety of alliances with other mestizo-dominated parties both at the national and provincial level.

Like the MAS, Pachakutik employed traditional populist rhetoric and strategies to win nonindigenous as well as indigenous votes. Pachakutik attacked the existing economic and political establishment and focused its campaigns on the popular sectors. It supported political outsiders for president, fashioning its campaigns around their personalities and accomplishments. Pachakutik also opposed privatization, foreign debt payments, and a free trade agreement with the United States, and it called for the closing of the US military base in Manta, Ecuador.

These policies largely paid off. Pachakutik won approximately 10 percent of the legislative vote and 15 to 20 percent of the first-round presidential vote between 1996 and 2002. Moreover, its presidential candidate, Lucio Gutiérrez of the PSP, was elected president in 2002, though Pachakutik's alliance with Gutiérrez and the PSP fractured within the year. Pachakutik's success was due in large part to its strong performance in urban, mestizo-dominated areas. Its presidential candidate won an average of 21 percent of the vote in 1996 and 27 percent in 2002 in counties where the indigenous represented a minority of the population (Madrid 2012: 87). It performed even better in rural indigenous areas, but these areas contained only a small minority of Ecuador's total population. Indeed, in the 1996 elections, Pachakutik won an average of 34 percent in counties where the indigenous represented a majority, and in the 2002 elections, it won an average of 53 percent of the vote in these majority indigenous counties (Madrid 2012: 87).

The alliance with Gutiérrez undermined Pachakutik's ethnopopulist brand, however. In the wake of the 2002 elections, Gutiérrez shifted to the right, implementing a program of market-oriented reforms and forging strong ties to the United States. Although Pachakutik eventually left Gutiérrez's government, it nevertheless had tarnished its reputation in the eyes of many of its populist supporters. As Lupu (2013; Chapter 3, this volume) argues, the behavior of parties must be consistent with their platform in order for them to maintain their brand.

To make matters worse, beginning with the 2006 elections, Pachakutik shifted in a more ethnocentric direction, abandoning the ethnic inclusiveness that is one of the hallmarks of the ethnopopulist brand. It started to focus more on indigenous issues and paid less attention to the populist agenda that had won it support in previous elections. The party also forsook alliances that year and opted to run an internal candidate, the indigenous leader Luis Macas, for president. In addition, the party nominated fewer nonindigenous people for other key positions and, as a result, many of the white and mestizo leaders and organizations that had formerly supported the party began to abandon it.

The shift took place for several reasons. Certainly, the failure of Pachakutik's pact with Gutiérrez soured the party on alliances. Many party leaders felt that Gutiérrez had used Pachakutik to get elected and then abandoned it. In addition, some indigenous leaders in Pachakutik wanted the party to focus more on indigenous issues and had grown frustrated with its tendency to award many of the key candidacies and leadership positions to whites and mestizos. In a 2007 interview with the author, Ramsés Torres, a member of Pachakutik's 2007–2011 delegation, complained: "There are indigenous leaders who have a perspective that is very ethnic and not pluralistic."

Not surprisingly, the ethnocentric strategy failed. The party fared much worse in 2006 than it had in previous elections, winning only 2.2 percent of the presidential vote and 4.1 percent of the legislative vote. It fared particularly poorly in white and mestizo-dominated counties. Since that time the party has continued to focus mostly on indigenous issues and run indigenous candidates for the most part, and has won few votes outside of some indigenous areas.

Pachakutik's ethnocentric turn points to one of the main difficulties for ethnic parties in implementing ethnopopulist strategies: these strategies may not be popular among many of the group's core leaders and supporters. Indeed, some indigenous members of both the MAS and Pachakutik have resisted their parties' efforts to ally with nonindigenous organizations and recruit whites and mestizos for key candidacies and leadership positions. Most indigenous parties in Latin America have arisen in large part because of concerns that the existing parties are dominated by whites and mestizos and do not address indigenous needs and demands. As a result, there has been a natural inclination on the part of these parties to focus on indigenous concerns and to reserve the key candidacies and leadership positions for indigenous people. Moreover, indigenous parties often have mixed feelings about allying with nonindigenous parties, organizations, or movements. Indigenous organizations have feared being co-opted, marginalized, and exploited, and the leaders of some indigenous parties that have forged alliances with major nonindigenous parties, such as Pachakutik in Ecuador and the Movimiento Revolucionario Tupak Katari de Liberación (MRTKL – Tupak Katari Revolutionary Movement of Liberation) in Bolivia, have complained that they received relatively few benefits from these alliances. Thus, although an inclusive ethnopopulist strategy might be an electorally effective strategy for an ethnic party, it is not an easy strategy to sell internally.

UNSUCCESSFUL ETHNIC PARTIES

The MAS and Pachakutik have been the exception rather than the rule. Most ethnic parties in Latin America have had little success. The various *Katarista* and *Indianista* parties that emerged in Bolivia, for example, never managed to win many votes outside of the Aymara heartland where they were based. Nor have the indigenous parties that sprang up in Colombia, Ecuador, Guatemala, or elsewhere in Latin America had much electoral impact.

This section focuses on two indigenous parties – the MIP in Bolivia and Winaq in Guatemala – that were, perhaps, the most promising of all of these unsuccessful parties. These parties emerged in the two countries with the largest indigenous populations and they arose at a time of growing indigenous activism and consciousness. Moreover, they were created by charismatic indigenous leaders who were well known not only in indigenous communities, but among the population as a whole. As a result, many observers expected the MIP and Winaq to make an important electoral showing. Nevertheless, neither of the parties managed to make significant inroads among whites and mestizos, and even their support among indigenous voters was limited to certain communities.

I will argue here that these parties flopped in part because they did not have the backing of enough social movements to help them overcome the severe resource deficits they faced. Both the MIP and Winaq had the support of some sectors of their countries' indigenous movements, but they failed to assemble a broader coalition of social movements to back their candidates. Perhaps even more importantly, these parties failed to adopt the inclusive ethnopopulist brand that the MAS in Bolivia and, initially, Pachakutik in Ecuador employed to win support of whites and mestizos as well as indigenous people. Felipe Quispe and other leaders of the MIP focused their appeals mostly on ethnic demands and alienated whites and mestizos. Rigoberta Menchú and Winaq ran a more inclusive campaign, but they failed to use traditional populist appeals.

The MIP was founded in 2000 by Felipe Quispe, who had a long and storied trajectory as an indigenous leader. Quispe had been one of the founders of the Movimiento Indio Tupak Katari (MITKA – Tupak Katari Indigenous Movement), an Aymara-based party, which had participated in the 1978, 1979, and 1980 elections, never winning more than 2 percent of the vote. He subsequently formed a guerrilla organization, the Ejército Guerrillero Tupak Katari (Tupak Katari Guerrilla Army), and was captured by the Bolivian authorities in 1992 and sentenced to prison as a result of his involvement in this group. He left prison in 1997 and became involved again in Bolivia's largest indigenous federation, the CSUTCB. Quispe was elected secretary general of this organization in 1998 in part because of divisions between the two main candidates, Evo Morales and Alejo Véliz.

In 2002, Quispe ran for president as the candidate of the MIP. The MIP was initially viewed as a major threat to the traditional parties because of the large indigenous population in Bolivia, the traditionally high levels of indigenous organization in the country, and Quispe's charismatic leadership. In fact, many observers initially believed that the MIP represented a larger threat to the existing parties than did the MAS.

The MIP had relatively few resources to devote to the campaign, however. In a 2004 interview with the author, Quispe complained:

The MIP lives in poverty. It doesn't have economic resources. It's not a movement of businessmen. It's of the *lumpenproletariat* – those who sleep in the street. So this does not permit us a national campaign. We don't have money to do advertisements.

According to one source, the party and its candidates spent only $15,000 on its 2002 campaign (Van Cott 2005: 92).

The MAS also had relatively few financial resources, but it had an extensive network of allied social organizations that it could use to compensate for its lack of financial resources. Quispe, however, was a polarizing figure and had not established ties to many politicians and organizations outside of the Aymara heartland in the Department of La Paz. Quispe and the MIP did have close links to some sectors of the indigenous movement, and various indigenous organizations and leaders supported his campaign. By 2002, however, the indigenous movement, including the CSUTCB, was severely divided, and most sectors of the indigenous movement backed Evo Morales. In the 2004 interview with the author, Quispe bemoaned the divisions within the indigenous movement:

We have an enemy. The enemy is Evo Morales. The enemy of the Indian is an Indian himself. We [the MIP] have not managed to have a national presence – just in La Paz. We would have done better without Evo. They try to destroy us. We are a bother. They don't let us win. They have their own CSUTCB, their own landless movement and women's movement.

As a result of the divisions within the indigenous movement, Quispe could not even count on organizational support in most indigenous communities.

To make matters worse, Quispe scared off many voters with his incendiary ethnonationalist rhetoric and demands. Quispe employed some traditional populist rhetoric – he denounced US imperialism, neoliberal policies, and the traditional parties – but his principal demands were ethnic. The platform of the MIP called for the "reconstitution of our historical territories" and the refounding of Bolivia as a communitarian indigenous nation named "Qullasuyu" (Movimiento Indígena Pachakuti 2005). Quispe himself made it clear: "we want our own state, controlled by us, not a white state" (Cúneo 2011: 57). Quispe was not even particularly committed to the democratic process. As he told the author in 2004: "I continue to think that we can capture the state through armed struggle, but the masses prefer the legal path."

This type of rhetoric and demands alienated most whites and mestizos, not to mention many indigenous people. In the 2002 elections, Quispe and the MIP fared well in Aymara areas, winning 26 percent of the vote in provinces where a majority of the population spoke Aymara. But the MIP fared poorly elsewhere, earning only 1.4 percent of the vote in provinces where a majority of the population spoke Spanish and 2.4 percent of the vote in provinces where most people spoke Quechua. Nationwide, the MIP captured 6.1 percent of the vote and won six seats in the legislature, but this was not enough to give the party much policy influence. Moreover, from the outset, the party was torn by internal divisions and a number of prominent figures within the party ended up abandoning it. Quispe and the MIP ran again in the 2005 general elections, but fared even worse, winning only 2.2 percent of the vote. The MIP has since disappeared altogether.

Winaq, which was founded by Rigoberta Menchú in 2007, also had a great deal of promise at the outset. Menchú, the winner of the Nobel Peace Prize, is a well-known figure in Guatemala who has a vast array of high-level contacts both inside and outside the country. Moreover, by most accounts, Guatemala has the second highest proportion of indigenous people after Bolivia, which makes it a potentially fruitful site for an indigenous party. According to the 2002 census, approximately 41 percent of the population self-identify as indigenous (mostly Maya), and self-identified indigenous people represent a majority of the population in nine of the country's twenty-one departments. Finally, disenchantment with the existing parties has been quite high in Guatemala in recent decades, which has provided an opening for new parties. Indeed, Guatemala had the second highest level of electoral volatility in Latin America during the 1980s and 1990s, and various new parties emerged during this period (Madrid 2005).

Winaq, however, failed to live up to expectations. Menchú did not have time to register Winaq as a political party in 2007, so she instead forged an alliance with a center-left party, Encuentro por Guatemala (EG – Gathering for Guatemala), and ran as its presidential candidate. Menchú won only 3.1 percent of the presidential vote nationwide in 2007, finishing a distant seventh. EG fared somewhat better in the legislative elections that year, winning 6.2 percent of the valid vote and four seats, but overall the election was a disappointment for both Menchú and EG.

Menchú fared poorly in 2007 in part because she did not assemble a broad coalition of social movements to back her campaign. According to an analysis by a prominent Guatemalan research organization:

Her candidacy was not the result of a process of construction of a wide alliance of political forces of the center and left, of small and medium businessmen, of a broad support network of organizations of peasants, indigenous people, youth, and women, of labor unions, and professional associations. (Instituto Centramericano de Estudios Políticos 2007: 2)

Neither Menchú nor EG started out with extensive ties to grassroots social movements. EG was an urban-based party of professionals and intellectuals without links to the popular sectors. Menchú, who ran a foundation in the capital, did have ties to indigenous leaders and Mayan intellectuals, especially in the capital, but, in contrast to Morales and Quispe in Bolivia, she did not preside over a grassroots movement and she had only weak ties to grassroots social movements and leaders (Bastos 2009; Falla 2007). Nor were Menchú and Winaq able to successfully forge these ties during the campaign, in part because they entered the electoral contest at a relatively late stage.

Menchú was not even able to win the support of many of the country's most important indigenous and peasant organizations, which are smaller and less powerful than their counterparts in Bolivia and Ecuador in any event. For example, the Coordinadora Nacional de Organizaciones Campesinas (CNOC – National Coordinator of Peasant Organizations) declined to endorse Menchú's candidacy in 2007. According to Basilio Sánchez, the leader of the CNOC, the organization "never felt her support. She has not gotten close to the social movements" (Ortiz Loaiza

et al. 2008: 16). Without the support of a broad coalition of social movements, Menchú did not have the organizational resources to run a successful national campaign. Moreover, she lacked the funding to run a
major media campaign and the party organization necessary to mobilize
voters throughout the country. Indeed, EG spent only six million quetzales on the 2007 election campaign, whereas the three main parties all
spent more than 100 million quetzales (Ortiz Loaiza et al. 2008: 11).

Another reason that Menchú and EG had relatively meager results in
2007 was that they declined to employ traditional populist strategies.
Menchú did not attack the traditional economic and political elites.[13] To
the contrary, she invited a prominent member of the business community,
Luis Fernando Montenegro, to serve as her vice-presidential candidate.
Nor did Menchú criticize the market-oriented policies that Guatemala
had implemented during recent decades. Indeed, in a 2008 interview
with the author, Montenegro said that he only agreed to participate in
the campaign when he was assured that it would not be a campaign
against the private sector and that he would not be obliged to support
land redistribution.

Instead, Menchú pursued a centrist campaign in 2007, one that
Montenegro described as ideologically between liberalism and social
democracy.[14] Throughout the campaign, she avoided identifying herself with leftist or populist ideologies, arguing that ideologies were the
source of the many problems that Guatemala had experienced in the
past (Falla 2007; Mack 2007). Menchú, in fact, rejected an alliance with
the far left party led by former guerrillas, the Unidad Revolucionaria
Nacional Guatemalteca (URNG – Guatemalan National Revolutionary
Unity), because she feared alienating the majority of Guatemalans who
disapproved of the guerrillas. The EG, by contrast, was a moderate,
technocratic center-left party that she believed would appeal to most
Guatemalans.

This centrist campaign, however, failed to inspire voters, especially the
poor and politically disenchanted Guatemalans who comprised most of
the electorate. Like Morales in Bolivia, Menchú waged an inclusive campaign, seeking the support of whites and mestizos as well as indigenous
people, but her bland campaign gave them little reason to vote for her.
Even indigenous people failed to mobilize behind her. In fact, she won

---

[13] Menchú had served as Peace Ambassador for the incumbent government of Óscar Berger,
which made it difficult for her to criticize the outgoing administration too severely.

[14] Interview with the author, 2008.

only 4.4 percent of the vote in municipalities where indigenous people represented more than 90 percent of the population (Mirador Electoral 2007). The winner of the 2007 election was Álvaro Colom, who ran a populist campaign in which he promised massive social spending.[15]

Thus, Menchú and Quispe fared poorly in part because they failed to follow the path of successful indigenous parties such as the MAS and Pachakutik. Neither Menchú nor Quispe assembled broad coalitions of social movements to back their campaigns, nor did they embrace the ethnopopulist brand. Whereas Quispe alienated whites and mestizos with his exclusionary rhetoric, Menchú failed to inspire them with her cautious centrist platform and rhetoric.

CONCLUSION

Although numerous ethnic parties have emerged in Latin America in the last several decades, the vast majority of these parties have performed poorly at the ballot box. Successful ethnic parties have been rare in Latin America for two main reasons: the low level of ethnic consciousness in the region, and the scarcity of party-building resources in those communities that have created ethnic parties. As we have seen, many people of indigenous and Afro-Latino descent do not self-identify as such and, as a result, it has been difficult to mobilize them with ethnic appeals alone. Moreover, the ethnic parties that have emerged in Latin America have suffered from severe resource deficits because of the widespread poverty afflicting the indigenous and Afro-Latino populations in the region. The ethnic parties that have emerged from these communities have not had funds to hire campaign staff, conduct polls, invest heavily in campaign propaganda, or carry out nationwide advertising campaigns.

The successful ethnic parties, namely the MAS in Bolivia and, initially, Pachakutik in Ecuador, have overcome these obstacles in two main ways. First, they have forged close ties to a variety of social movements, which have provided them with human and material resources, including activists, candidates, campaign posters, meeting venues, and the organization's

[15] Menchú ran for president again in 2011, this time as the head of a left-wing alliance that included Winaq, the URNG, and another left-wing party, the Alianza Nueva Nación (New Nation Alliance). Menchú made greater efforts to reach out to social organizations in 2011 and adopted a more populist discourse, but these efforts proved insufficient. In 2011, she fared only marginally better than in 2007, winning a mere 3.3 percent of the vote and coming in sixth place. Winaq, meanwhile, won 3.2 percent of the vote and three seats in that year's legislative elections.

seal of approval. Second, they have sought to appeal not just to people who identify as indigenous, but to whites and mestizos as well. This has been made feasible by the low level of ethnic polarization and the fluidity of ethnic boundaries in the region. In order to appeal across ethnic lines, the successful indigenous parties have recruited white and mestizo leaders, forged ties to nonindigenous organizations, and adopted highly inclusive rhetoric. In addition, they have developed broad-based platforms and used traditional populist appeals to woo voters of all ethnicities.

Most ethnic parties, however, have failed to employ these strategies. The MIP, for example, never reached out to nonindigenous voters, leaders, and organizations, and Winaq did not forge a broad coalition of social movements or employ traditional populist appeals. As a result, neither of these parties fared well. A similar ethnocentric focus has hamstrung other indigenous parties, such as the *Katarista* and *Indianista* parties in Bolivia, the Movimiento Independiente Amauta Jatari in Ecuador, and Yapti Tasba Masraka Nanih Asla Takanka (YATAMA – Organization of the Children of Mother Earth) in Nicaragua. These parties were formed specifically to represent indigenous interests and their leaders consequently focused on indigenous issues and demands. As the case study of Pachakutik makes clear, inclusive strategies are often unpopular among indigenous leaders and activists who distrust nonindigenous parties and organizations, and who prefer to reserve the key candidacies and leadership positions for themselves. Moreover, building ties with a broad variety of social movements is a difficult, long-term process that involves developing personal relationships and demonstrating a willingness to reciprocate.

The initial success of the MAS and Pachakutik shows that ethnic parties can win in Latin America, but it is not clear how long they will endure. As we have seen, Pachakutik has already fallen on hard times and the MAS, too, faces considerable internal tensions and organizational challenges. The coalition-building strategy of the MAS, like that of Pachakutik, has created resentment among some indigenous leaders who have complained that whites and mestizos are taking over the MAS. The MAS has successfully managed these internal tensions so far, but it has been able to do so in large part because Morales wields unchallenged authority within the party and he appears to be fully committed to ensuring that the MAS is ethnically inclusive.

To date, Morales, like other populist leaders, has demonstrated little interest in party-building, however. Indeed, he has blocked the creation of any autonomous party structures and leadership that might challenge his dominance of the party. Nevertheless, his personal popularity has contributed mightily to the success that his party has enjoyed so far, and his antiestablishment rhetoric and policies may contribute to party-building in the long term by creating the kind of polarized environment that strengthens partisan identities and promotes intraparty cohesion. Thus, the MAS may end up illustrating what Levitsky, Loxton, and Van Dyck refer to in Chapter 1 as the "paradox of populism": populist leaders sometimes create powerful parties even though they have no intention of doing so.

Party-Building in Brazil

The Rise of the PT in Perspective

David Samuels and Cesar Zucco Jr.

How does mass partisanship develop, particularly in the absence of deep socioeconomic or cultural cleavages? We attempt to explain variation in the evolution of mass partisanship in Brazil, focusing on the growth of the Workers' Party (PT). After two decades of military rule, Brazil returned to competitive elections in 1985. Twenty-five years later, it had below-average aggregate levels of mass partisanship (Huber et al. 2005) – about 35 percent of Brazilians identified with one of Brazil's many parties by 2010.

However, this below-average level is misleading, as most parties never acquired substantial numbers of adherents. Figure 12.1 shows the proportion of voters who identify with any party (the top line), as well as the share of Brazilians who have identified with the PT, Party of the Brazilian Democratic Movement (PMDB) and Party of Brazilian Social Democracy (PSDB).[1] Since 1989 (when surveys started consistently asking a partisanship question), only these parties have ever commanded the sympathy of more than 5 percent of voters – and only the PT has managed to capture a significant number of partisans.[2]

The PT was granted legal recognition in 1982. By 1989, about 5 percent of Brazilians identified as *petistas*. The proportion of *petistas* peaked at 25–30 percent in 2012; although the figure has since declined to 15–20 percent, it still accounts for about half of all partisan identifiers in Brazil. Meanwhile, since 1989, the PMDB – the successor to the party

---

[1] Data are from surveys conducted by Datafolha, one of Brazil's largest polling companies, which since 1989 has routinely asked voters the open-ended question, "Which is your preferred political party?" A collection of these surveys is available from UNICAMP's Center for the Study of Public Opinion (CESOP).

[2] The Figure shows a moving average (by semester) of levels of party identification, as computed by Datafolha.

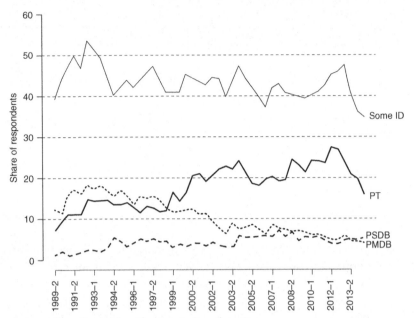

FIGURE 12.1 Party identification in Brazil, 1989–2011.
Source: Datafolha.

that served as the official opposition during the military regime – has
steadily lost identifiers, and despite holding the presidency from 1995
to 2002, the PSDB (which formed in 1988) has never attracted more
than a small number of partisans. The PSDB's main coalition partner –
the Democrats (DEM, formerly the Party of the Liberal Front, or PFL) –
which was once the largest conservative party in the legislature, does not
even register on this figure.

The PT's decline since 2013 may be temporary, due to economic stag-
nation and/or corruption scandals. It is too early to tell. In any case, at the
time of this writing, the PT still claimed a far larger number of partisan
supporters than any other party. Although many Brazilian parties can
claim electoral success, why has the PT been the only party to capture the
partisan loyalties of a sizable slice of the electorate?

In other research, we confirmed that partisanship has the same meaning to Brazilians as it does to voters elsewhere – it solidifies voters' attachment to a party's candidates, and acts as a perceptual filter through which
partisans understand politics, at least for the Brazilians that identify with
one of the main parties (Samuels and Zucco 2015). But an important
caveat applies: relatively few Brazilians have ever been partisans of any
party other than the PT.

The growth of party ID from zero to one in four voters within a single generation is a remarkable achievement for any party. How did the PT grow from a footnote in Brazil's party system in the early 1980s to a key player, winning four presidential elections and laying down roots in Brazilian society? Why have other parties not laid down similar roots in voters' minds?

The emergence of widespread partisanship for the PT is theoretically puzzling because comparative research predicts weak partisanship for *all* Brazilian parties. When asked, most voters place themselves around the center of the political spectrum, and their ideological self-placements in any case only weakly predict party ID (Samuels 2006). In addition, in contrast to many other new democracies, Brazil's parties have not organized along pro- and anti-old regime lines, and social cleavages such as class, ethnicity, religion, or region are comparatively shallow (Kitschelt et al. 2010; Mainwaring and Scully 1995). Finally, even if such social cleavages existed, Brazil's political institutions fragment the party system and enhance individualistic political behavior on the campaign trail, making it hard for voters to understand where parties stand on the issues and limiting the impact of party brand names as "cues" that can guide voter behavior (Ames 2001; Mainwaring 1999; Samuels 1999).

Given all of this, explaining the weakness of partisanship for the PFL/DEM, PSDB and PMDB seems fairly easy. But if Brazil's social and political context fosters weak partisanship, how can we explain the PT? Elsewhere in this volume, Noam Lupu suggests that diluting a party's established brand name – its public image, i.e., what voters generally think of when they hear or see the party's name – by abandoning long-held policy positions and by allying with ideologically strange bedfellows can, under certain conditions, lead to a *collapse* of party ID. This makes sense: scholars do not expect parties with obscure platforms to gain partisan adherents in the electorate. It is paradoxical, then, that the PT's base of partisan supporters grew even as its leaders abandoned its leftist positions and entered a confusing array of electoral coalitions.

We do not believe that *petismo* grew among Brazilian voters simply because the PT won four presidential elections since 2003 or because it held power initially during relatively good economic times. If that were the case, then the PSDB should also have been able to build its brand and gain adherents when it held the presidency. The key to party-building in Brazil, it seems, has less to do with social cleavages, party ideology, or success in office than with party organizational attributes. Clearly, the PT did something different from its competitors, and we believe that identifying this organizational factor could help understand the process of party-building across Latin America.

The PT has certainly changed a great deal since its origins, both programmatically and organizationally. However, *petismo* grew in the electorate because the PT remained true to its roots in a key way. Like most other Brazilian parties, the PT has a powerful central organization. However, most Brazilian parties embody a centralized Duvergerian "elite" model – they are electoralist machines with few programmatic commitments and whose leaders invest little to nothing in brand development.

In contrast, since its origin the PT has sought to avoid the supposed inevitability of Robert Michels's "Iron Law of Oligarchy" by institutionalizing opportunities for grassroots political participation in party affairs. For example, although the party has grown more centralized, it maintained formal structures for civil society participation, institutionalized thematic groups at all levels, and promoted direct internal elections. These efforts differ from Leninist parties' traditional democratic centralism and seek to demonstrate the PT's commitment to its version of democracy, which involves greater bottom-up participation from diverse segments of organized civil society.

Despite evolving a great deal, becoming embroiled in deep corruption scandals and consequently losing the support of many of its early adherents, the PT has maintained a distinct organizational profile, which has helped it spread its image throughout Brazilian society. This "branding" effort has borne fruit, as partisanship for the PT among Brazilian voters – *petismo* – grew up through 2013 and still remains a powerful brand. The success of the PT brand rests with the fact that, in contrast to Brazil's other parties, the PT combined organizational cohesiveness with member inclusiveness. Variation in organizational investment strategies explains variation in party-building in the electorate.

PARTY ORGANIZATION AND PARTY-BUILDING IN BRAZIL: BACKGROUND

In the years immediately following redemocratization, scholars concurred that Brazil's main parties were largely personalistic elite vehicles, in which informality superseded the written rules (Freidenberg and Levitsky 2006; Mainwaring 1999). It is important to recall that the PT was a bit player until 1989, when Lula ran a close second in the first competitive presidential election held since 1960. Much has changed since then. The PT controlled the government since. To what extent do the past and current organizational characteristics of *all* of Brazil's main parties explain why only the PT has managed to grow both in terms of votes and partisan identifiers?

Contemporary debate about Brazil's parties turns on how to interpret their "strength." Of course, different definitions of strength, or different views about what is important for generating strength, will generate different interpretations. For example, although Brazil's parties appear cohesive in the legislature (Figueiredo and Limongi 1999), such behavior may be a chimera, a function not of *partisan* activity or incentives, but of presidential influence (Zucco 2008), or of a legislative process that weeds out most controversy before votes are taken. Consider as well the fact that Brazil's parties claim literally millions of registered members (Speck 2013). Of course, membership may not indicate "strength," because joining a party requires simply signing a card, perhaps in exchange for a politician's promise of a small favor, and sometimes even without informed consent (Bramatti and Dualibi 2012). Our concern is with a particular understanding of party strength – the extent of affective psychological attachments in voters' minds. This facet of party strength has limits, too, but is widely acknowledged as a relatively durable measure of parties' representational links to voters. Mass partisanship matters because it tells us the extent to which parties help shape voters' preferences and influence their political behavior.

To assess the degree to which Brazil's parties have evolved organizationally – and then connect parties' structures to their ability to cultivate partisan attachments – we must first set the stage. In 1979, Brazil's military regime passed a law that set the template for party organizations as the country returned to democracy. This law tweaked the existing 1971 law, which in turn had tweaked the framework in effect prior to the 1964 coup. The 1979 law left very little room for organizational creativity, and as a result, upon redemocratization party organizations both resembled each other and resembled parties that had existed in earlier eras.

The 1979 framework privileged elected officials – particularly state and federal legislators, who dominated party organizations at the expense of individual members, leaders of organized ideological factions, or party bureaucrats (Ribeiro 2010: 233). The law made elected officials automatic (*nato*) and permanent members of state and national party "conventions," the events where parties made key decisions, such as choosing candidates and alliance partners, preparing platforms, and selecting their own leaders. In short, the 1979 law squeezed Brazil's parties into a "elitist but decentralized" mold, in which state-level political dynamics dominated and state-level party organs constituted the principal locus of power, relative to municipal as well as national organizations (Ribeiro 2010: 234).

The notion that in the 1980s and into the 1990s, Brazilian national parties constituted federations of state-level politicians, and that national-level coordination sometimes took a back seat to state-level interests, resonated with Brazilian history (Abrucio 1998; Hagopian 1996; Samuels 2003). After all, legislators whose careers depended on how well their party performed at the *state* rather than the national level controlled *national* party organs.

Because it wanted to project a distinct profile, the PT deliberately developed a different structure than what the 1979 law mandated (Keck 1992; Meneguello 1989; Ribeiro 2010; Samuels 1999, 2004). For example, in order to attract nontraditional candidates for office, the PT required all of its elected officials and government appointees to donate a portion of their salary to the party, and it threatened to expel elected officials who bucked the party line after an internal vote (the party followed through on this threat on several occasions). Rules such as these dissuaded all but the most committed politicians from joining.

As part of its effort to construct a different image, the PT also created a more elaborate organizational structure than the law required. This aspect of its organizational strategy did not primarily aim at dissuading politicians who lacked commitment to the PT's principles from entering the party, but rather sought to attract individual adherents. The goal was to create a "nonelite" organizational profile, and to do so the party focused on opening channels for grassroots participation in party affairs. In its early years the PT explicitly drew upon a Gramscian notion of gaining "hegemony in social movements" (Ribeiro 2010: 16), and cultivated connections to NGOs, labor unions, Catholic activists and other civil society organizations. Local-level supporters could engage the party through its "base nuclei" (*núcleos de base*), organized party units below the legally required municipal level. Although base nuclei are no longer relevant to the party's internal governance, they symbolized the PT's commitment to grassroots participation.

Early on the PT also created "sectoral" secretariats, through which members could engage on topical issues such as labor or women's rights, and institutionalized the participation of ideological factions, which gained the rights to present and debate proposals at party meetings and to proportional representation on party directories and executives. The party also created a system of regularly held "meetings" at the municipal, state and national levels of organization. These were separate from the legally mandated annual party "conventions." Meetings involved deliberation as well as taking decisions about party leadership and the party's platform.

Importantly for our comparison with Brazil's other main parties, PT meetings were highly inclusive. Relative to other parties, the PT's rules limited the influence of elected officials, and granted individual party members a relatively greater role. For example, the election of delegates to state-level meetings depended on the number of active members in each municipality, whereas in other parties *nato* members at one level (elected officials and party leaders) were then *nato* members at the next higher organizational level. To conform to the law, PT elected officials and leaders had the right to voice – but not vote – at the next higher meeting level (Ribeiro 2010: 236).

The 1979 Party Law deliberately recreated the structure of political parties that had existed both under the 1945–1964 period as well as under the military regime – relatively weak organizations that would be subordinate to a powerful executive branch of government. The PT succeeded in bucking the incentives of this institutional framework. However, even in 1990, no one predicted that the PT would become the key player in Brazil's party system. The party owes its electoral success to many factors, in particular voters' growing affective attachment to the party – not just its leader, Lula. We suggest that the explanation for this development owes much to the party's early efforts to differentiate itself organizationally.

Of course, most of Brazil's main parties have changed their statutes since 1979, and in 1995, the 1979 law was reformed and replaced. As with previous iterations of the party law, this one did not wipe the slate completely clean. For this reason, many parties' statutes remain virtually identical today – some even continue to reproduce stretches from the 1971 law (Ribeiro 2010: 238). Still, we are interested in the long-term impact of organizational structure on how parties engage the electorate – and why one party has succeeded while others failed to cultivate broad partisan attachments. To explain this variation, we now consider more recent organizational developments in Brazil's main parties.

PARTY-BUILDING AND ITS CONSEQUENCES: THE PATHS PARTIES TOOK – AND DID NOT TAKE

The organizational paths that Brazil's main parties took since the 1980s help explain why only the PT gradually gained partisan adherents. Brazil's

TABLE 12.1 *Organizational structure of Brazil's major parties*

	Centralized	Decentralized
Inclusive	PT	–
Exclusive	PSDB, PFL/DEM	PMDB

parties followed one of three organizational paths since 1979, varying on two dimensions: centralization/decentralization and exclusiveness/inclusiveness (Ribeiro 2010). The PT remained distinct because only it took taken the path that combines centralization with a considerable degree of inclusiveness – and it is this organizational structure that cultivates affective partisan attachments (Table 12.1).

The first path is the PMDB's. In organizational terms the PMDB continues to embody the old conventional scholarly wisdom about Brazilian parties, as it remains an "elite" party, albeit a relatively decentralized one. The party is a strong local election competitor in almost all regions of the country, even if very few Brazilians claim to "identify" with the PMDB.

The PSDB and PFL/DEM took a second path. These parties diverged from the PMDB's model by growing relatively *more* centralized and exclusive over time, enhancing the power of national party leaders and reducing the autonomy of municipal and especially state-level party leaders. As such, they have come to conform even more closely to the "elite" party model, dominated by elected officials with few connections to organized civil society and with limited opportunities for member participation.

The PT took a third path. It began as a fairly centralized party, in comparison with Brazil's other parties circa 1980, and has remained so over time. However, in contrast to Brazil's other parties, it has also remained relatively inclusive. This combination of an increasingly dominant cohesive central organization with the persistence of some degree of member participation continues to distinguish the PT from Brazil's other parties.

It is true that the PT has come to resemble Brazil's other parties in some respects – centralizing internal authority at the top and coming to rely on government funding for its organization and on corporate funding for its campaigns, for example. However, if the PT had grown wholly indistinct from Brazil's other parties by the 2000s, we would lack an explanation for the growth of *petismo* in the electorate during that decade. Contrary to Hunter's (2010) suggestion, the PT remains something of an anomaly in the Brazilian party system, as it has made different organizational choices from Brazil's other main parties. Its difference today must be contrasted not just against its own starting point but also against how Brazil's other main parties have evolved.

The PMDB

Under the military, the MDB (Brazilian Democratic Movement) was the only legally sanctioned opposition party. When the regime passed the party law in 1979, the MDB added "P" for Party to its name, and changed little else. Indeed, the MDB had been stitched out of state-level political groups that either did not fit or did not want to fit into the structure of the National Renewal Alliance (ARENA), the official "proregime" party. Since it has changed its organizational structure relatively little since redemocratization, in some senses the PMDB of today is not just similar to the PMDB of 1979, but also resembles parties that existed circa 1959. Like those parties, it wins votes as a relatively decentralized federation of state-level electoral machines, dominated by self-appointed cliques of politicians who cultivate personalistic and/or clientelistic relationships with groups of voters, and who make relatively few efforts to engage organized civil society or involve individual members in party affairs. For example, relative to Brazil's other parties, the PMDB has a more cumbersome process for higher-level party "intervention" in lower-level decisions, and key organizational decisions such as candidate selection and alliance decisions (outside of presidential elections) remain in the hands of lower-level party organs.

Under the military regime, the MDB attracted adherents ranging from radical leftists to fairly conservative politicians who found no place in ARENA. There was some degree of unity in this diversity, as everyone in the party knew that the party's *raison d'être* was "opposition to the regime." In 1986, a year after the military returned power to civilians, the PMDB won a landslide electoral victory, and it has been part of every government since then. Still, after the reestablishment of democracy, the PMDB lost its unifying cause, and since then it has never invested resources in developing a distinct "brand." That is, the PMDB's brand was situational, not bred in the bone. It stood up for democracy during a difficult period, but time has gradually weakened the memory of the PMDB's origins under the military regime, and it now seeks votes on its wide network of well-financed and experienced local and state political machines. As such, links to groups in organized civil society in the PMDB are relatively weak, and party organizational activity tends to ebb and flow with the electoral calendar.

The PMDB's organizational inertia is due to the fact that it remains a successful electoral machine. It has made good use of its inherited organizational structure, which guarantees a presence across the country, and its size guarantees substantial resources from the taxpayer-financed party fund, as well as access to regular and free TV airtime. This makes the PMDB an attractive option for office-seeking politicians. However, the PMDB's decision (largely by omission) to leave well enough alone organizationally – it remains relatively decentralized and thus lacks a clear brand – helps explain why mass partisanship for the PMDB has gradually dissipated.

The PSDB

The PSDB emerged in 1988 from a factional dispute within the PMDB and adopted both the *de facto* and *de jure* structure of its parent party, becoming a relatively loose association of professional politicians with relatively few connections to organized civil society and few opportunities for grassroots engagement (Roma 2002). In addition, in contrast to the PT, the PSDB was born a resource-rich party, dominated by experienced officeholders from the state of São Paulo, Brazil's largest and wealthiest. This, together with its meteoric success – winning the presidency only six years after its foundation – generated powerful *disincentives* for party leaders to invest in organizational development (Roma 2006).

The PSDB's fortunes have declined since Fernando Henrique Cardoso left office at the end of 2002, yet the party has made no effort to emulate the PT's organizational strategy. Instead, it has centralized decision making far more than the PT, and invested little in creating spaces for substantive participation. For example, the PSDB national executive committee can and does regularly remove recalcitrant state and municipal-level party leaders, and interferes regularly with candidate selection and alliance decisions at the state and municipal level (Ribeiro 2010: 241–242). The party has also increased the number of *nato* members on its national executive committee (Ribeiro 2010: 246), concentrating internal power among just a handful of senior leaders.

The PSDB remains a viable player because it continues to command several key state and municipal governments, providing a set of viable presidential candidates. However, its choice to become even *more* of an "elite" party has had consequences for its ability to cultivate mass partisan attachments. The party has never invested in developing a compelling programmatic vision for Brazil, and it has made little effort to forge lasting links with elements of organized civil society.[3] Former President Cardoso even chastised his own party publicly for its apparent inability to reach out to a broader base (Cardoso 2011). In an interview, he lamented that the PSDB brand is difficult to convey to the public. "We stand for adapting institutions to a globalized world and reforming the economy to improve efficiency and create jobs – but these are difficult concepts," he complained. Cardoso expressed pride in his administration's capacity to find solutions to complex challenges, but then noted that, "The problem for us was not putting ideas into practice – remember, we were the ones who started all these great policies – *Fome Zero*, *Bolsa Escola*, expanding health and education – but we didn't *tell a story*. It's not that we didn't tell the story well, we didn't even tell one. We had a pretty good idea of what to do when we got into office, but we never politicized our ideas, never made them into partisan issues."

Cardoso was able to clearly delineate the distinct paths the PSDB and PT have taken in this respect. While complaining that the PT has merely built on policies his government initiated, Cardoso acknowledged that Lula and the PT succeeded where he and the PSDB had failed, in terms of cultivating partisan attachments. Although the PT appropriated policies that his government had started, he said, it convinced voters that the policies were the PT's creations. "We lost the ideological battle to the PT," he noted. "What we lack is the combination of leaders and ideas. They're doing what they long claimed to stand for, but we were unable to make our ideas appeal to 'Average Joes' (*fulanizar as nossas idéias*) like the PT has. Lula has the capacity to speak the language of the people, and the discourse of the PT is the discourse of the average person – against the elites. They know how to define their enemies well, but we don't."[4] In short, partly to resolve intraparty political battles, the PSDB has become more of an elite party since it was founded. Although it had great success as Brazil's governing party from 1995 to 2002, it was unable to transform this considerable political capital into a mass partisan following.

[3] Interview with Maria de Lourdes Tavares Henriques, Secretary General of the Rio de Janeiro State PSDB, January 15, 2013.
[4] Interview with former President Fernando Henrique Cardoso, São Paulo, March 18, 2013.

The PFL/DEM

Just as the PSDB had emerged from a split in the PMDB, the opposition party under the military regime, the PFL emerged in the mid-1980s in a split from the PDS, the descendant of ARENA. The PFL wanted to distance itself from the legacy of authoritarian rule, in order to remain a viable potential member of future governing coalitions. Like the PMDB, the sources of its electoral success lay with its pool of career politicians and their entrenched local-level networks, rather than with a clear ideological or programmatic image. Unlike the PMDB but like the PSDB, however, the PFL's leaders have deliberately modified the party's statutes to further centralize intraparty power. Yet unlike both the PMDB and the PSDB, the PFL also deliberately engaged in a process of "rebranding," which involved changing the party's name. This effort failed, and the former-PFL-now-DEM has seen its fortunes decline precipitously.

In terms of organizational evolution, in 1999, the PFL centralized additional power in the hands of a smaller number of members of its national executive committee. At that time, the national executive committee gave itself the authority to distribute party fund resources to lower levels of the party's organization as it saw fit, as well as to determine local, state and national electoral coalitions. In 2007, the party's national leaders further reduced the influence of state-level leaders in national party affairs, and further enhanced the power of a small number of unelected notables on the party's national executive committee (Ribeiro 2010: 239–240, 246). The central leadership has in recent years also frequently deposed municipal- and state-level party officials who refuse to toe the national line (Ribeiro 2010: 251).

As the PFL was becoming more of a centralized, elite party, its leaders decided to engage political consultants in a rebranding effort. Through this process, they discovered that a plurality of Brazilians still associated the PFL with the military regime, believed that the party embodied a personalistic and corrupt style of politics, and had a poor impression of the party's leaders (Ribeiro 2010: 61–66). The consultants discovered that Brazilian voters most preferred a party that advocated and defended the principles of equality and participation, and convinced the PFL's leaders in 2007 to change the party's name to the Democrats and to issue a new platform that would articulate a long-term vision for the party's future along these principles.

This effort not only failed to attract new voters, but backfired badly, as the DEM has shrunk even in its traditional bailiwicks in smaller cities in Brazil's northeastern region. Dozens of PFL/DEM elected officials have also switched to other parties, a process that accelerated rapidly when Lula and the PT won in 2002 and the PFL/DEM decided to go into opposition (92 percent of those who left the PFL/DEM went to parties that entered Lula's government) (Ribeiro 2010: 81). The DEM's rebranding effort seems foolhardy in retrospect because the party's rhetoric in support of liberal economic principles and democratic values did not match its organization or its actions. In truth, although the DEM advocates liberal democratic and economic principles, it remained entirely dependent on access to government resources to maintain its network of patron–client ties (Ribeiro 2010: 78). Because clientelism and economic liberalism are incompatible in both theory and practice, the party's new brand failed to resonate. The DEM survives as a highly centralized and exclusive elite party, but its political future remains uncertain.

The PT

Given the centrality of the PT to this chapter's argument, we will spend more time discussing its organizational evolution. Since the mid-1990s, the PT has abandoned many of its more radical programmatic commitments, and since Lula took office in 2003, it has also had to confront a question it has grappled with since its founding: how to use control over the institutions of government to implement its ideals.[5] We suggest that despite a considerable degree of organizational centralization, a greater degree of ideological moderation, a good deal of lost political capital due to corruption scandals, and the powerful disincentives to engage in grassroots mobilization that come with controlling the government, the PT brand remains potent thirty-five years after its founding because the party has *avoided* normalization, relative to other Brazilian parties, in organizational terms. The party hardly embodies a utopian ideal of "participatory democracy," but it still remains far less of an elite electoralist vehicle than Brazil's other main parties. In what follows, we explore how several interrelated elements of the PT's organization facilitate its goal of cultivating mass partisanship, even after Lula took office: (1) expansion of its municipal-level organizational presence; (2) persistent efforts to recruit new members; and (3) creation of channels for members to participate in party politics.

---

[5] The PT discussed these issues early on, as well. See, for example, Pomar (1986).

Organizational Expansion

After its formation, the PT struggled to expand organizationally at the local level beyond its base in Brazil's wealthiest urban industrial centers. By 1985, for example, the PT had a party office (*diretório municipal* [DM]) in only about 25 percent of Brazil's municipalities – and many of these had a precarious existence. For example, between 1982 and 1984, the PT added 102 DMs – but it also closed 94.[6] Since its formation, the party has constantly sought to build its municipal-level "organizational capillarity" (Amaral 2010: 73; PT 2007b: 104; Ribeiro 2010: 252), which its leaders believed would bring in new members, win more votes, and cultivate deeper partisan attachments (Genoíno 2004). By 1989, the PT had a DM in 44 percent of Brazil's municipalities – but it was not until 2009 that the party could claim to be fully nationalized, having established an organizational presence in 96 percent of municipalities (Amaral 2010: 77).

Until 1995, the party's efforts at organizational expansion foundered due to lack of financial resources. That year, party moderates regained control over the PT's national directorate. Coincidentally, as noted above, that year the Brazilian Congress also revised the party law. Among the changes implemented was a tripling of the amount of taxpayer money deposited in the party fund, which distributes money to parties annually based on their size in the lower legislative chamber. As the PT grew from election to election, the party fund became its most important source of revenue (see Bruhn, Chapter 8, this volume).[7]

Investment in this organizational expansion effort took off – and paid off – after the party reformed its statute in 2001. That year the PT national directory directed its state directories to prioritize establishment of DMs in municipalities where the party had failed to meet its own requirements for holding its first direct internal leadership election (discussed later) (PT 2001a: 45, 2001b). The PT's national leaders strategically placed the party's most experienced organizers and technical staff in one of 400 "macro-regional poles," which were responsible for organizing DMs in up to fifteen municipalities. The party paid for new computers and

---

[6] In Mato Grosso do Sul in 1982, there were fifteen DMs, but none in 1984. The same occurred in Alagoas, where the PT went from twenty-two to zero DMs in the same period. In Pará and Goiás, there were not even enough affiliates to legally establish a *state*-level directory at that time, meaning the party was reduced to "provisional" status in those states. See Lemos (1986).

[7] This is also important to mention because it underlines that the PT's growth – as an organization and in terms of partisanship – was not simply a product of the resources that flooded the party after Lula took office in 2003.

TABLE 12.2 *Type of organizational presence, 2012*

	PT	PMDB	PSDB	DEM
Municipal directories (#)	4443	3357	2589	1093
Provisional committees (#)	937	1571	2195	3265
% of Municipalities with Party Offices	96.7	88.6	86.0	78.3
% of Party Offices That Were Provisional Committees	17.4	31.9	45.9	75.9

Source: Ribeiro (2013), Table 1, from Brazil's *Tribunal Superior Eleitoral.*

telecommunications equipment, and systematized its internal communication system to nationalize its electoral and branding campaigns, in an effort to "guarantee the PT symbol of quality" (Pereira 2004).

As Table 12.2 shows, all of Brazil's main parties have a local-level organizational presence in at least 78 percent of the country's 5,500+ municipalities. However, the PT's *use* of its local-level organization differs from Brazil's other parties – and this difference helps explain the growth of *petismo*. First, in contrast to other parties, the PT has required and continues to require that individuals interested in forming a DM must have an obvious affinity with the party and its principles, typically by having worked within a civil society organization allied with the party (PT 1988: 8). As Luiz Dulci, a former National Executive Committee member explained, organizing a DM remains a bottom-up process in the PT.[8] Individuals interested in forming a DM must meet with state-level party officials, and then hold a public meeting in their town that has been publicized in local media and among local social movements and unions. The state-level party directory typically coordinates this initial meeting, and requires that the agenda include a discussion of what the PT is and why the municipality needs to have the PT present locally.

Other parties are known as *partidos de cartório* – "notary public parties," legal fictions in which higher-level party elites file papers at the courthouse and parachute someone in to take over. But in the PT, as one party official noted, "If you don't have local leaders who are willing to take on the job of organizing the party, there's no way a DM will take root in that town. We don't go out and say, 'Hey, lets get this person or that person.' Someone who has no affinity with the party won't last long

[8] Interview with Luiz Dulci, former PT Secretary General, São Paulo, March 20, 2013.

in the PT. There has to be a group that emerges that has an affinity with us."[9] Throughout the process of local-level organizational expansion, the PT remained concerned with maintaining its brand, by restricting its local-level leadership to like-minded individuals, who are also typically already active in some civil society organizations. The PT, in other words, mobilized those who were already mobilized.

Second, the PT has adopted the distinct and deliberate tactic of opening *permanent* local-level party offices. In Brazil, the state and national electoral courts afford newly opened party offices (at any level of government) status as "provisional committees." Relative to a *diretório*, these lack legal and therefore political autonomy from higher-level party organs. A party can then choose to change a provisional committee into a *diretório* or not, by fulfilling several legal and bureaucratic requirements. To a greater degree, leaders of Brazil's other main parties have deliberately chosen not to request this change, because leaving municipal-level organs as "provisional" gives national party leaders the authority to "intervene" in local branches. As suggested, intervention allows national leaders to nominate and/or depose recalcitrant local party officials, make nomination and electoral alliance decisions, and even close local branches.

Table 12.2 reveals that the PT has the clearest strategy of opening directories rather than provisional committees. Although this reduces the national party leadership's ability to intervene in municipal party affairs, it makes its presence at the grassroots level less about personalities, and suggests that the party branch will be open for business not just during campaign season, but will also serve as a channel for a broader form of political participation. When the PT establishes a DM, it publicizes that it will soon have an election for local leadership. Members who show up can vote for president of the party at the local, state and national levels, and can participate in setting the party's local priorities. In terms of attracting members, "This is what is worth gold to us," one PT activist explained: "Anyone who comes to a party meeting can raise their hand and give their opinion."[10]

The PT's National Secretary of Organization explained that the creation of fully fledged DMs is part of the party's strategy to attract members and develop ties to society: "Provisional committees don't have any autonomy, don't have any real partisan life. All they have are personalities.

---

[9] Interview with Florisvaldo Souza, PT National Secretary of Organization, São Paulo, March 20, 2013.

[10] Interview with Glauco Piái, former PT São Paulo Municipal Secretary of Organization, São Paulo, March 14, 2013.

Average members don't see what the party does, they only see what the personalities do." Establishing a DM, in contrast, "Gives us certain capillarity for direct member participation, which the other parties lack."[11] The PT's effort to plant its flag across Brazil's cities – large and small – is part of a broader strategy to disseminate its brand as the "party of participation." Opening municipal directories – rather than provisional committees – is part and parcel of this distinct approach.

Membership Recruitment

A second element of the PT's effort to disseminate its brand as the party that offers average Brazilians meaningful participatory opportunities involves how it recruits new members. On paper at least, as of 2012, fully 10.7 percent of Brazilian citizens were legally members of a political party – a relatively high rate in comparative perspective (Speck 2013: 39). The PMDB claims 1.7 percent of all Brazilian voters as members (about two million people); the PSDB 1.0 percent; the DEM 0.8 percent, and the PT 1.1 percent (Speck 2013: 43). As Speck notes, given the conventional wisdom that Brazilian parties have shallow roots in society, these numbers are surprising. Yet the question is, what do they signify?

Aggregate party membership totals do correlate with and indicate electoral strength. However, they likely signify the end product of local-level intraparty competition, not national-level interparty competition. In most parties, individual politicians rather than party organizations seek out new recruits in order to demonstrate the breadth and depth of their own political networks at local nominating conventions. Recruits are asked little in return – and many do not even realize they are joining a party, believing instead they are merely showing support for their preferred candidate. As the PT's National Secretary of Organization explained, people join other parties because, "They're friends with someone who's running for city council, or because they're going to get something in return, from some leader who's connected to some candidate who needs electoral support. It has nothing to do with ideology. It has to do with receiving some kind of direct benefit."[12] For most of Brazil's parties, membership has an electoral significance, but little more.

In contrast, membership has electoral significance for the PT – but it also has a deeper meaning. The PT seeks new members in order to

---

[11] Interview with Florisvaldo Souza, PT National Secretary of Organization, São Paulo, March 20, 2013.

[12] Interview with Florisvaldo Souza, PT National Secretary of Organization, São Paulo, March 20, 2013.

cultivate affective attachment *with the party*, not simply so that individual politicians can indicate their likely electoral strength. For example, a 2002 pamphlet urging PT activists to pursue and sign up new members also reminded them that, "The party member is not just a number. We always seek to encourage the active participation of our members in partisan activities ... It's critical that our local organs not just find more members, but create a strategy to stimulate their participation" (PT 2002: 2).

Over the years, the PT has held several membership drives – in 2003 and 2006, for example. Although it has eased membership criteria since 2001, it still tends to seek out a particular type of individual – someone who is interested in getting involved in the party (PT 2003: 6). To this day, the PT requires new members to complete a "political formation" class within a year of joining to maintain active membership. While the possibility of participating in party activities attracts many,[13] this requirement (which involves learning about the PT brand and its history), along with the social pressure on new members to get involved in party activities beyond showing support for this or that individual candidate for local office, only appeals to a certain kind of voter, and has the effect of narrowing down the potential pool of new members.[14]

The targets of the PT's recruitment efforts have remained consistent over the years. To attract members in its early years, the PT drew on its connections to social movements, labor unions, and Catholic activists, largely in and around major cities in Brazil's south and southeast. This connection between PT membership and civil society persisted even after the party took control of the government. For example, among delegates to the 2007 PT National Conference, delegates' age did not predict whether they were involved in an NGO prior to joining the party. The proportion remained constant at slightly above 80 percent, regardless of whether the delegate had joined in 1980 or 2005 (Amaral 2010: 99).

After a decade of governing, and after massive protests rocked Brazil in mid-2013, it remains clear that the PT has not reached all elements of Brazilian society. In particular, the protests revealed that while the party has gained support from the rural poor, it has lost significant support from better-educated, urban middle classes. Ironically, the risk for the PT is to fall victim of its own success and

---

[13] Interview with Jorge Coelho, National Secretary of Mobilization, São Paulo, March 20, 2013.
[14] Interview with Edinho Silva, President of the São Paulo State Legislative Assembly, São Paulo, March 15, 2013.

watch a "movement against parties in general" become a movement against the PT.

A particular challenge is reaching out to younger Brazilians, who only became politically aware after the PT had won control of government – and long after the party had moderated, reformed its internal organization, and acquired substantial financial backing.[15] Likewise, the party is still attempting to figure out how to reach nontraditional civil society organizations in poorer communities. Luiz Dulci, former PT Secretary General, noted the difficulty of reaching mothers' groups (*associações de mães*), samba or rap music clubs, and local sports team leagues, for example. These "are not necessarily claim-making (*reivindicatória*) organizations, and we don't have a long tradition of dialogue with these kind of groups," he explained. However, "they are fantastic at organizing and mobilizing their communities, in *favelas*, or wherever. As the government party, we have to dialogue with these segments of society – not just to give them things, but to ask them what they want, and to visibly *include* them."[16]

The PT's Secretary of Social Mobilization added that, although PT government policies are partly responsible for improvements in these groups' welfare, they "represent a challenge for us, because although they used to be really poor, they have reached a higher level of income with no tradition of organized intermediation between their interests and the government – nothing that provides them with any sort of political awareness. They are unlikely to be union members; they're not in progressive churches; they're not in organized urban social movements, and not in a political party. It's a challenge to explain what our political project is – there's nothing automatic about this awareness. We have to show them how Brazil has changed, how rapidly it has changed, and what the PT's role has been. If we don't do the political-ideological work to reach out to them, they'll be lost to us."[17]

It is telling that the PT leadership is not only aware of this challenge, but is actively seeking to reach out to both established and new elements of Brazilian civil society. Nothing guarantees that its success in cultivating affective attachments will continue as it has since 1980 – in fact, the recent decline suggests that *petismo* may be relatively shallow

[15] Interview with Renato Simões, PT Secretary of Popular Movements, São Paulo, March 18, 2013.
[16] Interview with Luiz Dulci, former PT Secretary General, São Paulo, March 20, 2013.
[17] Interview with Renato Simões, PT Secretary of Popular Movements, São Paulo, March 18, 2013.

among some of the party's supporters – but the PT remains the only party that tries to reach out to diverse elements of Brazilian society. It seeks to cast a wide net, recruiting Brazilians whose only common characteristic appears to be that they are already politically engaged and believe in the political efficacy of participation. The party seeks members not simply as part of the electoral process, but to cultivate affective attachments – and these results appear to have borne fruit: although *petistas* today do not differ much from other Brazilians in terms of ideology, they do differ in terms of their understanding of and willingness to engage in politics. For example, according to a 2006 survey (Fundação Perseu Abramo 2006), *petistas* differ from nonpartisans as well as partisans of other parties in agreeing that "politics is important to me," and "participatory processes are important." *Petismo* is a vision of how politics should work – and the party actively seeks out Brazilians who share this view.

Participatory Opportunities

Thus far we have suggested that the PT's distinctiveness lies with how it *uses* its organizational apparatus. When it opens a local-level office, it gives that office real life as a center of partisan activities. When it recruits new members, it seeks out "activist" Brazilians, those interested in more than merely demonstrating enthusiasm for a particular local-level candidate. But this leads to a question – what sorts of participatory opportunities does the party offer? If the party's rhetoric does not match its actions, we would not expect its efforts to cultivate mass partisanship to succeed. Since its founding, the PT has created institutional spaces for members to get involved – whether in the running of the party itself, or in turning their social activism into political activism. These participatory opportunities – which are largely absent from Brazil's other major parties – are crucial for the PT's efforts to turn electoral support into lasting affective attachments.

As it grew and moderated, the PT faced the challenge of maintaining the enthusiasm that activists bring to politics. Moreover, internal factional disputes have resulted in "centrists" triumphant and "radicals" disappointed. Since 1995, Lula's faction and its allies have been able to impose their strategic vision on the party. This has reduced the influence of radical factions within the party, and has circumscribed the organizational channels through which radical factions exerted influence in the party's structure. Debate exists both within the party and among observers as to whether the PT's internal reforms since 2001 have sacrificed activism and militancy for a participatory façade.[18] Yet despite the changes in organizational structure and ideological content, the PT remains *relatively* true to its origins, and far more open to participation than any other main party in Brazil.

In this light, consider one of the most important changes to the PT's organization: the 2001 implementation of direct internal leadership elections at all levels, and internal primary elections for selection of mayoral, gubernatorial and presidential candidates (the *Processo de Eleições Diretas* [PED]). Prior to the advent of the PED, individual party members could only directly vote for party leaders at the municipal level. Each municipal-level meeting also elected delegates to the state meeting, where participants then elected delegates to the national meeting, where an election was held between different slates of candidates (representing different factions) for leadership slots. Individual party members in this system had no direct role at the more important, higher levels of party organization.

Just as leaders of the PT's moderate factions had desired (Ribeiro 2010), the PED reshaped both the perception and the actual nature of participation in the party.[19] It ostensibly empowered individual party members at the expense of nationally organized factions – mainly those with more radical political agendas, which had long played a prominent role in the party organization but, as both moderates and radicals had known, had relatively limited support among the party's broader membership base. The PED consolidated moderates' hold over the party while demonstrating that the PT remained committed to members' participation in shaping the party's direction (Amaral 2010: 84). Even though Ribeiro (2010) is far more skeptical than Amaral about how "participatory" the PT is today, he nonetheless acknowledges that the PT remains the only party with such a high degree of member participation in the process of choosing leaders and candidates at all levels. In the other parties, *natos* – unelected leaders – dominate these processes to a far greater degree.

Another participatory channel involves what the PT calls "sectoral" groups (*setoriais*). Sectoral groups – which are formal elements of party organization at the municipal, state and national levels – are organized around particular issues. Although the 1979 party law did not facilitate

---

[18] Compare, for example, Meneguello and Amaral's (2008) optimism against Ribeiro's (2010) skepticism.

[19] Interview with José Dirceu, former PT National President, São Paulo, March 18, 2013.

their formation, the PT's first statute included *setoriais* – and by the 1980s, the PT had well-organized sectoral groups for Agriculture, Labor, Student and Popular Movements. The party later added institutional spaces for Youth, Combat against Racism, Environment, and Women, and other protosectoral groups were placed under the umbrella of the party's National Secretariat for Social Movements: education, health, sport and leisure, community communication, disabled people, LGBT issues, religion, children and adolescents, urban policy, social assistance, indigenous affairs, and urban transportation.

The party's 2001 statute reform reduced sectorals' formal role in the party organization – like the PED, moderates pushed this reform to reduce radical factions' influence, because they had long been entrenched in some sectorals. The 2013 protests that exploded across Brazil illustrate the continued challenge the PT confronts in terms of reaching out, listening to, and acting upon the concerns of civil society. Nonetheless, sectorals remain the primary way that the PT engages civil society, even though they are all but absent from the structure of all other parties, even left-leaning ones.

As former PT President José Genoíno (a moderate within the party) argued in a 2003 interview, "We need to create a sort of militancy that goes beyond election campaigns," by "engaging people in topical issues of importance to them" (De Azevedo 2003). The sectorals serve this purpose. They create a partisan structure parallel to the main issues that mobilize Brazilians, and this gives the party an image of being open to average Brazilians' concerns. They also channel party activists toward civil society, connecting party members with like-minded nonmembers who are nonetheless active in social movements and civil society organizations. Ten years after Genoíno made this statement, the PT's National Secretary of Social Movements explained that the sectorals remain crucial to the PT's efforts to reach out to politically engaged citizens: "Whatever the issue, members can attend the sectoral meetings, participate in the debates, make contacts, and then tell people outside the party about what the PT is doing on that issue. That way, interested individuals have a person to contact, and they have a phone number. That's how it works, creating these ties."[20]

The statutes of the PSDB and PMDB do contain language about sectoral organizations (called "secretariats" in the PSDB), but a check on

---

[20] Interview with Jorge Coelho, PT National Secretary of Social Movements, São Paulo, March 20, 2013.

both parties' websites suggests that their sectoral groups are moribund. The PT remains distinct not just because it has created institutionalized channels that connect the party to virtually the entire spectrum of issues in organized civil society in Brazil (Ribeiro 2010: 165), but because the sectorals continue to play an important role in cultivating affective attachments between individuals and the party.[21]

CONCLUSION

How do we explain party-building – defined in this chapter as cultivating mass partisan attachments – in contemporary Brazil? Only the PT has cultivated a relatively broad base of partisan support – an affective attachment to the party and what it stands for, rather than to political personalities. As Panebianco (1988) would predict, all of Brazil's parties retain traces of their organizational roots, and our answer to this question focuses on variation across Brazil's parties in terms of this institutional inheritance. The PT remains different because its organization is different, and because what it does with its organization is different.

In the PFL/DEM, PSDB, and PMDB (as in most of Brazil's other parties), intraparty politics is an informal, personalistic and exclusive affair that favors established politicians and tightly constrains the role of individual members. These parties' structures are not designed to promote abstract affective attachments to an organization and what it stands for, and as such their brands have failed to resonate. All parties, in short, use their organization to contest elections, and many Brazilian parties are relatively successful in doing so. However, only the PT uses its organization to foster links with organized civil society groups and, consequently, to create affective partisan attachments.

In another work (Samuels and Zucco 2014), we found that all major parties in Brazil gain votes after establishing a local organizational presence, but only the PT gains *partisans* as well as votes. However, the "creation" of *petistas* only occurs where civil society is organizationally dense. Where organized civil society is thin on the ground, no party can cultivate partisanship by establishing a local organizational presence. We suggest that the PT succeeds in cultivating partisans where civil society is dense because its organizational outreach efforts are more likely to

---

[21] For additional insight into how the PT cultivated connections to civil society during the Lula and Dilma administrations, see Pogrebinschi and Samuels (2014) and Gómez-Bruera (2013: chs. 7–9).

pay off where there are large numbers of citizens who are already active
in social and political affairs. In this sense, the Brazilian case provides
another example of the importance of civil society to party-building
efforts, as Chapters 5 and 11 in this volume by Van Dyck and Madrid,
respectively, also suggest.

What makes the PT distinct is that it retained a good deal of its organizational "DNA" even as it grew beyond its niche roots. This trajectory,
however, does not fit comfortably with Greene's argument elsewhere in
this volume. According to Greene, niche parties institutionalize internal
structures and practices to preserve the party's identity, such as high barriers to membership, organizational leadership or electoral candidacies.
This characterization echoes the way scholars have long described the
PT, particularly in its early years. The PT, however, broke out of its niche
to win national power, something Greene suggests is very difficult to do,
given (à la Panebianco) the difficulty any party faces in radically transforming the organization it is born with. Granted, the 2013 protests in
Brazil suggest that the PT might not be as permeable to civil society as it
once was. Still, there is no comparison between the level of engagement
the PT maintains with civil society and that of other parties.

The PT's persistent investment in *projecting* rather than merely *protecting* its public image explains its ability to break out of its niche. In
all of its organizational reform efforts – expanding the local-level party
organization, recruiting members, and reforming the party's internal
structure – the PT has maintained a distinct profile. While some other
parties have chosen greater centralization and exclusivity, PT leaders recognized that the party cannot continue to grow unless is builds on and
opens new channels to organized civil society. The party has certainly
not engaged in single-minded pursuit of these goals, but political participation has long been an element of the so-called "PT way of governing"
(*modo petista de governar*), and the party continues to cultivate mass
partisan attachments by seeking out Brazilians who are engaged in some
form of social and/or political activism.

The PT is also a puzzling case for Lupu's argument (Chapter 3, this
volume) about party "brands," because the more the PT cast off and/or
moderated its programmatic profile and allied with ideological strangers,
the more *petismo* grew in the electorate. The party's evolution evinced the
weakening of the two factors Lupu regards as crucial for brand maintenance: intraparty consistency and interparty differentiation. In our view,
what continues to distinguish the PT – and what has enabled it to cultivate partisan support – is not its ideological profile or its choosiness in

terms of alliance partners, but its organization, which combines a relatively extensive and highly institutionalized formal organization with a relatively high degree of inclusiveness in partisan affairs, when compared against its competitors. In this sense, contra Hunter (2010), the PT remains an organizational anomaly in the Brazilian party system.

We agree that the PT has become relatively more centralized and less participatory since its origins (Ribeiro 2010). However, the way that Meneguello described the PT in its early years remains accurate: the PT's novelty is that it developed formal rules to foster a different way of conducting party politics, one that sought to cultivate and consolidate a lasting connection between the party, organized civil society, and individual members (1989: 90). To this day, only in the PT do individual members have substantive opportunities to participate in internal deliberations and otherwise engage in meaningful organizational activities. PT activism today is certainly less intense than in the 1980s, but on the other hand, the PT's recent reforms have also *opened up* the party to new members, who come from demographic sectors outside the party's initial urban, middle-class base. In abandoning its radical ideological roots but maintaining some semblance of its public profile, the PT actually made itself *more* attractive to some voters. The persistence of the party's relative organizational distinctiveness, in our view, helps explain the party's branding efforts.

13

The Organizational Foundations
of Corporation-Based Parties

William T. Barndt

By all accounts, stable new parties have been rare in Latin America in recent decades. As Chapter 1 of this volume rightly notes, most new parties in the region have lacked clear brands, failed to develop territorial organizations, or been unable to avoid internal schisms. Consequently, they have been fleeting. Of the handful of new parties that have survived over time, almost all were forged in the exceptional circumstances of polarization and civil war. This begs the question: Are there *any* standard roads to durable party organization in Latin America that do not run through intense conflict or violence?

In recent years, one group of new parties have attempted to blaze just such a path. These new parties have become viable through an intense reliance on particular business corporations, including breweries, retail chains, industrial and agroindustrial firms, and financial and media conglomerates. Using this new party-building strategy, these "corporation-based parties" have come to control presidencies, legislatures, governorships, and big city mayoralties across the region, including in Argentina, Bolivia, Brazil, Chile, Colombia, Guatemala, Panama, and Peru. And while no corporation-based party has yet cleared the threshold of success laid out in Chapter 1 (10 percent of the vote for five consecutive legislative elections), the novelty and potential of this new strategy merit its careful consideration as an alternative form of party-building in Latin America today.

How is this happening? Why are new political parties being built on existing business conglomerates? The answer is *organization*. Latin American corporations often have access to five organizational resources that are critical to launching new parties: finance, infrastructure, personnel, advertising and publicity assets, and mass networks. Given weakly regulated political finance, many major business firms and conglomerates find themselves in the unique position of being able to provide some or all of these resources directly to a political party. Thus, particular Latin American corporations with ready access to these resources may be able to sponsor their own electorally viable parties (Barndt 2014).

The major contribution of the chapter is thus to shed new light on one of the central dilemmas posed by this volume: that new parties often fail to take root because politicians lack the incentives or means to build organizations. This dilemma is discussed not only in Chapter 1 but also by many other chapters, including those by Bruhn, Eaton, Levitsky and Zavaleta, Loxton, Madrid, and Van Dyck. What this chapter suggests is that corporation-based party-building may provide one possible, partial, and problematic response to this dilemma. By building their own parties on their own infrastructures, major economic conglomerates have (initially and incompletely) begun to overcome one of the biggest problems in Latin American party-building: the absence of organizational resources.

Take, for example, the Democratic Change party in Panama (one case discussed in this chapter). Instead of building a party from scratch, the founders of Democratic Change constructed it around the Super 99 supermarket chain. From top to bottom, Democratic Change is *organizationally fused* to that supermarket chain. Super 99 markets across Panama act as nodes of party activity: they have served as local party offices and hosted party events, provided specialized personnel and staff to the party, repurposed their publicity assets for party advertisements, and expanded the party's geographic reach using their transportation and distribution networks. Democratic Change, that is, has been effectively sponsored by Super 99. In 2009, Ricardo Martinelli, the party's candidate – and the owner of Super 99 – captured the presidency of Panama. In 2014, it won a plurality (43 percent) of seats in the Panamanian legislature.

Of course, creating an electorally viable party is not the same thing as creating a *successful* party, as defined in the introductory chapter of this volume. Again, no corporation-based party has yet won 10 percent of the vote for five consecutive legislative elections. Yet they seem increasingly common in the region. Of the 307 new parties listed in Appendix I of Chapter 1, at least sixteen (5 percent) seem to have been at least partially sponsored by a corporation.[1] While ten of those sixteen have failed, the

---

[1] This figure was reached by comparing the census of corporation-based parties provided by Barndt (2014) with the census of new parties listed in Appendix I of Chapter 1.

future of the remaining six remains unknown.[2] Interestingly, those six parties constitute more than 10 percent of the "incomplete" cases listed in Appendix I – that is, 10 percent of the new parties in Latin America that have not yet succeeded or failed have depended on particular business corporations for organizational resources. This fact alone makes the strategy worth examining. That no corporation-based party has yet succeeded could simply be an artifact of the recentness of the strategy in this volume's universe of cases.

Moreover, there is *theoretical* reason to expect that corporation-based parties may eventually succeed (see also Levitsky and Zavaleta, Chapter 15, this volume). Specifically, this chapter suggests that the organizational inheritance that corporation-based parties receive from their business sponsors endows them with precisely the attributes this volume associates with successful party-building: territorial organizations, clear brands, and internal unity. Consider each of these three attributes in turn.

First and foremost, many corporations possess both the incentives and the means to invest in party organizations.[3] Since broad-based probusiness parties have generally failed in the region (Gibson 1996;

According to Barndt (2014), evidence suggests that the following new parties were at least partially sponsored by a particular corporation: Cambio Democrático (Democratic Change), Movimiento de Renovación Nacional (MORENA – Movement of National Renovation), Solidaridad (Solidarity), and Partido Liberal Nacional (National Liberal Party) in Panama; Unidad Cívica Solidaridad (UCS – Civic Solidarity Unity), Conciencia de Patria (CONDEPA – Conscience of the Fatherland), and Unidad Nacional (National Unity) in Bolivia; Todos por el Perú (Everyone for Peru)/Coordinadora Nacional de Independientes (National Coordinator of Independents), and Alianza para el Progreso (APP – Alliance for Progress) in Peru; Renovação /Reconstrução Nacional (National Reconstruction) and Partido Progressista/Popular (Progressive/Popular Party) in Brazil; Partido Renovador Institucional Acción Nacional (PRIAN – Institutional Renewal Party of National Action) in Ecuador; Encuentro Nacional (National Encounter) in Paraguay; Propuesta Republicana (PRO – Republican Proposal) in Argentina; Unión de Centro Centro (UCC – Union of the Centrist Center) in Chile; and Partido de la U (PSUN – Social Party of National Unity) in Colombia. The analysis excludes cases in which a corporation sponsors a particular party faction.

[2] The ten parties that seem to have failed are MORENA, Solidarity, and the National Liberal Party in Panama; UCS and CONDEPA in Bolivia; Everyone for Peru/National Coordinator of Independents in Peru; National Reconstruction in Brazil; UCC in Chile; National Encounter in Paraguay; and PRIAN in Ecuador. The six parties whose future remains unclear as of this writing are Democratic Change in Panama; National Unity in Bolivia; PRO in Argentina; PSUN in Colombia; APP in Peru; and the Progressive Party in Brazil.

[3] For other organizations that have sponsored parties in the region, see Loxton (Chapter 9), Madrid (Chapter 11), and Samuels and Zucco (Chapter 12) in this volume.

Middlebrook 2000),[4] particular corporations regularly find themselves without sufficient access to the state to achieve their policy goals. Faced with this situation, those corporations sometimes explore the idea of building their *own* parties. Transforming this idea into reality is easier for corporations than for most other social groups, given that they have a preexisting infrastructure upon which to build their parties: the corporation itself. Corporate assets can provide a new party with myriad resources critical to organization-building, including finance, clientelist networks, and media.[5] In short, corporations may be able to use their existing assets as the kind of organizational platform that Chapter 1 associates with the creation of successful parties.

Second, corporations enter into party politics with their own preexisting brands: brands associated with the goods and services they produce. Especially when those goods and services are produced for mass consumer markets – e.g., beer, processed food, retail chains – their brands already exist prominently in the popular consciousness. Consequently, corporations that choose to build their own parties may *begin* with a brand connected to a popular set of products: good beer, healthy food, efficient check-out lines. As shown below, corporations usually work hard to make sure that the voting public ascribes the same positive qualities to their new parties that it already associates with their popular brands. When consumers identify the product brands they like with the tickets they vote for, corporation-based parties do well. Corporation-based party-building, that is, provides a ready mechanism to endow parties with clear brands.

Third and finally, corporations can often build their own parties around an existing base of supporters. Within the corporation, loyal personnel can be repurposed as party activists, leaders, and candidates. Outside the corporation, employee and consumer networks can be repurposed as partisan bases. Corporations that bring their management, employees, and consumers together in support of the parties they sponsor may enjoy a level of cohesion that many other new parties lack. Along with clear brands, this internal support should make corporation-based parties more likely to avoid the kinds of schisms that have devastated many other new parties in the region.

---

[4] Though see Luna and Kaltwasser (2014) on some recent successful attempts to build broad-based parties of the right in Mexico, Chile, and El Salvador.

[5] As other contributors to this volume have also noted (see especially Bruhn (Chapter 8) and Muñoz and Dargent (Chapter 7)), such resources are critical to party-building.

In short, there seems to be a theoretical affinity between corporation-based party-building and the development of attributes that this volume associates with party success. As such, there is good reason to study the rise of corporation-based party-building in the region, even if no corporation-based party has yet cleared the threshold of success as defined in Chapter 1 of this volume.

The chapter proceeds as follows. Section I provides evidence for these arguments through case studies of the three parties that have depended most heavily on corporations for their organizational infrastructure: Democratic Change in Panama, the Institutional Renewal Party of National Action (PRIAN) in Ecuador, and the Civic Solidarity Unity (UCS) in Bolivia (see Table 13.1). By drawing heavily on the organizational infrastructure of its sponsoring corporation, each of these parties began its life with a clear brand, territorial organization, and internal cohesion. Though none has yet succeeded by the standards laid out Chapter 1 of this volume, each illustrates how the organizational inheritance of a business conglomerate can launch parties toward potential success.

Of course *potential* is the key word here. Like all new parties, most new corporation-based parties will fail. Moreover – and again like many other new parties – corporation-based parties often initially seem to be little more than the personalistic campaign devices of particular individuals: the owners of their sponsoring corporations. The second section of this chapter, therefore, is devoted to analyzing if and how corporation-based parties might overcome this profound challenge and become durable organizations. Corporation-based party-building is a new development in Latin America – and its future remains unclear. Yet for all the reasons laid out by this volume and this chapter, it is well worth considering if and how it might eventually succeed.

THREE CORPORATION-BASED PARTIES

Democratic Change was founded in 1998 by Ricardo Martinelli, who controls a diversified set of businesses in Panama centered on the Super 99 supermarket chain. During the 1990s, Martinelli expanded his business holdings into agricultural, financial, media, and industrial enterprises. Since its founding, Democratic Change has participated in four elections (1999, 2004, 2009, and 2014).[6] The party first presented its

---

[6] On the Panamanian party system, see Pérez (2000). On Democratic Change, see also Barndt (2014, n.d.).

own presidential candidate (Martinelli himself) in 2004, though it took only 5.3 percent of the vote. In the 2009 elections, Democratic Change increased its vote share six-fold and Martinelli was elected President of Panama. In 2014, the party ran a new presidential candidate, a cabinet minister, José Domingo Arias. Though the party's presidential vote share dropped from 32 to 26 percent, its share of the legislative vote shot up dramatically as it captured more than 40 percent of the seats in the National Assembly.[7]

Ecuador's PRIAN was formed in 2002 by Álvaro Noboa, who owns more than 100 firms in the agricultural, financial, mining, real estate, and transport sectors. After unsuccessfully campaigning for president as the candidate of the Ecuadorian Roldosista Party (PRE) in 1998, Noboa founded his own party, PRIAN, and ran again in 2002. Though Noboa lost that race in the second round, PRIAN won a respectable ten seats in the legislature. Four years later Noboa lost the presidency again, but PRIAN took the most votes in the first round of voting and the most seats (twenty-seven) of any party in the legislature. PRIAN continued to be an electoral force to be reckoned with throughout the 2000s. In recent years, however, the party has faced enormous challenges, due to the seeming determination of the government of Rafael Correa to push it out of existence.

Bolivia's UCS was formed in 1989 by Max Fernández, a businessmen who had recently (1987) taken control of the Cervecería Boliviana Nacional (CBN – National Bolivian Brewery).[8] Though the UCS was excluded from the 1989 presidential contest,[9] it won mayoralties in four of the ten major Bolivian cities that year. In the 1991 municipal elections, the UCS captured nearly a quarter of the national vote and consolidated its position as an ascendant political force. In the general elections of 1993, Fernández and the UCS took a strong 16 percent of the vote, which gave the party twenty congressional deputies. After Fernández died in an airplane crash in 1995, however, control of his businesses and the UCS passed to his son, Jhonny, who reduced the close connections between the

---

[7] Note that postelection conflicts reduced the number of seats that Democratic Change actually occupied.

[8] As extensively documented in the remarkable work of Fernando Mayorga (1991, 1993, 2002).

[9] Government attempts to stymie Fernández's attempts to found his own party led to his short-lived alliance with the Falange Socialista Boliviana (Bolivian Socialist Falange) in 1988.

TABLE 13.1 *Three corporation-based parties*

Party	Democratic Change	PRIAN	UCS
Country	Panama	Ecuador	Bolivia
Founding leader	Ricardo Martinelli	Álvaro Noboa	Max Fernández
Signature corporation (business group)	Super 99 (Grupo Martinelli)	Exportadora Bananera (Grupo Noboa; Corporación Noboa; Grupo de Empresas de Álvaro Noboa)	CBN
Founding year	1998	2002	1989
Presidential elections: percent votes, first round	1999: 2.8 2004: 5.3 2009: 32.1 2014: 26.1	2002: 17.4 2006: 26.8 2009: 11.4 2013: 3.7	1993: 14.3 1997: 16.1 2002: 5.5
Legislative elections: percent seats, lower house or constituent assembly	1999: 2.8 2004: 2.8 2009: 16.9 2014: 42.3	2002: 10.0 2006: 24.0 2007: 6.2 2009: 6.4 2013: 0.0	1993: 15.4 1997: 16.2 2002: 3.8

two.[10] By 2003, the CBN had been sold to an Argentine company, and ties between it and the UCS had withered (Ballivián 2003: 89).

In what follows, I trace how exactly these three parties depended on their associated business conglomerates for five resources they needed to become viable: finance, personnel, infrastructure, media, and a mass base (Barndt 2014). In accumulating these resources, each party also developed the winning combination of a clear brand, a territorial organization, and party unity.[11] Though these attributes were insufficient to save the UCS from collapse, they aided PRIAN in its struggle to survive

[10] In 1997, the party took 16 percent of the vote, with businessman Ivo Kuljis as its presidential candidate. During the 1990s, Jhonny won the important post of mayor of Santa Cruz.

[11] The observations that underlie these case studies were developed, in part, during author field trips to Bolivia (February–March 1998, June–July 1998, January 1999, July–August 2001), Ecuador (September–December 2003, March 2006, July 2007), and Panama (August–September 2009, March 2014).

recent assaults by the Correa government, and have allowed Democratic Change to win the presidency and subsequently a plurality of legislative seats in Panama.

Finance

Of all the resources that businesses can bring to parties, finance is noted most often. And, indeed, the UCS, Democratic Change, and PRIAN all clearly relied heavily on financial resources derived from their founders' business conglomerates. By providing extensive finance to their parties, these conglomerates provided one critical – and often scarce – resource necessary to building a party organization.

To begin, overwhelming evidence exists that the UCS depended on the financial support of the CBN. Fernández himself stated that the work of the UCS was "financed by my own business" (Mayorga 1991: 99; 2002: 176). Indeed, Fernández transferred at least 120,000 dollars a month from the brewery to the party, invested five million dollars in his own presidential campaign, and spent 800,000 dollars on municipal races during 1989 (García Montero 2001: 141–142; Mayorga 1991: 99). Like Fernández, Noboa invested "part of his fortune" in founding PRIAN and the party continued to receive funds from Noboa's businesses through at least 2006.[12] In practice, Noboa has also financed most of his own campaign costs, allowing him to "outspend all of his rivals."[13] Democratic Change, too, depended on financing derived from Martinelli's businesses (Rodríguez Garibaldo 2009: 251). In 2008–2009, for example, Martinelli spent more than sixteen million dollars on preelectoral and electoral expenses for Democratic Change (Porcell Alemán 2009: 78). In sum, each party's dependence on the finances of its founders' economic holdings was substantial. Yet expanding the analysis beyond financial resources makes even clearer the potential value of a corporate organizational inheritance.

---

[12] "Elecciones 2002: Álvaro Noboa Pontón," *El Hoy* (Quito), September 25, 2002; "Precandidatos dan pistas de sus círculos íntimos," *El Universo* (Guayaquil), January 29, 2006; Ray (2009).

[13] Njaim (2005: 253); de la Torre and Conaghan (2009: 7); "Álvaro Noboa, ocho años en campaña," *El Hoy* (Quito), January 24, 2006. Data on donations by individual businesses within the Noboa group are sparse, though a recent legal case revealed heavy donations by CONAPLAS, a Noboa Group plastics manufacturer, to the Noboa campaign in 2009 (Corte Nacional Electoral 2010; "El control del gasto no cubre todos los egresos," *El Hoy* [Quito], November 15, 2006.

Infrastructure

All three parties depended heavily on the infrastructural resources of their sponsoring conglomerates. At its simplest, this meant offices – party headquarters could be regularly found in the office buildings of the business – and the information technologies that accompany them (computers, telephones, etc.). But it also included the use of company property such as local branches (to organize local party events) or logistical resources (like transportation). Infrastructural resources transferred from the corporation allowed all three parties to construct territorial organizations and to build connections between themselves and their sponsoring corporations' popular brands.

This dynamic was most clearly evident for Democratic Change. The party's national headquarters were established on the second floor of the Costa del Este Super 99 in Panama City,[14] and local party headquarters were located in local branches of the supermarket.[15] Party membership drives sometimes took place inside local Super 99s.[16] Super 99s also served as critical meeting points for supporters during campaigns: political caravans that wound through cities and localities often began at Super 99s.[17] And Super 99 trucks were used to hand out campaign propaganda, including shirts, hats, and flags.[18] Indeed, the branch structure of the supermarket chain was particularly useful during electoral campaigns: twenty separate Super 99s are located in Panama City alone, allowing the party to expand its geographical reach throughout the capital district. The infrastructure of Super 99 was, in large part, the infrastructure of Democratic Change.

Max Fernández also put the infrastructure of the CBN at the service of the UCS. To begin, the distribution and transportation infrastructures of the business were critical components of campaign and party-building strategies: local beverage distributors and delivery services gave the UCS an "enormous geographic capacity," increasing the "territorial radius"

[14] After Martinelli's election, politicians came here to look for appointments in his administration (Lynch 1999).
[15] José González Pinilla, "La rápida evolución de CD," *La Prensa* (Panama City), December 11, 2009; "El primer traspaso acelerado de mando," *La Prensa* (Panama City), May 16, 2009; and author's interview with Raúl Leis, Panama City, September 2009.
[16] Kemy Loo Pinzón, "Partidos comienzan a inscribir adherentes," *La Prensa* (Panama City), August 2, 2009.
[17] For example, an April 19, 2009 caravan gathered at the Costa del Este Super 99.
[18] José González Pinilla, "Avalancha de 'locos' en Amador," *La Prensa* (Panama City), April 27, 2009.

of its electoral appeal (Mayorga 1991: 98–99, 1993: 55–57). Moreover, party rallies and meetings were managed by the CBN's Department of Events and often took place under the auspices of the brewery. For example, the party's "re-foundation" in 1989 took place "on the door-step of the *Cervecería Boliviana Nacional*" (Mayorga 1991: 73–74, 2002: 176). And the UCS headquarters was eventually moved to the seat of the central offices of the CBN (Mayorga 2002: 178). As with Democratic Change and Super 99, the infrastructure of the UCS and the CBN were practically interchangeable.

Noboa's use of business resources to provide infrastructural support for his party has been more indirect than that of either Fernández or Martinelli. This is because, as discussed below, PRIAN's infrastructural resources come more from the Fundación Cruzada Nueva Humanidad (Crusade for a New Humanity Foundation), a "charitable" foundation funded by Noboa's conglomerate, than from the conglomerate itself. For the most part, it is this foundation, rather than the particular assets of Noboa's businesses, that provide the types of infrastructural resources – such as transport[19] – that Democratic Change and the UCS received directly from their sponsoring conglomerates. In part, this is because the Noboa conglomerate simply lacks the retail branch structure that Martinelli and Fernández readily repurposed as party infrastructure. Nonetheless, Noboa has not shied away from deploying the infrastructural resources of his businesses in support of PRIAN. He has, for example, hosted campaign events on business properties and used his businesses' transportation services to move candidates and resources around the country.[20]

In short, all three of these parties relied on business assets for infrastructural resources, resources that contributed to the strength of each party's territorial organizations and of its brand. For the UCS and Democratic Change, these assets came straight out of their founders' business holdings. For PRIAN, as discussed below, they more often came through the foundation that Noboa's businesses funded. The availability of infrastructural resources was, that is, conditioned by the type of business that sponsored the party. Those conglomerates with important holdings in consumer retail (Martinelli's and Fernández's) could provide infrastructural resources more directly than those groups that lacked such holdings (Noboa) – a point to which I return in the conclusion of this chapter.

---

[19] "Electorales," *El Universo* (Guayaquil), March 15, 2006.
[20] "Ejecutivo irrespeta reglas de campaña," *El Hoy* (Quito), March 17, 2009; "El cierre de campaña en dos ciudades," *El Hoy* (Quito), July 10, 1998; "Medios de comunicación analizan franjas," *El Hoy* (Quito), August 28, 2006.

Personnel

All three parties depended on personnel from their associated conglomerates to act as staff, officials, candidates, and (following successful elections) government appointees. Specialized personnel were also transferred from businesses to parties: lawyers, accountants, advertising and publicity professionals, and administrators. By repurposing their own loyal (and dependent) employees as party officials and candidates, these corporations helped forestall the kinds of conflicts associated with internal schisms in other new parties.

Since its founding, many of PRIAN's key officials have been employees of the Noboa conglomerates. Iván Carmigniani, the manager of Mercanoboa, the Noboa Group's advertising agency (discussed later), engineered the publicity for PRIAN's electoral campaign in 2002.[21] Four of the seven other most important figures in Noboa's 2002 presidential campaign also worked or had worked for the Grupo Noboa: Wilson Sánchez Castello, external assessor for the Noboa Group and Noboa Corporation; Sylka Sánchez Castello, previously head of the Noboa Group's legal department, then the director of Noboa's holding company Fruit Shippers Ltd., and eventually a vice director of the Noboa Corporation; Ernesto Weisson Pazmiño, director of the international division of the Noboa Corporation; and Nicanor Moscoso Pezo, the campaign treasurer who served as a manager of Promandato Global and director of Industrial Molinera, both Noboa businesses.[22] During the 2006 campaign, the Sánchez "clan" remained and were joined by Arturo Yzcaza, manager of Exportadora Bananera Noboa, and Vicente Taiano, Noboa's vice-presidential candidate, who had worked since 1994 as a legal assessor to the Noboa Corporation. During 2006, Taiano's son served as director of PRIAN's "Youth Front" while running the vice-presidential candidate's law firm, which continued to manage Noboa's firms (OCPAL 2006). As of 2009, many of these individuals continued to be central figures in the party,[23] even as other new employees were incorporated: for example, Yuliana Paola Triviño, an auditor in the Noboa Group, served as campaign treasurer during the 2009 campaign.[24] Throughout PRIAN's existence, moreover, personnel from the Noboa Group's charitable foundation played key roles in electoral campaigns and party-building.

[21] This was also true in 1998, when Noboa ran with the PRIAN ticket.
[22] "El equipo de Noboa," *El Universo* (Guayaquil), November 23, 2002; Ray (2009: 16).
[23] Vicente Taiano, for example, had become national director of PRIAN.
[24] "La acción de tesoreros de campaña, regulada," *El Hoy* (Quito), March 23, 2009.

Ricardo Martinelli adopted a personnel strategy for Democratic Change that closely resembled Noboa's for PRIAN. When the party was founded, Martinelli chose trusted employees to help lead it: both Federico Torres Vásquez (a vice president of the party's 1997 provisional junta) and David Virzi (party director, 2000–2009) came out of Martinelli's sugar manufacturing business, Azucarera La Victoria.[25] Over time, this personnel strategy became even more pronounced: employees of the Martinelli conglomerate were appointed to key positions in party finance, legal strategy, public relations, and organizational development. Frank de Lima, who served as financial secretary of the party and campaign spokesman during the 2009 run, was Project Manager at Super 99 (Ministerio de Economía y Finanzas 2009). Giaconda Torres de Bianchini, Super 99's chief internal auditor, became the party's treasurer in 2003.[26] Julio Abrego, subsecretary of party organization, was also a manager at the supermarket.[27] Roberto Moreno, a party director, worked at Importadora Ricamar. Alma L. Cortés (party director and subsecretary general, 2003–2009) served as chief counsel for the Martinelli business group.[28] In addition, employees from Martinelli's businesses ran as candidates for office in both the Panamanian interior (Leis 2009) and metropolitan area (e.g., Julio Abrego in District 8-6). Several of these individuals – de Lima, Bianchini, Cortes, Abrego, Moreno – along with other Super 99 employees, were then appointed to government positions when Martinelli won in 2009.[29] For example, Jaime Trujillo, head of security for Super 99, became Chief of the National Security Counsel and Aixa Santamaría, who had worked as a Super 99 administrator in Chiriquí, was appointed governor of that province.[30]

The UCS also relied on personnel from Max Fernández's CBN. Less specific information was available for the UCS – even when requested from party officials themselves – due to the passage of time and internal

[25] Ismael Hernández A., "Conflicto por supuesta compra de acciones de Ingenio La Victoria," *La Prensa* (Panama City), January 26, 2004; Carolina Freire, "'Las islas van,'" *La Prensa* (Panama City), August 3, 2000.
[26] Elena Morales Gil and José González Pinilla, "De Bianchini, a la Contraloría," *La Prensa* (Panama City), October 15, 2009.
[27] "Órgano Ejecutivo," *Panamá América* (Panama City), June 27, 2009.
[28] Neir Carrasco Kerekes, "Murcia desata guerra política," *La Estrella* (Panama City), March 15, 2009.
[29] Elena Morales Gil and José González Pinilla, "El círculo de Martinelli llega al poder," *La Prensa* (Panama City), May 13, 2009.
[30] Flor Mizrachi Angel, "Renuncia titular del Mida," *La Prensa* (Panama City), June 30, 2010.

changes since the party's heyday (1989–1993). That said, prominent examples exist of employee transfers from the business into the party.[31] For example, both Mario Galindo Decker and Adolfo Gonzales Mier, executives of the CBN, became key figures in the party in the late 1980s and early 1990s. Galindo was the regional head of the UCS in Cochabamba, while Gonzales was a member of the party's National Directorate; both ran for office in Cochabamba (Mayorga 1991: 103–104, 1993: 55). Gustavo Medinacelli and Jorge Pacheco (vice president of the CBN) were key members of the UCS inner circle (Mayorga 2002: 221–222). And Roberto and Jhonny Fernández, Max's sons, each had important positions in both the CBN and the UCS (Mayorga 2002: 188). According to Mayorga, the party leadership was "superimposed" on the leadership of the CBN (2002: 177): in repurposing brewery staff to the UCS, Fernández sought to impose the same sort of executive control over his employees in the party that he maintained over them in his business operations. In all three parties, the transfer of loyal (or dependent) personnel from the corporation was a critical component of the organizational inheritance.

Mass Bases

All three parties also used corporate assets to develop mass support among the voting public. At least three different tactics were employed, each of which drew heavily on conglomerate resources. First, where possible, parties repurposed existing supplier and customer networks as networks of partisan support. Second, all three parties sought to mobilize voters through the clientelist distribution of corporate goods and services. Sometimes this occurred directly, with businesses providing goods and services to prospective partisans and voters. But it also happened indirectly, through the work of corporation-financed charitable foundations,[32] whose clientelist practices could be framed in terms of "corporate social responsibility" or philanthropy. Finally, conglomerate employees – managers and workers alike – were sometimes persuaded to vote for the

---

[31] Mayorga observed two decades ago that "the relationship between [the UCS and CBN] ... is manifested in terms of the composition of the lists of candidates in different elections and in the composition of national and regional [party] directorates: some employees of the business replicated their [business] positions in the internal organization of the party" (1991: 103).

[32] This also occurred through conglomerate transportation networks, which were used to distribute resources to supporters at election time.

party their employer sponsored.[33] These practices not only helped the parties build coherent territorial organizations, but also provided them with another source of party unity: the beginnings of a mass partisan base.

The CBN itself was the primary means through which the UCS acquired networks of local partisans. Between 1989 and 1991, Fernández used brewery resources to initiate more than a thousand community projects in hundreds of localities (Mayorga 1991: 83). Local factories served to build new patron–client relationships at the local level. By reactivating a facility in Sucre and installing a new factory in Trinidad, for example, Fernández successfully constructed local support for the UCS in those cities (Mayorga 1991: 86).[34] More broadly, the CBN's distribution routes acted as a "network of party affiliates, enabling a continuous and permanent presence of [party] activists" at the local level, including local merchants who sold the very popular CBN brands of beer. Indeed, employees of the CBN developed what one official described as a "cult-like"[35] relationship with the party, providing it with a loyal core of voters throughout the late 1980s and early 1990s (Mayorga 1991: 98–99).

To build networks among potential voters, Democratic Change relied on a variety of institutions and practices. To begin, the customer base of Super 99 provided Martinelli with a ready base of likely voters: wards where Super 99s provided voting blocs for Democratic Change (Barndt n.d.). Yet the most visible way that Democratic Change built partisan networks was through two ostensibly charitable foundations: the Super 99 Foundation (est. 1991) and the Ricardo Martinelli Foundation (RMF, est. October 2004). Both foundations are officially nonprofit organizations, charged with distributing scholarships to low-income Panamanian students. Nonetheless, the two foundations are clearly sponsored by Martinelli's businesses. In 2006, for example, Martinelli stated that Super 99 donated more than one-and-a-half million dollars a year to charity, much of which went to the RMF.[36] Martinelli himself is the RMF's "founder and benefactor," his wife is the Foundation's president,

---

[33] No survey data exists on this phenomenon. Anecdotal support of voting by conglomerate employees was reported in author interviews in both Panama and Ecuador.

[34] In Trinidad, "profits [*beneficios*]" from the new factory "were to be directed to 'preserving health and fomenting education'" (Mayorga 1991: 73).

[35] This description is from an anonymous official from the State Department, whom I interviewed in La Paz, Bolivia, in February 1998.

[36] And three other nonprofit organizations: Nutre Hogar (Nourishment Home), Casa Esperanza (Hope House), la Fundación Ofrece un Hogar (Home Away From Home Foundation). Super 99 also financed three eateries for low-income children ("Intentan recuperar El Machetazo," *La Prensa* [Panama City], November 13, 2006).

and (like the party itself) the RMF's headquarters have been located at the Costa del Este Super 99 in Panama City. Tellingly, when accusations emerged in 2006 that Martinelli's business-sponsored charitable foundations were spending vast amounts of money to benefit the party, it was the president of the party's Political Committee who responded – rather than a Foundation official.[37]

Together, the Super 99 Foundation and the RMF awarded thousands of scholarships a year during the 2000s: the RMF awarded more than 20,000 in the first half of 2008 alone.[38] Given that a key component of Democratic Change's electoral strategy was to appeal to the youth vote,[39] those scholarships represented a clear way to build electoral support. The party's campaign propaganda regularly focused on the activities of these foundations, which have headquarters in key provinces, including Chiriquí, Colón, Bocas del Toro, Herrera, and Los Santos.[40] Indeed, Martinelli himself *openly recognizes* the political benefits of the foundations. When asked in 2004, "What will you do to keep yourself in the mind of the voters during these five years [until the 2009 elections]?," Martinelli responded, "I have made a foundation with my own resources … to help the most needy of this country."[41] Through these two foundations, Martinelli's business conglomerate enabled Democratic Change to establish new relationships with the voting population it sought to target. This interlocking network of party and foundations, all sponsored by Super 99 and related businesses, allowed Martinelli and his supporters to forge a viable electoralist organization in remarkably short order.[42]

Like Martinelli, Álvaro Noboa used both his conglomerate and his business-sponsored foundation (Fundación Cruzada Nueva Humanidad) to build political support for PRIAN.[43] Yet it is the work of the Foundation, which draws openly on Noboa's financial and business resources,[44] that

---

[37] Roberto Henríquez, "Los plomeros de Panamá," *La Prensa* (Panama City), April 9, 2006.

[38] "Reseña," *La Prensa* (Panama City), June 23, 2008.

[39] Author's interview with Raúl Leis, Panama City, September 2009; author's interview with Roberto Henríquez, Panama City, September 2009; and Porcell Alemán (2009).

[40] www.ricardomartinelli.org/es/provincias.html. Accessed February 22, 2012.

[41] "Intentan recuperar El Machetazo," *La Prensa* (Panama City), November 13, 2006.

[42] There is a clear parallel between this infrastructure and that developed by PRIAN in Ecuador (see de la Torre and Conaghan 2009).

[43] de la Torre and Conaghan (2009); "Noboa continuará con brigadas," *El Universo* (Guayaquil), November 29, 2002.

[44] The work of the foundation began in 1976, though it was formally founded in 1981. The Foundation is headed by Noboa's wife, Anabella Azín, a doctor who works in the Foundation's "Medical Brigades," which provide medical services to low-income

has been most prominent. With annual spending of (as of 2002) more than a million dollars,[45] the Foundation distributes a variety of goods and services, including free medical clinics, food,[46] microcredits, wheelchairs,[47] clothing, computers, community libraries, and housing.[48] During the second round of the 2006 campaign, Noboa even handed out five-hundred-dollar gifts to beneficiaries of Foundation programs.[49] Noboa himself frequently travels with the Foundation, establishing direct links between it, PRIAN, and his candidacy.[50] Moreover, the Foundation has served as a device to consolidate PRIAN's territorial reach by "providing money to local organizers to establish [PRIAN] neighborhood committees."[51] And, as noted below, Noboa has used the foundation's work to keep himself and the party constantly in the media.[52]

Beyond the Foundation, PRIAN drew directly on networks maintained within Noboa's businesses. For example, PRIAN enjoyed the support of conglomerate employees, who numbered some 35,000 as of 2002. Such support may not have always been entirely voluntary: reports exist of local plantations threatening workers who did not join PRIAN

Ecuadorians ("Doctora y maestro son las compañeras de presidenciables," *El Universo* [Guayaquil], November 5, 2006).

[45] "A. Noboa pagó más por sus votos," *El Universo* (Guayaquil), October 22, 2002; "$4.5 millones en campaña," *El Universo* (Guayaquil), November 28, 2002.

[46] The food distributed is often produced by Noboa's companies ("Los otros protagonistas," *El Universo* [Guayaquil], November 20, 2006).

[47] The Foundation also has programs, run by Mariano Santos, whose office is in the Banco del Litoral, which was founded by Noboa and holds the Foundation's checking account ("Los otros protagonistas," *El Universo* [Guayaquil], November 20, 2006; "Álvaro Noboa recorrió Babahoyo," *El Universo* [Guayaquil], November 12, 2002).

[48] "Noboa promete subir el bono con los recursos del petróleo," *El Universo* (Guayaquil), October 21, 2006; "Noboa rifa viviendas populares," *El Universo* (Guayaquil), March 12, 2006; "Álvaro Noboa se promociona; Hurtado-Gallardo, en Quito," *El Universo* (Guayaquil), July 23, 2002; "Vivienda: Un ofrecimiento pendiente por años," *El Universo* (Guayaquil), November 8, 2006.

[49] Distribution of the money was coordinated by Santos ("Estrategia electoral con variaciones," *El Universo* [Guayaquil], November 11, 2006).

[50] "Prian promueve plan de Noboa en España," *El Universo* (Guayaquil), June 3, 2006. During 2006, the Guayaquil daily *El Universo* noted: "There is no political gathering in which ... Noboa does not 'award' a loan, in the name of his Fundación Cruzada Nueva Humanidad" ("A propósito del Nobel de la Paz y el Banco Grameen," *El Universo* [Guayaquil], October 30, 2006).

[51] De la Torre and Conaghan (2009: 7) observe that "The foundation became an organizational pillar in Noboa's campaign [in 2006]. It channeled resources to PRIAN's grassroots organizing efforts, providing money to local organizers to establish neighborhood committees. PRIAN estimated that at least 8,500 such groups were operating in Guayaquil in late October 2006" (see also Ray 2009: 16).

[52] "Noboa decidirá su propaganda," *El Universo* (Guayaquil), August 27, 2006.

(Bacon 2002). Conglomerate-owned plantations also distributed food to potential voters, while Mercanoboa openly distributed PRIAN-branded clothing and posters (Ronquillo 2002).[53] Between the indirect work of the Foundation and the direct work of businesses in the conglomerate, PRIAN developed a robust network of partisans and voters throughout the country. In all three parties, this combination of direct and indirect corporate support for party-building provided a novel organizational platform and a potential foundation for developing a loyal party base.

Publicity

Publicity resources are critical to the success of new parties. Unsurprisingly, therefore, Noboa, Martinelli, and Fernández all turned the publicity assets of their conglomerates to partisan purposes. At its most brazen, this entailed conglomerate-owned radio and television stations providing friendly reporting or editorial coverage for the party. More mundanely, the imagery – colors, icons – associated with conglomerates played an important role in party advertising. Businesses within the conglomerates also regularly devoted their normal advertising time to their parties during campaigns. And specialized advertising and polling assets of the groups were put at the service of the political parties as well. Through these activities, corporations helped their parties begin to forge a mass following – a following that associated those parties with well-established and popular corporate brands.

PRIAN has relied heavily on two publicity resources from the Noboa conglomerate. Most importantly, the Noboa conglomerate includes a publicity agency, Mercanoboa, that serves the party during electoral campaigns (de la Torre and Conaghan 2009). In 2002, for example, the agency was contracted to help organize and control Noboa's presidential campaign, as well as produce campaign spots.[54] As noted above, Iván Carmigniani, the manager of Mercanoboa, designed the party's campaign publicity that year.[55] In 2006, the Guayaquil daily *El Universo* described the relationship between Noboa and Mercanoboa during PRIAN's electoral campaigns as follows:

---

[53] Gisella Ronquillo, "El Partido millonario de Noboa," *El Universo* (Guayaquil), April 9, 2002.
[54] "Prian no reportó $302.963 de la campaña, según TSE," *El Hoy* (Quito), November 25, 2003; "La campaña de los finalistas dio un giro," *El Hoy* (Quito), November 16, 2002.
[55] This was also the case in 1998, when Noboa ran with the PRE.

There are days when Álvaro Noboa Pontón says that he wakes up "inspired." So he calls his collaborators from the publicity agency Mercanoboa on the phone and asks that they send the cameramen because he wants to tape a spot. The *muchachos* edit the images and, if he likes the composition – which he himself generally thinks up – he orders its release to the press.[56]

Mercanoboa has also allowed Noboa to lump together his political and business polling. According to Sylka Sánchez, one of the party's key leaders and a longtime employee of the conglomerate: "The polls [about PRIAN] are not by the party. They are business polls. They ask how goes the market for Quaker [as in Quaker Oats, produced by Noboa's Molinera Industrial] and also who would you vote for if the elections were tomorrow. It's not a big expense. They are Mercanoboa polls."[57] In addition to Mercanoboa, Noboa founded a monthly magazine in 1988, unironically titled La Verdad (The Truth), that he uses for his own "personal promotion" (Njaim 2005: 251). In the last issue published before the 2006 election (August, no. 217), for example, seven of the eight lead articles were about PRIAN, and Noboa himself used the magazine's editorial to make a pitch for himself and PRIAN (La Verdad 2006). Moreover, the portal of the magazine's website included (as of 2011) a direct link to both the PRIAN website and Álvaro Noboa's personal website. Both these assets, though especially Mercanoboa, have been consistent and important components of PRIAN's publicity campaigns.

Martinelli also transferred the publicity resources of Super 99 to Democratic Change, especially during the 2009 election. Most blatantly, the television airtime normally reserved for Super 99 advertisements was simply reallocated to the campaign (Leis 2009). But the party relied on Super 99 for much more than airtime: billboards next to Super 99s were plastered with party propaganda and Super 99s themselves were painted in the party's colors.[58] During the campaign, a variety of party advertisements drew freely on Super 99 imagery. The most direct of these was the campaign's "Biography Spot," which focused on Martinelli's success

---

[56] "Precandidatos dan pistas de sus círculos íntimos," *El Universo* (Guayaquil), January 29, 2006. Combining group media and network assets, PRIAN developed television spots over the course of the 2006 campaign that focused heavily on the charitable work of the Noboa Foundation (discussed previously) and on Noboa agricultural plantations ("PC reclama sobre la publicidad de precandidatos presidenciales," *El Universo* [Guayaquil], February 7, 2006).

[57] Gisella Ronquillo, "Prian admite que Noboa puede ceder candidatura," *El Universo* (Guayaquil), May 15, 2006.

[58] Silvio Sirias, "Balbina Herrera's head start," *The Panama News* (Panama City), November 22, 2008; and author's interview with Raúl Leis, Panama City, September 2009.

in expanding the Super 99 chain. Yet perhaps more daring was the campaign's "Video Jingle Hip Hop," which emphasized Super 99's humble beginnings and reminded voters that it was still there for them after the destructive US invasion of 1989 ("Ricardo Martinelli 2009" 2009a, 2009b). The Super 99s also allowed the party's associated charitable foundations to publicize their activities more effectively. According to party leader Roberto Henríquez, "The publicity that the [Ricardo Martinelli] Foundation produces to broadcast its actions and to congratulate new beneficiaries costs almost nothing, because Martinelli's businesses are big advertisers in the media and this allows [the foundation] very reasonable rates that translate into almost free airtime."[59] That is, the Foundation receives discounted publicity, which benefits Democratic Change politically, because of its close connections to Martinelli's businesses. Finally, it is notable that Martinelli is a shareholder in TVN-2, a major Panamanian television station. Though evidence does not exist that the station openly favored the party, the campaign posted favorable news coverage from TVN-2 journalists on its website, and the Martinelli administration hired prominent station personnel upon taking office.

When the UCS emerged, Max Fernández did not yet own important media outlets.[60] As such, the advertising resources of the CBN itself were deployed in support of the UCS. In the run-up to the 1989 election, for example, the television and print advertising reserved for Paceña, the CBN's flagship brand, was replaced by campaign spots (Mayorga 1991: 100–101, 1993: 56). Television spots contained the phrase, "*Pida empresa y tomará presidencia*," a take-off on a CBN slogan, "*Pida Paceña, y tomará cerveza*" (Mayorga 1993: 102).[61] Like Martinelli, moreover, the advertising strategy of Fernández's presidential campaign was based on the notion that his success at leading the CBN would translate easily into success at leading the country (Mayorga 1993: 119–120). Indeed, this conceit was a regular part of Martinelli's and Noboa's campaigns, as well – part of the brand that all three corporations successfully

---

[59] Henríquez, who also responded because he was named in other accusations that were then circulating, observed that the RMF awarded scholarships regardless of a recipient's political affiliation (Roberto Henríquez, "Los plomeros de Panamá," *La Prensa* [Panama City], April 9, 2006).

[60] Though the conglomerate came to own a radio station (12 Emisoras), a television network (Sitel), and a major newspaper (La Estrella del Oriente) in Santa Cruz and Beni.

[61] Roughly translated, the former means "ask for business and you'll take the presidency," and the latter means "ask for Paceña and you'll drink beer." The wordplay works well in Spanish.

transferred to their parties, repurposing mass support for product brands into mass support for their parties.

In sum, Democratic Change, PRIAN, and the UCS depended heavily – indeed, were sponsored by – particular business conglomerates.[62] Collectively, the resources provided to parties by their corporate sponsors allowed those parties to develop a clear brand, to develop a territorial organization, and to construct partisan bases that could help maintain party unity. Corporation-based party-building thus provided a way to imbue these new parties with many of the characteristics associated with other more successful parties in Latin America. As a result, each of these three parties survived and prospered – for a while.

THE DIFFICULTY OF SUSTAINING CORPORATION-BASED PARTIES

Of the three corporation-based parties discussed here, only Democratic Change clearly remains a viable contender into the future. This raises a critically important question: can corporation-based parties last? Numerous pitfalls exist, perhaps none more serious than the high degree of personalization in many corporation-based parties, including the three discussed here.

The UCS, Democratic Change, and PRIAN were not simply parties built on and by corporations. They were parties built on corporations by the *owners* of those corporations, owners who went on to lead their parties and run for president on their parties' tickets. From one perspective, the leaders of these three corporation-based parties literally *owned* the parties. Given this tight connection between corporate and political leadership, all three parties have frequently been dismissed as personalistic electoral vehicles: cases of wealthy businessmen briefly drawing on their own resources to finance their own campaigns, doomed to die with their founders' ambitions.

This high degree of personalism is worth dwelling on, given that personalism is often thought to be associated with fragile party structures. The most severe examples of this tendency have been the fleeting electoral devices hastily registered and equally hastily disbanded by outsider candidates like Peruvian president Alberto Fujimori (Levitsky and Cameron 2003). Roberts (2006) refers to them as "electoral populist" vehicles. Kitschelt et al. (2010) do not even consider them in their

---

[62] Of course, this is not to say that the overlap between business and party was total or exact. These three parties also drew on resources that were unconnected to their associated conglomerates and not all business assets were turned to the purposes of the parties.

landmark study of Latin American party systems. Consensus exists that such parties are usually temporary features of the electoral landscape. They take to an extreme the weaknesses of brand, organization, and cohesion that the introductory chapter of this volume argues have been so detrimental to party persistence. If corporation-based parties are the businessman's equivalent of Fujimori's electoral devices, they are (to say the least) unlikely to last.

Of course, it bears repeating that most corporation-based parties will fail in short order regardless. In this, they are no different than any other kind of new party. At the same time, however, corporation-based parties accrue advantages that most new parties lack. As this chapter has demonstrated, corporation-based party-building can endow new parties with attributes – brands, territorial organizations, and unity – that other new parties struggle to develop.

Another way to put this is that the corporation-based parties discussed in this chapter are often both highly personalist *and* in possession of the attributes this volume associates with party durability. This is a curious situation. While only time will tell whether these parties will last, it is worth remembering that some of the most successful parties in Latin America during the twentieth century maintained their highly personalist character for decades. (As Chapter 1 argues, we may well be paying insufficient attention to how leaders may *contribute* to party-building.) Unlike many personalist parties from earlier eras, however, corporation-based parties already have powerful *organizations*, inherited from the corporations that have sponsored them.

Indeed, the fact that corporation-based parties remain dependent on the corporation that sponsors them may actually help to reduce their personalization over time. Corporate owners may well be willing to relinquish their formal place at the head of their parties' tickets – this began to happen in Democratic Change in 2014[63] – as long as they maintain firm control over the corporations on which those parties depend. There are clear advantages to the corporate owners relinquishing formal leadership within the parties their corporations have sponsored, most importantly a degree of separation from the day-to-day political infighting

---

[63] While José Domingo Arias was nominated as the party's presidential candidate, Marta Linares de Martinelli, First Lady of Panama and head of the RMF, was nominated as vice-presidential candidate. The internal contention that surrounded the eventual decision to accept Martinelli's wife as the party's vice-presidential candidate provides clear evidence of the kinds of tensions that surround attempts by businesspeople party-builders to retain influence over the parties they build.

that characterizes parties-in-government. From this vantage point, the key characteristic of contemporary corporation-based parties may be less their personalization and more their lack of autonomy from their sponsoring corporations (Mainwaring and Scully 1995).

Depersonalized corporation-based parties may actually be more common in the region than we currently believe. All three corporation-based parties discussed in this chapter could be easily identified precisely because the owners of their sponsoring corporations also led the parties – all three ran for president at the head of their party's ticket. Corporation-based parties are much more difficult to identify where such clear ties between corporate and political leaderships are lacking. More research is needed on the possibility that existing parties in Latin America are corporation-based in the way this chapter describes, yet not formally led by corporate owners. Panamanian and Guatemalan parties seem an especially promising starting place for exploring this possibility (Barahona 2008).

It is also worth considering the possibility that corporation-based party organizations may endure independently of the party they initially inhabit. In other words, the parties named PRIAN and Democratic Change may well disappear – the UCS certainly has – while the underlying corporation-based party organizations endure. That is, corporation-based party organizations may persist as political mobilizing structures across time while taking on different party names at different moments.[64] Such corporation-based organizations would represent quite a powerful new type of "informal" party organization (Levitsky and Freidenberg 2007).[65]

Indeed, observers of corporation-based party-building in Latin America might do well to focus less on the particular partisan shells that corporation-based organizations temporarily inhabit and more on the extent to which the underlying organizations persist as meaningful partisan actors over time, shaping the political arena just below the surface of traditional (formal, autonomous) party politics. It seems entirely plausible that some party systems in Latin America will, over time, become constituted in part by competition between the most successful of these informal organizations. Arguably, this has already occurred in Panama, and perhaps in Guatemala as well.

[64] In some ways, this is not so different from earlier generations of party formation (and reformation). The histories of Latin American party systems are filled with examples of groups of partisan elites withdrawing themselves and their resources from particular parties, only to reintroduce themselves (and their resources) under a new name in a subsequent election.

[65] This seems a better description of the organizations described here than the otherwise quite useful idea of "party substitutes" (Hale 2006).

It seems less likely that corporation-based parties will transform themselves into the kinds of conservative parties that have traditionally populated Latin America. Such classic conservative parties sought to bring together and represent broad swaths of upper-class interests. Yet as Gibson (1996) and Schneider (2004) have rightly noted, business historically has been at best an aloof ally of such parties in Latin America. Few parties in the region have been able to count on the lasting support of the business class, organized or unorganized.

This has not been for lack of trying. In country after country over the last three decades, conservative factions have tried to come together and build national conservative parties with broad support in the business class (see Eaton, Chapter 14, this volume). In very few places, however, has a lasting and united conservative party been forged in this way.[66] This is because efforts to build such broad-based conservative parties rest on the willingness of *multiple* business conglomerates (along with other upper-class interests) to pool their resources and cooperate. As demonstrated in this chapter, however, *individual* businesses regularly control sufficient resources to form viable parties on their own. When serious conflict emerges within broad-based conservative parties, therefore, particular corporations have the option of defecting and forming their own individual parties – parties more likely to develop clear brands, coherent organizations, and internal unity.

Note the dilemma here: the very qualities that make a corporation-based party more likely to endure depend on its remaining grounded in one particular corporation. Attempts by a corporation-based party to broaden its base necessarily dilute its brand, organization, and mass support. For corporation-based parties, that is, the kind broadening of support that would normally be interpreted as an indicator of party institutionalization (Mainwaring and Scully 1995) instead increases the likelihood of party destabilization. Consequently, corporation-based parties are unlikely to evolve into the more classic and broad-based conservative parties discussed by Gibson (1996) and Middlebrook (2000).

This may well be the story of the Republican Proposal party (PRO) in Argentina.[67] The party's founder, Mauricio Macri, scion of the SOCMA[68] business conglomerate, has tried to chart a middle ground between basing

---

[66] El Salvador's Nationalist Republican Alliance (ARENA) and Independent Democratic Union (UDI) are regularly cited as possibilities (see Loxton, Chapter 9, this volume).

[67] See also Morresi and Vommaro (2014).

[68] SOCMA stands for the Sociedad Macri (the Macri Partnership), a business operation linked to the Grupo Macri (Macri Group).

the party in corporate-related assets – notably personnel – while simultaneously forging alliances with other conservative interests. In 2005, for example, the party forged an alliance with several small conservative party factions, and over the next decade, the party sought to broaden its appeal by allying with other factions in the Argentine provinces. PRO did fairly well in its first election (2007), and Macri himself won the presidency of Argentina in 2015.

Yet into the future, PRO's base-broadening strategy may not prove as fruitful for a variety of reasons, some particular to the Argentine context. From a more general perspective, the success of the party will depend on whether its broader base compromises its internal unity, coherent organization, and clear brand – the attributes associated with "purer" forms of corporation-based party-building. The experience of PRO, that is, raises questions about whether corporation-based parties can easily or naturally transform themselves into broader instruments of upper-class representation. In trying to do so, they may undermine the qualities that make them potentially durable in the first place.

Despite all these difficulties, it seems likely that at least some of these parties will become lasting features of the political landscape. As this chapter has argued, there is a clear theoretical affinity between corporation-based party-building and the development of attributes associated with party durability. Consequently, the phenomenon should be expected to persist and perhaps even expand in the future (see also Levitsky and Zavaleta, Chapter 15, this volume). Widespread privatization, the continued dominance of national economic conglomerates in many countries (as detailed by Schneider 2013), and the post-2002 economic boom have all reinforced the kinds of businesses that are best suited to repurpose their organizational assets into political parties.

Indeed, the potential of corporation-based parties (formal or informal) has only increased with the growth of the Latin American middle class. This is because, as the three cases discussed in this chapter have all suggested, the attributes we associate with party durability are most likely to be transferred to parties by corporations whose economic activities center *on mass consumption*. Corporations capable of grounding parties in the corner stores where people buy beer (UCS), in the supermarkets where they shop for food (Democratic Change), or even in the private universities where they go to college (as in the case of the Alliance for Progress [APP] in Peru[69]) will, on average, be better able to endow their

---

[69] See Levitsky and Zavaleta (Chapter 15, this volume). Martinelli's Democratic Change also sought to develop a mass base among students (as discussed above).

parties with the brands, organization, and mass networks that are critical to party durability. Moreover, the breadth of party-relevant resources – finance, infrastructure, personnel, mass networks, and publicity – available to consumer-oriented corporations reduces their need to reach out and form potentially destabilizing alliances with other conservative factions and organizations.

Conversely, corporations that lack extensive assets in consumer retail will be less capable of bringing popular brands, extensive branch organization, and robust partisan networks to their parties. And in their search for outside resources, such corporation-based parties are more likely to try to build broader-based, and thus less stable, instruments of representation. Such parties – PRIAN may be a good example here – are less likely to endure.

Given the different party-building capacities of these different kinds of corporations, it is worth noting that corporation-based parties may become most prominent in those countries that have growing (or extensive) consumer retail sectors. Liberalization, as Baker (2009a) has convincingly argued, may well be replacing the classic Latin American worker–capitalist cleavage with a new consumer–producer cleavage. If economies of consumption continue to take off in Latin America (World Bank 2013), more corporation-based parties should be expected to emerge: parties sponsored by corporations with popular consumer brands, branch organizations, and interests closely attuned to middle-class consumer bases.

Of course, most corporation-based parties will fade quickly – and most will likely continue to emerge in smaller countries with weakly institutionalized party systems. It is no doubt easier in these kinds of countries for a corporation to have the resources and networks to launch a new party. Given these hard constraints, however, there is good reason to think that the phenomenon of corporation-based party-building will remain part of the Latin American political landscape into the future.

PART IV

FAILED CASES (AND A FUTURE ONE)

14

Challenges of Party-Building in the Bolivian East

Kent Eaton

In the conflict-centered approach developed in Chapter 1 of this volume, Steven Levitsky, James Loxton, and Brandon Van Dyck argue that polarization creates favorable conditions for party-building because it helps to forge party brands, generate organizational resources and create internal cohesion. This chapter examines the theoretical framework in light of the Bolivian case, one of the starkest cases of polarization in the recent past in Latin America. In Bolivia, extreme regional polarization between the eastern and western halves of the country in the years after 2000 appeared to generate all three critical ingredients for party-building, but without resulting in the emergence of a successful party to represent the east.

What explains the failure of party-building despite the existence of brand attachments forged in the movement for eastern autonomy, a vibrant and extensive set of territorial and functional organizations, and high levels of cohesion among eastern political and economic elites? Although focused on only one subnational region in just one Latin American country, this chapter responds to the editors' insistence that failures of party-building can be as theoretically significant as successes. I use the surprising failure in Bolivia to develop two related theoretical arguments. The first has to do with timing and persistence; just as important as the extent of polarization is how long it lasts. While Bolivia experienced rising and eventually acute levels of polarization between 2003 and 2008, rapid depolarization after 2008 effectively undercut the bases for eastern party-building. The second has to do with the interconnected

For helpful comments on this chapter, I am grateful to Jennifer Cyr, Jorge Domínguez, Tasha Fairfield, Candelaria Garay, Steven Levitsky, James Loxton, Brandon Van Dyck and two anonymous reviewers.

nature of the relationship between the three ingredients that promote party-building. When internal elite cohesion unraveled in the Bolivian east, due to the exogenous and endogenous pressures examined below, this setback had dire consequences both for brand identification and for the ability to leverage organizational resources. Elite schisms raised difficult questions about who could interpret the party brand and which resources could be used to build a party.

In the opening decade of the twenty-first century, Bolivia experienced a turbulent and at times violent period of polarization along a single territorial cleavage between east and west. The chief protagonists of this polarization were two social movements with different regional bases of support and dramatically different visions for Bolivia. In the west, the Movimiento al Socialismo (MAS – Movement toward Socialism) won control of the national government and set out on a far-reaching process of constitutional revision designed to establish a plurinational state, reverse centuries of indigenous political subordination, and shift Bolivia away from neoliberalism. In the east, a conservative autonomy movement developed under the direction of opposition governors and socioeconomic elites, who opposed the new constitution, resisted the shift toward greater state involvement in the economy, and advocated instead for the autonomy to maintain a more market-oriented development model.

Although this territorial cleavage between the western highlands and the eastern lowlands predated the presidency of Evo Morales, his rise to power seemed to represent a significant new threat to the economic interests that dominate eastern departments and that previously enjoyed great influence in the national government. Antagonized by the overthrow of President Gonzalo Sánchez de Lozada in 2003 and by the landslide election of Morales in 2005, political and economic elites responded by leading a movement for autonomy in the east that succeeded in mobilizing thousands of lowland residents. Using classic social movement tactics such as signature gathering campaigns, public rallies, mass demonstrations and even hunger strikes, this conservative autonomy movement emerged as a major new actor in Bolivian politics and as a force that an otherwise hugely popular president had to take seriously (Eaton 2011). By 2008, the movement's growing strength brought Bolivia to a standstill, marked by successful (though unconstitutional) referenda on autonomy in four lowland departments in May and June, the takeover and/or sacking of a number of national government institutions in September, and a blockade of Santa Cruz enforced by over 30,000 members of highland Bolivia's most powerful union federation, the Confederación Sindical Única de Trabajadores Campesinos de Bolivia (CSUTCB – Unitary Syndical Confederation of Rural Workers of Bolivia). In the attempt to walk Bolivia back from the brink of still more violence, and as a reflection of the strength of the eastern autonomy movement, Morales agreed in October 2008 to substantive changes to nearly a quarter of the articles of the draft constitution that the MAS had approved the previous November in Oruro.

Bolivia's conservative autonomy movement succeeded in extracting meaningful concessions from a powerful president, but it failed to create a political party that could give representation to the interests, actors and demands that found expression in this movement. Herein lies the puzzle at the heart of this chapter. Why hasn't the movement that brought Bolivia to the verge of civil war in 2008 succeeded in party-building in the years since then? Why was Bolivia's moderately multiparty system replaced with a one-party dominant system rather than a competitive two-party system, one that would reproduce in the national party system the same polarization that characterized the larger political system?

This failure is especially puzzling for two reasons. First is the reality that indigenous movements within the same country successfully managed just such a transition by creating a party instrument able to compete in departments across Bolivia (Anria 2010; Madrid 2011; Van Cott 2005; Vergara 2011). Even more significantly, this transition occurred without access to the level of financial resources presumably available to the eastern autonomy movement. Why were indigenous Bolivians able to make the transition "from movement to party," while their counterparts in the conservative autonomy movement have so far failed at party-building? Second is the reality that conservative opposition governors in Bolivia created a much stronger coalition in defense of subnational prerogatives than their peers in Ecuador and Venezuela, who tried but failed in their efforts to coalesce against the left turn in their own countries (Eaton 2014). Why were opposition political elites in Bolivia able to ally and coordinate as movement leaders, unlike their peers in Ecuador and Venezuela, and yet not leverage this greater success into more robust party-building efforts?

My answer to these questions, which is based on research in La Paz and Santa Cruz in August/September 2012 and February/March 2014, comes in two parts. First, since 2008 the national government under President Morales has succeeded in weakening the internal cohesion of the eastern opposition by driving a wedge between the political and economic elites in the *Media Luna* (and especially in Santa Cruz), whose former cohesion fueled the movement for autonomy, and whose apparent divorce has compromised eastern party-building. At the heart of the "divide and rule" strategy adopted by Morales is the differential treatment of eastern economic and political elites. Whereas Morales has pursued a truce with large agribusinesses and adopted policies that assuage many of their core concerns, he has acted aggressively against political elites in the east, including opposition governors and mayors who would presumably play leading roles as party-builders. Offering carrots to economic elites and chiding them to attend to their businesses rather than to politics, Morales in contrast has used sticks vis-à-vis eastern political elites and directly sought to obstruct their ability to build parties. Here I emphasize a number of maneuvers by the national government that have targeted political elites and confounded opposition party-building, including the elimination of public funding for political parties, the judicial persecution of elected officials who belong to opposition parties, and a number of legislative and administrative changes since 2009 that make it very difficult for governors to behave in ways that would promote party-building.

Second, as the terrain has become less hospitable due to exogenous constraints imposed by the Morales government, the more endogenous fragmentation of political elites *within* the movement has also prevented successful party-building. For instance, rivalries among opposition governors prevented the organization that they built in 2008 – the Consejo Nacional Democrático (CONALDE – National Democratic Council) – from serving as the basis for a pan-departmental eastern opposition party. Competitive pressures fractured not just the alliance of opposition governors, but also solidarity within Santa Cruz among movement leaders who offered rival interpretations of the "autonomy" brand and who jockeyed for electoral advantage in national and subnational races. Some movement leaders adopted deeply ambivalent positions vis-à-vis political parties, due in part to the sharp conflict that developed between governors and the party politicians who represented eastern departments in the national legislature, and who were accused of privileging partisan over departmental interests. Finally, one especially important internal obstacle to party-building has been the weakening of the Comité Pro-Santa Cruz (CPSC – Pro-Santa Cruz Committee), a once well-financed organization at the heart of the autonomy movement that might have served as a mobilizing structure for a new political party, but that has failed to perform this function due to worsening internal divisions and disputes.

Before turning to theoretical expectations about party-building and failures thereof in Bolivia, the importance of these failures for Bolivian democracy is a point that deserves further elaboration. First and most broadly stated, the eastern departments are too significant to be so poorly integrated into the country's party system. Together they form 70 percent of the national territory and an increasingly large share of the national population, with the city of Santa Cruz doubling in population in the last decade. The east is also home to the country's most productive and efficient agribusinesses and important generators of export revenue, even if those achievements are sometimes overstated by the region's boosters. The underrepresentation of eastern economic interests in the country's party system makes for highly unstable politics. Second, the path taken in 2008 by Bolivia's conservative autonomy movement speaks to the importance of building viable political parties. Consider, for example, the violence that occurred in Santa Cruz in September and October of that year, when the most extreme members of the movement under the leadership of CPSC president Branko Marinkovic attacked government institutions and police installations in the attempt to ignite civil conflict. In a moment of great fluidity and uncertainty, the less extreme leaders of this movement, including Santa Cruz Governor Rubén Costas himself, were powerless to stop the violence. Relative to social movements, parties offer more institutionalized means for the expression of territorial interests and demands.

THEORETICAL EXPECTATIONS

Most of the comparative literature on party system development would lead us to expect greater party-building success in the Bolivian east than in fact has occurred. Consider, for example, traditional structural theories that emphasize the role of cleavages in explaining party behavior (Cox 1997; Lipset and Rokkan 1967). With respect to European polities, Seymour Martin Lipset and Stein Rokkan argued that cross-national party system variation reflected four types of underlying cleavages: center–periphery, church–state, land–industry, and capitalist–worker. Given its deep divisions between the western Andean highlands and eastern Amazonian lowlands, Bolivia is an important case for this structuralist approach. Sharp topographical differences have generated distinct sub-national regions, along with salient regional identities and grievances; while residents in western Bolivia claim that their former resource wealth financed infrastructural improvements in the now more vibrant east, residents in eastern Bolivia complain that the subsidies run in the opposite direction. Just as important, Bolivia's core territorial cleavage overlaps to a certain degree with an ethnic cleavage that pits mestizos and whites in the east against Aymara- and Quechua-speaking groups in the west. Applied to the Bolivian case, cleavage-based theories would predict significant party-building in the east in response to the tremendous electoral successes of indigenous party-building in the west, culminating in the 2005 election and 2009 and 2014 reelections of President Evo Morales.

A different kind of structural account in the party literature focuses not on underlying cleavages but on the availability of mobilizing structures, including preexisting organizational networks upon which party-builders can draw. According to Adrienne LeBas's explanation of variation in the emergence of political parties in Africa, "where opposition movements lack a strong organizational base, popular resistance tends to either splinter or fade" (2011: 36). The nature of the relevant organization can vary across cases. LeBas emphasizes trade unions, which gave the opposition parties that co-opted them the ability to connect with voters across ethnic lines (2011: 37). Beyond unions, David Samuels and Cesar Zucco (2014: 4) emphasize the importance of local links to organized civil society in accounting for the rise of the Workers' Party (PT) in Brazil, but note that "concrete political sentiments will only bear fruit if their targets are already politically active and actively engaged in civil society, often for reasons not directly related to partisan politics." In Bolivia, one would hypothesize that nonpartisan, territorially embedded and business-financed civic committees in the eastern departments could function as effective mobilizing structures for opposition party-building. This is related to but analytically distinct from the "corporation-based parties" identified by William Barndt (Chapter 13, this volume), in which businesses themselves form parties rather than financing more collective efforts. Given their dense organizational networks of affiliates (including economic, social, cultural, professional, sporting, and religious organizations), and their many decades of efforts as aggregators and defenders of regional interests vis-à-vis the central government, civic committees should be appealing to would-be party leaders as the building blocks upon which they could erect an eastern opposition party.

In addition to tapping extant organizational networks, accessing resources is also critical for successful party-builders. Resources can take a number of forms: fiscal, material, or even in-kind contributions. According to James Loxton (Chapter 9, this volume), parties that emerge from authoritarian regimes often inherit "a number of valuable resources that can help them to flourish under democracy," including the ability to finance the material benefits that are then delivered in clientelistic exchanges with poor voters. Observing that the lack of resources can be a significant obstacle to party-building, Raúl Madrid (Chapter 11, this volume) argues that ethnic parties like the MAS in Bolivia and Pachakutik in Ecuador "compensated for their lack of resources by relying heavily on in-kind contributions by members of the indigenous movement," such as food, free labor, and transportation. For the opposition in Bolivia, resources secured through the control of the four eastern departments, most of which were governed by the opposition between the introduction of gubernatorial elections in 2005 and 2010, should have provided a boost to party strengthening. Just as municipal decentralization in the 1990s created new opportunities for the MAS to emerge (Moira Faguet, and Bonifaz 2012), decentralization to the departmental level in theory should have created important access points for eastern opposition forces, especially considering the 2005 passage of legislation that gave departments over half of the revenue from the new Impuesto Directo a los Hidrocarburos (IDH – Direct Tax on Hydrocarbons).

Finally, a fourth approach in the party-building literature that emphasizes the significance of ideological conflict would also predict more robust party development in the Bolivian east. Scholars like Stathis Kalyvas have sought to shift the debate from structuralist accounts that privilege the role of underlying cleavages to more agency-based and contingent understandings that emphasize ideational struggles between political actors. Critical in the development of the Christian Democratic parties that Kalyvas studies, for example, was the emergence of attacks on the Catholic church by liberal anticlerical groups, which set in motion "the creation of a new political identity among lay Catholics and the formation of confessional parties" (1996: 6). Similarly, in his study of new left party survival and collapse in Latin America, Brandon Van Dyck (Chapter 5, this volume) finds that struggles against dictatorship facilitate party-building by creating electoral incentives for territorial organization, selection pressures for activist commitment, and the kinds of "higher causes" necessary to fuel mass activism. In Bolivia, the polarizing divide between the market-oriented conservative autonomy movement on the one hand, and Evo Morales's indigenous and statist (if not socialist) movement on the other, amounted to sharp ideological conflict of the sort that should have incentivized party-building in the east.

FROM MOVEMENT TO PARTY?

That opposition party-building has so far failed in the Bolivian east can
be seen in a number of dimensions. First is the disappearance of Poder
Democrático Social (PODEMOS – Social Democratic Power), a party
that attracted politicians from Acción Democrática Nacionalista (ADN –
Nationalist Democratic Action) upon the 2002 death of its founder Hugo
Banzer, and that represented a center-right alterative in the 2005 presidential elections lost by PODEMOS candidate Jorge Quiroga. PODEMOS
candidates won elections for prefect in two of the four eastern lowland
departments in 2005, but the party then evaporated, largely due to the
controversies surrounding its support for the August 2008 recall elections discussed below. Second, as seen in Table 14.1, is the proliferation
in the east of political entities called "citizen groupings" (*agrupaciones
ciudadanas*), which are recognized in the 2004 electoral law, but which
are not considered parties because they are only organized at the department level. In regional elections in 2010, when the MAS gained control of one of the lowland departments (Pando), a different *agrupación*
won the gubernatorial election in each of the three remaining lowland
departments. Rather than invest in a common party that could transcend
their departments, Governors Mario Cossío, Rubén Costas and Ernesto
Suárez all opted to go their own way in the electoral sphere by establishing distinct political entities. Not unlike the "partisan free agents" in Peru
described by Steven Levitsky and Mauricio Zavaleta (Chapter 15, this
volume), going it alone proved to be personally advantageous for these
three leaders of the autonomy movement, who were the only governors
to be reelected in Bolivia in 2010.

Comparing partisan dynamics on the right with party-building efforts
on the left in Bolivia reveals a much stronger disconnect between the
national and subnational levels for parties and politicians on the right. On
the left, the MAS has been able to win national elections while simultaneously building its presence at the subnational level. For example, MAS
gubernatorial candidates came in second in Beni, Santa Cruz, and Tarija
in the 2010 regional elections, and the MAS has won municipal elections
in all nine departments. According to Alberto Vergara, the MAS was able
to penetrate the subnational sphere because of the profound nature of
Bolivia's ideological debate; "the more intense the political debate in a
society, the better the chances of building political parties that represent
at subnational levels the national ideas in conflict" (2011: 67). But this
begs the question: why didn't the country's deep ideological conflict also

TABLE 14.1 *Partisan fragmentation in Bolivia's* Media Luna

	2005 elections (prefect)	2010 elections (governor)
Beni	PODEMOS (Ernesto Suárez)	Primero el Beni (Beni First) (Ernesto Suárez)
Pando	PODEMOS (Leopoldo Fernández)	MAS (Luis Adolfo)
Santa Cruz	Autonomía para Bolivia (APB – Autonomy for Bolivia) (Rubén Costas)	Verdad y Democracia Social (VERDES – Truth and Social Democracy) (Rubén Costas)
Tarija	Movimiento Nacionalista Revolucionario (MNR – Revolutionary Nationalist Movement) (Mario Cossío)	Camino al Cambio (Mario Cossío)

enable the other side in the debate – the opposition to Evo Morales – to successfully engage in party-building? Whereas the MAS won the 2009 presidential elections with 64 percent of the vote and captured six of nine departments in gubernatorial elections the following year, the fragmented opposition came together in the makeshift Plan Progeso para Bolivia–Nueva Convergencia (PPB-NC – Plan of Progress for Bolivia-New Convergence) in 2009 and then participated in the 2010 regional elections via multiple, department-only groupings.

Partisan fragmentation has also taken place within departments in the east, and not just across these departments. Consider the most important case of Santa Cruz, where the movement for autonomy was centered and where the political elites most closely associated with this movement have opted to pursue separate political projects. Most important here is Rubén Costas, who established Autonomía para Bolivia (APB – Autonomy for Bolivia) to contest the 2005 departmental elections and then abandoned it to create his Verdad y Democracia Social (VERDES – Truth and Social Democracy). Former CPSC president Germán Antelo broke with Costas and formed Nuevo Poder Ciudadano (NPC – New Citizen Power) to successfully contest the 2009 senate elections in association with PPB-NC, while former PODEMOS senator Oscar Ortiz affiliated with Consenso Popular (Popular Consensus) and lost his bid for the senate that same year. Meanwhile the movement's foremost intellectual leader Juan Carlos Urenda created a distinct group to compete in subnational elections, Todos por Santa Cruz (All for Santa Cruz), which failed to win any seats in either the departmental legislature or municipal council. While the movement's leadership has fragmented, Costas is clearly dominant among them; his VERDES organization controls a majority within the departmental legislature (currently composed of twelve VERDES legislators, nine MAS legislators, two Movimiento Nacional Revolucionario (MNR – Revolutionary Nationalist Movement) legislators, and five legislators representing the major lowland indigenous groups). Anticipating presidential elections in 2014, Costas announced plans in August 2012 to merge VERDES with Consenso Popular (which is organized as a party with representation beyond Santa Cruz) and to form a new party called Movimiento Demócrata Social (MDS – Social Democratic Movement), though ultimately Costas decided not to contest the presidency and to support instead the noneastern candidacy of Samuel Doria.[1]

As the political leaders who led the conservative autonomy movement in Santa Cruz have mostly gone their separate ways in terms of party-building, the internal opposition to these political elites within the department has also fragmented. Noteworthy here is the case of Santa Cruz Somos Todos (SCST – We're All Santa Cruz), an attempt in 2007 and 2008 by centrist and leftist intellectual and political figures to contest the hegemonic position of the socioeconomic elites who continue to dominate politically both at the department level and in the municipal government of Santa Cruz. Some members of SCST hoped that it could come to represent a viable alternative to both the MAS and to local elite-led projects, but the organization divided over whether to become a political party and how to participate in the 2008 autonomy referenda, and then collapsed after the departure of several high-profile members who assumed positions within the Morales administration.[2] In the absence of credible alternative options like the SCST, the MAS has been able to establish a strong presence in Santa Cruz, winning 42 percent of the vote in the 2009 presidential election, 37 percent in the 2010 gubernatorial election (in addition to control over twenty-four of the department's fifty-six municipalities), and 49 percent of the vote in the 2014 presidential

[1] According to Vladimir Peña, there was an internal discussion within VERDES about the possibility of pursuing the so-called Catalonia model (i.e., a strong regional party that enters into an alliance with a national party) but realized that this was not an option for them given the absence of a viable national party other than the MAS. This analysis informed the decision to create the MDS as a national alternative. Interview with Vladimir Peña, Secretario de Gobierno, Gobierno Autónomo Departamental de Santa Cruz, September 3, 2012, Santa Cruz.

[2] These include Gisela López as Coordinator of the Autonomy Ministry in Santa Cruz, Jerjes Justiniano as Ambassador to Brazil, and Claudia Peña as Minister of Autonomy. Interview with Helena Argirakis, former participant in SCST, September 4, 2012, Santa Cruz.

election. According to Gustavo Pedraza (2011: 14), unity among the opposition to the MAS will be critical if it is to hold on to political control of Santa Cruz.

While there is little doubt that leaders of the eastern autonomy movement felt the party-building imperative acutely, and while their party-building efforts have been sufficiently serious to ask why they failed, it is also important to note that not all movement leaders wanted to build a party or prioritized this goal.[3] In the wake of the collapse of Bolivia's traditional party system in the 2000s, parties were highly unpopular and widely mistrusted. Furthermore, forming a party raised the difficult question of whether and how to incorporate traditional party politicians, whose skills and experience could be of great use but who were often deemed insufficiently committed to the regional cause by civic leaders. A few leaders objected to the idea of enlisting the CPSC in any party-building project. Notwithstanding this ambivalence toward parties, it remains important to ask why those who wanted to build a party nevertheless failed, even though they appeared to be favored by internal cohesion, organizational resources, and a vibrant brand.

DIVIDE AND RULE: CARROTS AND STICKS IN THE BOLIVIAN EAST

Would-be party-builders in the east of Bolivia faced a number of exogenous constraints as they have attempted to transition from movement to party. Many of the most significant obstacles have been erected by Evo Morales and the MAS, who as political adversaries have proven to be adept and innovative in their varied efforts to complicate party-building by the opposition. Most important are Morales's concerted attempts since 2008 to dismantle the previously solid coalition between eastern economic and political elites, especially in Santa Cruz. The section below documents various signs of the reconciliation that has taken place between the Morales government and eastern economic interests, before examining the antagonism that continues to characterize the relationship between Morales and eastern political elites. One important caveat is in order before proceeding with this line of argument: as seen in the fact that some leading political leaders in the east are themselves significant landowners (e.g., Rubén Costas, Branko Marinkovic), differentiating between political and economic elites is not always straightforward. The

---

[3] I am grateful to Jennifer Cyr for help in thinking through this point.

key point is that those socioeconomic elites who have agreed to keep their heads down and focus on economic pursuits have been rewarded, while elites who have refused to give up on their political aspirations have been penalized.

Courting Eastern Economic Elites

One of the most important exogenous constraints on party-building in the east, and certainly one of the most surprising recent developments in Bolivia considering the depth of the country's polarization circa 2008, is the degree of reconciliation that has taken place between the Morales government and eastern economic elites. The same elites who financed the conservative autonomy movement, who led the struggle against the new constitution, and who would presumably bankroll opposition party-building have largely reconciled themselves to the government and to the post-2005 *"proceso de cambio"* (process of change) that culminated in the new constitution, all in exchange for a variety of policy concessions from Morales. By calling a truce with agrarian businesses, and by enabling them to prosper economically so long as they stay out of politics, Morales has provoked a sharp rupture between economic and political elites in the east, thereby reducing significantly the chances of successful opposition party-building. In effect, just as conflict over Morales's proposed highway through the Territorio Indígena y Parque Nacional Isiboro-Sécure (TIPNIS – Isiboro Sécure National Park and Indigenous Territory) reserve has ruptured the governing MAS coalition by pitting highland and lowland indigenous groups against one another, so has conflict between political and economic elites in the east weakened the opposition coalition. Bolivia therefore has moved from a period of polarization between east and west, one that had the effect of strengthening and unifying each coalition (either pro- or anti-Morales), to a period in which each of these coalitions has begun to unravel.

A lessening in the hostility of economic elites toward Evo Morales is palpable in Santa Cruz, and observable in a number of areas. In the words of one national government official, "economic growth and economic stability under the current government have greatly eased the earlier concerns of eastern economic interests."[4] But in addition to a general sense of improved economic opportunity, Morales has actively sought to cultivate

---

[4] Anonymous interview with bureaucrat in the Ministry of Foreign Affairs, August 27, 2012.

(if not co-opt) economic elites and to allay business concerns through specific interventions and concessions. Having received $1 billion more in gas revenue in 2012 than it received in 2011,[5] the national government has certainly enjoyed resources sufficient to build a more cooperative relationship with agrarian elites, whose alleged underproduction for the domestic market has caused food shortages (especially oil and sugar) that Morales would like to avoid.[6] Though gas revenues give the president significant scope to cultivate agrarian elites, some of the most important measures have cost the government in symbolic rather than fiscal terms.

The most significant changes have to do with national government policy vis-à-vis the structure of land-owning, and build on the significant concession that Morales already made in October 2008 when he accepted that new constitutional limits on the size of landholding would be future-oriented and not retroactive, in effect protecting existing agribusinesses. Limiting the size of landholdings to 5,000 hectares was a major victory for the MAS, along with the rule introduced in the 2006 Ley de Reconducción de la Reforma Agraria that the Instituto Nacional de Reforma Agraria (INRA – National Agrarian Reform Institute) would determine whether land was fulfilling an economic and social purpose (FES – Función Económica Social) on a two year cycle (Valdivia 2010).[7] Over the last several years, in addition to lifting all price controls and export restrictions, the Morales government has also agreed to shift FES reviews onto a five-year cycle and promised to increase land-owning limits to 8,000 hectares.[8] Vice President Álvaro García Linera has also conducted lengthy meetings with the agrarian business chamber (Cámara Agropecuaria del Oriente [Eastern Agricultural Chamber]), after which he announced that the national government would deal harshly with land invasions of productive farms, and accepted an invitation to attend

---

[5] "El país recibirá este año $US 1.000 mil millones más por renta petrolera," *La Razón*, August 28, 2012.

[6] In one particular sign of the end of hostilities between Santa Cruz businesses and the national government, the chief representative of the latter in the department emphasizes the frequency with which agribusinesses now seek to work through her office to assure La Paz that they will continue to provision the domestic market. Interview with Gisela López, Coordinadora del Ministerio de Autonomía en Santa Cruz, September 5, 2012, Santa Cruz.

[7] Before 2006, these technically complicated tasks were contracted out to private companies; they are now performed by INRA itself, which often lacks the institutional capacity to carry them out successfully (Chumacero 2009).

[8] Interview with Gustavo Pedraza, Regional Director, Fundación Boliviana para la Democracia Multipartidaria, August 30, 2012, Santa Cruz.

the important ExpoCruz fair in Santa Cruz in September 2012. Just as symbolically important, in January 2012 eastern business chambers participated in formal conversations billed as a "Gran Acuerdo Nacional" with the national government in Cochabamba. In the words of one eastern politician, "Evo has stolen the liberals' banner" – with devastating consequences for a brand that had identified autonomy as necessary for continued economic success in the east.[9]

While agrarian policy looms large in the truce that has taken place between Morales and eastern economic interests, it is also important to note other policy fields in which the stance of the national government has dovetailed with these interests. For example, despite the high-profile "nationalization" of hydrocarbons that took place early on under Morales, in fact the MAS government has refrained from carrying out wholesale nationalizations in other key sectors. Due largely to the opposition of mining cooperatives, the government has so far been unable to introduce a new regulatory framework in the mining sector, which is increasingly moving into the east, and which is still governed by the highly permissive regulations of the Sánchez de Lozada era (Marston 2013).

The cultivation of eastern economic interests who are willing to give up political activity has been all the more effective because of the speed with which Morales has moved against those individual economic elites most closely associated with extremist political positions within the autonomy movement. Most important here is the high-profile expropriation of landholdings belonging to the Monasterio and Marinkovic families in the aftermath of the violence in September and October 2008. Likewise, after the discovery of an apparent terrorist cell in Santa Cruz in April 2009, Morales moved quickly against individuals charged with responsibility for the plan to arm and finance a local militia group, including the part owner of the PAT television channel known for its critical reporting vis-à-vis the national government, as well as thirty other individuals now awaiting trial. But most businesses have escaped this kind of harsh treatment.[10]

Neither Morales's cultivation of economic elites nor the reality that agribusinesses are indeed profiting under the current government has gone unnoticed among political elites in the east. One of the clearest signs

[9] Interview with Alejandro Colanzi, member of the "mesa clandestina" (secret negotiating table) that ironed out the October 2008 compromise, September 1, 2012, Santa Cruz.
[10] Other business owners fear that involvement in politics could result in their becoming targets of judicial persecution by the national government. Anonymous interviews, September 6 and 9, 2012, Santa Cruz.

of the division between economic and political elites is that the former are no longer contributing financially to the CPSC. At a time when several CPSC leaders have fled into exile (over their alleged involvement in the April 2009 terrorism plot), many businesses have decided to no longer support the committee or to attend its meetings and events, either because of disagreements over the direction that it is taking (discussed later) or out of fear that support for the CPSC would put into jeopardy this new period of détente with the national government. According to the President of the CPSC, Herland Vaca Díez Busch, the younger generation of economic elites in Santa Cruz are "neoliberals," interested merely in making money and not motivated to defend their identities as *cruceños*. Stating that agribusinesses are making "more money under Evo than they ever did under Goni," Vaca Diez struggled to keep the CPSC afloat without the levels of financial support from Santa Cruz businesses that it has traditionally received.[11] As a further reflection of the divide between economic and political elites, Governor Rubén Costas has publicly complained that he feels abandoned by some of Santa Cruz's leading economic interests.

Constraining Eastern Political Elites

While Morales's courting of eastern economic elites has indirectly (and negatively) affected the political elites who are grouped in the CPSC, he has also pursued a number of other measures that more directly put eastern political elites on the defensive, including new rules governing the funding of political parties, the suspension of subnational elected officials, and the sharing of fiscal revenues with subnational governments.

One potentially significant challenge faced by new political parties or would-be parties in Bolivia is the elimination of public financing for parties in the aftermath of the 2009 Constitution.[12] At the insistence of the MAS, public financing was withdrawn in the 2009 Transitory Electoral Law, the negotiation of which proved to be nearly as divisive as the constitutional revision that preceded it and that made such a law necessary (Ayo 2011). Ending the prior system of public support for parties is especially negative for new, opposition parties that do not yet control offices within the state. Although this change is perhaps less important

---

[11] Interview with Herland Vaca Díez Busch, President of the CPSC, September 7, 2012, Santa Cruz.

[12] On the majoritarian features of the new constitution, which may be said to worsen the challenges facing new parties, see Centellas (2013).

for parties likely to count on socioeconomic elites as their core constituents, the hiatus that has opened up between political elites and economic elites in Santa Cruz means that this constraint may prove to be a not altogether insignificant one. In addition to the elimination of public financing, fewer external organizations now offer support for party-building and training of party leaders than was the case in the past. For example, USAID stopped its extensive funding of democratic governance programming in the wake of the conflict with the Bolivian government over the expulsion of US ambassador Philip Goldberg in 2008. Of the thousands of NGOs that operate in Bolivia, few focus on governance issues, and only two offer significant party-building support: Fundación IDEA and Fundación Boliviana para la Democracia Multipartidaria (FBDM – Bolivian Foundation for Multiparty Democracy) (financed by the United Nations Development Program).[13]

A more threatening rule change that has diminished the prospects for party-building in the east was put into place with the 2010 Ley Marco de Autonomías y Descentralización (Framework Law for Autonomy and Decentralization). Designed as a law that would clarify the various features of the new autonomy regime left unspecified in the 2009 Constitution, the law includes an article that enables the suspension of elected subnational officials whenever charges are filed against those officials by a public prosecutor (rather than when a final sentence is issued, which is the requirement stipulated in the constitution). The interpretation of the law is ambiguous and its constitutional status has been contested; Article 144 states that governors, mayors, departmental legislators, and municipal councilors *can* be suspended (*podrán*) when they are formally accused, while Article 145 identifies the procedures that the prosecutor *must* follow (*necesariamente deberá*) to suspend the official.[14] Regardless of the confusion, the law was deployed to suspend from office popular opposition figures who might have used their election (and reelection) as governors to launch more sustained efforts at party-building – even if initially only in the form of department-specific "*agrupaciones ciudadanas.*" Until Bolivia's Plurinational Constitutional Tribunal ruled in February

[13] FBDM offers technical assistance and leadership training to three national parties (Unidad Nacional [National Unity], MAS, and the Movimiento Sin Miedo [Movement without Fear]) and three Santa Cruz organizations (Consenso Popular, VERDES, and NPC). Interview with Mariela Loeza, Program Officer, FBDM, August 30, 2012, Santa Cruz.

[14] Interview with Eliane Capobianco, Directora de Desarrollo Autonómico, Departamento de Santa Cruz, September 5, 2012.

2013 against the constitutionality of these articles, the suspension of elected subnational officials operated as a significant constraint on party-building at a crucial moment for the opposition.

Institutional rules that allow the suspension of opposition officials have devastated the eastern opposition. Of the four governors who led the eastern movement for autonomy between 2005 and 2008, only Santa Cruz Governor Rubén Costas remains in his position. Since 2008, Pando Governor Leopoldo Fernández has sat in a La Paz prison awaiting trial on charges that he authorized the September 2008 massacre of fifteen MAS supporters in his department. In December 2010, Tarija Governor Mario Cossío was suspended from his position over corruption charges and replaced by a MAS governor selected by the departmental legislature. One year later, Beni Governor Ernesto Suárez was suspended from office due to irregularities in the construction of a road in his department and in the purchase of an electricity generator for a private cooperative. In contrast to Tarija, an interim MNR governor replaced Suárez in Beni in a deal struck between the MNR and the MAS that reflects Morales's willingness to negotiate with traditional parties in the attempt to assert political control over proautonomy departments (though the opposition to Morales subsequently recaptured the governorship in Beni in a special election held in January 2013).

To date, President Morales has failed in his attempt to likewise suspend Rubén Costas in Santa Cruz, who stands accused of improprieties in the financing of the May 2008 referendum that approved the department's autonomy statute. The charges in this case are particularly significant because the national government's acknowledgment of the May and June 2008 referenda in the four lowland departments was a significant part of the October 2008 compromise over the constitution, which stipulated that the autonomy statutes approved in the lowland departments could stand so long as they were adjusted to fit the new constitution, a process referred to as *adecuación*.[15] The failure so far of efforts to suspend Costas can be understood in part as a result of the majority he controls in the departmental legislature (the absence of which facilitated the suspension of his counterparts in Beni and Tarija), and in part due to the reality that Costas can still mobilize significant popular support, as seen in the 20,000 *cruceños* who filled the city's stadium in July 2012 to protest his attempted suspension. Despite his survival, Costas's legal problems inhibit party-building and help explain his August 2012 decision

---

[15] Interview with Alejandro Colanzi.

to merge VERDES with Consenso Popular in the attempt to build an organization that could compete in national elections.[16]

Moving from the departmental level to the municipal level, the ability to suspend subnational officials also enabled Morales to intervene within Santa Cruz in ways that challenge the governing VERDES organization and put it on the defensive politically. Nationally appointed prosecutors have suspended VERDES-allied mayors in Warnes, Buena Vista and La Guardia, the latter of which had the reputation of being one of the best governed municipalities in the country.[17] Given that "partisan" linkages between VERDES mayors and the VERDES departmental government might be one way to strengthen and build upon this new "*agrupación ciudadana*," the removal of VERDES mayors should be understood as a setback for that effort. Within the department of Santa Cruz, the replacement of VERDES mayors with MAS mayors is particularly troubling for the political opposition to Morales because the national MAS can then engage directly with and provide logistical and financial support to these mayors in ways that bypass Costas and circumvent the departmental government.[18] In this sense, until they were declared unconstitutional in 2013, Morales's sweeping powers to suspend subnational officials directly threatened efforts by opposition parties like VERDES to expand their territorial organization.

In addition to rule changes that eliminated public financing of parties and facilitated the suspension of elected political elites, the Morales government has also introduced other legislative and administrative changes that hamstring governors and limit significantly their ability to leverage governing authority for partisan purposes. Given its higher levels of capacity relative to other lowland departments, that decentralization has not provided a more significant boost for party-building in Santa Cruz is especially noteworthy. Although departmental officials in the governor's office have prepared drafts of ten bills for discussion in the legislature, the attempted suspension of the governor has paralyzed its activity, in addition to the prosecution of the legislature's president, Alcides Villagómez, who spent three months of 2012 in jail.[19] When the

---

[16] Meeting with Consenso Popular youth activists, party headquarters, September 3, 2012, Santa Cruz.

[17] Interview with Yalila Casanova, former member of SCST and Professor of Sociology at UAGRM, September 3, 2012, Santa Cruz.

[18] Interview with Gonzalo Plaza, Project Director, Pastoral Social Caritas, Santa Cruz, September 4, 2012.

[19] Interview with Capobianco.

departmental legislature has acted, as in the passage of laws governing reserved seats and the election of representatives to a Tribunal Electoral Departamental (Departmental Electoral Tribunal), the national government has responded by arguing that these laws are unconstitutional and that the department must focus on adjusting its autonomy statute to conform to the constitution before it begins legislating.[20] This places Santa Cruz Governor Costas in a difficult political bind; his legislative powers are in doubt unless and until the department adjusts its autonomy statute, but adjusting the statute is politically unpalatable given the symbolic importance of its approval in the May 2008 referendum.[21]

A number of other rule changes in fiscal and administrative dimensions have also prevented opposition governors from using state resources in ways that might facilitate party-building. In 2007, Morales cut IDH transfers to departments (but not municipalities) by 70 percent in order to finance the Renta Dignidad (Dignity Pension), in addition to other subsequent cuts that have financed other national-level social policy innovations like the Juancito Pinto program and a new education fund. Despite the fact that Santa Cruz (like all departments) is now officially "autonomous," finance specialists within the department's government describe a budgetary and financial system that is in many ways less autonomous than before political decentralization in 2005. Examples include heavy earmarking, the elimination of (public) departmental financial institutions like the Financiera de Desarrollo de Santa Cruz (FINDESA – Development Finance Company of Santa Cruz) (which financed the construction of Santa Cruz's industrial park in the 1980s and 1990s), and requirements that the department contribute funds to new (national) state-owned enterprises like the Agencia Boliviana de Carreteras (Bolivian Highway Agency), which makes unilateral decisions about roads and highways.[22] Furthermore, the aggressiveness of anticorruption measures by the national government coupled with the perceived lack of judicial independence seem to have had a chilling effect vis-à-vis the willingness of departmental employees to design and execute new

---

[20] See the comments of then Autonomy Minister Carlos Romero, "Desafío: estatutos autonómicos con pactos sociales," *El Cambio*, January 16, 2011, p. 11.

[21] While NGOs and groups within the Universidad Autónoma Gabriel René Moreno (UAGRM) initiated discussions over a "*plataforma ciudadana para adecuarse*" Costas refused to move on the issue of *adecuación*.

[22] As a sign of the lack of independence, departmental officials even need to get permission to make minor changes in computer software that is controlled by the Ministry of Economy. Interview with Carlos Schlink Ruiz, Director de Tesoro, Gobierno Autónomico Departamental de Santa Cruz, September 5, 2012.

projects. Nearly 60 percent of the royalty transfers to Santa Cruz went unspent in 2011, a telling indicator of the limits to the governor's governing authority.[23]

Finally, Morales's genius in discovering ways to punish eastern political elites while simultaneously cultivating compliant economic elites is on full display in the controversial case of Bolivia's diesel fuel subsidies. The size of these subsidies has been a long-standing concern for Morales, both because of the drain on the national budget that they represent, and because they transfer income to the eastern agribusinesses that previously financed the autonomy movement. When Morales proposed the elimination of these subsidies in 2010 he was greeted with the so-called "*gasolinazo*," which paralyzed economic activity across Bolivia. After weeks of conflict, the President agreed to restore the subsidies, but decided to pay for them by taking the revenue from the governors. Specifically, revenues from the Impuesto Especial a los Hidrocarburos (Special Tax on Hydrocarbons), which is a separate tax from the IDH whose revenues were already recentralized in 2007, are no longer shared with the departments and instead are being used to fund the diesel subsidies. In other words, not only did Morales relieve himself of the burden of financing diesel subsidies, but he also managed to shift the bill onto subnational political elites, pleasing the agrarian elites he has sought to cultivate and antagonizing the governors he has sought to chasten.

ENDOGENOUS CHALLENGES TO PARTY-BUILDING IN THE BOLIVIAN EAST

The external obstacles to opposition party-building that are described above have been formidable, but they only tell half of the story. The puzzle of why Bolivia's powerful conservative autonomy movement has failed to generate a viable political party can be more fully unraveled by appreciating the nature of challenges internal to the movement. Due to the conflict that has emerged between economic and political elites in the east, the ability of the latter group to close ranks has become all the more important, and yet here we see multiple forms of elite fragmentation since 2008. Rather than unify, the political elites who championed the movement for autonomy have fallen out in a number of dimensions, including

[23] As a result of these many constraints on the governor in Santa Cruz, Alejandro Colanzi argues that "de hecho, la gobernación es la vieja prefectura" (i.e., the elected governor has no more power than the appointed prefect did). Interview with Colanzi.

conflicts between regional leaders and traditional party politicians, conflicts among regional leaders (i.e., individual governors and mayors), and conflicts within the CPSC. The latter are particularly significant both because they have prevented the CPSC from serving as an effective mobilizing structure, and because of the role the CPSC previously played as the undisputed interpreter of the autonomy brand in the east.

Conflicts between Regional Leaders and Party Politicians

One of the core internal obstacles to party-building in the Bolivian east is the mutual suspicion and animosity that developed between regional leaders on the one hand and legislators from parties like PODEMOS who represented eastern departments within the national legislature. In the aftermath of the collapse of Bolivia's traditional party system, governors and other regional leaders have often looked down on party leaders and tried to avoid the taint associated with parties. Thus the individuals best positioned to build parties – the governors – have displayed varying degrees of reluctance about parties.[24]

This general inclination to avoid associations with politicians from existing parties like PODEMOS became more specific and acute in the difficult period during which the new constitution was written. This highly conflictive period (2006–2008) revealed not just conflict between supporters and opponents of the MAS government, but worsening grievances between the party politicians from PODEMOS who had been elected to represent the lowlands in the constituent assembly, on the one hand, and regional leaders (prefects/governors) who were enjoying a burst of legitimacy following their first ever direct election in 2005, on the other.[25] For instance, PODEMOS assembly members and regional leaders split over the "*capitalidad*" question that roiled the assembly for much of its life, with PODEMOS politicians mostly opposing the proposed shift of the capital to Sucre.

More important still is the angry response of the four lowland prefects when PODEMOS legislators supported the holding of a simultaneous recall vote vis-à-vis all prefects and President Morales in August 2008,

[24] A belief that the end of "*democracia pactada*" (pacted democracy) after 2005 would limit the power of opposition parties has also likely inhibited opposition party-building (even if party pacts, as in the October 2008 constitutional compromise, continue to occur in Morales's Bolivia).

[25] According to Zegada (2010: 214), prefects acted like "political virgins" relative to party politicians, and not a single legislator was ever invited to meet with CONALDE.

proposed as a means of resolving the stalemate that had developed after the approval of autonomy statutes in the *Media Luna*.[26] Though each of the lowland prefects survived the recall, Morales emerged in a strengthened position (with 64 percent support), infuriating the prefects and setting the stage for the violence of September and October 2008. Regional leaders were also highly critical of the October 2008 compromise that party politicians like Carlos Bohrt and Alejandro Colanzi ironed out with the government in order to avoid further violence.[27] Only two *cruceño* legislators (Branko Marinkovic and Gaby Pereira) voted against the constitutional compromise, further deepening the sense in the lowlands that most party politicians had privileged party interests over regional interests.[28] Together with its position over the *capitalidad* question, the support of PODEMOS legislators for the recall proposal and the constitutional compromise greatly diminished its potential as a party that could harness the eastern autonomy movement.

This discord and resentment between right-of-center parties and the leaders of the autonomy movement stands in contrast to dynamics on the left in Bolivia, where "experienced candidates" from leftist parties brought "organizational skills to the often less experienced indigenous organizations seeking to enter formal politics" (Van Cott 2005: 38).

Conflicts among Regional Leaders

In the east, the struggle against Morales's *"proceso de cambio"* was characterized by high levels of cooperation among lowland governors. This took organizational expression in CONALDE, which the governors used to strategize and coordinate their proautonomy activities, and to negotiate with Morales as a single collective actor rather than on a bilateral basis. In the years since the compromise of October 2008, however, personal rivalries and competitive pressures have widened the distance between the governors, decreasing the possibility that CONALDE could serve as the organizational precursor of a pan-departmental political party. The most important leadership conflict pitted Costas against Cossío. While Cossío was widely understood to have a stronger technical team and a

---

[26] Note, however, that some PODEMOS legislators, including the head of its bloc in the constituent assembly, Rubén Darío Cuellar, said that they responded not to the head of the party (Jorge Quiroga) but to "*la institucionalidad cruceña*" (Zegada 2010).

[27] To this day, many regional leaders oppose the process of *adecuación*, which was the logical result of the October 2008 compromise.

[28] Interview with Alejandro Colanzi.

better command of policy, Costas had a natural advantage as the governor of the most important lowland department and as a "civic" leader without a traditional party past (in contrast to Cossío's membership in a traditional party, the MNR).

If rivalries among governors prevented the conversion of CONALDE into a political party, rivalries among leaders within Santa Cruz have prevented the effective concentration of political forces within the department. Personalism is a powerful force in Santa Cruz and conflicts between political personalities have fragmented the political opposition to Morales in the department. Costas is the dominant force there, a leader forged in the struggle for autonomy who has come into conflict with other important figures. One such dispute, noted above, led to his abandonment of APB and the decision to form VERDES. Many of these personal disputes are exacerbated by individual leaders' affiliations with one of the two main "*logias*" (lodges) within Santa Cruz: Caballeros del Oriente and Toborochi.[29] Different lodge affiliations allegedly played a role in the falling out that occurred between Costas (who belongs to Caballeros del Oriente) and Germán Antelo (who belongs to Toborochi).[30] Costas and Oscar Ortiz (both from Caballeros del Oriente) have joined forces in the new MDS, while Antelo has created a distinct organization (NPC).

Another important division has taken place within the department between Costas and the Mayor of Santa Cruz, Percy Fernández. Though an erstwhile ally of Costas and himself a long-standing political figure among the local elite, Fernández sought an alliance with MAS councilors in order to secure a two-thirds majority on the city council. Specifically, Fernández allied with MAS councilor (and former MNR member) Freddy Soruco, which led to an institutional crisis in the city of Santa Cruz. The MAS alliance with Percy Fernández, whom Evo Morales called the best mayor in Bolivia in his 2014 presidential campaign, has troubled the traditionally smooth relations between city and department that were long the hallmark of elite rule in Santa Cruz. The mayor was noticeably absent from the large public assembly in July 2012 that was called to protest the attempted suspension of Costas from the governorship.

In addition to a tendency toward infighting, the generation of leaders who cohered around the struggle for autonomy also seem to have obstructed processes of leadership renewal. One can observe a pattern

[29] Interview with Reymi Ferreira, former rector of the UAGRM, August 31, 2012, Santa Cruz.

[30] Despite this falling out, Antelo did attend the July 2012 rally in opposition to the attempted suspension of Costas.

of inflexible if not hostile treatment of a younger generation of dynamic leaders deemed insufficiently orthodox on the question of autonomy. In the words of *cruceña* scholar and Minister of Autonomy Claudia Peña, "the civic leaders have eaten their young."[31]

Conflicts within the CPSC

In theory, one of the factors that would appear to augment the chances of successful party-building in the Bolivian east is the existence of the department-level civic committees that played such important roles as mobilizing structures for the autonomy movement, especially in Santa Cruz. Precisely because building organizations from scratch is quite difficult, as Levitsky, Loxton, and Van Dyck (Chapter 1, this volume) note, these civic committees should have been a boon to party-building. Originating in the aftermath of and in resistance to the 1952 Revolution, the CPSC brought together local elites who opposed the MNR. Later in the 1950s, it led a successful movement to secure regional control over a greater percentage of oil royalties – the so-called "*lucha por el 11%*" (the struggle for 11%) – which earned for the committee enormous local legitimacy and enabled it to emerge as the department's leading political space. Over the succeeding decades, the committee built a sophisticated internal organizational structure and maintained its formal position as a nonpartisan, purely civic entity. Despite its civic status, in fact the CPSC functioned at times like a parliamentary bloc for Santa Cruz in the sense that it brought together relevant political and socioeconomic actors and sought to lobby for more departmental resources and authority vis-à-vis La Paz (Sivak 2007). Its president, always drawn from the socioeconomic elite and always a member of one of the two dominant *logias*, operated as one of the most influential political figures in the department. The CPSC would receive high scores on the two variables Van Cott (2005) considers in her analysis of the organizational features that facilitate party-building; the CPSC was characterized by both "organizational maturity" and "dense organizational networks of affiliates."[32]

---

[31] Interview with Peña, La Paz, August 28, 2012. Asked to identify the chief factors that have prevented the eastern opposition from building a national party, Peña responded that Costas and the traditional elite of Santa Cruz are so ignorant of the rest of Bolivia that they could not possibly build a viable national party: "Not only do they know nothing about Oruro, but they don't want to know anything about Oruro."

[32] Van Cott (2005) found on average a fourteen-year lag between movement formation and the formation of indigenous parties; the CPSC is more than sixty years old.

Although the CPSC served as the central mobilizing structure for the autonomy movement, a number of factors prevent it from playing a similarly leading role in the incubation of a new political party. First is the express opposition of Santa Cruz leaders like Germán Antelo and Gabriel Dabdoub (former head of the industrial chamber CAINCO), who are on record for opposing the transformation of any civic committee into a political party. One can take issue with claims of CPSC leaders that the committee is apolitical and still agree that its nonpartisan orientation might have played an important role in giving the CPSC its tremendous power to convene *cruceños*, on full display in the well-attended *cabildos* of 2004, 2005, 2006, and 2008. In addition to disputes over the appropriate role of the CPSC vis-à-vis the establishment of a new partisan instrument, internal disagreements have also emerged within the committee over how to interpret its brand: should the committee emphasize the (continued) struggle for autonomy, the establishment of federalism, or the defense of democracy? While many remain focused on autonomy as the core rallying cry, others are seeking to reframe the struggle around demands for federalism. For example, departmental civic committees met in 2012 in Cochabamba to demand that Bolivia adopt federalism and introduce subnational judiciaries, which they argue is the only way to protect subnational governments from judicial persecution by the MAS. Still others have argued that something much deeper than autonomy or federalism is now at stake in Bolivia, and that a new party should prioritize the protection of democracy from the authoritarian maneuvers of the president.[33]

Beyond internal disagreements about branding, a second constraint is the sharp decline in the legitimacy of the CPSC and in levels of public support for the committee. In a 2001 survey, when asked to identify the institution that best represented them, 43 percent of *cruceños* named the CPSC and only 5 percent named the departmental prefecture. By 2009, the number for the CPSC had fallen to 26 percent and increased for the departmental prefecture (now a separately elected government) to 38 percent (Peña 2011: 71). While part of this reversal of fortune can be explained by the 2005 introduction of direct elections for departmental governors, much of the decline in support for the CPSC is likely a function of its role in the violence of September and October 2008, widely believed to have been coordinated and financed by CPSC President Branko Marinkovic.

---

[33] Meeting with youth activists in Consenso Popular.

Third, Herland Vaca Díez Busch, who served as CPSC President in
2011 and 2012, sought to improve the committee's image both by being
the first president ever to criticize publicly the *logias*, and by seeking to
expand the committee's engagement of migrants in the city's poorest
neighborhoods, including Plan 3000.[34] Shifting the CPSC in this direction has alienated some of the committee's traditional elite families and
financiers, opening up a set of internal conflicts that have weakened the
committee.[35] Equally fraught have been attempts to bring into the CPSC
representatives from five lowland indigenous groups (Guaraní, Moxeño,
Ayoreo, Guarayo, and Yuracuré). As of 2012, only the Moxeño representative, David Pérez Rapu, remained in the committee.[36] Overtures to
nonelites, declining financial contributions from traditional supporters,
and associations with the violence of 2008 have all lessened the CPSC's
appeal as a mobilizing structure upon which a new party might emerge.

CONCLUSION

The Bolivian case is an important one for the theoretical framework articulated by Levitsky, Loxton, and Van Dyck in Chapter 1 of this volume.
As of 2008, when Bolivia appeared on the verge of civil war, several years
of increasing polarization and conflict had generated all three of the conditions hypothesized to enable new parties to take root and become successful. In the eastern struggle for territorial autonomy between 2003 and
2008, classic social movement activities had created strong attachments
among participants that presumably could have sustained a robust party
brand for the opposition. Long-standing, well-resourced, and territorially extensive civic committees in the eastern departments appeared to
offer an ideal stock of organizational capacity for party-building. Just as
importantly, the ideological challenges to eastern political and economic
elites posed by President Evo Morales's historic rise to power should have
served as the critical source of elite cohesion that new parties need in
order to prosper.

[34] Interviews with Nicolás Ribera, First Vice President, and David Pérez Rapu, Director del CPSC por los Pueblos Indígenas, Santa Cruz, September 6, 2012.
[35] Interview with Marcelo Dabdoub, Secretario de Desarrollo Autónomico, Gobierno Autónomo Departamental, Santa Cruz, September 5, 2012.
[36] Interview with David Pérez Rapu, Director del CPSC por los Pueblos Indígenas, Santa Cruz, September 6, 2012.

In an outcome that supports rather than challenges this theoretical framework, Bolivia since 2008 has experienced a rapid process of depolarization and, along with it, greatly diminished prospects for party-building by the opposition. The last decade in Bolivia demonstrates that just as political entrepreneurs can fan the flames of polarization, so too can they act rapidly, aggressively, and effectively to reduce the scope of polarization. For polarization to generate its theorized effects, it must not merely be sufficiently deep but also relatively enduring. Both dimensions matter. Consider other left-turn cases of polarization that are often compared to Bolivia. In Venezuela, polarization proved to be as acute as in Bolivia, but much longer-lived. Hugo Chávez and his successor Nicolás Maduro have refrained from the kinds of substantive concessions and rhetorical overtures to the opposition that have done so much to reduce polarization in Bolivia and to cobble opposition party successes. It took over a decade, but persistent polarization in Venezuela eventually did produce important movement toward party-building in the Mesa de la Unidad Democrática (MUD – Democratic Unity Roundtable) alliance that emerged to contest the 2012 presidential election. In Ecuador, polarization has also endured due to Rafael Correa's decision not to copy from Morales's reconciliation playbook, and instead to continue to attack traditional economic elites located in Guayaquil. Ideological polarization, however, has been less extreme in Ecuador than in either Bolivia or Venezuela. Compared to the strong reaction that Morales's original project triggered in the Bolivian east, Correa's Citizen Revolution has provided much weaker incentives for party-building in Guayaquil and on the Ecuadorian coast.

Now that Bolivia's acute period of polarization has passed, eastern elite cohesion has been replaced by five important forms of elite fragmentation, each of which appears to constrain possibilities of party formation for those who led and financed the autonomy movement and who would need to lead and finance an eastern opposition party. In this sense, the Bolivian case offers additional evidence in support of Gibson's (1996) argument that elite fragmentation is one of the core challenges facing conservative party development.

First, political elites have fragmented *across* the four eastern departments, as directly reflected in the collapse of the governors' coalition in response to both external factors (i.e., the judicial persecution of individual governors) and internal factors (i.e., competitive pressures and resentments among the governors themselves). Second is the fragmentation of political elites *within* the critical department of Santa Cruz; individual leaders who gained prominence during the struggle for autonomy have now fallen out over personal and political disputes, and the now directly elected governor has eclipsed the president of the CPSC as the department's most important political figure. Third is continued division between *regional* leaders of the autonomy movement and *party* leaders in right-of-center parties; the latter were accused of being insufficiently committed to regional interests in the October 2008 constitutional compromise, and the former can now point to the lack of real autonomy in the wake of the new constitution to validate the more hardline position they took in 2008. Fourth is fragmentation among *economic* elites in the east; while a few have experienced expropriation and arrest by the national government over their roles in the violence of 2008 and 2009, most large agribusinesses appear to be prospering under Morales. Finally, a fifth form of fragmentation has occurred between political elites in the once powerful CPSC and the economic elites who have reconciled with Morales, and who no longer contribute to or even attend committee meetings. While the departure of economic elites might not be fatal to the long-term chances of creating a party on the right (Mizrahi 2003), in the short term business disinterest has restrained party-building.

Against this fractured landscape, it is possible to imagine two scenarios that might create opportunities for opposition party-building in the east, although each seems quite unlikely. First is the fallout from the historic rupture that has taken place within the governing MAS coalition now that such strong opposition to Morales has emerged among some eastern lowland indigenous communities over the TIPNIS conflict. Could this rupture lead to a territorial realignment of forces such that eastern indigenous communities on the one hand and eastern socioeconomic and political elites on the other might come together in common cause? Lowland indigenous leaders in the past who have negotiated with and/ or supported lowland elites have immediately lost credibility within their communities, but will this change if those communities move into the opposition against Morales?

Second is the possibility that an economic downturn triggered by a decline in the international price of gas could challenge Morales's continued ability to finance the concessions that have won the support of lowland agribusinesses. Even if prices remain high, recent studies suggest that the size of Bolivia's gas reserves may have been vastly overstated and that gas discoveries in Argentina and Brazil will reduce its markets in those countries in the years to come. Despite the possibility of this scenario, it is important to note that the concessions that have gone the furthest to reduce the hostility of eastern business interests do not appear to have a high (fiscal) price tag, including harsh language by the national government toward would-be land invaders, more lax monitoring of agribusiness productivity, and increases in the effective upper limit on the size of landholdings. Concessions like these do not depend on the price of gas, and they have gone a long way in encouraging businesses to accept Morales's invitation to focus on their businesses rather than on politics.

15

Why No Party-Building in Peru?

Steven Levitsky and Mauricio Zavaleta

Peru may be the most extreme case of party collapse in Latin America. The breakdown of the Peruvian party system and democracy in the early 1990s has been widely studied.[1] What is striking, however, is that a quarter of a century after the initial collapse, and fifteen years after redemocratization, the process of party decomposition continues. Notwithstanding initial expectations that redemocratization would trigger party rebirth (Kenney 2003), no successful party-building has occurred. All parties created after 1990 have collapsed,[2] failed to achieve national electoral significance,[3] or remained strictly personalistic vehicles.[4] Most politicians are now partisan free agents who create their own tickets or negotiate positions on others' tickets at each election. Thus, parties have been replaced by "coalitions of independents," or tickets composed of free agents that are cobbled together for elections and then dissolve (Zavaleta 2014a).

This chapter examines why parties have not reemerged in post-Fujimori Peru. We argue that this outcome is partly explained by the theoretical framework presented in Chapter 1, but that party decomposition also generated a self-reinforcing dynamic. After parties collapsed, politicians developed alternative strategies (such as party-switching and

---

[1] See Cameron (1994), Cotler (1995), Kenney (2004), Tanaka (1998, 2005b), Lynch (1999), Levitsky and Cameron (2003), Planas (2000), Roberts (1995, 1998, 2006), Seawright (2012), and Vergara (2009).

[2] Examples include the Union for Peru (UPP), We are Peru (SP), and the Independent Moralizing Front (FIM).

[3] Examples include the Socialist Party (PS), the New Left Movement (MNI), and Social Force (FS).

[4] Examples include *Fujimorismo*, National Solidarity, the Nationalist Party, and Possible Peru.

the deployment of party substitutes) that enabled them to win elections without parties. By facilitating politicians' efforts to "go it alone," the diffusion of these alternative strategies further weakened incentives for party-building. Moreover, electoral competition appears to select for politicians who make effective use of these nonparty strategies and technologies. Hence, there may be a path-dependent logic to party system collapse.

PARTY DECOMPOSITION IN POST-FUJIMORI PERU

The Peruvian party system collapsed in the late 1980s and early 1990s under the weight of a hyperinflationary crisis and the devastating Shining Path insurgency.[5] The four parties that dominated Peruvian politics in the 1980s – American Popular Revolutionary Alliance (APRA), the Popular Christian Party (PPC), Popular Action (AP), and the United Left (IU) – declined from 97 percent of the vote in 1985 to just 6 percent in 1995. Party collapse permitted the election of a political outsider, Alberto Fujimori, in 1990 (Cameron 1994). After his 1992 presidential coup, Fujimori governed without a party, relying on state institutions – particularly the intelligence agencies – as a substitute (Roberts 1995; Rospigliosi 2000). He created a new personalistic vehicle at every election: Change 90 in 1990, New Majority in 1992 and 1995, Let's Go Neighbor in 1998, and Peru 2000 in 2000.

Peru's established parties decomposed during Fujimori's eight-year authoritarian rule (1992–2000) (Lynch 1999; Tanaka 1998). Scores of ambitious politicians abandoned the so-called "traditional parties" and declared themselves "independents" (Planas 2000). No established party was able to seriously contest the 1995 presidential election.[6] Politicians from diverse partisan backgrounds formed the Union for Peru (UPP), which backed the candidacy of former United Nations Secretary General Javier Pérez de Cuéllar. Pérez de Cuéllar lost decisively to Fujimori, however, and the UPP quickly decomposed (Meléndez 2007: 231). Two embryonic national party organizations emerged in anticipation of the 1998 municipal elections: Fujimori's Let's Go Neighbor (Vamos Vecino, or VV) and Lima mayor Alberto Andrade's We are Peru (Somos Perú, or SP). However, both parties collapsed after the election. Fujimori abandoned VV for another personalistic vehicle (Peru 2000) prior to the 2000

[5] For analyses of this collapse, see Cameron (1994), Lynch (1999), Roberts (1998), and Tanaka (1998).
[6] APRA and AP won four and two percent of the vote, respectively, in 1995, while the PPC declined to field a presidential candidate and won three percent of the legislative vote.

election, and Andrade's decline in the polls triggered a wave of defections that reduced SP to minor party status. By 2000, party-building efforts had effectively ceased. The top five candidates in the 2000 presidential race (Fujimori, Andrade, Alejandro Toledo, Federico Salas, and Luis Castañeda) all headed personalistic vehicles.

The 2000–2001 democratic transition raised expectations of a return to parties. Scholars viewed the strong performance of established party candidates Alan García (APRA) and Lourdes Flores (PPC) in the 2001 presidential election as evidence of a traditional party comeback (Kenney 2003; Schmidt 2003).[7] APRA also performed well in the 2002 local elections, capturing twelve of twenty-five regional governments.[8] At the same time, a series of electoral reforms were undertaken in order to strengthen parties (Tuesta 2005; Vergara 2009). For example, the Fujimori-era electoral system, in which all 120 legislators were elected from a single national district, was replaced by one in which candidates were elected from 25 districts, which reduced the average district magnitude from 120 to 5 (Tanaka 2005b: 105, 125). Another reform established a minimum threshold of 5 percent of the vote for entry into Congress. Finally, the 2003 Political Parties Law banned independent candidacies, granted national parties a monopoly over legislative representation, and established a set of organizational requisites for national parties: to be legalized, new parties would require signatures from 135,000 supporters, as well as sixty-seven provincial branches – each with at least fifty activists – in two-thirds of the country's regions (Vergara 2009: 23).

Yet neither democratization nor institutional engineering halted the process of party decomposition. The "rebirth" of established parties proved illusory. The revival of APRA and the PPC was driven almost entirely by the electoral performance of García and Flores, respectively. In 2011, when neither García nor Flores was a candidate, both parties' electoral performance plummeted.[9] New national parties that emerged in the 2000s – such as Alejandro Toledo's Possible Peru (PP), Luis Castañeda's National Solidarity Party (PSN), and Ollanta Humala's Nationalist Party (PNP) – were little more than "name plates" for personalistic candidates (Planas 2000: 38). Indeed, every new party that

---

[7] García and Flores finished second and third, respectively.

[8] UPP won two regions, while SP, Toledo's PP, the FIM and MNI each won one. The other seven regions were captured by regional movements.

[9] Neither the PPC nor APRA fielded a presidential candidate in 2011, and the parties won six and four (out of 130) seats, respectively, in Congress. The two parties formed an alliance in 2016 but won only five seats in Congress. The other major parties from the 1980s either disappeared (IU) or survived as a minor party (AP).

won at least 4 percent of the national vote between 1995 and 2011 was a personalistic vehicle: a party created by, and exclusively for, a single presidential aspirant.[10] The extent of party collapse was made manifest in the 2011 presidential election, in which every major candidate either led a personalistic vehicle (Humala, Keiko Fujimori, Toledo, Castañeda) or had no party at all (Pedro Pablo Kuczynski).[11]

Although national parties survive, at least nominally (due to a law requiring presidential and congressional candidates to run on party tickets), they exist largely on paper. Parties' local linkages disintegrated during the 2000s (see Muñoz and Dargent, Chapter 7, this volume), and as a result, they largely disappeared at the grassroots level. As Table 15.1 shows, national parties have increasingly been displaced by provincial or regional "movements," or parties that compete exclusively in provincial and regional elections (De Gramont 2010; Zavaleta 2014a). The national parties' share of the vote in regional and provincial elections fell from 78 percent in 2002 to just 38 percent in 2014.[12] Whereas national parties captured seventeen of twenty-five regional governments and 110 of 195 provincial governments in 2002, they won only six of twenty-five regional governments and forty-eight of 195 provincial governments in 2014. By 2014, most national parties – including APRA and the governing PNP – had ceased to even run candidates in a majority of regional and provincial races.[13]

The success of new regional movements contributed little to party-rebuilding. Efforts to coordinate across regions or to scale up into national organizations failed (De Gramont 2010; Muñoz and Dargent, Chapter 7, this volume). Moreover, most of the regional movements that emerged in the 2000s were as loosely organized, personalistic, and ephemeral as the national parties they displaced (Tanaka and Guibert 2011; Zavaleta 2014a).[14] As a result, local and regional politics grew

[10] These include Toledo's PP, Andrade's SP, Castañeda's PSN, Humala's PNP, Humberto Lay's National Restoration (RN), and Cesar Acuña's APP. We treat *Fujimorismo* (created in 1990) as a single party, even though it changed names six times between 1990 and 2013.

[11] Kuczynski, known by his initials PPK, was backed by an alliance of parties. He later created a personalistic vehicle called Peruanos por el Kambio (PPK).

[12] Jurado Nacional de Elecciones and Oficina Nacional de Procesos Electorales online databases.

[13] Taken from Vera (2010), Coronel and Rodríguez (2011), Remy (2010), and Tanaka and Guibert (2011). In 2014, APRA ran candidates in twelve of twenty-five regions and barely a quarter of Peru's provinces. The PNP ran no candidates in the regional election.

[14] An exception is the Chim Pum Callao machine in Callao (Muñoz and Dargent, Chapter 7, this volume).

TABLE 15.1 *Provincial and regional governments won by national parties and regional movements, 2002–2010*

	2002		2006		2010		2014	
	Regions	Provinces	Regions	Provinces	Regions	Provinces	Regions	Provinces
National parties	18	110	7	109	6	72	6	47
Regional/provincial movements	7	84	18	86	19	123	19	148

Sources: Vera (2010); Coronel and Rodríguez (2011); Tanaka and Guibert (2011).

increasingly fragmented and fluid. An average of twelve parties contested each regional election in 2010 (Seifert 2014: 53–54), and few of these parties endured beyond a single election or two. Manuel Seifert (2014) measured regional "party volatility" by dividing the number of new parties by the overall number of parties in each regional election. In 2006, the average level of party volatility was 63.2, meaning that most of the parties competing in that year's regional election were new (Seifert 2014: 45). In 2010, the figure increased to 68.3, meaning that on average, more than two-thirds of the parties in each region were new (Seifert 2014: 52).

Far from experiencing a rebirth in the 2000s, then, Peru's party system decomposed further still. Not only were established parties displaced by personalistic vehicles, but at the local level, national parties of all types were displaced by short-lived, candidate-centered "movements." The result was a level of partisan fragmentation and fluidity that is unparalleled in Latin America.

A DEMOCRACY WITHOUT PARTIES: FREE AGENTS, *TRANSFUGUISMO*, AND COALITIONS OF INDEPENDENTS

Post-Fujimori Peru is thus a democracy without parties (Levitsky and Cameron 2003). Electoral politics is organized around individual candidates. National parties' capacity to channel political careers has evaporated. From the perspective of individual candidates, national parties no longer provide resources that can help them win public office (Muñoz and Dargent, Chapter 7, this volume). Gutted of their local organizations, most parties lack activists, campaign infrastructure, or financial or patronage resources to offer local candidates. Moreover, because partisan identities have largely evaporated, national party labels lack value; local politicians thus "prefer their own label."[15] Without resources or an attractive brand, national parties are, in the words of PPC leader Lourdes Flores, "completely unable to recruit good candidates. The good ones all want to go it alone."[16]

Most contemporary Peruvian politicians are thus partisan free agents. New entrants to the political arena do not expect to build a career within a

---

[15] Author's interview with PPC President Lourdes Flores, Lima, March 30, 2011.
[16] Author's interview with PPC President Lourdes Flores, Lima, March 30, 2011. Also author's interviews with AP legislator Víctor Andrés García Belaúnde (Lima, May 5, 2011) and former PP leader Juan Sheput (Lima, May 5, 2011).

single party, working their way up from local to national-level politics. Those seeking major executive posts (such as the presidency, regional governorships,[17] or big city mayoralties) create and lead their own personalistic vehicle. National-level examples include Alejandro Toledo (PP); Ollanta Humala (PNP); former Lima mayors Alberto Andrade (SP) and Luis Castañeda (PSN); former Prime Ministers Federico Salas (Let's Advance), Pedro Pablo Kuczynski (Peruanos por el Kambio [PPK – Peruvians for Change]), and Yehude Simon (Humanist Party); and evangelical leader Humberto Lay (National Restoration).

Lower-tier politicians – those running for Congress, regional legislatures, city council, and most mayoralties – negotiate, at each election, positions on other politicians' slates. Many candidates purchase their place on legislative lists, with payments reportedly ranging from $20,000 to $120,000.[18] Although most politicians formally affiliate with the party whose list they join, such "partisan affiliations" are, in reality, short-term contacts that cover a single election cycle. Because parties that are viable in one election are often not viable in subsequent ones, ambitious politicians must constantly renegotiate their partisan affiliations.

This practice of party-switching – known as *transfuguismo* – first gained notoriety in 2000, when Fujimori's spymaster, Vladimiro Montesinos, forged a congressional majority by bribing eighteen opposition legislators (known as *tránsfugas*, or "turncoats") to join the *Fujimorista* ranks. A leaked video of one of these bribes triggered Fujimori's fall, and the original *tránsfugas* fell into disgrace. However, the practice of *transfuguismo* diffused widely in the post–Fujimori era. By 2014, many politicians had affiliated with five or more parties (former Vice President Máximo San Román had belonged to eight!). Take Tito Chocano. Originally elected mayor of Tacna in 1986 as a member of the PPC, Chocano was subsequently reelected with three different parties: the Union of Tacna Independents in 1989; Fujimori's Change 90/ New Majority in 1993; and his own vehicle, Strength and Development,

---

[17] Between 2002 and 2014, elected regional executives were called regional presidents. A 2015 electoral reform changed the title to governor. To avoid confusion, we use the term governor to refer to all regional executives elected since 2002.

[18] Author's interviews with ex-legislator José Barba Caballero, May 4, 2011; ex-PP politician Juan Sheput, May 5, 2011; PNP legislator Sergio Tejada, May 23, 2013; and PSN legislator Heriberto Benítez, May 27, 2013. According to Sheput, candidacies are "auctioned off." Parties will take "anyone who is willing to pay." These claims were confirmed in numerous interviews with party leaders.

in 1995. In 2000, Chocano was elected to Congress with SP, and when new elections were held in 2001 after Fujimori's fall, he was reelected with Lourdes Flores's National Unity (UN). In 2010, Chocano won Tacna's governorship as the candidate of AP. Thus, Chocano won elections with six different parties between 1986 and 2010.

Another example is Moquegua politician Jaime Rodríguez. Rodríguez first ran for office in Mariscal Nieto province in 1989, as the candidate of Mario Vargas Llosa's Democratic Front (FREDEMO) coalition. He then ran (unsuccessfully) for mayor of Mariscal Nieto in 1993 – this time with AP. In 2001, Rodríguez ran for Congress (again unsuccessfully) with National Unity. In 2002, Rodríguez competed for the Moquegua governorship with a regional movement called Commitment and Development. He lost, but in 2006, he won the governorship as candidate of another regional movement: Our Ilo-Moquegua. Rodríguez left office in 2010, but in 2014, he was reelected governor of Moquegua – this time as candidate of yet another regional movement: Kausachun. Rodríguez thus ran for office six times, with six different parties, between 1989 and 2014.

Chocano and Rodríguez are by no means exceptional. Indeed, *transfuguismo* – or the renegotiation of partisan affiliations at each election – became a routinized practice in post-Fujimori Peru. Politicians – particularly those who entered politics after 1990 – no longer develop stable partisan ties, but rather negotiate short-term contracts with parties prior to each election. An examination of the partisan trajectories of the ninety-three candidates who finished first or second in gubernatorial elections between 2002 and 2010 found that they had belonged to an average of 2.3 parties (which, given that many were first-time candidates, is a strikingly high number). Data from the 2014 elections reveal a similar picture. Of the fifty winners and runners-up in that year's regional elections, thirty-five had belonged to two or more parties, eighteen had belonged to three or more parties, and eight had belonged to four or more parties.[19] Likewise, of the 195 provincial mayors elected in 2014, 168 (86 percent) had belonged to two or more parties, 101 (52 percent) had belonged to three or more parties during their career, and forty-eight (25 percent) had belonged to four or more parties. In Lima, thirty-four of the forty-two district-level mayors elected in 2014 had belonged to two or more parties, twenty had belonged to three or more parties, and

---

[19] Tacna runner-up Jacinto Gómez had belonged to seven parties, while Pasco runner-up Klever Meléndez had belonged to six.

eleven had belonged to four or more parties. On average, the district-level mayors elected in Lima had belonged to 2.6 parties.

Similar patterns emerge in legislative elections. Of the ninety-eight legislators elected in 2011 who had previously run for public office, forty had switched parties since the last election. Another analysis found that 63 percent of all legislative candidates in 2011 had no prior affiliation with the party that nominated them.[20] Overall, we found that legislators elected between 2001 and 2011 had, on average, run for office under two-party labels. Given that a quarter of these legislators were first-time candidates, this figure is, again, strikingly high.

The dynamics of *transfuguismo* are nicely illustrated in Villa El Salvador (VES), a lower-income Lima district that was a bastion of the IU in the 1980s. IU politician Michel Azcueta served as mayor of VES between 1984 and 1990. After IU collapsed, Azcueta formed Democratic Platform to run (unsuccessfully) for mayor of Lima in 1993. In 1995, Azcueta recaptured the VES mayoralty, but now as candidate of Lima mayor-elect Alberto Andrade's We Are Lima (later SP). In 1998, he again ran for higher office and was succeeded by Martín Pumar, another former IU cadre who had joined SP. In 2002, with SP in decline, Pumar ran for reelection with Peru First, but he lost to Jaime Zea, another ex-IU member who ran with Lima mayoral candidate Luis Castañeda's UN. Azcueta, meanwhile, left SP to run for mayor of Lima on Toledo's PP ticket. In 2006, Zea was reelected with Humberto Lay's RN. He defeated Azcueta, who had left the weakened PP for Trust Peru. In 2010, the VES mayoral race was won by Santiago Mozo, a businessman who ran unsuccessfully with Always United in 2006 and joined PP after failing to gain the endorsement of Radical Change (CR). Mozo defeated the incumbent, Zea, who had jumped from National Restoration to UN; Pumar, who had left Peru First for CR; and Azcueta, who ran with Alliance for Progress (APP).[21] Since 1990, then, every mayor of VES has been a *tránsfuga*, and the district's three leading politicians – Azcueta, Zea, and Pumar – have each switched parties *five* times.

If an increasing number of politicians are *free agents*, parties increasingly take the form of what Zavaleta (2014a) calls "coalitions of independents." National, regional, and local-level politicians who create personalistic vehicles in pursuit of executive office fill their legislative

---

[20] *Diario 16*, February 26, 2011, p. 8.
[21] In 2011, Mozo was removed from office and replaced by vice mayor Guido Iñigo. Iñigo was reelected in 2014 with his own movement, Villa Changes.

slates with free agents (either *tránsfugas* or amateurs without partisan backgrounds), most of whom lack real ties to the party.[22] Party leaders recruit individuals who can contribute either votes (e.g., well-known personalities) or money to the campaign (Rozas 2012). Partisan history and activism are secondary criteria.[23] As former PP politician Juan Sheput put it, "parties recruit people who have money. And party activists don't have much money."[24]

Individual politicians seek to join tickets with the greatest electoral potential, which tend to be those headed by the front-running candidates for executive office. Thus, they identify potential "locomotives," or top-of-the-ticket candidates with powerful coattails, and seek to negotiate their way aboard the train they are pulling.[25] Again, partisan ties are nearly irrelevant.[26] Although most candidates nominally affiliate with the party they run with (by law, only 20 percent of parties' legislative candidacies may go to independents), such affiliations are generally one-shot deals that cover a single election cycle: after the election, coalitions of independents disintegrate and candidates regain their free agent status.

An example of a coalition of independents is Radical Change (CR), a Lima-based party created and led by former congressman José Barba Caballero. The party has no membership or activist base, but rather is (in Barba's words) merely a "platform in search of candidates."[27] When CR ran in the 2010 municipal election in Lima, it awarded all of its candidacies – including the mayoral candidacy – to outsiders and free agents, using polling and candidates' ability to make financial contributions as selection criteria.[28] As Barba put it, "It doesn't matter who the [candidates] are or which party they come from, as long as they can

[22] Based on author's interviews with ex-Congressman José Barba Caballero, May 4, 2011; Possible Peru leader Juan Sheput, May 5, 2011; PPC leader Lourdes Flores, March 30, 2011; AP leader Víctor Andrés García Belaúnde, May 5, 2011; and VES district councilor Genaro Soto, July 20, 2013.

[23] Based on author's interviews with ex-Congressman José Barba Caballero, May 4, 2011; Possible Peru leader Juan Sheput, May 5, 2011; PPC leader Lourdes Flores, March 30, 2011; and AP leader Víctor Andrés García Belaúnde, May 5, 2011.

[24] Author's interview, May 5, 2011.

[25] Author's interviews with Lourdes Flores, March 30, 2011; José Barba Caballero, May 4, 2011; and VES district councilor Genaro Soto, July 20, 2013.

[26] According to Lourdes Flores, who was the "locomotive" for the PPC in Lima's 2010 mayoral race, prior to her entry into the race, when Alex Kouri was the frontrunner, PPC district mayoral candidates threatened, en masse, to defect to his party, Radical Change (CR). Asked how many PPC candidates would have defected had she not jumped into the race, Flores answered: "all of them" (author's interview, March 30, 2011).

[27] Author's interview with José Barba Caballero, May 4, 2011.

[28] Author's interview with José Barba Caballero, May 4, 2011.

win."[29] Thus, CR's slate of district-level mayoral candidates was composed almost entirely of *tránsfugas*, most of whom abandoned the party after the election.[30]

Another example is Social and Economic Participation Integration Andean Regional Reform (RAICES), a Puno-based regional movement that was created in 2009 by ex-Puno mayor Mariano Portugal. Prior to the 2010 local and regional elections, Portugal filled RAICES' candidate slate with *tránsfugas* and high-profile newcomers, including local university president Juan Luque, who was RAICES' regional presidential candidate. Three-quarters (nine of twelve) of RAICES' provincial mayoral candidates were *tránsfugas* from other parties (Zavaleta 2014a: 86). RAICES won five of the twelve mayoral races it contested, and Luque qualified for the regional presidential runoff. Immediately after the first round vote, however, provincial candidates – who were no longer on the ballot – abandoned the party (refusing, e.g., to support Luque in the second round), and after Luque lost the runoff, RAICES collapsed.[31] Four years later, Luque won the governorship with a new coalition of independents, Integration Project for Cooperation, none of whose candidates (except for Luque) had ties to RAICES (Zavaleta 2014b).

Coalitions of independents have emerged as the predominant form of electoral organization in post-Fujimori Peru (Zavaleta 2014a). We examined all political organizations that finished first or second in Peru's twenty-five regional elections in 2006 and 2010. Organizations in which at least half of mayoral candidates had previously run for office under the same label were scored as parties, while organizations in which a majority of mayoral candidates were either outsiders (i.e., did not previously belong to a party) or *tránsfugas* (i.e., defected from another party) were scored as coalitions of independents. By this measure, only 16 percent of the winners and runners-up in the 2006 and 2010 regional elections represented parties (of these, ten were APRA candidates). By contrast, 70 percent of winners and runners-up finishers led coalitions of independents (another 14 percent were pure independents, in that their ticket did not run mayoral candidates or ran them in fewer than half the region's provinces). In the 2014 regional elections, twenty-two of the twenty-five

---

[29] Author's interview, May 4, 2011.

[30] Author's interview with José Barba Caballero, May 4, 2011. *Tránsfugas* included Gustavo Sierra from PSN; Carlos Lazo from Trust Peru; Adolfo Ocampo from *Fujimorismo*; and Salvador Heresi Luis Bueno, Ricardo Castro, Luis Dibos, and Pedro Florian from PPC/ UN.

[31] In 2011, Portugal was elected to Congress on the PP ticket.

winning candidates either led coalitions of independents (seventeen) or were pure independents (five).

In post-Fujimori Peru, then, party politics decomposed down to their most basic unit: the individual candidate. Politicians became free agents, renegotiating their partisan affiliation at each election, and short-lived coalitions of independents became the primary mechanism through which politicians organized to compete in elections. Whether these coalitions of independents can be labeled parties is open to debate. Anthony Downs (1957: 25) famously defined a political party as "a team of men seeking to control the governing apparatus by gaining office in a duly constituted election." Strictly speaking, coalitions of independents meet these criteria. On election day, they are Downsian parties. However, if teams of politicians must be even minimally stable to qualify as parties, then coalitions of independents should be viewed as an alternative form of electoral organization.

EXPLAINING THE ABSENCE OF PARTY-(RE) BUILDING

Why, nearly a quarter of a century after the collapse of the party system and more than a decade after redemocratization, has virtually no party-building occurred in Peru? The Peruvian case suggests that democracy and electoral competition, by themselves, do not generate sufficient incentives for party-building. It also raises questions about the impact of electoral design. As noted above, the 2000–2001 transition gave rise to a series of electoral reforms aimed at strengthening parties, including adoption of a lower district magnitude, a minimum threshold for entry into Congress, and a new Parties Law that banned independent presidential candidacies, granted national parties a monopoly over legislative representation, and established tough new requisites for legal registration. Not only did institutional reforms fail, but as Muñoz and Dargent (Chapter 7, this volume) argue, some of them may have made party-building more difficult.

The absence of party-building in post-Fujimori Peru can be explained, in part, by the theoretical framework outlined in Chapter 1. For one, conditions for brand development were unfavorable. An elite consensus around neoliberal economic policies – rooted in the hyperinflationary crisis of the late 1980s and the success of neoliberal reforms in the 1990s – left little room for programmatic differentiation. None of Fujimori's main rivals in 1995 (Pérez de Cuéllar) and 2000 (Andrade, Castañeda, and Toledo) challenged his economic program. After Fujimori's fall, the

Toledo government (2001–2006) maintained his orthodox policies, and although Alan García (2006–2011) and Ollanta Humala (2011–2016) criticized neoliberal policies as opposition candidates, they continued them while in office (Cameron 2011; Vergara 2011). Thus, new parties such as Pérez de Cuellar's UPP, Andrade's SP, Castañeda's PSN, and Toledo's PP all failed to differentiate themselves from Fujimori on the left–right axis. Although Humala's PNP initially positioned itself on the left, it diluted its brand by shifting rightward in 2011.

Peru also lacked favorable conditions for organization-building. Particularly after 2000, politicians enjoyed open access to the media, and most new parties of significance enjoyed some access to the state, either at the local or the national level.[32] Following Van Dyck (Chapter 5, this volume), then, politicians lacked strong incentives to invest in organization. They also lacked the means. Civil society organizations, which served as a platform for party-building elsewhere in Latin America (see Madrid, Chapter 11, and Van Dyck, Chapter 5, this volume), were weak in Peru. Both the labor movement and the progressive church weakened during the 1990s, and unlike Bolivia and Ecuador, there were no national peasant or indigenous organizations for new parties to build upon (Yashar 2005). Both the Shining Path, which penetrated and destroyed many popular sector organizations, and the state counterinsurgency, which reduced the space for political activity during the 1990s, had a dampening effect on associational life (Rénique 2004; Yashar 2005; Burt 2006).

The Shining Path insurgency was, of course, a major instance of violent conflict. However, the party-building effects of this conflict were limited by the fact that, unlike the FMLN in El Salvador (Holland, Chapter 10, this volume), the Shining Path was a narrowly based organization which, due in part to its use of brutal violence against civilians, lacked broad public support.[33] Thus, when a Shining Path front organization, the Movement for Amnesty and Fundamental Rights (MOVADEF), attempted to register as a party in 2012, public opinion surveys found 85 percent opposition to its legalization.[34] Hence, even if MOVADEF

---

[32] PP and the PNP each controlled the presidency for five years, while SP and PSN each governed Lima for eight years. Access to state resources was enhanced by the creation of elected regional governments in 2002 (Vergara 2009).

[33] See Del Pino (1998), Degregori (2010), and Gavilán (2012). According to the final report of Peru's Truth and Reconciliation Commission, the Shining Path was responsible for 54 percent of the estimated 69,259 deaths that occurred during the insurgency.

[34] *Perú 21*, January 27, 2012. Another survey found that nearly 90 percent of Peruvians viewed a *Senderista* party as a national threat (*El Comercio*, November 18, 2012).

had registered as a party (its petition was denied), it is unlikely to have emerged as a viable electoral contender.

Following the Shining Path's defeat, levels of polarization and conflict in Peru were limited. The opposition to Fujimori was weak and fragmented throughout the 1990s, and levels of anti-Fujimori mobilization were low (Levitsky and Cameron 2003). Even the protests triggered by the flawed 2000 election were short-lived; it was ultimately an internal crisis that toppled Fujimori later that year (Cameron 2006). Perhaps as a result, the anti-*Fujimorista* opposition never gave rise to a party. During the 2000s, politics polarized briefly around presidential campaigns (in 2006 and 2011), but this polarization was confined to elite and media circles; neither populist candidate Ollanta Humala nor his opponents mobilized a substantial number of activists. Finally, although post-Fujimori Peru experienced a series of intense local-level conflicts (e.g., the 2002 *Arequipazo*, the 2009 Bagua incident, the Conga mining conflict in Cajamarca in 2011), these crises did not scale-up into national-level conflicts (Meléndez 2012).

Yet the causes of nonparty-building go beyond the absence of the conditions outlined in Chapter 1. The Peruvian case suggests that party collapse may itself be self-reinforcing (Levitsky and Cameron 2003; Sánchez 2012). In the aftermath of party collapse, politicians develop expectations, strategies, norms, and technologies that allow them to succeed in a context of elections without parties. Politicians who win public office without parties have little incentive to invest in them. Over time, the strategies, norms, and technologies of party-less politics may diffuse and even institutionalize. Moreover, electoral competition may select for politicians with the will, know-how, and resources to "go it alone." Thus, in the absence of the kind of polarization and conflict that generates collective mobilization and new partisan identities, the prospects for party-rebuilding may decline over time. This, we argue, is what occurred in post-Fujimori Peru.

The Emergence of a New Model

Peru's party system collapse became self-reinforcing via several steps. First, politicians learned that they could succeed without parties (Levitsky and Cameron 2003). This learning process began with television personality Ricardo Belmont's victory in the 1989 Lima mayoral race and was reinforced by Fujimori's 1990 presidential victory. The crisis of the "traditional" parties had reduced the perceived value of established party labels,[35] and Fujimori demonstrated that party organization was not necessary to win the presidency. Fujimori's subsequent political success – culminating in his landslide reelection in 1995 – thus triggered a bandwagoning dynamic, as politicians abandoned established parties for personalistic vehicles (euphemistically called "independent movements") (Planas 2000). Many of these politicians were successful. Alberto Andrade (ex-PPC) and Luis Castañeda (ex-AP) were elected mayor of Lima, and both emerged as major presidential contenders; Alex Kouri (ex-PPC) was elected mayor and then governor of Callao; and José Barba Caballero (ex-APRA) was twice reelected to Congress after forming his own party in 1992. (Barba claims he was inspired by his friend Rafael Rey, who had abandoned the Liberty Movement and created National Renewal: "I thought to myself, 'If that fool can form a political party, why can't I?'".[36]) At the same time, new politicians – those entering politics after 1990 – eschewed existing parties for personalistic vehicles, effectively launching their careers as outsiders. Prominent national-level examples include Toledo, Humala, and evangelical pastor Humberto Lay. Hundreds of other cases exist at the local and regional levels.

The rise of outsider politics generated a set of widely diffused practices and shared expectations that, over time, crystallized into informal institutions. These include:

Partisan Free Agency. Outside of APRA, politicians are no longer expected to establish enduring partisan ties or to pursue careers within a particular party. Rather, it is widely understood that politicians will act as partisan free agents, pursuing their career outside of parties and adopting partisan labels on a temporary basis in order to compete in elections.

Transfuguismo. It is also widely expected that politicians will routinely switch partisan affiliations, often renegotiating their party ties at each election cycle. This strategy of permanent *transfuguismo* is viewed by politicians as necessary for political survival. In the aftermath of party collapse, politicians learned that in a context of extreme volatility, loyalty to one's original party could derail a political career. Over the course of the 1990s, it became clear that continued political success required securing, at each election, position on a ticket headed by a viable "locomotive."[37] By the mid-2000s, *transfuguismo* had achieved taken-for-granted status, particularly among new politicians.

[35] As PPC leader Lourdes Flores put it, "the problem is that when we construct a solid label, voters reject it" (personal interview, March 30, 2011).
[36] Personal interview with José Barba Caballero, May 4, 2011.
[37] Author's interview with VES district councilor Genaro Soto, July 20, 2013.

Coalitions of Independents. The parties led by presidential and guber-natorial candidates are not expected to nominate longtime activists and members for lower level candidacies. Rather, they select candidates – either outsiders or *tránsfugas* who can provide either the most votes or the largest financial contribution. These candidacies are expected to be short-term contracts that effectively expire after the election.

The norms of partisan free agency, *transfuguismo*, and the forma-tion of coalitions of independents diffused widely during the 1990s and 2000s, eventually becoming (informally) institutionalized. In Villa El Salvador (VES), for example, local politicians were surprised in 1993 when the candidate linked to the long-dominant IU lost to the candidate sponsored by Lima mayor Ricardo Belmont's party, Public Works.[38] They quickly learned the new rules of the game, however, and in 1995, mayoral aspirant Michel Azcueta worked hard to secure the candidacy of We are Lima, the party led by Lima mayoral front runner Alberto Andrade.[39] With Azcueta's victory, "the idea of the locomotive took hold" in VES.[40] By the early 2000s, it was widely known that anyone seeking to win the mayoralty had to align him or herself with a viable Lima-wide candi-date. At the same time, informal rules emerged regarding the formation of coalitions of independents, such as the "four by four," in which the Lima-wide locomotive and the local mayoral candidate each name four district councilor candidates.[41]

Norms of partisan free agency, *transfuguismo*, and coalitions of inde-pendents are not fully institutionalized. APRA and (to a lesser extent) PPC politicians continue to pursue partisan careers, and the rules of the game of nonparty electoral politics have not gained broad normative acceptance (indeed, *transfuguismo* generates widespread public disap-proval). In practice, however, such practices have become widely known, accepted, and even taken for granted, particularly among politicians who began their careers after 1990.

New Technologies: Party Substitutes

Nonparty electoral strategies are reinforced by the fact that ambitious politicians have developed a range of "substitutes" (Hale 2006) for

---

[38] Author's interview with VES district councilor Genaro Soto, July 20, 2013.
[39] Author's interview with VES district councilor Genaro Soto, July 20, 2013.
[40] Author's interview with VES district councilor Genaro Soto, July 20, 2013.
[41] Author's interview with VES district councilor Genaro Soto, July 20, 2013.

traditional party structures.[42] Four party substitutes merit particular attention. One is private firms. Following the pattern of "corporation-based" party organization described by Barndt (Chapter 13, this volume), many successful businesspeople have mobilized the resources, employees, infrastructure, and distribution networks of their firms for electoral purposes, effectively transforming their firms into campaign organizations.[43]

A prominent example of business party-building is César Acuña, the wealthy owner of a consortium of private universities whose hub lies in Peru's northern coast.[44] After being elected to Congress with PSN in 2000 and UN in 2001, Acuña created Alliance for Progress (APP) prior to the 2002 local elections. APP was based almost entirely on Acuña's business empire. Acuña's universities were APP's principle source of finance (Barrenechea 2014: 54–55). University profits were used to pay campaign workers and finance campaigns, and the universities themselves provided infrastructure such as printing presses, media outlets, and meeting space (Barrenechea 2014: 55–60). The universities were also a source of selective incentives to recruit candidates and activists (Meléndez 2011; Barrenechea 2014: 60–65). Most APP leaders and candidates held university posts,[45] and many lower-level cadres and activists held university scholarships (Barrenechea 2014: 65). Finally, Acuña's Clementina Peralta Foundation, a charitable foundation funded by profits from the universities, operated a vast network of child care centers, health clinics, and other social services, many of which are staffed by APP activists (Meléndez 2011; Barrenechea 2014: 65–70). The Foundation's activities serve as the bases for clientelist electoral mobilization (Meléndez 2011; Barrenechea 2014: 65–70).

Acuña's business party strategy proved quite successful. In 2006, he was elected mayor of Trujillo, and in 2010, APP won 7.7 percent of the national vote, capturing fourteen provincial governments and the regional government of Lambayeque (Barrenechea 2014: 33–34). In 2014, Acuña was elected governor of La Libertad, displacing APRA from its longtime stronghold, and APP captured nineteen of Peru's 194 provincial governments – more than any other party.[46]

---

[42] This section draws heavily on Zavaleta (2014a).
[43] See Muñoz (2010, 2014) and Zavaleta (2010, 2014a).
[44] On Acuña's party-building project, see Meléndez (2011) and Barrenechea (2014).
[45] Examples include Humberto Acuña, Luis Iberico, Manuel Llempen, Gloria Montenegro, and Walter Ramos (Barrenechea 2014: 60–61).
[46] Acuña ran for president in 2016 but was disqualified by the electoral authorities for vote-buying.

Acuña was not alone in deploying his business as a party substitute. The number of "business parties" increased markedly in the 2006 and 2010 local and regional elections.[47] In Ayacucho, for example, both the winner (Wilfredo Oscorima) and the runner-up (Rofilio Neyra) in the 2010 gubernatorial race were successful businessmen who, lacking parties,[48] drew from their own business empires to finance lavish campaigns (Zavaleta 2014a: 104–106). Likewise, Maciste Díaz (Huancavelica), Luis Picón (Huánuco), and Martín Vizcarra (Moquegua) used private firms as springboards to win or retain the governorship in 2010, while several other business-based candidates (Máximo San Román in Cusco, Fernando Martorell in Tacna) finished second. A stunning eleven of the twenty-five successful candidates in the 2014 gubernatorial elections were businessmen. Other business-based candidates won election to Congress. Examples include Julio Gagó, a photocopy machine vender who used his firm's advertising and profits to raise his electoral profile and negotiate his way onto *Fujimorismo*'s congressional list in 2011, and José Luna Gálvez, owner of a private distance learning firm (and self-proclaimed "king of technical education") whose lavish spending earned him a spot on Castañeda's PSN ticket in 2011.

A second type of substitute employed by Peruvian candidates – especially at the local level – is media outlets. As Zavaleta (2010, 2014a) shows, local radio station owners and prominent radio hosts frequently use radio as a means to appeal to mobilize votes in the absence of on-the-ground organization.[49] In Puno, for example, outsider Hernán Fuentes used his Juliaca-based radio station, Radio Perú, as a springboard to the governorship in 2006 (Zavaleta 2010, 2014a: 94). Fuentes's party, Forward Country (AP, Avanza País), had no grassroots organization, but he gained public recognition by using Radio Perú to repeatedly attack incumbent governor David Jiménez. Fuentes won the governorship with less than 20 percent of the vote, nearly all of which was concentrated in areas covered by Radio Perú (Zavaleta 2014a: 94). Fuentes was succeeded in 2010 by Mauricio Rodríguez, the founder of Radio Pachamama, the most successful station in Puno. Rodríguez's coalition of independents, Political Project HERE (Proyecto Político AQUÍ), had

[47] See Ballón and Barreneachea (2010), Muñoz (2010), Meléndez (2011), and Muñoz and García (2011).

[48] Oscorima ran with (but quickly abandoned) APP, whereas Neyra created his own "Everyone with Ayacucho" movement.

[49] Media substitutes have been particularly widespread in the southern regions such as Cusco, Madre de Dios, and Puno.

no real organization, but Radio Pachamama – one of the few radio stations whose signal spanned Puno – allowed him to mobilize votes across the region (Zavaleta 2014a: 94–95). Likewise, Puno-based congressman Mariano Portugal used his radio station, Radio Samoa, as a platform for his electoral career (Zavaleta 2014a: 95). Radio-based candidates have also proliferated at the municipal level. In Puno alone, Zavaleta (2014a: 95) identified at least ten radio owners or journalists who finished either first or second in the 2010 mayoral elections. Four years later, popular radio journalist Oswaldo Marín was elected mayor of Juliaca, Puno's largest city. Indeed, the use of media outlets as electoral springboards became so widespread that one Puno-based politician, Efraín Pinazo, observed that "if you want to be a candidate, you don't create a party. You open a radio station."[50]

Media-based candidates have succeeded in other regions as well. For example, television and radio journalists such as Carlos Cuaresma and Hugo Gonzales Sayán used their media presence to capture Cusco's governorship in 2002 and 2006, respectively (Muñoz 2010). In Madre de Dios, the winner of the 2010 regional presidential election (Luis Aguirre) was a radio journalist, while the runner-up (Simón Horna) was a local television broadcaster (Vilca 2011: 203).

Third, politicians turn to local "operators" as a substitute for party organization (Zavaleta 2014a). Operators are independent agents who orchestrate the grassroots campaign activities that are normally carried out by local party activists: they recruit candidates to fill out party tickets; build ties to local business, farmers, or neighborhood associations; organize meetings and rallies; organize the distribution of clientelist goods; and recruit and coordinate personnel to carry out key campaign activities, such as painting graffiti, putting up posters, and distributing fliers (Zavaleta 2014a: 99–102).[51] Many operators are experienced former partisan cadres (often from leftist parties) who, in the absence of stable parties, turned to contracting out their services at each election (Zavaleta 2014a: 99). Like subcontractors, they maintain small networks of clients or hired hands which they can mobilize for activist work during campaigns.[52] This enables local politicians to essentially "rent" the organization that in most democracies is supplied by parties. Rather than

---

[50] Quoted in Zavaleta (2014a: 94).
[51] Also author's interview with Genaro Soto, district councilman in VES, Lima, July 20, 2013.
[52] Zavaleta (2014a: 99–102). Also author's interview with Genaro Soto, district councilman in VES, Lima, July 20, 2013.

invest in grassroots organizations, then, local politicians simply rent them for campaigns. When the election is over, the contracts expire and the organizations dissolve.

Finally, an alternative nonparty strategy is the use of notables, or celebrity candidacies, as a substitute for a partisan brand. Thus, prominent athletes, soccer club owners, television personalities, religious figures, and other notables are routinely recruited onto candidate lists as a means of winning votes. In 2011, for example, four ex-members of Peru's prestigious national women's volleyball team were elected to Congress (with four different parties), as were two prominent sports commentators and two well-known religious leaders. In 2014, a former beauty queen, Yamila Osorio, was elected governor of the important southern region of Arequipa.

In sum, Peruvian politicians have developed a set of organizational substitutes that enable them to win elections in the absence of parties. The diffusion of these new electoral technologies makes it easier for individual politicians to opt for partisan free agency rather than join existing parties or invest in new ones.

The turn to nonparty politics in Peru has been reinforced by the fact that electoral competition selects for individuals who can win on their own. Thus, individuals who can deploy their firms or media outlets as substitutes for party structures and celebrity candidates who can substitute their own "brand" for that of a party appear to have an electoral advantage over professional politicians. Because traditional party politicians lack strong brands or organizational resources, they have difficulty competing against outsiders wielding party substitutes: they are outspent by businesspeople; they cannot reach voters as efficiently as radio-based candidates; and they lack the name recognition of celebrities and local notables.[53]

The number of amateur politicians – individuals who accumulate resources and/or name recognition outside the political arena and deploy them as party substitutes in pursuit of public office – has increased steadily over time. We operationalize amateur politicians as candidates who, prior to running for public office, were established private business owners or managers, media figures (owners or journalists), or well-known religious, military, sports, or entertainment figures. In 2002, twenty-one of the fifty winners and runners-up in the gubernatorial elections were

[53] Author's interviews with PPC leader Lourdes Flores (March 30, 2011) and former PP politician Juan Sheput (May 5, 2011).

amateur politicians; in 2006, the figure increased to twenty-four of fifty; in 2010, it reached thirty-one of fifty, and in 2014, it reached thirty-nine. Likewise, the number of amateur politicians elected to Congress was fifty-four (of 120) in 2001, fifty-one (of 120) in 2006, and a striking seventy-four (of 130) in 2011. By 2010–2011, then, nearly 60 percent of the leading candidates for Congress and governor were businessmen, media figures, or celebrities.

Electoral competition may, therefore, have a selection effect that reinforces party decomposition. Candidates who win election via substitutes are particularly unlikely to invest in party-building. The ascendance of such politicians, together with the institutionalization of norms of partisan free agency, *transfuguismo,* and coalitions of independents may thus be self-reinforcing, diminishing the probability of party-rebuilding over time.

THE PARADOX OF *FUJIMORISMO*: AN EXCEPTIONAL CASE OF PARTY-BUILDING?

Fujimorismo may constitute an exception to the pattern of nonparty-building that characterized post-1990 Peru (Urrutia 2011a, 2011b).[54] After collapsing in the wake of Alberto Fujimori's fall from power, *Fujimorismo* reemerged as a major political force in the mid-2000s. Although Fujimori was imprisoned in 2007 for corruption and human rights violations, *Fujimorismo,* led by his daughter, Keiko, performed increasingly well in elections. After two *Fujimorista* parties won a combined 8.4 percent of the legislative vote in 2001, a united *Fujimorismo* won 13 percent of the legislative vote in 2006, 23 percent of the legislative vote in 2011, and 36 percent of the legislative vote in 2016. Moreover, Keiko Fujimori nearly captured the presidency in 2011 and 2016.

Fujimorismo possesses a relatively solid partisan base. Surveys consistently find that more Peruvians self-identify as *Fujimorista* than any other party, leading some scholars to describe *Fujimorismo* as a "nascent brand" (Meléndez 2010: 12). Based on a survey experiment carried out in 2011, Carlos Meléndez classified 6 percent of Peruvian voters as "core" *Fujimorista* supporters and an additional 10 percent as *Fujimorista* "leaners" (2012: 12). Though modest, these figures exceed those of any

---

[54] *Fujimorismo* has had eight different names since its foundation in 1990: Change 90, New Majority, Let's Go Neighbor, Peru 2000, Popular Solution, He Delivers, Force 2011, and Popular Force. We treat them as a single entity.

other Peruvian party, including APRA, which has long been considered Peru's largest party.[55]

The possible consolidation of a *Fujimorista* party is a surprising – indeed, paradoxical – outcome. Alberto Fujimori openly disparaged parties and never invested in one of his own. He created and discarded four different parties during his presidency and opposed his daughter's efforts to institutionalize *Fujimorismo* after his imprisonment.[56] According to Keiko Fujimori, her father "doesn't believe in parties. Like a good *caudillo*, he doesn't like to cede power. And to build a party organization, you have to cede power."[57]

Yet several factors may facilitate *Fujimorismo*'s consolidation. One is its condition as an authoritarian successor party (see Loxton, Chapter 9, this volume). Fujimori's authoritarian regime left several legacies that facilitated subsequent party-building efforts. One is an established brand. Due to his government's success in stabilizing the economy and defeating the Shining Path, Fujimori was enormously popular in the mid-1990s and retained substantial support through the end of his presidency (Carrión 2006).[58] Even after revelations of massive corruption and abuse of power triggered his fall from the presidency, Fujimori retained the support of an important segment of the electorate. In a 2006 survey, for example, 48 percent of respondents expressed a positive view of his presidency.[59] In 2011, 30 percent of respondents ranked the Fujimori government as the most effective in the last fifty years (Ipsos 2011), and a 2013 survey found that 42 percent of Peruvians viewed the performance of the Fujimori government as "good" or "very good."[60] Thus, *Fujimorismo* retained a potential base upon which to build.

Fujimori's authoritarian regime also left behind a patchwork of local patronage networks that could be used for party-building. Although Fujimori was notoriously reluctant to build a party organization, he made an exception in 1997, when he delegated to Absalón Vásquez the task of preparing a party – Let's Go Neighbor (VV) – to compete in the 1998 municipal elections. Vásquez used state resources to recruit

---

[55] According to Meléndez's survey research (personal communication), 2.0 percent of Peruvian voters are hardcore *Apristas*, while 6.3 percent "lean APRA."
[56] Author's interview with Keiko Fujimori, July 25, 2013.
[57] Author's interview with Keiko Fujimori, July 25, 2013.
[58] When Fujimori was sworn in for an illegal third term in August 2000, his approval rating stood at 45 percent (Carrión 2006: 126).
[59] Ipsos Apoyo survey, January 2006.
[60] GfK survey, June 18–19, 2013.

dozens of mayors and city council members into a "Tammany Hall-like" machine."[61] Although Fujimori subsequently abandoned Vásquez's project, VV networks provided a critical foundation for party-rebuilding in the mid-2000s.[62]

A third authoritarian legacy that facilitated party-rebuilding was clientelist linkages. Fujimori's heavy investment in politicized social programs gave rise to extensive clientelist networks (Roberts 1995; Schady 2000). Lacking a party, Fujimori created these linkages via the state (Roberts 1995), establishing strong ties to soup kitchens (*comedores*), mothers' clubs, and squatters' associations, particularly in the lower-income districts surrounding Lima.[63] Many of these networks survived – albeit in a weakened state – after Fujimori's fall from power, and *Fujimorista* leaders viewed them as the "organizational pillars" of their party-building project.[64] Though modest, the network of soup kitchens provided *Fujimorismo* with an organizational platform that was unavailable to most new parties.

Fujimorista party-building was also facilitated by polarization and conflict. For *Fujimoristas*, the 2000 transition ushered in a period of conflict and struggle that they universally describe as the "era of persecution" (Urrutia 2011a). Fujimori supporters were treated as pariahs, scorned by much of the media, and occasionally insulted in public.[65] More than 200 *Fujimorista* officials were prosecuted for corruption or human rights violations in the early 2000s.[66] Many of them were convicted and imprisoned,[67] and dozens of others were investigated, charged but not convicted,

---

[61] Author's interviews with *Fujimorista* advisor Guido Lucioni, June 16, 2011; also author's interview with ex-legislator Martha Moyano, May 5, 2011.

[62] Author's interviews with Guido Lucioni, June 16, 2011, and Keiko Fujimori, July 25, 2013.

[63] Author's interviews with ex-*Fujimorista* legislator Martha Moyano, May 6, 2011, and *Fujimorista* parliamentary advisor Guido Lucioni, June 16, 2011.

[64] Author's interview with Guido Lucioni, June 16, 2011. Also interview with Martha Moyano, May 6, 2011. Keiko Fujimori called the soup kitchens were "our principal base organization" (author's interview, July 25, 2013).

[65] As Keiko Fujimori put it, "the media ignored us ... We practically did not exist. And that created more solidarity among us" (author's interview, July 25, 2013). Also author's interview with ex-*Fujimorista* legislator Martha Moyano, May 6, 2011.

[66] According to Adriana Urrutia, 217 *Fujimoristas* faced "constitutional accusations" between July 2000 and July 2003 (Urrutia 2011a: 102).

[67] These included ex-intelligence advisor Vladimiro Montesinos, ex-prime minister Víctor Joy Way, ex-interior minister Juan Briones, ex-intelligence chief Julio Salazar Monroe, and ex-attorney general Blanca Nélida Colán.

or given suspended sentences.[68] In 2002, three prominent *Fujimorista* legislators, including former President of Congress Martha Chávez, were expelled from Congress. Finally, Fujimori himself was tried and convicted in 2007. Although Fujimori's conviction was generally perceived (in Peru and abroad) as legitimate, *Fujimoristas* viewed it as an act of political persecution.[69]

The perceived persecution of 2001–2007 helped to unify and revitalize *Fujimorismo*.[70] As *Fujimorista* Jorge Morelli put it, "there is no better glue for a political movement than a feeling of injustice … We were like Christians in Rome."[71] Likewise, Keiko Fujimori observed that although *Fujimorismo* was "badly divided" in the wake of Fujimori's fall, "once they started arresting people, persecuting people, we united."[72]

Fujimorismo thus reemerged in the early 2000s as a loosely organized social movement seeking Fujimori's return. Fragmented into several organizations, including *La Resistencia* and the *Comandos del Chino*, the movement was composed of an estimated 800 hardcore activists, many of whom were former military personnel angered by human rights investigations and trials.[73] The early movement mobilized against the prosecution of Fujimori government officials, the expulsion of *Fujimorista* legislatores, and the Truth and Reconciliation Commission and other transitional justice measures.[74] *Fujimoristas* also broadcasted radio

---

[68] These include ex-ministers Luis Salas, Carlos Boloña, César Saucedo, Absalón Vásquez, and Jaime Yoshiyama, ex-president of Congress Martha Chávez, Fujimori's brother and advisor, Santiago, and Fujimori's daughter Keiko.

[69] Also author's interviews with Jorge Morelli, Lima, June 18, 2011, Martha Moyano, May 6, 2011, and Santiago Fujimori, Lima, March 24, 2011. Also Navarro (2011: 53–54) and Urrutia (2011b).

[70] See Novarro (2011) and Urrutia (2011a, 2011b). Also author's interview with ex-legislator Martha Moyano, Lima, May 6, 2011.

[71] Author's interview, Lima, June 18, 2011. Indeed, *Fujimorista* leaders began to use the "persecution" to mobilize activists. A common chant at *Fujimorista* rallies was "more persecution, more *Fujimorismo*" (author's interviews with Keiko Fujimori, July 25, 2013). According to Keiko Fujimori, when she speaks to new activists, "I tell them about the persecution…. It generates solidarity, commitment and pride" (author's interview, July 25, 2013).

[72] Author's interview, July 25, 2013. According to *Fujimorista* politician Martha Moyano, "We went through ten years of the [anti-*Fujimoristas*] calling us corrupt, calling us killers. But the attacks made us much stronger. So I guess we need to thank [the anti-*Fujimoristas*]. They gave us the tools we needed to rebuild" (author's interview, May 6, 2011).

[73] Author's interview with Keiko Fujimori, July 25, 2013. Also Urrutia (2011a: 108–111).

[74] Author's interviews with Jorge Morelli, Lima, June 18, 2011; Martha Moyano, May 6, 2011; Guido Lucioni, June 16, 2011; Santiago Fujimori, Lima, March 24, 2011; and Keiko Fujimori, July 25, 2013.

programs (such as the Hour of the *Chino*) with messages from Fujimori, held events to celebrate important *Fujimorista* anniversaries, and organized meetings across the country in which the exiled Fujimori communicated with locals via radio (and later, Skype).[75] Although the movement was relatively small, it was characterized by a strong identity and subculture (Navarro 2011; Urrutia 2011b), rooted primarily in the shared experience of the 1990s counterinsurgency.[76]

Fujimorismo began to take on a party-like form in 2005, when the exiled Fujimori created Yes He Delivers (*Sí Cumple*) in the hope of returning to Peru to run for president in 2006.[77] Built upon political networks from the old VV machine,[78] and with about 3,000 core activists, *Sí Cumple* dedicated much of 2005–2006 to a grassroots "Fujimori is Coming" campaign, mobilizing supporters around the idea of Fujimori's return and eventual candidacy.[79] After Fujimori was detained in Chile, the party nominated hardline *Fujimorista* Martha Chávez as its presidential candidate. Chávez won only 7.4 percent of the vote, but *Fujimorismo* captured 13 percent of the legislative vote and Keiko Fujimori was elected to Congress with more votes than any other candidate. Keiko's performance established her as a viable presidential candidate and a unifying figure within the movement.

After 2006, *Fujimorismo* lost much of its pariah status and gained far greater access to the media. Nevertheless, it maintained a foot in the social movement arena, mobilizing protests against Fujimori's extradition, trial, and conviction in 2006–2007.[80] At the same time, the party continued to build up its organization, establishing a significant presence in the urban popular sectors (Urrutia 2011b). In 2011, Keiko Fujimori

---

[75] Author's interviews with Jorge Morelli, Lima, June 18, 2011; Martha Moyano, May 6, 2011; Santiago Fujimori, Lima, March 24, 2011; and Keiko Fujimori, July 25, 2013.

[76] All *Fujimoristas* embraced hardline counterinsurgency positions and deeply distrusted human rights advocacy, which they viewed as soft on (and potentially sympathetic to) terrorism. Thus, all *Fujimoristas* rejected human rights trials, the Truth and Reconciliation Commission, and other transitional justice measures as unjust – even treasonous – attacks on the armed forces. Based on author's interviews with Jorge Morelli, Lima, June 18, 2011; Martha Moyano, May 6, 2011; and Guido Lucioni, June 16, 2011. On the importance of ideology for party cohesion, see Hanson (2010).

[77] Author's interview with Keiko Fujimori, July 25, 2013.

[78] Author's interviews with *Fujimorista* politicians Guido Lucioni, June 16, 2011 and Keiko Fujimori, July 25, 2013.

[79] Author's interview with Martha Moyano, May 6, 2011.

[80] According to ex-*Fujimorista* legislator Martha Moyano, Fujimori's trial was a "powerful tool" for mobilizing activists and unifying the movement (author's interview, May 6, 2011).

nearly won the presidency and *Fujimorismo* became the second largest party in Congress. Following the election, *Fujimorismo* (now renamed Popular Force) launched a new organization-building effort. By 2013, the party had provincial offices in 100 of 195 provinces, as well as 160 fully operational "base committees" in Lima.[81] Popular Force was one of the few national parties to compete seriously in the 2014 regional elections, winning three governorships (more than any other party).

Fujimorismo's future prospects remain uncertain. The party remains highly personalistic, and at times, it has been paralyzed by conflict between *Albertistas*, who remain strictly devoted to a movement-like defense of Alberto, and *Keikistas*, who, without openly opposing Alberto, seek to build a party that will survive him. It is not clear that *Fujimorismo* will survive Alberto Fujimori's departure from the political scene. Thus, one possible scenario remains something akin to the Odriísta National Union (UNO), ex-dictator Manuel Odría's party, which remained strong in the decade following his 1956 fall from power (finishing third, with 28 percent of the vote, in the annulled 1962 election), but weakened and eventually disappeared after his death.[82] Even if *Fujimorismo* does survive Alberto, it is likely to confront many of the same organization-building challenges facing other Peruvian parties. For example, a majority of the *Fujimorista* legislators elected in 2011 and 2016 were either political amateurs or *transfugas*, which suggests that Popular Force may be vulnerable to defection in the future. Given its solid base and Keiko Fujimori's emergence as an electorally viable leader, however, *Fujimorismo* stands a reasonable chance of consolidating as party.

CONCLUSION

Peru is an extreme case of party decomposition. Nearly twenty-five years after the collapse of the party system, Peruvian politicians have not rebuilt the old parties or constructed new ones. The Peruvian case suggests that there may be a self-reinforcing logic to party collapse. Peruvian politicians learned how to win elections without parties and have developed a set of informal norms, practices, and organizational substitutes to facilitate such efforts. Indeed, electoral competition appears to be selecting

[81] Author's interview with Keiko Fujimori, July 25, 2013.
[82] Other parties led by former dictators that enjoyed initial success but then collapsed include Gustavo Rojas Pinilla's National Popular Alliance (ANAPO) in Colombia and Hugo Banzer's Nationalist Democratic Action (ADN) in Bolivia (Loxton and Levitsky 2015).

for partisan free agents, or those with the skills and resources needed to win elections in the absence of parties. To the extent that free agents and "coalitions of independents" displace party politicians, the prospects for a "return to parties" are likely to decline.

What can be done to rebuild parties? Although Peruvian observers continue to focus on institutional solutions, such as electoral reform and a stricter Political Parties Law, we are skeptical that parties can be "engineered" in this way. Electoral rules do not create effective party brands or enduring partisan identities. Activist bases cannot be legislated into existence.

One reform that might help, however, is the introduction of a system of public finance.[83] Public finance cannot create parties, but as Bruhn's chapter (Chapter 8, this volume) shows, it may help them consolidate. Peru's national parties lack effective labels and the resources necessary to induce local-level politicians to join (and remain in) their ranks. Public finance cannot resolve the former problem, but it might help to attenuate the latter one. If national parties possessed resources to offer individual politicians, the incentives to go it alone would likely weaken. Publicly financed parties would not have to rely on candidates who purchase their way onto legislative lists.[84]

There are two problems with a public finance-based solution, however. First, as Bruhn notes, public finance cannot create strong partisan attachments. Thus, in the absence of conditions that give rise to new party-building projects, the contribution of public finance may be limited. Second, given widespread public distrust of parties and politicians, a system of public finance would likely be highly unpopular. And given the notorious weakness of the Peruvian state, it is likely that voters would quickly associate public finance with political scandals and corruption – thereby reinforcing public hostility toward parties. Thus, when systems of public financing are associated in voters' minds with corruption and "partyarchy," they may ultimately have a boomerang effect, undermining, rather than strengthening, parties. Given the extraordinarily high levels of public distrust in Peru, it is not difficult to imagine such a scenario.

To conclude on more theoretical terms, our analysis adopts a middle ground between the optimism of scholars who view party-building

---

[83] A 2015 electoral reform introduced a relatively modest system of public funding for parties in Congress, which is expected to begin in 2017.

[84] The growing practice of candidates purchasing legislative candidacies appears to have opened the door to candidates linked to drug trafficking and other illicit activities.

as highly likely under conditions of stable electoral competition,[85] and the pessimism of scholars who argue that due to the influence of mass media technologies, contemporary party-building is exceedingly difficult.[86] The case of *Fujimorismo* suggests that party-building remains possible even where conditions for party-building are unfavorable. However, the Peruvian case also makes clear the incentives for party-building are weaker today, and that electoral competition is insufficient to create such incentives. Rather, strong parties emerge out of structural conditions – such as periods of intense social and political conflict – that emerge only infrequently. In the absence of such conditions, party collapse may indeed have a Humpty Dumpty effect: once parties disappear and politicians develop the means to win elections without them, all of the electoral engineering in the world may be insufficient to put them back together again.

---

[85] These include Aldrich (1995), Brader and Tucker (2001), and Lupu and Stokes (2010).
[86] See, for example, Levitsky and Cameron (2003) and Mainwaring and Zoco (2007).

16

Past the Poof Moment

Cuba's Future Political Parties

Jorge I. Domínguez

Cuba's last freely competitive multiparty election was held in 1948. Today's octogenarians and nonagenarians may remember it, but probably with not as much enthusiasm as their first spin on a Model-T Ford. Thus the title for this chapter must be whimsical because no one has a good account of how or when this conceptual moment might be reached: the "poof moment" will be evident when the old political regime will have changed enough, or would have been replaced, to permit multiparty politics and freely competitive elections again. No Cuban alive at that time is likely to remember prerevolutionary elections.

Communist regimes in Europe *c.* 1990 collapsed without much scholarly anticipation. There is a vast retrospective scholarship on how the political regime transition took place but not a persuasive anticipatory scholarship. In East Asia, other than North Korea the remaining communist regimes have enacted market economy changes in order to avoid political regime changes, and in so doing also provide little comparative guidance for Cuba's imagined multipartisan future. Cuba's market economy transition is, at best, at its earliest stages and economic growth rates have remained anemic since the 2008–2009 worldwide economic crisis, which curtailed Venezuela's support for the Cuban economy.

The most intriguing anticipatory imagination of a nonexistent multiparty system was Juan Linz's (1967: 264–275) endeavor to characterize Spain's multiparty system one decade before Francisco Franco's death. A giant in the scholarly study of comparative politics during the second half of the twentieth century, Linz concluded that Spain's

I am grateful to Anna Grzymała-Busse, Alejandro de la Fuente, and my co-editors of this book for comments on an earlier draft. Mistakes are my responsibility alone.

postauthoritarian political system would be in the hands of two comparably very large parties: the Communists and the Christian Democrats. Yet, Communists and Christian Democrats would turn out to be minor political actors in post-Franco Spain. Linz's effort remains valuable, however, because he asked the right questions, asking scholars to:

- look at the political cleavages built on social cleavages;
- consider societal changes that may blur inferences from the past;
- look at the political parties of the last preauthoritarian period;
- take into account the possible electoral law; and
- compare to "most similar" cases (in Linz's case, Italy).

In this analysis, I expect to show that Cuba has had no experience of politicizing social cleavages to build or sustain political parties. Racial and social class differences impinged on party formation and development only in a limited way before the revolution; it is unlikely that they would be used to build new parties in the future. The prospects for parties built on regionalism or religion are even worse. Societal changes in the intervening decades have not altered the likelihood of successful conversion of social into political cleavages and have decimated the prospects for the rebirth of any of the old parties, save the Communists. The one salvageable political cleavage from before the revolution is the politics of intransigence, albeit not a good augur for democratic politics.

The most durable organizational legacy from before the revolution is the "party of power," which the Liberal Party was before 1959 and, after revolutionary victory, the Communists became. By "party of power" I mean a political party without which it is very difficult to organize and sustain an effective governing coalition. Such a party need not win a majority of the votes, but it is one without which no government will last long in power. In the future, much will depend on the internal evolution of the ruling Cuban Communist Party (PCC) and the rules and laws that may be constructed at or following the poof moment.[1]

In this book, thinking about Cuba's possible future party system allows us to consider a wider array of possible party outcomes. The book examines what makes some new parties successful while most new parties fail. This chapter ponders what may be the basis for new parties that could

---

[1] There is a vast literature outside Cuba fantasizing about a Cuba that does not exist. I have contributed to some of it (Domínguez 2006). There is, however, little political science work published by Cuban scholars who live and work in Cuba regarding their country's future circumstances. One such, on the political economy of future property ownership and the role of cooperatives, is Piñeiro Harnecker (2013).

grow out of an authoritarian regime, which is one of the key concerns of Chapter 1 of this volume.

POLITICAL PARTIES BEFORE THE 1959 REVOLUTION

Cuba's last freely competitive presidential election, held in 1948, characterized well the nation's politics at the time (Stokes 1951). Cuba's parties and party system had jelled in time for the 1940 presidential election and become fairly stable. In the four freest national elections (1944 and 1948 for president and Congress, and 1946 and 1950 for Congress), between 42 and 56 percent of members of the Chamber of Deputies had been reelected (computed from Riera 1955). These were not transient parties but, rather, well organized and durable political organizations that reelected their parliamentarians.

In 1948, there were four principal parties or party coalitions contending for the presidency. Cuba had six provinces. None of the presidential candidates won an outright majority in any province except for the governing Auténtico-Republican coalition which won big in Matanzas province. There was, therefore, substantial national electoral uniformity – Cuba had no Quebec, no Bavaria, no Catalonia, and no Scotland, each of which has a local party representing its interests while lacking significant strength in every other region.

In Cuba, national parties ran national campaigns. The winning Auténtico-Republican presidential candidate, Carlos Prío, for example, won a high of 54.5 percent in Matanzas and a low of 41.5 percent in La Habana provinces. The Auténtico-Republican coalition had become principally a clientelistic machine, disbursing goodies across the country. To the extent that the Auténticos had a political profile, they were mildly nationalist, and they had led Cuba's opposition to Fulgencio Batista's rule between 1933 and 1944.

Second, the Liberals and the Democrats coalesced. They overperformed in Pinar del Río province, but in the other five provinces these two parties came within 3 percentage points of their national average of 30.4 percent. They were also clientelistic machines. The Liberals had been Cuba's nearly indispensable ruling party. They had staffed Gerardo Machado's presidency-turned-dictatorship in the 1920s; they had stabilized Batista's rule prior to his convening the convention that would write the 1940 Constitution. Though defeated by the Auténticos in 1944 as part of Batista's coalition, the Liberals crossed the aisle to join the Prío government soon after the 1948 election and would in the end, after Batista overthrew Prío by coup, support Batista's dictatorship in the 1950s. In 1948, the Liberals and the Democrats (the latter, a conservative party) proved, by running as an opposition alliance, that they could perform well without the spigot of resources from the national treasury. To the extent that these parties had a political profile, they supported US interests in Cuba.

The two weakest parties ran alone, and both ran better in La Habana and Oriente provinces. The Ortodoxos (one-sixth of the national vote, one-fifth each in La Habana and Oriente provinces) had one platform plank: they opposed corruption. Their slogan was "honor against money;" their symbol, a broom. Theirs was a party of principle, vociferous in protesting against corruption and how Cuba was governed. In its advocacy, it was "intransigent" – a word its presidential candidate, Eduardo Chibás, cherished (Grupos de Propaganda Doctrinal Ortodoxa 1951). One of its deputy candidates for the 1952 elections (cancelled because of Batista's coup in March 1952) was Fidel Castro.

Finally, the prerevolutionary communist party, the Popular Socialist Party (PSP, est. 1925), earned 7.5 percent of the national vote, making it one of the more electorally successful communist parties in Latin America (only Chile's Communists would have a stronger electoral history). It won nearly one-tenth of the votes in La Habana province, although it also did well in Oriente where it had unionized many sugar mill workers. The Communists became a lawful party as Batista's allies at the end of the 1930s and were defeated as part of his coalition in 1944. In 1948, they ran alone – their one and only solo contest in a competitive election. The Communists had been skilled parliamentarians at the constitutional convention and in Congress. Although only 5.5 percent of the members of Congress, they accounted for 15.5 percent of the bills submitted; only one of the thirty-five bills submitted by Communist parliamentarians sought particularistic benefits for a single person, in contrast to a pattern common for other parties. Communist parliamentarians caucused regularly, worked as a team on legislation, sponsored and listened to a research advisory commission, drafted member speeches in caucus, and tithed a part of their salary to the party. They voted with high party discipline (Escalante and Marinello 1945). They contributed Cabinet Ministers to the Batista presidency (1940–1944). They founded the Cuban Labor Confederation (CTC, Central de Trabajadores de Cuba) and supported the Batista coalition and the US–Soviet alliance in World War II. Organized labor and university intellectuals were prominent in its leadership.

There are three implications from this account of the party system. First, there were too few votes to be gained either in regionalist representation (despite mild regional variation in voting patterns), or in labor union representation and responsible behavior in parliament that earned the Communists only one out of fourteen nationally cast votes.

Second, the politics of principled intransigence, with support from a sixth of the electorate, has an uncut umbilical cord with the revolutionary regime that came to power in 1959 – repudiating decadent tourism, proclaiming the worth of moral incentives and the construction of a "new man," in the mid-1960s dispatching homosexuals to hard-labor camps in the hopes of converting them into heterosexuals, and even (briefly) seeking to substitute nonalcoholic malt for beer for the sake of productivity. There may be a good future for a party of intransigents.

Third, the Liberals were Cuba's first "party of power." They were part of the government coalition under seven of the ten Cuban presidents elected to a term between 1902 and 1958, including two whose elections were marred by fraud (Machado, Batista). They were masters of clientelist programming and appeals. They could be loyal, or cross the aisle, in search of political advantage. And only they and the Communists successfully appealed across racial lines.

SOCIAL CLEAVAGES IN SEARCH FOR A POLITICAL PARTY?

There were social class differences in the Cuban electorate. In December 1951, in anticipation of the 1952 presidential election (cancelled because of Batista's coup), a public opinion survey ascertained that upper-class Cubans favored the Auténtico candidate, Carlos Hevia, by approximately three-to-one over Batista, who was once again running for president. The Auténticos were also well ahead of the Ortodoxos among the upper class. Among the lower class, the election was much closer, with Hevia ahead of Batista but within the statistical margin of error, and the Ortodoxos coming in third (Goldenberg 1965: 111). Nevertheless, no candidate or their parties made distinctive social class appeals to the electorate. Only the Communists did, but to little effect.

At the 1940 constitutional convention, the Communists had proposed various restrictions on schools run by Roman Catholic religious orders; the Roman Catholic Church resisted successfully (Amigó 1947). The Church had relatively modest social support, however. In 1954, the University of Havana Catholic Students Association conducted a national survey (N = 4000). It found that only 24 percent of Catholics attended Church services regularly and only 16 percent of all marriages were formalized in church (Jover Marimón 1971: 400–401). Cuba had already become secular in advance of the 1959 revolution. A small Cuban Christian Democratic party was founded in the 1950s but it never contested a free competitive election.

Cuba's most significant latent social cleavage pertained to race relations (de la Fuente 2001). A party based on race – the Independent Party of Color – was founded in 1908, following Cuba's independence in 1902, but it was crushed militarily in 1912. Cuban parties based on race have been legally banned ever since. Since the early twentieth century, the Liberal Party encouraged the election of Afro-Cuban politicians to the senate and the house on the party's ticket; one of them, senator Martín Morúa, sponsored the law that prohibited race-based political parties. In time, other parties also appealed to Afro-Cubans. Fulgencio Batista, himself a mulatto, included various Afro-Cuban politicians in his coalition, principally from the Liberal and communist parties. Blas Roca, long-serving communist party general secretary, was a mulatto and a close Batista ally from 1939 to 1945 (*Fundamentos 1944*). Through its leadership of the labor confederation (CTC), the Communists helped to narrow the wage gap between white and black skilled workers. In the 1943 census, blacks scored lower in all income categories, controlled for all occupations, but the white–black gap was narrowest among the skilled workers (República de Cuba 1945: 1203–1205). Nevertheless, from the late 1930s onward no Cuban party, not even the Communists, operated as a race-based party or made its principal appeals on the basis of race-based politics. The Communists focused on class-related policies, though in the expectation that "correct" class policies would also reduce the gaps between Cubans across the color spectrum.

In short, there were plausible social bases to establish political parties on the basis of race, though probably not on the basis of religion, and no party succeeded on either of these bases. Only the Communists focused on class-based policies, and they were the smallest of the parties in Congress.

TRENDS BEARING ON SOCIAL CLEAVAGES AFTER 1959

In over the half-century since 1959, have social changes increased the likelihood of transforming social differences with regard to region, social class and inequality, religion, and race into political cleavages on which parties may be built? No.

Regional differences persisted after the revolution, and still exist. But, except for the obviously better circumstances of life in the city of Havana, the differences across Cuba's provinces have been modest and are an unlikely basis for new regionalist parties (Martín Posada and Núñez Moreno 2012).

Income inequality and inequality in access to goods and services widened dramatically after 1990, following the end of subsidies from the Soviet Union. Poverty reappeared amid about a fifth of the population. Since 1990, downward social mobility greatly outstripped instances of upward social mobility; the mix further deepened inequalities. As before 1959, social class will likely have an impact on voting behavior but will also be an unlikely basis for a principally class-based party. Since the 1960s, the Cuban Communist Party (PCC, est. 1965) has appealed broadly for national support, not just for support from the proletariat or income-disadvantaged groups. The government's emphasis on universal rights of access to education, health care, and welfare subsidies stresses the commonality of Cubans in their nationhood (Espina Prieto 2004; Espina Prieto and Togores González 2012; Togores and García 2004). Cubans have never responded predominantly to partisan appeals based on social class differences.

The government and the PCC confronted organized religion, and especially the Roman Catholic Church, in the 1960s. A half-century later, the controls on organized religion had relaxed and the Cardinal Archbishop of Havana, Jaime Ortega, played an important role in 2011 to facilitate the freeing of most remaining prisoners of conscience. Various Catholic dioceses publish magazines and there is increasingly open missionary work. Yet, interviews with leading church figures suggest that the proportion of Cubans who attend Roman Catholic mass on a regular basis remained a single-digit number, though perhaps 15–20 percent of the population identified with some community of faith (Centro de Investigaciones Psicológicas y Sociológicas 1993). Only the Roman Catholic Church has the territorial organization to pose a civil society challenge to the PCC but the number of priests remains only about 300 in a country of just over eleven million people. Moreover, led by Cardinal Ortega for a third of a century until 2016, the Bishops have resisted behaving as a party or becoming its sponsors. A Catholic Party still seems unlikely, though more Catholic associations would likely spring up.

Cuba's racial circumstances have changed over the past several decades. By the early 1980s, racial differences between blacks and whites had disappeared in estimates of life expectancy and high school completion – outcomes far better than in other racially heterogeneous societies such as Brazil and the United States. Racial differences persisted in the geography of housing and the likelihood of imprisonment (Meerman 2001; de la Fuente 2001: 309–316). And, at the start of the 2010s, there were two other underaccomplishments. One was membership in the key political institutions, such as the Political Bureau of the PCC chosen in 2016 (five Afro-Cubans out of seventeen members) and the executive committee of the Council of Ministers (none of the eight is Afro-Cuban). The other was explicitly expressed racial prejudice. In a comparative study of such discursive behavior, Sawyer et al. (2004) found that such racism was significantly higher in Cuba than in the United States, Puerto Rico, or the Dominican Republic. Since the start of the 1960s, Cuba's official leadership claimed to have solved the race problem; hence, it became counterrevolutionary to discuss it in public.

Cuba's official silence on race prevented the lawful formation of independent civil society Afro-Cuban associations as well as the construction of race-based parties. It delayed by a half-century a Cuba-wide conversation on race. Yet, at the margin of official Cuba, such a conversation has begun, and Afro-Cuban identity affirmation has strengthened through music, the plastic arts, literature, Afro-Cuban religiosity, and to some extent (Cubans have very limited access) via the Internet (de la Fuente 2012). There is, however, no race-based opposition political movement. There are Afro-Cuban leaders and members of human rights, dissident, and opposition organizations, but they demand their rights as citizens, less so as minorities with race-dependent rights. Loyal intellectual critics of aspects of official policies (Morales Domínguez 2007) want the political and social regimes to live up to their principles in order to strengthen, not to topple, them. Past the poof moment, a race-based political party is unlikely.

The comparative evidence in this book bolsters this conclusion. No chapter discusses Afro-Latin parties in other Latin American countries. Raúl Madrid's thoughtful chapter (Chapter 11, this volume) on ethnopopulism focuses on indigenous communities in their wider contexts in Bolivia, Ecuador, and Guatemala, but not on Afro-Ecuadorans who are numerous but do not coalesce in a party. Latin America's most likely locale for a racially based party is Brazil, yet in this book you will not read about Afro-Brazilian parties. Scott Mainwaring's magisterial study of party systems, with special attention to Brazil, allocates less than a page to the possibility of race-based parties in Brazil (1999: 46). The most intellectually stimulating study of a race-based political party in Brazil – Brazilian Black Front, or *Frente Negra Brasileira* – explains why the party was so short-lived, why it collapsed, and why it was never revived (Fernandes 1969; see also Telles 2004). Race in Latin America has not produced race-based parties, nor are such parties likely.

In conclusion, the patterns from the prerevolutionary and revolutionary time periods are likely to endure. Past the poof moment, Cuba will likely remain bereft of parties that frame mass appeals based on region, religion, social class, or race, even if some parties will draw greater or lesser shares of support from these social categories.

FROM A "PARTY OF POWER" TO THE FOUR FACES OF THE PCC

Any thinking about Cuba's partisan future must examine its Communist Party (est. 1965). Opposition contestation in Cuba has been remarkably limited for a half-century. The most effective Cuban opposition politician, capable of gathering thousands of signatures on a petition for political reform, Oswaldo Payá, died in 2012. No other Cuban opposition politician, party, or political organization has been able to mobilize more than a few hundred adherents. Chapter 1 of this volume looks out for new party formation under authoritarian rule, but Cuba's authoritarian regime – unlike Brazil's from the 1960s to the 1980s or Mexico's for seventy decades – has made opposition party construction unsafe and impossible.

Absent significant contestation, the Communist Party, under its own or a different name, is likely to be a "party of power," as in Russia and China – ideology may slacken, policies and party names may change, but the leaders of the former Communist Party hold onto power. Russia's Vladimir Putin well exemplifies the establishment of such a party. The Russian Communist Party, as such, is in the opposition to Putin but many of the former elites of the once-ruling Communist Party – Putin among them – have joined the new "party of power," no matter the changes in its name (Colton 2007). One of Putin's political resources has been the restoration of pride in nation and Russia's role in the world. Ideology otherwise matters little and policies are pragmatic. The Chinese Communist Party is another "party of power," which has successfully changed economic policies dramatically, transited to a political system that has brought prosperity to many through its adoption of many market economy features, won nationalist support, earned a leading place in world politics and economy, and not hesitated to repress opposition or civil society (Friedman 2008). China's is an economically transformed still-authoritarian political regime. Russia's is a more open but still semiauthoritarian political regime with many fewer economic accomplishments. In both, a "party of power" rules, and opposition electoral prospects are weak.

The PCC already resembles such a "party of power," holding together various tendencies that promote or resist market-oriented policy changes, seek or repel accommodation with the United States, and embrace or shun the liberalization of social and political rules toward homosexuals. As with the contemporary Chinese Communist Party, and Putin's rule, the Cuban Communists are proud of having defied the United States and upheld Cuban sovereignty notwithstanding adversity, played an outsized worldwide role, outlived the collapse of the Soviet Union and East Central European communist regimes, constructed a feeling of pride in being a Cuban, and built the means of social cohesion through various social policies, including the narrowing racial gaps noted above. Cuba's Constitution (Article 5) describes the PCC as the "organized vanguard of the Cuban nation." In 2013, Raúl Castro announced that he would step down as Cuba's president in 2018 and designated Miguel Díaz Canel (born 1960) as his first vice president and successor. Thus the party's most likely near-term future, still seeking to avoid a freely competitive election, is to consolidate as a de-ideologized party of power, enacting further market reforms in the search for prosperity, and sustaining a few politically liberalizing initiatives to defuse conflicts.

Past the poof moment, however, this party of power will face options with regard to its future and also face internal fissiparous strains. What may be learned from the experience of communist parties in East Central Europe that transited toward democratic political systems? "One of the bigger surprises of the communist collapse in East Central Europe in 1989," writes Anna Grzymała-Busse, "was the persistence of the former ruling political parties ... In all but Estonia and Latvia, these parties survived, competed in democratic elections, and in some cases reinvented themselves as moderate democratic parties that went on to win elections, govern, and successfully oversee both economic and political reform" (Grzymała-Busse 2008: 91). The likelihood of such an outcome, she argues, is enhanced if the Communist Party had started along this path before the transition to democratic politics. Pragmatic reformers, accustomed to political negotiations, thus acquired a "usable past" for the time after the regime change transition; in East Central Europe before

1989, the Polish and Hungarian Communist Parties had experimented the most with market mechanisms and, within the context of a communist political regime, were the most "liberal." They made among the most successful transitions to become social-democratic-enough parties after the regime change, embracing both economic and political change (see also Grzymała-Busse 2002).

Led by President Raúl Castro since 2006, the PCC has embarked on a process of significant but gradual reforms. The most politically noteworthy changes are the rise of private agriculture and of small and medium sized businesses; the number of "self-employed" persons nearly tripled from September 2010 to July 2014, reaching 471,085 in a population of 11.2 million people (Pérez Villanueva 2016: 37). These changes remain contentious within the party. Thus far, Raúl Castro is their main supporter under his official slogan, a "prosperous and sustainable socialism," with socialism understood as central planning and state property, and prosperity and sustainability with market policies and disciplined budgets. On the side of political liberalization, policies that once repressed homosexuals have been cancelled, and there is wider space for academic debate in universities and think-tanks and less censorship of magazines published by Roman Catholic Bishops. On the economic side, this is far less than the changes enacted in Poland or Hungary before regime transition at the end of the 1980s, or in China since the end of the 1970s. On the political side, the changes also fall far short compared to the Polish or Hungarian experiences before the transition.

"Third wave democratization," Samuel Huntington (1991: 182) once argued, "moved forward on the false confidence of dictators" that they could win a competitive election. Indira Gandhi in India in 1977, Augusto Pinochet in 1988, Wojciech Jaruzelski in Poland in 1989, Daniel Ortega in Nicaragua in 1990 – all of these and others made these mistakes.

Since its postrevolutionary foundation in the 1960s, the PCC has not developed the skills to solicit the votes of citizens. Its organization is designed to rule; it has run many campaigns in support of the rulers but it lacks the experience of democratic competitive elections. However, at the municipal level, there have been multicandidate single-party elections since the mid-1970s. Research on these elections shows that only 2 percent of 150 voters surveyed mentioned membership in the Communist Party as a "desirable" quality in a municipal assembly candidate. The main motivation of voters in local elections was whether local candidates had a reputation for honesty, good neighborliness, and humane sensibilities. Cubans voted for their friends and neighbors. It is noteworthy, therefore, that most elected local officials are party members, held in high regard even if the PCC as an institution is not (Dilla, González, and Vincentelli 1992). This is not good news for the PCC but it is for party members likely to be elected no matter on which party name they run.

Within the framework of Chapters 1 and 3 of this volume, the Cuban Communist Party's brand adds little value on election day. Suppose, therefore, this Cuban party of power makes a similar mistake and holds a free election. It may lose because the Party lacks experience to elicit voter support in competitive elections, the brand attracts few voters, and its potential candidates may defect given the brand's weakness. The party could splinter into its various tendencies, whereupon the party's four faces are likely to emerge.

A partisan core would struggle to remain the indispensable party of power in any political coalition – not unlike the prerevolutionary Liberal Party – but this party of power would not have the monopoly clout that the PCC has hitherto had. The social democrats long harbored in the PCC, and motivated by a wish to take quicker advantage of the US market for economic growth, may be one splinter, perhaps evoking the traditions of Cuba's prerevolutionary Communist Party. For these social democrats, Raúl Castro has been constructing a usable past of market-oriented policies and some social and political liberalization.

Two other responses are possible, as Daniel Ziblatt (1998) and John Ishiyama (1999), among others, have noted for East Central Europe. One is "leftist retreat" (Czech Communist Party), which involves the successor party privileging its historic ideology, rejecting the free market, repudiating US influences, and becoming an antisystem party in the new democratic regime. Another is the "national-patriotic" response, common in the Balkans and the former Soviet Union, with an emphasis on the defense of the nation and deep suspicion of external influences. Fidel Castro and those most committed to his personal legacy illustrate both tendencies. To the very end of his presidency, he deemphasized market mechanisms, relied upon public exhortations and mass mobilizations, and railed against US imperialism on behalf of Cuba's honor everywhere. National-patriotic or principled-leftist Fidelista offshoots of the Communist Party are plausible. The first may seek to prevent US dominance. The second would relaunch the intransigence of the prerevolutionary Ortodoxos. (Fidel Castro would never associate with the word "retreat" but he may cherish a leftist intransigence.)

It is easier to imagine a coalition between the party of power and the social democrats and an alternative coalition between the national-patriots and the leftist-intransigents. The first would be the legacy of Raúl Castro's search for prosperity. The second evokes two slogans that Fidel Castro made famous, respectively, early in revolutionary rule and immediately following the collapse of the Soviet Union: "Fatherland or Death" and "Socialism or Death." Both might evolve as niche parties, as Greene presents them in Chapter 6 (this volume). But, as a hypothesis, the party of power could coalesce with any, given that principles do not restrain it.

THE POPULAR BASES OF THE POSTPOOF PARTIES
AND THE ELECTORAL LAW

The party of power, the national-patriotic party, and the leftist-intransigent parties would compete for a demographically well-defined segment of Cuba's population. At the start of the second decade of the twenty-first century, the largest Cuban quinquennial cohort was between ages forty-five and forty-nine; the size of this cohort was nearly twice the size of the cohort age five and below. Over a quarter of Cuba's population will be above age sixty by 2025. In 2011, life expectancy at birth was seventy-eight years (Oficina Nacional de Estadísticas e Información 2012: Cuadros 3.2, 3.12, 3.17). In short, Cuba will be a paradise for a party that represents the rights of pensioners. But Cuba's prospective elderly may not just be greedy for pensions. Cubans already in their sixties were socialized as young revolutionaries during the 1960s, the most formative moment of the country's and their own experiences. Cubans from the lead quinquennial cohort ages 45–49 witnessed the relative economic prosperity of the 1970s, the consolidation of successful state policies in health care and education, and the global spread of Cuban influence during the 1970s and 1980s. As embodied in the designated successor, First Vice President Miguel Díaz Canel, they may want to fix the problems with government policies, not overturn the political regime. And, in a postpoof Cuba, they could readily support any of the three parties closest to the Cuba of their youth.

If Cuba's elderly split their votes between the leftist-intransigents, the national-patriots, and the party of power – the pensioners voting for the latter's efficacy, the more ideologically motivated dividing their votes between the two other parties – Cuba's future social democrats may have a chance to win a disproportionate share of voters born after 1985, which was the last year of a period of sustained economic growth. The social democrats may be able to coalesce with the party of power. (As with the prerevolutionary Liberals, or the Institutional Revolutionary

Party in Mexico after 2000, or the Brazilian Democratic Movement Party (PMDB) in Brazil since 1985, the party of power need not be the largest party – the key is that a government coalition is very difficult to sustain without its partnership.) If so, the prospects for wider and deeper political and economic liberalization look good.

Cuba has had a large diaspora, geographically concentrated in southern Florida, which has become both economically prosperous and politically influential. The Cuba Research Institute from Florida International University has been polling the southern Florida Cuban-origin population for two decades. In 2014, its poll showed that 84 percent of respondents preferred to get their news in Spanish. Compare two categories. One is US citizen Cuban-Americans long resident in the United States; only 23 percent of these would "invest in a private business in Cuba if given the opportunity" and only 21 percent of them are likely to "return to Cuba to live" under "a more democratic form of government." The other category is the immigrants who arrived since the US–Cuban 1994 migration agreement; 56 percent of these would invest in a private business in Cuba and 34 percent of the total would return to live in Cuba (Cuban Research Institute 2014). In terms of the wisdom of investing, the Cuban diaspora is already divided. In terms of the likelihood of returning to Cuba to live, the diaspora is rather homogenous: no.

Miami elites have long sought to influence events in Cuba and would likely seek the same in the future. They will support market policies and sustained political liberalization. As in Miami today, so too in Cuba's future, they are likely to split between a center-right politically and economically "business" or "liberal" party versus a revanchist party that seeks the recovery of properties expropriated by the revolutionary government in 1959–1961 and to indict, convict, and imprison agents of the old regime. Because the diaspora is, by definition, not in Cuba, its influence is likely to be indirect, spending on television advertising and programming and funding the campaigns of new parties, some staffed by the minority of Cubans who would repatriate. One or both diaspora-supported parties could be large because some significant fraction of Cuban voters will look to Miami in search of economic growth.

Finally, Cuba's postpoof electoral law would have to change to permit free competitive elections. One feature could persist, however. Even in the February 2013 National Assembly elections in which the number of candidates equaled the number of posts to be filled, Cuban electoral districts are multimember. A voter may vote for the "united slate" (the Communist Party's preference), or vote blank or null or selectively. In the 2013 election, 23.5 percent of voters cast a nonconforming vote, that is, they voted null, blank, or selectively, for example, for some but not all of the candidates on the ballot (calculated from *Granma* 2013). To be elected, a deputy candidate must receive half of the votes. Thus a multiparty system could develop, resting on open-list proportional representation – what Cuban voters already face in multicandidate municipal elections with runoff options. Runoff provisions may help the party of power, the social democrats, and the center-right Miami-supported party, to the detriment of the left-intransigents, the national-patriots, and the revanchists.

THE POSTPOOF TRANSITION

In this chapter, I have stayed close to the knowable empirical evidence as informed by comparative political science. It is likely, however, that the specific paths to be followed may be greatly affected by the yet unknowable details of the postpoof transition. Consider three paths that comparative scholarship highlights.

One is a conflict path. Suppose the US government (under a post-2016 US president who reverses the US policy opening toward Cuba authorized in December 2014) and the revanchist political minority of the diaspora sustains a hardline. Suppose the post-Chávez political leadership in Venezuela can no longer bankroll Cuba's party of power. Would an economic crisis in Cuba intensify conflict, weaken the party of power severely, and leave a stark political confrontation between national-patriots, left-intransigents, and revanchists – for example, a domestic Cold War? Would such conflict, as the book's introduction and conclusion suggest, deepen polarization, heighten cohesion for each party, and lead to a few but strong successful parties, each espousing a clearly defined brand? Or would a persisting confrontation with a revanchist diaspora and the US government prevent the fractionalization of the ruling PCC and sustain its cohesion even longer?

The second approach constructs an electorally competitive dominant party. Suppose, instead, the Raúl Castro reforms raise economic standards and prolong the rule of the party of power. Would it delay a full transition to competitive democratic politics? Or would an economically stronger PCC follow a concede-to-thrive strategy, that is, from a position of newer economic strength further open up the political system in order to compete more successfully in prospective democratic elections, hoping to win and rule, even if no longer in authoritarian fashion (Slater and Wong 2013)?

A third option is a more open democratic transition. Levitsky and Way (2010) argue that competitive authoritarian regimes, which Cuba's may have become by that time, are more likely to democratize if there is high transnational linkage without many sanctions (i.e., carrots, not sticks). Suppose the US government, building on President Barack Obama's December 2014 policy shift toward the Cuban government, and the non-revanchist center-right of the Miami diaspora invest in Cuba and become the bankers of the economic transition. Would the ties of family affection and the rising high linkage of economic interest improve the opportunities for a democratic coalition between the social democrats and the center-right?

I do not know which of these scenarios is correct. But the general argument presented here implies a gradual political economic and political transition, already under way, en route to a splintering of the Communist Party because the social democrats want to accelerate the political and economic transition through economic growth linked to the US market, which other factions would resist. The alternative scenarios, above, could derail this process by weakening the party of power much earlier or discrediting a Cuban party excessively friendly to the US government or the diaspora. The concede-to-thrive strategy is to some extent also already under way, but it is unlikely to speed up the political opening. The PCC resisted the geopolitical shock of the collapse of the Soviet Union as well as the repeated shocks of economic slowdowns – two likely triggers of the concede-to-thrive strategy. From this ruling party's perspective, and certainly under Raúl Castro's presidency, "slow" is the approach. Yet, Raúl Castro is also constructing a "usable past" for the party of power and the social democrats still in its midst. His partisan offspring may be electorally competitive.

CONCLUSION

Juan Linz asked the right questions. Look at social and political cleavages before the installation of the authoritarian regime. Look at societal changes that may have affected such cleavage formation and development. Examine the political parties before the revolution. Look to comparative experiences. Consider possible implications of the electoral system and the electoral institutions with which voters are familiar. Applying this approach to Cuba, it seems highly likely that a key feature of the prerevolutionary political system would resurface, namely, Cuba will likely not have significant parties that frame their principal appeals based on politicized social cleavages such as region, religion, race, or social class.

The interaction between prerevolutionary traits and the experience of a half-century of PCC rule under Fidel and Raúl Castro is likely to sustain a party of power that will use and abuse state resources to get its candidates elected, and also a social democratic offshoot that supports reform. There may be a significant minority of the Cuban electorate that is nationalist, leftist, and intransigent under the legacies of the Ortodoxos and their once deputy candidate, Fidel Castro.

PCC–originated candidates have a high chance of being elected in a postpoof Cuba but the PCC brand seems weak, making it possible for the party to splinter into its principal tendencies. The demographics of the Cuban electorate give an edge to prospective social democrats and to a "party of power," with the latter remaining indispensable for government formation.

The Cuban diaspora, wealthy and politically engaged, will most likely be influential in Cuba's postpoof future but it is already split. A significant fraction of Cuban-origin Miami residents will likely engage with Cuba in business but the diaspora is unlikely to be the public face of the party that will next govern Cuba.

The most open question is whether the actual process of regime transition will witness intense conflict, a dominant party emphasis, or a more open process of change. Consistent with the introduction and conclusion to this book, the intense conflict path may be the more likely to lead to successful parties. Yet, in contemporary Cuba, one thinkable alternative is that Raúl Castro has been constructing a "usable past" for a more moderate big "center" of Cuban politics, designed to outlive him, a "party of power" along the lines noted in Loxton's chapter (Chapter 9, this volume) regarding conservative parties. And if he succeeds, then his legacy on Cuban politics may linger longer than his brother's.

17

Conclusions

Latin American Parties, Past and Present

Jorge I. Domínguez

Why do some old political parties endure while others fade? Why do some new parties succeed while others fail? This book has focused on new parties that emerged during Latin America's so-called third wave of democratization, starting approximately in 1978, and it seeks to explain the variation between new party success and failure. Chapter 1 by Levitsky, Loxton, and Van Dyck (LLV) asks readers to think about the new successful parties in the context of variation in outcomes, looking not just at successful new parties but also being mindful of new post-1978 parties that have failed. Party success, LLV tell us, is defined as winning at least 10 percent of the national vote in at least five consecutive national legislative elections.

This chapter widens the set of outcomes in two directions in order to assess whether the book's key arguments address other cases well. First, I relax the constraint of focusing only on new parties. LLV identify eleven parties formed since 1978 that have received at least 10 percent of the vote in five or more consecutive national legislative elections. In this chapter, I do not restrict my attention to parties formed since 1978. Instead, I also consider older parties that remained above the 10 percent standard for a century, or nearly so, to understand success independent of its "newness." My list of centenarians includes eight parties. Second, I relax the constraint that parties must reach the 10 percent threshold and, instead, examine parties that received many fewer votes, but that nevertheless endured for many decades: communist parties. Losing elections need not cast a party to the dustbin of history – surely not if in losing we find further reason to pledge our lives and our honor to the party's cause. In widening the book's scope here, I examine similarities and differences among Latin American parties, still active today, across a longer span of time: why have older parties succeeded and why have many unsuccessful parties endured as well?

I argue, first, that the microfoundations for partisan continuity need attention, that is, the mechanisms whereby citizens are socialized into partisanship and sustain collective conversations on which parties depend. These collective conversations may encompass many in mass membership parties, or just the few key party elites in electoral-professional parties, but no party survives without at least the latter kind of internal life. These internal features enable party leaders to map strategies for power. All successful parties, I argue, nurture identitarian attachments for partisanship. Some party strategies also emphasize content, at risk of permanent exclusion from presidential power, which I will illustrate through Latin America's opposition communist parties. Party brand (Chapters 1 and 3, this volume) matters above all to answer the question: who am I? It matters less for the question: what should I think?

Second, LLV's explanatory variable "territorial organization" should not be limited to the construction of party branches but, rather, encompass any means to sustain parties in localities, including family ties, patronage, and friendship networks. Third, I will show, with regard to some of Latin America's longest surviving and still-influential parties, that brand management and brand loyalty are malleable in the hands of masterful politicians, for whom brand dilution (but not brand abandonment) is a source of utility and pride as a strategy to reposition the party in its aim for perpetual power. Fourth, I emphasize two sources of partisan elite cohesion: we come from the same family or we have been a persecuted party (on the latter, see LLV). Either source of cohesion may suffice for long endurance even in the absence of much electoral success.

This chapter will then turn to the rupture of democratic regimes in the 1960s and 1970s, namely, the wave of military coups that injured and at times killed many parties. Thereafter, I inquire about three classic sources of new party formation. First, are there social cleavages on which parties may be built? Do differences regarding geographic territory, race, ethnicity, social class (workers, businesses) or religion give rise to political parties? Second, do severe political cleavages between elite politicians launch parties? Do civil wars, revolutions, and heroic contestation over the fate of authoritarian regimes give rise to parties? Third, do ambitious content-free politicians scour for votes, adopting and adapting their ideas successfully to clear the political market of the day?

Once old parties survive or new parties are established, how do they further survive and win? I examine party financing, private or public, the usable pasts of parties associated with discredited regimes, and the value of partisan organization nationwide and subnationally, seeking to avoid both the perils of niche parties and the severing of vertical partisan ties between national and local leaders. I conclude by examining some keys to successful party consolidation, with attention to timing and strategy.

LATIN AMERICA'S CENTENARIAN POLITICAL PARTIES: THE JURASSICS AND THE COMMUNISTS

Nearly a half-century ago, Charles Anderson (1967) famously argued that Latin American politics resembled a "living museum." Notwithstanding significant conflict and economic and social change, key political structures and behaviors endured. Anderson's observation applied best to the centenarian and quasi-centenarian political parties in Colombia, Honduras, Uruguay, Paraguay, and Mexico. Admittedly, the Colombian Liberal Party of Carlos Lleras Restrepo (1966–1970) was more of an economic modernizer than its predecessors, and the Institutional Revolutionary Party (PRI) of Gustavo Díaz Ordaz (1964–1970) had demilitarized decades earlier. But as will be clear in the next section, more than the labels had endured in this partisan recreation of a movie fantasy, where the dinosaurs of yesterday remain alive and powerful today – *Jurassic Park*.

The world has few centenarian political parties but Latin America has several: Colombia's Liberals and Conservatives, Honduras' Liberals and *Nacionales*, Uruguay's Colorados and Blancos, and Paraguay's Colorados, while Mexico's PRI was founded under a different name in the 1920s. Since their foundation to the end of the twentieth century, no other party governed these countries. Colombia, Honduras, and Uruguay had partisan duopolies; Paraguay's Colorados and Mexico's PRI ruled for decades in authoritarian regimes. I will call these eight the Jurassic parties.

Moreover, several Latin American countries also nurtured nearly centenarian communist parties, founded following the Bolshevik revolution in imperial Russia. The Cuban Communist Party rules Cuba. Chilean Communist Party student leaders played a significant role in organizing university student protests against President Sebastián Piñera's government and in the 2012 election were elected congressional deputies.

These quite different partisan dinosaurs are still alive and often influential. For all, political socialization and interpersonal communication – bonding – are keys to party survival and cohesion. All have changed the substantive meaning of their brand over time: brand maintenance required brand change. The Jurassics and the communists differ on a key point: the communists rarely reach the LLV standard while the Jurassics always have.

The communists have been much more programmatic and had until the 1980s preferred to be principled losers than influential winners. The communists changed their brand during and after the 1980s, anticipating or immediately following the collapse of European communism and the shifts in Chinese communism. The noncommunist Jurassics, never ideological, nevertheless further changed their brands in response to the economic crisis of the 1980s. The Jurassic parties have been clientelist and power-focused above all other considerations; principles, programs, and policies mattered only to suit the moment. Their territorial presence has been their defining trait.

"Strict" Aldrichistas

Political parties regulate competition and channel the ambitions of politicians who seek elective office. They start within their internal ranks, and they then contest other parties. To win election, a party coordinates collective action to persuade voters to support its candidates. Once in office, parties coordinate the collective choices that officeholders must make. In addressing these challenges, politicians and parties may or may not be motivated by principles, programs, or policies on specific issues, but they are surely motivated by ambition. John Aldrich (1995: 18–27) articulated this view of parties to explain the rise and consolidation of parties in the United States. His analysis fits parties more widely. I will call "strict" *Aldrichistas* those Latin American parties that are motivated mainly by ambition, not by principles, programs, or policies.

Mexico's PRI exemplifies a strict *Aldrichista* political party – it has wanted to win and rule. Full stop! The PRI adapted from its origins as a deal between military chieftains, persecuted the Roman Catholic Church at one moment and made it its informal ally at another, designed successful and long-lasting import substitution policies at one time and vanguard neoliberal economic policies at another, and opposed US economic sanctions on Cuba at the same time that it cooperated with the US Central Intelligence Agency to spy on Cuban officials. Generations of impressive PRI leaders mainly wanted to win. In 2012, their approach was again vindicated when their candidate, Enrique Peña Nieto, was elected president of Mexico, campaigning from the opposition while saying almost nothing about the great issues of the day.

Colombia's Liberals and Uruguay's Colorados were similarly, albeit at different historical junctures, architects of import substitution policies and dismantlers of such policies, adversaries of the Conservatives and the Blancos in their respective countries, and ordinarily coalescent with the same Conservatives and the same Blancos for many decades, at times under schemes formally enshrined in the respective national constitutions, and at times out of simple electoral calculation.

Strict *Aldrichista* parties in Latin America invoked principles, programs, and policies regarding issues, but did so vaguely and flexibly. Their internal structure often made it difficult to articulate a singular party program. Uruguay's electoral law long ensured that formal factions could run their own lists under the same party label; the electoral law's double simultaneous vote aggregated the votes for the otherwise independent lists of the same party to determine who won the most votes for the executive (sometimes a collegial entity, sometimes a president) and the legislature. Colombia's National Front, founded in 1958, lasted four presidential elections. Constitutionally it wedded the Liberal and Conservative parties to each other, compelling them to split seats in Congress and terms in the presidency. These strict *Aldrichista* parties did not care much for principles, programs, and policies, and even if they had, they could not have articulated and implemented them.

However, the strict *Aldrichista* parties were not born this way. In the nineteenth century, Colombia's Liberals and Conservatives constructed political differences and nurtured political loyalties and interests regarding the role of the Roman Catholic Church and the relationship between state and economy. Similarly, at the start of the twentieth century, Uruguay's Colorados and Blancos constructed their basis of support around the differences between town (Montevideo) and country. In both examples, these attachments were forged at war and sealed in blood. Significant traces of those birth marks would endure for decades. And this shared bonding in war and suffering is common to many of the successful "new" parties, as LLV and other authors in the volume note – shared victimization birthed and sustained the PT (Workers' Party) (Van Dyck, Chapter 5, this volume), the FMLN (Farabundo Martí National Liberation Front) (Holland, Chapter 10, this volume), the FSLN (Sandinista Front for National Liberation), and the PRD (Party of the Democratic Revolution) (Van Dyck, Chapter 5 and Greene, Chapter 6, this volume), and, in their own self-construction, the UDI (Independent

Democratic Union) (Loxton, Chapter 9 and Luna, Chapter 4, this volume), and ARENA (Nationalist Republican Alliance) (Loxton, Chapter 9, this volume). In the language of Lupu's chapter, each had an "appealing, consistent, and differentiable party brand."

How did the Jurassic parties change from ancient blood-oath fraternities into strict *Aldrichistas* and how did they survive as civil wars ended? How did one become a partisan, not merely a warrior? Strict *Aldrichista* parties find it difficult to formulate national appeals to voters. They are not membership parties; members rarely, or never, meet to discuss policies. Party primaries came late in their histories. Internal party life was thin or nonexistent. Adherents knew their attachments; they did not require impersonal discussions with strangers. Colombia's Liberal Party held its first presidential primary only in 1990 (Martz 1999–2000).

Pork, parents, parlors, and power are the four pillars on which these parties built the engines for change and the prospects for survival post–civil war. The centenarian and quasi-centenarian parties were clientelist (pork). They distributed government jobs to supporters, allocated resources to the localities that supported them disproportionately, and gave handouts to motivate voters and grease the wheels of local political machines. The Colombian and Uruguayan Jurassics at various times agreed to share those resources through public deals.

In the United States, two explanations long accounted for the survival of comparably long-lived parties, the Democrats and the Republicans. One is political socialization (parents) and the other is interpersonal communication (parlors). Political socialization starts with parents and the transmission of political ideas from parent to child. It emphasizes how society has significant effects on molding a child's political views and how a child's own personal growth leads to a personal political identity. Adults resist pressures to change their partisan attitudes (allowing for variation, of course). Resocialization in adulthood demands what Sears calls "an exacting and unusually powerful social situation" (Sears 1975: 135; see also Greenstein 1965; and for children's political socialization in Mexico, see Segovia 1975).

Reflecting upon the first century of Colombia's Liberals and Conservatives, Dix (1967: 211–216) noted their "hereditary hatreds," often manifested territorially. Colombian parties emerged from the nineteenth-century civil wars and politically homogenized across territories. In the 1960s, still one-third of Colombia's municipalities reported electoral margins for one over the other party of at least ten to one, and another 28 percent of the municipalities showed margins of at least three to one. Such territorial political homogeneity sustained these parties. Merely to call the Liberals and Conservatives clientelist misses the blood and guts that shaped them. Hartlyn (1988: 155–156) has shown other continuities: 89 percent of the municipalities voting Conservative in 1946 did so as well in 1978, with 63 percent being the equivalent number for the Liberals.

Political socialization of elites in strict *Aldrichista* parties may also explain the grip of family dynasties, such as the Roosevelts, the Kennedys, and the Bushes in modern US parties, just as it does in Latin American parties. Thus, in Uruguay, President Lorenzo Batlle Grau (1868–1872) was the father of President José Batlle Ordóñez (1899; 1903–1907; 1911–1915), who was the uncle of President Luis Batlle Berres (1947–1951; 1955–1956) and great-uncle of President Jorge Batlle Ibáñez (200–2005). In Colombia, among the Liberals, President Alberto Lleras Camargo (1945–1946; 1958–1962) was the cousin of President Carlos Lleras Restrepo (1966–1970). President Alfonso López Pumarejo (1934–1938; 1942–1945) was the father of President Alfonso López Michelsen (1972–1976). President Eduardo Santos (1938–1942) was the great-uncle of incumbent President Juan Manuel Santos (2010–). Among the Conservatives, President Mariano Ospina Pérez (1946–1950) was the nephew of President Pedro Nel Ospina (1922–1926) and the grandson of President Mariano Ospina Rodríguez (1857–1861). President Misael Pastrana (1970–1974) was the father of President Andrés Pastrana (1998–2002). Loyalty to party, politician, family, friend, community coalesced to define political life.

The circumstances in which the first Batlle and the last Batlle governed were utterly different. Uruguay was riddled by internal warfare until the first Batlle and it was a stable democracy under the latter. Colombia enjoyed one of its least violent historical moments since the 1940s under the elder Pastrana and one of the most violent under the younger Pastrana. The Batlles and the Pastranas inherited and transmitted the familiar propensities of partisanship and ruling.

Interpersonal political communication – parlors among elite and the rural poor – collectivized the effects of childhood and early adult socialization. The politically like-minded speak with each other with greater frequency. Such "bonding" social capital (Putnam 2000: 21–23) facilitates participation at the cost of democratic deliberation (Mutz 2006). Bonding social capital in political contexts bolsters partisanship. It reminds us why we belong together politically, why we co-own the party brand.

Political socialization and participatory-bonding social capital are produced in localities. Parties that have strong geographic bases draw strength from them. For much of the twentieth century, Uruguay's Colorados were dominant in the city of Montevideo and the Blancos in rural areas (Vanger 1963; Weinstein 1975; González 1995). Colombia's parties, as noted, have also a long tradition of geographic fiefdoms. Similarly, Baker (2009b) has shown for Mexico that political discussion networks help to explain the regionalization of Mexican politics – politically like-minded Mexicans talk to each other in the localities in which they live and as a result reinforce and sustain their partisanship. The territorial bases of the traditional parties were built and sustained through political socialization and interpersonal communication in geographic locations.

Finally, these parties focused on power, arranging constitutional and electoral laws to sustain themselves. In Mexico and Paraguay, the PRI and the Colorados were the lords in authoritarian political systems; the laws and the uses and abuses of power kept them entrenched for decades. In Uruguay, the electoral law – double simultaneous vote – made it almost impossible for a party other than the Blancos and Colorados to win in presidential (none did until the twenty-first century) or legislative elections and made it easier to co-opt newcomers to politics. In Colombia, in 1957 the Liberals and the Conservatives amended the Constitution to ensure that only members of their parties could be elected to public office for four rounds of quadrennial elections.

Pork, parents, parlors, and power rendered the strict *Aldrichista* parties successful. Sometimes they warred on each other. Sometimes they engineered peace and public order through pact-making and coalitions. They often reduced the prospects of popular participation, except to mobilize supporters to confront The Other. Over the decades, they implemented quite different economic strategies. In the social realm, Uruguay built a welfare state; Honduras remained poor and implemented rudimentary social policies. For decades as well as today, Uruguay has been in many respects an exemplary liberal democracy, whereas Colombia until the twenty-first century had been governed principally in liberal albeit oligarchic fashion, and Paraguay and Mexico as authoritarian regimes. Principles, programs, and policies tell us little about the transformation and endurance of strict *Aldrichista* parties. Pork, parents, parlors, and power tell us why they populated for so long Latin America's living museum, its very own Jurassic Park.

Pork and unprogrammatic traits made these parties distinctive but political socialization and interpersonal communication are the microfoundations of party-building and survival. In today's Latin America, Chile's UDI and El Salvador's ARENA parents pass on their beliefs to their children and send them to elite private schools. Brazil's PT members play soccer with each other and reinforce their partisan commitments through these networks of social capital. Mexico's PRD members, concentrated territorially in Mexico City, intensify their bonds arguing and arguing. The tools of party-building long ago invented on other continents worked for Latin America's Jurassics and today's new successful parties.

Lessons from the Jurassics also shed light on some of the reasons for new party failure in more recent times. The Colombian Liberals, the Mexican PRI, and other Jurassics did not disconnect the national from the local. When it happened for a brief period of time in Colombia (Muñoz and Dargent, Chapter 7, this volume), the parties suffered badly, and quickly moved to repair those links. When parties form at the national level without the territorial organization of localities, families, and conversation parlors – as Front for a Country in Solidarity (FREPASO) in Argentina (Van Dyck, Chapter 5, this volume) and Democratic Alliance M-19 (AD M-19) in Colombia (Holland, Chapter 10, this volume) – the party is likely to fail, as FREPASO and AD M-19 did in due course. Where the provincials reject a national alliance, the party is likely either to remain purely local (provincial parties in Argentina) or fragment and fail as in Eastern Bolivia (Eaton, Chapter 14, this volume). Family socialization and interpersonal communication matter as the building blocks of parties that operate locally but also to win national power.

The "best practices" of successful parties are, therefore:

- Be loyal to your ancestors, and socialize your kids politically.
- Be loyal to your friends, and talk with them about shared political bonds.
- Be loyal to your locality.
- You may not know what to think, but you know who you are.
- Win, no matter how.

The Communists

No Latin American communist party has ever won the presidency in a free competitive election, although the Chilean and Cuban communists were members of "popular fronts" with the incumbent president in the late 1930s and early 1940s, and the Chilean communists again in 1970–1973, and "popular front" is one way to describe the Broad Front (FA) at its launch in the early 1970s. Yet, the communist parties have existed in Latin America for as long as they have elsewhere. They have been persistently small but not transient, and often factionalized but rarely without some influence (Alexander 1957). They have been poor in financial resources or media access but often have star politicians who garner more attention than votes; Chile's Pablo Neruda, Nobel Prize in Literature, was a Chilean Communist Party senator and presidential candidate.

Latin American communists were not motivated principally by ambition for office. For many of them, principles mattered (Sutton 1990). These have been parties of expressive belief and ideological commitment – Here I stand, for I can do no other. Communist parties sought to regulate left candidacies but were not good at it because factionalism split the left over both principles and personalities. They had little hope of coordinating public policy choices and their expectation for success in mobilizing collective action was tempered by recurrent failures. Across much of the continent, communist parties were legally prohibited from contesting elections. Many communists suffered from state violence, formally or through extrajudicial executions and torture. Where they were lawful, in the peak years of the Cold War, the 1960s and the 1970s, only the Chilean Communists won as much as a sixth of the votes; the communist parties in Mexico, Costa Rica, Peru, Uruguay, and Venezuela won 5–10 percent of the votes, entering parliament under proportional representation electoral laws (Blasier 1987: 84).

Communist parties have had a paradoxical relationship to democratic politics. They ought to value it. Under authoritarian regimes, communists were often murdered, jailed, tortured, or exiled. Yet in the 1960s the communist parties of Venezuela and Colombia endorsed the use of political violence against the democratic regimes in their countries (as did the Guatemalan communist party against a much less open regime). Cuba's communist party established an authoritarian regime and jailed, executed, or exiled its opponents. In the 1980s, the resort to political violence by communists in Chile and El Salvador probably retarded the democratic transition in both. At their worst (Franco 2013: 120–151), communists were intolerant, narrow-minded, and turned on each other to commit acts of cruelty, most tragically so in the case of Peru's Shining Path (Theidon 2000).

Yet, at their best Latin American communist parties facilitated democratic transitions and tilted public policy to help lower-income citizens. They did so first in Chile and in Cuba at the end of the 1930s, when their joining respective "popular fronts" widened the public arena, established greater freedom for labor unions, and tilted social policy toward lower-income receivers (see Chapter 16, this volume).

Communist parties have much in common with noncommunist niche parties, as, Chapter 6 by Greene discusses them. Both kinds of parties create partisans, territorial organizations, and internal cohesion. Both kinds survive for many elections. Communist parties emerged facing unequal and unfair competition in barely democratic political systems. Communist parties vetted members, not just leaders, for ideological compatibility, and valued the party's identity and ideas. Faced with a hostile environment, their protective shells were built during long periods when governments banned them from operating lawfully. Designed to endure authoritarianism, they are less effective at adapting to the more open politics of democratic regimes.

Mexico's communists twice contributed to open up the political system, notwithstanding their persistent distrust of elections as a source of state legitimacy. In advance of the 1979 legislative election, the party was legalized (having been banned for thirty years), ran candidates for Congress, and became the third largest in the Chamber of Deputies. Then, in anticipation of the future fate of several European communist parties, in 1981, in 1987, and in 1989 Mexican communists joined other small left parties, dissolving the Mexican Communist Party (PCM) into the United Socialist Party of Mexico (PSUM), then into the Mexican Socialist Party (PMS), and finally as co-founders of the PRD. PSUM party leader, José Woldenberg, became the first president of the Federal Electoral Institute – a key architect of a key institution in enacting Mexico's democratic transition. PSUM leader Amalia García would be elected PRD governor of the state of Zacatecas.

The Communist Party of El Salvador, as a member of the FMLN, was a co-architect of the pact to end the domestic and international wars in El Salvador. The Communists became FMLN political party activists (see Holland, Chapter 10, this volume). In 1995, the FMLN convention dissolved the parties that had founded it and transformed them into mere "*tendencias*" within a single FMLN party. In 2004, long-time Communist leader Schafik Handal was the FMLN presidential candidate. The old Communists contributed to the organizational capacity of the FMLN but detracted from its appeals to more centrist voters; Handal was badly defeated in 2004 but the FMLN won the presidency in 2009 with a more centrist candidate, and in a tight election in 2014 it elected former FMLN military commander Salvador Sánchez Cerén as president. The postwar Communists in the FMLN sustained the peace in El Salvador, rendering its once revolutionary left allegiant to the democratic political system.

Brazil had two communist parties (Chilcote 1974) but the miniscule PCB (Brazilian Communist Party) renounced communism in the early 1990s. The PCdoB (Communist Party of Brazil), Maoist in the 1960s, engaged briefly in guerrilla warfare, broke with the Chinese and embraced Albania's Enver Hoxha as their own new leader within world socialism, becoming a lawful party allied to the PMDB (Brazilian Democratic Movement Party) upon the transition from military rule. The PCdoB nudged the PMDB government in the State of São Paulo to expand day care centers (Alvarez 1989: 227–228) and played a role in the changes in labor unions. In 1988, the PCdoB broke with the PMDB and allied with PT, eventually joining PT administrations. In the 2010 election, the PCdoB received 2.7 million votes (2.8 percent of the votes cast) and elected fifteen deputies to the federal chamber (http://electionresources.org/br/deputies.php?election=2010&state=BR). In the past three decades, the Communists helped to make the once violent and extremist left allegiant to the democratic regime.

Finally, the Chilean Communist Party, as noted, may have retarded the transition to democracy in the 1980s through its resort to political violence to oppose the Pinochet dictatorship. In 1990, its former allies joined the wide coalition of Christian Democrats and Socialists, leaving the Communists alone. In parliamentary elections since 2000, Communists, alone or in coalition, got 5–6 percent of the votes, in 2009 electing three deputies for the first time in thirty-seven years. These Communists also modified their brand, edging toward the center. In 2009, they endorsed Christian Democrat Eduardo Frei for the second round of the presidential election; in 2013, the Communists endorsed Socialist Michelle Bachelet in advance of the first round of the election. Young party leaders played key roles in the massive university student mobilizations against the Sebastián Piñera administration. Communist Camila Vallejo was elected president of the university students' federation. Alas, her own biography pays tribute to political socialization and interpersonal political bonding – both her parents were longtime Communist Party members, and so was her partner.

In these four examples, the Communists changed their historic preference for principles and chose one of two paths. The party dissolved in Mexico and El Salvador, joining larger coalitions where communist leaders and factions would play leading roles, often as left political moderates. These larger polyvalent parties twice have won the presidency of El Salvador and in 2006 nearly did so in Mexico. In Brazil and Chile, the communist parties moderated – relatively early in Brazil, but only in the twenty-first century in Chile – and joined other left and center parties in successful coalitions. In all but Chile, communist parties contributed to the transition from authoritarian rule; and in all four, they helped to make the left, including former violent revolutionaries, allegiant to democracy. Democratic stability requires counting the Communists in.

Nothing keeps a party smaller but more cohesive than state persecution. Murder of its militants worked to keep communist parties alive. Sacrificing for beliefs was a source of personal and collective strength. Communists at times split in multiple ways (again akin to Greene's niche parties), paralyzing their own efforts, but often their democratic centralism sustained their social capital, and thus their cohesion. When they privileged principles, programs, and policies above all, the Communists were dogmatic losers. When they resorted to political violence, they alienated most citizens and sometimes murdered each other. But, beginning in the 1980s in Brazil and Mexico, and in the 1990s elsewhere, they changed the content of the brand. Some Communists became statesmen during Mexico's democratic transition, co-architects of democratic peace in El Salvador, and elsewhere agents to secure the allegiance of the far-left to liberal democratic politics.

The guidelines for communist party endurance notwithstanding relentless electoral defeat may be:

- Suffer for the cause.
- Talk about the cause – to your children, your friends, and your lover(s).
- Change the cause to become influential in due course.
- But never lose sight that Communists care about a cause.

That same principled cohesion helps to explain the success of Brazil's PT and Mexico's PRD, which suffered actual hardship at the hands of the state (Van Dyck, Chapter 5, this volume), but it travels just as well to explain the origins of the strong parties of the right, UDI and ARENA, in Chile and El Salvador respectively – for the latter two spun founding myths about their victimization (Loxton, Chapter 9, this volume). The same skillful brand repositioning elected Lula president of Brazil in 2002 and nearly elected Andrés Manuel López Obrador president of Mexico in 2006. There is, however, a specific challenge on the left. Paraphrasing Marx and Engels's (1959: 6) 1848 *Communist Manifesto* – A specter is haunting Latin America's left – the specter of communism. It is the

specter of nearly a century of communist party defeat. How, then, can
the noncommunist left sustain what it shares with the Communists: the
belief in, and the commitment to, a cause? How may it become more
democratic than the Communists in its internal party life in order to better engage its membership? And how may the left win without betraying
its principles?

THE DEMOCRATIC REGIME RUPTURE AND
THE PARTIES

Latin America's first military coup wave, in the 1920s and 1930s, along-
side the worldwide economic depression in the 1930s, swept away many
parties. Latin America's second military coup wave in the 1960s and
1970s significantly disarticulated the party systems. As Remmer (1985)
showed, the longer the period of dictatorship, the greater the changes in
the party system, with Colombia and Honduras among the least changed
party systems. The impact of Latin America's second Great Depression in
the 1980s further damaged parties. In the previous discussion of political
socialization, I quoted Sears's argument to the effect that resocialization
in adulthood demands "an exacting and unusually powerful social situation." That is exactly what these accumulated calamities portended for
Latin America's parties, a reason for the emergence of new parties since
the late 1970s (see Roberts, Chapter 2, this volume), and the consolidation of this book's eleven LLV superstars. How did this rupture affect the
parties (for elaboration, see Domínguez 2013)?

Retrospective voting implies that voters hold rulers accountable for
performance in office. Voters punish politicians and parties when outcomes are bad and reward them when outcomes are good. This is not
the only explanation for voting behavior, of course. In previous pages,
clientelism, loyalties to families and friends, territorial organization, principles and persecutions, among others, also motivate citizens to support
or to withhold support from parties. But retrospective voting is, indeed, a
powerful explanation (Baker and Greene 2011; Lora and Olivera 2005;
Murillo, Oliveros, and Vaishnav 2010; Weyland 2000). Punitive retrospective voting is one element in the collapse of Venezuela's Democratic
Action (AD) and COPEI (Independent Electoral Political Organization
Committee) and Peru's APRA (American Popular Revolutionary Alliance)
in the 1990s and, after 2000, for the collapse of Argentina's Radical Civic
Union (UCR) and of all of the parties in Bolivia that had elected a president in the preceding two decades.

Positive retrospective voting – in particular, the China-generated positive exogenous shock on commodity exports that blessed Latin American economies and presidents after 2000 – also in part helps to explain three consecutive Peronist victories in Argentine presidential elections; the reelections of Bolivia's President Evo Morales heading the Movement toward Socialism (MAS); four consecutive PT presidential election victories in Brazil; three victories of the FA in Uruguay's presidential elections; and the personalist reelections of Hugo Chávez in Venezuela and Álvaro Uribe in Colombia.

Latin America's eight big Jurassic parties were also affected by punitive retrospective voting. That helps to explain in the twenty-first century the first victory of the FA over the Colorados and Blancos in Uruguay. In Colombia, the extremely high levels of violence help to explain the Liberal Party's defeat in 1998 and the Conservative Party's defeat in 2002, and as noted the election and reelection of President Uribe. Considerations of liberal democracy also weigh in. Paraguay's Colorados and Mexico's PRI lost when voters turned their back on authoritarian rule.

More generally, Michael Coppedge (1994) argued for Venezuela that long-established parties had created an oligopoly of power and employed the electoral laws and incumbent resources to sustain their grip on public office, which he called a "partyarchy." Coppedge used this framework to explain the defeat and subsequent collapse of Venezuela's AD and COPEI. The same scheme may be applied to the significant electoral setbacks for Colombia's Liberals and Conservatives and for Uruguay's Blancos and Colorados since 2000. Yet, Colombia's Liberals and Conservatives, and Uruguay's Blancos and Colorados, remain significant parties, still exceeding the 10 percent vote and seat thresholds in the most recent (2014) parliamentary elections that this book's first chapter requires to call a party successful. Those two political systems have undergone partisan realignment, not partisan collapse. In Venezuela, where party collapse did take place, an opposition coalition reformed in time to contest vigorously the 2010 and win the 2015 legislative elections, and nearly to win the first post-Chávez presidential election (Álvarez 2013).

Only in Peru did the party system collapse following the 1990 election, not to be replaced. Levitsky and Zavaleta, in Chapter 15, argue that the collapse may be explained employing the same variables as indicated in LLV: dilution and then abandonment of party brands, destruction of and barriers to party organizational construction, and decline in political polarization. They note the rise of party substitutes (business funds, media access, and celebrity politics) and the evolution of internal

norms that persistently set and kept Peru sliding on a path without parties – Latin America's sole remaining no-party system among the larger
countries.

Prolonged dictatorship and poor economic performance killed some
Latin American parties but none of the eight Jurassic parties that family and interpersonal communication sustained. It weakened others and
opened opportunities for some new parties. We turn now to the new
successful parties.

Social Cleavages in Search of Political Parties

A start for the scholarship on party formation focuses on social cleavages
(Lipset and Rokkan 1967) that may be politicized, as Chapter 1 argues,
becoming the conflict battleground to shape politics. Geography, ethnicity, social class and religion are four candidates for cleavage formation,
each of which this book addresses.

Between 2003 and 2008 in Bolivia, political preferences and regionalism overlapped closely and delineated political contestation – a South
American first since the Uruguayan party settlement early in the twentieth century. Chapter 14 by Kent Eaton studies this intense regional political polarization in Bolivia, which crystallized political attitudes on both
sides of this geographic divide. Across the generations, family socialization conversations can emphasize pride of place. Yet, unlike Uruguay's
Blancos facing Colorados – two parties whose discourse and electoral
constituencies approximated the city versus rural areas framing – a century ago, Bolivia's eastern provinces fell prey to political fragmentation
for various reasons: personalist, economic, interprovincial within the
east, and also between the provincial and national leaders in opposition
to President Evo Morales. As Eaton notes, Morales's own coalition has
undergone fissures; there could be wider fragmentation across the political spectrum. Another outcome could be an eastern coalition to make
common cause across economic and ethnic interests to take advantage of
Morales's loss of political support. Bolivia may still resurrect the grand
territorial political cleavage that once seemed possible but became blurred
from the internal fissures – or eastern Bolivia might aspire at most to the
independent provincial parties that are evident in some Argentine provinces (Gibson 2012). No new successful parties are based principally on
territorial cleavages, however, in Bolivia or elsewhere in Latin America.

National-scope ethnic-based parties arose in the late 1980s in Latin
America for the first time since the 1930s when the Getúlio Vargas's

government crushed the Brazilian Black Front (*Frente Negra Brasileira*) [Fernandes 1969: 187–233]. If grievances give rise to politicized social cleavages, surely race and ethnicity in Latin America should produce parties. Ethnicity or race emphasizes lineage descent and the cross-generational family socialization conversations that sustain pride and prejudice. In fact, ethnic- and race-based parties have been and remain rare. They have not been the arenas for explicit interpartisan conflict or state-wide civil violence. Chapter 11 by Madrid examines the variation between successful and unsuccessful ethnic parties. Successful ethnic parties build networks that cut across ethnic and other nonethnic communities. Their ethnopopulist appeals include deliberate efforts to reach out to nonindigenous peoples. In contrast, unsuccessful ethnic parties appeal just to their own kind and do not build wider coalitions.

Social class has been a workhorse of analyses regarding social cleavages yet most chapters in this book believe it explains little about new party formation after 1978. One of the most successful new parties, the PT, has governed Brazil. Yet Samuels and Zucco emphasize the PT's organizational strategy, not social class or other social cleavages, to evaluate its success. Chapter 5 by Van Dyck on new left parties concurs, emphasizing foundational variables (lack of access to state or media resources, high polarization, and also partisan organization) other than social class for these parties. Chapter 9 by Loxton on right-wing parties privileges the utility of legacies from a preceding authoritarian regime to launch and sustain such parties, only one of which is tethered to business elites. Chapter 4 by Luna examines the growth of Uruguay's FA as it veered toward a catchall multiclass party, appealing well beyond its original urban organized labor supporters – indeed, the Broad Front broadened. These nationwide parties did not go *mano-a-mano* over social class disputes.

Only Chapter 13 by William Barndt on corporation-based political parties privileges social class by his choice of topic. Barndt demonstrates how such parties may be created and grown – though none successfully enough to be included in the star set in Chapter 1. Corporation-based parties have been significant in elections in Bolivia and Ecuador and, in 2009, CEO Ricardo Martinelli was elected President of Panama, but none has demonstrated electoral staying power. Corporation-based parties are common though less significant in other Latin American countries.

Class-based conservative parties remain rare and corporation-based parties have been transient. Barndt, Loxton, and Eaton show how difficult it has been to engage business leaders and companies to create and sustain new conservative parties that meet the success standards of this book's Chapter 1; only El Salvador's ARENA and Chile's UDI qualify for inclusion as successful new conservative parties that, among other objectives, represent business interests. Barndt notes that corporation-based parties are more likely to succeed if they are based on just one corporation, which would fund it and staff it, than if its leaders seek to coordinate the business community to establish a business-anchored conservative party.

Democratic politics, as Lindblom (1977, Part V) argued, is marked by "the privileged position of business" because business executives are public officials in the market system and because business executives are also public officials in government and politics. Corporation-based parties in Latin America, therefore, are simply at the tail end of a worldwide distribution of parties linked to business.

Finally, what about religious cleavages? No LLV-anointed new successful party formed in Latin America since 1978 is Christian Democratic, even though Latin America was once home to significant and, for a time, growing Christian Democratic parties (Williams 1967). By the end of the twentieth century, once significant Christian Democratic parties had collapsed in Venezuela, El Salvador, Guatemala, and Peru; Christian Democrats had once been elected president in the first three of these countries (Mainwaring and Scully 2003). Three Christian Democrats were elected presidents of Chile; two of the three were father and son (in echoes of the Jurassic party success formula – party politics is the family business). But the last Christian Democrat president of Chile was elected in 1994. No Christian Democratic party has governed a Latin American country in this century. Evangelicals have formed parties but none that meets the LLV standard of success. Religion has attenuated as a basis for sharp political conflict, and thus it has attenuated as a basis for partisanship.

Social cleavage analysis contributes little, therefore, to the understanding of party systems in contemporary Latin America. Successful parties based on region could form in Bolivia but have yet to do so. Parties based on ethnicity can be successful but must appeal beyond their ethnic constituencies; none has met the 10 percent vote share in five consecutive elections. Religion is a less reliable basis for new parties than it once was. Social class helps to explain how voters may allocate their votes on election day but none of the qualifying parties (10 percent, five elections) is principally a social class–based party, none is a worker-dominant party, and only some transient parties are corporation-based. Look elsewhere to explain new party success.

Political Cleavages Generating Political Parties

The reason the Bolivian revolution of the 1950s fizzled and the country stumbled into stability, Samuel Huntington (1968: 315–334) once argued, is that, unlike in Mexico, political conflict in Bolivia was too tame and insufficiently violent. Intense and at times violent conflict cleaved Latin American polities in the 1970s and 1980s. Chapter 5 by Van Dyck and Chapter 1 by LLV argue that authoritarian regimes are the apt cauldron for new democratic left parties, such as Mexico's PRD and Brazil's PT, which had to rely on their own partisan organizational resources and access to civil society organizations to compensate for the lack of funding at their foundation and for the lack of access to television, which shunned them. Not only the new left felt aggrieved but, Loxton argues, so too did the new right, the UDI in Chile and ARENA in El Salvador. Both new major parties in El Salvador, ARENA and the FMLN (see Holland, Chapter 10, this volume), stem from a prolonged violent civil war. Nicaragua's only sustained new party, the FSLN, grew out of a revolutionary insurgency. In this respect, the experience of Latin America's communist parties – suffer for the cause – was generative for new parties on the left and the right. And the origins of these new parties recall the nineteenth-century civil war origins of the Jurassics in Colombia and Uruguay; the wars that enveloped Honduras also in the nineteenth century; and comparable violence from the Mexican Revolution during the first two decades of the twentieth century, which shaped the PRI's ancestor party, founded as a peace-making deal in 1929. The new parties (Van Dyck's and Loxton's chapters), just like the old ones at their origins, battled over the electorate.

Nothing is so helpful to new party formation as cohesion built around the intense support for, and fierce opposition to, authoritarian regimes, or birthed from the womb of internal war or, as in the case of Panama's PRD (Democratic Revolutionary Party), born again out of opposing US military invasion. In the LLV pantheon of successful parties, this Huntingtonian explanation fits well. First, shed your blood, then vote for me.

It becomes harder, however, to understand why "sufficiently" brutal dictatorships in Argentina and Guatemala, both of which met the Huntingtonian brutality standard, did not generate new successful parties, in contrast to Brazil, Chile, and El Salvador, each of which did on both the right and on the left. Similarly, it is odd that, in Nicaragua, a new party consolidated only on the left, not on the right. Levitsky and

Zavaleta argue that a *Fujimorista* party may be emerging belatedly from Peru's 1990s as a new party for the 2010s, nurtured in brand grievance over the jailing of Fujimori and building on a Loxton-like usable past of a dictatorship that defeated the Shining Path insurgency and tamed inflation. It is less clear why an anti-*Fujimorista* party has not emerged as well, given that antidictatorship parties exist amid Peru's neighboring countries.

Chapter 1 warns us to focus not just on new parties that succeed but also on new parties that failed soon enough. The unresolved challenge is to focus not just on the positive matches between a theoretical argument and its expected empirical prediction but also to consider when there is no such match. Latin America is understaffed in terms of political parties. The poor and the darker-skinned are not well enough represented in the party system. Given the reasons presented in the introduction and in various chapters, there should be more new successful parties. We now turn away from the parties there might be to the few successful parties that there are.

Political Parties Catch Supporters

Anthony Downs's rightly famous work, *An Economic Theory of Democracy*, was kidnapped by Americanists decades ago to shed light just on the US two-party system. Yet Downs also argued that "parties in a multi-party system try to remain as ideologically distinct from each other as possible" (Downs 1957: 115). That is what Latin American communist parties used to do and why they lost. Downs's hypothesis is nowhere true in Latin America today, even among communists; it is important to know why.

In Downs's scheme, German social democrats should not appeal to the business community and no blue-collar worker should vote Tory in the United Kingdom. Dutch Christian Historicals would rather be hysterical than join with Roman Catholics in a Christian Democratic Party. Alas, Downs was also wrong in these cases for reasons that Otto Kirchheimer explained, and lamented, for European parties. Catchall parties, Kirchheimer argued, had slackened their programmatic commitments, loosened their anchor in their mass membership, weakened their constituency appeals to reach out to everyone, and simplified their internal structures to emphasize popular candidates (Kirchheimer 1966). So too we read in our book. (The communist parties in Latin America were defeated because they refused to become catchall parties.)

How, then, do the new parties move toward catchall status? One general argument is to mimic the Jurassic parties and their "strict" *Aldrichista* strategies while avoiding the strategies of the historic communist parties. Therefore, deemphasize ideology, build the brand on long ties of family and friendship, serve your core constituents, and broaden your appeal.

* Forget dogmas, but know who you are.

The success of the FA and the UDI, Luna argues in Chapter 4, stems from each party reaching well beyond their founding bases. Key leaders know who they are (small elite for the UDI, elites and cadres for the FA). The Chilean business community was cash-rich but vote-poor and, Luna observes, through the UDI it invested its funds for clientelist appeals to the popular sectors, not just for programmatic ends. The FA's more decorous approach is constituency service, but to all constituents, as well as the broad personal appeal of its candidates. FA candidates appeal not just to the militant reds and ideologues but also to informal sector voters.

* Talk out of both sides of your mouth: segment and target the appeal.

This leads Luna to argue, insightfully, that Latin America's most successful catchall parties pursue segmented strategies. They narrow-cast their messages. They target their strategies. A former Tupamaro guerrilla can put on a jacket and tie to explain why Uruguay is a great investment site for businesses weary of unpredictable Argentine Peronists. A multimillionaire Chilean can run as a populist, promising to the rich, order, to the poor, jobs, and to all prosperity. The politics of valence issues – vote for me because I am more competent at delivering on the values and interests on which we all agree, such as prosperity – trumps the electoral politics of positional issues.

What, then, about the important argument regarding party brands, presented in Chapter 3 and echoed in Chapter 1 and other chapters? Brands certainly matter for successful parties. The Jurassics and the communists are the gold standard of successful brand survival. In Chapter 3, Lupu argues that partisanship responds to the actions of party elites, as the voters observe them. Parties whose brands become more diluted are likely to see their partisan ranks erode. As parties converge, voters become unable to distinguish between brands, and partisanship declines. Therefore, successful party-building and sustenance requires intraparty brand consistency and interparty brand differentiation. As Chapter 1 points out, Argentina's FREPASO, Ecuador's Pachakutik, and Bolivia's Movement of the Revolutionary Left (MIR) diluted their brand and were severely punished by voters in the subsequent elections. So did Venezuela's AD and Peru's APRA earlier in the 1990s. Levitsky and Zavaleta present extreme brand dilution as a key explanation for the lack of parties in Peru.

Nevertheless, some of Latin America's most successful politicians and parties have been sterling examples of some brand dilution. Fernando Henrique Cardoso and his Brazilian Social Democracy Party (PSDB) moved from the center-left through to the center-right in the quarter century that followed the PSDB's foundation in the late 1980s. Cardoso was twice elected Brazil's president. The PSDB has ranked first or second in every Brazilian presidential election since 1994. Lula and the PT followed a comparable path: they won the presidency in 2002, and the next three consecutive presidential elections, only because they shifted to the political center (Hunter 2010). In Mexico in 2006, Andrés Manuel López Obrador was at the center of the political spectrum, dragging his PRD there (Bruhn 2009). Earlier, Chile's Socialists blazed the path in their construction of a durable centrist democratic coalition that won every presidential election but one since 1989. The Colombian Liberals and Conservatives converged across nearly all policy issue areas by the late 1950s, and would remain the only parties capable of winning the presidency through the end of the century.

In this book, Samuels and Zucco explicitly disagree with the argument regarding brand dilution. The PT, they note, moderated and the policy gap between its own and the PSDB's presidencies is nowhere as wide as it may have been imagined in the mid-1990s. Instead, Samuels and Zucco argue, the PT tamed its ideological profile and policies and allied publicly and formally with ideological strangers – intraparty brand inconsistency and attenuated interparty brand differentiation helped the PT win and govern. The "petista way of governing" (*modo petista de governar*) combines two recipes for winning elections and governing Brazil: develop and keep highly institutionalized formal organization to coordinate all of the party's multiple and highly diverse constituents and develop and sustain opportunities for widespread and meaningful participation within the party – organizational cohesiveness and member inclusiveness through interpersonal communication. Or, to put it perhaps too simply, when two petistas meet and encounter three opinions, hug.

I am not an academic magician and cannot pretend that there are no differences on this question in this book. But a plausible hypothesis is that voters today, as over the past century, care less about program and more about identity. If so, then the key insight of the Jurassic parties remains pertinent: you may not know what to think about dogma but you know who you are. Lupu and others, after all, emphasize partisan *attachments*, not partisan theology. Some parties – Mexico's National Action Party (PAN) among them (Mizrahi 2003), not just the communists – rely on doctrinal socialization to create identity and hence attachment, but others may generate the same without the need for ideological orthodoxy: I love Brazil's PT or Chile's UDI or the Jurassic parties because I was born into a family of partisans, played soccer with the kids of party members, and went to picnics and outings only with friends and families sharing the same partisan attachments. René Descartes once notably argued, *cogito ergo sum* – I think, therefore I am.

• For Latin America's party brand attachments, *ergo sum* often suffices.

Surviving and Winning

Once launched on the right and with access to the business community, as Loxton, Luna, and Barndt indicate, parties such as ARENA, UDI, National Renovation (RN), and the corporation-based parties obtain funds from the business community. But, for parties on the left, financing is a challenge. At t–1, parties of the left toughened their souls and revved their militants because they had no access to state or business resources to finance party organization; the shared sufferings from exclusion fostered bonding, telescoping what the Jurassic parties had required a century to achieve. Then, Bruhn shows, at t+1 the early winners among left parties instituted public financing of campaigns to solve two problems. One is their own financing. And, because public funds are allocated as a function of votes cast in a previous election, funds go disproportionately to the parties that already did well, entrenching the old parties that had survived and the new parties that broke in, thereby disadvantaging yet newer parties.

Chapter 8 by Bruhn thus shows how Mexico's PRD, Brazil's PT, and Uruguay's FA gained disproportionately from the introduction of generous public financing. Such public funds do not account for the origins of new left parties but they help to explain why some new left parties met the LLV threshold for success (lots of public financing) in some countries while new parties have not been successful in Peru (no public financing) or Argentina and Colombia (limited public financing). The resulting cartel of parties risks the taint of partyarchy that has hurt the Jurassic parties as well as COPEI and Acción Democrática in Venezuela, but the temptation to survive outweighs the risk of that taint.

- Win early, get access to the state (pork or public funds), and thus win often.

Loxton and Barndt remind us that business forms few parties and note the rarity of new successful conservative parties, that is, parties that exceed the 10-percent voting threshold for five consecutive elections. But, Loxton argues, new conservative parties competing in democratic regimes are effective if they deploy their "usable past" from the preceding nondemocratic regime – to borrow from Grzymała-Busse's (2002) similar argument to explain successful post-1989 communist party survivors in Eastern Europe. Beyond the business ties, Loxton points to the utility of inherited clienteles and organizational infrastructure, credibility in demonstrated competence, and the cohesion born from the struggle to become respectable in the new regime, having already struggled in the past against godless anticapitalist communism.

Latin America's Jurassic parties felt no shame in embracing their long-inherited clienteles, enabling family and friendship networks, and emphasizing identitarian attachments. The new democratic offspring of nondemocratic ancestry are following along this well-trod path. The PT members may thrive at a neighborhood football game while its UDI counterparts may forego the game but sponsor a football league to cluster their popular-class supporters. The usable past enables the new right to contest the new left in their respective mass appeals.

Chapter 6 by Greene also makes the important cautionary point that parties may have useless or counterproductive pasts. Niche parties, he argues, are created by outsiders in competitive authoritarian regimes, built to survive in difficult conditions, and thus they rely upon inward-looking practices. They value longevity in activism and sacrifice for the cause – Latin America's communist parties have long been exemplar niche parties, doomed to lose and proud to protest. Greene also notes that some niche parties may acquire significant size in new democratic regimes, yet they continue to produce candidates whose policy preferences are out of step with most voters. In this respect, niche parties behave as Downs, quoted above, would expect them – catering just to their niche – but for a different reason from Downs's. Niche parties are not strategic vote maximizers; rather, niche parties are navel-gazers. Niche parties may temporarily shed the useless past, with the PAN following Fox to victory in 2000 and the PRD following López Obrador to near victory in 2006 but, absent leaders to drag them to the center, niche parties seek political "comfort food" in their niche.

How, then, to gaze not just upon inner sources of party pride – as recurrently defeated communist parties and other niche parties have long done – but on the prospects of electoral victory? One approach, just noted, is for very popular leaders to drag the once niche party toward the political center, becoming a catchall party. An alternative is for a niche-oriented national leadership to invest in subnational election victories where, in small communities, niche party supporters suffice to win democratic elections or, more commonly, where ideology matters little for municipal administration and voters support the nice boys and girls whom everyone knows locally (and where their guerrilla pasts do not frighten). That is the case of the FMLN in El Salvador for its first two decades contesting elections, as Chapter 10 shows. Holland points out that this strategy resembles that of Brazil's PT and Uruguay's FA in their investments in subnational elections. But it differs from the PT and the FA in that the FMLN continued to bristle with militant ideology: it lost national elections for that reason and won elections in local niches for that reason. At the national level, the FMLN preferred doctrinal discipline, expelling treacherous parliamentarians, over influencing national policy. Holland argues that the subnational strategy earns administrative and reputational capital – a former guerrilla commander may make a good town mayor. The FMLN won the presidency for the first time in 2009 when, learning from left parties in Brazil and Mexico, its presidential candidate ran as a moderate center-leftist. It won again in 2014 when its former guerrilla commander presidential candidate learned to speak as a moderate. These triumphs came because the FMLN had accustomed voters that it could govern competently – as it had in municipalities, including the capital city.

In contrast to the investments in impressive subnational resources in El Salvador, Brazil, and Uruguay, Muñoz and Dargent describe the wider disconnect between national and local politics in Colombia and, especially, in Peru. Reformists undercut the power of regional bosses in Colombia and Peru; they may have overachieved. Municipalization was the form of decentralization in both countries. It resulted in greater independence for municipal leaders but also greater difficulty in linking the national and local levels. In Peru, in addition, municipalization reforms created obstacles and disincentives for coordination between local politicians, either to create new regional parties or to link with national parties. The Peruvian municipalization implementation took place after the national parties had collapsed, thereby making it more difficult to create new parties.

The Colombian decentralization had two somewhat contradictory effects. First, the decentralization reform shook up the Jurassic parties and opened up possibilities for party realignment. Second, the coordination challenges between the local and national levels also made it difficult to create new parties. Therefore, after the disruptive realignment juncture at the start of the twenty-first century, by 2010 a new Colombian party system had settled in. The largest party in Congress had been created by the highly popular President Álvaro Uribe, the Social Party of National Unity or Party of the U (PSUN), with twenty-eight senators and forty-seven deputies. The next two biggest parties, however, remained the Jurassics: Conservatives (twenty-two senators, thirty-seven deputies) and the Liberals (seventeen senators, thirty-five deputies). There were three other new parties, of which the largest, Radical Change, had half of the senators and deputies of the third-placed Liberals and the other two had even fewer (Posada 2013). In the 2014 Congressional elections, the Liberals and the Conservatives again exceeded the 10-percent threshold of votes and seats; they ranked second and third in the Chamber of Deputies and third and fourth in the Senate. Muñoz and Dargent show the wide gap in Green Party performance at the national and subnational levels in the 2010 election: very good national performance of its presidential candidate who went on to the presidential second-round election, but a poor subnational and also legislative performance, ranking sixth in the senate and the chamber.

The decentralization scheme in Peru thus blocked party aggregation between the local and the national. In Colombia, the decentralization scheme ensured that the only parties that succeeded were those in the cartel of the already powerful: the "party of power" (the Party of the U), which could use the resources of the state, and the Jurassics, which notwithstanding decentralization were better positioned to link the national and the subnational. Decentralization made it harder to launch new successful parties in Colombia and, as a result, made it possible for the Jurassics to be born yet again.

Successful political parties build territorial organizations, a point that LLV make forcefully in their introduction and that is echoed throughout the chapters: Build at the national and subnational levels and coordinate between the two levels. If the attempt is made to build solely at one level, the effort at party formation and consolidation will likely fail (Argentina's FREPASO and Colombia's AD M-19 just at the national level; Eastern Bolivia's politicians and Peruvian efforts just at the local levels).

Van Dyck emphasizes that exclusion from state resources and from the media motivates parties to invest in organization. Samuels and Zucco build their case for the PT's successful inculcation of party attachments on the PT's effective, expansive, and inclusionary organization. Holland shows how the FMLN turned itself into a party from its bases as a guerrilla organization. Luna demonstrates how parties employ segmented organizational approaches in their strategies. Greene analyzes niche parties' propensity for inward-looking practices precisely because these parties worship at the altar of their own organization. Van Dyck, Luna, and Madrid emphasize the great value for parties that can make use of ready-made organizational allies in civil society. Barndt and Loxton point to business as investing its funds to build organizations for business-friendly parties, and Bruhn shows how public finance can contribute to the same end on the left. These party organizations are very different – from President Roberto Martinelli's checkbook to the legions of PT militants. But on the right and the left and in the center, the mass membership and the elite-led parties, all agree with the concluding eight words of Huntington's *Political Order in Changing Societies* (1968):

- "He controls the future who organizes its politics."

Strategies for Catchall Party Consolidation: Conclusion

Historical timing, Roberts explains in Chapter 2, may be decisive for successful party formation. He focuses on the two epochal transitions in the last quarter of the twentieth century, namely, from authoritarian rule and from import-substitution industrialization economic strategies. The first gave a new opportunity to parties to regulate competition and channel the ambitions of politicians who seek elective office. The second gave parties a new opportunity to disagree over economic policy. Roberts argues that, where right or center-right parties implemented market-oriented policies, then left or center-left parties opposed those policies, and both on the right and the left successful parties emerged and consolidated – Brazil, Chile, El Salvador, and Uruguay, as other chapters in this book also make clear. Roberts contends that where center-left or populist parties implemented the market-oriented policies, then market liberalization blurred the distinctions between parties and dealigned the party systems – Argentina, Bolivia, Costa Rica, Ecuador, and Venezuela. Center-left party brands were thus protected in the first set of countries because left parties opposed the economic transformation when it was enacted, but center-left and populist parties were injured in the second set because supporters could not understand what happened to the brand.

Now we may distinguish between brand dilution and brand abandonment. Brazil's PT, Chile's Socialists, El Salvador's FMLN, and Uruguay's FA won the presidency only following, and because of, brand dilution. What skewered the populist and center-left parties in the countries that witnessed deeper and widespread dealignment was brand abandonment. Susan Stokes (2001) first named this problem when she called it "neoliberalism by surprise." The problem is not the gradual, sustained, transparent, change in the content of the brand, publicly announced during an election campaign, as the PT, the Chilean Socialists, the FMLN, and the FA did. The problem is a sudden, dramatic change in brand content that is kept hidden from the electorate during the campaign and revealed only after the hitherto center-left party gains power. Brand dilution is about modulating ideas; thus it adjusts, retains, and expands brand loyalty. Brand abandonment is about treason to the base; it cuts the heart out of identitarian attachments and may kill the party. FREPASO's brand abandonment is what Lupu illustrates so well in his chapter: it killed FREPASO.

There is, therefore, a five-fold pattern to successful parties. First, there is timing: parties formed during or at the conclusion of war have an edge. That is the case of the Colombian Liberals and Conservatives, the Honduran Liberals and *Nacionales*, the Paraguayan Colorados, and the Uruguayan Colorados and Blancos as they crossed from the nineteenth to the twentieth centuries; the Colombian Jurassics also killed each other in large numbers during the La Violencia years in the 1940s and 1950s. It is also the case for Mexico's PRI, born under a different name and internal structure as a deal between military chieftains to end the political violence of the Mexican Revolution. Another example of great timing, Roberts indicates, are the two coinciding epochal transitions of the late twentieth century, especially if the right implemented the market reforms and the left opposed them at first. That delineated and consolidated parties on the right and the left – the gold-star winners in LLV's Chapter 1 in Brazil and Chile. And, evoking the same bellicose origins that once gave birth to the Jurassic parties, war was also the midwife of parties in El Salvador and Nicaragua in the 1980s and 1990s.

Second, give us an adversary but not an enemy; we do not want war or its recurrence (the Jurassics, FMLN, FSLN). Give us someone that frightens us in order to unite and, if necessary, discipline the base. Help us bond as friends and partisans but do not give us real cause to be afraid or cowed, for we want not to return to dictatorship. Brazil, Chile, El

Salvador, and Uruguay, as Roberts well points out, exemplify the sustained political differences that nurture party competition. Sustaining interparty differentiation guards the line between possibly useful brand dilution and suicidal brand abandonment.

Third, do the party's internal work. The Jurassics teach us well. Foster family transmission of partisan attachments. Foster bonding opportunities to reinforce such attachments through interpersonal communication. Picnics, sports, community activities, and other similar communicative and bonding endeavors create identitarian attachments and do not require ideological elaboration, positional issue commitments, or risk theological splintering over doctrine (thus avoiding the mistake of communist parties). Make sure the party members know who they *are*; it matters much less what they think.

Fourth, as the family-reliant Jurassics were the first to learn, feed the organization that you have. Fund a cartel of political parties (Bruhn, Chapter 8, this volume). When the left wins, enact generous public financing to remain viable and make it harder for another leftist party to outflank it. When the right wins, enact liberal rules to enable business financing (Barndt, Chapter 13 and Loxton, Chapter 9, this volume) of parties through individuals and corporations.

Finally, as Cuba's President Ramón Grau San Martín (1944–1948) once put it, "Let there be candy for everyone." Once in power, Grau abhorred good government types who sought to root out clientelist practices. Clientelism is the candy on which the Jurassics built their longevity. Clientelism has helped the UDI and Renovación Nacional in Chile (Luna, Chapter 4 and Loxton, Chapter 9, this volume), and the PFL (Liberal Front Party) in Brazil (Samuels and Zucco, Chapter 12, this volume), turn funds into votes; it enables corporation-based parties to compete. Alas, even parties of the left once in power, as the PT showed spectacularly during the Lula presidency, and the FSLN demonstrated in Nicaragua during the Daniel Ortega presidency in the twenty-first century, resort to clientelism.

Fear but not too much, build your organization, enjoy lawful access to public or private resources, and be relaxed toward the use of the resources of power at the right juncture – thus construct and sustain catchall parties. That is what the communist parties never learned. That is what the Jurassic parties always knew. That is what fills the LLV pantheon of post-1978 consolidated party heroes.

Bibliography

Abal Medina, Juan. 2009. "The Rise and Fall of the Argentine Center-Left: The Crisis of Frente Grande." *Party Politics* 15 (3): 357–375.

Abente, Diego. 1995. "A Party System in Transition: The Case of Paraguay." In Scott Mainwaring and Timothy Scully, eds. *Building Democratic Institutions*, 298–320. Stanford: Stanford University Press.

Abramo, Fundação Perseu. 2006. "Pesquisa de Opinião Pública." Dataset available at www.fpa.org.br.

Abrucio, Fernando. 1998. *Os Barões da Federação*. São Paulo: Editora Hucitec.

Achen, Christopher. 1992. "Social Psychology, Demographic Variables, and Linear Regression: Breaking the Iron Triangle in Voting Research." *Political Behavior* 14 (3): 195–211.

Albó, Xavier. 2002. *Pueblos indios en la política*. La Paz: Plural Editores.

Albright, Jeremy. 2009. "Does Political Knowledge Erode Party Attachments? A Review of the Cognitive Mobilization Thesis." *Electoral Studies* 28 (2): 248–260.

Aldrich, John. 1995. *Why Parties? The Origin and Transformation of Political Parties in America*. Chicago: University of Chicago Press.

2011. *Why Parties? A Second Look*. Chicago: University of Chicago Press.

Alesina, Alberto and Stephen Spear. 1988. "An Overlapping Generations Model of Electoral Competition." *Journal of Public Economics* 37 (3): 359–379.

Alexander, Robert. 1957. *Communism in Latin America*. New Brunswick: Rutgers University Press.

Alianza Republicana Nacionalista (ARENA). 2011. *30 años trabajando por El Salvador, 1981–2011: Historia política de ARENA*. San Salvador: Editorial Cinco.

Allison, Michael. 2006a. "Leaving the Past Behind? A Study of the FMLN and URNG Transitions to Political Parties." Ph.D. Dissertation, Department of Political Science, Florida State University.

2006b. "The Transition from Armed Opposition to Electoral Opposition in Central America." *Latin American Politics and Society* 48 (4): 137–162.

2010. "The Legacy of Violence on Post-Civil War Elections: The Case of El Salvador." *Studies in Comparative International Development* 45 (1): 104–124.

Allison, Michael and Alberto Martín Álvarez. 2012. "Unity and Disunity in the FMLN." *Latin American Politics and Society* 54 (4): 89–118.

Altman, David. 2004. "Redibujando el mapa electoral chileno: Incidencia de factores socioeconómicos y género en las urnas." *Revista de Ciencia Política* XXIV (2): 49–66.

2012. "Political Recruitment and Candidate Selection in Chile, 1990 to 2006: The Executive Branch." In Peter Siavelis and Scott Morgenstern, eds. *Pathways to Power: Political Recruitment and Candidate Selection in Latin America*, 241–291. University Park: Pennsylvania State University Press.

Altman, David and Rossana Castiglioni. 2006. "The 2004 Uruguayan Elections: A Political Earthquake Foretold." *Electoral Studies* 25 (1): 147–154.

Álvarez, Ángel. 2013. "Venezuela: Political Governance and Regime Change by Electoral Means." In Jorge I. Domínguez and Michael Shifter, eds. *Constructing Democratic Governance in Latin America*, 316–339. Fourth edition. Baltimore: Johns Hopkins University Press.

Álvarez, Chacho and Joaquín Morales Solá. 2002. *Sin excusas*. Buenos Aires: Editorial Sudamericana.

Álvarez, Sonia. 1989. "Politicizing Gender and Engendering Democracy." In Alfred Stepan, ed. *Democratizing Brazil: Problems of Transition and Consolidation*, 252–296. New York: Oxford University Press.

Amaral, Oswaldo. 2010. "As Transformações na Organização Interna do Partido dos Trabalhadores entre 1995 e 2009." Ph.D. Dissertation, Department of Political Science, Universidade Estadual de Campinas.

2011. "Ainda conectado: o PT e seus vínculos com a sociedade." *Opinião Pública* 17 (1): 1–44.

AmericasBarometer. "El Salvador," The Latin American Public Opinion Project (LAPOP), www.lapopsurveys.org.

Americas Watch. 1991. *El Salvador's Decade of Terror: Human Rights since the Assassination of Archbishop Romero*. New Haven: Yale University Press.

Ames, Barry. 2001. *The Deadlock of Democracy in Brazil: Interests, Identities, and Institutions in Comparative Politics*. Ann Arbor: University of Michigan Press.

Amigó, Gustavo. 1947. "La iglesia católica en Cuba." *Revista javeriana* 28: 138.

Anderson, Charles. 1967. *Politics and Economic Change in Latin America*. Princeton: Van Nostrand.

Andolina, Robert James. 1999. "Colonial Legacies and Plurinational Imaginaries: Indigenous Movement Politics in Ecuador and Bolivia." Ph.D. Dissertation, Department of Political Science, University of Minnesota.

Anria, Santiago. 2010. "Bolivia's MAS: Between Party and Movement." In Maxwell Cameron and Eric Hershberg, eds. *Latin America's Left Turns*, 101–126. Boulder: Lynne Rienner Press.

2013. "Social Movements, Party Organization, and Populism: Insights from the Bolivian MAS." *Latin American Politics and Society* 55 (Fall): 19–46.

Araoz, Mercedes and Roberto Urrunaga. 1996. *Finanzas municipales: inefi-ciencias y excesiva dependencia del gobierno central.* Working Paper 25, Centro de Investigación de la Universidad del Pacífico and Consorcio de Investigación Económica y Social.

Archer, Ronald. 1995. "Party Strength and Weakness in Colombia's Besieged Democracy." In Scott Mainwaring and Timothy R. Scully, eds. *Building Democratic Institutions: Party Systems in Latin America,* 164–199. Stanford: Stanford University Press.

Archer, Ronald and Matthew Soberg Shugart. 1997. "The Unrealized Potential of Presidential Dominance in Colombia." In Scott Mainwaring and Matthew Soberg Shugart, eds. *Presidentialism and Democracy in Latin America,* 110–160. New York: Cambridge University Press.

Arnson, Cynthia. 2000. "Window on the Past: A Declassified History of Death Squads in El Salvador." In Bruce Campbell and Arthur D. Brenner, eds. *Death Squads in Global Perspective: Murder with Deniability,* 85–124. New York: St. Martin's Press.

Arriola, Leonardo. 2013. *Multiethnic Coalitions in Africa: Business Financing of Opposition Election Campaigns.* New York: Cambridge University Press.

Artiga González, Álvaro. 2001. "El Salvador." In Manuel Alcántara and Flavia Freidenberg, eds. *Partidos Políticos de América Latina: Centroamérica, México y República Dominicana,* 137–178. Mexico City: Instituto Federal Electoral and Fondo de Cultura Económica.

2006. "El FMLN. Entre la oposición y el gobierno tras doce años de elec-ciones." *Revista Centroamericana de Ciencias Sociales* 3 (2): 49–84.

Arzheimer, Kai. 2006. "Dead Men Walking? Party Identification in Germany, 1977–2002." *Electoral Studies* 25 (4): 791–807.

Austin, Reginald and Maja Tjernström. 2003. *Funding of Political Parties and Election Campaigns.* Stockholm: International Institute for Democracy and Electoral Assistance (IDEA).

Auyero, Javier. 2000. *Poor People's Politics.* Durham: Duke University Press.

Ayo, Diego. 2011. *Autonomías, control social y democracia en la Bolivia de Evo Morales.* Unpublished book manuscript.

Bacon, David. 2002. "Blood on the Bananas." Unpublished essay. http://dbacon. igc.org/.

Bailey, Stanley. 2009. *Legacies of Race: Identities, Attitudes, and Politics in Brazil.* Stanford: Stanford University Press.

Baker, Andy. 2009a. *The Market and the Masses in Latin America: Policy Reform and Consumption in Liberalizing Economies.* New York: Cambridge University Press.

2009b. "Regionalized Voting Behavior and Political Discussion in Mexico." In Jorge I. Domínguez, Chappell Lawson, and Alejandro Moreno, eds. *Consolidating Mexico's Democracy: The 2006 Presidential Campaign in Comparative Perspective,* 71–88. Baltimore: Johns Hopkins University Press.

Baker, Andy and Kenneth Greene. 2011. "The Latin American Left's Mandate: Free-Market Policies and Issue Voting in New Democracies." *World Politics* 63 (1): 43–77.

Balcells, Laia. 2012. "The Consequences of Victimization on Political Identities. Evidence from Spain." *Politics & Society* 40 (3): 309–345.

Ballón, Eduardo and Rodrigo Barrenechea. 2010. "Especial Poder Regional: El poder desde las regiones." *Revista Poder* 22 (December).

Baloyra, Enrique. 1982. *El Salvador in Transition.* Chapel Hill: University of North Carolina Press.

Barahona, Marco Antonio, ed. 2008. *Guatemala: Monografía de los partidos políticos 2004–2008.* Guatemala City: Asociación de Investigación y Estudios Sociales, Departamento de Investigaciones Sociopolíticas.

Barndt, William. 2014. "Corporation-Based Parties: The Present and Future of Business Politics in Latin America." *Latin American Politics & Society* 56 (3): 1–22.

n.d. "Democracy for Sale: Corporation-Based Parties and the New Conservative Politics in the Americas." Book manuscript in progress.

Barnes, William. 1998. "Incomplete Democracy in Central America: Polarization and Voter Turnout in Nicaragua and El Salvador." *Journal of Interamerican Studies and World Affairs* 40 (3): 63–101.

Barozet, Emmanuelle and Marcel Aubry. 2005. "De las reformas internas a la candidatura presidencial autónoma: Los nuevos caminos institucionales de Renovación Nacional." *Revista Política* 45: 165–197.

Barr, Robert. 2009. "Populists, Outsiders and Anti-Establishment Politics." *Party Politics* 15 (1): 29–48.

Barrenechea, Rodrigo. 2014. *Becas, bases y votos. Alianza para el Progreso y la política subnacional en el Perú.* Lima: Instituto de Estudios Peruanos.

Barrett, Patrick. 2000. "Chile's Transformed Party System and the Future of Democratic Stability." *Journal of Interamerican and World Affairs* 42 (3): 1–32.

Bartle, John and Paolo Bellucci. 2009. *Political Parties and Partisanship: Social Identity and Individual Attitudes.* New York: Routledge.

Bartels, Larry. 2000. "Partisanship and Voting Behavior, 1952–1996." *American Journal of Political Science* 44 (1): 35–50.

2006. "Three Virtues of Panel Data for the Analysis of Campaign Effects." In Henry Brady and Richard Johnston, eds. *Capturing Campaign Effects,* 134–163. Ann Arbor: University of Michigan Press.

Bartolini, Stefano and Peter Mair. 1990. *Identity, Competition, and Electoral Availability: The Stabilisation of European Electorates 1885–1985.* Cambridge: Cambridge University Press.

Bastos, Santiago. 2009. "Guatemala: los límites de la política multicultural tras la tierra arrasada." Paper Presented at the Congress of the Latin American Studies Association, Rio de Janeiro, Brazil, June 11–14.

Baumer, Donald and Howard Gold. 1995. "Party Images and the American Electorate." *American Politics Research* 23 (1): 33–61.

Beccassino, Angel. 1989. *M-19, El heavy metal latinoamericano.* Bogotá: Fondo Editorial Santodomingo.

Berglund, Frode, Sören Holmberg, Hermann Schmitt, and Jacques Thomassen. 2006. "Party Identification and Party Choice." In Jacques Thomassen, ed. *The European Voter,* 106–124. Oxford: Oxford University Press.

Beyond Citizen Kane. Prod. John Ellis. Dir. Simon Hartog. BBC television documentary. Accessed on December 16, 2014. www.youtube.com/watch?v=77TKLQ10p34.

Birnir, Jóhanna Kristín. 2004. "Stabilizing Party Systems and Excluding Segments of Society? The Effects of Formation Costs on New Party Foundation in Latin America." *Studies in Comparative International Development* 39 (3): 3–27.

Blasier, Cole. 1987. *The Giant's Rival: The USSR and Latin America.* Revised edition. Pittsburgh: University of Pittsburgh Press.

Boas, Taylor C. 2005. "Television and Neopopulism in Latin America: Media Effects in Brazil and Peru." *Latin American Research Review* 40 (2): 27–49.

Bom, Djalma. 2008. "Interview with Editors." In Marieta De Moraes and Alexandre Fortes, eds. *Muitos caminhos, uma estrela: memórias de militantes do PT*, 79–103. Sao Paulo: Editora Fundação Perseu Abramo.

Booth, Eric and Joseph Robbins. 2010. "Assessing the Impact of Campaign Finance on Party System Institutionalization." *Party Politics* 16: 629–650.

Borjas, Adriana. 2003. *Partido de la Revolución Democrática: Estructura, organización interna y desempeño público, 1989–2003.* Mexico City: Ediciones Guernika.

Botero, Felipe. 2006. "Reforma política, personalismo y sistema de partidos. ¿Partidos fuertes o coaliciones electorales?" In Gary Hoskin and Miguel García, eds. *La reforma política de 2003*, 139–159. Bogotá: Universidad de los Andes, Konrad Adenauer.

Botero, Felipe and David Alvira. 2012. "Fulano de tal va por su aval. Desconexión entre los niveles nacionales y locales de los partidos políticos en Colombia." In Laura Wills-Otero and Margarita Battle, eds. *Política y territorio: análisis de las elecciones subnacionales en Colombia 2011*, 131–161. Bogotá: Programa de las Naciones Unidas para el Desarrollo, International Institute for Democracy and Electoral Assistance (IDEA), Netherlands Institute for Multiparty Democracy.

Botero, Felipe and Juan Carlos Rodríguez. 2008. "Ceticismo otimista: a reforma eleitoral colombiana de 2003." In Carlos Santander and Nelso Panteado, eds. *Os Processos Eleitorais Na América Latina*, 25–35. Brasília: Editorial LGE.

Boudon, Henry Lawrence. 1997. "New Party Persistence and Failure: A Comparative Analysis of Colombia's M-19 Democratic Alliance and Venezuela's Radical Cause." Ph.D. Dissertation, Department of International Studies, University of Miami.

2000. "Party System Deinstitutionalization: The 1997–98 Colombian Elections in Historical Perspective." *Journal of Interamerican Studies and World Affairs* 42 (3): 33–57.

2001. "Colombia's M-19 Democratic Alliance: A Case Study in New-Party Self-Destruction." *Latin American Perspectives* 28 (1): 73–92.

Brader, Ted and Joshua Tucker. 2001. "The Emergence of Mass Partisanship in Russia, 1993–1996." *American Journal of Political Science* 45 (1): 69–83.

2008. "Reflective and Unreflective Partisans? Experimental Evidence on the Links between Information, Opinion, and Party Identification." Unpublished manuscript.

Bramatti, Daniel and Julia Dualibi. 2012. "Filiados tucanos desconhecem partido." *Estado de São Paulo* (January). Accessed June 29, 2013. www.estadao. com.br/noticias/impresso,filiados-tucanos-desconhecem-partido-,828549,0. htm.

Brancati, Dawn. 2007. "The Origins and Strengths of Regional Parties." *British Journal of Political Science* 38 (1): 45–70.

Bruhn, Kathleen. 1997. *Taking on Goliath: The Emergence of a New Left Party and the Struggle for Democracy in Mexico.* University Park: Pennsylvania State University Press.

 2004. "The Making of the Mexican President, 2000: Parties, Candidates, and Campaign Strategy." In Jorge I. Domínguez and Chappell Lawson, eds. *Mexico's Pivotal Democratic Election*, 92–122. Stanford: Stanford University Press.

 2006. Bruhn, Kathleeen and Kenneth F Greene. The Mexico 2006 Candidate Study [datafile]. University of California, Santa Barbara and University of Texas at Austin.

 2009. "López Obrador, Calderón, and the 2006 Presidential Campaign." In Jorge I. Domínguez, Chappell Lawson, and Alejandro Moreno, eds. *Consolidating Mexico's Democracy: The 2006 Presidential Campaign in Comparative Perspective*, 169–188. Baltimore: Johns Hopkins University Press.

Bruhn, Kathleen and Kenneth Greene. 2007. "Elite Polarization Meets Mass Moderation in Mexico's 2006 Elections." *PS: Political Science and Politics* 40: 33–38.

 2009. "The Absence of Common Ground between Candidates and Voters." In Jorge I. Domínguez, Chappell Lawson, and Alejandro Moreno, eds. *Consolidating Mexico's Democracy: The 2006 Presidential Campaign in Comparative Perspective*, 109–128. Baltimore: Johns Hopkins University Press.

Buenahora Febres-Cordero, Jaime. 1997. *La democracia en Colombia: Un proyecto en construcción.* Bogotá: Imprenta de la Contraloría de la República.

Budge, Ian, Ivor Crewe, and Dennis Farlie. 1976. *Party Identification and Beyond: Representations of Voting and Party Competition.* New York: John Wiley and Sons.

Buquet, Daniel, ed. 2005. *Las claves del cambio: ciclo electoral y nuevo gobierno 2004/2005.* Montevideo: Banda Oriental – Instituto de Ciencia Política.

Burnell, Peter and Alan Ware, eds. 1998. *Funding Democratization.* New York: Manchester University Press.

Burt, Jo-Marie. 2006. "'Quien Habla es Terrorista': The Political Use of Fear in Fujimori's Peru." *Latin American Research Review* 41 (3): 32–62.

Buxton, Julia. 2001. *The Failure of Political Reform in Venezuela.* Farnham: Ashgate.

Calvo, Ernesto and Marcelo Escolar. 2005. *La nueva política de partidos en la Argentina: Crisis política, realineamientos políticos y reforma electoral.* Buenos Aires: Prometeo.

Calvo, Ernesto and Maria Victoria Murillo. 2007. "How Many Clients Does It Take to Win an Election? Estimating the Size and Structure of Political Networks in Argentina and Chile." Working Paper Presented at the Elections and Distribution Workshop at Yale University, New Haven, Connecticut, October.

Cameron, Maxwell. 1994. *Democracy and Authoritarianism in Peru: Political Coalitions and Social Change.* New York: St. Martin's Press.

    2006. "Endogenous Regime Breakdown. The Vladivideo and the Fall of Peru's Fujimori." In Julio Carrión, ed. *The Fujimori Legacy: The Rise of Electoral Authoritarianism in Peru.* University Park: Pennsylvania State University Press.

    2009. "El giro a la izquierda frustrado en Perú: El caso de Ollanta Humala." *Convergencia: Revista de Ciencias Sociales* (1): 275–302.

    2011. "Peru: The Left Turn That Wasn't." In Steven Levitsky and Kenneth M. Roberts, eds. *The Resurgence of the Latin American Left.* Baltimore: Johns Hopkins University Press.

Campbell, Angus, Philip Converse, Warren Miller, and Donald Stokes. 1960. *The American Voter.* New York: John Wiley and Sons.

    1980. *The American Voter.* Chicago: University of Chicago Press.

Campello, Daniela. 2015. *Globalization and Democracy: The Politics of Market Discipline in Latin America.* Cambridge: Cambridge University Press.

Carrión, Julio. 2006. "Public Opinion, Market Reforms, and Democracy in Fujimori's Peru." In Julio F. Carrión, ed. *The Fujimori Legacy: The Rise of Electoral Authoritarianism in Peru*, 126–149. University Park: Pennsylvania State University Press.

Caramani, Daniele. 2006. *The Nationalization of Politics: The Formation of National Electorates and Party Systems in Western Europe.* New York: Cambridge University Press.

Cardoso, Fernando Henrique. 2011. "O Papel da Oposição." Available at http://oglobo.globo.com/pais/noblat/posts/2011/04/12/o-papel-da-oposicao-374379.asp, August 27, 2011.

Carey, John. 2003. "Presidentialism and Representative Institutions." In Jorge I. Domínguez and Michael Shifter, eds. *Constructing Democratic Governance in Latin America*, 11–42. Second edition. Baltimore: Johns Hopkins University Press.

Carreras, Miguel. 2012. "Party Systems in Latin America after the Third Wave: A Critical Re-assessment." *Journal of Politics in Latin America* 1: 135–153.

Casas, Kevin. 2005. "State Funding and Campaign Finance Practices in Uruguay." In Eduardo Posada-Carbó and Carlos Malamud, eds. *The Financing of Politics: Latin American and European Perspectives*, 189–228. London: Institute for the Study of the Americas.

Casas, Kevin and Daniel Zovatto. 2011. "Para llegar a tiempo: Apuntes sobre la regulación del financiamiento político en América Latina." In Pablo Gutiérrez and Daniel Zovatto, eds. *Financiamiento de los partidos políticos en América Latina* (Serie Doctrina Jurídica #594), 17–67. Mexico City: International Institute for Democracy and Electoral Assistance (IDEA), Organization of American States, and Universidad Nacional Autónoma de México.

Casas-Zamora, Kevin. 2005. *Paying for Democracy: Political Finance and State Funding for Parties.* Colchester: ECPR Press.

Castiglioni, Rossana. 2001. "The Politics of Retrenchment: The Quandaries of Social Protection under Military Rule in Chile, 1973–1990." *Latin American Politics and Society* 43 (4): 37–66.

Cavarozzi, Marcelo and Juan Abal Medina. 2002. *El asedio a la política. Los partidos latinoamericanos en la era neoliberal.* Buenos Aires: Politeia.

Centellas, Miguel. 2013. "Bolivia's New Multi-Cultural Constitution: The 2009 Constitution in Historical and Comparative Perspective." In Todd Eisenstadt, ed. *Latin America's Multicultural Movements and the Struggle between Communitarianism, Autonomy and Human Rights,* 88–110. New York: Oxford University Press.

Centro de Estudios de la Realidad Contemporánea (CERC). 2013. *A cuarenta años del golpe militar.* Santiago: Centro de Estudios de la Realidad Contemporánea.

Centro de Investigaciones Psicológicas y Sociológicas. 1993. *La religión: Estudios de investigadores cubanos sobre la temática religiosa.* Havana: Editora Política.

Chalmers, Douglas, Mario do Carmo Campello de Souza, and Atilio Borón. 1992. "Introduction: The Right and Latin American Democracies." In Douglas Chalmers, Mario do Carmo Campello de Souza, and Atilio Borón, eds. *The Right and Democracy in Latin America,* 1–9. New York: Praeger Publishers.

Chandra, Kanchan. 2011. "What Is an Ethnic Party?" *Party Politics* 17 (2): 151–169.

Cheresky, Isidoro. 2003. "Las elecciones nacionales de 1999 y 2001: Fluctuación del voto, debilitamiento de la cohesión partidaria y crisis de representación." In Isidoro Cheresky and Jean-Michel Blanquer, eds. *De la ilusión reformista al descontento ciudadano: Las elecciones en Argentina, 1999–2001,* 19–51. Buenos Aires: Homo Sapiens Ediciones.

Chhibber, Pradeep and Ken Kollman. 1998. "Party Aggregation and the Number of Parties in India and the United States." *American Political Science Review* 92 (2): 329–342.

2004. *The Formation of National Party Systems: Federalism and Party Competition in Canada, Great Britain, India, and the United States.* Princeton: Princeton University Press.

Chilcote, Ronald. 1974. *The Brazilian Communist Party: Conflict and Integration, 1922–1972.* New York: Oxford University Press.

Chong, Dennis. 1991. *Collective Action and the Civil Rights Movement.* Chicago: University of Chicago Press.

Chumacero, Juan Pablo. 2009. "Trece años de reforma agraria en Bolivia." In Chumacero, Juan Pablo, ed. *Informe 2009: Reconfigurando Territorios,* 11–38. La Paz: Fundación Tierra.

Ciudadanos al Día (CAD). 2008. *Financiamiento Municipal: El Fondo de Compensación Municipal (Foncomun).* Lima: Ciudadanos al Día.

Collier, David. ed. 1979. *The New Authoritarianism in Latin America.* Princeton: Princeton University Press.

Collier, Ruth Berins and David Collier. 1991. *Shaping the Political Arena: Critical Junctures, the Labor Movement, and Regime Dynamics in Latin America.* Princeton, NJ: Princeton University Press.

Collins, Jennifer. 2006. "Democratizing Formal Politics: Indigenous and Social Movement Political Parties in Ecuador and Bolivia, 1978–2000." Ph.D. Dissertation, Department of Political Science, University of California.

Colton, Timothy. 2007. "Putin and the Attenuation of Russian Democracy." In Dale Herspring, ed. *Putin's Russia: Past Imperfect, Future Uncertain*, 37–52. Lanham: Rowman and Littlefield.

Conaghan, Catherine and James Malloy. 1994. *Unsettling Statecraft: Democracy and Neoliberalism in the Central Andes*. Pittsburgh: University of Pittsburgh Press.

Constable, Pamela and Arturo Valenzuela. 1991. *A Nation of Enemies: Chile under Pinochet*. New York: W.W. Norton and Co.

Contreras, Carlos. 2004. *El aprendizaje del capitalismo*. Lima: Instituto de Estudios Peruanos.

Converse, Philip. 1969. "Of Time and Partisan Stability." *Comparative Political Studies* 2 (2): 139–171.

Coppedge, Michael. 1994. *Strong Parties and Lame Ducks: Presidential Partyarchy and Factionalism in Venezuela*. Stanford: Stanford University Press.

1998. "The Evolution of Latin American Party Systems." In Scott Mainwaring and Arturo Valenzuela, eds. *Politics, Society, and Democracy: Latin America*, 171–206. Boulder: Westview Press.

Córdova Vianello, Lorenzo. 2011. "El financiamiento a los partidos políticos en México." In Pablo Gutiérrez and Daniel Zovatto, eds. *Financiamiento de los partidos políticos en América Latina* (Serie Doctrina Jurídica #594), 351–368. Mexico City: International Institute for Democracy and Electoral Assistance (IDEA), Organization of American States, and Universidad Nacional Autónoma de México.

Corte Nacional Electoral de Ecuador. 2010. *Informe No. 004-DFFP-CNE-2009*. Quito: Corte Nacional Electoral de Ecuador.

Cotler, Julio. 1995. "Political Parties and the Problems of Democratic Consolidation in Peru." In Scott Mainwaring and Timothy Scully, eds. *Building Democratic Institutions: Party Systems in Latin America*, 323–353. Stanford: Stanford University Press.

Cox, Gary. 1997a. *Making Votes Count: Political Economy of Institutions and Decisions*. Cambridge: Cambridge University Press.

1997b. *Making Votes Count: Strategic Coordination in the World's Electoral Systems*. Cambridge: Cambridge University Press.

Crisp, Brian and Rachael Ingall. 2002. "Institutional Engineering and the Nature of Representation: Mapping the Effects of Electoral Reform in Colombia." *American Journal of Political Science* 46 (4): 733–748.

Cuban Research Institute. 2014. *2014 FIU Cuba Poll*. Miami: Florida International University. http://worldmountain.com/cp14/polltables.htm.

Cúneo, Martín. 2011. "Felipe Quispe: el último Mallku." *El Viejo Topo* 284: 51–57.

Cyr, Jennifer. 2012. "From Collapse to Comeback? Explaining the Fates of Political Parties in Latin America." Ph.D. Dissertation, Department of Political Science, Northwestern University.

Dalton, Russell. 1984. "Cognitive Mobilization and Partisan Dealignment in Advanced Industrial Democracies." *Journal of Politics* 46 (1): 264–284.

Daly, Sarah Zukerman. 2016. *Organizational Violence after Civil War: The Geography of Recruitment in Latin America*. New York: Cambridge University Press.

Dargent, Eduardo and Paula Muñoz. 2011. "Democracy against Parties? Party System Deinstitutionalization in Colombia." *Journal of Politics in Latin America* 3 (2): 43–71.

2012. "Perú 2011: Continuidades y cambios en la política sin partidos." *Revista de Ciencia Política* 32 (1): 245–268.

Dargent, Eduardo and Alberto Vergara. 2012. "Decentralization against Parties? The Effects of Decentralization on Political Parties." Paper Presented at the Conference *Ruling Politics: The Formal and Informal Foundations of Power in New Democracies*, Harvard University, November 20–22.

Dávila, Andrés. 2013. "El Partido Verde: entre el umbral, los egos y la reencarnación del M-19." *Razón Pública*. http://razonpublica.com/index.php/politica-y-gobierno-temas-27/7130.

Dávila, Andrés and Natalia Delgado. 2002. "La metamorfosis del sistema político colombiano: ¿clientelismo de mercado o nueva forma de intermediación?" In Francisco Gutiérrez, ed. *Degradación o cambio: evolución del sistema político colombiano*, 317–355. Bogotá: Norma.

De Azevedo, Ricardo. 2003. "Entrevista com Jose Genoino." *Teoria e Debate* 53: 6–8.

De Gramont, Diane. 2010. "Leaving Lima Behind? The Victory and Evolution of Regional Parties in Peru." Undergraduate thesis, Harvard College.

De la Fuente, Alejandro. 2001. *A Nation for All: Race, Inequality, and Politics in Twentieth Century Cuba*. Chapel Hill: University of North Carolina Press.

2012. "'Tengo una raza oscura y discriminada.' El movimiento afrocubano: hacia un programa consensuado." *Nueva Sociedad* 242: 92–115.

De la Torre, Carlos. 2000. *Populist Seduction in Latin America: The Ecuadorian Experience*. Athens: Ohio University Center for International Studies.

De la Torre, Carlos and Catherine Conaghan. 2009. "The Hybrid Campaign: Tradition and Modernity in Ecuador's 2006 Presidential Election." *International Journal of Press/Politics* 14 (3): 335–352.

De Zeeuw, Jeroen. 2008. *From Soldiers to Politicians: Transforming Rebel Movements After Civil War*. Boulder: Lynne Rienner Publishers.

Degregori, Carlos Iván. 2010. *Qué difícil es ser Dios: el Partido Comunista del Perú-Sendero Luminoso y el conflicto armado interno en el Perú: 1980–1999*. Lima: Instituto de Estudios Peruanos.

Del Castillo, Pilar. 2005. "Financing Political Parties in Spain." In Eduardo Posada-Carbó and Carlos Malamud, eds. *The Financing of Politics: Latin American and European Perspectives*, 93–103. London: Institute for the Study of the Americas.

Del Pino, Ponciano. 1998. "Familia, cultura y revolución: vida cotidiana en Sendero Luminoso." In Steve Stern, ed. *Los senderos insólitos del Perú*, 161–191. Lima: Instituto de Estudios Peruanos.

Delli Carpini, Michael and Scott Keeter. 1996. *What Americans Know about Politics and Why It Matters*. New Haven: Yale University Press.

Di Tella, Torcuato. 1971–1972. "La búsqueda de la fórmula política argentina." *Desarrollo Económico* 11 (42–44): 317–325.

Dilla, Haroldo, Gerardo González, and Ana Vincentelli. 1992. "Cuba's Local Governments: An Experience beyond the Paradigms." *Cuban Studies* 22: 151–170.

Dinas, Elias. 2014. "Does Choice Bring Loyalty? Electoral Participation and the Development of Party Identification." *American Journal of Political Science* 58 (April): 449–465.

Dix, Robert. 1967. *Colombia: The Political Dimensions of Change.* New Haven: Yale University Press.

   1979. "Political Opposition under the National Front." In Albert Berry, Ronald Hellman, and Mauricio Solán, eds. *Politics of Compromise: Coalition Government in Colombia,* 131–164. New Brunswick: Transaction Publishers.

   1989. "Cleavage Structures and Party Systems in Latin America." *Comparative Politics* 22 (1): 23–37.

   1992. "Democratization and the Institutionalization of Latin American Political Parties." *Comparative Political Studies* 24 (January): 488–511.

Domínguez, Jorge I. 1998. "Free Politics and Free Markets in Latin America." *Journal of Democracy* 9 (4): 70–84.

   2006. *Cuba hoy: Analizando su pasado, imaginando su futuro.* Madrid: Editorial Colibrí.

   2013. "Conclusion: Early Twenty-First Century Democratic Governance in Latin America." In Jorge I. Domínguez and Michael Shifter, eds. *Constructing Democratic Governance in Latin America,* 340–364. Fourth edition. Baltimore: Johns Hopkins University Press.

Domínguez, Jorge I. and James McCann. 1996. *Democratizing Mexico: Public Opinion and Electoral Choices.* Baltimore: Johns Hopkins University Press.

Domínguez, Jorge I., Omar Everleny Pérez Villanueva, and Lorena Barberia, eds. 2004. *The Cuban Economy at the Start of the Twenty-First Century.* Cambridge: Harvard University Press.

Dowd, Robert and Michael Driessen. 2008. "Ethnically Dominated Party Systems and the Quality of Democracy." Afrobarometer Working Papers 92.

Downs, Anthony. 1957. *An Economic Theory of Democracy.* New York: Harper and Row.

Dunkerley, James. 1982. *The Long War: Dictatorship and Revolution in El Salvador.* London: Junction Books.

Durand, Francisco. 1997. "The Growth and Limitations of the Peruvian Right." In Maxwell Cameron, ed. *The Peruvian Labyrinth: Polity, Society, Economy,* 152–175. University Park: Pennsylvania State University Press.

Duverger, Maurice. 1951. "The Influence of Electoral Systems on Political Life." *International Social Science Bulletin* 3: 314–352.

   1954. *Political Parties: Their Organization and Activity in the Modern State.* London: Methuen; New York: Wiley.

Eaton, Kent. 2006. "The Downside of Decentralization: Armed Clientelism in Colombia." *Security Studies* 15 (4): 533–562.

   2011. "Conservative Autonomy Movements: Territorial Dimensions of Ideological Conflict in Bolivia and Ecuador." *Comparative Politics* 43 (3): 291–310.

   2014. "Recentralization and the Left Turn: Explaining Divergent Outcomes in Bolivia, Ecuador and Venezuela." *Comparative Political Studies* (47) 8: 1130–1157.

Enelow, James and Melvin Hinich. 1982. "Nonspatial Candidate Characteristics and Electoral Competition." *Journal of Politics* 44: 115–130.

Erikson, Robert. 1978. "Constituency Opinion and Congressional Behavior: A Reexamination of the Miller-Stokes Representation Data." *American Journal of Political Science* 22 (3): 511–535.

Escalante, Aníbal and Juan Marinello. 1945. "El trabajo de los socialistas en la última legislatura." *Fundamentos* 41 (5): 8–16.

Espina Prieto, Mayra. 2004. "Social Effects of Economic Adjustment: Equality, Inequality and Trends toward Greater Complexity in Cuban Society." In Jorge I. Domínguez, Omar Everleny Pérez Villanueva, and Lorena Barberia, eds. *The Cuban Economy at the Start of the Twenty-First Century*, 209–243. Cambridge: Harvard University Press.

Espina Prieto, Mayra and Viviana Togores. 2012. "Structural Change and Routes of Social Mobility in Today's Cuba: Patterns, Profiles, and Subjectivities." In Jorge I. Domínguez, Omar Everleny Pérez Villanueva, Mayra Espina Prieto, and Lorena Barberia, eds. *Cuban Economic and Social Development: Policy Reforms and Challenges in the 21st Century*, 261–289. Cambridge: David Rockefeller Center for Latin American Studies.

Fairfield, Tasha. 2010. "Business Power and Tax Reform: Taxing Income and Profits in Chile and Argentina." *Latin American Politics and Society* 52 (2): 37–71.

Falla, Ricardo. 2007. "Rigoberta Menchú: A Shooting Star in the Electoral Sky." *Revista Envío* 312 (July). Online. www.envio.org.ni/articulo.php/3606.

Falleti, Tulia. 2010. *Decentralization and Subnational Politics in Latin America.* Cambridge: Cambridge University Press.

Fedelino, Annalissa. 2010. *Making Decentralization Work: Cross-Country Experiences.* Washington, DC: International Monetary Fund.

Fernandes, Florestan. 1969. *The Negro in Brazilian Society.* New York: Columbia University Press.

Fernandes Veiga, Luciana. 2011. "O partidarismo no Brasil (2002/2010)." *Opinião Pública* 17 (2): 400–425.

Fernández, Sergio. 1994. *Mi lucha por la democracia.* Santiago: Editorial los Andes.

Figueiredo, Argelina and Fernando Limongi. 1999. *Executive e legislativo na nova ordem constitutional.* Rio de Janeiro: Editora FGV.

Finkel, Steven. 1995. *Causal Analysis with Panel Data.* Thousand Oaks: Sage Publications.

Fiorina, Morris. 1981. *Retrospective Voting in American National Elections.* New Haven: Yale University Press.

Fish, Steven. 2005. *Democracy Derailed in Russia: The Failure of Open Politics.* Cambridge: Cambridge University Press.

Fisher, Justin and Todd Eisenstadt. 2004. "Introduction: Comparative Party Finance: What Is To Be Done?" *Party Politics* 10: 619–626.

Flanagan, Scott and Russell Dalton. 1984. "Parties under Stress: Realignment and Dealignment in Advanced Industrial Societies." *West European Politics* 7 (1): 7–23.

Fontaine Talavera, Arturo. 2000. "Chile's Elections: The New Face of the New Right." *Journal of Democracy* 11 (2): 70–77.

Franco, Jean. 2013. *Cruel Modernity.* Durham: Duke University Press.

Freidenberg, Flavia. 2003. "Ecuador." In Manuel Alcántara and Flavia Freidenberg, eds. *Partidos políticos de América Latina: Países andinos,* 235–406. Mexico City: Instituto Federal Electoral, Fondo de Cultura Económica.

Freidenberg, Flavia and Steven Levitsky. 2006. "Informal Institutions and Party Organization in Latin America." In Gretchen Helmke and Steven Levitsky, eds. *Informal Institutions and Democracy: Lessons from Latin America,* 178–200. Baltimore: Johns Hopkins University Press.

Frieden, Jeffry A. 1991. *Debt, Development and Democracy: Latin America, 1965-1985.* Princeton: Princeton University Press.

Friedman, Edward. 2008. "Why the Dominant Party in China Won't Lose." In Edward Friedman and Joseph Wong, eds. *Political Transitions in Dominant Party Systems,* 252–268. New York: Routledge.

Fundamentos. 1944. "Una carta del Partido Socialista Popular a Batista." *Fundamentos* 4 (31): 375–376.

Galeas, Geovani. 2004. *Mayor Roberto D'Aubuisson: El rostro más allá del mito.* San Salvador: La Prensa Gráfica.

Galeas, Geovani and Marvin Galeas. 2009. *Las claves de una derrota: Cómo y por qué ARENA perdió las elecciones.* San Salvador: Editorial Cinco.

Galeas, Marvin. 2011. *Sol y acero: La vida de don Guillermo Sol Bang.* San Salvador: Editorial Cinco.

Gamboa, Laura. 2010. "Competing with Empty Pockets. Why the Liberal Party Wins Regional Elections in Colombia." Master's thesis, University of Texas at Austin.

García Durán, Mauricio, Vera Grabe, and Otty Patiño. 2008. "The M-19's Journey from Armed Struggle to Democratic Politics." Working Paper, Berghof Research Center for Constructive Conflict Management, Berlin, Germany.

García Lema, Alberto. 1994. *La reforma por dentro: la difícil construcción del consenso constitucional.* Buenos Aires: Planeta.

García Montero, Mercedes. 2001. "Bolivia." In Manuel Alcántara Sáez and Flavia Friedenberg, eds. *Partidos políticos de América Latina: Países andinos,* 33–148. Salamanca: Ediciones Universidad de Salamanca.

Garretón, Manuel Antonio. 2000. "Cambio, continuidad y proyecciones de las elecciones presidenciales de fin de siglo." In *Nuevo gobierno: Desafíos de la reconciliación,* 97–107. Santiago: La Facultad Latinoamericana de Ciencias Sociales.

  2003. *Incomplete Democracy: Political Democratization in Chile and Latin America.* Chapel Hill: University of North Carolina Press.

Gaspar Tapia, Gabriel. 1989. *El Salvador: El ascenso de la nueva derecha.* San Salvador: Centro de Investigación y Acción Social.

Gavilán, Lurgio. 2012. *Memorias de un soldado desconocido.* Lima: Instituto de Estudios Peruanos.

Geddes. Barbara. 1994. *Politician's Dilemma: Building State Capacity in Latin America.* Berkeley: University of California Press.

Genoíno, José. 2004. "A tática eleitoral do PT." *Teoria e Debate* 59. Accessed August 15, 2012. www.fpabramo.org.br/o-que-fazemos/editora/teoria-e-debate/edicoes-anteriores/nacional-tatica-eleitoral-do-pt.

Gerchunoff, Pablo and Juan Carlos Torre. 1996. "La política de liberalización económica en la administración de Menem." *Desarrollo Económico* 36 (143): 733–768.

Gibson, Edward. 1990. "Democracy and the New Electoral Right in Argentina." *Journal of Interamerican Studies and World Affairs* 32 (3): 177–228.

 1992. "Conservative Electoral Movements and Democratic Politics: Core Constituencies, Coalition Building, and the Latin American Electoral Right." In Douglas Chalmers, Maria do Carmo Campello de Souza, and Atilio Borón, eds. *The Right and Democracy in Latin America*, 13–42. New York: Praeger.

 1996. *Class and Conservative Parties: Argentina in Comparative Perspective.* Baltimore: Johns Hopkins University Press.

 1997. "The Populist Road to Market Reform: Policy and Electoral Coalitions in Mexico and Argentina." *World Politics* 49 (3): 339–370.

 2005. "Boundary Control: Subnational Authoritarianism in Democratic Countries." *World Politics* 58 (1): 101–132.

 2012. *Boundary Control: Subnational Authoritarianism in Federal Democracies.* Cambridge: Cambridge University Press.

Gilbert, Dennis. 1988. *Sandinistas.* New York: Basil Blackwell.

Gillespie, Charles Guy. 1991. *Negotiating Democracy: Politicians and Generals in Uruguay.* Cambridge: Cambridge University Press.

Gingerich, Daniel. 2009. "Corruption and Political Decay: Evidence from Bolivia." *Quarterly Journal of Political Science* 4 (1): 1–34.

 2010. "Bolivia: Traditional Parties, the State, and the Toll of Corruption." In Charles Blake and Steven Morris, eds. *Corruption and Politics in Latin America: National and Regional Dynamics*, 55–88. Boulder: Lynne Rienner.

 2013. *Political Institutions and Party-Directed Corruption in South America: Stealing for the Team.* New York: Cambridge University Press.

Goldenberg, Boris. 1965. *The Cuban Revolution and Latin America.* New York: Praeger.

Gómez, Silvia. 1997. *La transición inconclusa: Treinta años de elecciones en México.* Mexico City: El Colegio de México, Centro de Estudios Sociológicos.

Gómez-Bruera, Hernán. 2013. *Lula, the Workers' Party and the Governability Dilemma in Brazil.* London: Routledge.

Gonzáles, Luis. 1995. "Continuity and Change in the Uruguayan Party System." In Scott Mainwaring and Timothy Scully, eds. *Building Democratic Institutions: Party Systems in Latin America*, 138–163. Stanford: Stanford University Press.

González Trujillo, Miguel Ángel, Onel Ortíz Fragoso, Gabriela Rojo Rosas, and Rubén Sánchez Martínez. 2010. "Los Congresos Nacionales." In González Trujillo, Miguel Ángel, Onel Ortíz Fragoso, Gabriela Rojo Rosas, and Rubén Sánchez Martínez, eds. *20 Años: Un futuro con historia*, 61–88. Mexico City: Agencia Promotora de Publicaciones.

Graham, Carol and Cheikh Kane. 1998. "Opportunistic Government or Sustaining Reform? Electoral Trends and Public-Expenditure Patterns in Peru, 1990–1995." *Latin American Research Review* 33 (1): 67–104.

Green, Donald Philip, Bradley Palmquist, and Eric Schickler. 2002. *Partisan Hearts and Minds: Political Parties and the Social Identities of Voters.* New Haven: Yale University Press.

Greene, Kenneth. 2000. *Mexico Party Personnel Surveys, 1998–1999.* Data file.

　　2007. *Why Dominant Parties Lose: Mexico's Democratization in Comparative Perspective.* New York: Cambridge University Press.

　　2008. "Dominant Party Strategy and Democratization." *American Journal of Political Science* 52 (1): 16–31.

　　2011. "Campaign Persuasion and Nascent Partisanship in Mexico's New Democracy." *American Journal of Political Science* 55 (2): 398–416.

Greene, Kenneth, Jorge I. Domínguez, Chappell Lawson, and Alejandro Moreno. 2012. *The Mexico 2012 Panel Study.* Data file available at the Inter-University Consortium for Political and Social Research, University of Michigan.

Greenstein, Fred. 1965. *Children and Politics.* New Haven: Yale University Press.

Grindle, Merilee. 2000. *Audacious Reforms: Institutional Invention and Democracy in Latin America.* Baltimore: Johns Hopkins University Press.

　　2012. *Jobs for the Boys: Patronage and the State in Comparative Perspective.* Cambridge: Harvard University Press.

Grupos de Propaganda Doctrinal Ortodoxa. 1951. *Doctrina del Partido Ortodoxo.* Havana: Fernández.

Grynaviski, Jeffrey. 2010. *Partisan Bonds: Political Reputations and Legislative Accountability.* Cambridge: Cambridge University Press.

Grzymala-Busse, Anna. 2002. *Redeeming the Communist Past: The Regeneration of Communist Parties in East Central Europe.* Cambridge: Cambridge University Press.

　　2008. "The Communist Exit in East Central Europe and Its Consequences." In Edward Friedman and Joseph Wong, eds. *Political Transitions in Dominant Party Systems*, 91–105. New York: Routledge.

Guerrero Cazar, Fernando and Pablo Ospina Peralta. 2003. *El poder de la comunidad: Ajuste estructural y movimiento indígena en los Andes ecuatorianos.* Buenos Aires: Consejo Latinoamericano de Ciencias Sociales.

Gutiérrez, Francisco. 2007. *¿Lo que el viento se llevó? Los partidos políticos y la democracia en Colombia, 1958–2002.* Bogotá: Grupo Editorial Norma.

Gutiérrez, Francisco and Andrés Dávila. 2000. "Paleontólogos o politólogos: ¿qué podemos decir hoy sobre los dinosaurios?" *Revista de Estudios Sociales* 6: 39–49.

Gutiérrez, Pablo and Daniel Zovatto, eds. 2011. *Financiamiento de los partidos políticos en América Latina* (Serie Doctrina Jurídica #594). Mexico City: International Institute for Democracy and Electoral Assistance (IDEA), Organization of American States, and Universidad Nacional Autónoma de México.

Guzmán Mendoza, Carlos Enrique and Ermício Sena de Oliveira. 2003. "Brasil." In Manuel Alcántara and Flavia Freidenberg, eds. *Partidos políticos de América Latina: Cono sur*, 117–242. Mexico City: Instituto Federal Electoral, Fondo de Cultura Económica.

Hagopian, Frances. 1996. *Traditional Politics and Regime Change in Brazil*. Cambridge: Cambridge University Press.

Hagopian, Frances, Carlos Gervasoni, and Juan Andres Moraes. 2009. "From Patronage to Program: The Emergence of Party-Oriented Legislators in Brazil." *Comparative Political Studies* 42 (3): 360–391.

Hagopian, Frances and Scott Mainwaring, eds. 2005. *The Third Wave of Democratization in Latin America: Advances and Setbacks*. New York: Cambridge University Press.

Hale, Henry. 2004. "Yabloko and the Challenge of Building a Liberal Party in Russia." *Europe-Asia Studies* 56 (7): 993–1020.

2006. *Why Not Parties in Russia? Democracy, Federalism, and the State*. New York: Cambridge University Press.

Hall, Gillette and Harry Anthony Patrinos, eds. 2006. *Pueblos indígenas, pobreza y desarrollo humano en América Latina*, 1994–2004. Bogotá: Banco Mundial.

Hanson, Stephen. 2010. *Post-Imperial Democracies: Ideology and Party Formation in Third Republic France, Weimar Germany, and Post-Soviet Russia*. Cambridge: Cambridge University Press.

Harbers, Imke. 2009. "Decentralization and the Development of Nationalized Party Systems in New Democracies: Evidence from Latin America." *Comparative Political Studies* 43 (5): 606–627.

Harnecker, Marta, Federico Fuentes, and Santos Ramírez. 2008. *MAS-IPSP: instrumento político que surge de los movimientos sociales*. Caracas: Centro Internacional Miranda.

Hartlyn, Jonathan. 1988. *The Politics of Coalition Rule in Colombia*. Cambridge: Cambridge University Press.

Hawkins, Kirk. 2010. *Venezuela's Chavismo and Populism in Comparative Perspective*. New York: Cambridge University Press.

Herman, Edward and Frank Brodhead. 1984. *Demonstration Elections: U.S.-Staged Elections in the Dominican Republic, Vietnam, and El Salvador*. Boston: South End Press.

Hetherington, Marc. 2001. "Resurgent Mass Partisanship: The Role of Elite Polarization." *American Political Science Review* 95 (3): 619–631.

2011. "Resurgent Mass Partisanship: The Role of Elite Polarization." In Richard G. Niemi, Herbert F. Weisberg, and David C. Kimball, eds. *Controversies in Voting Behavior*, 242–265. Washington, DC: CQ Press.

Hicken, Allen. 2009. *Building Party Systems in Developing Democracies*. New York: Cambridge University Press.

Hicken, Allen and Erik Martinez Kuhonta, eds. 2015. *Party System Institutionalization in Asia: Democracies, Autocracies, and the Shadows of the Past*. New York: Cambridge University Press.

Highton, Benjamin and Cindy Kam. 2011. "The Long-Term Dynamics of Partisanship and Issue Orientations." *Journal of Politics* 73 (1): 202–215.

Hinnich, Melvin and Michael Munger. 1994. *Ideology and the Theory of Political Choice*. Ann Arbor: Michigan University Press.

Hirschman, Albert. 1970. *Exit, Voice, and Loyalty: Responses to Decline in Firms, Organizations, and States.* Cambridge: Harvard University Press.

Hogg, Michael, Dominic Abrams, Sabine Otten, and Steve Hinkle. 2004. "The Social Identity Perspective: Intergroup Relations, Self-Conception, and Small Groups." *Small Group Research* 35 (3): 246–276.

Hogg, Michael A., Elizabeth A. Hardie, and Katherine J. Reynolds. 1995. "Prototypical Similarity, Self-categorization, and Depersonalized Attraction: A Perspective on Group Cohesiveness." *European Journal of Social Psychology* 25 (2): 159–177.

Holland, Alisha. 2013. "Right on Crime? Conservative Party Politics and *Mano Dura* Policies in El Salvador." *Latin American Research Review* 48 (1): 44–67.

Holmsten, Stephanie, Robert Moser, and Mary Slosar. 2009. "Do Ethnic Parties Exclude Women?" *Comparative Political Studies* 43 (10): 1179–1201.

Hopkin, Jonathan. 2004. "The Problem with Party Finance: Theoretical Perspectives on the Funding of Party Politics." *Party Politics* 10: 627–651.

Hoskin, Gary. 1998. "Urban Electoral Behavior in Colombia." In Henry Dietz and Gil Shidlo, eds. *Urban Elections in Democratic Latin America*, 91–118. Wilmington: Rowman and Littlefield.

Huber, Evelyne and John Stephens. 2012. *Democracy and the Left: Social Policy and Inequality in Latin America.* Chicago: University of Chicago Press.

Huber, John, Georgia Kernell, and Eduardo Leoni. 2005. "Institutional Context, Cognitive Resources and Party Attachments across Democracies." *Political Analysis* 13 (4): 365–386.

Hug, Simon. 2001. *Altering Party Systems: Strategic Behavior and the Emergence of New Political Parties in Western Democracies.* Ann Arbor: University of Michigan Press.

Huneeus, Carlos. 2000. "Technocrats and Politicians in an Authoritarian Regime. The 'Odeplan Boys' and the 'Gremialists' in Pinochet's Chile." *Journal of Latin American Studies* 32 (2): 461–501.

2003. *Chile, un país dividido: La actualidad del pasado.* Santiago: Catalonia.

2007. *The Pinochet Regime.* Boulder: Lynne Rienner Publishers.

Hunter, Wendy. 1997. *Eroding Military Influence in Brazil: Politicians against Soldiers.* Chapel Hill: University of North Carolina Press.

2007. "The Normalization of an Anomaly: The Workers' Party in Brazil." *World Politics* 59 (3): 440–475.

2010. *The Transformation of the Workers' Party in Brazil, 1989–2009.* New York: Cambridge University Press.

Hunter, Wendy and Timothy Power. 2007. "Rewarding Lula: Executive Power, Social Power, and the Brazilian Elections of 2006." *Latin American Politics and Society* 49 (1): 1–30.

Huntington, Samuel. 1968. *Political Order in Changing Societies.* New Haven: Yale University Press.

1970. "Social and Institutional Dynamics of One-Party Systems." In Samuel Huntington and Clement Moore, eds. *Authoritarian Politics in Modern Society: The Dynamics of Established One-Party Systems*, 3–47. New York: Basic Books.

1991. *The Third Wave: Democratization in the Late Twentieth Century.* Norman: University of Oklahoma Press.

Inglehart, Ronald. 1977. *The Silent Revolution: Changing Values and Political Styles among Western Publics*. Princeton: Princeton University Press.

Ignazi, Piero, Luciano Bardi and Oresti Massari. 2010. "Party Organisational Change in Italy (1991–2006)." *Modern Italy* 15: 197–216.

Instituto Centramericano de Estudios Políticos. 2007. *Ganadores y perdedores políticos de la primera vuelta*. Guatemala: Instituto Centroamericano de Estudios Políticos.

Instituto Universitario de Opinión Pública (IUDOP). 1994–2012. *Public Opinion Survey Series*. San Salvador: IUDOP.

Ipsos, Apoyo. 2006. "La elección se polariza." *Resumen de Encuestas a la Opinión Pública* 6 (65). Lima: Ipsos Perú.

2011. "Avanza Keiko." *Resumen de Encuestas a la Opinión Pública* 11 (140). Lima: Ipsos Perú.

Ishiyama, John. 1999. "Discussion and Conclusions." In John Ishiyama, ed. *Communist Successor Parties in Post-Communist Politics*, 223–230. Commack: Nova Science Publishers.

James, Daniel. 1988. *Resistance and Integration: Peronism and the Argentine Working Class, 1946-1976*. New York: Cambridge University Press.

Jiménez Pozo, Wilson, Fernando Landa Casazola, and Ernesto Yáñez Aguilar. 2006. "Bolivia." In Gillette Hall and Harry Anthony Patrinos, eds. *Pueblos indígenas, pobreza y desarrollo humano en América Latina: 1994-2004*, 45–73. Bogotá: Banco Mundial.

Johnson, Kenneth. 1998. "Between Revolution and Democracy: Business Associations and Political Change in El Salvador." In Francisco Durand and Eduardo Silva, eds. *Organized Business, Economic Change, and Democracy in Latin America*, 123–146. Miami: North-South Press.

Joignant, Alfredo and Patricio Navia. 2003. "De la política de individuos a los hombres del partido: Socialización, competencia política y penetración electoral de la UDI (1989–2001). *Estudios Públicos* 89: 129–171.

Jones, Mark. 1996. "Assessing the Public's Understanding of Constitutional Reform: Evidence from Argentina." *Political Behavior* 18 (1): 25–49.

Jones, Mark and Wonjae Hwang. 2005. "Provincial Party Bosses: Keystone of the Argentine Congress." In Steven Levitsky and Mara Victoria Murillo, eds. *Argentine Democracy: The Politics of Institutional Weakness*, 115–138. University Park: Pennsylvania State University Press.

Jones, Mark and Scott Mainwaring. 2003. "The Nationalization of Parties and Party Systems: An Empirical Measure and an Application to the Americas." *Party Politics* 9 (2): 139–166.

Jover Marimón, Mateo. 1971. "The Church." In Carmelo Mesa-Lago, ed. *Revolutionary Change in Cuba*, 399–426. Pittsburgh: University of Pittsburgh.

Jozami, Eduardo. 2004. *Final sin gloria: Un balance del Frepaso y de la Alianza*. Buenos Aires: Editorial Biblos.

Kalyvas, Stathis. 1996. *The Rise of Christian Democracy in Europe*. Ithaca: Cornell University Press.

2006. *The Logic of Violence in Civil War*. Cambridge: Cambridge University Press.

Karl, Terry Lynn. 1987. "Petroleum and Political Pacts: The Transition to Democracy in Venezuela." *Latin American Research Review* 22: 63–94.

2004. "The Vicious Cycle of Inequality in Latin America." In Susan Eva Eckstein and Timothy Wickham-Crowley, eds. *What Justice? Whose Justice?*, 133–157. Berkeley: Berkeley University Press.

Katz, Richard and Peter Mair. 1995. "Changing Models of Party Organization and Party Democracy: The Emergence of the Cartel Party." *Party Politics* 1: 5–28.

Kayser, Mark Andreas and Christopher Wlezien. 2011. "Performance Pressure: Patterns of Partisanship and the Economic Vote." *European Journal of Political Research* 50 (3): 365–394.

Kaztman, Rubén. 1999. *Activos y estructuras de oportunidades. Estudios sobre las raíces de la vulnerabilidad social en Uruguay*. PNUD-CEPAL, Montevideo.

Keck, Margaret. 1992. *The Workers' Party and Democratization in Brazil*. New Haven: Yale University Press.

Kenney, Charles. 1998. "The Second Round of the Majority Runoff Debate: Classification, Evidence, and Analysis." Paper Presented at the XX International Congress of the Latin American Studies Association (LASA), Chicago, IL, September.

2003. "The Death and Rebirth of a Party System, Peru 1978–2001." *Comparative Political Studies* 36 (10): 1210–1239.

2004. *Fujimori's Coup and the Breakdown of Democracy in Latin America*. Notre Dame: The Notre Dame University Press.

Kirchheimer, Otto. 1966. "The Transformation of Western European Party Systems." In Joseph La Palombara and Myron Weiner, eds. *Political Parties and Political Development*, 177–200. Princeton: Princeton University Press.

Kitschelt, Herbert. 1989. *The Logics of Party Formation: Ecological Politics in Belgium and West Germany*. Ithaca: Cornell University Press.

1994. *The Transformation of European Social Democracy*. Cambridge: Cambridge University Press.

2000. "Linkages between Citizens and Politicians in Democratic Polities." *Comparative Political Studies* 33 (6–7): 845–879.

Kitschelt, Herbert, Kirk A. Hawkins, Juan Pablo Luna, Guillermo Rosas, and Elizabeth J. Zechmeister, eds., 2010. *Latin American Party Systems*. New York: Cambridge University Press.

Kitschelt, Herbert, Zdenka Mansfeldova, Radoslaw Markowski, and Gábor Tóka. 1999. *Post-Communist Party-Systems: Competition, Representation, and Inter-Party Cooperation*. New York: Cambridge University Press.

Kitschelt, Herbert and Steven Wilkinson. 2007. *Patrons, Clients and Policies: Patterns of Democratic Accountability and Political Competition*. New York: Cambridge University Press.

Klarén, Peter. 2012. *Nación y sociedad en la historia del Perú*. Lima: Instituto de Estudios Peruanos.

Klein, Marcus. 2004. "The Unión Demócrata Independiente and the Poor (1983–1992): The Survival of Clientelistic Traditions in Chilean Politics." *Jahrbuch fur Geschichte Lateinamerikas* 41: 301–324.

Koivumaeki, Riita-Ilona. 2010. "Business, Economic Experts, and Conservative Party-building in Latin America: The Case of El Salvador." *Journal of Politics in Latin America* 2 (1): 79–106.

2014. "El Salvador: Societal Cleavages, Strategic Elites, and the Success of the Right." In Juan Pablo Luna and Cristóbal Rovira Kaltwasser, eds. *The Resilience of the Latin American Right*, 268–293. Baltimore: Johns Hopkins University Press.

Krouwel, André. 2006. "Party Models." In Richard Katz and William Crotty, eds. *Handbook on Party Politics*, 249–269. London: Sage.

Lanzaro, Jorge, ed. 2004. *La izquierda uruguaya: Entre la oposición y el gobierno.* Montevideo: Instituto de Ciencia Política.

Larrea, Carlos and Fernando Montenegro Torres. 2006. "Ecuador." In Gillette Hall and Harry Anthony Patrinos, eds. *Pueblos indígenas, pobreza y desarrollo humano en América Latina, 1994–2004*, 75–117. Bogotá: Banco Mundial.

Latinobarometer. 1998. Latinobarometer Survey (Mexico) [datafile]. Available from http://www.latinobarometro.org/lat.jsp

Lawson, Chappell. 2002. *Building the Fourth Estate: Democratization and the Rise of a Free Press in Mexico.* Los Angeles: University of California Press.

Lawson, Chappell, et al. 2007. *The Mexico 2006 Panel Study* [datafile]. http://mexicopanelstudy.mit.edu/

Lawson, Kay. 1980. *Political Parties and Linkage: A Comparative Perspective.* New Haven: Yale University Press.

Layman, Geoffrey and Thomas Carsey. 2002. "Party Polarization and Party Structuring of Policy Attitudes: A Comparison of Three NES Panel Studies." *Political Behavior* 24 (3): 199–236.

LeBas, Adrienne. 2011. *From Protest to Parties: Party-Building and Democratization in Africa.* New York: Oxford University Press.

LeoGrande, William. 2000. *Our Own Backyard: The United States in Central America, 1977–1992.* Chapel Hill: University of North Carolina Press.

Lemos, Rubens. 1986. "Balanço mostra um desafio para o Partido: Ou o PT cresce construindo ou apenas existe sem crescer." *Boletim Nacional* (January): 6–7.

Levitsky, Steven. 2003. *Transforming Labor-Based Parties in Latin America: Argentine Peronism in Comparative Perspective.* New York: Cambridge University Press.

2013. "Peru: Challenges of a Democracy without Parties." In Michael Shifter and Jorge I. Domínguez, eds. *Constructing Democratic Governance in Latin America. Fourth edition*, 282–315. Baltimore: Johns Hopkins University Press.

Levitsky, Steven and Maxwell Cameron. 2003. "Democracy without Parties? Political Parties and Regime Change in Fujimori's Peru." *Latin American Politics and Society* 45 (3): 1–33.

Levitsky, Steven and Flavia Freidenberg. 2007. "Organización Informal de los Partidos en América Latina." *Desarrollo Económico* 46: 539–568.

Levitsky, Steven and James Loxton. 2013. "Populism and Competitive Authoritarianism in the Andes." *Democratization* 20 (1): 107–136.

Levitsky, Steven and María Victoria Murillo. 2003. "Argentina Weathers the Storm." *Journal of Democracy* 14 (4): 152–166.
Levitsky, Steven and Kenneth M. Roberts, eds. 2011. *The Resurgence of the Latin American Left*. Baltimore: Johns Hopkins University Press.
Levitsky, Steven and Lucan Way. 2002. "The Rise of Competitive Authoritarianism." *Journal of Democracy* 13 (2): 51–65.
    2010. *Competitive Authoritarianism: Hybrid Regimes after the Cold War*. New York: Cambridge University Press.
    2012. "Beyond Patronage: Violent Struggle, Ruling Party Cohesion, and Authoritarian Durability." *Perspectives on Politics* 10 (4): 869–889.
    2013. "The Durability of Revolutionary Regimes." *Journal of Democracy* 24 (3): 5–17.
Lijphart, Arend. 1994. *Electoral Systems and Party Systems: A Study of Twenty-Seven Democracies, 1945–1990*. Oxford: Oxford University Press.
Lindblom, Charles. 1977. *Politics and Markets*. New York: Basic Books.
Lindo-Fuentes, Héctor and Erik Ching. 2012. *Modernizing Minds in El Salvador: Education Reform and the Cold War, 1960–1980*. Albuquerque: University of New Mexico Press.
Linz, Juan. 1967. "The Party System of Spain: Past and Future." In Seymour Lipset and Stein Rokkan, eds. *Party Systems and Voter Alignments: Cross-National Perspectives*, 197–282. New York: The Free Press.
    1973. "The Future of an Authoritarian Situation or the Institutionalization of an Authoritarian Regime – The Case of Brazil." In Alfred Stepan, ed. *Authoritarian Brazil: Origins, Policies, and Future*, 233–254. New Haven: Yale University Press.
Lipset, Seymour and Stein Rokkan, eds. 1967. *Party Systems and Voter Alignments: Cross-National Perspectives*. New York: The Free Press.
Loaeza, Soledad. 1999. *El Partido Acción Nacional: la larga marcha, 1939–1994. Oposición leal y partido de protesta*. Mexico City: Fonda de Cultura Económica.
López, Claudia. 2010. "La Refundación de La Patria. De La Teoría a La Evidencia." In Claudia López, ed. *Y refundaron la patria: de cómo mafiosos y políticos reconfiguraron el estado colombiano*, 29–78. Bogotá: Corporación Nuevo Arco Iris.
López Alves, Fernando. 2000. *State Formation and Democracy in Latin America, 1810–1900*. Durham: Duke University Press.
Lora, Eduardo and Mauricio Olivera. 2005. "The Electoral Consequences of the Washington Consensus." *Economía* 5 (2): 1–45.
Loveman, David and Thomas Davies, Jr., eds. 1997. *The Politics of Antipolitics: The Military in Latin America*. Lanham: SR Books.
Loveman, Mara. 2014. *National Colors: Racial Classification and the State in Latin America*. New York: Oxford University Press.
Loxton, James. 2014a. "Authoritarian Inheritance and Conservative Party-Building in Latin America." Ph.D. Dissertation, Department of Government, Harvard University.
    2014b. "The Authoritarian Roots of New Right Party Success in Latin America." In Juan Pablo Luna and Cristóbal Rovira Kaltwasser, eds. *The*

Resilience of the Latin American Right, 117–140. Baltimore: Johns Hopkins University Press.

2015. "Authoritarian Successor Parties." *Journal of Democracy* 26 (3): 157–170.

Loxton, James and Steven Levitsky. 2015. "Personalistic Authoritarian Successor Parties in Latin America." Paper Presented at the Conference *Life after Dictatorship: Authoritarian Successor Parties Worldwide*. Kellogg Institute for International Studies, University of Notre Dame, Notre Dame, Indiana, April 17–18.

Lucero, José Antonio. 2008. *Struggles of Voice: The Politics of Indigenous Representation in the Andes*. Pittsburgh: University of Pittsburgh Press.

Luna, Juan Pablo. 2007. "Frente Amplio and the Crafting of a Social-Democratic Alternative in Uruguay: Electoral Success and Forthcoming Challenges." *Latin American Politics and Society* 49 (4): 1–30.

2010. "Segmented Party Voter Linkages in Latin America: The Case of the UDI." *Journal of Latin American Studies* 42 (2): 325–356.

2014. *Segmented Representation. Political Party Strategies in Unequal Democracies*. Oxford: Oxford University Press.

Luna, Juan Pablo and David Altman. 2011. "Uprooted but Stable: Chilean Parties and the Concept of Party System Institutionalization." *Latin American Politics and Society* 53 (2): 1–28.

Luna, Juan Pablo and Fernando Rosenblatt. 2012. "¿Notas para una autopsia? Los partidos políticos en el Chile actual." In Javier Díaz and Lucas Sierra, eds. *Democracia con partidos. Informe para la reforma de los partidos políticos en Chile*, 115–268. Santiago: CEP/CIEPLAN.

Luna, Juan Pablo and Cristóbal Rovira Kaltwasser. 2014. "The Right in Contemporary Latin America: A Framework for Analysis." In Juan Pablo Luna and Cristóbal Rovira Kaltwasser, eds. *The Resilience of the Latin American Right*, 1–22. Baltimore: Johns Hopkins University Press.

Lupu, Noam. 2013. "Party Brands and Partisanship: Theory with Evidence from a Survey Experiment in Argentina." *American Journal of Political Science* 57 (1): 49–64.

2014. "Brand Dilution and the Breakdown of Political Parties in Latin America." *World Politics* 66 (4): 561–602.

2015a. "Partisanship in Latin America." In Ryan Carlin, Matthew Singer, and Elizabeth Zechmeister, eds. *The Latin American Voter: Pursuing Representation and Accountability in Challenging Contexts*, 226–245. Ann Arbor: University of Michigan Press.

2015b. "Party Polarization and Mass Partisanship: A Comparative Perspective." *Political Behavior* 37 (2): 331–356.

2016. *Party Brands in Crisis: Partisanship, Brand Dilution, and the Breakdown of Political Parties in Latin America*. New York: Cambridge University Press.

Lupu, Noam and Jonas Pontusson. 2011. "The Structure of Inequality and the Politics of Redistribution." *American Political Science Review* 105 (2): 316–336.

Lupu, Noam and Susan Stokes. 2009. "The Social Bases of Political Parties in Argentina, 1912–2003." *Latin American Research Review* 44 (1): 58–87.

2010. "Democracy, Interrupted: Regime Change and Partisanship in Twentieth-Century Argentina." *Electoral Studies* 29 (1): 91–104.

Lynch, Nicolás. 1999. *Una tragedia sin héroes: la derrota de los partidos y el surgimiento de los independientes, Perú 1980–1992.* Lima: San Marcos.

Lyne, Mona. 2005. "Parties as Programmatic Agents: A Test of Institutional Theory in Brazil." *Party Politics* 11 (2): 193–216.

Lyons, Terrence. 2005. *Demilitarizing Politics: Elections on the Uncertain Road to Peace.* Boulder: Lynne Rienner.

Mabry, Donald. 1973. *Mexico's Acción Nacional: A Catholic Alternative to Revolution.* Syracuse: Syracuse University Press.

Mack, Luis Fernando. 2007. "La participación política de los grupos étnicos de ascendencia mayense: Algunas reflexiones." In *Multiculturidad y partidos políticos: Estudios sobre organización y participación de los pueblos indígenas,* 11–69. Guatemala: Organización de los Estados Americanos.

Madrid, Raúl. 2005. "Ethnic Cleavages and Electoral Volatility in Latin America." *Comparative Politics* 38 (1): 1–20.

2008. "The Rise of Ethnopopulism in Latin America." *World Politics* 60 (3): 475–508.

2011. "Bolivia: Origins and Policies of the Movimiento al Socialismo." In Steven Levitsky and Kenneth M. Roberts, eds. *The Resurgence of the Latin American Left,* 239–259. Baltimore: Johns Hopkins University Press.

2012. *The Rise of Ethnic Politics in Latin America.* New York: Cambridge University Press.

Magaloni, Beatriz, Alberto Diaz Cayeros, and Federico Estévez. 2007. "Clientelism and Porfolio Diversification: A Model of Electoral Investment with Applications to Mexico." In Herbert Kitschelt and Steven Wilkinson, eds. *Patrons, Clients, and Policies: Patterns of Democratic Accountability,* 182–205. New York: Cambridge University Press.

Magaloni, Beatriz, Alberto Diaz Cayeros, and Federico Estévez, eds. Forthcoming. *Strategies of Vote Buying: Democracy, Clientelism and Poverty Relief in Mexico.* New York: Cambridge University Press.

Mahoney, James. 2001. *The Legacies of Liberalism: Path Dependence and Political Regimes in Central America.* Baltimore: Johns Hopkins University Press.

Mainwaring, Scott. 1999. *Rethinking Party Systems in the Third Wave of Democratization: The Case of Brazil.* Stanford: Stanford University Press.

2006. "The Crisis of Representation in the Andes." *Journal of Democracy* 17 (3): 13–27.

Mainwaring, Scott and Frances Hagopian. 2005. "Introduction: The Third Wave of Democratization in Latin America." In Frances Hagopian and Scott Mainwaring, eds. *The Third Wave of Democratization in Latin America,* 1–13. Cambridge: Cambridge University Press.

Mainwaring, Scott and Mark Jones. 2003. "The Nationalization of Parties and Party Systems." *Party Politics* 9 (2): 139–166.

Mainwaring, Scott and Aníbal Pérez-Liñán. 2005. "Latin American Democratization since 1978: Democratic Transitions, Breakdowns, and Erosions." In Frances Hagopian and Scott Mainwaring, eds. *The Third*

Wave of Democratization in Latin America: Advances and Setbacks, 14–59. New York: Cambridge University Press.

2013. *Democracies and Dictatorships in Latin America: Emergence, Survival, and Fall.* New York: Cambridge University Press.

Mainwaring, Scott and Timothy Scully. 1995. *Building Democratic Institutions: Party Systems in Latin America.* Stanford: Stanford University Press.

1995. "Introduction: Party Systems in Latin America." In Scott Mainwaring and Timothy R. Scully, eds. *Building Democratic Institutions: Party Systems in Latin America,* 1–34. Stanford: Stanford University Press.

2003. *Christian Democracy in Latin America: Electoral Competition and Regime Conflicts.* Stanford: Stanford University Press.

Mainwaring, Scott and Edurne Zoco. 2007. "Historical Sequences and the Stabilization of Interparty Competition: Electoral Volatility in Old and New Democracies." *Party Politics* 13 (2): 155–178.

Manning, Carrie. 2004. "Armed Opposition Groups into Political Parties: Comparing Bosnia, Kosovo, and Mozambique." *Studies in Comparative International Development* 39 (1): 54–76.

2007. "Party-Building on the Heels of War: El Salvador, Bosnia, Kosovo and Mozambique." *Democratization* 14 (2): 253–272.

Martín Posada, Lucy and Lilia Núñez Moreno. 2012. "Geography and Habitat: Dimensions of Equity and Social Mobility in Cuba." In Jorge I. Domínguez, Omar Everleny Pérez Villanueva, Mayra Espina Prieto, and Lorena Barberia, eds. *Cuban Economic and Social Development: Policy Reforms and Challenges in the 21st. Century,* 291–320. Cambridge: Harvard University Press.

Marston, Andrea. 2013. "Bolivia: Underground Cooperatives." *Berkeley Review of Latin American Studies* (Fall): 43–47.

Martínez, Víctor. 2005. *Fisiones y fusiones, divorcios y reconciliaciones: La dirigencia del Partido de la Revolución Democrática (PRD) 1989–2004.* Mexico City: Plaza y Valdés.

Martz, John D. 1999–2000. "Political Parties and Candidate Selection in Venezuela and Colombia." *Political Science Quarterly* 114 (4): 639–659.

Marx, Karl and Friedrich Engels. 1959. "Manifesto of the Communist Party." In Lewis S. Feuer, ed. *Marx and Engels: Basic Writings on Politics and Philosophy.* New York: Anchor Books.

Matanock, Aila. 2014. "Bullets for Ballots: Electoral Participation Provisions in Peace Agreements and Conflict Recurrence." Working Paper.

Mateos Díaz, Araceli and Manuel Alcántara Sáez. 1998. *Los diputados ecuatorianos: Actitudes, valores y percepciones políticas.* Quito: PASGD.

May, John. 1973. "Opinion Structures and Political Parties: The Special Law of Curvilinear Disparity." *Political Studies* 21: 135–151.

Mayorga, Fernando. 1991. *Max Fernández, la política del silencio: Emergencia y consolidación de Unidad Cívica Solidaridad.* La Paz: Instituto Latinoamericano de Investigaciones Sociales.

1993. "UCS y Max Fernández: Incertidumbre Estratégica y Flexibilidad Táctica." In Carlos Toranzo Roca, ed. *Los Nuevos Actores Políticos en Bolivia,* 51–66. La Paz: Instituto Latinoamericano de Investigaciones Sociales.

2002. *Neopopulismo y Democracia: Compadres y Padrinos en la Política Boliviana*. La Paz: Centro Boliviano de Estudios Multidisciplinarios.

McClintock, Cynthia. 1998. *Revolutionary Movements in Latin America: El Salvador's FMLN and Peru's Shining Path*. Washington, DC: US Institute of Peace Press.

McClintock, Michael. 1985. *The American Connection, Volume One: State Terror and Popular Resistance in El Salvador*. London: Zed Books.

McGuire, James. 1997. *Peronism without Perón: Unions, Parties, and Democracy in Argentina*. Stanford: Stanford University Press.

McIlwaine, Cathy. 1998. "Contesting Civil Society: Reflections from El Salvador." *Third World Quarterly* 19 (4): 651–672.

Meerman, Jacob. 2001. "Poverty and Mobility in Low-Status Minorities: The Cuban Case in International Perspective." *World Development* 29: 1457–1482.

Meguid, Bonnie. 2008. *Party Competition between Unequals: Strategies and Electoral Fortunes in Western Europe*. Cambridge: Cambridge University Press.

Meléndez, Carlos. 2007. "Partidos y sistema de partidos en el Perú." In Rafael Roncagliolo and Carlos Meléndez, eds. *La política por dentro: Cambios y continuidades en las organizaciones políticas de los países andinos*, 213–272. Lima: International Institute for Democracy and Electoral Assistance (IDEA).

2010. "¿Cómo escapar del fatalismo de las estructuras? Marco para entender la formación del sistema de partidos en el Perú." In Carlos Meléndez and Alberto Vergara, eds. *La iniciación de la política. El Perú político en perspectiva comparada*, 161–182. Lima: Pontificia Universidad Católica del Perú.

2011. "Del Shambar al 'Sancochado:' El Proyecto Político de César Acuña." In Carlos Meléndez, ed. *Anti-candidatos: guía analítica para unas elecciones sin partidos*, 173–186. Lima: Mitin.

2012. *La soledad de la política: Transformaciones estructurales, intermediación política y conflictos sociales en el Perú (2000–2012)*. Lima: Mitin.

2014. "Is There a Right Track in Post-Party System Collapse Scenarios? Comparing the Andean Countries." In Juan Pablo Luna and Cristóbal Rovira Kaltwasser, eds. *The Resilience of the Latin American Right*, 167–193. Baltimore: Johns Hopkins University Press.

Melo, Carlos Ranulfo and Rafael Câmara. 2012. "Estrutura da Competição pela Presidência e Consolidação do Sistema Partidário no Brasil." *Dados* 55 (1): 71–117.

Mendilow, Jonathan. 1996. "Public Party Funding and the Schemes of Mice and Men: The 1992 Elections in Israel." *Party Politics* 2: 329–354.

Meneguello, Rachel. 1989. *PT: A formação de um partido, 1979–1982*. São Paulo: Paz e Terra.

Meneguello, Rachel and Oswaldo Amaral. 2008. "Ainda Novidade: uma revisão das transformações do Partido dos Trabalhadores no Brasil." Occasional Paper 02–08, Oxford University Brazilian Studies Programme.

Michels, Robert. 1962. *Political Parties: A Sociological Study of the Oligarchical Tendencies of Modern Democracy*, translated by Eden and Cedar Paul. New York: Free Press.

Middlebrook, Kevin, ed. 2000. *Conservative Parties, the Right, and Democracy in Latin America.* Baltimore: Johns Hopkins University Press.

Mieres, Pablo. 1994. *Desobediencia y lealtad. El voto en el Uruguay de fin de siglo.* Montevideo: Editorial Fin de Siglo.

Mijeski, Kenneth and Scott Beck. 2011. *Pachakutik and the Rise and Decline of the Ecuadorian Indigenous Movement.* Athens: Ohio University Press.

Ministerio de Economía y Finanzas de Panamá. 2009. "Frank George de Lima Gercich." Ministerial Profile. Accessed December 19, 2009. www.mef.gob. pa/Portal/Vice-Economia.html.

Mirador Electoral. 2007. *La participación indígena en el proceso electoral Guatemala 2007: Una tarea inconclusa.* Guatemala: Mirador Electoral.

Miranda, Roger and William Ratliff. 1993. *The Civil War in Nicaragua: Inside the Sandinistas.* New Brunswick: Transaction Publishers.

Mizrahi, Yemile. 2003. *From Martyrdom to Power: The Partido Acción Nacional in Mexico.* Notre Dame: University of Notre Dame Press.

Moira Zuazo, Jean-Paul Faguet and Gustavo Bonifaz, eds. 2012. *Descentralización y democratización en Bolivia.* La Paz: Friedrich Ebert Stiftung.

Molina, José, Janeth Hernández Márquez, Ángel E. Álvarez, Margarita López Maya, Henry Valvads, and Valia Pereira Almao. 2003. "Venezuela." In Manuel Alcántara and Flavia Freidenberg, eds. *Partidos Políticos de América Latina: Países Andinos,* 478–606. Mexico City: Instituto Federal Electoral and Fondo de Cultura Económica.

Molinar, Juan and Jeffery Weldon. 1994. "Electoral Determinants and Consequences of National Solidarity." In Wayne A. Cornelius, Ann L. Craig, and Jonathan Fox, eds. *Transforming State-Society Relations in Mexico: The National Solidarity Strategy,* 124-141. La Jolla: Center for U.S.-Mexican Studies, University of California at San Diego.

Mora y Araujo, Manuel. 1995. "De Perón a Menem: Una historia del peronismo." In Atilio Borón, ed. *Peronismo y menemismo: Avatares del populismo en la Argentina,* 47–66. Buenos Aires: Ediciones El Cielo Por Asalto.

Morales, Mauricio. 2008. "La primera mujer presidenta de Chile: ¿Qué explicó el triunfo de Michelle Bachelet en las elecciones de 2005–2006?" *Latin American Research Review* 43 (1): 7–32.

Morales, Mauricio and Rodrigo Bugueño. 2001. "La UDI como expresión de la nueva derecha en Chile." *Estudios Sociales* 107: 215–248.

Morales Domínguez, Esteban. 2007. *Desafíos de la problemática racial en Cuba.* Havana: Fundación Fernando Ortiz.

Moreira, Constanza. 2000. "Las paradojales elecciones del fin de siglo uruguayo: comportamiento electoral y cultura política." In Instituto de Ciencia Política, ed. *Elecciones 1999/2000,* 87–110. Montevideo: Ediciones de la Banda Oriental.

2005. "El voto moderno y el voto clasista revisado: explicando el desempeño electoral de la izquierda en las elecciones de 2004 en Uruguay." In Instituto de Ciencia Política, ed. *Las claves del cambio: ciclo electoral y nuevo gobierno 2004/2005,* 27–43. Montevideo: Ediciones de la Banda Oriental.

Moreno, Alejandro. 2003. *El votante mexicano: Democracia, actitudes políticas y conducta electoral.* Mexico City: Fondo de Cultura Económica.

Moreno Morales, Daniel, Eduardo Córdova Eguívar, Vivian Schwartz Blum, Mitchell Seligson, Gonzalo Vargas Villazón, and Miguel Villarroel Nikitenko. 2008. *The Political Culture of Democracy in Bolivia, 2008.* Nashville: Latin American Public Opinion Project.

Morgan, Jana. 2011. *Bankrupt Representation and Party System Collapse.* University Park: Pennsylvania State University Press.

Morgan, Jana, Jonathan Hartlyn, and Rosario Espinal. 2011. "Dominican Party System Continuity and Regional Transformations: Economic Policy, Clientelism, and Migration Flows." *Latin American Politics and Society* 53 (1): 1–32.

Morgenstern, Scott and Richard F. Potthoff. 2005. "The Components of Elections: District Heterogeneity, District-Time Effects, and Volatility." *Electoral Studies* 24 (1): 17–40.

Morley, Samuel, Roberto Machado, and Stefano Pettinato. 1999. *Index of Structural Reform in Latin America.* Serie Reformas Económicas 12. Santiago: Comisión Económica Para América Latina y el Caribe.

Morner, Magnus. 1967. *Race Mixture in the History of Latin America.* Boston: Little, Brown and Company.

Morresi, Sergio and Gabriel Vommaro. 2014. "Argentina: The Difficulties of the Partisan Right and the Case of Propuesta Republicana." In Juan Pablo Luna and Cristóbal Rovira Kaltwasser, eds. *The Resilience of the Latin American Right,* 319–445. Baltimore: Johns Hopkins University Press.

Moser, Robert. 2001. *Unexpected Outcomes: Electoral Systems, Political Parties, and Representation in Russia.* Pittsburgh: University of Pittsburgh Press.

Moser, Robert and Ethan Scheiner. 2012. *Electoral Systems and Political Context: How the Effects of Rules Vary Across New and Established Democracies.* New York: Cambridge University Press.

Mossige, Dag. 2013. *Mexico's Left: The Paradox of the PRD.* Boulder: Lynne Rienner.

Movimiento Indígena Pachakuti. 2005. *Programa de Gobierno: Plan Pachakuti, 2006–2011.* La Paz: MIP.

Muñoz, Paula. 2005. *El diseño institucional municipal 1980–2004 y sus implicancias para las zonas rurales.* Lima: Asociación SER.

2007. *La incertidumbre de la política regional. Estudio sobre la articulación entre el gobierno regional y los gobiernos locales de Puno.* Lima: Asociación SER.

2010. "¿Consistencia política regional o frágiles alianzas electorales? El escenario cuzqueño actual." *Revista Argumentos* 4 (3). Online http://revistaargumentos.iep.org.pe/articulos/consistencia-politica-regional-o-fragiles-alianzas-electorales/.

2013. "Campaign Clientelism in Peru: An Informational Theory." Ph.D. Dissertation, Department of Government, University of Texas at Austin.

2014. "An Informational Theory of Campaign Clientelism: The Case of Peru." *Comparative Politics* 47 (1): 79–98.

Muñoz, Paula and Andrea García. 2011. "Balance de las elecciones regionales 2010: Tendencias, particularidades y perfil de los candidatos más exitosos." In María Ana Rodríguez and Omar Coronel, eds. *El nuevo, poder en las regiones: análisis de las elecciones regionales y municipales 2010,* 8–17. Lima: Pontificia Universidad Católica del Perú.

Muñoz-Pogossian, Beatriz. 2008. *Electoral Rules and the Transformation of Bolivian Politics: The Rise of Evo Morales*. New York: Palgrave Macmillan.

Murillo, María Victoria, Virginia Oliveros, and Milan Vaishnav. 2010. "Electoral Revolution or Democratic Alternation?" *Latin American Research Review* 45 (3): 87–114.

Mustapic, Ana María. 2005. "Inestabilidad sin colapso: La renuncia de los presidentes: Argentina en el año 2001." *Desarrollo Económico* 45 (178): 263–280.

Mustillo, Thomas. 2007. "Entrants in the Political Arena: New Party Trajectories during the Third Wave of Democracy in Latin America." Ph.D. Dissertation, Department of Political Science, University of North Carolina at Chapel Hill.

2009. "Modeling New Party Performance: A Conceptual and Methodological Approach for Volatile Party Systems." *Political Analysis* 17: 311–332.

Mutz, Diana. 2006. *Hearing the Other Side: Deliberative versus Participatory Democracy*. New York: Cambridge University Press.

Nairn, Allan. 1984. "Behind the Death Squads." *The Progressive* (May): 20–29.

Nasi, Carlos. 2007. *Cuando callan los fusiles: Impacto de la paz negociada en Colombia y en Centroamérica*. Bogotá: Grupo Editorial Norma.

Nassmacher, Karl-Heinz. 2009. *The Funding of Party Competition: Political Finance in 25 Democracies*. Baden-Baden: Nomos.

Navarrete, Carlos. 2010. Interview with editors in "Conversaciones" section. In González Trujillo, Miguel Ángel, Onel Ortíz Fragoso, Gabriela Rojo Rosas, and Rubén Sánchez Martínez, eds. *20 Años: Un futuro con historia*, 263–267. Mexico City: Agencia Promotora de Publicaciones.

Navarro, Melissa. 2011. "La organización partidaria fujimorista a 20 años de su origen." Undergraduate thesis, Department of Social Science, Pontificia Universidad Católica del Perú.

Navarro Wolff, Antonio. 2001. "La desmovilización del M-19 diez años después." In Cynthia Arnson and Fernando Cepeda Ulloa, eds. *Haciendo paz: reflexiones y perspectivas del proceso de paz en Colombia*. Bogotá: El Ancora Editores.

Navarro Wolff, Antonio, and Juan Carlos Iragorri. 2004. *Mi guerra es la paz*. Bogotá: Planeta.

Negretto, Gabriel. 2001. "Negociando los poderes del presidente: reforma y cambio constitucional en la Argentina." *Desarrollo Económico* 41 (163): 411–444.

Nickson, Andrew. 1995. *Local Government in Latin America*. Boulder: Lynne Rienner Publishers.

Njaim, Humberto. 2005. "Financiamiento político en los países andinos: Bolivia, Colombia, Ecuador, Perú, y Venezuela." In Steven Griner and Daniel Zovatto, eds. *De las normas a las buenas prácticas: El desafío del financiamiento político en América Latina*, 235–270. San José: Organization of American States.

Nogueira-Budny, Daniel. 2013. "From Marxist-Leninism to Market-Liberalism? The Varied Adaptation of Latin America's Leftist Parties." Ph.D. Dissertation, University of Texas at Austin.

Nohlen, Dieter, ed. 1993. *Enciclopedia electoral latinoamericana y del Caribe*. San José: Instituto Interamericano de Derechos Humanos.

Nohlen, Dieter. ed. 2005. *Elections in the Americas: A Data Handbook: Volume 2: South America*. Oxford: Oxford University Press.

Novaro, Marcos. 2009. *Argentina en el fin de siglo: democracia, mercado y nación (1983–2001)*. Buenos Aires: Paidós.

Novaro, Marcos and Vicente Palermo. 1998. *Los caminos de la centroizquierda: Dilemas y desafíos del Frepaso y de la Alianza*. Buenos Aires: Editorial Losada.

Observatorio Cambios Políticos Latinoamericanos [OCPAL]. 2006. "Perfil Vicente Taiano." Quito: Pontificia Universidad Católica del Ecuador. Available online at: www.puce.edu.ec/sitios/ocpal/an_taiano.htm.

O'Donnell, Guillermo. 1973. *Modernization and Bureaucratic-Authoritarianism: Studies in South American Politics*. Berkeley: Institute of International Studies, University of California.

O'Donnell, Guillermo and Philippe Schmitter. 1986. *Transitions from Authoritarian Rule: Tentative Conclusions about Uncertain Democracies*. Baltimore: Johns Hopkins University Press.

Oficina Nacional de Estadísticas e Información. 2012. *Anuario estadístico de Cuba 2011*. www.one.cu/aec2011.htm.

Ortiz Loaiza, Paola, María Alejandra Erazo, Silvia Montepeque, and Sara Sapón. 2008. "22 años después: lo inédito del proceso electoral 2007." In *Cuadernos de información política*, Cuaderno No. 14. Guatemala: Facultad Latinoamericana de Ciencias Sociales.

Ostiguy, Pierre. 2009a. "The High and the Low in Politics: A Two-Dimensional Space for Analysis in Comparative Politics and Electoral Studies." Kellogg Institute Working Paper #360. Kellogg Institute for International Studies, University of Notre Dame, July.

2009b. "Argentina's Double Political Spectrum: Party System, Political Identities, and Strategies, 1944–2007." Kellogg Institute Working Paper #361. Kellogg Institute for International Studies, University of Notre Dame, October.

Oxhorn, Phillip. 2005. *Organizing Civil Society: The Popular Sectors and the Struggle for Democracy in Chile*. University Park: Pennsylvania State University Press.

Paige, Jeffery M. 1997. *Coffee and Power: Revolution and the Rise of Democracy in Central America*. Cambridge: Harvard University Press.

Panebianco, Angelo. 1988. *Political Parties: Organization and Power*. Cambridge: Cambridge University Press.

Partido dos Trabalhadores, Diretório Nacional. 1988. *Boletim Nacional (Edição Especial: Eleições)*. São Paulo: Partido dos Trabalhadores.

2001a. *Resoluções do XII Encontro Nacional*. São Paulo: Partido dos Trabalhadores.

2001b. *Informe SORG #36*. São Paulo: Partido dos Trabalhadores.

2002. *Por dentro da campanha de filiação do PT*. São Paulo: Partido dos Trabalhadores.

2003. *Começa a campanha de filiação*. São Paulo: PT Noticias, Partido dos Trabalhadores.

2007. *Resoluções do III Congresso do Partido dos Trabalhadores.* Porto Alegre: Partido dos Trabalhadores.

Pasotti, Eleonora. 2010. *Political Branding in Cities: The Decline of Machine Politics in Bogotá, Naples, and Chicago.* Cambridge: Cambridge University Press.

Patiño, Otty. 2000. "Armas versus política." In Carlos Eduardo Jaramillo Castillo, ed. *De las armas a la democracia,* 31–95. Bogotá: Instituto Luis Carlos Galán para el Desarrollo de la Democracia.

Payne, Mark, Daniel Zovatto, Fernando Carrillo Flórez, and Andrés Allamand Zavala. 2002. *Democracies in Development: Politics and Reform in Latin America.* Washington, DC: Inter-American Development Bank.

Pazos, Luis and Sibila Camps. 1995. *¿Ladran, Chacho: ¿Quién es Carlos "Chacho" Álvarez, Líder del Frente Grande?* Buenos Aires: Editorial Sudamericana.

Pedersen, Mogens. 1983. "Changing Patterns of Electoral Volatility in European Party Systems, 1948–1977." In Hans Daalder and Peter Mair, eds. *Western European Party Systems: Continuity and Change,* 29–66. London: Sage Publications.

——— 1983. "Changing Patterns of Electoral Volatility in European Party Systems, 1948-1977." In Hans Daalder and Peter Mair, eds. *Western European Party Systems: Continuity and Change,* 29–66. Beverly Hills, CA: Sage.

Pedraza, Gustavo, et al. 2011. *Hacia un sistema político subnacional: ¿Son posibles los partidos subnacionales?* La Paz: Fundación Boliviana para la Democracia Multipartidaria.

Peña, Claudia. 2011. *¿Vos confías? Capital social, identidad y desarrollo en Santa Cruz.* La Paz: Friedrich Ebert Stiftung.

Pereira, Silvio. 2004. "PT se organiza para as eleições." *Teoria e Debate* 57. Accessed August 15, 2012. www.fpabramo.org.br/o-que-fazemos/editora/teoria-e-debate/edicoes-anteriores/nacional-pt-se-organiza-para-eleicoes.

Pérez, Orlando J. 2000. *Post-Invasion Panama: The Challenges of Democratization in the New World Order.* Washington, DC: Lexington.

Perz, Stephen, Jonathan Warren, and David Kennedy. 2008. "Contributions of Racial-Ethnic Reclassification and Demographic Processes to Indigenous Population Resurgence: The Case of Brazil." *Latin American Research Review* 43 (2): 7–33.

Petit, Pere. 1996. *A esperança equilibrista: a trajetória do PT no Pará.* So Paulo: Boitempo.

Piñeiro Harnecker, Camila. 2013. "Cuba's New Socialism: Different Visions Shaping Current Changes." *Latin American Perspectives* 40 (May): 107–126.

Pinto, Carolina. 2006. *UDI: La conquista de corazones populares (1983-1987).* Santiago: A&V Comunicaciones.

Pizarro, Eduardo. 2002. "La atomización partidista en Colombia: el fenómeno de las microempresas electorales." In Franciso Gutiérrez, ed. *Degradación o cambio: evolución del sistema político colombiano,* 357–401. Bogotá: Norma.

Planas, Pedro. 1998. *La descentralización en el Perú republicano (1821–1998).* Lima: Municipalidad Metropolitana de Lima.

2000. *La democracia volátil: movimientos, partidos, líderes políticos y conductas electorales en el Perú contemporáneo*. Lima: Friedrich Ebert Stiftung.

Pogrebinschi, Thamy and David Samuels. 2014. "The Impact of Participatory Democracy: Evidence from Brazil's National Public Policy Conferences." *Comparative Politics* 46 (3): 313–332.

Poiré, Alejandro. 2006. "In the Public Interest or a Poisoned Subsidy? Public Funding of Political Parties: Subnational Evidence from Mexico." Paper Presented at the Annual Meeting of the American Political Science Association, Philadelphia, Pennsylvania, August 30.

Pollack, Marcelo. 1999. *The New Right in Chile, 1973–1997*. London: Palgrave Macmillan.

Pomar, Vladimir. 1986. "Vamos nos preparar para o poder municipal." *Boletim Nacional* (January): 13.

Porcell Alemán, Jaime. 2009. *De 'Ricardito' a Presidente*. Panama City: Producciones e Impresiones Rivera.

Porto, Mauro. 2003. "Mass media and politics in democratic Brazil." In Maria D'Alva and James Dunkerley, eds. *Brazil Since 1985: Economy, Polity and Society*, 288–313. London: Institute of Latin American Studies, University of London.

2012. *Media Power and Democratization in Brazil: TV Globo and the Dilemmas of Political Accountability*. New York: Routledge.

Posada-Carbó, Eduardo. 2008. "Democracy, Parties, and Political Finance in Latin America." Kellogg Institute Working Paper #346. Kellogg Institute for International Studies, University of Notre Dame.

2013. "Colombia: Democratic Governance amidst an Armed Conflict." In Jorge I. Domínguez and Michael Shifter, eds. *Constructing Democratic Governance in Latin America*. Fourth edition, 233–252. Baltimore: Johns Hopkins University Press.

Posada-Carbó, Eduardo and Carlos Malamud, eds. 2005. *The Financing of Politics: Latin American and European Perspectives*. London: Institute for the Study of the Americas.

Posner, Paul. 1999. "Popular Representation and Political Dissatisfaction in Chile's New Democracy." *Journal of Interamerican Studies and World Affairs* 41 (1): 59–85.

2004. "Local Democracy and the Transformation of Popular Participation in Chile." *Latin American Politics and Society* 46 (3): 55–81.

Powell, Eleanor Neff and Joshua Tucker. 2009. "New Approaches to Electoral Volatility: Evidence from Postcommunist Countries." Paper Presented at the Annual Meeting of the American Political Science Association, Toronto, Ontario, September 3–6.

Power, Margaret. 2002. *Right-Wing Women in Chile: Feminine Power and the Struggle against Allende, 1964–1973*. University Park: Pennsylvania State University Press.

Power, Timothy. 1998. "Brazilian Politicians and Neoliberalism: Mapping Support for the Cardoso Reforms, 1995–1997." *Journal of Interamerican Studies and World Affairs* 40 (4): 51–72.

2000. *The Political Right in Postauthoritarian Brazil: Elites, Institutions, and Democratization*. University Park: Pennsylvania State University Press.

2008. "Centering Democracy? Ideological Cleavages and Convergence in the Brazilian Political Class." In Peter Kingstone and Timothy Power, eds. *Democratic Brazil Revisited*, 81–106. Pittsburgh: University of Pittsburgh Press.

Power, Timothy and Cesar Zucco. 2009. "Estimating Ideology of Brazilian Legislative Parties, 1990–2005: A Research Communication." *Latin American Research Review* 44 (1): 218–246.

2013. "Bolsa Família and the Shift in Lula's Electoral Base, 2002–2006." *Latin American Research Review* 48 (2): 3–24.

Pribble, Jennifer. 2013. *Welfare and Party Politics in Latin America.* New York: Cambridge University Press.

Przeworski, Adam. 1985. *Capitalism and Social Democracy.* Cambridge: Cambridge University Press.

Przeworski, Adam and John Sprague. 1986. *Paper Stones: A History of Electoral Socialism.* Chicago: University of Chicago Press.

Putnam, Robert. 2000. *Bowling Alone: The Collapse and Revival of American Community.* New York: Simon and Schuster.

Puyana Valdivieso, José Ricardo. 2005. "El Proceso de selección de los candidatos a diputados del FMLN en 2005." Working Paper. Universidad de Salamanca, Instituto Interuniversitario de Iberoamérica Observatorio de Partidos Políticos de América Latina.

Pyes, Craig. 1983. *Salvadoran Rightists: The Deadly Patriots.* Albuquerque: Albuquerque Journal.

Rahn, Wendy. 1993. "The Role of Partisan Stereotypes in Information Processing about Political Candidates." *American Journal of Political Science* 37 (2): 472–496.

Ray, Kenneth. 2009. "Establishing 'Anti-Establishment' Party Organization in the Central Andes." Paper Presented at the Congress of the Latin American Studies Association, Rio de Janeiro, June.

Remmer, Karen. 1985. "Redemocratization and the Impact of Authoritarian Rule in Latin America." *Comparative Politics* 17 (2): 253–275.

1991. "The Political Impact of Economic Crisis in Latin America in the 1980s." *American Political Science Review* 85 (3): 777–800.

2008. "The Politics of Institutional Change: Electoral Reform in Latin America, 1978–2002." *Party Politics* 14 (1): 5–30.

Remy, María Isabel. 2004. *Los múltiples campos de la participación ciudadana en el Perú.* Lima: Instituto de Estudios Peruanos. Online http://revistaargumentos.iep.org.pe/articulos/crecientes-distancias-entre-la-politica-nacional-y-la-politica-regional/.

2010. "Crecientes distancias entre la política nacional y la política regional." *Revista Argumentos* 4 (5).

Rénique, José Luis. 2004. *La batalla por Puno: Conflicto agrario y nación en los Andes peruanos.* Lima: Instituto de Estudios Peruanos, SUR, and Centro Peruano de Estudios Sociales.

República de Cuba. 1945. *Informe general del censo de 1943.* Havana: P. Fernández y Cia.

Ribeiro, Pedro Floriano. 2010. *Dos sindicatos ao governo: a organização nacional do PT de 1980 a 2005.* São Carlos: Editora da Universidade Federal de São Carlos.

2013. "Organização e poder nos partidos brasileiros: uma análise dos estatutos." *Revista Brasileira de Ciência Política* 10 (1): 225–265.

2014. "An Amphibian Party? Organisational Change and Adaptation in the Brazilian Workers' Party, 1980–2012." *Journal of Latin American Studies* 46 (1): 87–119.

Ribeiro, Ricardo. 2011. "A decadência longe do poder: refundação e crise do PFL." Master's thesis, Department of Philosophy, Universidade de São Paulo.

Ricardo, Martinelli. 2009a. "Cuña Biográfica." Video accessed on campaign website, September 20, 2009: www.youtube.com/watch?v=KYEASKO3Apg&lr=1.

2009b. "Video Jingle Hop Hop Ricardo Martinelli," Video accessed on campaign website September 20, 2009: www.youtube.com/watch?v=rBBFrxf79ro&lr=1.

Rice, Roberta Lynne. 2006. "From Peasants to Politicians: The Politicization of Ethnic Cleavages in Latin America." Ph.D. Dissertation, Department of Political Science, University of New Mexico.

Riedl, Rachel. 2014. *Authoritarian Origins of Democratic Party Systems in Africa*. New York: Cambridge University Press.

Riera, Mario. 1955. *Cuba política, 1899–1955*. Havana: Impresora Modelo.

Rincón, Omar. 2011. "Mucho ciberactivismo... pocos votos. Antanas Mockus y el Partido Verde colombiano." *Nueva Sociedad* 235: 74–89.

Roberts, Kenneth M. 1995. "Neoliberalism and the Transformation of Populism in Latin America: The Peruvian Case." *World Politics* 48 (1): 82–116.

1998. *Deepening Democracy? The Modern Left and Social Movements in Chile and Peru*. Stanford: Stanford University Press.

2002. "Social Inequalities without Class Cleavages in Latin America's Neoliberal Era." *Studies in Comparative International Development* 36 (4): 3–34.

2006. "Populist Mobilization, Socio-Political Conflict, and Grass-Roots Organization in Latin America." *Comparative Politics* 38 (2): 127–148.

2014. *Changing Course: Parties, Populism, and Political Representation in Latin America's Neoliberal Era*. New York: Cambridge University Press.

Roberts, Kenneth M. and Moisés Arce. 1998. "Neoliberalism and Lower-Class Voting Behavior in Peru." *Comparative Political Studies* 31 (2): 217–246.

Roberts, Kenneth M. and Erik Wibbels. 1999. "Party Systems and Electoral Volatility in Latin America: A Test of Economic, Institutional, and Structural Explanations." *American Political Science Review* 93 (3): 575–590.

Rodríguez, María Ana and Omar Coronel. 2010. "Introducción." In María Ana Rodríguez and Omar Coronel, eds. *El nuevo poder en las regionales: análisis de las elecciones regionales y municipales 2010*, 3–7. Lima: Pontificia Universidad Católica del Peru.

Rodríguez, Tania. 2010. "Estrategias políticas, desafíos organizacionales y campañas presidenciales en democracias emergentes: los casos del Partido dos Trabalhadores y del Partido de la Revolución Democrática." Ph.D. Dissertation, Colegio de México.

Rodríguez Garibaldo, Belisario. 2009. *Las elecciones en Panamá: descripción política y periodística de los procesos electorales de Panamá 1984–2004*. Panama City: Cultural Portobelo.

Rodríguez, Juan Carlos. 2002. "¿Cambiar todo para que nada cambie? Representación, sistema electoral y sistema de partidos en Colombia." In Franciso Gutiérrez, ed. *Degradación o cambio: evolución del sistema político colombiano*, 221–260. Bogotá: Norma.

2006. "Voto preferente y cohesión partidista." In Gary Hoskin and Miguel García, eds. *La reforma política de 2003. ¿La salvación de los partidos políticos colombianos?*, 161–189. Bogotá: Universidad de los Andes/Konrad Adenauer.

Rojas, José Carlos. 2011. "Fiesta y regalo: los vínculos clientelares y la maquinaria política de Chimpum Callao." Undergraduate thesis, Pontificia Universidad Católica del Perú.

Roma, Celso. 2002. "A institucionalização do PSDB entre 1988 e 1999." *Revista Brasileira de Ciências Sociais* 17 (49): 71–92.

2006. "Organizaciones de partido en Brasil: El PT y el PSDB bajo perspectiva comparada." *América Latina Hoy* 44: 153–184.

Romero, Mauricio. 2011. *La economía de los paramilitares: redes de corrupción, negocios y política.* Bogotá: Debate.

Romero Ballivián, Salvador. 2003. "CONDEPA y UCS: El declive del neopopulismo boliviano." *Revista de Ciencia Política* 23 (1): 67–98.

2011. "La corta y sobresaltada historia del financiamiento público a los partidos políticos en Bolivia." In Pablo Gutiérrez and Daniel Zovatto, eds. *Financiamiento de los partidos políticos en América Latina*, 93–117. Mexico City: International Institute for Democracy and Electoral Assistance (IDEA), Organization of American States, and Universidad Nacional Autónoma de México.

Roper, Steven. 2008. "Introduction: The Influence of Public Finance on Post-Communist Party Systems." In Steven Roper and Jānis Ikstens, eds. *Public Finance and Post-Communist Party Development*, 1–9. Burlington: Ashgate.

Ropigliosi, Fernando. 2000. *Montesinos y las Fuerzas Armadas: cómo controló durante una década las instituciones militares.* Lima: Instituto de Estudios Peruanos.

Rosenblatt, Fernando. 2013. "How to Party? Static and Dynamic Party Survival in Consolidated Latin American Democracies." Ph.D. Dissertation, Political Science Institute, Pontificia Universidad Católica de Chile.

Rosenstone, Steve, Roy Behr, and Edward Lazarus. 1984. *Third Parties in America.* Princeton: Princeton University Press.

Rospigliosi, Fernando. 2000. *Montesinos y las Fuerzas Armadas: cómo controló durante una década las instituciones militares.* Lima: Instituto de Estudios Peruanos.

Rozas, Lucila. 2012 "Trayectorias de postulación y carreras políticas en el Perú: un estudio comparado de Puno y La Libertad." Undergraduate thesis, Department of Social Science, Pontificia Universidad Católica del Perú.

Sabatini, Christopher. 2003. "Decentralization and Political Parties." *Journal of Democracy* 14 (2): 138–150.

Samuels, David. 1999. "Incentives to Cultivate a Party Vote in Candidate-Centric Electoral Systems: Evidence from Brazil." *Comparative Political Studies* 32 (4): 487–518.

2002. "Presidentialized Parties: The Separation of Powers and Party Organization and Behavior." *Comparative Political Studies* 35(4): 461–483.

2003. *Ambition, Federalism and Legislative Politics in Brazil.* New York: Cambridge University Press.

2004. "From Socialism to Social Democracy: Party Organization and the Transformation of the Workers' Party in Brazil." *Comparative Political Studies* 37 (9): 999–1024.

2006. "Sources of Mass Partisanship in Brazil." *Latin American Politics and Society* 48 (2): 1–27.

2008. "Brazil: Democracy under Lula and the PT." In Jorge I. Domínguez and Michael Shifter, eds. *Constructing Democratic Governance in Latin America.* Third Edition, 152–176. Baltimore: Johns Hopkins University Press.

Samuels, David and Matthew Shugart. 2010. *Presidents, Parties, and Prime Ministers: How the Separation of Powers Affects Party Organization and Behavior.* New York: Cambridge University Press.

Samuels, David and Cesar Zucco. 2010. "The Roots of *Petismo*, 1989–2010." Unpublished manuscript.

2014. "The Power of Partisanship in Brazil: Evidence from Survey Experiments." *American Journal of Political Science* 58 (1): 212–225.

2015. "Crafting Mass Partisanship at the Grass Roots." *British Journal of Political Science* 45(4): 755–775.

Sánchez, Enrique and Paola García. 2006. "Los Afrocolombianos." In Josefina Stubbs and Hiska Reyes, eds. *Más allá de los promedios: Afrodescendientes en América Latina.* Washington, DC: World Bank.

Sánchez, Marco Aurelio. 1999. *PRD, la élite en crisis: Problemas organizativos, indeterminación ideológica y deficiencias programáticas.* Mexico City: Plaza y Valdés.

Sánchez, Omar. 2009. "Party Non-Systems: A Conceptual Innovation." *Party Politics* 15 (4): 487–520.

2012. "The 2011 Presidential Election in Peru: A Thorny Moral and Political Dilemma." *Contemporary Politics* 18 (1): 109–126.

Sánchez López, Francisco and Flavia Freidenberg. 1998. "El proceso de incorporación política de los sectores indígenas en el Ecuador: Pachakutik, un caso de estudio." *América Latina Hoy* 19: 65–79.

Sanders, Arthur. 1988. "The Meaning of Party Images." *Political Research Quarterly* 41: 583–599.

Sandoval Panamá, David Ernesto. 2005. *Guerreros de la libertad.* Andover: Versal Books.

Sartori, Giovanni. 1976. *Parties and Party Systems: A Framework for Analysis.* New York: Cambridge University Press.

Sawyer, Mark, Yesilernis Peña, and James Sidanius. 2004. "Racial Democracy in the Americas: A Latin and U.S. Comparison." *Journal of Cross-Cultural Psychology* 35: 749–762.

Scarrow, Susan. 1996. *Parties and their Members: Organizing for Victory in Britain and Germany.* New York: Oxford University Press.

Schady, Norbert. 2000. "The Political Economy of Expenditures by the Peruvian Social Fund (FONCODES), 1991–95." *American Political Science Review* 94 (2): 289–304.

Schattschneider, Elmer Eric. 1942. *Party Government*. New York: Farrar and Rinehart.

2004. *Party Government: American Government in Action*. New Brunswick: Transaction Publishers.

Schedler, Andreas. 2002. "The Menu of Manipulation." *Journal of Democracy* 13 (2): 36–50.

ed. 2006. *Electoral Authoritarianism: The Dynamics of Unfree Competition*. Boulder: Lynne Rienner Publishers.

Schlesinger, Joseph. 1991. *Political Parties and the Winning of Office*. Ann Arbor: University of Michigan Press.

Schmidt, Gregory. 2003. "The 2001 Presidential and Congressional Elections in Peru." *Electoral Studies* 22: 344–351.

2006. "Institutional Engineering in a Least-Likely Case: The Peruvian Ley de Partidos and the 2006 Election." Paper Presented at the XXVI Meeting of the Latin American Studies Association, San Juan, Puerto Rico, March 15–18.

Schmitt, Hermann and Sören Holmberg. 1995. "Political Parties in Decline?" In Hans-Dieter Klingemann and Dieter Fuchs, eds. *Citizens and the State*, 95–133. Oxford: Oxford University Press.

Schmitt-Beck, Rüdiger, Stefan Weick, and Bernhard Christoph. 2006. "Shaky Attachments: Individual-level Stability and Change of Partisanship among West German Voters, 1984–2001." *European Journal of Political Research* 45 (4): 581–608.

Schmitter, Philippe. 2001. "Parties Are Not What They Once Were." In Larry Diamond and Richard Gunther, eds. *Political Parties and Democracy*, 67–89. Baltimore: Johns Hopkins University Press.

Schneider, Ben Ross. 2004. *Business Politics and the State in Twentieth-Century Latin America*. New York: Cambridge University Press.

2010. "Business Politics in Latin America: Patterns of Fragmentation and Centralization." In David Coen, Wyn Grant, and Graham Wilson, eds. *The Oxford Handbook of Business and Government*, 307–329. New York: Oxford University Press.

2013. *Hierarchical Capitalism in Latin America*. New York: Cambridge University Press.

Schumpeter, Joseph. 1947. *Capitalism, Socialism, and Democracy*. New York: Harper.

Scully, Timothy. 1992. *Rethinking the Center: Party Politics in Nineteenth and Twentieth Century Chile*. Stanford: Stanford University Press.

Sears, David. 1975. "Political Socialization." In Fred Greenstein and Nelson Polsby, eds. *Handbook of Political Science: Micropolitical Theory*, 93–153. Reading: Addison-Wesley.

Seawright, Jason. 2012. *Party System Collapse: The Roots of Crisis in Peru and Venezuela*. Stanford: Stanford University Press.

Secco, Lincoln. 2011. *História do PT (1978–2010)*. São Paulo: Ateliê Editorial.

Segovia, Rafael. 1975. *La politización del niño mexicano*. Mexico: El Colegio de México.

Segura, Renata and Ana María Bejarano. 2004. "¡Ni Una Asamblea Más Sin Nosotros! Exclusion, Inclusion, and the Politics of Constitution-Making in the Andes." *Constellations* 11 (2): 217–236.

Seifert, Manuel. 2014. *Colapso de los partidos nacionales y auge de los partidos regionales. Las elecciones regionales y municipales 2002–2010*. Lima: Escuela de Gobierno y Políticas Públicas, Pontificia Universidad del Perú.

Seligson, Mitchell, Abby B. Córdova, Juan Carlos Donoso, Daniel Moreno Morales, Diana Orcés, and Vivian Schwartz Blum. 2006. *Democracy Audit: Bolivia 2006 Report*. Nashville: Latin American Public Opinion Project.

Shefter, Martin. 1977. "Party and Patronage: Germany, England, and Italy." *Politics and Society* 7 (December): 403–451.

1994. *Political Parties and the State: The American Historical Experience*. Princeton: Princeton University Press.

Shirk, David. 2005. *Mexico's New Politics: The PAN and Democratic Change*. Boulder, CO: Lynne Rienner Publishers.

Shugart, Matthew Soberg. 1992a. "Guerrillas and Elections: An Institutionalist Perspective on the Costs of Conflict and Competition." *International Studies Quarterly* 36 (2): 121–151.

1992b. "Leaders, Rank and File, and Constituents: Electoral Reform in Colombia and Venezuela." *Electoral Studies* 11 (1): 21–45.

Sichar Moreno, Gonzalo. 1999. *Historia de los partidos políticos guatemaltecos: Distintas siglas de (casi) una misma ideología*. Quetzaltenango: Editorial Los Altos.

Sidanius, Jim, Yesilernis Peña, and Mark Sawyer. 2001. "Inclusionary Discrimination: Pigmentocracy and Patriotism in the Dominican Republic." *Political Psychology* 22 (4): 827–851.

Silva, Eduardo. 1996. *The State and Capital in Chile: Business Elites, Technocrats, and Market Economics*. Boulder: Westview Press.

2009. *Challenging Neoliberalism in Latin America*. New York: Cambridge University Press.

Sivak, Martín. 2007. *Santa Cruz: una tesis. El conflicto regional en Bolivia (2003–2006)*. La Paz: Plural.

Slater, Dan. 2010. *Ordering Power: Contentious Politics and Authoritarian Leviathans in Southeast Asia*. New York: Cambridge University Press.

Slater, Dan and Erica Simmons. 2008. "Critical Antecedents and Informative Regress." *Qualitative Methods* 6 (1): 6–13.

2016. "The Power of Counterrevolution: Elitist Origins of Political Order in Postcolonial Asia and Africa." *American Journal of Sociology* 121(5): 1472–1516.

Slater, Dan and Joseph Wong. 2013. "The Strength to Concede: Ruling Parties and Democratization in Developmental Asia." *Perspectives on Politics* 11: 717–732.

Smith, Benjamin. 2005. "Life of the Party: The Origins of Regime Breakdown and Persistence under Single-Party Rule." *World Politics* 57 (3): 421–451.

Soderberg Kovacs, Mimmi. 2007. "From Rebellion to Politics: The Transformation of Rebel Groups to Political Parties in Civil War Peace Processes." Ph.D. Dissertation, Department of Peace and Conflict Research, Uppsala University.

Soto Gamboa, Ángel. 2001. "La irrupción de la UDI en las poblaciones 1983–1987." Paper Presented at the Meeting of the Latin American Studies Association, Washington, DC, September 6–8.

Sousa Braga, María do Socorro and Jairo Pimentel, Jr. 2011. "Os partidos políticos brasileiros realmente não importam?" *Opinião Pública* 17 (2): 271–303.

Sniderman, Paul and Edward Stiglitz. 2012. *The Reputational Premium: A Theory of Party Identification and Policy Reasoning*. Princeton: Princeton University Press.

Speck, Bruno. 2013. "Nem ideológica, nem oportunista: A filiação partidária no contexto pré-eleitoral no Brasil." In José Carneiro and Bruno Speck, eds. *Candidatos, partidos e coligações nas eleições municipais de 2012*, 37–60. Rio de Janeiro: Fundação Konrad Adenauer.

Stanley, William. 1996. *The Protection Racket State: Elite Politics, Military Extortion, and Civil War in El Salvador*. Philadelphia: Temple University Press.

Stefanoni, Pablo and Hervé Do Alto. 2006. *Evo Morales, de la coca al palacio: una oportunidad para la izquierda indígena*. La Paz: Malatesta.

Stokes, Donald. 1963. "Spatial Models of Party Competition." *American Political Science Review* 57 (2): 368–377.

Stokes, Susan. 2001. *Mandates and Democracy: Neoliberalism by Surprise in Latin America*. Cambridge: Cambridge University Press.

2005. "Perverse Accountability: A Formal Model of Machine Politics with Evidence from Argentina." *American Political Science Review* 99 (3): 315–325.

2009. "Pork, by Any Other Name: Building a Conceptual Scheme of Distributive Politics." Paper Presented at the Annual Meeting of the American Political Science Association, Toronto, Ontario, September 3–6.

Stokes, Susan, Thad Dunning, Marcelo Nazareno, and Valeria Brusco, eds. 2013. *Brokers, Voters and Clientelism: The Puzzle of Distributive Politics*. New York: Cambridge University Press.

Stokes, William. 1951. "The 'Cuban Revolution' and the Presidential Elections of 1948." *Hispanic American Historical Review* 32: 37–79.

Sutton, Francis. 1990. *Ideology and Social Structure: A Study of Radical Marxism*. New York: Garland Press.

Szwarcberg, Mariela. 2012. "Political Parties and Rallies in Latin America." *Party Politics* 20 (3): 456–466.

Tanaka, Martín. 1998. *Los espejismos de la democracia. El colapso del sistema de partidos en el Perú*. Lima: Instituto de Estudios Peruanos.

2002. *La dinámica de los actores regionales y el proceso de descentralización*. Working Paper 125. Lima: Instituto de Estudios Peruanos.

2005a. "Los sistemas de partidos en los países andinos: autoritarismos competitivos y reformismo institucional." In Daniel Zovatto and Kristen Sample, eds. *Democracia en la región andina*, 31–60. Lima: Asociación

Civil Transparencia, International Institute for Democracy and Electoral Assistance (IDEA).

2005b. *La democracia sin partidos. Perú 2000–2005: los problemas de representación y las propuestas de reforma política.* Lima: Instituto de Estudios Peruanos.

2007. "El sistema de partidos 'realmente existente' en el Perú, los desafíos de la construcción de una representación política nacional, y cómo enrumbar la reforma poítica." Working Paper. Consorcio de Investigación Económica y Social.

Tanaka, Martín and Yamilé Guibert. 2011. "Entre la vaporización de los partidos y la debilidad de los movimientos regionales." In María Ana Rodríguez and Omar Coronel, eds. *El nuevo poder en las regiones: análisis de las elecciones regionales y municipales 2010*, 18–28. Lima: Pontificia Universidad Católica del Perú.

Tanaka, Martín and Carlos Meléndez. 2013. "The Future of Peru's Brokered Democracy." In Diego Abente and Larry Diamond, eds. *Clientelism, Social Policy, and the Quality of Democracy: Evidence from Latin America, Lessons from Other Regions*, 65–87. Baltimore: Johns Hopkins University Press.

Tarrow, Sidney. 1998. *Power in Movement: Social Movements and Contentious Politics.* Cambridge: Cambridge University Press.

Tavits, Margit. 2013. *Post-Communist Democracies and Party Organization.* New York: Cambridge University Press.

Taylor-Robinson, Michelle. 2010. *Do the Poor Count? Democratic Institutions and Accountability in a Context of Poverty.* University Park: Pennsylvania State University Press.

Telles, Edward. 2004. *Race in Another America: The Significance of Skin Color in Brazil.* Princeton: Princeton University Press.

2014. *Pigmentocracies: Ethnicity, Race, and Color in Latin America.* Chapel Hill: University of North Carolina Press.

Theidon, Kimberly. 2000. "How We Learned to Kill Our Brother? Memory, Morality and Reconciliation in Peru." *Bulletin de l'Institut Français d'Études Andines* 29 (3): 539–554.

Thomassen, Jacques. 1976. "Party Identification as a Cross-National Concept: Its Meaning in the Netherlands." In Ian Budge, Ivor Crewe, and Dennis Farlie, eds. *Party Identification and Beyond: Representations of Voting and Party Competition*, 63–79. New York: John Wiley and Sons.

Togores, Viviana and Anicia García. 2004. "Consumption, Markets, and Monetary Duality in Cuba." In Jorge I. Domínguez, Omar Everleny Pérez Villanueva, and Lorena Barberia, eds. *The Cuban Economy at the Start of the Twenty-First Century*, 245–296. Cambridge: Harvard University Press.

Tuesta, Fernando. 2005. *Representación Política: La Reglas También Cuentan.* Lima: Pontificia Universidad Católica del Peru/Fundación Friedrich Ebert.

Tuesta Soldevilla, Fernando. 2011. "El financiamiento de los partidos políticos en el Peru." In Pablo Gutiérrez and Daniel Zovatto, eds. *Financiamiento de los partidos políticos en América Latina (Doctrina Jurídica #594)*, 445–482. Mexico City: International Institute for Democracy and Electoral Assistance (IDEA), Organization of American States, and Universidad Nacional Autónoma de México.

Turner, John C. 1987. *Rediscovering the Social Group: A Self-Categorization Theory*. New York: Blackwell.

1999. "Some Current Issues in Research on Social Identity and Self-Categorization Theories." In Naomi Ellemers, Russell Spears, and Bertjan Doosje, eds. *Social Identity: Context, Commitment, Content*, 6–34. Malden: Blackwell.

UN Truth Commission on El Salvador. 1993. *From Madness to Hope*. Report of the Commission on the Truth for El Salvador S/25500.

Universidad de los Andes. 2010. *De Convergencia al PIN*. Lima: Congreso Visible.

University of Salamanca. 2013. *Encuesta de Élites Parlamentarias de El Salvador*. Salamanca: University of Salamanca.

Urrutia, Adriana. 2011a. "Que la Fuerza (2011) esté con Keiko: el nuevo baile del fujimorismo. El fujimorismo, su organización y sus estrategias de campana." In Carlos Meléndez, ed. *Post-Candidatos: Guía analítica de sobrevivencia hasta las próximas elecciones*, 91–120. Lima: Aerolíneas Editoriales.

2011b. "Hacer campaña y construir partido: Fuerza 2011 y su estrategia para (re)legitimar al fujimorismo a través de su organización." *Argumentos* 5 (2). Online http://revistaargumentos.iep.org.pe/articulos/hacer-campana-y-construir-partido-fuerza-2011-y-su-estrategia-para-relegitimar-al-fujimorismo-a-traves-de-su-organizacion/.

UTEC. 2003. "Resultados de la XXXI Encuesta de Opinión Pública, 28, 29 y 30 de noviembre de 2003." Centro de Investigación de la Opinión Pública Salvadoreña (CIOPS), Universidad Tecnológica de El Salvador (UTEC).

Valdivia, Gabriela. 2010. "Agrarian Capitalism and the Struggle for Hegemony in the Bolivian Lowlands." *Latin American Perspectives* 37 (4): 67–87.

Valdivia, Verónica. 2008. "Los guerreros de la política: La Unión Demócrata Independiente, 1983–1988." In Verónica Valdivia, et al., eds. *Su revolución contra nuestra revolución. Vol. II. La pugna marxista-gremialista en los ochenta*, 139–180. Santiago: LOM Ediciones.

Valenzuela, Arturo. 1977. *Political Brokers in Chile: Local Government in a Centralized Polity*. Durham: Duke University Press.

1978. *The Breakdown of Democratic Regimes: Chile*. Baltimore: Johns Hopkins University Press.

1995. "The Military in Power: The Consolidation of One-Man Rule." In Paul Drake and Iván Jaksić, eds. *The Struggle for Democracy in Chile, Revised Edition*, 21–72. Lincoln: University of Nebraska Press.

Valenzuela, J. Samuel. 1992. "Democratic Consolidation in Post-Transitional Settings: Notion, Process, and Facilitating Conditions." In Scott Mainwaring, Guillermo O'Donnell, and J. Samuel Valenzuela, eds. *Issues in Democratic Consolidation: The New South American Democracies in Comparative Perspective*, 57–104. Notre Dame: University of Notre Dame Press.

Van Biezen, Ingrid. 2000. "Party Financing in New Democracies: Spain and Portugal." *Party Politics* 6: 329–342.

2004. "Political Parties as Public Utilities." *Party Politics* 10: 701–722.

Van Biezen, Ingrid and Petr Kopecký. 2007. "The State and the Parties: Public Funding, Public Regulation, and Rent-Seeking in Contemporary Democracies." *Party Politics* 13: 235–254.

Van Cott, Donna Lee. 2005. *From Movements to Parties: The Evolution of Ethnic Politics.* New York: Cambridge University Press.

Van der Borgh, Chris. 2004. *Cooperación externa, gobierno local y reconstrucción posguerra: La experiencia de Chalatenango, El Salvador.* Amsterdam: Rozenberg Publishers.

Van Dyck, Brandon. 2014a. "Why Party Organization Still Matters: The Workers' Party in Northeastern Brazil." *Latin American Politics and Society* 56 (2): 1–26.

2014b. "The Paradox of Adversity: New Party Survival and Collapse in Latin America." Ph.D. Dissertation, Department of Government, Harvard University.

Vanger, Milton. 1963. *José Batlle y Ordóñez of Uruguay: The Creator of His Times, 1902–1907.* Cambridge: Harvard University Press.

Vera, Sofía. 2010. "Radiografía a la política en las regiones: tendencias a partir de la evidencia de tres procesos electorales (2002, 2006 y 2010)." *Revista Argumentos* 4 (5). Online http://revistaargumentos.iep.org.pe/articulos/radiografia-a-la-politica-en-las-regiones-tendencias-a-partir-de-la-evidencia-de-tres-procesos-electorales/.

Vergara, Alberto. 2007. *Ni amnésicos ni irracionales: las elecciones peruanas de 2006 en perspectiva histórica.* Lima: Solar Central de Proyectos.

2009. "El choque de los ideales: reformas institucionales y partidos políticos en el Perú post-fujimorato." Working Paper. Lima: International Institute for Democracy and Electoral Assistance (IDEA).

2011. "United by Discord, Divided by Consensus: National and Sub-national Articulation in Bolivia and Peru, 2000–2010." *Journal of Politics in Latin America* 3 (3): 65–93.

Vilca, Paulo. 2011. "Por las rutas de la política regional." In Carlos Meléndez, ed. *Anti-candidatos: Guía analítica para unas elecciones sin partidos,* 178–209. Lima: Mitin.

Villamizar Herrera, Darío. 1995. *Aquel 19 será: una historia del M-19, de sus hombres y sus gestas.* Bogotá: Planeta.

Villanueva, Pérez and Omar Everleny. 2016. "La economía cubana: Evolución y perspectivas." *Cuban Studies* 44: 19–42.

Wantchekon, Leonard. 1999. "Strategic Voting in Conditions of Political Instability: The 1994 Elections in El Salvador." *Comparative Political Studies* 32 (7): 810–834.

Ward, Ian. 1993. "'Media Intrusion' and the Changing Nature of the Established Parties in Australia and Canada." *Canadian Journal of Political Science* 26 (3): 477–506.

Ware, Alan. 1996. *Political Parties and Party Systems.* New York: Oxford University Press.

Webre, Stephen. 1979. *José Napoleón Duarte and the Christian Democratic Party in Salvadoran Politics, 1960–1972.* Baton Rouge: Louisiana State University.

Weinstein, Martin. 1975. *Uruguay: The Politics of Failure.* Westport: Greenwood Press.

Weyland, Kurt. 1996. "Neo-Populism and Neo-Liberalism in Latin America: Unexpected Affinities." *Studies in Comparative International Development* 32 (3): 3–31.

1998. "Swallowing the Bitter Pill: Sources of Popular Support for Neoliberal Reform in Latin America." *Comparative Political Studies* 31 (5): 539–568.

1999. "Neoliberal Populism in Latin America and Eastern Europe." *Comparative Politics* 31 (4): 379–401.

2000. "A Paradox of Success? Determinants of Political Support for President Fujimori." *International Studies Quarterly* 44: 481–502.

White, Alastair. 1973. *El Salvador.* Boulder: Westview Press.

Williams, Edward. 1967. *Latin American Christian Democratic Parties.* Knoxville: University of Tennessee Press.

Willis, Eliza, Christopher Garman, and Stephan Haggard. 1999. "The Politics of Decentralization in Latin America." *Latin American Research Review* 34 (1): 7–56.

Wills-Otero, Laura, Margarita Battle, and Fredy Barrero. 2012. "Candidaturas y partidos: los procesos de selección de candidatos en las elecciones subnacionales de Colombia." In Laura Wills-Otero and Margarita Battle, eds. *Política y territorio: análisis de las elecciones subnacionales en Colombia 2011,* 63–104. Bogotá: Programa de las Naciones Unidas para el Desarrollo, International Institute for Democracy and Electoral Assistance (IDEA), Netherlands Institute for Multiparty Democracy.

Wills-Otero, Laura and Christian Iván Benito. 2012. "De Uribe a Santos: cambios y continuidades de la política colombiana en 2011." *Revista de Ciencia Política* 32 (1): 87–107.

Wolf, Sonja. 2009. "Subverting Democracy: Elite Rule and the Limits to Political Participation in Post-War El Salvador." *Journal of Latin American Studies* 41 (3): 429–465.

Wood, Elizabeth. 2000a. *Forging Democracy from Below: Insurgent Transitions in South Africa and El Salvador.* New York: Cambridge University Press.

2000b. "Civil War and the Transformation of Elite Representation in El Salvador." In Kevin Middlebrook, ed. *Conservative Parties, the Right, and Democracy in Latin America,* 223–254. Baltimore: Johns Hopkins University Press.

2003. *Insurgent Collective Action and Civil War in El Salvador.* New York: Cambridge University Press.

World Bank. 2013. *Economic Mobility and the Rise of the Latin American Middle Class.* Washington, DC: World Bank.

Wright, William. 1971. "Comparative Party Models: Rational-Efficient and Party Democracy." In William Wright, ed. *A Comparative Study of Party Organization,* 17–54. Columbus: Merrill.

Yaffé, Jaime. 2005. *Al centro y adentro: La renovación de la izquierda y el triunfo del Frente Amplio en Uruguay.* Montevideo: Linardi y Risso.

Yashar, Deborah. 1995. *Contesting Citizenship in Latin America: The Rise of Indigenous Movements and the Postliberal Challenge.* New York: Cambridge University Press.

Zambrano, Jesús. 2010. Interview with editors in "Conversaciones" section. In González Trujillo, Miguel Ángel, Onel Ortíz Fragoso, Gabriela Rojo Rosas, and Rubén Sánchez Martínez, eds. *20 Años: Un futuro con historia,* 283–286. Mexico City: Agencia Promotora de Publicaciones.

Zamora, Rubén. 1998. *Heridas que no cierran: Los partidos políticos en la post-guerra*. San Salvador: La Facultad Latinoamericana de Ciencias Sociales.
  2003. *La izquierda partidaria salvadoreña: entre la identidad y el poder*. San Salvador: La Facultad Latinoamericana de Ciencias Sociales.
Zas Fris, Johnny. 2005. *La insistencia de la voluntad. El actual proceso de descentralización política y sus antecedentes inmediatos (1980–2004)*. Lima: Defensoría del Pueblo, Society for Ecological Restoration.
Zavaleta, Mauricio. 2010. "¿Cómo se compite sin partidos? Política electoral en Cusco y Puno." *Revista Argumentos* 4 (5). Online http://revistaargumentos. iep.org.pe/articulos/como-se-compite-sin-partidos-politica-electoral-en-cusco-y-puno/.
  2014a. *Coaliciones de independientes: Las reglas no escritas de la política electoral en el Perú*. Lima: Instituto de Estudios Peruanos.
  2014b. "Todo se transforma: la articulación de la oferta política en el Perú subnacional." *Argumentos* 8 (5). Online http://revistaargumentos.iep.org. pe/articulos/todo-se-transforma-la-articulacion-de-la-oferta-politica-en-el-peru-subnacional/.
Zechmeister, Elizabeth. 2015. "Ideology." In Ryan Carlin, Matthew Singer and Elizabeth Zechmeister, eds. *The Latin American Voter: Pursuing Representation and Accountability in Challenging Contexts*, 195–225. Ann Arbor: University of Michigan Press.
Zegada, Claure and María Teresa. 2010. "El rol de la oposición política en Bolivia (2006–2009)." In Luis Alberto García Orellana and Fernando Luis García Yapur, eds. *Mutaciones del campo político en Bolivia*, 151–239. La Paz: United Nations Development Programme.
Ziblatt, Daniel. 1998. "The Adaptation of Ex-Communist Parties to Post-Communist East Central Europe: A Comparative Study of the East German and Hungarian Ex-Communist Parties." *Communist and Post-Communist Studies* 31: 119–137.
  Forthcoming. *Conservative Political Parties and the Birth of Modern Democracy in Europe, 1848–1950*. New York: Cambridge University Press.
Ziegfeld, Adam. Forthcoming. *Why Regional Parties? Clientelism, Elites, and Party System Formation in India*. New York: Cambridge University Press.
Zolberg, Aristide. 1966. *Creating Political Order: The Party-States of West Africa*. Chicago: Rand McNally.
Zucco, Cesar. 2008. "The President's 'New' Constituency: Lula and the Pragmatic Vote in Brazil's 2006 Presidential Election." *Journal of Latin American Studies* 40 (1): 19–49.
  2013. "When Payouts Pay Off: Conditional Cash-Transfers and Voting Behavior in Brazil 2002–2010." *American Journal of Political Science* 57 (4): 810–822.
Zucco, Cesar and Benjamin Lauderdale. 2011. "Distinguishing Between Influences on Brazilian Legislative Behavior." *Legislative Studies Quarterly* 36 (3): 363–396.
Zuckerman, Alan, Josip Dasović, and Jennifer Fitzgerald. 2007. *Partisan Families: The Social Logic of Bounded Partisanship in Germany and Britain*. New York: Cambridge University Press.

Index

Made in the USA
Monee, IL
26 August 2021

76536922R00333